Business Process Engineering
Study Edition

Reference Models for Industrial Enterprises

Springer
Berlin
Heidelberg
New York
Barcelona
Budapest
Hong Kong
London
Milan
Paris
Santa Clara
Singapore
Tokyo

August-Wilhelm Scheer

Business Process Engineering Study Edition

Reference Models for Industrial Enterprises

With 554 Figures

 Springer

Prof. Dr. Dr. h.c. August-Wilhelm Scheer
Universität des Saarlandes
Institut für Wirtschaftsinformatik
Postfach 151150
D-66041 Saarbrücken
Germany

ISBN 3-540-63867-9 Springer-Verlag Berlin Heidelberg New York

Library of Congress Cataloging-in-Publication Data
Die Deutsche Bibliothek – CIP-Einheitsaufnahme
Scheer, August-Wilhelm: Business process engineering: reference models for industrial enterprises /
August-Wilhelm Scheer. – Study ed. – Berlin; Heidelberg; New York; Barcelona; Budapest; Hong
Kong; London; Milan; Paris; Santa Clara; Singapore; Tokyo: Springer, 1998
    ISBN 3-540-63867-9

© Springer-Verlag Berlin · Heidelberg 1998
Printed in Germany

The use of general descriptive names, registered names, trademarks, etc. in this publication does
not imply, even in the absence of a specific statement, that such names are exempt from the relevant protective laws and regulations and therefore free for general use.

Hardcover-Design: Erich Kirchner, Heidelberg

SPIN 10660967   42/2202-5 4 3 2 1 0 – Printed on acid-free paper

Preface

The 1st study edition is based on the 2nd hardcover edition of "Business Process Engineering". Several inconsistencies and minor modifications have been carried out. This study edition is a response to many requests for a budget-priced edition for students.

This edition pursues a holistic descriptive approach that is based on the Architecture of Integrated Information Systems (ARIS) developed by the author. In addition to the data view, this approach also comprises the function, organization and control views, and encompasses all phases of the information system lifecycle - from analysis, requirements definition and design specification to implementation. The reference models developed here can thus serve as initial models for concrete applications.

The illustrations are oriented strongly toward standard software in order to reflect their significance in terms of real-world representations. In particular, the discussion applies examples from the R/3 system from SAP AG and from the systems from IDS Prof. Scheer GmbH, build on concepts developed by the author. No "user description" of concrete systems is provided; instead, general foundations are laid in order to facilitate a deeper understanding of the application logic that is reflected in standard software. An attempt is made to close the gap between business administration theory and the "operating instructions" of standard software.

An intensive discussion of the options for terminological generalization and specialization serves to incorporate a significant property of object-oriented systems design into the model - namely, class formation. Typical applications for object-oriented representations are embedded in the ARIS concept.

The author's recent books on business information science conform to the basic principle shown in Figure 01.

Business information science serves as a facilitator between business applications and information technology.

However, dual relationships exist between these two elements. On the one hand, information technology has to be analyzed as to the extent to which new technological developments can lead to new application concepts. This "direction of influence" is represented by the arrows shown on the left side of Figure 01. The description of the entire panorama of information technology is not the primary focus of business information science; instead, it concerns itself only with the segment that leads to changes in business application concepts. And it is on this area that business information science must concentrate particularly.

The arrows on the right side of the diagram are intended to illustrate the influence the DP-oriented business concepts exert on information technology. They show that DP-oriented application concepts place demands on the further development of information technology to provide effective support for it.

These types of general concepts are implemented by means of information systems. Information systems thus serve as concrete facilitators between general business concepts and information technology. Since information systems involve both the business-related subject level as well as information technology, they are correspondingly complex; as a result, they are categorized in order to reduce this complexity.

The author's ARIS architecture - developed in "Architecture of Integrated Information Systems", which was published in English in 1992 - represents an effort to address these issues.

The present book "Business Process Reengineering - Reference Models for Industrial Enterprises", pursues these views and levels of information systems as they relate to an industrial enterprise.

The business-related relevance of the tier concept for information systems decreases as one moves closer to the technical implementation of phase. At the same time, the stability of the concepts decreases, since

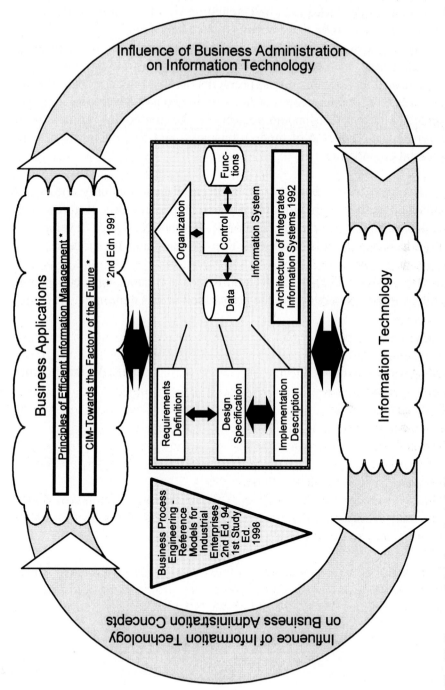

Fig: 01: Framework for the author's books

information technology, with its breathtaking pace of development, primarily influences the technical implementation of information systems. This principle is reflected by the problems treated here.

On the whole, the objective of this book is to illustrate the multitude of informational and organizational problems involved in an industrial enterprise in a more modern form, while simultaneously developing new DP-oriented solutions. This should not only be the function of business information science, but also of modern business- and manufacturing-oriented industrial engineering.

The content of this book has been prepared hypermedially and is now available together with video sequences of the author's lectures under *http://lehre2000.iwi.uni-sb.de*. The ARIS-Internet-Navigator developed by IDS Prof. Scheer GmbH enables the user to manipulate the models.

I wish to thank Dipl.-Kfm. Roland Rolles and cand. rer. oec. Michael Genth for their support during the preparation of this edition.

Saarbrücken, January 1998   August-Wilhelm Scheer

Overview

Contents

Part B: Logistics Processes   86

Part A: Architecture and Description of Integrated Information Systems

This book primarily discusses information systems for industrial operations. Nonetheless, the title "Business Process Engineering" would appear to be appropriate, as business administration has traditionally focused on the complexity of industry, and industrial solutions frequently set the pace for applications in other areas.

As elementary school students learn to work with computers, technical knowledge of DP fundamentals continues to lose significance in designing application systems. As a result, this book will not go into detail on the technical basics of hardware and software. These topics are treated in many introductory publications (e.g., the comprehensive discussion in *Hansen, Wirtschaftsinformatik I 1996; Stahlknecht, Wirtschaftsinformatik 1995*). The importance of adequately **translating** business application knowledge into DP-suitable structures, on the other hand, is increasing. This problem will therefore be the focus of the discussion.

Screens provide the typical user interface to a business information system (see the accounting system screens in Figures A.01,a and A.01,b and *SAP, System R/3 - Funktionen im Detail, pp. 3-16*). These screens display a variety of system aspects such as technical DP commands (user commands), functions, data and organizational concepts.

Users are able to understand a screen's contents only if their familiarity with the business background allows them to interpret the information contained in the screens. By itself—i.e., without contextual information—the screen is essentially meaningless.

The inability of screens to communicate information intuitively becomes more apparent when a business process sequence must be determined from a series of screens, as shown in the relationship between Figures A.01,a and A.01,b. In practice, therefore, users are trained in the subject background. This training, however, is geared toward specific systems and does not provide a generic view on the level of business theory.

The information system interfaces themselves are inadequate to describe the actual business situation represented by information systems;

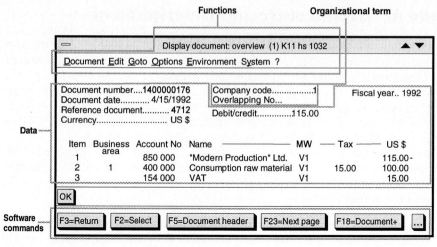

Fig. A.01,a: Screen "Display document"

Fig. A.01,b: Screen "Display document item"

rather, this necessitates specialized descriptive views and languages geared toward the business problem areas involved.

In order to ensure that these descriptions are complete, the subject being described must first be developed and structured into its descriptive components. The components of an information system and their interrelationships are referred to as architecture. This book will discuss a concept introduced in the Architecture of Integrated Information Systems (ARIS).

After the architecture has been stipulated, adequate descriptive methods are selected. Software engineering provides numerous design and development techniques for DP systems (see *Balzert, Die Entwicklung von Software-Systemen 1982; Österle, Informationssysteme 1981; Lehner et al., Organisationslehre für Wirtschaftsinformatiker 1991; Mertens et al., Lexikon der Wirtschaftsinformatik 1990*). A selection must be made from these in order to guarantee a form of representation that is both as uniform as possible throughout and that also ensures that it is no more difficult to learn the methods of representation than it is to learn the content.

First, therefore, the subject to be described in this book will be specified, the proposed architecture developed, and finally these elements will be built upon to select and present the descriptive methods that will be used throughout the remainder of the book.

A.I Architecture of Integrated Information Systems (ARIS)

A.I.1 Integrated Information Systems

Computer-supported business information systems provide the vehicle for linking business application concepts with information technology.

In dealing with business application systems, a distinction is frequently made between **administrative, scheduling, planning** and **control systems** (see *Mertens, Integrierte Informationsverarbeitung I 1993, pp. 10 ff.*). This definition is based on the type of business task involved.

A DP system that is used simply as a "quick calculator" for mundane large-scale tasks such as printing addresses or listings is categorized as an administrative data processing system.

A DP system that is used to control short-term, well-structured processes within an organization—e.g., order processing or sales/marketing—is called a scheduling system.

A system that supplies information to executives is called a management information system.

Planning systems are used for long-term, typically poorly structured activities.

Management information systems rely on scheduling systems to create the database that is accessed by appropriate consolidation procedures to provide management information. On the other hand, scheduling systems such as order processing also contain simple processing functions such as order writing, which belong to administrative systems. Thus, there is no hard and fast separation between the concepts. Information systems, therefore, serve as a superordinate concept for administrative, scheduling, management information and planning systems.

A further delineating criterion in information systems is the distinction between operative information systems that are closely linked to the production of goods and services and value-oriented job accounting and controlling systems. A closer look, however, shows the increasing interdependence between quantity-oriented and value-oriented IS aspects. For example, a purchasing system provides important data to Accounts Payable, and a sales system supplies data to Accounts Receivable. Withdrawals from inventory are also immediately recorded in the inventory control system as quantity-related data and in inventory accounting as value-related data.

The classification of information systems according to their emphasis—either operative or value-oriented—should thus be understood solely as a

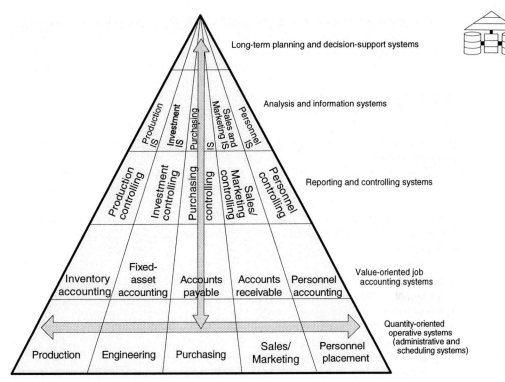

Fig. A.I.01: Integrated information systems

didactic, conceptual aid. This is how the information pyramid depicted in Figure A.I.01 should be viewed.

Because it is difficult to make a distinction between administrative and scheduling systems, the pyramid consolidates them under the concept of "operative systems," which encompass quantity-oriented processes that are closely associated with the production of goods and services. Typical departments in this category are Production, Engineering, Purchasing, Sales/Marketing and Personnel Placement.

These quantity-oriented processes are tracked by value-oriented job accounting systems in order to reveal their business implications. Theoretically, these value-oriented systems can be conceptually distinguished from the quantity-oriented systems since they build upon one another, but in practice, they are closely interlinked in terms of structural organization and data creation. Figure A.I.01 shows this clearly by assigning every operative function to a corresponding value-oriented job accounting system.

In the third level, information for reporting and controlling systems is transferred from the quantity- and value-oriented systems. Specialized controlling systems can also be assigned to departments.

In the next level of consolidation, analysis and information systems are created that incorporate data from external sources along with the consolidated data from the operative and job accounting systems. These systems can also be organized according to organizational departments. Examples of this are marketing information systems, purchasing information systems and production information systems.

Planning and decision-support systems constitute the highest level of consolidation. These systems primarily provide support for long-term planning and decision making. They are also called executive information systems (EIS).

The vertical structure in Figure A.I.01 shows the different operational views of information systems. At the same time, it illustrates increasing levels of data consolidation. The data from the operative function-oriented information systems are increasingly consolidated into interfunctional evaluative views until an enterprise-wide management information system is achieved.

The principle illustrated in the horizontal structure according to organizational functions is typical in the articulation of corporate organizational structures as well as in the classification of subjects within the science of business administration. This principle is not, however, the only criterion for structuring an industrial organization to reduce the complexity of its problems.

In industrial organizations, when a problem's complexity is defined by the effort a human being has to expend in order to solve it, this complexity is the result of the multitude of functions to be processed and the large number of goods and services to be scheduled (materials, component parts, assemblies, all the way to end products). Figure A.I.02 compares these two dimensions, with the size of the area representing the overall complexity. These functions include several operative and "higher-level" functions from the pyramid in Figure A.I.01.

Dividing this "complexity" area into individual sections serves to reduce the overall complexity. A vertical structure would group together all functions associated with a particular group of objects. In terms of structural organization, this approach could lead to an object-oriented (divisional) organizational structure. The broken lines in Figure A.I.02 illustrate this principle.

The predominant form of structuring, however, is function-oriented. In this approach, organizational units are formed for functional units that are responsible for the overall spectrum of products and services. This principle is illustrated in Figure A.I.02 by horizontal lines. Since this structural principle was the prevailing organizational form in the early days of electronic data processing, DP structures reflect horizontal compartmentalization schemes. This is how information systems for supporting production, purchasing, sales/marketing and accounting first came into being—a trend that can easily be verified in standard software

Functions   **Objects/Outputs = Products**

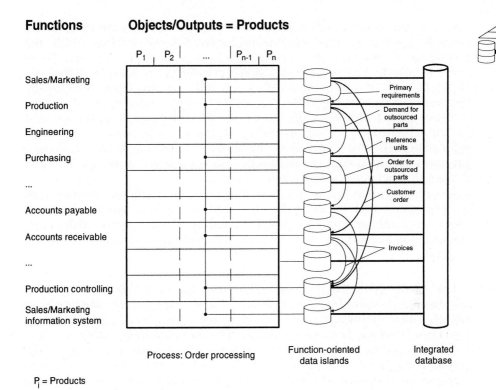

P$_i$ = Products

Fig. A.I.02: Reduction of complexity

catalogs listing vendors who have specialized in specific functions. As a rule, these function-oriented information systems contain their own databases, as illustrated in Figure A.I.02, which leads to the well-known problem of function-oriented data islands.

A closer look, however, shows that these business functions are linked by decision and process relationships: When objects (or outputs) are processed, they typically pass through several functions; for example, an order passes from Sales through Production and Purchasing to Accounts Receivable and is processed further in the controlling and sales/marketing information systems. Figure A.I.02 shows several examples of the data transfer process.

If each function manages its own data, the object relationship of processes results in redundancy because data that belong to one object are stored by several functions. Although this leads to increased physical storage requirements, the primary problem is one of logical data consistency, because the data definitions would not necessarily have to be consistent if each function defines its data according to its own requirements. Transferring data between functions becomes problematic because each function interprets data differently. Therefore, an integrated database is necessary to ensure that all enterprise-wide data definitions are consistent, and to minimize redundancy when data are entered, stored and processed.

An approach of this type overlays a process-oriented view across the functions. The process view provides the basis for integrating information systems. Integrated information systems thus encompass the two directions of integration illustrated in the information pyramid. The horizontal arrow at the operative system level shows consistent information streams that follow the flow of materials or the production process in an industrial organization. The vertical arrow shows the close relationship between quantity and value.

In summary, it is fair to say that integrated information systems follow an object-oriented—i.e., process-oriented—design paradigm. Business processes combine operative functions and operative systems with value-oriented job accounting systems to create planning and decision support systems.

During the MIS debate that lasted from the mid 1960s to the early 1970s, the Cologne Integration Model (KIM) had already attempted to design a descriptive model of an enterprise's integrated data processing (see *Grochla et al., Gesamtmodelle der Datenverarbeitung 1974*).

Without considering enterprise-specific circumstances, this model records both the most important tasks that can be completed with the help of data processing and the information flow between them. As a result, the descriptive language is primarily function-oriented.

KIM uses input/output analysis to determine the relationships between the individual data processing tasks. For every task, the model first determines the input data necessary to complete the task and then determines the processes that create these data. The same is true for the output data and the processes that receive them. Figure A.I.03 shows an excerpt from KIM, which is an example from Production.

Data processing tasks are represented by rectangles. If, for example, "production scheduling" (where the model begins) makes changes to the corresponding production plan because of product design changes, it initiates the function for the "production plan update service." The link between "production scheduling" and "production plan update service" is represented by Arrow 68. In KIM terminology, arrows are also called channels, and their meaning is called channel content. Arrow 68 (Channel 68) means (see *Grochla et al., Gesamtmodelle der Datenverarbeitung 1974, p. 259*): "update notices concerning new and/or existing bills of materials." Channel 908 routes the changes to the "production plans" file, which is then updated. These update notices are also routed to other departments and functions.

If all these relationships were entered into the overall diagram in their entirety for all implemented data processing tasks, it would be unintelligible. Therefore, only the most important links are entered directly. The other links are indicated by connectors. The numbers entered

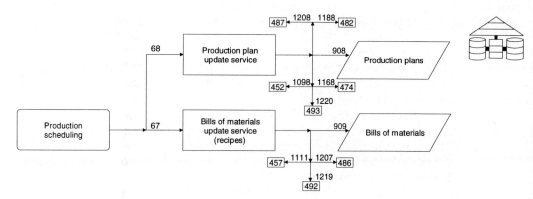

Fig. A.I.03: Excerpt from KIM (Kölner/Cologne Integration Model)

in the connectors indicate the destination for each channel. The connector at Channel 1168 is numbered 474. It is possible to look up the numbers in the KIM connector list to verify if new information is being routed to the "optimal lot size analysis data processing task."

The Cologne Integration Model contains approximately 350 data processing tasks that are linked by more than 1,500 channels (see *Schareck/Schmitz, Dokumentationsverfahren betrieblicher Informations- systeme 1975, p. 21*). To improve the overview, the graphical representation of the overall model is divided into 14 individual views. These views are supplemented by task description lists, channel description lists and connector lists.

The high expectations that KIM would be able to serve as the basis for concrete system developments have not been met. One reason might be that KIM is still oriented too much toward traditional business administration concepts, and it placed excessive demands on the technical DP capabilities available at the time. For example, the development of database systems was still in its infancy. Moreover, today it is apparent that the attempt to refine the model even further by focusing on individual industry characteristics—e.g., with the help of the MIDAM (Model of Integrated Data Processing in Mechanical Engineering) Project—has failed (see also *Poths, Integrierte Gesamtmodelle 1978*).

Despite this, KIM offers an important contribution to the discussion of integrated business application systems and still provides an interesting complement to the view of information modeling developed in this book.

The methods of information modeling chosen in this book use largely standardized means of representation, in contrast to KIM, which developed its own methodology.

A.I.2 The ARIS Approach

The Architecture of Integrated Information Systems (ARIS) concept follows the previously developed integration concept in that it supports existing business processes.

The first step involves developing a model for business processes. Because it is highly complex, the model is divided into different views. This makes it possible to describe individual views using specialized methods without having to incorporate the corresponding relationships to the other views. Ultimately, however, the relationships between the views are reintroduced.

In addition to this division, the second basic thrust of ARIS involves a concept of different descriptive levels. Information systems can be described with respect to their proximity to information technology. Development of a lifecycle concept ensures a consistent description from the business problem all the way to DP implementation.

The architecture strives to holistically describe an information system for supporting business processes (from all views and across all phases of development). *Scheer, Architecture of Integrated Information Systems, 1992* gives a more precise derivation and portrayal of ARIS. It also describes other architectures such as CIM-OSA and compares them with ARIS.

A.I.2.1 Descriptive Views

Figure A.I.04,a illustrates an excerpt from the "order processing" business process, which serves to illustrate the concept of views.

The process is triggered by the "customer order received" event, which in turn initiates the "order confirmation" function. Condition descriptions for the relevant operation environment are necessary in order to process this operation—in this example, conditions affecting the customer and the articles contained in the order. The conditions can be changed during workflow processing, for example, if the stock on hand data are updated by reservations.

The event still has to be processed by a human being. This person is assigned to a department, which is equipped with information technology resources such as PCs, access to databases, etc.

Order confirmation is the result of workflow processing. The "order confirmation" event can initiate additional operations such as "order tracking" and "production planning." In return, condition descriptions as well as human and technical resources are necessary to process these operations. At the same time, relationships to other activities can result in

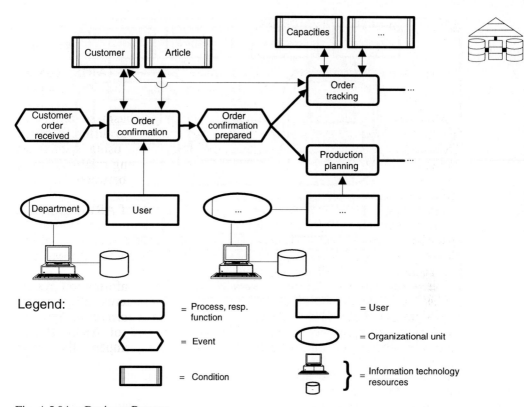

Fig. A.I.04,a: Business Process

the same condition descriptions being required or the same resources being used. In the example, this is indicated by the use of the same customer data for receiving and tracking orders.

The components and their interrelationships to be described in a computer-supported business process include processes, activities, events, conditions, users, organizational units and information technology resources. Considering all the effects on all the elements of the process when designing an information system would severely complicate the design process.

In order to reduce this complexity, the model is divided into individual views (see Figure A.I.04,b) that represent discrete design aspects and can be handled (largely) independently, which simplifies the task.

When determining which views to use, it is necessary to note that relationships <u>within</u> the views are very high and the relationships <u>between</u> the views are relatively simple and loosely linked. Only under these conditions does it make sense to break them down.

Events such as "customer order received," "completion notice received," or "invoice written" are information objects that are represented by data. Reference field conditions such as "customer status"

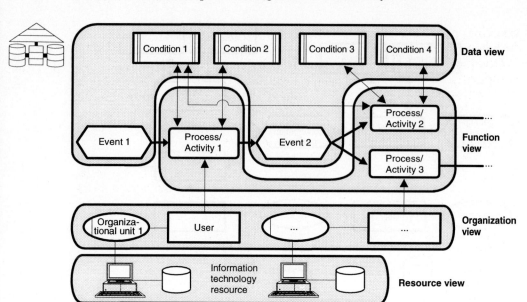

Fig. A.I.04,b: Views of the process model

and "article status" are also represented by data. Conditions and events thus form the **data view**.

In traditional data processing, event data are designated as transaction data, while the reference environment is described by master data that are continually updated and thus provide a current representation of the condition.

The functions to be performed and their relationships form a second view, the **function view**. It contains the description of the function itself, the enumeration of the individual subfunctions that belong to the overall relationship, and the positional relationships that exist between the functions.

Because of their close relationship, the "user" and "organizational unit" components are consolidated into **one** descriptive view. Users are assigned to organizational units, which are formed according to criteria such as "same function" or "same work object." Thus, the structure and relationships between users and organizational units constitute the **organization view**.

Information technology components constitute the fourth descriptive object, the **resource view**. This view, however, is significant for business considerations only insofar as it results in general conditions for describing the other components that are more strongly geared toward business. For this reason, descriptions for data, functions and organizational structure are differentiated on the basis of their proximity to information technology resources. In each view, the resources are treated at the level of the design specification and the implementation description. **The lifecycle model replaces the resource view as the independent descriptive object**.

Dividing the initial problem into individual views does reduce its complexity, albeit at the expense of the description of the relationships between the views as expressed by the arrows in the process model. For this reason, a "control view" is used to restore the relationships between the components. The control view is an essential ARIS component that distinguishes it from other proposed architectures.

By introducing the control view into the architecture, it is possible to retain the relationships between the views, although previously the views were isolated and could therefore be treated in a more simplified form. The subsequent explicit input of the relationships between the views makes it possible to systematically enter all the relationships.

This process results in the four ARIS views shown in Figure A.I.05, which will be discussed in more detail in later sections.

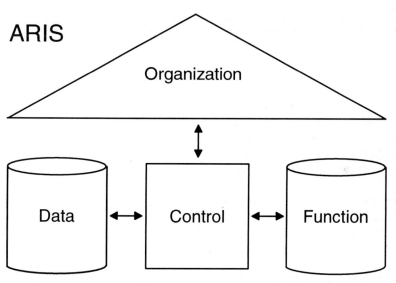

Fig. A.I.05: ARIS views of the process model

A.I.2.2 Descriptive Levels

The ARIS resource view is structured in accordance with a lifecycle concept of an information system's descriptive levels.

The implementation of business processes with the aid of information technology is generally described by differentiated lifecycle models in the form of levels or phases. In ARIS, however, the lifecycle does not have the significance of a procedural model for developing an information system; rather it defines the different levels based on their proximity to information technology. This follows a three-tier model (see Figure A.I.06).

The description of the operational business problem is the point of departure in systems development. This step incorporates the information technology options for supporting business processes and decisions through DP-oriented business administration (see *Scheer, Principles of Efficient Information Management, 1991*). The description encompasses rough business processes that are oriented very closely to user objectives and user language. Therefore, only semi-formal descriptive methods are used to represent the description of the business problem. Because of their lack of detail and their highly technical vocabulary, they cannot serve as a starting point for a formalized translation into implementation.

The requirements definition has to describe the business application to be supported in such formalized language so that it can be used as the starting point for a consistent translation into information technology. The requirements definition is very closely associated with the problem description, as expressed by the width of the double-headed arrow.

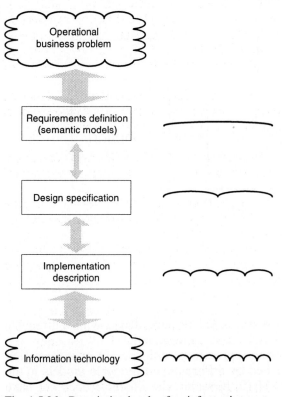

Fig. A.I.06: Descriptive levels of an information system

At the design specification level, the conceptual environment of the requirements definition is transferred to the categories of the DP conversion. The modules or user transactions that execute the functions are defined instead of the functions themselves. This level can also be thought of as an adaptation of the requirements description to general information technology interfaces. The requirements definition and the design specification should be loosely linked. This means that a design specification can be changed without modifying the requirements definition. This loose link should not mean, however, that the requirements definition and the design specification can be developed in isolation from one another. After completing the requirements definition, it is much more important that the business content be determined in such a way that DP-oriented considerations such as system output do not have an influence on the requirements content.

In the third step, the implementation description, the design specification is transferred to concrete hardware and software components, thus establishing the physical link to information technology.

The "waterfall" model for the development process should be avoided at all costs when defining these descriptive levels. It is much more important to distinguish between the architecture of an information system and the procedural model for developing an information model. It is common knowledge that phases can be networked in the form of overlaps and processing loops. At first glance, it would appear that prototyping— i.e., the rapid implementation of a technical concept to obtain an impression of its quality—would contradict the idea of a clear division of the descriptive levels.

This is also true of object-oriented approaches, for which consistency of the design objects from requirements definition to implementation description is an important paradigm (see *Heß, Wiederverwendung von Software 1993*).

Nevertheless, the different descriptive levels of an information system continue to exist, even if they do not lead to a sequential procedural model.

The levels are characterized by different update cycles (see Figure A.I.06). The updating frequency is highest at the information technology level and lowest at the requirements definition level.

The implementation description is very closely linked to the development of information technology and is thus subject to ongoing revision as a result of technological changes such as the development of new database systems, networks, hardware, etc.

The requirements definition level is particularly significant because it is both a long-term repository of collective business knowledge and at the same time a point of departure for further steps in generating the implementation description. For this reason, emphasis is placed on the view of developing requirements definitions or semantic models.

The focus is therefore on creating requirements definitions, since they possess the longest lifecycle within the information system, and through their close affinity to the description of the business problem they also document the heaviest use of the information system. The requirements definition is the link between users and the initial implementation of their problem description into a DP language.

The ARIS architecture is developed using the division process and the descriptive levels, including the initial business solution (see Figure A.I.07).

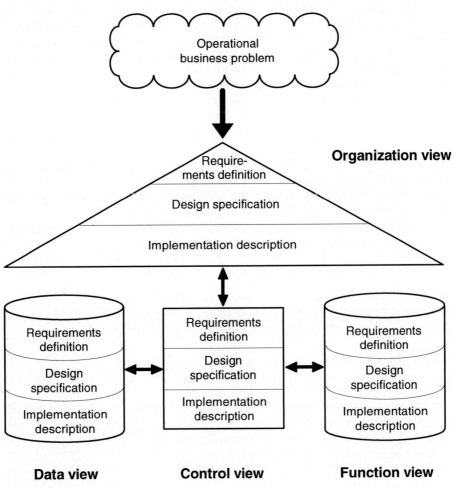

Fig. A.I.07: ARIS-Architecture

A.II Selecting and Representing the Description Methods Employed

The ARIS architecture's descriptive views and levels are fixed. Including the business problem description, which serves as the point of departure, they comprise thirteen components. What is now necessary is to select and portray suitable description methods for each component to the extent necessary for their use in this book. For a more in-depth discussion, see the relevant literature on computer-assisted software engineering (CASE) as well as *Scheer, Architecture of Integrated Information Systems, 1992*.

The criteria for selecting the methods are:
- Simplicity of the means of portrayal
- Suitability for the subject contents that are specifically to be expressed
- The ability to use consistent methods for all applications to be portrayed
- The existing or anticipated degree of familiarity with the methods and
- The degree of independence of the methods from technical developments in information and communication technology.

The initial business situation should show the weaknesses of the existing information system in condensed form and thus reveal those areas where improvements are necessary. The process chain diagram (PCD) provides a condensed representation of this relationship and an overview of the information (sub)system to be treated. The PCD contains all the ARIS descriptive views (functions, organization, data and their interaction). Figure A.II.01 illustrates an excerpt from a target concept for a customer order processing system.

The second and third columns list the functions of the business process together with the events they generate and through which they are initiated. The logical interdependencies can be illustrated with linking operators. The input and output data accessed by the functions are shown in the next column in the form of data clusters.

The "Type of Processing" column provides additional information about DP function support, i.e., whether processing is interactive or batch/automatic. The left column of the PCD specifies the organizational unit (department) responsible for each function.

Process chain diagrams are primarily geared toward representing the interaction between all ARIS components. They are thus created at a relatively high level of consolidation for describing the initial situation. Individual columns can also be masked.

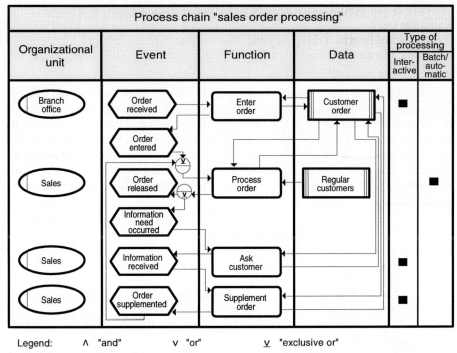

Legend: ∧ "and"   ∨ "or"   <u>∨</u> "exclusive or"

Fig. A.II.01: Process chain diagram

This book will use process chain diagrams to provide an initial overview of a new business process. They will also be used in an expanded form to represent links between ARIS levels within the framework of the control view.

A.II.1 Requirements Definitions

A.II.1.1 Requirements Definition: The Function View (Functional Structure, Process Sequence, Processing Forms)

There is a function for each process, which describes the "what" factor. It creates or modifies objects. A complex function can be broken down into subfunctions.

Breaking down functions serves to reduce their complexity. This process is concretized by the description methods of hierarchy diagrams or function trees.

Hierarchy diagrams are self-explanatory, as shown in the order handling example (from *Scheer, Principles of Efficient Information Management, 1991, p. 132*) in Figure A.II.02.

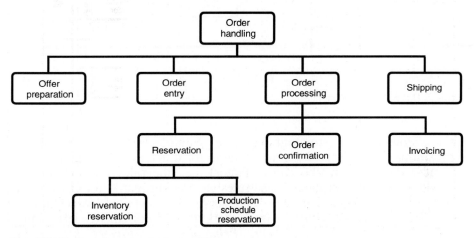

Fig. A.II.02: Function tree: Order handling

Functions are represented by round-cornered boxes and can be divided across several hierarchy levels, as illustrated by the subfunctions of "order processing" and "reservation." The division process ends when functions are reached that are processed in one job cycle, i.e., when it no longer makes sense from a business standpoint to divide them. These functions are termed elementary functions. There are frequently no clear criteria for determining the functional structure (see *Scheer, Architecture of Integrated Information Systems, 1992, p. 65*), although some possible breakdown criteria include the division of subfunctions according to their approximate temporal sequence, the fact that they process the same information objects or that they do so using the same operations.

The functional structure makes a complex function more manageable. It is, however, static—i.e., the order and the temporal sequence in which the subfunctions are processed in the process context is unclear. This process view is introduced by positional relationships, which are represented by arrows.

A process is a time-consuming event that is initiated by a start event and terminated by an end event. Depending on process events, different process branches and loops can follow a process.

These branches can be evaluated with respect to the probabilities of their occurrence—in addition, different logical relationships are possible within incoming and outgoing positional relationships (see *Scheer,*

Architecture of Integrated Information Systems, 1992, p. 70). Figure A.II.03 shows several representation elements.

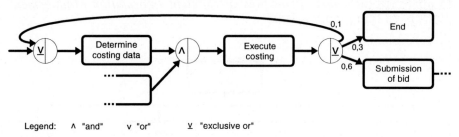

Fig. A.II.03: Process sequence

Nassi/Shneiderman structograms (see *Nassi/Shneiderman, Flowchart Techniques 1973, pp. 12 ff.*) are suitable for a detailed description of the functional execution (the "how" factor), i.e., the rules for transforming input data into output data. These rules are used primarily for creating the design specification, but they also serve as a detailed description of business algorithms within the framework of the requirements definition.

Figure A.II.04 (from *Scheer, Principles of Efficient Information Management, 1991, p. 133*) shows the control structure symbols used in the structogram and illustrates an excerpt from order processing.

Structograms are suitable for describing both global relationships as well as detailed processes. They are also suitable for differentiated representations of rules for business decisions.

When designing functions, it is necessary to determine how the user affects the process. There is a distinction between two basic forms of processing: automatic processing without user intervention and interactive processing.

In processing without user intervention, similar processes are grouped together and processed in a self-contained "lot" (batch processing).

Batch-oriented planning runs are frequently made at predetermined times (e.g., at the end of each week or at the end of each month) for the next planning period.

Because user-controlled processing is especially suitable for decision-oriented applications, it will be emphasized here. Automatic functions, on the other hand, frequently comprise additional processing of operation-related events in job accounting systems.

The criteria for case-oriented processing are:
-    Currency
-    Plausibility check
-    Iterative modification of an initial solution
-    Interactive decision process.

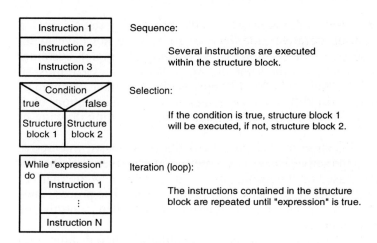

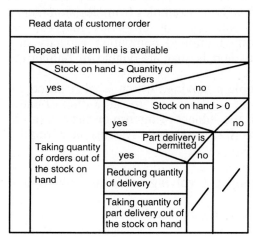

Fig. A.II.04: Control structures of structured programming and structogram of order processing

If data are unforeseeably or continuously required, they must be continually updated. This is particularly important for master data (data that are updated over an extended period of time) such as article, customer, vendor and employee data, which are accessed by many applications.

Master data administration is a typical interactive application because of the necessity of keeping master data up-to-date.

Interactive processing is advisable if data are entered and the system immediately executes a logical check by comparing them with master data, so that if there is an error, the user can instantly make corrections. The advantage of this type of processing is that the user is very familiar with the procedure and can therefore correct mistakes more easily in real time, as opposed to the post-processing corrections that were typical of batch-oriented processing and its output of awkward error listings.

Interactive processing allows users to save processing steps from an initial solution during iterative modification, so they do not have to re-enter data from scratch. For example, when creating a complex customer order, a previous order from the same customer can be accessed, most of its data imported and the necessary changes made. A further example of this is the iterative modification of a geometric representation of a customer-related order for a different version from an existing drawing of a similar part.

The interactive decision process is a particularly intensive interactive form with many interactive steps. Users define alternatives that the DP system evaluates. Based on the results, users can develop new alternatives and in turn allow the system to check their ramifications. The process ends when the user reaches a satisfactory solution, which then controls the further functional sequence.

Interactive problem solving is especially meaningful when dealing with poorly structured decision problems. Some examples from decision theory include problems with multiple objectives or problems that can be accurately solved only by applying unlimited computing capacity and therefore must resort to heuristic models that are viable in human/DP interaction.

In recent years, interactive problem solving, which is also based on highly user-oriented principles in comparison to algorithm-oriented optimization approaches, has been the subject of intense discussion in the area of decision support systems (DSS). Expert systems also require powerful interactive interfaces.

Figure A.II.05 shows an example involving both interactive and automatic processing.

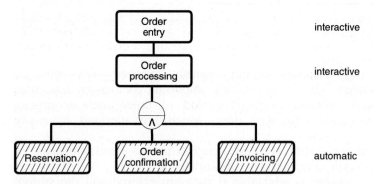

Fig. A.II.05: Example of interactive and automatic processing forms

A.II.1.2 Requirements Definition: The Organization View

Up to now, the role of the organizational structure was given little regard within the information system—functional requirements frequently dominate during its design. Many modern business concepts discussed under buzzwords such as "lean production" or "CIM," however, are very closely associated with the organizational structure. For this reason, the organizational structure was introduced into the ARIS architecture as an independent descriptive level.

In order for human beings to be able to handle complex social structures such as enterprises, these structures must be broken down into manageable units. The rules required for this process are referred to as "organization." If the structuring process relates to the company as a static system, the set of rules designed for this purpose is referred to as structural organization. If the structuring relates to tasks to be performed by the enterprise, the design of the rules for breaking down the tasks is referred to as procedural organization. ARIS deals with questions of procedural organization—e.g., forming process sequences for a task—in the function description. They are discussed again in the control section of the requirements definition along with questions involving the distribution of functions among task performers and event-driven process chains. Therefore, problems of structural organization are treated in this section.

The principal task of the organizational structure is coordinating as inexpensively as possible the communication needs that arise from breaking down a complex unit.

Organizations' coordination efforts are governed by their environmental conditions. For this reason, there is no generally "optimal" organizational structure. Picot (see *Picot, Organisationsstrukturen der Wirtschaft 1993, pp. 52 ff.*) cites the characteristics of the task as well its rate of change as influencing factors for organizational forms. Specificity is understood as the degree of uniqueness of the task. If both dimensions are categorized as "high" and "low" and compared to one another, the four-field case shown in Figure A.II.06 results.

Market-like relationships frequently develop when standardized tasks are performed that exhibit a low degree of specificity and are subject to few modifications over time. Coordination efforts are minimal here, since virtually no agreements are usually necessary between customers and vendors, and both can be exchanged without high coordination costs. If standardized tasks change frequently, framework contracts must be drawn up under which changing tasks can be performed. Figure A.II.06 terms this case a strategic network. Its practical importance is taking on increasing significance between producers and suppliers in the automotive industry.

While outsourcing frequently provides the most cost-effective solution for tasks with low specificity ratings, high-specificity tasks require an internal solution, i.e., in-house production. For tasks involving minimal change, a hierarchical organizational structure is the most cost-effective

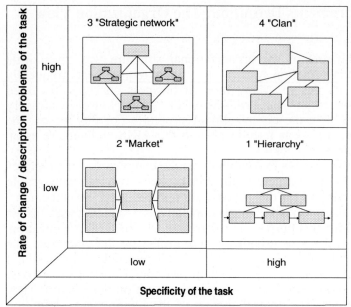

Fig. A.II.06: Organizational forms
(see *Picot, Organisationsstrukturen der Wirtschaft 1993, p. 53*)

solution with respect to coordination and communication costs. In this regard, strict rules governing the chain of command and reporting channels can be implemented so that the organization functions like a highly efficient machine (see *Robey, Designing Organizations 1990, p. 83*).

In a changing environment, for example, as a result of technical progress, the strict bureaucratic rules of a hierarchical organization are less appropriate. In this case, the organization must behave more organically, i.e., like a living organism (see *Robey, Designing Organizations 1990, p. 142*). Figure A.II.06 terms this the "clan" form. The basis of a clan is a strong, collectively produced, continually evolving culture (see *Picot, Organisationsstrukturen der Wirtschaft 1993, p. 53*). Coordination occurs because of the orientation toward common goals and ideas rather than because of strict bureaucratic rules. This organizational form is especially typical for solving ad hoc problems.

Because of the high degree of change in the business environment (market globalization, developments in technology, political developments), strategic networks and intercompany clans are expected to take on increasing importance as organizational forms.

A difference that is related to the difference between hierarchical and clan-oriented organizational forms is the one between a functional structure and a self-contained structure (see *Robey, Designing Organizations 1990, p. 233*). In a functional structure, several units participate in accomplishing an overall task, which results in considerable coordination and information effort between the functions. In a self-contained organizational structure, each organizational unit is functionally integrated within itself and can thus process a task in its entirety—but the units do require coordination.

In a functional structure, one department (Production, Engineering, Purchasing, Sales, Finance and Accounting) is given responsibility for all areas and products. The advantage of this approach is that employees can be highly specialized. A disadvantage of a highly departmentalized functional structure, however, is the high communication and coordination effort between the subfunctions.

Information systems design has long been oriented toward this broad functional organizational structure. In a structure of this type, however, the interrelationship between the individual functions is difficult to produce, for instance, by using the same data objects. For this reason, the discussion of integrated data processing led to the demand for a unified database for supporting the different functions (see Figure A.I.02). Functional integration, however, virtually eliminates the goal of complexity reduction inherent in the functional structure.

As a result, functional integration is accompanied by the process of dividing the complexity on the basis of other criteria, such as territories/locations or products (see Figure A.I.02).

Substructuring by territory is an especially good choice for sales functions in order to better address regional factors such as laws or languages.

In a product-oriented organizational structure, organizational units are formed for each product and/or product group. The structuring criteria of territories/locations and/or products are better suited for self-contained organizational forms.

As many functions as possible that are responsible for an object class are integrated within a product group. This makes it possible to decrease coordination and communication effort between the individual processing

Fig. A.II.07,a: Functional organizational structures

functions. At this stage, however, there is the problem of brokering between the object-oriented subsystems.

This is the reason for hybrid organizational forms. Figure A.II.07,a shows how a central purchasing department responsible for all products can be organized in a functional structure.

A purchasing event must pass through all subfunctions, which can result in significant coordination problems.

In a purely object-oriented structure (see Figure A.II.07,b), on the other hand, purchasing departments are set up for different product groups. These departments comprise self-contained groups that process all activities involved in a purchasing process. In this organizational form, however, synergy effects that arise **between** the product groups are not exploited. For example, during price negotiations with a supplier, only the orders from one group are taken into account instead of including all purchase orders.

	$P_1 ... P_g$	$P_h ... P_m$	$P_n ... P_r$	$P_s ... P_N$
Supplier selection				
Terms				
Planning				
Ordering				
Checking and auditing invoices				

Fig. A.II.07,b: Object-oriented organizational structure

	$P_1 ... P_g$	$P_h ... P_m$	$P_n ... P_r$	$P_s ... P_N$
Supplier selection				
Terms				
Planning				
Ordering				
Checking and auditing invoices				

Fig. A.II.07,c: Mixed (hybrid) organizational structure

In Figure A.II.07,c, therefore, the "supplier selection" and "terms" functions are performed centrally for all purchases and thus conform to a functional structure, while the functions of "planning," "ordering" and "checking and auditing invoices" are decentralized according to object-oriented structural criteria. The object-oriented units can plan and order the components tailored to their special needs quickly and in a process-oriented manner, while the central functions of "supplier selection" and "terms" reflect the synergy effects of the overall company vis-à-vis the suppliers.

As a result of the process view emphasized in this book, preference is given to flexible organizational structures. It should be added that several structural criteria for forming organizational structures can exist parallel to one another (e.g., function-, product- and territory-oriented views). In the case of job accounting views, this is necessitated by profit center concepts.

At the same time, the "clan" and "self-contained" organizational forms are followed, and independently operating organizational units are supported that are both decentralized and networked with each other so that they can operate with a high degree of functionality. The synergy effect between the decentralized units is also utilized, so that the organizational form represented in Figure A.II.07,c, which is designated as networked decentralization, is the organizational model used here (see also *Zülch/Grobel, Schlanke Produktion - eine Herausforderung an die Organisationsplanung 1993*).

Operatively, the processes are handled in the decentralized units. The relationships between the decentralized units are treated at the superordinate coordination level. As a rule, these problems are not as closely linked in terms of time as the processes within the process-oriented organizational unit. Further planning units can be formed that encompass several coordination units. The planning functions can also be coordinated at a superordinate level. This planning level principle in a process sequence is represented later in this book by the leitstand concept illustrated in Figure A.II.08.

The organizational chart is a typical form for representing organizational structures. It describes the organizational units (i.e., task performers) that are formed according to the corresponding criteria and their relationships (others are job descriptions, task structure diagrams and functional diagrams, see *Lehner et al., Organisationslehre für Wirtschaftsinformatiker 1991, pp. 264 ff.*).

Designating the chain of command within the organization establishes the links between the organizational units. This also determines the reporting channels within the organization. Figure A.II.09,a illustrates an organizational chart for a five-tier business organization showing the chain of command. If the respective functional responsibilities are noted for the units, the organizational chart illustrates the division of the business tasks.

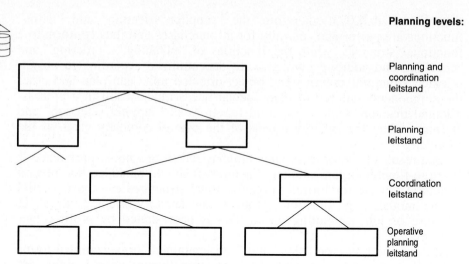

Planning levels:

Planning and coordination leitstand

Planning leitstand

Coordination leitstand

Operative planning leitstand

Fig. A.II.08: Four-tier leitstand concept

The differences between functional and process-oriented organizational views have already been mentioned. Figure A.II.09,b illustrates this once again by showing the order processing process in a function-oriented organizational chart. The order is entered in a sales office, the appropriate branch office is notified, the order is consolidated into a production plan along with other orders at the product area level, assigned to a specific plant and produced in a production area.

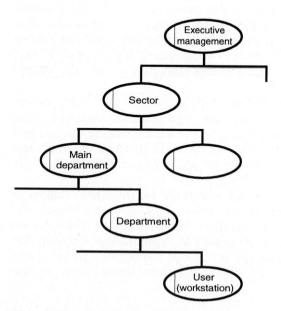

Fig. A.II.09,a: Organizational chart

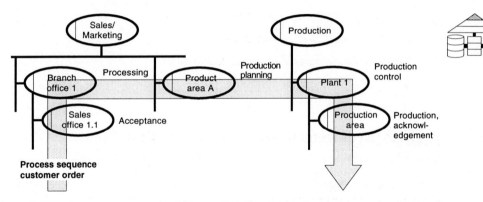

Fig. A.II.09,b: Process sequence within a function-oriented company organizational structure

This book will use the functional organizational chart in Figure A.II.10,a and the process-oriented organizational chart in Figure A.II.10,b as reference models. The principal business processes involved are logistics and product development, as well as information and coordination processes. The main outline of the book follows this structure, which will be elaborated in later sections.

The idea of networked decentralization according to the leitstand concept in Figure A.II.08 is followed for depicting the planning level within the business processes.

By comparing function-oriented and process-oriented organizational models, it is possible to:

Fig. A.II.10,a: Reference model of a function-oriented structural organization

-    Better illustrate the problems of functional structural organization with respect to process-oriented procedural organization

-    Illustrate the primacy of the structural organization over the procedural organization and

-    More accurately represent the requirements that changes in structural organization impose on business process analysis.

Fig. A.II.10,b: Process-oriented structural organization

A.II.1.3 Requirements Definition: The Data View

Methodically speaking, the description of the requirements definition of the data view is especially demanding. Whereas, for example, the function view requires only **one** concept, namely the function, many concepts are used within the data view, such as entity types, relationship types, attributes, domains, etc.

The function description requires only two types of relationships between the functions: hierarchical subordination and predecessor/ successor relationships. Many relationships that are significantly more difficult to classify can exist between data objects, however.

It has been found that the data requirements definition is playing an increasingly important role in information systems development. The easier it is to use higher programming languages to create supplemental functions in existing programming systems, the more important it becomes to provide these functions with the proper data structures. Moreover, considerable effort is involved in changing data structures.

These factors require that more attention be paid to the data view requirements definition. Chen's entity-relationship model is the most widespread designing method (see *Chen, Entity-Relationship-Model 1976*). The basic model will be discussed first, followed by a summary of the important extensions to it. A subsequent example will clarify the design process. Since alternative forms of graphical representation exist for the entity-relationship model, these will be compared to the representations used in this book.

A.II.1.3.1 The Basic ER Model

The ER model distinguishes between entities, attributes and relationships. All three concepts can be viewed at the instance level and at the type level. The type level represents sets.

Entities are real or abstract objects of interest for a given segment of an enterprise's tasks. This segment can, for example, be a business process. According to the structural model in Figure A.I.04, the data objects of interest are objects in the process chain environment or initial and/or resulting events. For the customer order processing process, these objects are, for example, customers, articles or orders. Entities are described by attributes. If the same entities are grouped into sets, they are designated as entity types. Entity types will be identified by capital letters and depicted as rectangular boxes in the ER model diagram.

Attributes are properties of entities, for example, the customer number, name and address of the entity type CUSTOMER. The difference between entity and attribute depends on the purpose within a given context. For example, in a different context, addresses can be used as entities and not as an attribute of CUSTOMER. The association between CUSTOMER and ADDRESS would then be produced from a relationship.

Since the difference between entity and attribute can only be determined from the context, design problems can occur. To avoid these problems, some models forego this distinction (e.g., the NIAM model, see *Nijssen/Halpin, Conceptual Schema and Relational Database Design 1989*). Distinguishing between entity and attribute can be helpful, however, since stronger classification of the design objects also supports the design process. For this reason, this book will make this distinction in the entity-relationship model.

The distinguishing feature between entity and attribute is that entities possess attributes. Attributes, on the other hand, cannot possess additional attributes. If a characteristic that is first identified as an attribute is described by further attributes, it becomes an entity type. One indicator that this is an entity type is if relationships extend from it to other entity types. In this case, the object does not need to possess any other attributes to qualify as an entity type.

A **relationship** is a logical link between two or more entities. While entities can exist in isolation, relationships can only exist in combination with the affected entities. A relationship type between CUSTOMER and ADDRESS could be RESIDES AT. Relationship types are also written in uppercase. They are represented in the ER model diagram by diamond-shaped boxes and linked to the corresponding entity types (see Figure A.II.11).

It is not always easy to distinguish between entity type and relationship type, as each situation depends on the context.

A guideline for distinguishing between entity type and relationship type is that entity types, as a rule, can only be expressed by nouns; relationships, on the other hand, only by verbs (see *Howe, Data Base Design 1983, p. 95*). A relationship type is written from left to right. Thus, Figure A.II.11 only makes sense when read as "customer resides at address" and not as "address resides at customer." CUSTOMER, therefore, is a subject entity type and ADDRESS is a predicate entity type. Frequently, however, it is not so easy to determine in which direction to

Fig. A.II.11: Representation of a relationship in the entity-relationship model (ERM or Chen Diagram)

read the model. This difficulty can only be overcome by carefully choosing superordinate concepts, for example, "belongs to" in this case.

Attributes can be assigned both to entity types and to relationship types (see Figure A.II.12).

Attributes are represented by circles in the ER model diagram. The value ranges of attributes are termed domains. The assignments between elements of the value range and elements of the entity and relationship types, in turn, are themselves relationships and are represented by lines, which are assigned names.

Relationship types are distinguished according to the number of entity types linked to them, i.e., unary, binary or n-ary relationships.

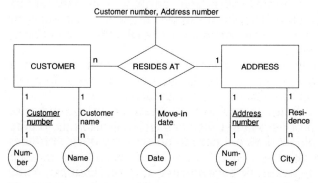

Fig. A.II.12: Assignment of attributes in the entity-relationship model

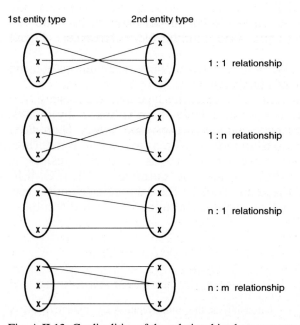

Fig. A.II.13: Cardinalities of the relationships between two entity types

The cardinality or degree of complexity of a relationship indicates how many other entities are assigned to a certain entity of a certain type. This is expressed by 1:1, 1:n, n:1 and n:m indicators (see Figure A.II.13).

In a 1:1 relationship, exactly one element of the second set is assigned to each element of the first set, and vice versa. In a 1:n relationship, exactly one element of the second set is assigned to each element of the first set, but n elements of the first set are assigned to each element of the second set. The n:1 relationship expresses the same situation in reverse order. In an n:m relationship, several elements of the second set are assigned to one element of the first set, and vice versa.

The cardinalities of this relationship type are shown in the lines of the entity-relationship diagram (see Figure A.II.12). A 1:1 relationship must exist between one entity type and at least one domain (value range of an attribute). The values of this domain can identify the entity instances; in the example, these are the customer number and the address number, which are therefore underlined.

Relationships are identified by merging the key values of the affected entity types—thus, the RESIDES AT relationship is identified by indicating the customer number and the address number.

Because parallel lines between an entity type and a relationship type are permissible (see the representation of bills of materials later in the book), role names must be assigned to the decision boxes.

The cardinalities of a relationship type are directed from the appropriate entity types to the number of relationships assigned to it. Thus, the "n" of the relationship type RESIDES AT in Figure A.II.12 indicates that a customer can take part in n instances of the relationship type RESIDES AT. From the point of view of the entity type "address," exactly one relationship that points to one customer is to be assigned to each address instance. Cardinality indicates how many relationship lines can proceed from one entity, as in Figure A.II.13.

It should be noted, however, that Chen's original work interpreted the cardinality indications in a different manner. In order to avoid unnecessary confusion, however, this book will use what is today the generally accepted, clearer formulation, particularly in cases in which more than two entity types are linked by a relationship type (see *Schlageter/Stucky, Datenbanksysteme 1983, p. 51*).

A.II.1.3.2 Extended ER Models

Chen's entity-relationship model, published in 1976, has undergone further development at many conferences and in numerous publications (see the collected works of Chen (*Chen, Entity-Relationship Approach 1981*), Davis/Jajodia/Ng/Yeh (*Davis/Jajodia/Ng/Yeh, Entity-Relationship Approach 1983*) as well as the proceedings from the Annual International Conference on the Entity-Relationship Approach).

This book will only discuss those extended models that are significant to this discussion.

A.II.1.3.2.1 Extending the Model with Design Operators

Data model design operators have been developed that provide formal support during the design process. Although the design is primarily an intellectual process, these operators help prevent random data structures. Their use ensures a systematic procedure and provides the viewer of an existing data structure with insights as to its creation.

Proceeding from existing concepts, new concepts are produced using design operators. The entire design process is carried out largely at the specialized knowledge level. This means that business administration knowledge is necessary during the entire design process when designing data structures for business applications. The ongoing reflection of business conditions from the point of view of their data structures leads designers either to redesign known conditions based on a new view or to create new business relationships. For the most part, this book uses the terms "design" and "modeling" synonymously, thereby avoiding the distinction emphasized by Wedekind (see *Wedekind, Datenbanksysteme I 1991, pp. 34 ff.*).

Design rules for supporting data structuring have been developed based on the works of Smith/Smith (see *Smith/Smith, Databases Abstractions 1977a* and *Smith/Smith, Databases Abstractions 1977b*). These rules have been supplemented and refined by other authors (see *Brodie, Database Abstraction 1981; Codd, Extending a Database Relation Model 1979; Hammer/McLeod, Database Description 1981; Ortner, Semantische Modellierung 1985; Wedekind, Datenbanksysteme I 1991*). Although overlaps exist between the different models due to concepts that are not yet fully developed, four basic design operators have been established: **classification, generalization, association** and **grouping**.

These operators will also be used in the subsequent discussion of object-oriented design.

Classification
In **classification**, the same elements are identified and assigned to a concept. In this sense, one element is identical to another if it can be described by the same properties (attributes). For example, if a person can be described by customer number, address, total sales, etc., he or she belongs to the "customers" class.

The classification operation serves to identify objects (entities) that belong to one object type (entity type).

Generalization/Specialization
Chen used generalization early on as an additional representational element (see *Dogac/Chen, Entity-Relationship Model 1983, p. 360*).

In **generalization**, similar object types are grouped under one superordinate object type (see Figure A.II.14). The object type CUSTOMER and the object type SUPPLIER are generalized under the generic concept BUSINESS ASSOCIATE. Properties that are common to the initial objects are transferred to the generic object type, so that they must be described only by attributes that deviate from them. The formation of the new concept BUSINESS ASSOCIATE is represented graphically by the additional triangle. This element is referred to as an "is-a" relationship.

The generalization process can also occur in reverse: **specialization**, in which a generic concept is divided into subconcepts (BUSINESS ASSOCIATE is split into CUSTOMER and SUPPLIER). For this reason, there are no directional arrows connecting the lines between the superordinate and subordinate concepts. Specialization involves the inheritance of properties from the generalized object type to the specialized object type, which can posses its own attributes or modify "inherited" ones.

While specialization supports a top-down data structuring approach by dividing up complex concepts, generalization involves a bottom-up approach, since in this case, superordinate objects are formed for existing detailed concepts.

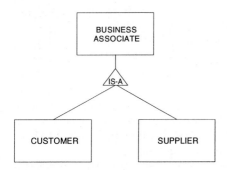

Fig. A.II.14: Generalization of subsets to main sets

A distinction can be drawn as to whether the formation of subsets must occur without overlaps, i.e., in disjunct sets, or whether overlaps are permissible. For example, a customer can also be a supplier. If overlaps are not allowed, this problem can be circumvented by introducing a third group "CUSTOMER as well as SUPPLIER."

In the formulation used later in this book, overlaps are permissible in the subsets since the explicit consideration of the "as-well-as classes" would unnecessarily inflate the representation. Sinz formulates stricter forms of requirements generalization (see *Sinz, Das Entity-Relationship-Modell 1990, p. 24*) and cites additional relevant literature.

Further examples of generalization are the superordinate concept ORDER and the subordinate concepts CUSTOMER ORDER, PURCHASE ORDER and PRODUCTION ORDER.

Parallel generalization criteria are also valid. For example, business associates can be divided into domestic and foreign associates (see Figure A.II.15).

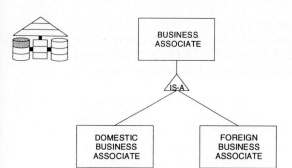

Fig. A.II.15: Generalization / Specialization

Subsequent representations will not always show all subsets of a superordinate concept in their entirety. Strict requirements of disjunction and completeness are therefore **not** explicitly specified.

Generalization/specialization activity reveals redundancies, for example, by identifying a concept that has been treated as independent in practice as in fact being a specialization of a superordinate concept. Thus, for example, the cost objective concept can be interpreted from the standpoint of cost accounting as a generalization of the concepts used in the operative systems: article, customers, area, etc.

Association

Association describes the formation of new concepts by combining the existing different object types. The new concept can be a repository of new properties.

As a combination of different concepts into one new concept, association is expressed in the ER model by the formation of relationship types. In this sense, a relationship type groups the entity types associated with it.

It can, however, also be applied to relationships, in that these relationships are viewed at one of the next levels as entity types and therefore can themselves be a starting point for relationships (see *Mayr/Dittrich/Lockemann, Datenbankentwurf 1987, p. 510; Knolmayer/Myrach, Anforderungen an Tools 1990, p. 93; Sinz, Das Entity-Relationship-Modell 1990, p. 24*).

The example in Figure A.II.16 should be interpreted as follows:

The first form of association discussed here is used to form the relationship type ORDER HEADER from the entity types CUSTOMER and TIME. The key attributes CUSTOMER NUMBER (CNO) and DATE form the complex key to the order header. Because one order can encompass several items that each relate to different ordered articles, the ORDER ITEM relationship exists between the entity types ORDER HEADER and ARTICLE. Since relationships can only exist between entity types, the original relationship type ORDER HEADER is reinterpreted as an entity type.

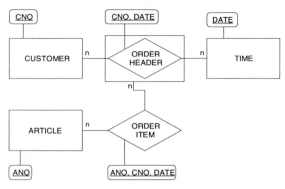

Fig. A.II.16: Reinterpretation of a relationship type

Figure A.II.16 represents this factor by boxing in the diamond. When forming further relationships to other entity types, this modified relationship type is treated as a normal entity type. This procedure is clarified graphically by expressing the development of the relationship type from the participating entity types by drawing the lines to the points of the diamonds. Instead of leading to the diamond, however, the lines from the reinterpreted entity types lead to the edge of the rectangle surrounding it.

Many publications merely interpret **pre-existing** entity relationship models. This book, however, demonstrates how an ER model is created. This creation process should also be traceable in the finished ER model, as this makes it easier to understand. It is especially important to introduce a concept as a relationship type and to clarify its resulting use as the point of departure for new relationships, since this leads to the formation of complex keys.

Basically, it is possible to abbreviate a complex key by assigning a simple key (e.g., a serial number).

The complete complex keys will be included, however, since they clarify the structural origin of the concepts.

The literature shows a deviation from Figure A.II.16 by illustrating a reinterpretation by enclosing all entity types associated with the relationship (see Figure A.II.17).

In this example, the customer and time data would be incorporated into the order header. This seems unnecessary for the situation illustrated here. The second type of representation is more suitable for explaining the formation of complex information objects that consist of different entity and relationship types. These complex information objects are treated as an entity type in subsequent data structuring. This form of representation thus forms the bridge to object-oriented models, which were developed in response to criticism of the relational data model (see *Härder, Grenzen und Erweiterungsmöglichkeiten relationaler Datenbanksysteme 1989* and *Dittrich, "Nachrelationale" Datenbanktechnologie 1990*).

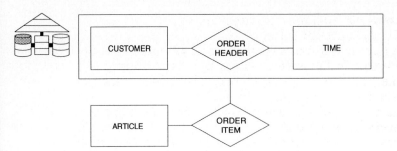

Fig. A.II.17: Alternative representation of the facts in Fig. A.II.16

Grouping

In **grouping**, groups are formed from the elements of an entity set. For example, a company's workstations can be grouped into departments. The new concept "department" is described by its own attributes, such as the name of the department manager or the number of employees in the department. Other examples of this operation include combining individual pieces of equipment into equipment groups or order line items into orders.

The grouping operation can be represented in the entity-relationship model by a 1:n relationship type (compare to Figure A.II.18 for the WORKSTATION and DEPARTMENT example).

Fig. A.II.18: Grouping: 1:n relationship between department and workstation

A.II.1.3.2.2 Event and Condition Representations

When deriving the data view from the process model (see A.I.04), it was stipulated that the data view encompasses the description of events and conditions.

Events are represented in the following ER models by a link with the entity type TIME. Thus, events always involve a relationship between the frame of reference in the microenvironment, as expressed by the status description, and the entity type TIME, whose key attribute "date" provides a unique identifier. The date is measured in the necessary time increment (day, hour, minute, etc.).

When using design operators, all data structures related to events can be recognized by the key attribute "date."

Classical data processing refers to event-oriented data as transaction data. These data are obvious from the data structure, as are the events in Figure A.II.16 ORDER and ORDER ITEM.

Conditions of the reference environment are represented either by entity types or relationship types. In this case, it is not necessary to provide a temporal reference, i.e., no date is necessary as an identifier. Classical data processing refers to these data as "master data."

Special symbols are used to distinguish between event data and status data (see *Campbell, Entity-Relationship Modeling 1992*). This seems unnecessary here, since the event, attribute or characteristic is clear from the temporal reference in the key.

The temporal concept can be applied in the context of data structures for changes in data that occur over time. Thus, each entity, relationship and attribute possesses a record of its creation, its changes and its deletion. The representation of this record is called version management (see *Wilkes, Versionsunterstützung in Datenbanken 1989*). This information is especially important for design data, but it can also play a role in business applications, for example, in the case of personnel data. Although the temporal concept is important in data structures, the rest of the book will only treat it peripherally.

A.II.1.3.2.3 Extended Cardinalities

One semantic elaboration involves specifying upper and lower limits for the number of permissible relationship instances a relationship may have (see *Schlageter/Stucky, Datenbanksysteme 1983, p. 50* or *Webre, An Extended Entity-Relationship Model 1983, p. 193*). The two letters (a, b) in Figure A.II.19 indicate that every entity of the entity type A must participate in **at least** a_1 and **at most** b_1 relationship instances of the type AB.

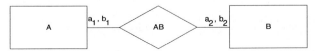

Fig. A.II.19: Representation of upper and lower limits for the number of permissible relationship instances

Every relationship is expressed by two (min, max) degrees of complexity. $0 \leq min \leq 1$ and $1 \leq max \leq *$ (where $*$ is a wildcard) define the range of values. The lower limit $min = 0$ can also indicate that an entity can participate in one relationship, but it is not mandatory.

If minimum and maximum values of only 0 or 1 and/or 1 or $*$ are permitted, the following abbreviations are customary for the four cases of a {min, max} notation (see *Schlageter/Stucky, Datenbanksysteme 1983, p. 51*):

(1, 1) corresponds to 1,
(0, 1) corresponds to c,
(1, *) corresponds to m,
(0, *) corresponds to mc.
(c = choice, m = multiple)

This book will for the most part forego the (min, max) notation and only distinguish whether an entity participates in one or more than one relationship—thus, only "1" and "n" are used as notations. More precisely, this means that "1" stands for {min = 0, max = 1} and "n" for {min = 0, max = n}.

Thus, not all possibilities for exact indication of integrity conditions are used. These frequently occur only with respect to a concrete application, so that it would hardly be possible to derive them from the general representation used here.

A.II.1.3.2.4 Identification and Existential Dependence

By definition, relationship types exist because of the existence of the entity types associated with them; thus, they do not exist in isolation. This also holds true for reinterpreted relationship types. These items are formally different from primary entity types because they are identified by a compound key instead of by a simple key attribute. Reinterpreted relationship types are thus dependent on other entity types both existentially and in terms of identification. They are thus called weak entity types.

In addition, there are entity types that do indeed possess a single key attribute and are still dependent on the existence of other entities (see Figure A.II.20).

These types of existential dependencies are, for example, evidenced by grouping operations. As a rule, dependencies exist in both directions. Thus, for example, a department is only meaningful if it contains at least one workstation, and in return, a workstation is only meaningful if it is assigned to a department.

Existential dependence is also expressed by degrees of complexity; thus, the (min, max) notation for the DEPARTMENT and WORKSTATION example would be expressed by (1, *) and (1, 1).

The definition of existential and identificational dependence results in the assignment of conditions of referential data integrity.

Fig. A.II.20: Existential dependence of department and workstation

A.II.1.3.3 Alternative Forms of Representation

In addition to the graphical representations selected here, which go back to Chen, there are other typical forms of representation in use.

Frequently, relationship types are not explicitly represented; rather, they are indicated by the lines between entity types. Relationship types that possess attributes are then introduced as (weak) entity types.

Many of these representations are oriented toward the elements developed by Bachman for network data models. According to Knolmayer/Myrach (see *Knolmayer/Myrach, Anforderungen an Tools 1990, p. 93*), these representations are inferior to those used in this book.

The table from Knolmayer/Myrach (see Figure A.II.21,a) provides a good overview of the alternative graphical representation options for relationship cardinalities; *Loos, Representation of Data Structures 1993* provides a further comparison.

Numerical notation	Crow's foot notation	Arrow notation	Bachman notation
(0,1)	A ⎯⎯⎯○+ B	A ⎯⎯⎯○▶ B	A ⎯⎯⎯ B
(1,1)	A ⎯⎯⎯++ B	A ⎯⎯⎯+▶ B	
(n,0)	A ⎯⎯○◀ B	A ⎯⎯○▶▶ B	A ⎯⎯⎯▶ B
(n,1)	A ⎯⎯+◀ B	A ⎯⎯+▶▶ B	

Fig. A.II.21,a: Alternative representation options for relationship cardinalities
(see *Knolmayer/Myrach, Anforderungen an Tools 1990, p. 93*)

In the SERM (structured entity-relationship model) approach developed by Sinz (see *Sinz, Das Entity-Relationship-Modell 1990*), the primary and dependent object types are visualized using directional graphs. This also provides a graphical representation of data structure development. The primary (strong) entity types are drawn on the left side, from which weak entity types and relationship types branch off to the right. The representation of the information objects is thus geared toward whether they are "dependent" or "independent" in nature. The corresponding design context determines whether a data object is independent of or dependent on other objects. This book subscribes more to the idea of making the design process traceable, but without emphasizing the result too rigidly as the only possible view. Thus, in the data models shown here, the information objects that belong to one business domain are represented adjacent to one another. Consequently, this practice reveals the design process in that the reinterpretation operation creates a clear record of the design of the information object. As a result, the main difference between the SER model and the model used in this book lies in the graphical representation.

The modeling technique developed by SAP within the framework of its SIMO information modeling technique links the concepts of the SER model with the extended ER model presented in this book (see *Keller/Hechler, Informationsmodell 1991*).

Figure A.II.21,b shows the symbols used in the SAP-ER model notation. No distinction is made between entity types and relationship types during object formation. The logical dependencies between the information objects are expressed by complex reference arrow representations. A distinction is made between hierarchical, aggregate and referential relationships. Hierarchical relationships express unilateral existential dependencies between information objects. Aggregate relationships correspond to the formation of relationship types based on the classical ER model. Referential relationships describe logical dependencies between reinterpreted entity types and primary entity types as exemplified by the extended ER model. Specialization is symbolized by a triangle, analogously to the extended ER model.

In order to convey an impression of the modeling technique, Figure A.II.21,b illustrates the introductory example for the extended ER model together with the symbols from the SAP-ER model. This transfer clearly shows that the fundamental subject contents can be transferred to this form of representation without any loss of information.

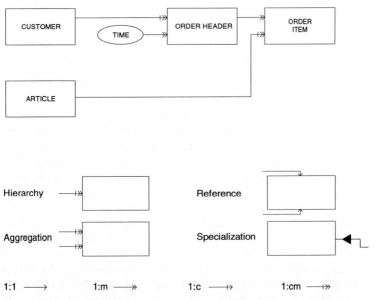

Fig. A.II.21,b: Example of a representation according to the SAP-ERM
(see *Seubert, SAP-Datenmodell 1991, p. 94*)

A.II.1.3.4 Establishing the Design Aids Used

Figure   A.II.22 summarizes the concepts and forms of representation taken from the design operators as well as from the essential structural elements of the ER model that will be used in this book.

Hereinafter, the discussion will focus on the design of entity and relationship types in designing data structures. Completeness in the representation of attributes is not the objective here, as they frequently have only explanatory functions.

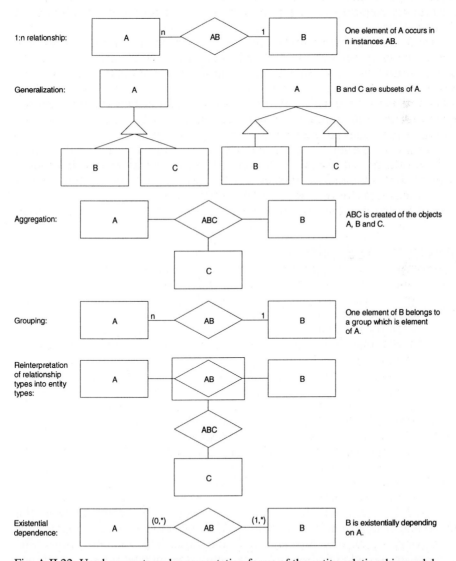

Fig. A.II.22: Used concepts and representation forms of the entity-relationship model

A.II.1.3.5 An Example

Designing a logical data structure is an intellectual process that can be methodically carried out using the design operators cited here. This process, however, does not necessarily lead to the same results if several colleagues perform the same task under the same conditions. To this extent, there is no one "correct" data model, rather only a correct data model for a given set of circumstances. If this set of circumstances is subject to interpretation, different developers will design different data models. The following brief example is intended to illustrate the development of a data model.

An entity-relationship diagram is to be set up for the following set of circumstances:

-       A company is identified by the company name and has additional characteristics such as a legal form, capital stock, etc.
-       A company can own several plants, but a plant can only belong to one company.
-       A plant is identified by the plant name and has characteristics such as location, number of employees, etc.
-       A plant can produce several articles; an article can be produced in several plants.
-       As a parent company, a company can hold an equity interest in other companies (subsidiaries) and at the same time be a subsidiary of one or more other companies.
-       A company can belong to a group, which is identified by the group name.

Hints for solving the problem:
1.   Underline the nouns, which can represent entity types. It is important to ensure that each entity type can be described by properties and/or can exist independently, i.e., does not depend on other concepts in the application environment.
2.   Identify the relationships between entity types by underlining the verbs that link subjects with objects (e.g., owns, belongs to, produces).
3.   Identify the cardinalities. The word "can" denotes undetermined relationships such as "can be 0 or more" or "can be 1 or more." Some indications are not directly expressed in the text, but must be inferred from the context. This is not always unambiguous. Consequently, the solution assumes that a company can exist without plants (thus, the simple cardinality "n"); however, if the concept "company" assumes that it must own at least one plant, this leads to the cardinality "(1,n)."

The models developed in this book relate to typical contents of industrial business administration. These contents are referred to as the contextual background for modeling. The correctness of the models thus refers only to the concurrence with the described contents. Since the contents are selected as broadly as possible, the models possess reference character for individual applications.

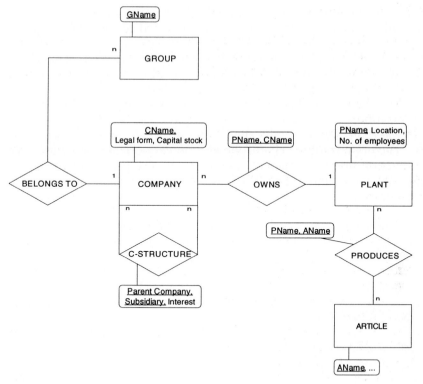

Fig. A.II.23: Solution

A.II.1.4 Requirements Definition: The Control View

The control view deals with the links between functions, organization and data. It reunites the design results, which were initially developed separately for reasons of simplification. The relationships result from the connecting lines between views of the process model in Figure A.I.04.

The discussion will first focus on the representation forms for relationships between two views at a time, and finally, between all three views.

A.II.1.4.1 Combining Functions with Organization

The link between the function view and the organization view first describes the allocation of process chain functions to organizational units in an organizational chart. This allocation determines the degree of functional integration, i.e., the functional steps in a process chain that are to be processed by an organizational unit. At the same time, the decision responsibility inherent in the functions is allocated to the organizational units.

A more detailed analysis shows that not only the functions themselves are allocated, but also their processing forms and thus the degree of user control (interactive or batch).

These stipulations further specify the process chain's structure within the organization.

Figure A.II.24 shows both allocations for the "order processing" process. The organizational chart follows a process-oriented structure. In a purely function-oriented structure, a process can also pass through several parallel functional units. This form of representation is also called a function tier model.

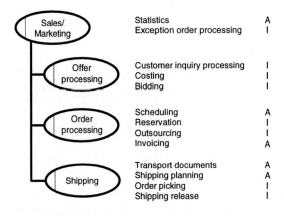

I = Interactive
A = Automatic/batch

Fig. A.II.24: Allocation of functions to processing forms

A.II.1.4.2 Combining Functions with Data

A.II.1.4.2.1 Event Control and Data Flow

Events are both the cause and the result of functions. An event can be defined as the occurrence of an object or the change in a given instance of an attribute. In contrast to an activity, which is a time-consuming occurrence, an event is limited to one point in time. Events are entered in the data view. To this extent, the description of process event control is a link between the data view and the control view.

Events are represented as hexagons. Several functions can originate in parallel from one event—conversely, the completion of several functions can lead to one event. Moreover, different logical relationships, as already described in the function view, can also be transferred to the refined representation form.

Logical operators describe the link between events. A distinction is made between the combination of inputs into an operator and the combinations of outputs. Inputs as well as outputs can be linked by logical "AND" (∧), "OR" (v) and "exclusive OR" (v̲) relationships. The node for representing the linking operators for input and output is divided: The upper area contains the logical symbols for the input links; the lower level, those for the output links. If only **one** input and/or output occurs, a logical symbol is eliminated. If only **one** input and **one** output exist, the node is eliminated. As long as probabilities can be linked with alternative outputs, they are entered into the output line. Figures 25,a-g show several cases of conceivable process structures.

In (d), which contains an "OR" link to the successors, the rule governing selection can be represented as an independent (decision) function, as shown in (e). Function F contains the rules for making decisions in an "OR" scenario, which lead to the intermediate events E3 and E4, which are followed by function F1 or F2. The representation shown in (d) is the preferred short form.

When more complex relationships exist between the completed and the starting functions, e.g., different logical relationships between groups of functions, an operator node can be backed by input and output decision tables.

Linking different operators is also permissible, as example (f) shows.

The logical relationships between functions and events can be explained analogously to the links between events and functions, as in example (d).

The order processing example presented in Figure A.II.03 is supplemented with events in Figure A.II.26,a and represented in an event-driven process chain (EPC). This chain is a link of conditional event networks according to the Petri network theory, for example, as used in the stochastic GERT networking plan technique (see *Pritsker, Papers-Experiences-Perspectives 1990, pp. 246 ff.*).

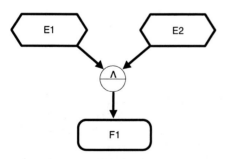

Fig. A.II.25,a: If the events E1 and E2 occur, function F1 starts.

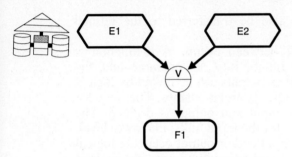

Fig. A.II.25,b: If the events E1 or E2 occur, function F1 starts.

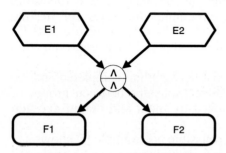

Fig. A.II.25,c: If the events E1 and E2 occur, the functions F1 and F2 start.

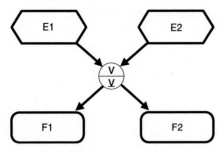

Fig. A.II.25,d: If the events E1 or E2 occur, either function F1 or F2 starts.

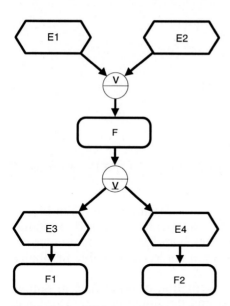

Fig. A.II.25,e: If the events E1 or E2 ccur, the decision function F starts in which the decision on the start of either event E3 or E4 is taken.

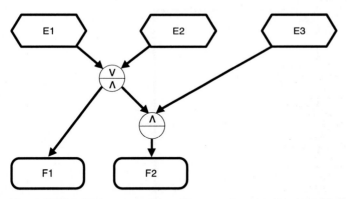

Fig. A.II.25,f: If the events E1 or E2 occur, function F1 starts; if the event (E1 or E2) and the event E3 occur, function F2 starts.

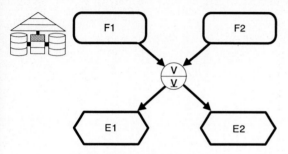

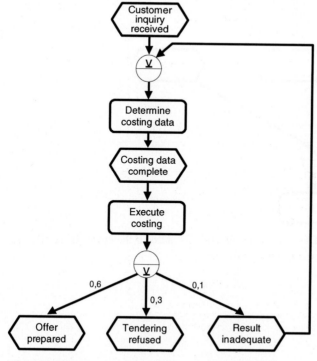

Fig. A.II.25,g: If the function F1 or F2 is completed, either the event E1 or the event E2 happens.

In addition to the graphical representation of event control (as in Figure A.II.26,a), the same set of circumstances can also be expressed in tabular form, as in Figure A.II.26,b. This book uses both forms of representation, although cycles and decision alternatives are not as manageable in tabular form.

In addition to event control, the transformation of input data to output data forms a link between the data view and the function view. DeMarco diagrams are suitable for representing this relationship. According to their basic principles, the EPC representation is supplemented by data flow. Only the most important attributes are indicated as input and output data

Fig. A.II.26,a: Event control (graphical representation)

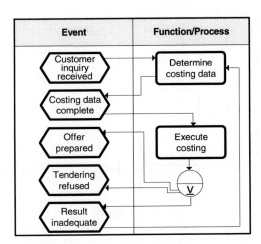

Fig. A.II.26,b: Event control (tabular representation)

for the information objects. Information objects are events that have already been indicated as well as conditions in the information environment. Figures A.II.27,a and A.II.27,b show the examples introduced above, supplemented by data flow.

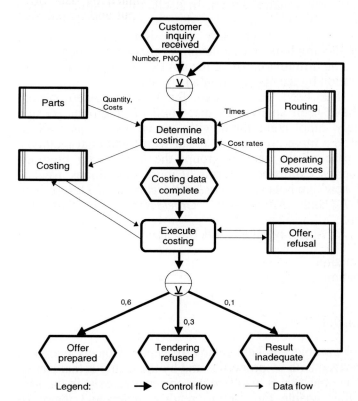

Fig. A.II.27,a: Adding the data flow to Fig. A.II.26,a (graphical representation)

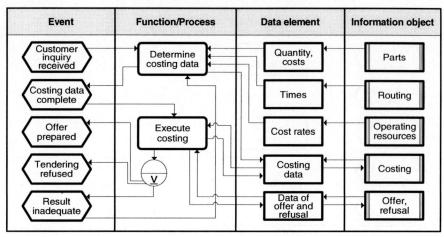

Event	Function/Process	Data element	Information object
Customer inquiry received	Determine costing data	Quantity, costs	Parts
Costing data complete		Times	Routing
Offer prepared	Execute costing	Cost rates	Operating resources
Tendering refused	V	Costing data	Costing
Result inadequate		Data of offer and refusal	Offer, refusal

Fig. A.II.27,b: Adding the data flow to Fig. A.II.26,b (tabular representation)

A.II.1.4.2.2 Object-Oriented Modeling

Object-oriented modeling transfers principles of object-oriented programming to software systems design. In itself, this statement shows that modeling is heavily influenced by design and implementation. Conversely, this leads to a consistency of design objects from the modeling level to the implementation level. Consequently, degrees of latitude that exist at the different levels of the development process are not taken into consideration by the object-oriented approach.

Thus far, there has been no standard for object-oriented system modeling. There have been approaches that build on traditional design methods and merely supplement them with special views, as well as proposals that lead to a more pronounced break with traditional methods. But even in the case of the second group, the break with previous techniques is frequently expressed in terms of more superfluous aspects, e.g., in the use of new symbols (see *Booch, Objectoriented Design with Applications 1991* and *König/Wolf, Objektorientierte Software-Entwicklung 1993*).

The main properties of object-oriented modeling are:

1.   Object formation
2.   Class formation
3.   Inheritance
4.   Polymorphism
5.   Dynamic linking

The definition of an object is kept relatively vague. Objects represent things that are described both by properties and by the methods that can be applied to them. The objective is to define the objects that exist in the user environment and thus enable the user to readily understand them. In contrast to the structuring principle, which reduces the complexity of a set of circumstances by dividing it into different aspects, the object-oriented approach strives to unify data and methods to characterize an object as especially understandable. The object "employee" can, for example, be described by the properties name or hire date and by the methods "calculate salary" or "calculate attendance."

Class formation groups similar objects into object classes. Relationships between classes are represented by lines that can be provided with a designator such as cardinalities (n corresponds to a solid circle at the end of the line, 1 to an empty circle). The role names of objects participating in a relationship can be specified further. Thus, in the example, the relationship "works for" is expressed by the role name "employee" from the point of view of the person and by the role name "employer" from the point of view of the company.

The principle of inheritance transfers methods and attributes of a superordinate class to a subordinate one. Multiple inheritances are also possible, i.e., the inheritance from several superordinate classes to a subordinate class, as well as reverse inheritance, i.e., the inheritance from a subordinate class to a superordinate class.

The polymorphism and dynamic linking properties describe more technical DP properties. Polymorphism expresses the fact that a method can be carried under different names. Dynamic linking means that the components of a system are not merged until runtime.

Of these properties, only inheritance is seen as a genuine contribution of object-oriented design (see *Korson/McGregor, Understanding Object Oriented 1990, p. 42*).

The similarity between the ER model that has been extended by specialization and generalization and the object-oriented view is particularly clear in the design concept introduced by Rumbaugh et. al (see *Rumbaugh, Object-Oriented Modeling and Design 1991*).

Figures A.II.28,a and b illustrate an example of this similarity. The entity types of the ER model correspond to the object types of the OMT

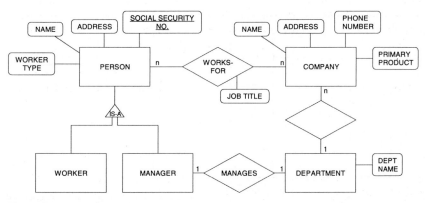

Fig. A.II.28,a: ER Model
(source *Rumbaugh, Object-Oriented Modeling and Design 1991, p. 6*, slightly altered by the author)

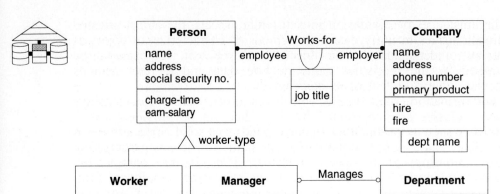

Fig. A.II.28,b: Object diagram
(source *Rumbaugh, Object-Oriented Modeling and Design 1991, p. 84*)

object-oriented approach. Attributes are also used; only the methods are modified. The object diagram is the significant form of representation for the object-oriented approach (see *Rumbaugh, Object-Oriented Modeling and Design 1991, p. 6*).

Figure A.II.29 integrates Rumbaugh's method into the ARIS concept. The object diagrams are components of the control level, since data (entity types and attributes) as well as functions (referred to as methods in the object-oriented model) come together in them.

The dynamic behavior of the system is formed by dynamic models, which describe condition changes. They consist of events and conditions. Conditions are represented by ellipses; events, by the arrows that link them. Conditions can be interpreted as functions that are triggered by events (see *Rumbaugh, Object-Oriented Modeling and Design 1991, p. 84*). For this reason, a close link exists to the event-driven process chains discussed earlier.

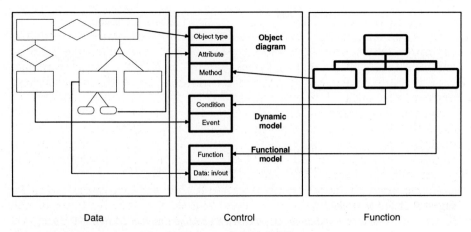

Fig. A.II.29: Integration of the OMT approach into ARIS

The rules governing transformations from input to output data are outlined in the function description. Thus, data flow charts are widely used to represent function models. These input/output relationships represent classical means for representing the system description, so that both the dynamic models as well as the functional models can be embedded into the ARIS concept by linking data views and function views.

ARIS was expressly developed to encompass the object-oriented approach to modeling. At the same time, however, it clearly shows that organizational aspects of the approach have been given little or no consideration. Rumbaugh's object-oriented approach is shown within the framework of requirements planning using an extensive example and citing particularly suitable applications, e.g., the geometrical description of products within the product development process chain.

A.II.1.4.3 Combining Organization with Data

Data can be assigned to a company's organizational units, just as functions can. In an industrial enterprise, it is important to determine which data should be managed on an enterprise-wide basis (e.g., customer and article data), which data should be managed at the plant level (e.g., tooling and maintenance data), which data should be managed at a plant department level (e.g., quality and DNC data), etc. The result is a data tier concept (see *Scheer, Architecture of Integrated Information Systems, 1992, p. 127*). The allocation of data to organizational units also encompasses stipulating permissible data manipulation (creating, deleting, amending or reading).

Data maintenance involves comprehensive responsibility, and therefore data are typically only allocated to one organizational unit per attribute group of an entity type. Nevertheless, weaker forms of manipulation involving different organizational units can be performed for the same data object.

In a mixed object- and function-oriented organizational structure (hybrid organization), the entities must be allocated and attributes must be assigned to organizational units. Figure A.II.30 shows one superordinate central purchasing department as well as two decentralized purchasing departments, each of which is responsible for a particular category of suppliers. Data subsets of a supplier data file are assigned to these organizational units. All entities (suppliers) are assigned to the central department, together with a set of global attributes. A subset of the suppliers, together with all its attributes, is assigned to each decentralized purchasing department. The subsets can also overlap.

At the level of the requirements definition, only two criteria must be determined for partitioning the data. The design specifications of the distributed database determine whether the physical data will be stored centrally or decentrally.

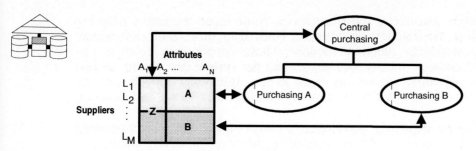

Fig. A.II.30: Interrelations between data and organizational units

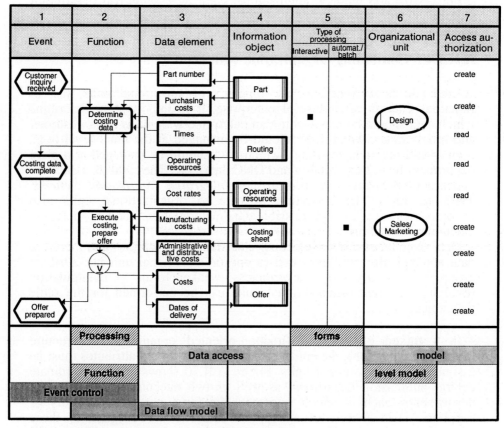

Fig. A.II.31: Process chain "order processing" (extract)
(see *Brombacher, Effizientes Informationsmanagement 1991, p. 129*)

The application control mechanism can also be stipulated by stipulating the data responsibilities of decentralized organizational units. Thus, when a requirement notification for an outsourced part is received, the system can use a supplier number to identify the appropriate purchasing department. Thus, event control can not only initiate the affected function, but also identify the department responsible for the process.

This information is evaluated within the framework of the design specification for trigger- and/or action-driven processing.

A.II.1.4.4 Functions - Organization - Data

The relationships between the design views, which have previously been viewed separately, are now condensed to show their interaction. This step re-creates the overall view of the process chain, which was intentionally divided into subaspects to reduce its complexity. The point of departure for the problem description was the subject-oriented view of a process chain, as it can be roughly represented in a process chain diagram (PCD). This process chain is now redisplayed in detailed form, although it does not include all details for the isolated processes that were processed on the individual levels. Figure A.II.31 shows the extended process chain model and indicates each level contained in it (see *Brombacher, Effizientes Informationsmanagement 1991, p. 128 f.*).

Columns 2 through 4 describe the data flow between information objects and functions. The first and second columns contain function event control. The combination of the second and the sixth columns forms the function level model. The combination of the third, fourth, sixth and seventh columns describes the access to information objects authorized by the organizational units.

Combining columns 2 and 5 shows the processing forms.

The process chain model thus provides a condensed overview of the context of a subject and is used for this purpose, even when an abbreviated form is being employed by masking columns.

A.II.2 Design Specifications

In the design specification, concepts related to the requirements definition are adapted to information technology interfaces. This book defines information technology interfaces as those descriptions that build on general information technology concepts without being geared toward concrete products. There is a trend toward defining standardized interfaces. Examples of this are the relational model that serves as the interface for relational database systems, module and transaction definitions that serve as interfaces for programming languages as well as network topologies that serve as interfaces for concrete network systems.

In contrast to the requirements definition, additional, new objectives are associated with the design specification. While the development of the requirements definition emphasized an understanding of the subject and formal exactness, objectives that are already oriented toward the properties of information technology now come to bear. Now, for example, the objective is to reduce redundancy in order to avoid foreseeable storage and processing expenses or to take obvious performance limits into consideration.

Differences in design objectives result in design objects that can stand in an n:m relationship to the design objects of the requirements definition.

In order to ensure content consistency between levels, the transformation rules are represented, and an effort is made to keep the cardinalities n and m as small as possible. In an object-oriented design, they should ideally equal 1.

Under the ARIS concept, the design requirements for functions, organization and data are initially handled in isolation so that they can be viewed together with their interrelationships in the control view.

A.II.2.1 Design Specification: The Function View (Module and Transaction Design)

The design specification for the function view encompasses module design (automatic processing modules and interactive modules), control structure design and input/output display in the form of screens and listings.

Within the framework of module and transaction design, the functions belonging to a module are defined and, if need be, refined in more detail than in the requirements definition.

The design objective is to keep as many actions within the module as possible, and as few as possible between the modules.

There are hierarchies within modules. A (user) transaction is an interconnected sequence of interactive steps for processing a task. A user transaction is thus a structural view of the subject environment, but it has great significance for the design requirement since it forms the basis for data integrity concepts. It ensures that if there are execution errors in the transaction, all data will be returned to their status at the beginning of the transaction.

The process chain in the sense of the requirements definition typically consists of several user transactions. For the user, one interactive step is the processing of a screen form (receiving a form, data entry, sending the form). This interactive step can require several system steps in the DP system in order, for example, to input data into the form, to transform them or to store them. Database transactions can also be executed within this system step.

Hence, the concepts of user transaction, interactive step and system step reflect this process. The actual processing logic is formulated in the

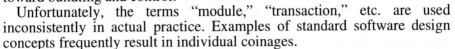

system steps, while the other units possess properties oriented more toward bundling and control.

Unfortunately, the terms "module," "transaction," etc. are used inconsistently in actual practice. Examples of standard software design concepts frequently result in individual coinages.

In the architecture of the R/3 system from SAP AG (see Figure A.II.32, after *SAP, SAP-System R/3 Architektur 1992, pp. 6-3*), the term MODULE is used only for the smallest unit, i.e., for a system step. Modules are combined to form an interactive program or a module pool.

The process control for an interactive step, i.e., the order in which the modules are called, is controlled by a DYNPRO (DYNAMIC PRO-GRAM). Therefore, under the principle of software reusability, a module can be called by several DYNPROs.

Each user transaction—i.e., a DYNPRO CHAIN—refers to a specific module pool.

The term "module" will be used in a more general manner in this book. It applies to an aggregate concept for transaction, program, program element or processing step, if these possess module properties—i.e., if they provide defined input/output for processing. Occasionally, a distinction is also made on the basis of processing mode (batch and interactive modules).

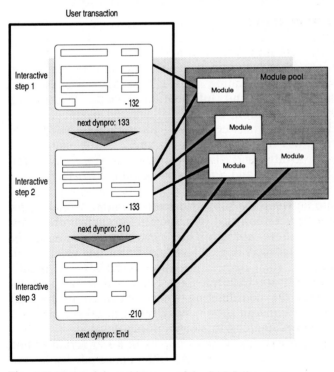

Fig. A.II.32: Module architecture of the SAP R/3 system
(see *SAP, SAP-System R/3 Architektur 1992*)

Because of the independent objectives of the module design, one function of the requirements definition can be supported by several modules, or several functions by one module.

The structograms introduced earlier provide a detailed representation of algorithms and the control flow (general programming).

User transaction design requires a high degree of representational detail. Since this book covers the numerous information processing tasks that an industrial operation involves, a description of processes and transactions is unsuitable. Consequently, transactions are described in more detail only where they serve as examples. Frequently, the transactions in an application are simply listed in order to give the reader an impression of the possible structure of the tasks as well as of the necessary degree of detail.

Within the framework of the requirements definition, examples of standard software products are used to derive contents for the requirements definition in a bottom-up procedure. Within the framework of the design specification, they are used to demonstrate concrete results, especially for screen forms.

A.II.2.2 Design Specification: The Organization View (Network Topology)

The organizational structure determined in the requirements definition produces demands on communication and coordination needs, i.e., demands on a communication and information system. Within the framework of a design specification, these are illustrated by the network topology. The relationship between the information needs of organizational structures has frequently been explored, as for example in Galbraeth, Huber or Draft and Lengel (see *Robey, Designing Organizations 1990, pp. 450 ff.* and *Picot, Organisationsstrukturen der Wirtschaft 1993*)

The interrelationship between the subject-oriented organizational model and the network topology is established by allocating organizational units to computer levels and/or nodes. The networked decentralized organizational model in Figure A.II.07,c leads to a two-tier model. The decentralized units can use their own information systems to meet their specific hardware and software requirements. These individual systems are then networked with the coordinating system because of the far-reaching information and communication needs of the central system.

Figure A.II.33 shows an example of this network topology.

Each computer node is networked with terminals in a star arrangement, while the computer nodes themselves are interconnected by a bus structure.

Central purchasing department

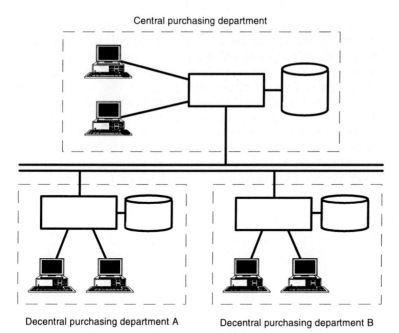

Decentral purchasing department A   Decentral purchasing department B

Fig. A.II.33: Networked decentralization

Component types (e.g., UNIX workstations, PCs) are also incorporated into the network topology description, but not existing concrete capacity characteristics, products or transfer protocols. These are not determined until the implementation description phase.

A.II.2.3 Design Specification: The Data View (Relational Model, Network Model)

Using the ER model to design the logical data structures is the first step in designing a database. In the next step, the data structure must be reformulated into a design specification data model.

A design specification data model is a form of description on which concrete database systems can be built. In addition to the hierarchical model, which is only of interest for historical reasons, the relational data model and the network model form the basis for database systems. The relational data model represents the state of the art—extensions and new concepts are leading toward object-oriented data models. These models are handled in non-standard applications, e.g., for engineering support. The network model is suitable for procedural applications (e.g., bill of materials explosions) and thus deserves a brief discussion.

The normalization theory developed within the framework of the relational data model is not represented. If the design operators discussed above are observed during ER model design, the data structure of the relational model derived from it will already be in a higher normal form (e.g., the third normal form). Readers interested in the normalization process should consult the wealth of literature on the relational model.

Figure A.II.34,a illustrates the data structure for CUSTOMER, ARTICLE and the n:m relationship between them and PURCHASE as an ER model; Figure A.II.34,b illustrates a 1:n relationship between ORDER and ITEM. The entity type ITEM possesses an identifying item number. These examples demonstrate the conversion into both data models.

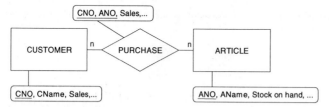

Fig. A.II.34,a: Data structure for CUSTOMER and ARTICLE in the entity-relationship model

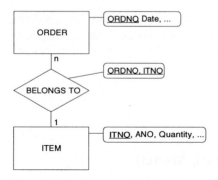

Fig. A.II.34,b: Data structure between ORDER and ITEM

A.II.2.3.1 The Relational Model

A relation describes an entity type by using its attributes. For exact mathematical formulations, see *Codd, Relational Model 1970, pp. 377 ff.; Schlageter/Stucky, Datenbanksysteme 1983, pp. 80 ff.; Vetter/Maddison, Database Design 1981, pp. 173 ff.; Wedekind, Datenbanksysteme I 1991, pp. 180 ff.* If the attribute names are designated as A_i and their value ranges (domains) as $W(A_i)$, relation R is a subset of the Cartesian product of the value ranges:

$$R(A_1, A_2, ..., A_n) \subseteq W(A_1) \times W(A_2) \times ... \times W(A_n)$$

If, for example, the attributes Name and City are given with their value ranges (Mason, Smith) and (Chicago, Detroit), the result is the Cartesian product in Figure A.II.35.

Since the instances (Mason, Detroit) and (Smith, Chicago) should not exist, only the first and the fourth lines from Figure A.II.35 remain as elements of the relation in Figure A.II.36.

Every line of the relation forms an n-digit tuple that is uniquely identified by an attribute and/or a combination of attributes. This attribute and/or attribute group forms the key and is underlined.

Written in a different notation (at the type level), a relation is represented by its relation names as well as by the enumeration of its attributes and by the underlining of its primary key attribute. If the persons entered are customers, the representation is:

R. CUSTOMER (Name, City).

Each entity type in the ER model constitutes a relation in the relational model. Since the relational model does not distinguish between entity and relationship, relationships are also represented as relations.

Name: {Mason, Smith}
City: {Chicago, Detroit}

Name	City
Mason	Chicago
(Mason	Detroit)
(Smith	Chicago)
Smith	Detroit

Fig. A.II.35: Cartesian product of the attributes Name and City

Relation:

Name	City
Mason	Chicago
Smith	Detroit

Fig. A.II.36: Relation to Fig. A.II.35

n:m relationships require their own relation, while 1:n relationships require no new relations. Instead, the relationship is expressed by adding the key attribute of the "superordinate" entity type to the relation of the "subordinate" entity type. It is then referred to as an external key.

The two examples of the n:m relationship between CUSTOMER and ARTICLE as well as of the 1:n relationship between ORDER and ITEM are each shown at the type level and at the instance level (see Figures A.II.37,a-b and A.II.38,a-b).

ENTITY TYPE LEVEL

R. CUSTOMER (<u>CNO</u>, CName, Sales,...)

R. ARTICLE (<u>ANO</u>, AName, Stock on hand,...)

R. PURCHASE (<u>CNO, ANO</u>, Sales, ...)

Fig. A.II.37,a: Data structure of CUSTOMER and ARTICLE in the relational model

ENTITY LEVEL

R. CUSTOMER

<u>CNO</u>	CName	Sales
1	K1	100
2	K2	200

R. ARTICLE

<u>ANO</u>	AName	Stock on hand
100	A1	5
101	A2	10

R. PURCHASE

<u>CNO</u>	<u>ANO</u>	Sales
1	100	1000
1	101	1050
2	100	2000
2	101	2050

Fig. A.II.37,b: Example of a CUSTOMER-ARTICLE database in the relational model at entity level

ENTITY TYPE LEVEL

R. ORDER (<u>ORDNO</u>, Date, ...)

R. ITEM (<u>ITNO</u>, ORDNO, ANO, Quantity, ...)

Fig. A.II.38,a: Data structure of ORDER and ITEM in the relational model

ENTITY LEVEL

R. ORDER

<u>ORDNO</u>	Date
1	03/15
2	04/16

R. ITEM

<u>ITNO</u>	ORDNO	ANO	Quantity
1	1	A5	10
2	1	A7	25
3	2	A18	40
4	2	A5	34
5	2	A8	15

Fig. A.II.38,a: Example of an ORDER-ITEM database at entity level

If an extended ER model is used that retains integrity conditions concerning the maximum and minimum number of permissible relationship instances or existential conditions affecting relationships and entity types, it cannot yet be represented in the relational model.

Extending the relational model with "triggers" can, however, also express such conditions of referential integrity (see *Dogac/Chen, Entity-Relationship Model 1983, pp. 358 ff.*).

The SQL language is closely associated with the relational model. SQL has come to be the standard for manipulation and data description (see *ANSI 1992*). The standard serves as the basis for vendor-oriented derivatives, and reference will be made to it in implementation description examples.

A.II.2.3.2 The Network Model

The network model has evolved primarily through the efforts of CODASYL (Conference on Data System Languages). CODASYL is an organization of DP producers and users, which published proposals for network data structures as early as 1969. The network model provides the foundation for many database systems that are still in use today. The central concept is the set, which describes a 1:n relationship between two entities.

At the type level, entities are represented by boxes and the 1:n relationship by an arrow, as indicated in Figure A.II.39,a for the relationship between ORDER and ITEM.

Each order is assigned one, none or several order items. The set header is referred to as the owner; the set body, as the member.

Figure A.II.39,b shows the instances of the two sets. An owner element or set points to the first member set and from there to the next member set in the 1:n relationship. The last or each individual member set can point to the owner set, so that a link exists from the subordinate set type to the superordinate set type.

In the network representation, m:n relationships are divided into two 1:n relationships, creating a new entity type for linking the output entity types.

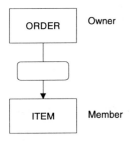

Fig. A.II.39,a: Data structure of ORDER and ITEM in the network model

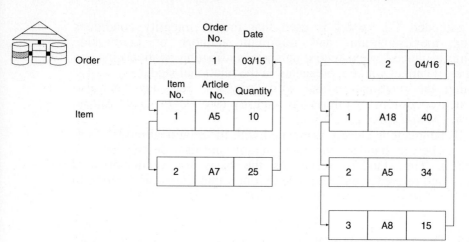

Fig. A.II.39,b: Set instances of the order database

In the m:n relationship between CUSTOMER and ARTICLE, a 1:n relationship leads from CUSTOMER and ARTICLE to the new entity type CUST-ART, which corresponds to the relation R. PURCHASE in the relational model (see Figure A.II.40,a).

The instance level for this example is shown in Figure A.II.40,b.

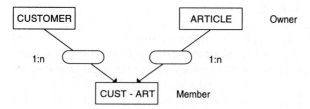

Fig. A.II.40,a: The m:n relationship in the network model at entity type level

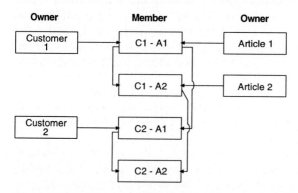

Fig. A.II.40,b: The m:n relationship in the network model at entity level

This also enables the ER model data structures to be readily transferred to a network model.

The relationships, i.e., the arrows, are physically implemented by address chains, by storing the address reference in chain tables or by physical adjacency. Generally, the network model possesses a closer proximity to the physical implementation than the relational model, which is free from access path considerations.

A.II.2.4 Design Specification: The Control View

As with the requirements definition, all the links between the ARIS components will not be treated in the same degree of detail. Thus, only the methods that will be discussed later will be treated in detail here. In order to retain the systematic structure, all the dual relationships are first discussed, then the interaction between all of the ARIS components.

A.II.2.4.1 Combining Functions with Organization

The modules and transactions designed within the framework of the design specification for the function view are assigned to computer topology nodes. In particular, this determines how the users assigned to the nodes can access concrete program modules, i.e., how user password authorization or other authorization can be controlled. An additional allocation affects the access of organizational units to screens. They create the user view at the level of the design specification for organizational units.

A.II.2.4.2 Combining Functions with Data

The data view design specification is represented by the relations that have been designed. If the relations are linked to the program modules, the segment required by the program is referred to as an external scheme. With the creation of this view, it becomes possible to rename names and transform sequences in the attributes.

The program modules access data via database transactions.

A database transaction transfers a database from one consistent condition into another consistent condition. In this context, "consistent" is understood as database correctness.

A database transaction forms an atomic unit. It can either be executed completely or not at all. Since it typically consists of several processing steps and database accesses, however, all previously executed changes must be undone if any inconsistencies occur during processing. For this reason, the transaction concept also provides the basis for integrity conditions to be monitored by a database as well as the foundation for error handling in database systems (see *Reuter, Fehlerbehandlung 1982*).

Numerous database accesses can be executed within a database transaction. The number of accesses is determined by the degree of integration of the information system.

The user transaction concept introduced in the function view is more comprehensive than that of a database transaction. A user transaction encompasses a coherent functional unit taken from the application view in which database transactions can **also** be carried out.

Database transaction handling within the control view emphasizes the link between functional and data aspects. In active database designs, functional operators are also treated as components of the data view. The ARIS concept, however, clearly separates the views and their links. This does not preclude the links shown in the control view from being assigned to the other views afterwards. This option is supported in active databases by the fact that primarily data-oriented functions—such as maintaining data integrity conditions—can also be assigned to the data view.

A.II.2.4.3 Combining Organization with Data

The central concern when combining the organization view with the data view involves detailing the data access authorization for organizational units as well as distributing data among the nodes on a computer network. Date (see *Date, Twelve Rules for Distributed Database System 1987*) has developed exhaustive criteria for distributed database requirements (see also *Scheer, Architecture of Integrated Information Systems, 1992, pp. 180 ff.*). The fundamental principle governing distributed databases is that they must appear to the user as a non-distributed—i.e., centralized—database. This principle is also referred to as transparency.

A distributed database with (intentional) redundancies places high demands on database coordination. For this reason, designs have been developed that allow simplified coordination mechanisms between distributed data, albeit at the expense of transparency. Examples of this are the blackboard architecture—which provides a centralized distribution and coordination function—and client/server architectures. Because they involve the distribution of data as well as the distribution of functions, client/server solutions will be discussed in the section on linking all three ARIS components.

A.II.2.4.4 Functions - Organization - Data

In viewing all three ARIS components at the design specification level, the process chain concept developed within the framework of the requirements definition will be adopted and expanded to include the concepts in the design specification. If both data and functions can be distributed among the different network nodes, this is referred to as distributed data processing.

A.II.2.4.4.1 Trigger and Action Control

In order to control a process chain, subprocesses must be initiated at the right time and assigned to the appropriate workstations (organizational units). Subprocesses can be executed automatically by the computer or controlled interactively by the user. Action messages and triggers facilitate the information flow between the processing programs and the users (see *Berthold, Aktionsdatenbanken 1983; Mertens, Integrierte Informationssysteme I 1991; Mertens/Hoffmann, Aktionsorientierte Datenverarbeitung 1983*). Action messages convey information to users; trigger notices, information to application programs.

The term "trigger" is used primarily in conjunction with so-called active database systems. A trigger describes an action together with the premise that initiates it. A trigger consists of a plurality of instructions that are executed when a condition is met. Triggers are used in active database systems to maintain consistency (e.g., in the SQL database system standard). Furthermore, triggers are increasingly being taken to mean a general control mechanism for program sequences (see *Kotz, Triggermechanismen in Datenbanksystemen 1989, p. 2*), whereby the modules to be controlled are only loosely coupled.

Trigger and action messages can thus also support hybrid, automatic and manual processing. Example a) in Figure A.II.41 shows purely program-controlled—i.e., automatic—processing in which the process branches are controlled by parameters. This form assumes the individual job handling alternatives are precisely defined and can be unambiguously controlled by the parameter list.

Processing form b) in Figure A.II.41, on the other hand, provides users with a screen display of Process 1. Users can input supplemental information during the process, abort the process because of missing information that cannot be supplied, or start Process 2 after the data are complete.

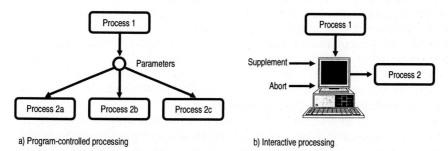

a) Program-controlled processing   b) Interactive processing

Fig. A.II.41: Program-controlled and interactive processing

Action- and trigger-controlled processing provides a suitable DP instrument for controlling complicated process chains that encompass both automatic and interactive steps.

Descriptive languages for providing exact descriptions of triggers have been developed at the design specification level; these languages are then translated into concrete program instructions during the implementation description phase. According to the event/trigger mechanism (ETM) (see *Kotz, Triggermechanismen in Datenbanksystemen 1989, pp. 54 ff.*), a trigger consists of an event and an action $T = (E, A)$ that function as a pair, which means that action A will be executed immediately when a type E event occurs.

An event indicates that a particular situation has been achieved, which can, for example, be the creation or deletion of an event instance. An action can be any executable module.

If, for example, a result verification procedure is to be initiated within a product development process after "Design Phase 1," this leads to the trigger (see *Kotz, Triggermechanismen in Datenbanksystemen 1989, p. 64*):

> EVENT end_of_design_phase_1 (design_object: DB_ID);
> ACTION verification_procedure_A (verif_obj: DB_ID)
>   = <verification of verif_obj>;
> TRIGGER T1 = ON end_of_design_phase_1
>   DO verification_procedure_A (design_object);

Events and actions contain identifiers for each object to be handled. In the example, a design object is designated as design_object with the database identifier DB_ID, and the object to be verified by an action as verification_object with the unique database identifier DB_ID.

By defining events, actions and triggers separately, different triggers can access the same events and action definitions. At the same time, different control processes are possible using event and action parameters given the same basic definition.

The above notation is still independent of concrete trigger systems in certain database systems or programming environments. For this reason, it resides at the design specification level. The notation outlined here is used in the subject-related segment, sometimes with free verbal formulation of the trigger designation. Concrete trigger controls, for example, are derived from them for selected database systems.

The E/A-T concept allows direct linkage to event-driven process chains. The events have already been entered in the EPCs, and "actions" correspond to the functional modules. The triggers describe the relationship between E and A and formally correspond to the lines connecting events and functions in the EPC.

The operations developed in EPCs and PCDs can thus be transferred directly to trigger and action control design specifications, although the module definitions introduced within the framework of the design specification functional analysis must be used. Not only is the logical process sequence taken from the EPC, but the organizational assignments and processing forms necessary for action control are taken from the PCDs. The EPC and PCD representations need only be supplemented with symbols from the design specification. Above all, this involves labeling the events that initiate triggers and action messages.

A.II.2.4.4.2 Distributed Data Processing

Distributed data processing involves distributing program execution and data storage among network nodes. General reasons for distributing these tasks to different computers include taking advantage of special hardware and software configurations, decreasing network traffic by decentralizing data management and processing functions, using electronic mail to take advantage of communication options, etc. As illustrated in the discussion of distributed databases, transparent distribution requires significant coordination functions. For this reason, special forms of distributed processing are common today that are not completely transparent, but nonetheless exhibit some of the cited advantages by distributing data and tasks. Client/server architectures are among these forms of distributed data processing. The loss of transparency is apparent in that one node cannot access all services on the other nodes as though these services were directly available to the node without restriction; rather, one node can only access another node via defined interfaces. The node whose services are being requested handles these tasks locally, and the process is not apparent to the user making the request. The partners in this relationship are designated as the client and the server. A client can thus request a server-defined service. The roles of the client and the server can change during the operation, since in a different processing step, a partner that was initially performing server functions can use the services of the partner that was previously acting as the client.

In contrast to central processing, a three-tier division of functions and data exists in a client/server architecture, as illustrated in Figure A.II.42. For additional models of client/server architectures, see *Houy/Scheer/ Zimmermann, Anwendungsbereiche von Client/Server-Modellen 1992* and *Plattner, Client/Server-Architekturen 1993*.

With centralized processing, the central computer controls data management, processing functions and input and output editing. In a three-tier client/server architecture, a central server manages the central data, which are used by many applications. Different processing servers access these data. They can manage their own data for individual processing steps and/or temporarily store central data. Display servers handle the presentation of data, especially support for complex user interfaces. Moreover, they can execute local applications such as word processing.

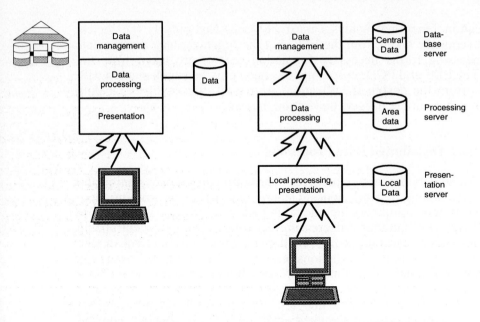

Central processing   3-tier client-server architecture

Fig. A.II.42: Division of functions and data

The illustration shows the advantages of client/server architectures. The database server is freed from processing tasks and the processing server from generating complex display presentations.

Client/server architectures are being supported by new hardware developments, which exhibit a significantly better price/performance ratio than traditional mainframes. Standardized interfaces for the server services can also support heterogeneous computer networks.

Distribution criteria must be established within the client/server architecture for distributing data and functions among the computer levels and thus among the computer types.

Both PCs and UNIX workstations can be employed as user-oriented systems. Typical operating systems here include MS-DOS, Windows, OS/2 and UNIX. Powerful UNIX workstations or traditional computers with proprietary operating systems can be used as back-end computers.

A.II.3 Implementation Description

Within the framework of the implementation description, the design specifications are transferred to concrete information technology products.

The main objective in this design phase is to take advantage of the performance characteristics of each component. This can necessitate modifications to the design specification, but any such modifications must not have repercussions that would affect the requirements definition.

Only portions of the implementation description will be discussed below.

A.II.3.1 Implementation Description: The Function View

Only a few examples will be provided to illustrate the transfer of the developed subject contents to concrete DP programs. This process will be represented using excerpted program elements themselves rather than by listing programming procedures, for which the interested reader should consult the appropriate standard literature.

A.II.3.2 Implementation Description: The Organization View

The network topology developed within the framework of the design specification is implemented using hardware, software and network protocols. This process primarily deals with questions of communication, i.e., with implemented network protocols in several key areas (see also CAM, and particularly MAP). The ISO/OSI model serves as a reference model for transfer protocols. Although there is a trend toward standardization among many vendors, a number of proprietary protocols still exist. Moreover, as time goes on, protocols stipulated by international standardization committees are being rendered obsolete by so-called industry standards. Industry standards frequently have the advantage of being less complicated and more quickly implemented because they do not have to undergo lengthy coordination processes. Figure A.II.43 shows a table of the different protocol families according to the ISO/OSI architecture. Subsequent sections of this book will refer back to this list at some points, for example, to illustrate standardization efforts.

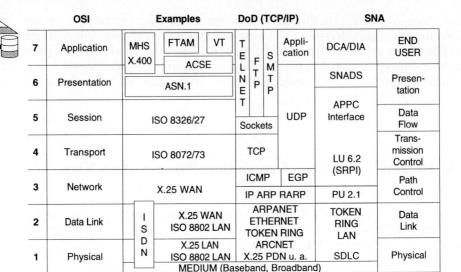

Fig. A.II.43: Protocol families and standardizations

A.II.3.3 Implementation Description : The Data View (Database Scheme)

A data description language is used to transfer the relational or network model to a concrete database system scheme.

Figure A.II.44 shows recent or frequently used database systems along with several of their characteristic features.

The transformation of a data model into concrete database systems is shown on the basis of the IBM DB2 **relational database** and the Siemens UDS **network database**. The "article-customer" relations and/or sets from Section A.II.2.3 serve as an example.

A.II.3.3.1 Relational Database Description

Figure A.II.45 shows the article-customer relationship for the DB2 relational database. Tables represent relations and relationships in DB2. The three tables ARTICLE, CUSTOMER and PURCHASE are based on the relational model in Figure A.II.37,a. The required attributes must be indicated when the table is defined. It is necessary to determine the class of variables to which the attributes belong (e.g., alpha characters, numeric characters or dates). The indication "not null" means that the corresponding attributes cannot be omitted at the entity level.

Product	Manufacturer	Type	Host computer	Microcomputer Workstation
ADABAS	Software AG	Relationally oriented	X	(X)
CLIPPER	Nantucket Corp.	Relationally oriented		X
DB 2	IBM	Relational	X	
dbase IV	Borland	Relational		X
DMS	Unisys	Network	X	
IDMS/SQL	Cullinet	Relational	(X)	
IMAGE/3000	Hewlett Packard	Network	X	
IMS/VS-DB	IBM	Network-oriented	X	
INFORMIX	INFORMIX Corp.	Relational	X	X
INGRES	Relational Technology	Relational		X
ORACLE	ORACLE	Relational	X	X
PISA	infodas	Relational	X	X
PROGRESS	PROGRESS	Relational		X
SOKRATES	gft	Relational		X
StarBase	COGNOS	Relational		X
Sybase	Sybase	Relational	X	X
UDS	Siemens	Network	X	
VAX Rdb/VMS	Digital Equipment	Relational	X	X

Fig. A.II.44: Survey of several database systems

```
CREATE TABLE ARTICLE
(ANO NUMBER (10) NOT NULL,
ANAME CHAR (20),
  ...              );

CREATE TABLE CUSTOMER
(CNR NUMBER (10) NOT NULL,
CNAME CHAR (20),
  ...              );

CREATE TABLE PURCHASE
(ANO NUMBER (10) NOT NULL,
CNR NUMBER (10) NOT NULL,
SALES NUMBER (5),
  ...              );
```

Fig. A.II.45: Scheme definition by using the data description language of the database system DB2

The <u>ANO</u> and <u>CNO</u> attributes in the PURCHASE table create the relationship between the ARTICLE and CUSTOMER tables.

A.II.3.3.2 Network Database Description

Figure A.II.46 shows the creation of the scheme in the UDS network database. In UDS, the scheme is provided in a data description language (scheme DDL), whose language elements rely heavily on the COBOL programming language. A database is defined by a scheme, which is identified by a scheme name. All entity types and their relationships contained in the database must be declared in the scheme. The AREA NAME is used to create logical subunits for the purpose of data protection, data integrity and processing contending access requests. The individual areas are stored in different system files.

The entity types are represented by records. The structure and definition of the attribute records resemble the file section in a COBOL program. When defining the records, only the user-dependent fields are defined. At the same time, access paths (LOCATION MODE), primary key attributes (DUPLICATES ARE NOT ALLOWED) and search terms (SEARCH KEY) can be agreed upon. In the example, the records ARTICLE,

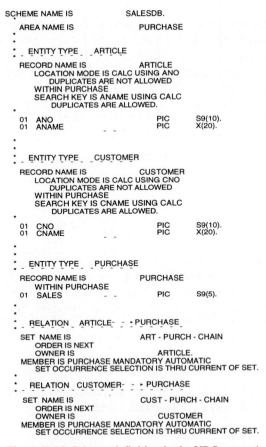

Fig. A.II.46: Scheme definition in the UDS network database

CUSTOMER and PURCHASE are created. The ART-PURCH-CHAIN set is defined for the ARTICLE to CUSTOMER relationship, and the CUST-PURCH-CHAIN set is defined for the CUSTOMER to PURCHASE relationship. Each owner and member of the set relationship must be indicated. At the same time, attributes of the chain (MANDATORY AUTOMATIC) are indicated. With the help of the set indicators, the database management system generates records that users cannot access directly (for a definition, see *Siemens, UDS Entwerfen und Definieren 1982*).

The scheme definitions of concrete database systems are used at some points for particularly interesting database systems.

A.II.3.4 Implementation Description: The Control View

The implementation description control view involves physically linking the component types defined in the design specification, which have already been concretized in their respective views at the implementation description level. This means, for example, that files are allocated to concrete data storage buffers, and programs are physically linked to data and network nodes. Concrete implementation examples will be used at some points to illustrate these relationships without going into systematic detail concerning their derivation and rationale.

A.III Further Procedures

A summary of the methods that have been developed for representing information systems within the ARIS architecture will now be presented. This will be followed by a brief overview of the tools the ARIS concept provides to support these methods; only tools that will be used in this book will be included. The section on design specifications for information management will present more far-reaching comments involving general tool use.

The structural criteria for the rest of the book are presented at the end of this chapter.

A.III.1 Summary of Methods Used

The major methods that have been developed are positioned in the ARIS concept in Figure A.III.01.

Where methods can be used in more than one field of the architecture, they are assigned to their principal application. The holds true, for example, for structograms that can be used to represent algorithms within the requirements definition but are the primary means of representation for "rough" programming in the design specification. In the same way, rough process chain diagrams are used to represent initial situations; however, they also serve to portray network views at the requirements definition level and can be used within the framework of the design specification (when extended to include DP elements such as screens).

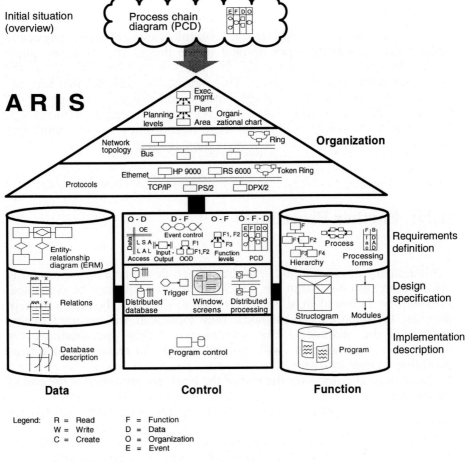

Fig. A.III.01: Summary of the ARIS methods used

Figure A.III.02 shows the levels of importance assigned to the ARIS tiers treated in the book. The main emphasis is placed on the representations on the requirements definition level, since this represents the closest relationship to business situations.

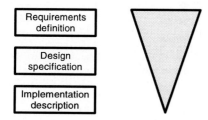

Fig. A.III.02: Importance of the ARIS representation levels

A.III.2 Tool Use

The term "tools" is employed here in the sense of computerized aids used to support the design methods cited. Their use can apply to the creation of designs within the individual ARIS fields or to the transformation of a design result to superordinate or subordinate levels (see Figure A.III.03).

Some graphical representations use special design tools specifically developed for ARIS methods of modeling the requirements definition (see *IDS, ARIS-Produkte 1997*).

In addition to the design support provided by descriptions, tools can also help navigate within and between the design results. The "ARIS Navigator," © IDS Prof. Scheer, provides developers with a product that makes it possible to skip from an object originating in one view to the situations associated with the object that are represented in the other views. The reference models for industrial enterprises developed in this book are documented on diskette and available for evaluation using the ARIS Navigator.

Tool application includes not only graphics support and storage of design results, but can also effectively support the design process by providing initial tentative solutions (reference models). The application of these types of reference models for function, organization, data and control views can significantly accelerate the design process (see *Scheer, Papierlose Beratung 1991*). The models developed later in this book can also serve as reference models for enterprise-specific applications.

The ARIS tools are geared toward storing and manipulating reference models.

The ARIS Analyzer system has been specially developed for analyzing and developing the initial business situation for industrial enterprises.

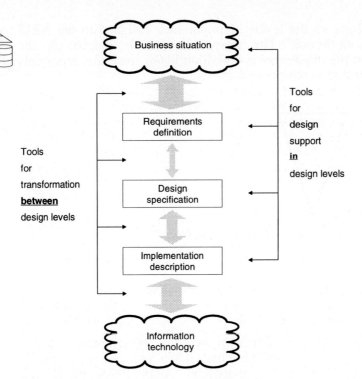

Fig. A.III.03: Tool support for system design

It features a knowledge base containing reference models for ARIS views and can be used for various structures of industrial companies (see *IDS, ARIS Analyser 1993; Jost/Keller/Scheer, Konzeption eines DV-Tools im Rahmen der CIM-Planung 1991; Jost, Rechnergestützte CIM-Rahmenplanung 1992*). Since it is the objective of this book to develop an ARIS-based information system for a general industrial company, the ARIS Analyzer will not be discussed in further detail here; however, elements of enterprise typology will be incorporated in generalized observations.

A.III.3 Structural Criteria and Book Format

The primary structural criterion used to present the information system is the concept of business processes (see Figure A.III.04). The most important business processes are:

1. Logistics
2. Product specification
3. Overlapping information and coordination systems.

Part B will develop information systems for logistics. Logistics generally encompasses the movement and storage of goods. In addition to this operative function, the planning and scheduling levels of logistics will also be discussed. Because they involve a different flow of goods, a distinction will be made between outbound logistics, inbound logistics and production logistics (see Figure A.III.04). As a result, logistics encompasses the movement of products between the company and its customers, the movement of goods within the company and the movement of production resources between suppliers and the company.

The processing order of this logistics chain follows didactic points of view. Therefore, this discussion will begin with production logistics, since this is where data structures that are needed by the other logistics chains are defined.

Part C of the book discusses the "product development" product chain. This part also discusses marketing aspects as well as the question of computer-aided design of technical product properties, which is an important issue in industrial enterprises.

Although Part D presents accounting as an important part of the overlapping information and coordination systems, close links to value-oriented views are already established within the operative analyses. As a result, the specific discussion of the accounting system will summarize the individual aspects of the finance and accounting system that are treated here in order to arrive at a general concept and will also treat enterprise-wide applications that go beyond the scope of this initial summary.

Information management is also included in the coordination process discussed in Part D.

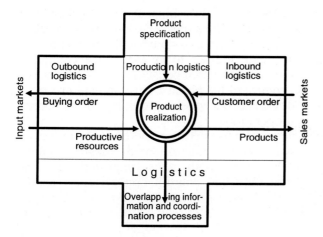

Fig. A.III.04: Business processes

The three logistical subprocesses are interlinked with one another. At the same time, logistics is also connected to the other product development business processes and to the information and coordination systems. The arrows in Figure A.III.04 indicate these relationships. The Y-CIM model in Figure A.III.05 again illustrates the interrelationships between the logistical subsystems and the product development process. The left branch of the Y describes the primary business/planning-oriented aspects of the production planning and control system (PPC). It encompasses the order processing functions controlled by order flow from requirements planning, time management, production control and factory data entry through shipping. Thus, production logistics is integrated into the outbound logistics functions of order processing and shipping. At the same time, requirements planning encompasses inbound logistics.

The upper area of the right branch of the Y describes the process of product development and engineering, including the necessary documentation. The link to logistics is primarily created by description data from product development in the form of bills of materials and routings. The computerized resources necessary for product implementation are listed in the lower part of the right branch of the Y. Control of these systems requires that the products to be produced be described on this system. In addition to this information relationship between product development and production, there is also a close relationship to short-term production control and factory data entry. The production orders defined within production logistics are merged with the description data from product development and executed on the production systems. Because of this close relationship between short-term production control and production resources, their description is treated there, inasmuch as they are necessary for an understanding of the primary business factors involved.

Since the inbound- and outbound-oriented processes also require the description data for the goods/services to be purchased/sold, there is a relationship here as well.

Figure A.III.05 also illustrates the relationships of the circumstances summarized in the Y model to the third business process. Financial accounting records the business processes associated with the company's environment (and is therefore also referred to as external accounting). Internal accounting records the value-oriented consumption of production resources for monitoring and control of the product development process.

Information management develops concepts for providing the resources, application systems, and their operation.

The many interdependencies that exist between the business processes and the different views (quantity- or value-oriented) make graphical representation difficult. The Y model—both in its simplified form and extended to include the information and coordination systems—should therefore only be understood as a rough graphical representation; despite the discussion of subprocesses, this book will subscribe to a holistically integrated viewpoint.

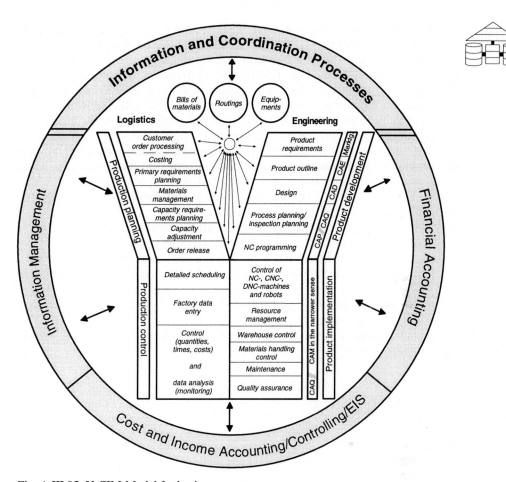

Fig. A.III.05: Y-CIM-Model for business processes

The representations strive for an average level of aggregation in order to counteract the risk of getting lost in the details of practical processes. On the other hand, the models should also exhibit a close link to reality in order to serve as reference models for concrete systems. Experience in numerous projects has shown that using the representation level selected here to illustrate practical applications results only in a doubling of the representation elements (e.g., functions or data objects). This doubling occurs in particular through further specialization of the elements used here, in that, for example, the concept of purchase order distinguishes between "intercompany orders" and "normal purchasing."

The structure of the detailed representation conforms to the ARIS model. First an overview of the process is provided for each subprocess, using process chain diagrams as a principal resource.

The detailed description is then discussed for each subprocess. In the process, the requirements definition is first created. In addition to the functional structure using a function tree, emphasis is placed on the design of the data structures. The relationship between functions and data is created using process chains. This descriptive form is followed for each function of the subprocess. After describing the last function of the subprocess, a summary of the requirements definition is provided that supplements any descriptive components that may still be missing. Finally, the design specification and implementation description are discussed. A comprehensive treatment is not provided for all ARIS components, in accordance with the level of emphasis chosen for this book. Figure A.III.06 shows the logical structural process with the corresponding descriptive methods being emphasized.

The following representation format is used to facilitate understanding:

-      In the data models, newly introduced objects are shaded.
-      On each left side of the Y model, the subject contents are shaded.
-      On each right side of the ARIS model, the view being discussed is shaded.
-      In the organization and function models, the uppermost hierarchy levels are shaded.
-      The color figures contain their own numbering scheme, which begins with "F."

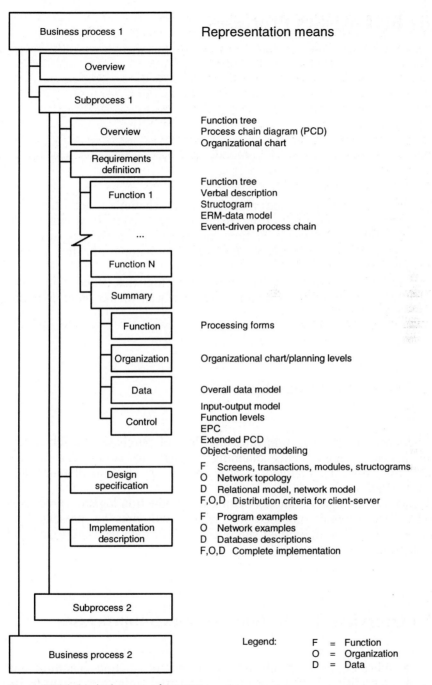

Fig. A.III.06: Logical structural process

Part B: Logistics Processes

Logistics encompasses the planning and scheduling activities that accompany an enterprise's flow of goods. Logistics is divided into inbound, outbound and production logistics. The term "logistics" is primarily used to underscore the process nature of the various presentations.

This discussion will begin with production logistics, since it involves significant structures that also serve as interfaces to the other logistics systems.

B.I Production Logistics

Production logistics accompanies the flow of purchase and job orders from primary requirements planning through to completion of the production order. This subject is also termed "production planning and control" (PPC).

Because of its highly complex nature, the production logistics process is divided into several subprocesses, which will first be presented in overview form. The individual subprocesses will then be categorized and discussed in greater detail.

B.I.1 Overview: Production Logistics Subprocesses

As a subcategory of production logistics, production planning and control is a traditional DP application in industrial companies. Reasons for this include the high volume of information that must be processed—bills of materials, routings and orders—as well as the high degree of planning complexity required within the framework of requirements and capacity planning.

Data management systems—e.g., the Bill of Materials Processor (BOMP)—were implemented early on to manage bills of materials, which

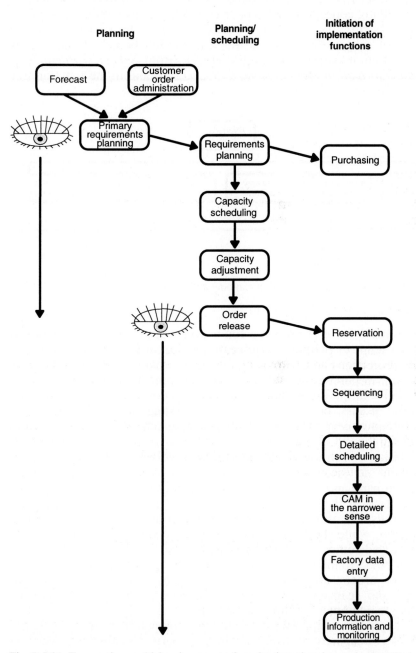

Fig. B.I.01: Forecasting multi-level concept of production planning and controlling

describe the composition of end products in terms of components and materials. These systems were the first step in the development of universal database systems. In large industrial enterprises, it is not uncommon for 100,000 parts records, several hundred thousand structural records and several hundred thousand operation records to be managed.

The planning concept of DP-supported PPC systems within the standard software systems that are on the market conforms to a largely uniform sequence of subprocesses, as illustrated in the left branch of the Y-CIM model in Figure A.III.06, in Figure B.I.01 (from *Scheer, Principles of Efficient Information Management, 1990, p. 204*) and in the function tree shown in Figure B.I.02.

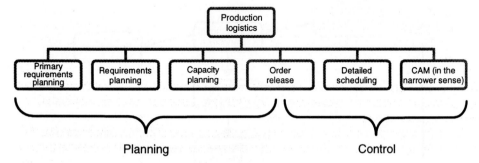

Fig. B.I.02: Function tree of production planning and control

The demand for end products for a given time frame is determined within the scope of **primary requirements planning**. This figure is based on sales projections and/or existing customer orders. Because of its close relationship to purchasing and sales, this planning step will be treated in Section B.IV in the discussion of general logistics concepts. This section will only discuss primary requirements **management**. The specified primary requirement initiates a sequence of planning and/or scheduling steps within the PPC system.

The task of **requirements planning** involves using the primary requirement to determine the demand for subordinate assemblies, component parts and materials based on quantity and requirement period. This results in both demand for in-house parts and for outsourced parts and materials. The in-house requirements are grouped into production lots (job orders), while the "purchasing" function compiles the requirements for outsourced components into purchase orders.

Within the framework of the **capacity planning** function, the production orders are assigned to processing capacities (equipment groups), and capacity scheduling allocates capacity requirements according to equipment groups and periods.

The **capacity adjustment** function compensates for potential bottlenecks or capacity peaks by employing alternate equipment, overtime and extra shifts, or by postponing orders.

The **order release** function reviews pending production orders to determine if the necessary materials, semi-finished products, tooling, NC programs and capacities are available. The orders are then released for processing. Order release constitutes the transition from the planning phase to implementation and initiates a series of implementation functions.

Within the framework of the **detailed scheduling** function, orders/operations are scheduled at the assigned equipment. This function also determines the sequence of orders (operations) upstream of the equipment.

The **factory data entry** function deals with information involving completed deadlines, quantities and/or incidental conditions and notifies Production Control as the initial basis for further control functions. In particular, it uses special terminals or data capture systems located directly at the machines to input current data about orders, personnel, equipment, materials and tools.

The databases created on the planning and control levels are made available to an analysis system. This **production information monitoring system** compares target data with actual data and provides up-to-date production control.

In contrast to many of the simultaneous business planning approaches employed in manufacturing, the PPC system outlined here conforms to a multi-level planning concept. This means that the results from the planning process on one level serve as the starting point for the planning considerations on the next level. Although reverse relationships can readily be indicated between requirements planning and capacity planning, it is very difficult for the planning system to process them. This is particularly true if the individual planning steps are processed in batch form, i.e., if large volumes of data are processed at predetermined times without user intervention.

An interactive production control system, on the other hand, provides the option of executing several planning cycles by interactively scheduling case-oriented processes and by repeating individual planning steps with updated data if unallowable or undesirable planning results are produced. The overall concept is more flexible because the resulting control loops are smaller. Despite this flexibility, the incompleteness of the multi-level planning concept leads to difficulties when the individual planning levels are coordinated.

The simultaneous approaches developed within the business administration framework primarily build on linear and integer optimization methods. The large volumes encountered in industrial enterprises, particularly in manufacturing, do not permit these techniques to be applied down to the degree of detail needed for the operations (see *Scheer, Produktionsplanung 1976*). For this reason, the sequential concept developed within the framework of the standard software literature must be viewed as an original and effective DP contribution to the development of application-oriented business solutions.

These solutions emphasize data integration, while business administration views integration as the integration of business decisions and virtually ignores the database aspect. Both approaches would thus appear to complement one another: DP-oriented production planning and control emphasizes data integration but generally fails to treat decision coordination; in business administration, on the other hand, integrated planning systems deal with the integration of decision aspects but do not address questions of data management. Section B.IV.1.3 will introduce an approach that links both of these planning concepts.

B.I.2 Primary Requirements Management

The primary requirement comprises requirements figures for end products, independently salable intermediate products and spare parts derived from sales plans and customer orders.

Primary requirements planning is the task of sales planning and/or marketing activities and is therefore discussed in greater detail within the framework of outbound logistics. In particular, sales planning can be preceded by extensive forecast and optimization calculations.

As illustrated in Figure B.I.01, the primary requirement determines requirements planning and capacity planning. Primary requirement data management is therefore closely linked with these functions—i.e., changes in the primary requirement initiate changes in requirements planning for subordinate parts.

The primary requirement is thus an important interface between inbound, outbound and production logistics.

Primary requirements management, which is discussed within the context of production logistics, represents only one aspect of primary requirements planning and is therefore not discussed in the same degree of detail as the other subprocesses.

Because primary requirements planning relates to several articles, the PRIMARY REQUIREMENTS PLAN is first defined as header information. On a given planning date, one organizational unit—e.g., Sales Planning—determines the requirement and forwards it to another organizational unit—e.g., Production Planning. Thus, both organizational units use the planning date (DATE) to define the PRIMARY REQUIREMENTS PLAN (see Figure B.I.03).

The objects associated with the primary requirement (end products, salable intermediate products and spare parts) are termed ARTICLE.

The requirements figures can either be allocated to a fixed frequency grid (see Figure B.I.04,a), or each requirements figure can be assigned the corresponding requirement deadline (see Figure B.I.04,b).

Both forms of representation in Figure B.I.04 lead to the same extension of the data structure. The article-oriented PRIMARY REQUIREMENT or

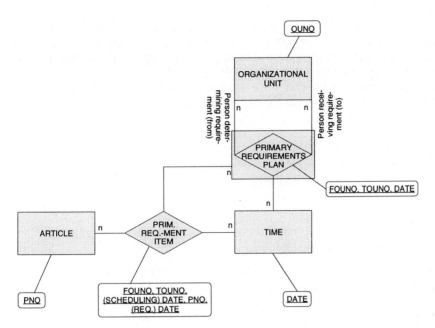

Fig. B.I.03: ERM to determine primary requirement

a)
	Period 1	Period 2	...	...	Period n	
	Require-ment figure 1					Primary requirement

b)
	Require-ment figure	Date

Fig. B.I.04,a-b: Representation forms of primary requirement

the primary requirement item is a relationship between the entity types TIME, as the requirement date, the primary requirement object ARTICLE and the associated PRIMARY REQUIREMENTS PLAN.

The entity type TIME is identified by a date, which can also designate frequency; the entity type ARTICLE is identified by the part number (PNO). Correspondingly, the PRIMARY REQUIREMENT is identified by the key attributes of the primary requirements plan and by indicating the part number and the date.

If the primary requirements coincide with customer orders, the identity between the primary requirement and the corresponding customer orders can be established using an "is-a" relationship to the CUSTOMER ORDER ITEM (see Figure B.I.05).

The representation is to be interpreted in such a way that an item in a customer order can be viewed as a requirement notification for end products. The other requirement origins are indicated in the figure by the second "is-a" relationship to FORECAST VALUE.

The data structure of the primary requirement will subsequently be integrated into the data structure of the general requirements management concept.

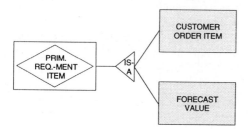

Fig. B.I.05: Subtypes of primary requirement

B.I.3 Requirements Planning

B.I.3.1 Overview: Requirements Planning

The concept of requirements planning involves determination of the in-house and outsourced parts needed to fulfill the primary requirement, as well as management of inventories and procurement of outsourced parts. Since the procurement function will be discussed in connection with the inbound logistics process chain, the scheduling functions of requirements planning will be discussed in conjunction with production logistics.

Within the framework of requirements planning, the demand for in-house and outsourced parts is determined and then compiled into orders (lots).

Sales planning provides the primary requirements for end products and independently salable parts, which serve then as the point of departure for requirements planning. Bills of materials are used to classify these primary requirements into requirements for assemblies, component parts and materials. The bill of materials master data are thus necessary for the requirements explosion. Bill of materials management is a fundamental function in connection with overall production planning and control as well as for additional business functions—e.g., Cost Accounting uses bills of materials for costing.

Thus, bill of materials management will be the first item discussed with reference to the function tree for the requirements planning concept shown in Figure B.I.06.

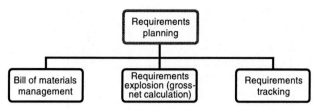

Fig. B.I.06: Function tree for requirements planning

Afterwards, the requirements explosion will be discussed in the context of gross-net calculation, along with inventory management functions. The lot sizing techniques used in DP systems for requirements planning will be briefly discussed as well.

Tracking information concerning the origins of the requirements is particularly significant in customer-order-oriented production and is therefore discussed in the section on requirements tracking.

This process is shown in Figure B.I.07 in the form of a process chain diagram (PCD), which includes the rough databases and the organizational units responsible for performing each function. In addition to primary requirements planning, which provides an interface to outbound logistics, bill of materials management also provides an interface to the enterprise's "product development" process. Production planning or job planning converts the drawings and engineering bills of materials generated by Design Engineering to production bills of materials. Virtually all functions are supported by interactive DP systems. Only the requirements explosion is illustrated as an automatic (batch) process, which also produces an automatic reconciliation of inventory levels. Moreover, interactive inventory-taking functions and case-oriented requirements explosions are also possible.

"Paper" drawings are also listed as data input in generating engineering drawings and bills of materials.

The process chain diagram reveals the way in which requirements planning is embedded in a wide range of departments and different areas within the enterprise. Figure B.I.08 shows the departments involved organized into a functional reference model of the organization (see also Figure A.II.10,a). The organizational units indicated here can be categorized further by classifying them under the main functions. In this connection, both the inventory functions performed by Marketing as well as those performed by Purchasing and Production are indicated for the various classes of parts (articles, outsourced parts and in-house parts). The system view must cross departmental boundaries because within the requirements explosion all three classes of parts are processed together with their inventory levels.

It should be noted, however, that the organizational chart shown here is not a model solution, but merely a frequently encountered organizational classification system. As a variation on Figure B.I.08, for example, it would also be possible for inventory management of all classes of parts to

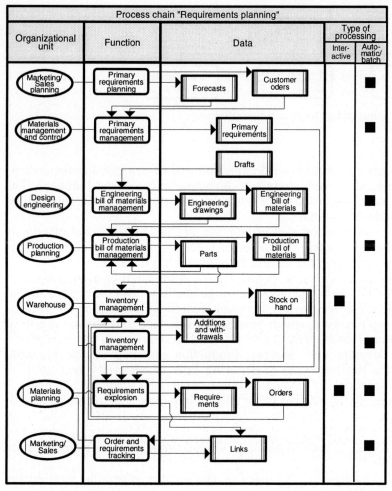

Fig. B.I.07: Process chain diagram for requirements planning

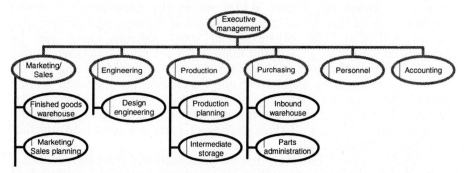

Fig. B.I.08: Organizational chart of organizational units involved in requirements planning

be organizationally assigned to a single department, e.g., to a central requirements planning unit.

Since the structure of the bill of materials is probably the most fundamental data structure in an industrial enterprise, it is presented in detail as a relational and network model within the framework of the design specification. This data structure is also discussed within the context of the implementation description both from the data view, by specifically embedding it in database systems, as well as from the function view, by using programming examples for bill of materials explosions. This complete analysis of bill of materials management from the requirements definition to the implementation description is, however, an exception to the rule, which is indicated only by way of example; the other subprocesses in this book will primarily be studied from the perspective of the requirements definitions.

B.I.3.2 Requirements Definitions for Requirements Planning

B.I.3.2.1 Managing Bills of Materials

Figure B.I.11 illustrates the major functions involved in managing bills of materials. When defining bills of materials, the objective is to determine the most suitable organizational form for a bill of materials for the product to be described, which involves distinguishing between a basic bill of materials and different variants. These variants sometimes lead to complicated data structures, which are discussed below. The basic bill of materials will be discussed first, after which extensions will be treated.

Bill of materials data management encompasses creating, updating and deleting data. In this connection, it is possible to make a distinction between complete bills of materials and individual components.

The analyses distinguish between the parts composition view (bill of materials view) and the parts utilization view.

Bill of materials management is the task of Production Planning.

As the name implies, Production Planning is responsible for designing and planning the production process. This refers primarily to the production and assembly of products. In addition to "Production Planning," other commonly used terms include "Job Planning," "Manufacturing Engineering," "Production Control," "Production Scheduling" and "Planning" (see *Eversheim, Organisation in der Produktionstechnik, Vol. 3, p. 2*). The term "Production Planning" will be used throughout the remainder of the book.

According to a definition by the German Committee for Cost-Efficient Manufacturing (AWF), production planning can be divided into process planning and production control. Process planning refers to planning activities that occur once and only involve the introduction of a part into

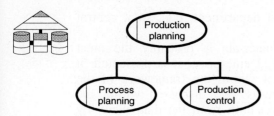

Fig. B.I.09: Organizational chart of production planning

the production program; production control refers to all tasks that are associated with the handling of an order. According to this definition, production planning processes the product descriptions from the production view, as illustrated in the upper right branch of the Y model, as well as overall production logistics (up to primary requirements planning). The corresponding organizational chart is shown in Figure B.I.09 (see also additional organizational models for production planning in *Wiendahl, Analyse und Neuordnung der Fabrik 1991, p. 23).*

Figure B.I.10 shows the events that initiate bill of materials management as a rough event-driven process chain. This figure illustrates that these events can occur in design engineering as well as in requirements planning or production planning.

The following detailed description of bill of materials management emphasizes the development of the data model.

Process-oriented production uses the term "recipe" to describe the composition of a product. Although they are not truly synonymous, the terms "bill of materials" and "recipe" are used interchangeably. The differences will be discussed in the later section on PPC systems for process-oriented production.

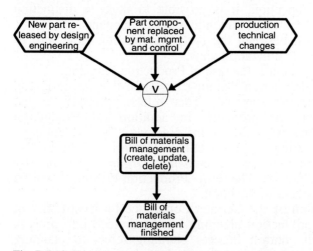

Fig. B.I.10: Event control of bill of materials management

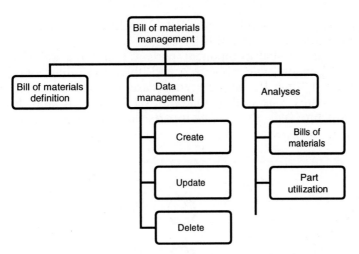

Fig. B.I.11: Functions involved in bill of materials management

B.I.3.2.1.1 The Basic Bill of Materials

The term "part" encompasses end products, assemblies, component parts and raw materials. End products are parts that the company does not process further. Assemblies consist of other parts (components) and are used, in turn, to produce further parts (assemblies or end products). Component parts are manufactured from a single material, e.g., by stamping or milling. Materials (raw materials) are basic materials that are typically not produced in-house. Except for materials, all other types of parts can usually be either produced in-house or outsourced (if they are end products, they would then be termed "merchandise"). There are other terms in addition to the definitions cited here. Thus, in the SAP application software environment, for example, the term "material" is used as a superordinate concept, which corresponds to the use of the term "part" in this book (see *SAP, System RM-PPS Funktionsbeschreibung 1993, p. 22*).

Diagrams can be used to provide a visual representation of how end products are composed of assemblies and component parts. Figure B.I.12 shows how end product P1 comprises component parts C1 and C2 as well as assembly A1. Assembly A1, in turn, consists of component parts C1 and C3. Component parts C1 and C3 are outsourced, while component part C2 is produced from material M1.

Production processes are associated with the production of a component part; production and assembly processes, with the production of an assembly. The problem description also determines whether a specific production condition is defined as an independent part or only as an intermediate result within an assembly or production process of a superordinate part.

Thus, the relationship illustrated in Figure B.I.12 could also result in the diagrams shown in Figures B.I.13,a and B.I.13,b.

Figure B.I.13,a assumes that component parts C1 and C2 are first assembled into independent assembly A2 and then assembled with assembly A1 to form product P1. In the second case, on the other hand, component parts C1 and C3 as well as material M1 go directly into the end product; the structure only shows which parts the entire end product comprises.

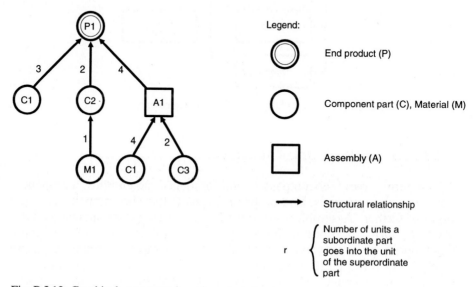

Fig. B.I.12: Graphical representation of product structure

An assembly must be defined if organizational departments have to identify it as a unit. There can be several reasons for this, as shown in Figure B.I.14 (see *VDI, Produktionsplanung 1974, p. 29*).

The horizontal rows show the different criteria that lead to the formation of assemblies; the vertical columns show the individual departments that apply these criteria. In actual practice, assembling components into a complete assembly—which then goes into several different superordinate parts—is the most frequent criterion encountered in defining assemblies, and it is used in all production-oriented departments. Thus, Design Engineering determines which end products these assemblies will be used in, Production Planning can schedule the superordinate parts based on production of the assemblies, while they function as cost objectives for Costing. Moreover, they are frequently put in buffer storage and can also be sold as spare parts.

The other criteria for forming assemblies are not required simultaneously by all production-oriented departments. This is especially true in the case of the closed-function criterion of a parts group that is

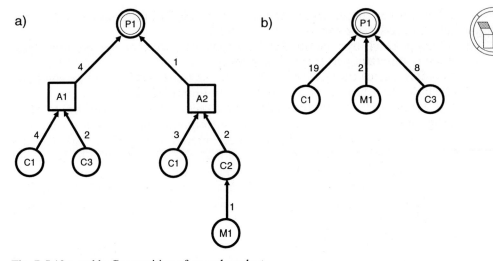

Fig. B.I.13,a and b: Composition of an end product

Departments that apply these criteria / Criteria for assembly formation	Design engineering	Production planning	Cost accounting (costing)	Inventory organization	Spare parts organization	Marketing/ Sales
Assembly goes into various super-ordinate parts as preassembly group	×	×	×	×	×	
Assembly is stored independently		×	×	×		
Assembly is available as spare or as independent sales group		×	×	×	×	×
Assembly comprises a closed function	×	×	(×)			

Fig. B.I.14: Criteria for forming assemblies

primarily used in Design Engineering. For example, Design Engineering can view the entire electronics system of an automobile as a unit, although it refers to totally different subsystems such as ignition and lighting and is not stocked as a closed group.

The different points of view of the various departments can lead to the formation of different assemblies. There are two options in this case: attempt to compromise with a unified product structure or create several parallel structures for each product, for example, on the basis of Marketing, Design Engineering and Production needs (see Section B.I.3.2.1.2.2 on combined bills of materials).

The further discussion assumes that the products are structured on the basis of production views.

The product tree illustrated in Figure B.I.12 contains redundancies. Thus, component part C1 is shown twice.

Redundancies can also occur between the trees for different products, as illustrated in reference to assembly A1 in Figure B.I.15.

If these parts structures were stored sequentially according to their design, then $7 + 5 = 12$ items of parts information and $6 + 4 = 10$ items of structure information would have to be entered. Component parts C1 and C3 would each be stored three times and assembly A1 would be stored twice. The structural information concerning the composition of A1 would also have to be entered twice. Aside from the aspect of special DP storage techniques, this redundant storage leads to a high degree of storage and updating effort.

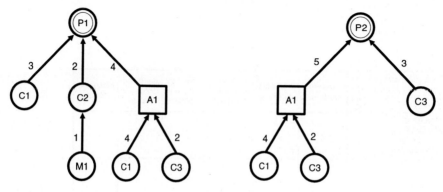

Fig. B.I.15: Product trees for two end products

This redundancy can be avoided if the data structure is stored as a gozinto graph rather than as separate trees. The gozinto graph records each part and each structural relationship only once (see *Vazsonyi, Planungsrechnung 1962*). Figure B.I.16 shows the gozinto graph for end products P1 and P2.

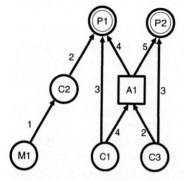

Fig. B.I.16: Gozinto graph for two end products

The gozinto graph serves as the point of departure for data modeling. It consists of the parts and their relationships. Thus, the entity type PART and the relationship type STRUCTURE can be seen directly in the gozinto graph in Figure B.I.17. Each part in the gozinto graph is an element of the entity type PART, and every arrow is an element of the relationship type STRUCTURE. Each part is identified by a part number PNO and every relationship by indicating the part numbers that link it as a source and a sink. For purposes of distinction, the part numbers are given the additional indicators H (higher) and L (lower). The cardinalities for the relationship type can also be shown clearly.

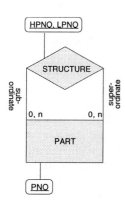

Fig. B.I.17: ERM of bill of materials

To do this, figure B.I.18 shows the parts of the gozinto graph in their "roles" as higher-level parts and lower-level parts together with their assignments. An assembly is both a higher-level part and a lower-level part. Since outsourced parts M1, C1 and C3 do not assume the role of a "higher-level part", and end products do not assume the role of a "lower-level part", no corresponding assignments lead to them. Several elements of the other sets can be assigned to elements of the "higher-level part" set and to elements of the "lower-level part" set. Thus, each case involves cardinalities of 0,n.

0 or any number of parts can be subordinate to a part—i.e., one part can be the starting point for 0 or an arbitrary number of lines, which lead from left to right in Figure B.I.18. The number 0 includes an important condition of integrity, since it shows that the case illustrated in Figure B.I.18 for C1, C3 and M1, which exhibits no relationships, is permissible.

By the same token, 0 or an arbitrary number of parts can be superordinate to a part.

Further data structures will omit the indication of minimal instances for the sake of simplicity and will conform to the simplified notation of cardinalities (see Section A.II.1.3.2.3). This leads to consistent cardinalities of n.

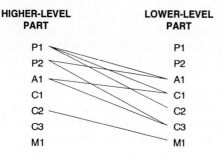

Fig. B.I.18: Relationships between higher- and lower level part

When defining the parts, a distinction is made between end products, assemblies, component parts and materials. At the same time, the parts can be classified as outsourced, in-house and sales parts. Since these types of parts initiate different planning processes and thus different data structures, Figure B.I.19 introduces a system of specialization with the subtypes MATERIAL, COMPONENT PART, ASSEMBLY and END PRODUCT (ARTICLE). A subtype relationship expresses the fact that each element of the subtype is also an element of the superordinate entity type. This type of specialization is free from overlaps, while the specialization into outsourced, in-house and sales parts shown in Figure B.I.20 is not.

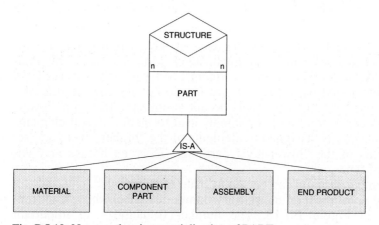

Fig. B.I.19: Non-overlapping specialization of PART

Articles and/or sales parts encompass all salable parts, i.e., end products, merchandise, spare parts and salable assemblies. Outsourced parts can be outsourced materials, outsourced component parts and outsourced assemblies. In-house parts are parts that must undergo at least one production or assembly process.

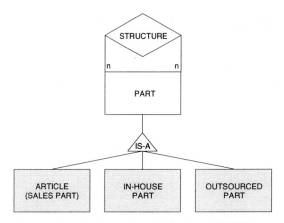

Fig. B.I.20: Overlapping specialization of PART

The specialized entity types ARTICLE, IN-HOUSE PART and OUTSOURCED PART are the respective reference objects for outbound, inbound and production logistics. Their mutual inclusion in the bill of materials structure once again clarifies their central importance.

Attribute types are assigned to the entity types and to the relationship type STRUCTURE. Although these properties can differ depending on the industry, type of enterprise and state of data processing, a relatively fixed catalog has been established (see *Grupp, Elektronische Stück-listenorganisation 1976, pp. 89 ff.; Mertens/Griese, Integrierte Informationssysteme II 1993, pp. 68 ff.; VDI, Produktionsplanung 1974, pp. 46 ff.*).

Several attribute types refer in general to the entity type PART, while others are assigned to the subtypes OUTSOURCED PART, IN-HOUSE PART and ARTICLE.

Figure B.I.21 shows typical attribute groups.

The planning data for Purchasing primarily refer to orders; the planning data for Production, to production orders; and the planning data for Sales, to customer orders. These will be discussed individually in the sections on their respective functions. Some attribute groups are assigned to separate entity and relationship types in the downstream data structuring process. Thus, only a general overview of the attribute types of relevance for bills of materials will first be provided.

Some of the attributes—e.g., their identification as A, B or C parts—are created by programs, while other data are manually taken from different departments such as Design Engineering, Production Planning and Cost Accounting.

The following list will include several attribute types of the general entity type PART, its subtypes OUTSOURCED PART, IN-HOUSE PART and ARTICLE, as well as the relationship type STRUCTURE and—to the extent necessary—provide a brief discussion of each.

Attribute groups	Occur for part type
Identification data	all
Classification data	all
Status data	all
Technical/physical data	all
Routings	in-house parts
Stock on hand data	all
Requirements data	all
Planning data for:	
Purchasing	outsourced parts
Production	in-house parts
Sales	end products
Cost data	all

Fig. B.I.21: Attribute groups

Many attributes will not be required until later sections, where they will be discussed in greater detail.

1) General attribute types related to the entity type PART:

Identification data: Serve as unique identifiers of the part in different files or catalogs.
Part number: Key to the entity type PART.
Drawing number: Key to the technical drawing of the part.
Number in sales catalog: ...
Part name: ...
Classification data: Serve to arrange the parts according to several predetermined properties. Parts having the same classification are identical with respect to these properties. Frequently, classifying information is incorporated into the part number. In this case, the part number consists of the identification number and the classification number, which is then termed the "locator number."
Part type: Identifier for end products, spare parts, assemblies or component parts.
Value: Identifier based on the result of an ABC analysis.

Planning level:	Number of the planning level on which the part occurs within the gozinto graph.
Requirement type:	Identifier indicating whether the part requirement is derived only from the superordinate parts requirement (secondary requirement), or if a primary requirement also exists.
Type of planning:	Identifier indicating whether the requirement should be determined using specific consumption-oriented forecasting techniques. The parameters necessary in this case, such as smoothing factors and previous forecast values, must then be stored as well.

Status data: Indicate the current status of the part in the manufacturing process.

State of production: Identifier that describes the current status of the part within its lifecycle, such as design phase, testing phase, pilot lot, production and discontinuation phase.

Use status: Identifier indicating whether the part is still being actively used in production, is being carried as a spare part or has been discontinued.

Date of update: Date of most recent technical change.

Technical/physical parameters: Unit of measure, weight, dimensions, space requirement, type of material, color and model.

Stock on hand data: Total inventory, storage area requirements.

Planning data: These data are required for planning and scheduling purposes.

Type of planning: Identifier indicating whether a part is subject to consumption-based planning, demand-based planning without requirements verification, demand-based planning with single-level requirements verification, or demand-based planning with multi-level requirements verification.

Cost data: Summary, parts-oriented cost variables that are necessary for optimization calculations within the planning system.

Date of update: Date of most recent cost update.

Fixed lot costs: Setup costs for in-house parts or fixed order costs for outsourced parts.

Storage cost rate: Global value used to calculate lot sizes. It can be further differentiated in the storage rates based on stock location.

Results of
cost accounting: Cost rates for the material and production costs for a part.

2) Attributes relating to special part types:

Type: OUTSOURCED PART

Ordering policy: Identifier for calculating the order size: Economic order quantity, fixed order size, unit period adjustment, requirement for a specific number of periods.

Limits: Upper and lower limits of the order size.

Delivery time: Average time between sending the order and receiving the goods.

Safety factor: Percentage factor used to compensate for requirement fluctuations during the delivery time.

Type: IN-HOUSE PART

Lot size: Minimum, optimum, maximum lot size.

Processing time: Average sum of production, setup and transfer times for a part order.

Routing: Production procedures, operation data with equipment classification.

Type: ARTICLE (SALES PART)

Selling price: Gross amount.

Rebate classification: Identifier for part-oriented rebate scales, which, together with the customer rebate identifier, determines the actual amount of the rebate.

Minimum package size: Lower limit for a shipping order.

3) Structural relationship attributes:

Type: STRUCTURE

Quantity:	Number of component units that go into a superordinate part unit (production coefficient). The dimensions in which each unit is measured are specified in the part master record.
Scrap rate:	Scrap rate for the components when manufacturing the superordinate part.
Lead time:	Number of time units between the start of production for a superordinate part order and the point in time at which the components are needed. If the components must be present at the start of the superordinate order, the lead time is 0.
Operation classification:	Operation number within the routing for the superordinate part for which the components will be used.
Validity date:	Date on which the structure becomes valid.
Expiration date:	Date on which the structure becomes invalid.
Type of bill of materials:	Designates in which product classifications (bills of materials) the structure occurs (bills of materials for production, engineering, sales, plant and spare parts).
Variant information:	Designates in which product variants the structure occurs.

Bill of materials management (creating, updating, deleting) is an aspect of Process Planning. Drawings and bills of materials created in Design Engineering provide initial information. The engineering bill of materials is structured according to function views, while the bill of materials from Production Planning conforms to production-oriented views. The section on the product development process chain will go into greater detail on the use of computer-aided design (CAD) systems in generating bill of materials information.

In addition to managing bill of materials data for in-house parts, bills of materials can also be maintained for outsourced parts. Thus, for example, bills of materials for outsourced assemblies can be maintained that help track down defective components in this assembly. Suppliers are increasingly providing these types of bills of materials in the form of data files that can be imported automatically. During the subsequent scheduling process, it is important to ensure that the components in outsourced assemblies are not scheduled. Suppliers can also supply bills of materials for systems (machines), for example, to identify necessary spare parts.

	Modular representation	Structural representation	Overview representation
Bills of materials for part P1	Part name Quantity C2 2 A1 4 C1 3	Part name Quantity C2 2 .M1 1 C1 3 A1 4 .C1 4 .C3 2	Part name Quantity C2 2 C1 19 A1 4 C3 8 M1 2
	Description: Directly subordinate parts (components) are listed along with the quantities in which they go into the part in question.	Description: Single-level bills of materials of all parts of the structure of the part considered are listed.	Description: Every part is listed along with the total quantity in which it go into the part in question.
	Use: Requirements explosion, process planning, assembly costing.	Use: Production planning, preparation of spare catalogs.	Use: Design changes, product costing.
Utilization lists for part C1	Part name Quantity P1 3 A1 4	Part name Quantity P1 3 A1 4 .P1 4 .P2 5	Part name Quantity P1 19 A1 4 P2 20
	Description: Directly superordinate parts are listed along with the quantities of the part in question that goes into them.	Description: Single-level utilization lists are listed for the entire production structure generated from this part.	Description: All parts the part goes into either directly or indirectly are listed along with their total quantities.
	Use: Process planning for delayed production orders, design changes.	Use: Design changes.	Use: To determine where and to what extent cost and design changes will have any effects.

Fig. B.I.22: Methods of evaluating the product structure

Both methods of viewing the data structure—viewing the composition of a superordinate part in terms of its components and viewing the way in which a part is used in superordinate assemblies—have led to corresponding ways of evaluating the data structure. In this connection, the list representing the composition of parts is referred to as the bill of materials; the list that documents their use, as the utilization list. Modular, structural and overview representations can be defined for both views, depending on whether the issue is solely the parts that are incorporated directly, the overall hierarchical structure of a product or only the overall relationships without additional structuring (see Figure B.I.22, which relates to a portion of Figure B.I.16).

B.I.3.2.1.2 Extensions of Bills of Materials

High degrees of redundancy can occur in data management when closely related product structures are represented as independent bills of materials. This is true in the case of product variants, in cases where the composition of a product is managed separately according to the viewpoints of Design Engineering or Production and according to production processes in different plants, and in the case of customer-oriented production in which every customer order can constitute its own bill of materials, although it differs only minimally from other customer orders.

When creating independent bills of materials for similar products, these cases lead to an unmanageable volume of data. Thus, special forms have been developed for managing similar bills of materials. The convenience of these options for master data management can be the decisive factor in the selection of a PPC system.

The treatment of cycles in the product structure is an important problem in some industries, e.g., the chemical industry.

B.I.3.2.1.2.1 Variants

From a marketing perspective, it can be advisable to manufacture different designs of a product. For example, a machine tool can be offered that is equipped with motors having different power ratings, or a consumer article can be offered in different colors. End product or assembly designs that differ in minimal ways are referred to as variants. Variant management is particularly important in connection with planning, since the number of possible product variants can often range anywhere from several hundred thousand to millions.

Thus, for example, several hundred thousand model variants can be formed by combining all possible configurations of an automobile model.

The following basic procedures exist for managing variant bills of materials:

(1)   Each design is managed as an independent part entity.

(2)   Bills of materials are defined only for **variant families**; however, each individual variant is defined implicitly and can be activated from the variant group by indicating an extra identifier in addition to the part number.

(3)   Product variants are no longer defined as part entities. Only parts "below" the product variants within the product structure are entered as entities. A particular product variant is only built from these components if it is needed.

The question of which procedure to use depends primarily on the number of variants to be taken into consideration. In the above enumeration, the procedures are classified according to their suitability for increasing numbers of variants. Significant consequences for scheduling options are linked to these procedures. The resulting data structures are demonstrated in Figures B.I.23,a through B.I.23,j on the basis of the gozinto graphs of three variants. Production coefficients are not indicated. Only the single-level bills of materials for the end product variants are taken into consideration. The procedures are, however, also applicable to subordinate assemblies.

In **Procedure (1)**, each variant is treated as an independent product and can therefore be scheduled independently. Thus, for example, requirement forecasts can be prepared, and the corresponding model parameters can be recorded as entity attributes.

In Figure B.I.23,a, this leads to a total of 8 part entities and 13 structural relationships. Since assemblies A1, A2 and A3 are used in all three variants, the structural relationships between them and the variants are largely identical.

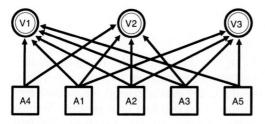

Fig. B.I.23,a: Redundant storage of product variants

In order to minimize this redundancy, the **identical-part bill of materials** is introduced. Those parts that are included in all variants are bundled into a new, fictitious "identical-part assembly" (see Figure B.I.23,b). A new part entity and three structural relationships are formed to define the identical-part group IP, but two structures are eliminated for

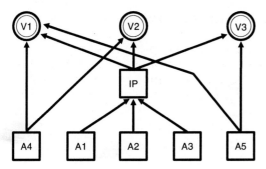

Fig. B.I.23,b: Identical-part bill of materials

each variant. A total of 9 part entities and 10 structural relationships is necessary. This data organization is only meaningful if the identical parts remain constant over an extended period of time, since all bills of materials are affected if they are changed.

Plus-minus bills of materials, on the other hand, are more flexible (see Figure B.I.23,c). A variant is defined as a basic product (V2 in this example). The differences between it and the other variants are expressed by plus parts and minus parts. In the structural records, the algebraic sign of the production coefficient indicates whether the part is being added to the basic product or whether "too much" was calculated there and must therefore be deducted. If many variants occur, this form of storage is very difficult to manage, even though it reduces the necessary scope of data to 8 part entities and 9 structural relationships in the example.

In the identical-part and plus-minus bills of materials, there is no change to the general ER model for the bill of materials in Figure B.I.17.

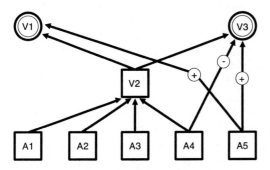

Fig. B.I.23,c: Plus-minus bill of materials

In **Procedure (2)**, only one part entity is initially formed for one variant family and linked with all assemblies that are included in the variant family (see Figure B.I.23,d).

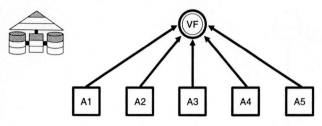

Fig. B.I.23,d: Variant family

This leads to 6 part entities and 5 structural relationships. The individual variants of the variant family are then classified, and links are defined from the variants to the structures applicable to them (see Figure B.I.23,e). The advantage of this form of management, which at first glance seems complicated, is that the actual attribute values for the parts and structural relationships are only represented once, while the variants and the relationships originating from them do not have to contain descriptive attributes. (It should be noted, however, that individual structural coefficients and other data can be stored in the variant structures.) This variant form is referred to as a **multiple bill of materials**, whose entity-relationship is illustrated in Figure B.I.23,f. If a known fixed upper limit can be indicated for the number of variants that apply to a variant family, the multiple bill of materials leads to a further significant simplification. For the ER model in Figure B.I.23,f, this case means that the cardinality n is determined from the start by a fixed value (n^*), e.g., as it is fixed at 3 in this example. In this case, the structure variant classifications are entered into the structural records as attributes, and the relationship type STRUCTURE-VARIANT-ASSIGNMENT is eliminated in the ER model.

Instead of **one** quantity field, a quantity field is created in each structural relationship for **each** variant (see Figure B.I.23,g), which indicates whether—and if so, in how many units—the subordinate component goes into a given variant. This reduces the data structure to 6 part entities and 5 (extended) structural relationships. In order to create the bill of materials for a variant, the part number of the variant family must first be given, followed by the variant key. Finally, every product structure is checked to determine if the component belongs to the variant and how many quantity units go into the variant. In Figure B.I.23,g, the use of an assembly as a variant is indicated by a "1" in the quantity fields.

This form of storage makes it particularly easy to represent so-called **quantity variants**. These occur when the variants are distinguished only by different production coefficients rather than by different **types of assemblies (structure variants)**. This form of storage complicates requirements planning, since the variant family for which only part data are managed is merely a fictitious part. For planning purposes, therefore, it may be meaningful to assign the variant attributes to the defined individual variant entities.

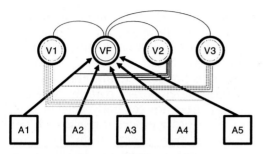

Fig. B.I.23,e: Multiple bill of materials

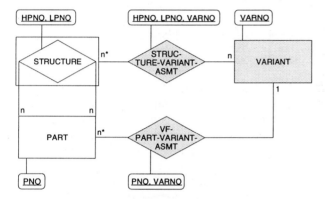

Fig. B.I.23,f: ERM for multiple bill of materials

Structural relationship	Quantity fields			Further user-dependent attributes
	V1	V2	V3	
A1 - VF	1	1	1	
A2 - VF	1	1	1	
A3 - VF	1	1	1	
A4 - VF	1	1		
A5 - VF	1		1	

Fig. B.I.23,g: Multiple bill of materials with a given quantity of variants

Another form of planning involves referencing the overall requirement to the variant family. In this case, the structural relationship contains an additional attribute for storing the percentage with which the component goes into each unit of the family. This coefficient must then be statistically tracked because it is influenced by shifts in demand between the variants.

Procedure (3) is used when an almost unmanageably large number of variants exists for each product type, as is the case, for example, for automotive manufacturing or during component part production when the variants consist largely of standard parts. What both cases have in common is that a specific product variant is not defined until the customer order is received for it. This variant forms a temporary part entity with a temporary single-level bill of materials. These are generally deleted from the active bill of materials inventory after order processing and archived for subsequent information functions for new orders from the same customer, for spare parts delivery or because of legal regulations. Only assemblies (together with their bills of materials) are maintained in isolation from one another as master entities (see Figure B.I.23,h).

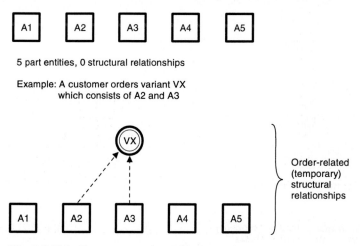

Fig. B.I.23,h: Temporary variant bill of materials

A customer order, therefore, indicates the type and quantity of the assemblies to be incorporated into the variant. The structural relationships are formed on the basis of this information. The decision table technique can be used to determine which parts must be present in the product in each case (so-called mandatory variants) and which parts cancel each other out. The use of expert systems is advisable in particularly complicated cases (see *Schönsleben, Flexible Produktionsplanung und -steuerung 1985, pp. 37 ff.*). In these approaches, the logic of the data structures is relocated into the application program, i.e., the function view.

These types of plausibility checks in compiling a bill of materials are particularly necessary in interactive solutions. A planner compiles the product requirements from existing requirements or even directly from the customer by repeatedly querying the requirements. *Wedekind/Müller, Stücklistenorganisation 1981* developed a systematic approach for this process.

But extensive variant solutions of the type that occur in actual practice can be created with the data structures represented here. This is particularly true if several of the cited variant representations are combined. Figure B.I.23,i shows a complex variant representation. A car model consists of three assemblies: "chassis," "body" and "engine." The engine forms a variant family with three different instances, of which one must be selected (mandatory variants). The body consists of the raw body and the side-view mirror attached to it. Both are, in turn, variant families. In both instances, the body can be selected as either white or red mandatory variants. There are two variants for the side-view mirror that refer to the strength of the springs contained in it. The spring strength is designed according to the anticipated wind resistance. The anticipated wind resistance is determined by the anticipated driving speed of the car

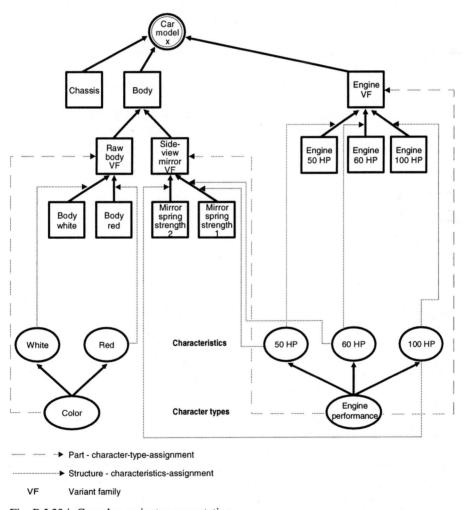

Fig. B.I.23,i: Complex variant representation

and thus by engine performance. It should be noted that this at first glance aberrant relationship between engine performance and side-view mirror deflection does, in fact, exist in practice and thus clearly illustrates the multiplicity of the many variant relationships that can exist.

The lower portion of Figure B.I.23,i shows both types of characteristic features, which determine variant selection, as Character Type 1 with color and Character Type 2 with engine performance. Characteristics are assigned to the character types. The engine performance character type determines engine and mirror variants.

The ER model for this example illustrated in Figure B.I.23,j is similar to the ER model for multiple bills of materials. In contrast to the multiple bill of materials, the individual variants are not explicitly defined. Instead, only character types are specified along with the characteristics assigned to them, by virtue of which a special variant is specified. Since the individual possible variants are no longer explicitly listed, a similarity to the temporary variant bill of materials also exists.

Character types used to provide detailed specifications for variant families are assigned to those families using the relationship type VF-PART-CHARACTER-TYPE-ASSIGNMENT. The characteristics belonging to one character type are entered via a 1:n relationship CHARACTER-GROUPING.

The relationship type STRUCTURAL-CHARACTERISTIC-ASSIGN-MENT links the bill of materials structures belonging to a characteristic, whereby limitation to a specific variant family is also expressed by the

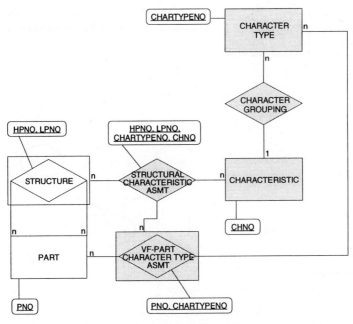

Fig. B.I.23,j: ERM for complex variant formation

link to VF-PART-CHARACTER-TYPE-ASSIGNMENT. The part number of the corresponding variant family is the same as the HPNO of the structural relationship.

The logic presented here encompasses significant properties of the sales group concept contained in the SAP RM-PPS and RV system, which is used in many industrial enterprises for managing variant problems (see *SAP, System RM-PPS Funktionsbeschreibung 1993, p. 34*).

B.I.3.2.1.2.2 Combined Bills of Materials

There are several criteria for categorizing a product into its components.

Design Engineering classifies the product according to functional groups, e.g., electronics, drive train or chassis.

Production, on the other hand, requires a bill of materials whose structure conforms to the sequence of production and assembly operations. These two types of structuring typically lead to different bills of materials. Design-related functional groups are frequently not assembled together and are thus not listed as an assembly on the production bill of materials, as shown by the example in Figure B.I.24 (see also *Kittel, PPS im Klein- und Mittelbetrieb 1982, p. 49*). From the design perspective, the automobile chassis window belongs to the "door" production group, but for safety reasons it is the final assembly step (after installing the door frame).

If an enterprise maintains only one engineering bill of materials, mistakes will occur in the scheduling of components, since the actual production flow deviates from the one that is represented. For this reason, the **production bill of materials** is an absolute necessity for Production Planning and Control.

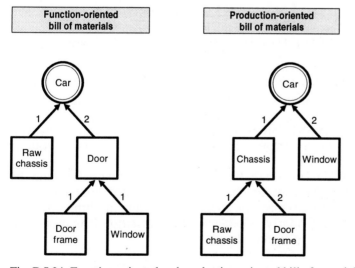

Fig. B.I.24: Function-oriented and production-oriented bill of materials

In addition to the classification perspectives of Design Engineering and Production, a product can also be subclassified on the basis of sales criteria, i.e., parts that are sold together form sales groups. These groups can be end product packages as well as spare parts sets that form a unit only from the perspective of Sales, but are neither designed nor produced together.

Figure B.I.25 shows one possible classification according to sales groups for product P1, which was classified in Figure B.I.12 from the perspective of Production. Component part C1 is sold separately as a spare part; four units from assembly A1 form spare part group S2, together with the two units C2. Different bills of materials for the same product can exist in a company, for example, if the product is produced in different plants using different production techniques, upon which the application of the component will depend. This scenario deals with "plant bills of materials."

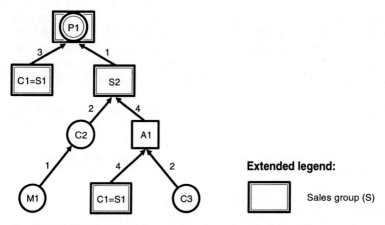

Fig. B.I.25: Composition of an end product classified according to sales groups

If several parallel product structures are to be maintained, there are two options:
(1)   The bills of materials are managed in separate databases; however, this leads to high storage and management costs if a large volume of data is involved.
(2)   Since the bills of materials for many parts are identical despite the different structural approaches, they are treated analogously to variants. A hybrid form of identical-part and multiple bills of materials is particularly suitable for this scenario. This procedure will be discussed in further detail.

One part entity is defined for all units that are necessary from the perspective of Design Engineering, Production or Sales. The link from the corresponding view is maintained in attributes of the structural relationship, i.e., *quantity in engineering bills of materials, quantity in production bills of materials, quantity in sales bills of materials, etc.*

If the corresponding quantity field equals 0, the component does not occur. A part entity and/or a structural relationship can be contained in one or more bills of materials.

Figure B.I.26 shows the gozinto graph for the combined bill of materials for product P1 according to production and sales group criteria, as discussed above in Figures B.I.12 and Figure B.I.25. Each line indicates in which quantity fields (P or S) the structural records for 0 different coefficients are stored. The design structure can also be illustrated in this way.

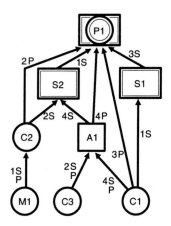

Fig. B.I.26: Combined bill of materials

B.I.3.2.1.2.3 Cycles

While the gozinto graphs for manufactured products are generally cycle-free, this is not true for recipes in the chemical industry, where end products or intermediate products themselves can be reused as raw materials, catalysts or additives in upstream production stages.

On the entity level, however, these types of cyclical diagrams lead to the same data structures at the type level as the ones discussed above. Figure B.I.27 shows a cyclical gozinto graph. One unit from A consists of 0.8 unit of component C as well as 0.2 unit of end product P. At the same time, one unit from A goes into one unit of P. The figure clearly shows that parts P and A are both higher-level and lower-level parts in their relationship to one another. Nevertheless, in principle the data structure cannot be distinguished from that of a typical bill of materials and thus leads to the data model for the type-level bill of materials discussed above.

Problems do indeed result from the requirements explosion of cyclical gozinto graphs: Many bill of materials processors and/or processing programs for bill of materials management frequently cannot process cyclical gozinto graphs. In the structural bill of materials explosion, the cycles execute continually unless, for example, identifiers are included that ensure that each part will only be processed once. In overview bills of materials, the overall requirement coefficient can be determined only by the explosion of an interdependent linear system of equations (see *Kloock, Input-Output-Analyse 1969; Vazsonyi, Planungsrechnung 1962*).

Within the framework of maintenance programs for bill of materials management, special programming functions frequently query whether cyclical structures may be stored.

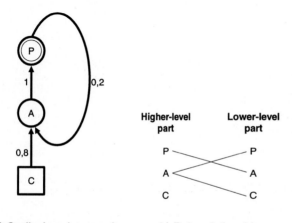

a) Cyclical gozinto graph   b) Role relationship

Fig. B.I.27: Representation of a cyclical product structure

B.I.3.2.2 Requirements Explosion

The requirements explosion derives the requirements for subordinate assemblies, component parts and outsourced parts from the primary requirements for salable products and compiles them into orders on the basis of optimal lot size.

In business administration literature, the requirements explosion is illustrated using matrix operations (see *Kloock, Input-Output-Analyse 1969, pp. 68 ff.*). The primary requirement is indicated by a vector that is multiplied by the direct requirement matrix. The direct requirement matrix contains the bill of materials structure from the gozinto graph. The coefficients for the bill of materials are imported into the matrix. One of its elements a_{ij} then indicates how many quantity units of part i go directly into part j (see Figure B.I.28,a).

The inverse matrix for D is technological matrix D^{-1}. If the technological matrix is subtracted from the unit matrix, the result is the total input matrix $(I-D^{-1})$ (see Figure B.I.28,b). One of its elements a_{ij} indicates how many quantity units of a part i are necessary for the production of a quantity unit of part j.

If the primary requirement vector is multiplied by the total input matrix, the result is the quantity of all parts that are necessary for the production of the primary requirements.

However, it is difficult, if not impossible, to take into account inventory levels, processing and lead times, reservations and lot sizing. Thus, a sequential process that is typical in DP systems is presented here.

	M1	C1	C2	C3	A1	P1	P2
M1			1				
C1					4	3	
C2						2	
C3					2		3
A1						4	5
P1							
P2							

Fig. B.I.28,a: Direct requirements matrix referring to the example of Fig. B.I.16

	M1	C1	C2	C3	A1	P1	P2
M1	1		1			2	
C1		1			4	19	20
C2			1			2	
C3				1	2	8	13
A1					1	4	5
P1						1	
P2							1

Fig. B.I.28,b: Total input matrix of the example of Fig. B.I.16

B.I.3.2.2.1 Planning Types - Planning Level - Production Level

Fundamentally, there are two procedures for determining parts requirements: **consumption-based** and **demand-based** materials planning (see Figure B.I.29). In consumption-based planning, a part requirement is derived from past consumption values using simple extrapolation, e.g., exponential smoothing. This statistical method of determining requirements involves procedure-related forecasting errors.

In demand-based planning, on the other hand, the part requirement is derived from the requirement figures for superordinate parts.

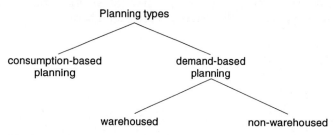

Fig. B.I.29: Planning types

The distinction between those parts that are consumption-based and those that are demand-based is made on the basis of the value of the parts and the regularity of their demand pattern. ABC analysis can aid in this process. This analysis is simple and requires only the consumption value per part for the last period (e.g., the last year). All parts are sorted in descending order according to their value. The cumulative quantities and value-oriented percentages are then compared in a Lorenz concentration graph (see Figure B.I.30).

Actual practice has shown that approximately 10 % of the parts frequently constitute 70 % of the annual consumption value. A further 20 % of the parts make up an additional 20 % of the annual consumption value, and the remaining 70 % of the parts constitute only 10 % of the annual consumption value. According to this grouping, the parts are referred to as A, B and C parts. ABC analyses must be repeated at specific intervals in order to verify the grouping.

A and B parts in particular are planned on the basis of the demand-based approach, since their inexact planning leads to higher inventory and shortfall costs. Particularly valuable A parts that are required only in small numbers per period can also be completely removed from the mechanical planning system and planned manually for each existing customer order. C parts, on the other hand, are planned in a consumption-based manner. It should be noted that demand-based planning is more precise, but it also requires more computation. The trend is toward using unified planning procedures, and therefore toward the increased use of demand-based

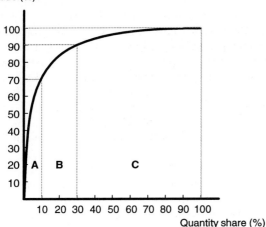

Percentage of consumption value (%)

Quantity share (%)

Fig. B.I.30: Lorenz graph for part classification

planning, in order to unify the organization. It is also practical to assume that only requirements with a stabile data pattern and a low consumption value are suitable for consumption-based planning (see Figure B.I.31 and *Grochla, Materialwirtschaft 1992, pp. 29 ff.*).

While consumption-based planning **schedules** the requirements using a retrograde calculation and thus follows the "fetch" principle, the **physical material flow** of the consumption-based planning process is controlled according to the "bring" principle. This means that a processing location has the completed lots transported to the next processing location. If a lot is intended for several downstream orders, it must be divided into different transport routes. The bring principle leads to difficulties if scheduling delays frequently occur with the components and an imperfect availability

Classi-fication \ Data pattern	Horizontal	Season and trend	Irregular
A	DB	DB	DB
B	DB	DB	DB
C	CB	CB	CB

Legend:

CB = Consumption-based planning
DB = Demand-based planning

Fig. B.I.31: Criteria to determine the planning type

check is conducted prior to the release of superordinate production orders. Such cases involve a great deal of effort in searching for missing in-process parts.

Under demand-based planning, a distinction can be made between warehoused and non-warehoused parts. The term "warehoused" means that finished parts are normally put into stock before they are processed further. Their respective quantities and locations are monitored through the stock-in and stock-out functions. Inventory management is particularly necessary when lots are formed, i.e., requirements are preproduced and warehoused. On the other hand, if parts are to be immediately processed further, tight order control of the material flow is necessary, but inventory management is not.

In order to avoid having to process a part redundantly during the requirements explosion because its requirement is derived from several superordinate parts, parts are handled in sequence according to their planning levels. A distinction must be made between the terms "planning level" and "production level" (see Figure B.I.32). "Production levels" refer to individual end product trees, while "planning levels" refer to gozinto graphs that are formed across all interrelated part relationships.

The highest production level within a product tree is the composition of the end product itself. This level is defined as 1 plus the number of lines in the longest path within the product tree that leads from the outsourced parts to the end product (see Figure B.I.32). The production level for a non-end product is computed by subtracting from the production level of the end product the number of lines in the path that lies between the given part and the end product. A part (here C1 and C3) can occur on several production levels.

The planning level of a part is defined as 1 plus the number of lines of the longest path within the overall gozinto graph that leads from the outsourced parts to the node for a given part. The planning levels are also indicated in Figure B.I.32. One unique planning level can be assigned to each part.

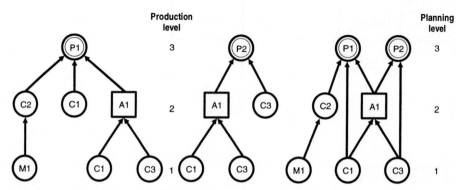

Fig. B.I.32: Explanation of production and planning level

Another common definition refers to the planning level as the numerically smallest production level on which a part occurs within product trees.

The definition used here, however, has the advantage that all outsourced parts are assigned to planning level 1, while in the second definition they belong to different planning levels. A 1:n relationship exists between the entity types PLANNING LEVEL and PART (see Figure B.I.33).

B.I.3.2.2.2 Secondary Requirements, Inventory, Orders

Within the requirements explosion, net requirements are computed from the gross requirements by subtracting inventory levels and are then compiled into orders (gross-net calculation). An inventory level refers to the item in inventory—i.e., to the part—and to the location designation—i.e., to the storage location. Requirements and orders are transaction data and refer to parts and time.

PART, STOCK LOCATION and TIME are thus defined as independent entity types in Figure B.I.35, while INVENTORY LEVEL, REQUIREMENT and ORDER are relationship types. The term "order" is used in a general sense and encompasses production orders as well as purchase orders. In the same way, the term "requirement" encompasses the primary requirement as well as the derived requirement. The information objects ORDER and REQUIREMENT follow the same logical structure as was developed for the primary requirement in Figure B.I.03. The relationship type ORDER HEADER is defined in Figure B.I.34 for the order. This relationship type is defined by the links to the customer, the order receiver and TIME (order date, DATE). The order date is, for example, the requirements planning date. In the case of internal orders (e.g., production orders), the customer and order receiver are organizational units in the enterprise (e.g., Production Planning and Production Control); in the case of external orders such as purchase orders and customer orders, one partner is external (customer or supplier) and one partner is an internal organizational unit (Purchasing or Sales). The

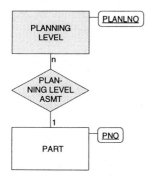

Fig. B.I.33: Assignment of planning levels

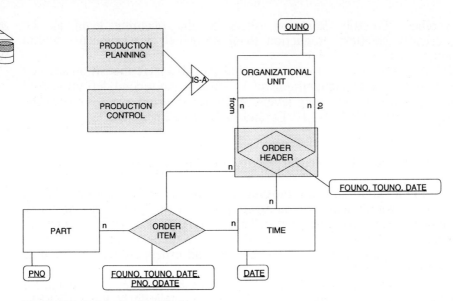

Fig. B.I.34: ERM of order definition

individual items in the order are assigned to the order header. The order items refer to the parts and are thus identified by the additional indication of the PNO and the completion date ODATE.

In the following discussions, the items are of primary importance for requirements and (purchase) orders. "Order" and "requirement" are thus understood to refer to items. For purposes of simplification, a (*) is substituted for the keys for customer, order receiver and order date.

Figure B.I.35 develops the requirements planning data structure. Since the information objects PART, STRUCTURE and PLANNING LEVEL have already been introduced, they are not shaded.

The cardinalities for INVENTORY LEVEL, REQUIREMENT and ORDER are of the nth degree:
-    A part can be stored in several storage locations, and several different parts can be in one storage location.
-    Several orders and requirements can exist for one part, and several orders and requirements can exist per time unit (instance of the entity type TIME).

The entity type STOCK LOCATION can be embedded in a multi-level hierarchy. If, for example, the stock location is interpreted as a bin in a high-rise shelf storage unit, the sequence of stock location (storage bin), storage system (shelving), storage area, storage building and storage location (city) can form a hierarchy within the warehouse department, whereby hierarchical n:1 relationships exist between each coordinate concept. This is briefly clarified in Figure B.I.35, in that a hierarchical n:1 relationship was formed from the entity type STORAGE AREA to the entity type STOCK LOCATION.

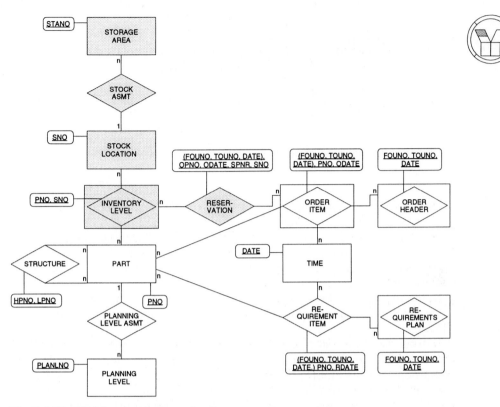

Fig. B.I.35: ERM for requirements planning

As previously mentioned in the context of the primary requirement, two procedures can be selected for entering the temporal classification of orders and requirements. In the first procedure, each individual requirement or order is entered with its exact requirement and/or completion time, as indicated in Figure B.I.36,a.

The second approach defines fixed periodic units. Requirements and orders whose due dates fall within a period are grouped together (see

Requirement/order

Part No.	Requirement/ order date	Quantity units
111	1/1	500
113	1/8	350
114	1/8	400
111	1/15	600
111	1/17	300

Fig. B.I.36,a: Day-specific entry of requirement/order

Requirement/order

Part No.	Period 1 (1/1-1/7)	Period 2 (1/8-1/14)	Period 3 (1/15-1/21)
111	500		900
113		350	
114		400	

Fig. B.I.36,b: Periodic entry of requirement/order

Figure B.I.36,b for part number 111 in period 3). The predefined time-slot grid makes temporal classification less precise, and problems of information tracking occur in forming the lots (see the discussion of requirements tracking). Because of the higher degree of data currency that is necessary in interactive processing, there is a tendency to use day-specific planning.

Both techniques, however, formally lead to the same data structure, since they are only distinguished by the **instances** of the entity type TIME.

Before an order is released to Production, the system must check whether the necessary resources (components, capacities, tools and equipment) are available. If so, the resources necessary for the order are reserved and thus become unavailable for other uses.

Figure B.I.35 shows RESERVATION as a relationship type between INVENTORY LEVEL and ORDER ITEM, which are defined as entity types for this purpose from the perspective of this additional design procedure. The cardinalities for RESERVATION equal n, since the inventory level of a component can be assigned to several superordinate orders, and in turn, several reservations for different components can be formed for a part order.

B.I.3.2.2.3 Gross-Net Calculation

Figure B.I.37 shows event control for this process in the form of a rough EPC. The event "occurrence of an original requirement" initiates the gross-net calculation. The event "occurrence of an original requirement" is the result of the consumption-based requirements forecast and/or primary requirements planning. An update in the primary requirement can, for example, be initiated by a customer order update.

In addition to the occurrence of an original requirement, events outside of requirements planning, such as bills of materials updates, supplier changes for outsourced parts, operational malfunctions or reaching a fixed planning date, can trigger replanning.

These events are analyzed to determine whether to perform period-oriented replanning using the reoptimization method or event-related

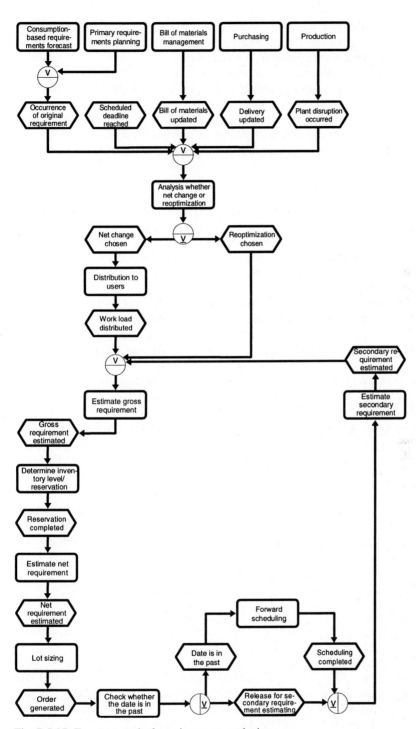

Fig. B.I.37: Event control of requirements explosion

planning using the net change method. In net change replanning, many functions are controlled interactively by users so that the task to be processed is assigned to a planner.

The logic of the gross-net calculation process is the same for automatic processing under the reoptimization principle and for the interactive net change method.

The EPC shows the fundamental logic between events and functions, but it does not contain the entire algorithmic control flow.

A calculation scheme is generated to represent the gross-net calculation (see Figure B.I.38). Primary requirements, consumption-based requirements and percentages for scrap allowances serve as the starting point for the calculation.

The part numbers for which a requirement was computed during upstream requirements planning are sorted by planning level.

The algorithm is thus verbally explained using the example in Figure B.I.38 and then summarized in a structogram in Figure B.I.41. The further contents of the event-driven process chain in Figure B.I.37 are then self-explanatory.

For every part for which a requirement is identified at transfer or during the requirements explosion, net requirements are computed from the gross requirements and compiled into lots. The parts are handled in the sequence of their planning levels, with the process beginning at the highest planning level. This procedure ensures that:

-       Only parts for which there is a demand are processed
-       Each part is processed only once (because it can belong to only **one** planning level)
-       When a part is processed, all superordinate parts have already been processed, and thus all secondary requirements have already been transferred (since superordinate parts belong to higher planning levels).

Figure B.I.39 shows the part structure that serves as the basis for the example. For parts P1, P2 and A, the requirement explosion is carried out completely, while for C1 and C2 only the secondary requirements are determined. Since the parts are exploded according to the planning level procedure, they are processed in the order P1, P2 and A.

This means that in Figure B.I.38, first the figures for P1 are processed, then for P2 and finally for A. The first column contains the names of the information objects from which existing data are taken. All other data are created within the framework of the calculation itself. Initial inventory levels and totals for each part are entered in a control column.

A planning operation is performed for six periods. This requires a fixed frequency grid. The process would not change if an individual requirement date were assigned to each individual requirement. In this case, the example would be interpreted as if six requirements with different base periods were defined for each part.

Planning level 3 (P1, P2) — **Planning level 2** (A)

Information objects	No.	Period	P1 Init. inv. (T)	P1·1	P1·2	P1·3	P1·4	P1·5	P1·6	P2 Init. inv. (T)	P2·1	P2·2	P2·3	P2·4	P2·5	P2·6	A Init. inv. (T)	A·1	A·2	A·3	A·4	A·5	A·6
Primary req.	1	Primary requirement	2655 T	100	200	1000	400	955	0	1620 T	50	70	300	500	400	300	0 T	0	0	0	0	0	0
Order	2	+Secondary req.	0 T	0	0	0	0	0	0	0 T	0	0	0	0	0	0	9966 T	0	5006	2640	2320	0	0
Primary req.	3	+Consumption-based requirement	400 T	50	50	100	100	50	50	300 T	50	50	50	50	50	50	600 T	100	100	100	100	100	100
Part	4	+Additional requirement (10%)	305 T	15	25	110	50	100	5	192 T	10	12	35	55	45	35	1056 T	10	510	274	242	10	10
	5	Total of lines 1 to 4 = gross requirement	3360 T	165	275	1210	550	1105	55	2112 T	110	132	385	605	495	385	11622 T	110	5616	3014	2662	110	110
Stock on hand	6	Stock on hand	320 I	320	295	20	20	20	20	200 I	200	240	108	73	30	30	1610 I	1610	450	100	100	100	100
Part	7	-Reserve stock	20 I	20	20	20	20	20	20	30 I	30	30	30	30	30	30	100 I	100	100	100	100	100	100
Order	8	+Released orders or outstanding orders	240 T	140	0	100	0	0	0	500 T	150	0	350	0	0	0	0 T	0	0	0	0	0	0
	9	Total of lines 6 to 8 = available stock	815 T	440	275	100	0	0	0	1001 T	320	210	428	43	0	0	1860 T	1510	350	0	0	0	0
Reservation	10	Reservations for released orders of superordinate parts	0 T	0	0	0	0	0	0	0 T	0	0	0	0	0	0	1250 T	1050	200	0	0	0	0
	11	Max 0, Lines 5+10 minus line 9 = net requirement	2820 T	0	0	1110	550	1105	55	1442 T	0	0	0	562	495	385	11362 T	0	5466	3014	2662	110	110
	12	Lot sizing (planned orders)	2820 T	0	0	1660	0	1160	0	1442 T	0	0	0	562	880	0	11362 T	0	8480	0	2882	0	0
Part	13	Lead time shift		1 Per.							2 Per.							1 Per.						
Product structure		Production coefficient		2							3							2 or 1						
Part / Product structure		Estimating second. req. of subordinate parts A	5640 T	0	3320	0	2320	0	—	4326 T	0	1686	2640	0	0	0	22724 T	16960	0	5764	0	0	0
		C1	0	—	—	—	—	—	—	0	—	—	—	—	—	—	11362 T	8480	0	2882	0	0	0
		C2	0	—	—	—	—	—	—	0	—	—	—	—	—	—							

Fig. B.I.38: Gross-net-calculation

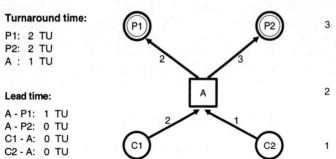

Fig. B.I.39: Part structure for Fig. B.I.38

Line 1:	Primary requirements are defined here only for parts P1 and P2.
Line 2:	The secondary requirement is derived from the superordinate parts requirement (Line 13). Therefore, it only occurs here for A (C1 and C2 are not analyzed further). Gross-net calculation cannot begin for A until it has been completed for P1 and P2.
Line 3:	Parts with a low consumption value (C parts) are generally consumption-based planned. Part of the requirement can be consumption-based planned for a demand-based part for certain market segments (e.g., spare parts). In this case, demand-based and consumption-based planning occur in parallel.
Line 4:	A percentage supplement can be allocated for scrap and inventory shrinkage. The percentage rate is assigned to the part entities.
Line 5:	The gross requirement per period results from the requirement figures in lines 1 through 4.
Line 6:	The stock on hand is defined as the quantity units of a part physically present in the warehouses at the beginning of a period. Quantities that are still present in the warehouse but allotted to (reserved for) specific production or customer orders are thus included in the stock on hand but are not taken into consideration until later (Line 10). The stock on hand is totaled from the inventory records for the part or taken from a total field of the part record and initially added to the first requirement period under consideration. If this stock on hand exceeds the requirement for the period, the remaining stock is carried forward to the next period.

Line 7:   The reserve stock is intended to compensate for unexpected fluctuations in requirements and must not be used for normal requirements.

Line 8:   Production orders released before the planning date and/or outstanding orders are recorded with their anticipated completion and/or delivery dates and are thus included in the available stock (Line 9) for this period. For P1, 140 quantity units are expected as additions to inventory from released orders during the first period, and 100 during the third period; for P2, 150 quantity units are expected during the first period, and 350 during the third period. Since the orders for the third requirement period have not been started (their processing time is two periods each), the required quantity units for A components have not yet been physically allocated to the orders.

Line 9:   The available stock (computed by adding the entries in lines 6 and 8 and subtracting line 7) can be used continuously for covering the gross requirement in line 5.

Line 10:   Orders released to Production prior to the planning date are entered in line 8 with their anticipated production completion date as an addition to inventory. Upon release, material withdrawal instructions are created for the required components. If components are not immediately physically taken from the warehouse, they must be labeled (reserved, noted) to prevent them from being allotted to any other orders. Since reservations are only possible for subordinate parts, they only occur for A in the example. The production coefficient of 2 indicates that the released order for 100 quantity units of P1 leads to a requirement of 200 QU for A. Because of the lead time of one time unit between A and P1, these 200 quantity units of A are not required until one TU after production begins on order P1; thus, 200 QU of A must be reserved at the start of the second period. The released order for P2, however, requires a reservation of $350 \times 3 = 1050$ quantity units of A in the first period.

The reservations in the example and in the data structure in Figure B.I.35 refer only to stock on hand. It is conceivable that released orders will be reserved for other released superordinate orders.

It is assumed that the components have already been physically removed from the warehouse for the incoming orders in period 1.

Line 11:   The net requirement is found by subtracting the available stock from the gross requirement plus the reservations. A negative net requirement is available as inventory for the next period.

Line 12:   The net requirement quantities for successive periods can be compiled into production lots and/or order quantities. This procedure is performed separately for each part, i.e., without taking into account the interdependence with parts that use the same production systems (sequence problem). The techniques applied and the problems involved will be discussed in more detail below. In the example, the lots have been formed arbitrarily.

An order entity of the type ORDER (ITEM) is created for each lot. On the one hand, typical order attributes include the identifying attributes FOUNO, TOUNO and DATE, which are taken from the order header, as well as PNO and ODATE; on the other hand, they include non-key attributes such as "quantity ordered" and "order status" (planned, scheduled, released, outstanding, processed).

Line 13:   When calculating the secondary requirement of the subordinate parts (A in reference to P1 and P2 as well as C1 and C2 in reference to A), the lead times of the superordinate parts must be considered. In order to calculate the lead time shifts, the turnaround time stored in the part record for the superordinate part must be subtracted from its requirement period. If a component need not be ready at the beginning of the first operation, but only after completion of several operations, this can be taken into account by the lead time between the components and the superordinate part, which is stored in the product structure record. Since the turnaround time and the lead time are each indicated in whole period units, significant inaccuracies can result from repeated rounding. They can, however, be partially corrected during subsequent planning steps involving capacity and operation planning. In the example, the relationships illustrated in Figure B.I.40 apply, whereby all reference points correspond to the starting points for the periods.

The secondary requirement for A of 5006 QU in the second period is computed from the lot of 1660 QU for P1 in the third period (one-period lead time shift) and the lot of 562 QU for P2 in the fourth period (two-period lead time shift).

The secondary requirement quantities computed by taking into account the lead time shift and the production coefficients are entered into the corresponding fields of the requirements records. At the same time, the accessed components are marked as requirement objects.

The structogram in Figure B.I.41 illustrates the gross-net calculation process, taking into account the calculation scheme discussed above. The

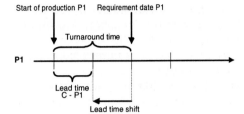

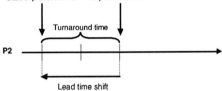

The lead time shift of a component is generally estimated as follows:
Lead time shift of a component   = Turnaround time of the superordinate part
                                  - Lead time of the component with respect
                                    to the superordinate part

Fig. B.I.40: Determination of the lead time shift of a component

Transfer primary requirements and order parts according to planning level

Repeat per part number until there are part numbers marked as requirements objectives

Transfer REQUIREMENTS and STOCK ON HAND to line 1, 2, 3, 4, 6, 7
Transfer released order quantities to line 8
Transfer reservations via the information relationship: PART, STOCK ON HAND, RESERVATION to line 10
For period = 1 to maximal period do

Estimate gross-net calculation (line 5, 9, 11) and transfer stock on hand to the subsequent periods

Repeat until net requirements exist which are not collected as lots

Estimate lot size (order quantity)
Repeat until there are non-processed components of a part using the bill of materials relationships

Multiply lot size by the production coefficient to determine the secondary requirement of components
Calculate lead time shifts
Transfer secondary requirement onto components
Mark part number of the component as requirements objectives and sort it according to its planning level

Fig. B.I.41: Structogram for gross-net calculation

structogram only contains concepts from the requirements definition level. The indication of line numbers refers to the calculation scheme in Figure B.I.38.

The results of the requirements calculation are summarized in the information objects REQUIREMENT and ORDER.

The attribute fields for REQUIREMENT are differentiated according to the lines and periods in the calculation scheme in Figure B.I.38 (see Figure B.I.42).

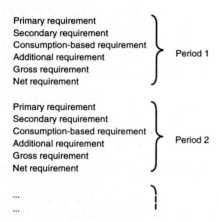

Fig. B.I.42: Extended attributes of the information object REQUIREMENT

Since primary requirements deadlines are the starting point for the requirements explosion, all component orders are geared to their latest permissible deadline in order to achieve the primary requirement on time. This reverse scheduling follows the pull concept since the components are "pulled" on schedule from the respective superordinate requirements to the primary requirement.

In the explosion, components may be scheduled in the "past," since the exact turnaround times were not known when the primary requirement quantities were determined.

The invalid start dates from the past can be corrected by shortening the component turnaround times.

For this purpose, the part entities can be assigned transfer-time-reduction factors that indicate the number of time units and/or the percentage by which the turnaround time can be reduced. However, the planning float times are lost when the transfer times are reduced. After reducing the transfer times—and consequently the turnaround times for critical orders—forward scheduling of the order network is carried out (with the earliest possible start date beginning in the present). This makes it possible to compute realistic deadlines all the way to the corresponding primary requirements. Even if this calculation means that the original primary requirement deadline cannot be met, at least realistic deadlines exist that must then be discussed with the corresponding planners who planned the primary requirement and/or accepted the customer order. If need be, forward and reverse scheduling must be performed several times.

B.I.3.2.2.4 Lot Sizing

The primary methods for calculating lot size in requirements planning are:
- Constant lot size
- Economic order quantity (EOQ)
- Adapted economic order quantity
- Unit period adjustment

The identifier for the method used for a part is treated as a part entity attribute.

Determination of the optimal lot size is a classic problem of business administration. The adapted EOQ and unit period adjustment methods were, however, developed as heuristic methods within the environment of DP-oriented solutions and only reluctantly accepted by traditional business administration.

The methods will first be introduced and then their methodological premises will be illustrated.

A specified constant lot size Y is generally not oriented toward cost considerations; instead, it is geared toward categories such as "one month's requirement," "two months' requirement," etc. Such a rule may not necessarily be the result of insufficiently cost-conscious procedures; it can also result from the realization that the narrow premises of the other methods do not permit a satisfactory optimum cost solution. Thus, a method is selected that is above all easy to manage from an organizational standpoint.

Methods geared toward computerized cost minimization require the following data:

R_h = Net requirement for subperiod h
C = Fixed lot and order costs
s = Storage cost rate [TU/(QU x subperiod)]

The net requirements are attributes taken from REQUIREMENTS; fixed lot and order costs as well as the storage cost rate are attributes of the entity type PART.

Rather than the individual subperiod requirements R_h, an average period requirement R is incorporated into the EOQ (see Figure B.I.43). The other methods, on the other hand, are based explicitly on the existing period requirements.

According to Figure B.I.44, the adapted EOQ method searches for the subperiod j^* at which the unit costs are lowest, as calculated from the lot for requirement periods i to j^*.

$$Y_{OPT} = \sqrt{\frac{2 \cdot C \cdot R}{s}}$$

Fig. B.I.43: Economic order quantity (EOQ)

$$j^* = \left\{ j \,\middle|\, k_{ij} = \underset{j'}{\text{Min}} \left\{ k_{ij'} \right\} \right\}$$

Fig. B.I.44: Economic order quantity - determination of the subperiod j^*

$k_{ij'}$ are the unit costs for a lot that is started in period i and contains the requirements up through period j'; in each case, i indicates the new starting period after determining a lot and is thus a date. The unit costs are computed according to the formula in Figure B.I.45,a.

If the condition in Figure B.I.44 is met for several values of j, it is necessary to determine which j should be selected as j^*; this can, for example, be the minimum value of j.

The unit period adjustment method shown in Figure B.I.46,a involves finding those period requirements at which the fixed lot costs equal the lot storage costs. These period requirements are then included in the lot. This condition is derived from the classic economic order quantity at which its optimum value is satisfied.

$$k_{ij'} = \frac{C + s \cdot \sum_{h=i}^{j'} R_h \cdot (h - i)}{\sum_{h=i}^{j'} R_h}$$

Fig. B.I.45,a: Adapted economic order quantity - determination of the product cost k_{ij}

Thus, subperiod j^* is sought according to the formula in Figure B.I.46,a.

Both sides of the inequality have the same dimension in the second formulation: QU x TU, i.e., quantity unit (UNIT) x time unit (PERIOD). This element inspired the name of the process.

Unit period adjustment can be further refined by conducting alternative comparisons (see *Scheer, Produktionsplanung 1976, p. 197*).

Applying the EOQ (see Figure B.I.43) requires a constant (stationary) period requirement R. In the case of an irregular demand pattern, an average value for R can be formally calculated based on past period requirements or forecast values, but the formula usually no longer leads to a minimum cost solution.

Example: C = 60 MU
s = 0.20 MU/(units * subperiod)

Subperiod = h	1	2	3	4	5
Period requirement = R_h	85	220	176	143	440

1st lot:	Fixed lot costs	60	0	0		
	Fixed storage costs	0	44	70.4		
	Cumulated costs	60	104	174.4		
	Product costs	0.706>	0.341<	0.363		
	Lot size $(R_1 + R_2)$	305				
2nd lot:	Fixed lot costs			60	0	0
	Fixed storage costs			0	28.60	176.0
	Cumulated costs			60	88.60	264.5
	Product costs			0.340>	0.277<	0.349
	Lot size $(R_3 + R_4)$			319		
3rd lot:	Lot size (R_5)					440

Fig. B.I.45,b: Example of the adapted economic order quantity

The other methods are based on varying requirement values, but the target size does not correspond to the minimized costs for each planning period. Rather, the costs are minimized per time unit for planning period sequences of different lengths. Even if unit period adjustment improves the solution through subsequent refinements, it still does not need to coincide with the exact optimal solution.

Dynamic optimization can be used to determine the exact optimal lot size (see *Wagner/Whitin, Economic Lot Size Model 1958*). The same data are necessary as before, but the model is much more computation-intensive.

The recursive formula (see Figure B.I.47) also provides the optimal solution for the example, which in this case coincidentally corresponds to the solution provided by the adapted EOQ. Simulation studies by DeMatteis (see *DeMatteis, Lot-sizing Technique 1968*) have shown that the unit period adjustment method (including the refinements cited) generally leads to better results than the adapted EOQ (see also *Ohse, Lagerhaltungsmodelle 1969*).

$$j^* = \text{Min} \left\{ j \mid C < s \sum_{h=i}^{j} R_h * (h-i) \right\} \quad \text{or}$$

$$j^* = \text{Min} \left\{ j \mid \frac{C}{r} < \sum_{h=i}^{j} R_h * (h-i) \right\}$$

i = Period of fixed lot size = starting period
j = Last requirement period for the lot

Fig. B.I.46,a: Unit period adjustment

Example: Unit period $\quad \dfrac{C}{s} = \dfrac{60}{0.2} = 300$

Subperiod = h	1	2	3	4	5
Period requirement = R_h	85	220	176	143	440

1st Lot:	Unit periods	0	220	572		
	Lot size $(R_1 + R_2 + R_3)$	481				
2nd Lot:	Unit periods				0	440
	Lot size $(R_4 + R_5)$				583	

Fig. B.I.46,b: Example of unit period adjustment

$$F(j) = \text{Min} \left\{ \underbrace{\text{Min}_{1 < i < j} \left\{ C + \sum_{h=i+1}^{j} R_h * (h-i) * s + P(i-1) \right\}}_{\substack{\text{Total costs of producing (ordering)} \\ \text{requirements } R_j \text{ in period i}}} ; \underbrace{C + P(j-1)}_{\substack{\text{Total costs of pro-} \\ \text{ducing (ordering)} \\ \text{requirements } R_j \text{ in} \\ \text{period j (i.e. new} \\ \text{lot formation)}}} \right\}$$

Fig. B.I.47: Recursive formula for dynamic optimization

It must be generally noted, however, that the product cost curve is very often flat in the vicinity of the optimal lot size. Thus, the other methods can also provide satisfactory solutions, especially considering that they require less computation.

Consequently, the effects of having to plan lot sizes for each part in isolation are significantly more important.

Incorporating a period requirement into the lot for a previous period influences not only the affected part, but also all subordinate parts because their completion is now derived from the requirement period for the lot instead of from the original requirement period. Ongoing lot formation, therefore, tends to lead to high current capacity utilization. Previous PPC systems failed to take into account these types of interrelationships in determining lot sizes.

Nor are the lot size models for multi-level production developed in the business administration literature very satisfactory because they do not include a capable, generally applicable solution (see *Crowston/Wagner/Williams, Lot Size Determination 1973; Scheer, Produktionsplanung 1976, pp. 92 ff.; Schneeweiß, Lagerhaltungssysteme 1981; Zimmermann, Produktionsplanung variantenreicher Erzeugnisse 1988; Tempelmeier, Material-Logistik 1992; Glaser/Geiger/Rohde, Produktionsplanung und -steuerung 1992, pp. 136 ff.*).

These approaches confirm the need for simultaneous product-structure-related planning. However, this is completely impossible when using the (planning) level-oriented requirements explosion.

A further point of criticism is that lots are formed for each part. Thus, the setup costs comprise the setup costs for all operations in a part routing, and the storage cost rate refers to storage of the finished part. The actual parameter for the changeover costs, however, is the machine. Within a part routing, operations can be performed on different machines; moreover, storage occurs between the operations. Thus, an additional operation-oriented lot size analysis can be performed within the lot to which the part pertains.

Although the literature has used this case as an example for a long time in lot size planning models for multi-level production, the approaches fail to provide a generally valid algorithm (see *Müller, Simultane Lagerdisposition und Fertigungsablaufplanung 1972; Müller-Merbach, Optimale Losgrößen 1965; Glaser/Geiger/Rohde, Produktionsplanung und -steuerung 1992, pp. 136 ff.*).

An operation-oriented analysis is meaningful when similar operations can occur for different parts. This case is, for example, typical for the variant and part family production described earlier. Overall setup costs can be reduced when the same operations for different parts are performed immediately one after another, i.e., operation-oriented lots are formed. This is referred to as "combining." These options cannot be used in part-oriented lot size formation, however, because the same operations can relate to parts from different planning levels. When analyzing a part, the requirement for parts with similar operations is thus not (or not completely) known.

Thus, operation-oriented planning is carried out within the framework of short-term production control.

The interdependencies to requirements planning can then no longer be incorporated, however, because of the level planning concept.

A further difficulty, which also originates from the multi-level nature of the problem, affects the calculation of the storage cost rate s that must be applied (see *Scheer, Produktionsplanung 1976, pp. 108 ff.*).

B.I.3.2.2.5 Inventory Management

The prerequisite for an exact gross-net calculation within requirements planning is maintaining up-to-date inventories for end products, intermediate products (assemblies), component parts and materials. Since warehousing functions occur in all logistic chains (sales (finished goods warehouse), production (intermediate storage), purchasing (received goods warehouse)), the basic tasks are illustrated (see Figure B.I.48).

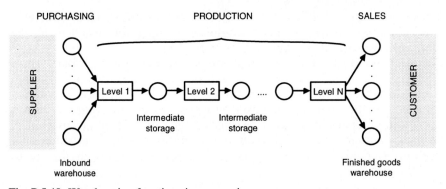

Fig. B.I.48: Warehousing functions in companies

A planning "account" is created for each part carried on stock. This account contains the scheduled additions and withdrawals along with the effective inventory levels (see Figure B.I.49).

In addition to the physical stock on hand that is updated by entering additions and withdrawals, the credit column contains the orders for outsourced parts with their expected arrival dates as well as the additions for production orders with their completion dates. The debit side contains reservations as well as scheduled withdrawals for scheduled production orders. Figure B.I.50 shows the event control for reservations.

Maintaining a planning account provides a current overview of requirements and inventories at all times, which can be used for scheduling new production orders or customer orders.

Planning account for part number xx at 4/15 ...

Inventory/Additions			Reservations/Withdrawals		
Inventory level	4/15	700	Inventory level	4/15	300
Planned additions	4/19	300	Planned withdrawals	4/18	200
Planned additions	4/15	760	Planned withdrawals	4/23	150

Fig. B.I.49: Planning account for inventory management

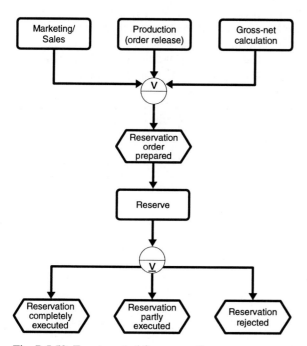

Fig. B.I.50: Event control for reservations

It is not necessary to introduce a new data structure to implement such an account, since it is already contained in the data structure in Figure B.I.35. Inventory, order and reservation data are accessible for any given part, so creating the account involves a simple analysis based on this data structure.

B.I.3.2.2.5.1 Data Entry Functions

Entering stock-in and stock-out data is essential for inventory management. Stock-in data are taken from information accompanying the delivery (bill of lading) or recorded by manual or automatic counting devices (for example, barcode readers) at an inventory point upstream of the warehouse. Correspondingly, stock-out data are registered by preparing a paper or electronic withdrawal document. The organizational structure must ensure that no unauthorized movement of goods can occur. Since one part can be maintained at several different storage locations, stock-transfer transactions must also be entered. Figure B.I.51 shows event control for a stock-in function.

If stock-out transactions are not kept up to date, they can be determined "retrogressively" on a specific closing date based on the number of completed production orders. In the case of a stock-in transaction for a finished part (assembly or end product), bills of materials are used to determine the target consumption for component parts and materials, and they are debited against the inventory level as a target stock-out. Such a procedure is meaningful despite the resulting inaccuracies if entering the actual consumption is not feasible due to organizational or cost considerations.

If quality inspection procedures are performed before physical stock-in and stock-out functions, a distinction can be made between an inventory

Fig. B.I.51: Event control for a stock-in function

level that has already been accepted within the warehouse and an inventory level within the inspection area. This must be taken into account during availability checks and reservations and is entered using status identifiers.

When transferring a production order to intermediate or end-product storage, the production order is identified as finished and its status updated accordingly.

In addition to entering the quantity-oriented transactions and inventory updates, values can also be entered and updated. This applies, for example, in the case of average purchase prices referenced to the inbound warehouse or in the case of cost values for intermediate and end products.

Inventory movements provide important information for accounting functions. When goods are received, the quantities recorded in the respective accounts are increased in the inventory accounting system, price differences are identified in the case of standard-price-controlled material and the goods/invoice received clearing account is updated.

Other material movements are also always entered in the appropriate inventory accounts.

At the same time, data are also collected for cost accounting, for instance, by debiting the requisitioning cost center and/or the requisitioning cost objective.

Because delivered quantities are counted in Receiving and evaluated according to their properties, important information becomes available that is necessary for Invoice Control, which is typically organizationally subordinate to Financial Accounting.

The warehouse department, however, does not merely supply data for downstream functions; it also uses previously entered data. For example, online display of order items provides important support in entering data for inbound goods. Because the ordered materials are typically delivered, the displayed data only need to be acknowledged when the incoming goods are inspected in order to then be automatically posted as an addition to inventory.

In addition to entering additions and withdrawals, the warehouse department also manages the reservations created during the requirement forecast. Reserved and free stock can be reassigned and reservations can be created outside a formal planning sequence.

B.I.3.2.2.5.2 Analyses

Interactive queries can also be performed if an online inventory management system is used. Displaying current inventory levels, outstanding orders and master data relating to suppliers, parts, etc., is especially suitable for this purpose.

In addition, period-oriented analyses are also useful; they are frequently processed as batch functions because they are highly computation-intensive:

-   Materials inventory lists (organized according to materials classes, inventory accounts, inventory value, etc.)
-   Inventory transaction ledger for a period (e.g., a month)
-   List of inactive inventory items, i.e., materials with a most recent order date and/or receiving date prior to a given date
-   ABC parts classification
-   Calculation of inventory endurance based on average consumption per time unit
-   List of material shortfalls, i.e., parts with an invalid negative available inventory.

B.I.3.2.2.5.3 Inventory

Stocktaking, i.e., taking a physical inventory on a specific closing date, is also an important function in a computerized inventory management system. It consists of providing support in selecting the parts to be inventoried and in inventory processing.

The user can specify the parts to be counted by indicating specific keys. Criteria can include the article number, storage location, the appropriate ABC identifier, the current inventory level or the type of procurement involved, as well as any combination of these elements. An online function can display the parts that have been entered using the selection

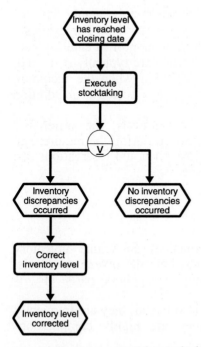

Fig. B.I.52: Event control for stocktaking

criteria input. It is only feasible to physically count parts with low inventory levels.

Continuously tracking the inventory levels provides a smooth transition to a perpetual inventory. Figure B.I.52 illustrates event control for stocktaking.

After selecting the parts to be counted, a list is generated with the target inventory as well as a blank field for entering the actual count. After entering the actual count, the system calculates variations between target and actual values and provides them to information functions. At the same time, accounting functions are initiated for reconciling inventory discrepancies.

B.I.3.2.3 Requirements Tracking

In the requirements explosion as it has been represented thus far, aggregates are formed when requirements are transferred to components and when lots are sized. These aggregates destroy the information relationships between requirements and orders under the following conditions:

1. Requirements planning using a fixed frequency grid combines requirements having different origins that are scheduled during the same period. Thus, the origin of such an aggregate requirement or order can no longer be identified. Moreover, under requirements planning with day-specific scheduling, the information relationships are lost as soon as the lots are formed.
2. Within the framework of primary requirements planning, aggregation interrupts the relationship between customer orders and the period-oriented requirements for each part.
3. When the secondary requirements are transferred, the information relationship between the secondary requirement and the subordinate parts order that created the requirement is lost. The secondary requirement for a period can be the result of several superordinate orders.
4. During lot formation, net requirements from different periods are combined. Thus, the actual requirement deadlines for the lot subsets are no longer visible.

The information flow between requirements and orders is, however, essential for controlling the flow of materials. For this reason, the above-indicated information relationships are maintained during the requirements explosion. The information relationships required for this purpose differ in storage- and search-intensiveness depending on the degree of detail required for tracking them.

Requirements tracking is a valid solution for the following reasons:

1.   Because of the trend in many industries toward customer-specific production, it is necessary to have access to the related component production orders for customer orders in order to provide information about their production status.

2.   After completing an order (lot), the system must also "know" which subsequent orders the lot goes into. If this information is missing, the "push" principle, which is frequently used for material control, cannot be applied, and the material flow can only be controlled via a "pull" function, which involves setting up an intermediate storage area.

3.   If a lot is delayed, the affected superordinate orders must be determined. At the same time, it is also necessary to determine which quantities of the lot are time critical and which subquantities were included solely for reasons of cost, but in reality possess float times.

4.   In capacity planning and production control, priority figures are frequently calculated that help assign orders to the capacities. When calculating the priority figures, information is used that pertains to the customer orders into which the production orders go. These types of variables, such as capital that is "tied up" in the customer order, customer importance, etc., can be determined if the relationship between the production order and the customer order can be established.

A distinction is made between single-level and multi-level requirements tracking procedures.

In single-level requirements tracking, only the link between two directly connected parts within the gozinto graph is analyzed, while multi-level requirements tracking analyzes the relationship between a production order and the initiating customer order or a primary requirement across **all** sublevels. In principle, both procedures facilitate the control of overall material flow from each production order to the initiating customer order or the primary requirement. Multi-level requirements tracking is data-intensive, while single-level requirements tracking requires significant search procedures in order to determine the relationship between a production order and the initiating customer order or the primary requirement.

B.I.3.2.3.1 Single-Level Requirements Tracking

B.I.3.2.3.1.1 Procedure

In designing the data structure, a distinction must be made between two cases:

Maintaining references to the work order when calculating the secondary requirement for a component based on a superordinate

part order, i.e., the requirements derivation relationship between **different** parts,
Tracking the relationship between the gross requirement and its derived material assignments and orders within the gross-net calculation for **one** part (requirements coverage).

Requirements Derivation
Figure B.I.53 shows a simple example designed to demonstrate requirements derivation. Based on the bill of materials relationship, two requirement figures consisting of 200 quantity units for A1 and 100 quantity units for A2 are derived from the order for 100 quantity units of end product P1 (see dotted lines). This shows once again that a plurality of requirements can arise from one order.

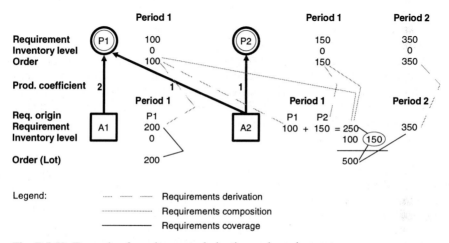

Fig. B.I.53: Example of requirements derivation and requirements coverage

Correspondingly, the requirement for P2 in period 1 yields a requirement of 150 for A2 and a requirement of 350 for A2 in period 2 (see dotted lines).
The requirement of 250 quantity units for A2 in period 1 in Figure B.I.53 is made up of orders for P1 and P2 (100 and 150 quantity units respectively). Thus, a requirement can result from several superordinate orders (see broken dotted lines).
The REQUIREMENTS DERIVATION thus forms an n:m relationship between the information objects ORDER and REQUIREMENT. In Figure B.I.35, in which the requirements planning data structure was designed, both ORDER and REQUIREMENT were stipulated as relationship types. They are now reinterpreted as entity types (see also Figure B.I.54). The information objects REQUIREMENT and ORDER represent item concepts.

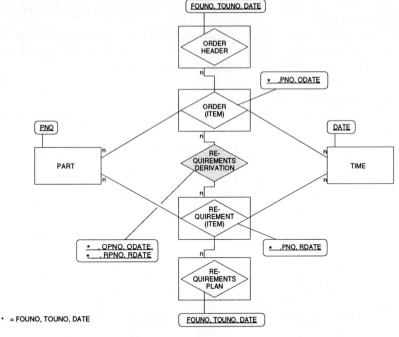

Fig. B.I.54: ERM of requirements derivation

Requirements Coverage

The gross-net calculation specifies how a gross requirement is covered by assigning inventories (actual inventory and/or anticipated inventory based on released orders) and orders. Lots are formed in order to cover several requirements with one order, as is the case in Figure B.I.53 for the order for 500 quantity units of A2 (after subtracting the inventory of 100) for the requirements in period 1 and period 2 (see solid lines). It would also be conceivable, for example, for the net requirement of 500 quantity units to be covered by a lot of 300 quantity units in period 2 and 200 quantity units in period 1 in order to take better advantage of transport capacities. In this case, there is an n:m relationship between the entity types ORDER and REQUIREMENT with respect to REQUIREMENTS COVERAGE as shown in Figure B.I.55.

When assigning inventories, it is possible for an inventory item to be assigned to several requirements (from different periods), and, conversely, for a requirement to be covered by several inventory items or different storage locations. Thus, an n:m relationship also exists for INVENTORY COVERAGE between INVENTORY and REQUIREMENT.

The overall data structure is summarized in Figure B.I.55, whereby the relationships to the entity types PART and TIME were omitted for the sake of simplicity.

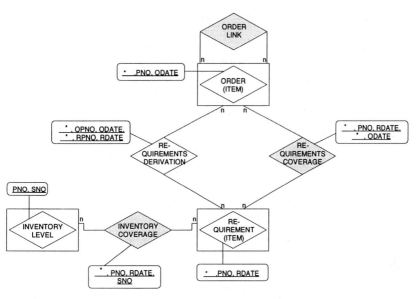

Fig. B.I.55: ERM of requirements tracking

In order to differentiate between key attributes that are formally the same, they are assigned reference objects using the first letter of the appropriate word: O (ORDER), R (REQUIREMENT), I (INVENTORY).

This data structure makes it possible to derive material flow relationships between orders. For example, REQUIREMENTS COVERAGE can be used to determine that the order for 500 quantity units of A2 is used to cover the gross requirements in period 1 and period 2. REQUIREMENTS DERIVATION can also be used to determine that the subquantity of 250 quantity units results from an order for 100 quantity units of P1 and from an order for 150 quantity units of P2.

Figure B.I.56 shows requirements tracking event control.

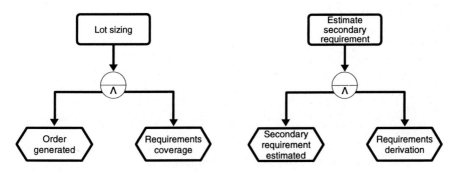

Fig. B.I.56: Event control of requirements tracking

Although the information relationship between **orders** for different hierarchical levels is not explicitly indicated in the data structure, it is implicitly available via the relationships REQUIREMENTS DERIVATION and REQUIREMENTS COVERAGE.

Another option for order tracking involves directly regenerating the relationships between material flow and orders. The relationship between orders is also n:m. On the one hand, an order can initiate several subordinate orders; on the other hand, it can go into several orders for superordinate parts. For all practical purposes, this procedure skips the levels of the gross-net calculation and represents only the informational relationships between orders. Figure B.I.57 shows this link between orders for the example.

The summary in Figure B.I.55 also shows the n:m relationship ORDER LINK between the orders, although it is already contained in the relationships REQUIREMENTS DERIVATION and REQUIREMENTS COVERAGE.

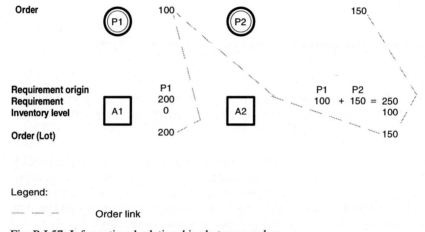

Fig. B.I.57: Informational relationships between orders

B.I.3.2.3.1.2 An Example

Since the informational relationships involved in requirements tracking are quite complicated, the principle developed here will now be summarized in a simple example. For purposes of simplification, the key attributes in the header information for REQUIREMENT and ORDER are omitted in the information objects. The following assumptions are made:

-    Consumption-based requirements and additional requirements are zero.
-    No inventories, released orders or reservations exist. Thus, the gross requirement equals the net requirement.
-    The (net) requirement for two periods is combined into one lot.

- The turnaround times for all parts amount to one time unit.
- The part names are used as part numbers (PNO).
- Representations at the entity level are in tabular form.

The part structure in Figure B.I.58 serves as the point of departure. Two customer orders of 100 and 200 quantity units exist for end product P; the orders are due in the third period. Because they refer to the same planning date, they are combined, and because they are the primary requirement, they constitute the point of departure for calculating the requirement. The

Planning level

CUSTOMER ORDER	Customer number CNO	OUNO	DATE	PNO	CDATE	Quantity
	1	A1	1	P	3	100
	2	A1	1	P	3	200
	=> Primary requirement			P	3	300

Fig. B.I.58: Example of single-level requirements tracking

customer reference is lost as a result of this aggregation. (The relationships to the customer orders are also examined in the next section, which discusses the multi-level requirements explosion.)

The first column in Figure B.I.59 indicates the sequence of the individual steps.

In the second processing step, a production order is formed on the basis of the existing primary requirement for end product P (first step). Since the gross requirement is assumed to be equal to the net requirement, the requirement quantities equal the order quantities.

Step 3 specifies that the production order will be used to cover the requirement for P, thus creating an instance of the relationship type REQUIREMENTS COVERAGE.

In step 4, the secondary requirement for subordinate part A is determined, entered in the REQUIREMENTS DERIVATION and added to the cumulative requirement record in step 5. Based on the turnaround time for product P, the planning date of the component is advanced by one time unit, as is period 2.

Processing step	REQUIRE-MENT (ITEM)	PNO	RDATE	Quantity	Remarks
1		P	3	300	Primary requirement
5		A	2	300	Transfer of P
7		C	2	600	Transfer of P
11		C	1	900	Transfer of A

Processing step	ORDER (ITEM)	PNO	ODATE	Quantity	Remarks
2		P	3	300	
8		A	2	300	
12		C	1	1500	

Processing step	REQUIRE-MENTS COVERAGE	PNO	RDATE	ODATE	Quantity	Remarks
3		P	3	3	300	
9		A	2	2	300	
13		C	2	1	600	
14		C	1	1	900	

Processing step	REQUIRE-MENTS DERIVATION	OPNO	ODATE	RPNO	RDATE	Quantity	Remarks
4		P	3	A	2	300	Transfer of P
6		P	3	C	2	600	Transfer of P
10		A	2	C	1	900	Transfer of A

Note: The key attributes of order header and requirements plan are disregarded to simplify matters.

Fig. B.I.59: Single-level requirements tracking for Fig. B.I.58

In steps 6 and 7, the same procedure is performed for the second subordinate component C.

At this point, the system has worked its way through planning level 3 and proceeds into the next lower planning level 2. All requirements for assembly A have been transferred. Since there are no inventories to consider, the requirement of 300 quantity units in the second period generates an order that is created in step 8. At the same time, step 9 results in requirements coverage. Because the production coefficient between C and A is 3, a requirement of (300 x 3) 900 quantity units of C is computed from the order for A in step 10, which is assigned to period 1 because of the lead time shift of one period. After the requirements derivation has been completed, the requirement is transferred to the requirement relation (step 11).

Two requirements exist for part C in periods 1 and 2. They are combined into one order in the first period because of the lot sizing rule (step 12). Now the requirements coverage relationship is more meaningful because it distributes the order quantity of 1500 among the two different requirements in steps 13 and 14.

In summary, single-level requirements tracking can be used to answer the following questions:

1. Which orders result from one requirement, or which requirements are covered by one order? (via the REQUIREMENTS COVERAGE relationship)
2. Which requirements are derived from a superordinate order, or into which superordinate orders does a specific component requirement go? (via the REQUIREMENTS DERIVATION relationship)
3. Into which superordinate orders does a component order go, or which subordinate orders are derived from a superordinate part order? (indirectly via the REQUIREMENTS COVERAGE and REQUIREMENTS DERIVATION relationships)

The answer to the third question, which is especially important for the production flow between orders, is represented in Figure B.I.60 as a network plan for tracking the order for 1500 quantity units of part C.

Again this demonstrates the fact that it is not necessarily mandatory to have a direct informational relationship between the orders like the one treated by the relationship type ORDER LINK in the data structure in Figure B.I.55.

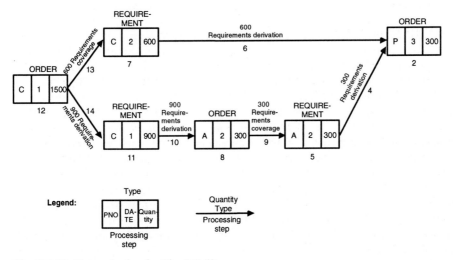

Fig. B.I.60: Network plan for Fig. B.I.58

In single-level requirements tracking, a large number of search procedures is necessary within the data structure. These procedures can be avoided if a company moves to a multi-level requirements tracking system, although this necessitates maintaining a more complex data system.

B.I.3.2.3.2 Multi-Level Requirements Tracking

B.I.3.2.3.2.1 Procedure

If a relationship to the customer orders is to be entered immediately for each production or purchase order, there are two options:
1.   All orders are scheduled in an extremely customer-oriented manner, i.e., each production order entity refers to a specific customer order. This rules out the practice of combining requirements from different purchase orders or for different periods into one lot.
2.   The relationship to the customer orders is always retained in the requirements tracking relationships. The requirements derivation and the requirements coverage relationships must be more sophisticated than in the case of single-level requirements tracking. On the other hand, the number of requirements entities and order entities remains the same, thus retaining the options of combining requirements and forming combined lots.

The following discussion will concentrate on the second procedure. The information objects CUSTOMER ORDER HEADER and CUSTOMER ORDER ITEM will be introduced in order to establish the relationship to the customer order. Both are treated as reinterpreted entity types.

The header information comprises the information object CUSTOMER ORDER HEADER. It is designed as a relationship type between the purchaser (customer), the order receiver (the sales department) and the time value, but it is treated here as a reinterpreted entity type. A more precise derivation will be provided in the section on outbound logistics.

The CUSTOMER ORDER ITEM possesses the key attributes *customer number*, *organizational unit number* and *date* as keys from the customer order header as well as *part number* and *requirement date* for the parts-oriented key information. When the concept of the primary requirement was introduced, it was emphasized that this requirement results from customer orders and forecast values and that the entity type CUSTOMER ORDER ITEM can therefore be interpreted as the requirements item. This interpretation has the advantage that a gross-net calculation can also be performed for CUSTOMER ORDER ITEM using the existing data structure without having to define individual relationship types for stock assignments, etc.

When creating lots on the end product level, the requirements coverage relationship determines to which customer order items (primary requirements) the production lot refers. During the subsequent requirements explosion from assemblies to component parts, the system determines which subsets of a gross requirement were derived from which superordinate production order and from which customer order items.

The data model is developed in Figure B.I.61. The requirements derivation and requirements coverage relationships are each linked to the entity type CUSTOMER ORDER ITEM. Several instances of the relationship types can exist based on one customer order item; this is true, for example, for the derived component requirements and orders. The connection to the customer orders significantly increases the number of relationship type instances as compared to single-level requirements tracking.

In practice, several approaches are used to limit the number of these relationships:

1.   Multi-level requirements tracking is used only for parts on higher planning levels; parts on lower planning levels are tracked using the single-level approach.

2.   Multi-level requirements tracking is used only for a single segment of the planning period; only single-level requirement relationships are derived from primary requirements or from customer orders with later requirements deadlines.

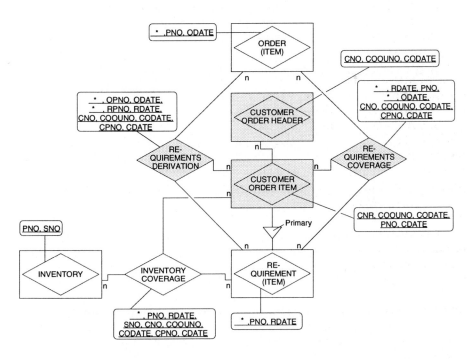

Fig. B.I.61: ERM of multi-level requirements tracking

3.   Requirements derivation and/or requirements coverage relationships are created using the multi-level approach, but only with the subset that refers to the earliest primary requirement or customer order; further processing of the remaining subset uses the single-level approach.

In any concrete application, it is necessary to carefully consider which of the three procedures should be used, either by itself or in which combination. In this case, a compromise must be found between the effort needed for information processing and the information requirement for information tracking into the production stage, specifically with respect to customer-oriented manufacturing.

B.I.3.2.3.2.2 An Example

Multi-level requirements tracking is illustrated in Figure B.I.62 based on the example already used for single-level requirements tracking. The example begins with the two customer order items from steps 1 and 2. Step 5 forms a combined primary requirement from the customer order quantities. The customer orders are thus sources of the primary requirement. The related requirements derivation relationships are created in steps 3 and 4. The key attributes of the "superordinate production order" are the same as the key attributes of the customer order items.

In the further explosion, the REQUIREMENTS COVERAGE and the REQUIREMENTS DERIVATION are alternately accessed to obtain the detailed transfers of the relationships to the customer order item. The tables for the information objects REQUIREMENT and ORDER remain the same as in single-level requirements tracking; only the relationships for REQUIREMENTS COVERAGE and REQUIREMENTS DERIVATION are differentiated in more detail.

The ensuing process, as illustrated in Figure B.I.62, is self-explanatory.

B.I.3.2.4 Summarizing and Supplementing the Requirements Definition for Requirements Planning

The following section will again systematically discuss all the ARIS components in the requirements definition for requirements planning, this time treating all representation methods.

B.I.3.2.4.1 Requirements Definition for Requirements Planning: The Function View

The major requirements planning functions discussed here are summarized in Figure B.I.63 in the form of a function tree. This figure illustrates that some functions, such as reservation, are treated in several

Processing step	CUSTOMER ORDER ITEM	CNO	COOUNO	CODATE	CPNO	CDATE	Quantity
1		C1	A	1	P	3	100
2		C2	A	1	P	3	200

Processing step	REQUIRE-MENT (ITEM)	PNO	RDATE	Quantity
5		P	3	300
11		A	2	300
14		C	2	600
20		C	1	900

Processing step	ORDER (ITEM)	PNO	ODATE	Quantity
6		P	3	300
15		A	2	300
21		C	1	1500

Processing step	REQUIRE-MENTS COVERAGE	CNO	COOUNO	CODATE	CPNO	CDATE	PNO	RDATE	ODATE	Quantity
7		C1	A	1	P	3	P	3	3	100
8		C2	A	1	P	3	P	3	3	200
16		C1	A	1	P	3	A	2	2	100
17		C2	A	1	P	3	A	2	2	200
22		C1	A	1	P	3	C	2	1	200
23		C2	A	1	P	3	C	2	1	400
24		C1	A	1	P	3	C	1	1	300
25		C2	A	1	P	3	C	1	1	600

Processing step	REQUIRE-MENTS DERIVATION	CNO	COOUNO	CODATE	CPNO	CDATE	OPNO	ODATE	RPNO	RDATE	Quantity
3		C1	A	1	P	3	P	3	P	3	100
4		C2	A	1	P	3	P	3	P	3	200
9		C1	A	1	P	3	P	3	A	2	100
10		C2	A	1	P	3	P	3	A	2	200
12		C1	A	1	P	3	P	3	C	2	200
13		C2	A	1	P	3	P	3	C	2	400
18		C1	A	1	P	3	A	2	C	1	300
19		C2	A	1	P	3	A	2	C	1	600

Note: The key attributes of order header and requirements plan are not regarded to simplify matter.

Fig. B.I.62: Example of a multi-level requirements tracking

branches of the function tree. Within the context of the requirements explosion, reservations are taken into account in the gross-net calculation. At the same time, reservations are maintained as assignments to released orders in inventory management. This, in turn, demonstrates that the function tree provides little information about the process-oriented positional relationships between functions.

Since requirements planning exhibits close relationships to closely-related logistics chains (inbound and outbound logistics), there are also overlaps to the function trees for these corresponding areas.

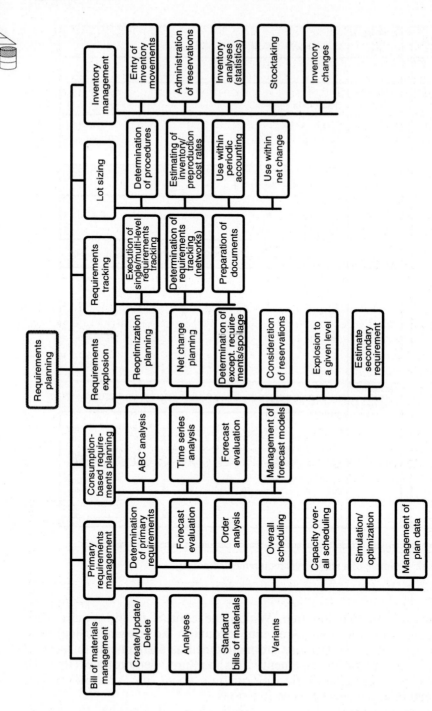

Fig. B.I.63: Function tree for requirements planning

The processing frequency—and thus the corresponding degree of user interaction—must be determined within the framework of the requirements definition for the function view.

Processing frequency distinguishes between time-period-oriented and case-oriented processing. These types of processing are closely associated with the "reoptimization" and "net change" planning principles.

On a given planning date, reoptimization releases all previously established temporal and quantitative assignments that have not yet been specified by binding decisions. This means, for example, that inventory assignments for planned but unscheduled orders are canceled, as are all lots for orders not yet released to Production.

When applying the net change principle, on the other hand, only the updates that have occurred since the last requirements planning session are included in the calculation in the form of new customer orders, new inventory notices, new bill of materials combinations, etc.. In strict form, the net change principle itself is self-controlling in that the planning dates are not specified; instead, changes that occur independently initiate replanning (case-oriented processing).

Interactive processing is required if the user wants to control the process. Batch processing, on the other hand, is typically time-period-oriented and runs without user intervention, i.e., automatically.

Figure B.I.64 examines the processing forms for major requirements planning tasks on the basis of interactive causes. Both processing forms, however, can be suitable.

Creating, updating and deleting in connection with **basic bill of materials data management** underscores the advantages of interactive processing in order to ensure that the information is up-to-date, to check plausibility and to use options for iterative data modification. An iterative modification can, for example, involve creating a bill of materials from a similar existing bill of materials.

Function	Subfunction	Reasons for interactive processing				Automatic/ batch
		Currency	Plausibility	Iterative modification	Interactive decision process	
Bill of materials management	Create/Delete	X	X	X		
	Update	X	X	X		
	Analysis of bills of mat.	X				X
Master schedule management	Import					X
	Update	X				
ABC analysis						X
Consumption-based planning	Create				X	X
	Update	X			X	
Gross-net calculation	Reoptimization					X
	Net change			X		X
Lot sizing	Reoptimization					X
	Net change				X	
Requirements tracking	Reoptimization					X
	Net change			X		X
Forward scheduling with turnaround time reduct.	Reoptimization			X		X
	Net change			X		
Stockkeeping	Additions/withdrawals	X	X			
	Stocktaking	X	X			X

Fig. B.I.64: Reasons for interactive processing of the functions of requirements planning

Individual bill of materials creation as an analysis function can be invoked interactively to ensure currency; because they are so computation-intensive, however, bill of materials catalogs are created in batch mode.

In **primary requirements management**, data from the upstream primary requirements planning process are imported in a batch run. Primary requirements changes, on the other hand, are entered on a case-oriented basis (interactively) to ensure currency.

ABC analysis involves processing all data, which makes it a typical batch function.

In **consumption-based planning**, the user interactively checks forecast data that have been created in a batch process. An interactive decision process can result if the user simulates multiple data configurations.

In consumption-based planning, requirement updates must also be entered immediately in order to continue to be able to track their consequences, if necessary.

In connection with the subfunctions for the **requirements explosion**, a distinction must be made between planning functions that are performed based on the reoptimization principle and those performed based on the net change principle. Net change functions lend themselves to interactive processing in those cases where they involve iterative modifications, which can even consist of an interactive decision process. If, on the other hand, only automatic functions are initiated, interactive processing is unnecessary.

A typical interactive function that meets the demands for iterative modification is the scheduling of individual requirements updates or customer orders including their gross-net calculation. The combination of individual lots within the framework of a net change planning process is also an interactive function in that plan updates are integrated into existing lots.

In specifically case-oriented processing, the overall gross-net calculation can be performed interactively for primary requirements. Lots can also be formed interactively by supplying the results of the requirements explosion to the planner level by level; the results, in turn, serve as the starting point for determining the secondary requirements for subordinate parts. These can be automatically triggered when a process is initiated, and the events can be transferred to the planner at the next planning level for lot processing using action databases.

Requirements tracking within the framework of reoptimization is a batch function. When working through plan updates using the net change method, interactive functions can result here as well, for example, by manually stipulating assignments. If the algorithm for requirements tracking is fixed, however, a batch process will only be initiated within the framework of the net change principle.

Within the framework of forward scheduling, both reoptimization and net change can be performed interactively by interactively modifying the affected order networks (turnaround time reduction, multiple forward and reverse scheduling).

Additions and withdrawals within the framework of the **stockkeeping function** are performed interactively in order to maintain currency and to correct errors; the same applies for posting inventory data. The creation of inventory lists, on the other hand, is a batch function.

B.I.3.2.4.2 Requirements Definition for Requirements Planning: The Organization View

Figure B.I.65 incorporates the organizational units involved in requirements planning into the functional reference organizational chart

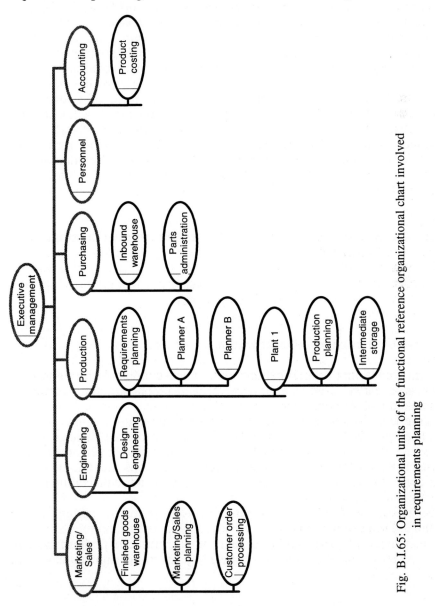

Fig. B.I.65: Organizational units of the functional reference organizational chart involved in requirements planning

from Figure A.II.10,a. Production is located in the center. Requirements Planning, however, also has many organizational interfaces to other main departments.

B.I.3.2.4.3 Requirements Definition for Requirements Planning: The Data View

Figure B.I.66 summarizes the data model developed for requirements planning. Where alternative options for representation exist (e.g., for representing variants and for requirements tracking), only those data structures used in the remainder of the book are illustrated.

The form of representation shown in Figure B.I.66 follows developmental logic commonly used in business administration, which primarily emphasizes the distinction between entity and relationship types as well as the representation of specialization/generalization operations.

Figure B.I.67 shows the same situation in the form of a structured entity-relationship model. Elements of the SER model approach (see *Sinz, Datenmodellierung im Strukturierten Entity-Relationship-Modell 1993*) and of the extended ER model are used, and the model is read from left to right. The SER model approach provides a manageable representation of a finished data model, while the extended ER model expresses the design process more graphically.

B.I.3.2.4.4 Requirements Definition for Requirements Planning: The Control View

This section will first systematically discuss all dual relationships and then the overall view of the ARIS components.

B.I.3.2.4.4.1 Functions - Organization

Static functional classification and process-oriented formation of planning levels are used to portray the organizational structure. These are then linked with the functions.

Figure B.I.68 incorporates the requirements planning functions into the organizational chart from Figure B.I.65. For reasons of manageability, however, only the major functions have been integrated here. The subfunctions contained within the principal functions are thus assigned implicitly. If only individual subfunctions apply for an organizational unit, they are indicated.

The bill of materials management functions primarily pertain to the production bill of materials.

It becomes apparent that an organizational unit can perform several functions and a function can be processed by several organizational units.

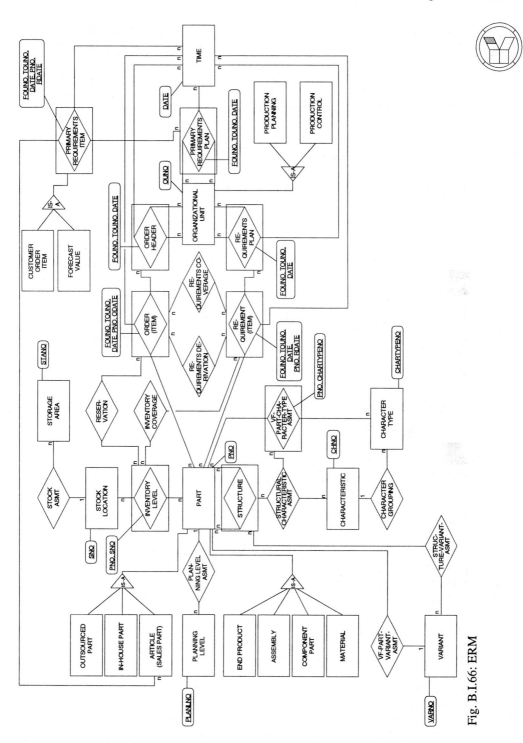

Fig. B.I.66: ERM

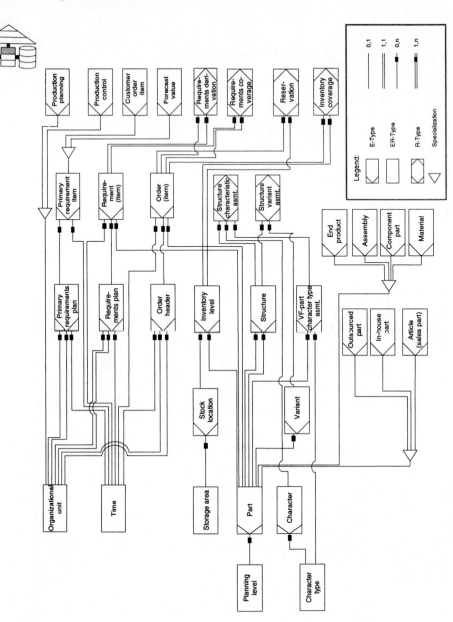

Fig. B.I.67: SERM as evaluation

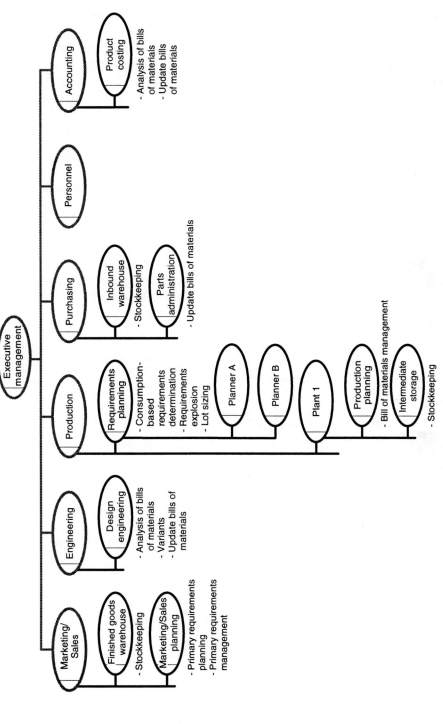

Fig. B.I.68: Assignment of requirements planning functions to organizational units

An example of the second case is bill of materials updating, which is performed by Engineering, Purchasing, Accounting and, within the framework of bill of materials management, by Production as well. The "update bills of materials" function can, however, also relate to different data groups in the bill of materials description. This relationship is established by the authorization relationships between the organizational unit and the data.

Figure B.I.69 shows requirements planning functions assigned to the planning levels, which are classified by logistics processes. The highest relevant functions are entered, and the relevant subfunctions are assigned implicitly.

Some functions, such as bill of materials management, can be assigned to several planning levels because, for example, sales-oriented updates are permissible at the product area level, and production-oriented updates are permissible at the plant level. Component reservations can be performed on the basis of their proximity to the start of the order, and can thus occur in increasing detail and with greater degrees of linking (e.g., planning reservation or physical reservation) at the plant, plant department or equipment group levels (see also the subsequent discussions of production control).

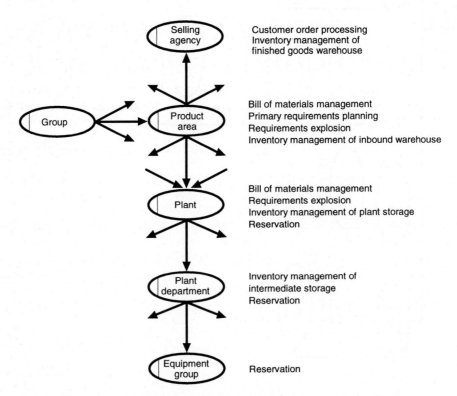

Fig. B.I.69: Assignment of requirements planning functions to planning levels

Whether the requirements explosion is carried out at the product area level or at the plant level depends on an enterprise's degree of decentralization as well as on its production structure. If the same parts can be produced in several plants, the production orders must be assigned to the plants within the framework of requirements planning and subsequent capacity planning. This situation suggests the advantage of centralized requirements planning at the product area level. In the case of frequent production-oriented replanning due to capacity or quality considerations, for example, it makes more sense to orient the requirements explosion more closely to production, and thus to the plant level. This holds true especially if a plant operates on a three-shift basis, and disruptions could also necessitate requirements replanning (in net change) during the night shift.

In the process industry, the requirements can frequently be classified only for each recipe level, since production results determine the application in which the resulting substances can be processed downstream, and only then are the recipes that are suitable for further explosion selected. This level-by-level requirements explosion, in turn, is closely linked to Production and is assigned to the plant level—and in some cases even to the plant department level.

B.I.3.2.4.4.2 Functions - Data

Event control as a significant link between data and functions was already treated with respect to the use of event-controlled process chains (EPC) for content representation. Figure B.I.70 provides a summary of all EPCs developed.

In the next section, the transformation of input data to output data will be illustrated within the context of process chain representation.

The object-oriented modeling approach is treated as a significant supplement to the data view and the function view. This approach represents a link between both views to the extent that the objects also function as objects in the data view and the methods assigned to the objects are defined as functions in the function view.

The object model for Rumbaugh's object modeling technique (OMT) shown in Figure B.I.71 (see Section A for symbol definitions) can be derived directly from the ER model for requirements planning.

The dynamic model in Figure B.I.72 shows all conditions (ovals) and events for status updating (arrows). A detailed notation system can use brackets to define conditions and indicate actions in order to formulate a complete event-condition-action chain.

The functional model in Figure B.I.73 describes input/output relationships between the data view and the function view for requirements planning.

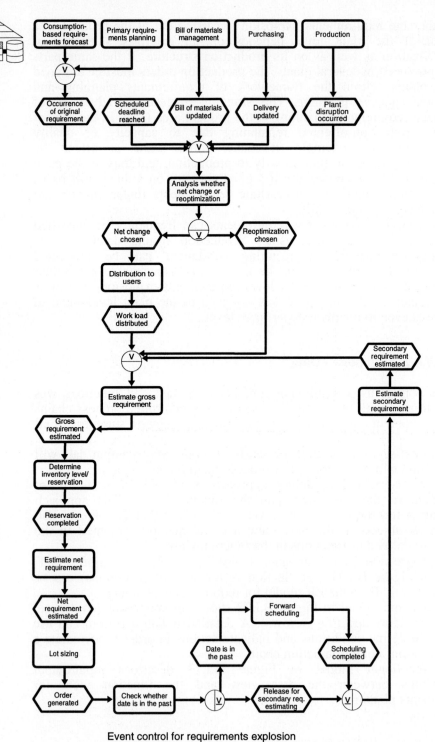

Event control for requirements explosion

Fig. B.I.70: Representation of all EPCs of requirements planning (part 1)

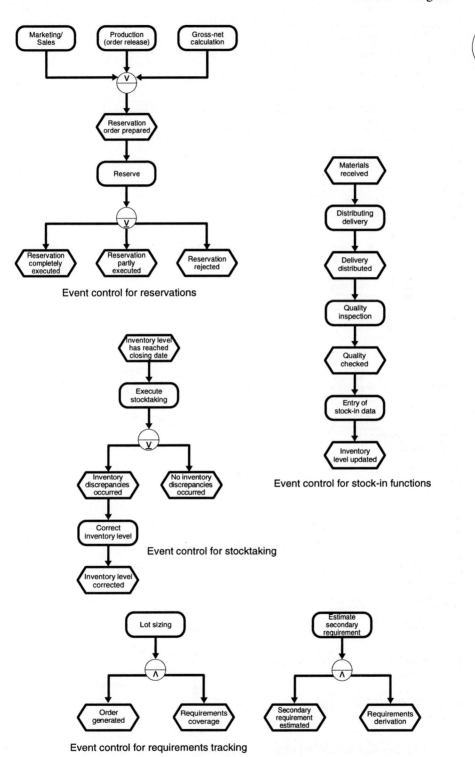

Event control for reservations

Event control for stock-in functions

Event control for stocktaking

Event control for requirements tracking

Fig. B.I.70: Representation of all EPCs of requirements planning (part 2)

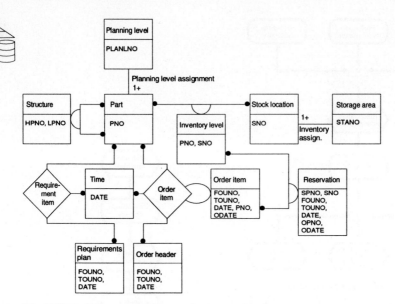

Fig. B.I.71: Object model for requirements planning

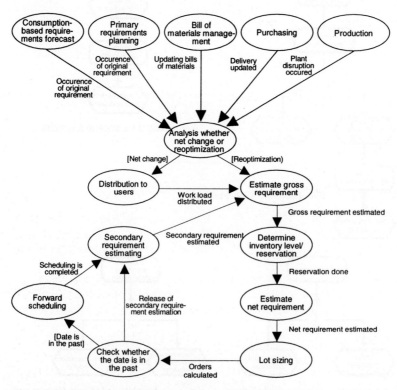

Fig. B.I.72: Dynamic model for requirements planning

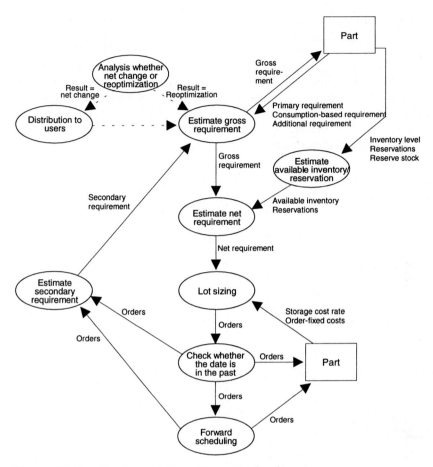

Fig. B.I.73: Functional model for requirements planning

B.I.3.2.4.4.3 Organization - Data

Figure B.I.74 uses an access table to express the relationship between organizational units and data. The authorization levels are indicated as C (Create), D (Delete), U (Update) and R (Read), with the highest levels in each case being shown.

The data view and the organization view are each represented by rough objects. It should be noted that in addition to data objects, a detailed analysis can also define access authorizations for attribute groups, attributes and even attribute instances (see *Scheer, Architecture of Integrated Information Systems, 1992, pp. 126 f.*). Only in the data cluster for PART is a distinction made between entity types and attributes. At the same time, the following distinction is made according to part type: ARTICLE (SALES PART), IN-HOUSE PART and OUTSOURCED PART.

The first row in Figure B.I.74 expresses the fact that only Marketing/Sales is authorized to create articles, while all other departments have read-only access to the part type ARTICLE (SALES PART). The fourth row shows that article attributes can be updated by Marketing/Sales, Engineering, Production and Accounting and can be read by Purchasing. Examples of update authorization include the following functions: Marketing/Sales: price changes; Engineering: technical descriptions of the article; Production: changes in turnaround time; Accounting: changes in cost data.

		Marketing/Sales	Engineering	Production	Purchasing	Personnel	Accounting
	Article	C	R	R	R		R
Objects of part	In-house parts	R	C	C	R		R
	Outsourced parts	R	R	R	C		R
	Article	U	U	U	R		U
Attributes of part	In-house parts	R	U	C	R		U
	Outsourced parts	R	R	R	U		U
Structural relationships		R	C	C	C		R
Requirements		C	R	C	C		R
Production orders		R	R	C	R		U
	Finished goods warehouse	C	R	R	R		R
Inventory	Intermediate storage	R	R	C	R		R
	Inbound warehouse	R	R	R	C		R
Requirements links		R	R	C	C		R

Legend: Create   C
           Delete   D
           Update   U
           Read   R

Fig. B.I.74: Access authorizations of requirements planning

		Production	
		Requirements planning	
		Planner A	Planner B
Parts		Part No. 1 - 999	Part No. 1000 - 5000

Fig. B.I.75: Allocation of task packages according to part numbers

Personnel has no access authorization to requirements planning data.

Access authorizations also control the allocation of task packages among organizational units. For example, different planners can be responsible for different part groups (according to part number ranges). In this case, there is a detailed responsibility relationship between the organizational unit and the part number ranges of the key for the entity type PART (see Figure B.I.75).

B.I.3.2.4.4.4 Functions - Organization - Data

The process chain diagram (PCD) in Figure B.I.76 shows the relationships between all ARIS components involved in requirements planning.

The PCD contains a rough representation of the previously discussed dual relationships and provides a condensed overview of the process sequence.

The input/output relationship between the data view and the function view is illustrated in columns 2 and 3 on the information object level. The direction of the arrows indicates whether instances or attributes of the information object are primarily read or updated/created.

The PCD focuses the representation on the <u>interaction</u> between the <u>three</u> ARIS components; the previously discussed representations are necessary for a detailed description of a view or a dual relationship.

B.I.3.3 Design Specification for Requirements Planning

The requirements definitions developed above are adapted to technical DP interfaces within the framework of the design specifications for requirements planning.

B.I.3.3.1 Design Specification for Requirements Planning: The Function View

The module is an important concept in the design specification for the function view. Module design classifies functions into units and concentrates particularly on the principles of multiple use and information hiding. Interactive and batch modules can be differentiated on the basis of the way in which they are processed (batch or interactive). A user transaction describes an interactive, holistic task from the perspective of the user and typically comprises several interactive steps. On the other hand, a business process encompasses a plurality of user transactions.

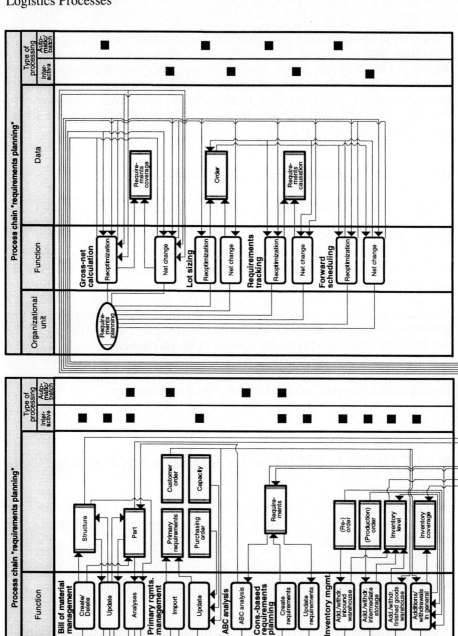

Fig. B.I.76: Process chain diagram for requirements planning

Since these terms are not standardized, standard software examples offer different interpretations.

In order to provide an impression of the degree of detail the design specification involves, Figure B.I.77 shows the menu for the online bill of materials management feature in the SAP R/3 standard PPC system.

Bill of Materials Menu

Bill of Materials
. Materials Bill of Materials
. . Create
. . Update
. . Display
Equipment Bill of Materials
. . Create
. . Update
. . Display
. End Bills of Materials
Bulk Change
. Materials
. . Replace
. . Delete
. . Create
Analyses
. Bill of Materials Explosion
. . Multi-level Modular
. . Multi-level Structural
. . Quantity Overview
. Utilization
. . Materials Utilization
. . . Direct Materials Utilization
. . . Multi-level Materials Utilization
. . . Materials Utilization Quantity Overview

Figure B.I.77: Bill of materials menu in the SAP R/3 standard PPC system

Submodules are assigned to each module, and transactions to each submodule. Transactions can be called by transaction codes. With the appropriate function codes, a transaction can thus be called by several (sub)modules.

B.I.3.3.2 Design Specification for Requirements Planning: The Organization View

From the perspective of the design specification, the subject-oriented organizational structure is depicted by a network topology, which conforms to the communication relationships identified in the requirements definition. Principal organizational criteria for the network topology are the planning levels organized according to the requirements planning process, as formed within the framework of the requirements definition in Figure B.I.69. The product planning level is transferred with interplant planning, and the plant planning level with plant-oriented planning.

This structure is illustrated in greater detail in Figure B.I.78 in the form of a client/server architecture by assigning stand-alone departmental computers to these departments for their functions, and by equipping all users with computer workstations having the appropriate graphical user interfaces and independent storage units for workstation-oriented data. Bus-type local area networks are used within a local unit.

This network topology serves as the basis for distributing functions and data, a subject that is discussed with respect to the design specification for control.

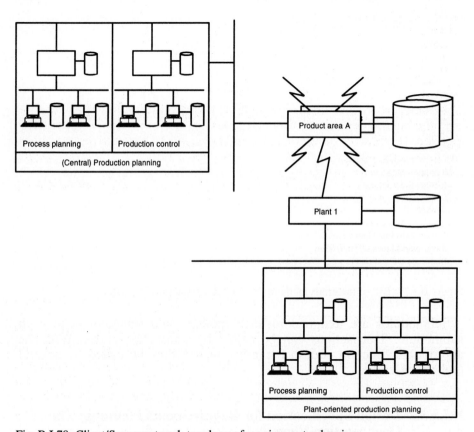

Fig. B.I.78: Client/Server network topology of requirements planning

B.I.3.3.3 Design Specification for Requirements Planning: The Data View

The ER data models for the requirements definition are transferred to the relational model representations and to the network model representations. The network model is especially important for bill of materials management, since bill of materials chaining has led to a form of data management that is also being refined by bill of materials processors within the framework of relational database systems.

Since transferring the ER data model to the relational model is a schematic process due to fixed transformation rules, it is more suited to a condensed representation of the information objects presented, including their key and descriptive attributes.

The portrayal follows the subareas of bill of materials management, requirements explosion and requirements tracking.

Bill of Materials Management

In contrast to the ER model approach, the **relational model** does not employ a graphical descriptive language. It makes no further distinction between entity types and relationship types. Consequently, in n:m relationships, a relation is set up for each entity type and relationship type. No specialized relation is set up for 1:1 and 1:n relationships.

The ER model structure in Figure B.I.17 yields the relations R. PART and R. STRUCTURE:

R. PART (<u>PNO</u>, designation, etc.)

R. STRUCTURE (<u>HPNO</u>, <u>LPNO</u>, quantity, etc.)

Role names (higher-level (H) part and lower-level (L) part) are assigned for the key attributes within the relation R. STRUCTURE.

These relations reflect the bill of materials structure. This is illustrated on the entity level in Figure B.I.79 using the gozinto graph in Figure B.I.16. The part numbers are taken from the abbreviations in that example.

The underlined key attributes correspond to those of the ER model approach. Special part relations with their own attributes can be set up for the subtypes introduced for the ER model approach. Importing the entire attribute catalog, including the repetition groups, would lead to an unnormalized relation. Applying the normalization steps would reduce this unnormalized relation to simpler relations, creating independent relations for the subtypes. Since only individual attributes are selected here, however, the normalization steps are not performed.

It is always ensured, however, that the data structures are in the third normal form for the explicitly cited attributes.

PART	PNO	DESIGNATION	...
	P1	End product 1	
	P2	End product 2	
	A1	Assembly 1	
	C1	Component part 1	
	C2	Component part 2	
	C3	Component part 3	
	M1	Material 1	

STRUC-TURE	HPNO	LPNO	Quantity	...
	P1	C2	2	
	P1	C1	3	
	P1	A1	4	
	P2	A1	5	
	P2	C3	3	
	A1	C1	4	
	A1	C3	2	
	C2	M1	1	

Fig. B.I.79: Relational model: product structure

Entity types in the **network model** are represented graphically by boxes, and 1:n relationships can only be represented by a set (owner-member set). An additional concept must be introduced for n:m relationships that divides the n:m relationship into two 1:n relationships. This process corresponds to the relationship type of the ER model approach.

Since the bill of materials structure itself is an n:m representation of the PART entity type, two boxes are necessary for PART and STRUCTURE, as well as two lines (see Figure B.I.80).

Fig. B.I.80: Network model: product structure

The bill of materials (BOM) represents the gozinto graph arrows that lead directly to a part, and the part utilization (PU) set represents the arrows that originate directly from a part.

Because of its historical significance as the precursor of general database systems, the chaining technique used in bill of materials processors is used to represent bills of materials on the entity level. The address references that are used should be understood as logical addresses that must be implemented in different physical forms to keep from leaving the design specification level.

On the entity level, every part and every arrow of the gozinto graph are represented by a PART or STRUCTURE record, respectively.

The records contain address reference fields (pointers) and application-oriented attributes. The address reference fields will be referred to as the record's system component; the attributes, as its the application component.

The system component of the part record contains two fields for the addresses of the first link record each of the bill of materials chain (BOMC) and of the part utilization chain (PUC) (see Figure B.I.81). If no chain originates from a part, the field contains an END character. Since only the address references of the direct structural relationships are entered, the chains represent so-called **single-level bills of materials** or **single-level part utilization lists**.

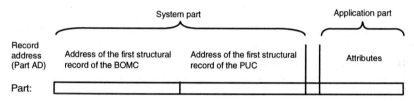

Fig. B.I.81: The part record in the network model

Bill of materials chains originate from end products, assemblies and component parts and link all records of the gozinto graph structural relationships that lead directly to the part. This process is illustrated in Figure B.I.16 for assembly A1 by arrows C1-A1 and C3-A1.

Part utilization chains originate from materials, component parts and assemblies and link all records of the gozinto graph structural relationships that originate directly from a part. For assembly A1, this is represented by the arrows A1-P1 and A1-P2.

The system component of the product structure record comprises link address fields for both sets and part record addresses for the respective superordinate and subordinate parts in the structural relationship, i.e., the addresses of the respective owner records. This relationship assumes that every link record points to the owner. This approach, in turn, is only **one** option for implementing the loop from members to owner; it has been selected here for the sake of simplicity. Other options include, for example, ring structures in which only the last link record of a chain refers to the owner.

In the bill of materials explosion, the superordinate part is the starting point of the analysis and is therefore known. The related part record refers to the first structural record of the bill of materials chain. The subordinate part address is taken from the first structural record of the bill of materials chain and the additional structural records.

The subordinate part is identified in the part utilization list. It refers to the first structural record of the part utilization chain. The superordinate part address is taken from it and the other structural records.

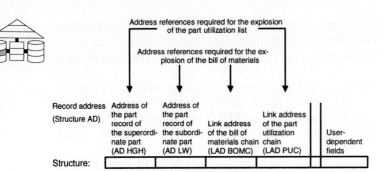

Record address (Structure AD)	Address of the part record of the superordinate part (AD HGH)	Address of the part record of the subordinate part (AD LW)	Link address of the bill of materials chain (LAD BOMC)	Link address of the part utilization chain (LAD PUC)	User-dependent fields
Structure:					

Fig. B.I.82: The product structure set within the network model

Strictly speaking, a BOM set forms the corresponding 1:n relationship of a single-level bill of materials. Figure B.I.83 shows the single-level bills of materials for the gozinto graph in Figure B.I.16.

The address references for the example are listed in their entirety in Figure B.I.84.

Although only the single-level bills of materials are represented directly, the other bills of materials, such as the structural bill of materials, can also be determined, since the single-level bills of materials are interlinked, and each component, in turn, can be the starting point for a new single-level bill of materials. In the example, assembly A1 is not only a component of the single-level bill of materials for P1 and P2, but also the starting point for its own bill of materials. The structural bill of materials can be specified by exploding the single-level bill of materials for an end product until a part is reached that, in turn, is the starting point for a single-level bill of materials, which is then exploded further. The process is continued where it was left off on the next higher level after the lowest level has been handled.

Figure B.I.85,a shows this process for structural bill of materials P1. The solid arrows indicate the address references for the single-level bill of materials sets. The broken arrows indicate address references to the owner records for the part utilization set; they serve to reach the subordinate part address from a structural relationship. Every structural relationship (arrow) is a member of a BOM set **and** a PU set, whereby the

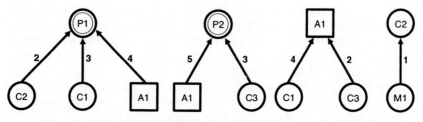

Fig. B.I.83: Single-level bills of materials of the Fig. B.I.16

Part records

Record address	Address of the first structural record of the bill of materials chain	Address of the first structural record of the part utilization list	Part name
1	10	END	P1
2	17	10	C2
3	END	11	C1
4	13	12	A1
5	15	END	P2
6	END	14	C3
7	END	17	M1

Structural records

Record address	Address of the record of the superordinate part	Adress of the record of the subordinate part	Link address of the bill of materials chain	Link address of the part utilization chain	Prod. coeff.	Corresponds to the arrow in Fig. B.I.16
10	1	2	11	END	2	C2-P1
11	1	3	12	13	3	C1-P1
12	1	4	END	15	4	A1-P1
13	4	3	14	END	4	C1-A1
14	4	6	END	16	2	C3-A1
15	5	4	16	END	5	A1-P2
16	5	6	END	END	3	C3-P2
17	2	7	END	END	1	M1-C2

———————————► Address references of the single-level bill of materials chain for P1
— — — —► Address references of the single-level bill of materials chain for A1
- - - - - ► Address references of the single-level bill of materials chain for P2
— · — · ► Address references of the single-level bill of materials chain for C1

Fig. B.I.84: Address references to Fig. B.I.14

a) Address references Structural bill of materials for P1

Record address item master	Record address of the product structure	
1	—	
2	10	1 Modular chain
3	11	
4	12	
3	13	2 Modular chain
6	14	
2	17	
7		

b) Address references Structural part utilization list for C1

Record address item master	Record address of the product structure
3	—
1	11
4	13
1	12
5	15

Fig. B.I.85,a-b: Address references for structural bill of materials and structural part utilization list superordinate part address is the owner of the BOM set and the subordinate part address is the owner of the PU set.

The same interrelationships that apply to the bill of materials relationships apply to part utilization. Thus, Figure B.I.85,b is analogous to the explosion of the structural part utilization list for C1.

The special forms of bill of materials management, e.g., variants, can also be depicted using relational and network models. Figure B.I.86 uses the cyclical gozinto graph from Figure B.I.27 to illustrate this example.

Network models frequently require a cycle-free schematic representation. This requirement is satisfied by using cyclical gozinto graphs since cycles only occur on the entity level and not on the type level.

a) Relational model

Part	(PNO ,	Name)		Structure (	HPNO,	LPNO.	Quantity)
	P	End product			P	A	1
	A	Assembly			A	P	0.2
	C	Component part			A	C	0.8

b) Network model

PART

AD	BOMC	PUC	Name
1	4	6	P
2	5	4	A
3	END	5	C

STRUCTURE

AD	AD HIGH	AD LOW	LAD BOMC	LAD PUC	Prod. coef.	Struct. rel.
4	1	2	END	END	1	A-P
5	2	3	6	END	0.8	C-A
6	2	1	END	END	0.2	P-A

Fig. B.I.86: Cyclical product structure in the relational and network model

Requirements Explosion

The data structure for the requirements explosion from Figure B.I.35 is transformed into the relational model in Figure B.I.87. The key attributes of the original entity types consist of simple terms. The STOCK LOCATION relation uses the warehouse number key for the superordinate relation on the basis of the 1:n relationship. R. ORDER and R. REQUIREMENT are each identified by part number and date. If several orders or requirements for the same part exist on the same date, the date must be defined more explicitly. The TIME relation contains predefined date categories. The RESERVATION relation combines the keys of the INVENTORY LEVEL and ORDER relations. Since subordinate components are always reserved for an order, the part numbers are distinguished by the letters S (stock location) and O (order).

In each case, the application-oriented attributes are merely suggested.

R. TIME (<u>DATE</u>)
R. PART (<u>PNO</u>, PLANLNO, name, ...)
R. STRUCTURE (<u>HPNO, LPNO</u>, production coefficient, ...)

R. STORAGE AREA (<u>STANO</u>, space capacity, ...)
R. STOCK LOCATION (<u>SNO</u>, STANO, space capacity, ...)
R. INVENTORY LEVEL (<u>PNO, SNO</u>, goods on hand, reserve stock, ...)
R. ORDER HEADER (<u>FOUNO, TOUNO, DATE</u>, status, ...)
R. REQUIREMENTS PLAN (<u>FOUNO, TOUNO, DATE</u>, ...)
R. ORDER (ITEM) (<u>FOUNO, TOUNO, DATE, PNO, ODATE</u>, quantity, ...)
R. REQUIREMENT (ITEM) (<u>FOUNO, TOUNO, DATE, PNO, RDATE</u>, quantity, ...)
R. RESERVATION (<u>FOUNO, TOUNO, DATE, OPNO, ODATE, SPNO, SNO</u>, quantity, ...)
R. PLANNING LEVEL (<u>PLANLNO</u>, number, parts, ...)

Fig. B.I.87: Relational model of requirements planning

Requirements Tracking

The relation R. REQUIREMENTS DERIVATION occurs as the first element in the requirements explosion. Its key comprises the keys for the superordinate order (work order) and the requirement. Each key consists of the part number and date as well as the keys for the following header information objects: distributing organizational unit, receiving organizational unit and distribution date. The keys are distinguished by using either O (order) or R (requirement) as the first letter of the relation name. The imported requirement record is maintained in the

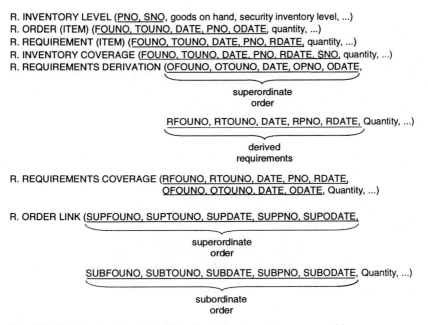

R. INVENTORY LEVEL (<u>PNO, SNO</u>, goods on hand, security inventory level, ...)
R. ORDER (ITEM) (<u>FOUNO, TOUNO, DATE, PNO, ODATE</u>, quantity, ...)
R. REQUIREMENT (ITEM) (<u>FOUNO, TOUNO, DATE, PNO, RDATE</u>, quantity, ...)
R. INVENTORY COVERAGE (<u>FOUNO, TOUNO, DATE, PNO, RDATE, SNO</u>, quantity, ...)
R. REQUIREMENTS DERIVATION (<u>OFOUNO, OTOUNO, DATE, OPNO, ODATE,</u>

superordinate
order

<u>RFOUNO, RTOUNO, DATE, RPNO, RDATE,</u> Quantity, ...)

derived
requirements

R. REQUIREMENTS COVERAGE (<u>RFOUNO, RTOUNO, DATE, PNO, RDATE,</u>
<u>OFOUNO, OTOUNO, DATE, ODATE</u>, Quantity, ...)

R. ORDER LINK (<u>SUPFOUNO, SUPTOUNO, SUPDATE, SUPPNO, SUPODATE,</u>

superordinate
order

<u>SUBFOUNO, SUBTOUNO, SUBDATE, SUBPNO, SUBODATE</u>, Quantity, ...)

subordinate
order

Fig. B.I.88: Relational model of the single-level requirements tracking

R. REQUIREMENTS COVERAGE relation and at the same time **totaled** in the R. REQUIREMENT relation.

The R. REQUIREMENTS COVERAGE and R. INVENTORY COVERAGE relations are generated in the coverage calculation. Their keys also result from the combination of keys from two relations. However, since the coverage calculation refers to the same part each time, the part numbers within the keys are identical and are therefore not listed twice. The origin of the key attribute can be identified by the first letter of the relation name.

The R. REQUIREMENTS COVERAGE relation assigns the order quantities to a requirement; these order quantities fulfill the requirement. The R. INVENTORY COVERAGE relation assigns the corresponding inventory quantities to a requirement.

The R. ORDER LINK relation is introduced if the material flow between the individual orders must be maintained directly. In this case, the subquantities that are derived from a superordinate order for subordinate orders are assigned to the superordinate order. On the other hand, this relation also allows the subquantities to be seen with which a subordinate order goes into superordinate orders. This means that it is possible to obtain a direct answer to the question of what is to happen to an order (lot) after it is completed. The keys are distinguished by SUP (superordinate) and SUB (subordinate).

The customer order reference is created by incorporating the key for R. CUSTOMER ORDER ITEM into the relation model for multi-level requirements tracking (see Figure B.I.89).

R. INVENTORY LEVEL (<u>PNO, SNO</u>, goods on hand, security stock level, ...)
R. ORDER (ITEM) (<u>FOUNO, TOUNO, DATE, PNO, ODATE,</u> quantity, ...)
R. REQUIREMENT (ITEM) (<u>FOUNO, TOUNO, DATE, PNO, RDATE,</u> quantity, ...)
R. CUSTOMER ORDER HEADER (<u>CNO, COTOUNO, CODATE,</u> status, ...)
R. CUSTOMER ORDER ITEM (<u>CNO, COTOUNO, CODATE, PNO, CDATE,</u> quantity, price, ...)
R. REQUIREMENTS COVERAGE (<u>RFOUNO, RTOUNO, DATE, RDATE, PNO,</u>

Requirements item

<u>OFOUNO, OTOUNO, DATE, ODATE,</u>

Order item

<u>CNO, COOUNO, CODATE, CPNO, CDATE,</u> quantity, ...)

Customer order item

R. INVENTORY COVERAGE (<u>FOUNO, TOUNO, DATE, PNO, RDATE, SNO,</u>
<u>CNO, COOUNO, CODATE, CPNO, CDATE,</u> quantity, ...)
R. REQUIREMENTS DERIVATION (<u>OFOUNO, OTOUNO, DATE, OPNO, ODATE,</u>
<u>RFOUNO, RTOUNO, DATE, RPNO, RDATE,</u>
<u>CNO, COOUNO, CODATE, CPNO, CDATE,</u> quantity, ...)

Fig. B.I.89: Relational model of the multi-level requirements tracking

B.I.3.3.4 Design Specification for Requirements Planning: The Control View

The ARIS function, organization and data components are linked within the framework of the control design specification.

B.I.3.3.4.1 Functions - Organization

The assignment of modules to network topology nodes specifies user group access authorization to transactions and assigns module execution to the appropriate host systems at the network nodes. Figure B.I.90 illustrates this principle for the client/server network topology shown in

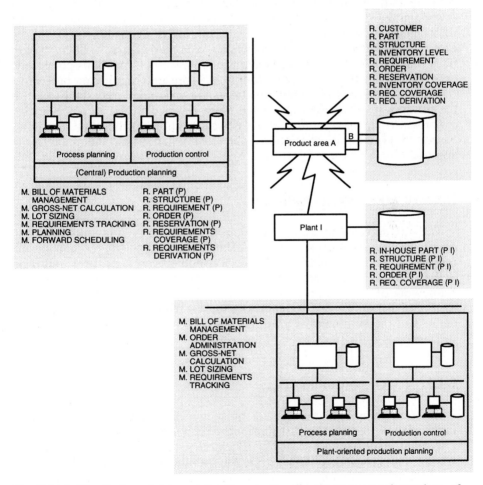

Fig. B.I.90: Distribution of data and functions in the client/server network topology of requirements planning

Figure B.I.78. For purposes of simplification, the module names correspond to the function names in the requirements definition; in a more detailed analysis, however, an n:m relationship can exist between modules and functions. The function names are preceded by "M." to indicate the independent design step of module formation.

The execution of some modules, such as bill of materials management, is distributed among several computer nodes, and access authorization can be different at each node. For example, the update service can have access to bills of materials on the plant level, but it cannot create new parts.

On the other hand, a transaction of a department that has access to an independent computer node can also be "switched through" to the higher-level computer, which is the case with respect to lot sizing for plant-oriented production planning. Based on detailed knowledge, lot replanning can be performed vis-à-vis central gross-net calculation.

Since no detailed branching of the transactions and modules occurs that is comparable to the division in the requirements definition structures, the information value of the functional structure used here is only very rough. In a realistic analysis, on the other hand, a higher degree of detail would be necessary. Coordinating redundant functions—i.e., functions performed at several nodes in the computer hierarchy—presents significant problems.

The requirements planning functions, for example, are established on the product level as well as on the plant level. Thus, it is possible, for example, to perform a quick gross-net calculation on the plant computer based on production disruptions—at least when using the net change approach.

B.I.3.3.4.2 Functions - Data

The link between modules and relations is represented by the transfer of event control to process control of modules using trigger and action messages. At the same time, relation attributes as well as the systems on which the files are kept must be assigned to the modules within the framework of input/output relationships. The input/output relationships, in turn, can be only very roughly analyzed and are discussed within the context of the summary of all three ARIS components. The same applies with respect to the discussion of the triggers.

B.I.3.3.4.3 Organization - Data

Without going into the special problems of data consistency checks, Figure B.I.90 shows the distribution of relations among network nodes. The plant level data are distributed centrally, and they can be distributed among the processing servers on the production planning department level, at least temporarily. As in module distribution, redundancies occur. These redundancies, however, can be attributed to the rough form of representation, since on the different levels, the same relation names can be understood as attribute segments of the comprehensive relation as well as tuple segments. Thus, only the orders that are produced in the plant are maintained on the plant level. Likewise, the plant is only assigned orders that have a bearing on its planning period, while orders that go beyond this period can be stored on the product level. Such a system of multi-level data management requires exact stipulation of update authorizations and database synchronization. The design specification is thus also responsible for formulating appropriate conditions for ensuring data integrity. Because this discussion concentrates on the higher descriptive levels, however, this problem will not be pursued further.

Figure B.I.90 adds the departmental abbreviations to the relation names to show the individualization of the relations on the basis of attribute selection and tuple selection.

B.I.3.3.4.4 Functions - Organization - Data

The discussion of the design specification linking all ARIS components will first concentrate on trigger and action control, since subsystems at different nodes can be controlled through the event-driven sequence of modules, thus also addressing organizational task distribution. In action control, the distribution of a task among the users—i.e., the organizational units—is a central function.

In order to demonstrate that modules will now be stipulated in the design specification EPC instead of the functions for the requirements definition, each function name taken from the requirements definition is preceded by "M." This indicates that a function can be classified into several modules within the framework of the design specification and also that a module can be utilized in several functions.

In the development of event-driven process chains (EPC), the events that control the functional sequence within requirements planning were identified within the context of the requirements definition. Within the framework of the design specification, these events are then analyzed on the basis of the extent to which they directly support technical DP control functions. Trigger and action control constitutes the basis of this analysis. Triggers are monitoring routines that analyze specific events within the system sequence and then react by activating automatic program steps. Action control, on the other hand, controls the interactive sequence in which processes are distributed among the users responsible for processing and "fill the mailbox" upstream of a workstation.

Within the framework of the design specification, therefore, events from the requirements planning EPCs are labeled on the basis of whether they are objects of the trigger check or assignments to users' mailboxes.

In Figure B.I.91, right-hand cross hatching is used to identify the events that initiate automatic processing for the requirements explosion (see Figure B.I.37 for the requirements definition).

190

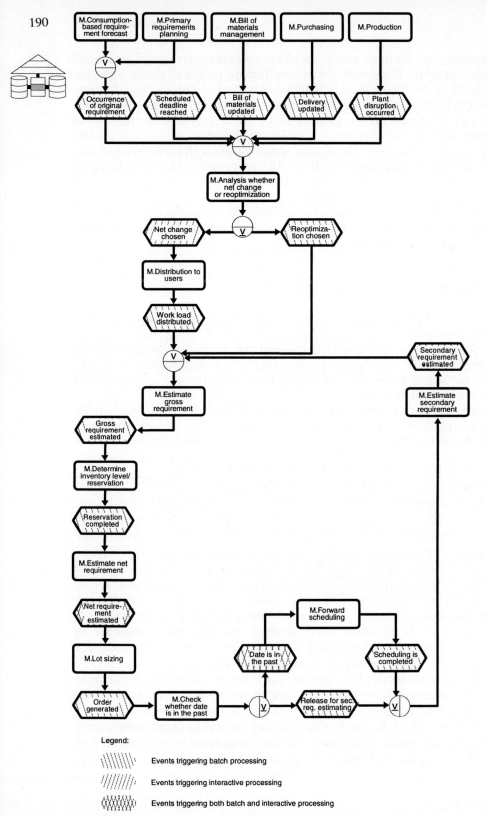

Fig. B.I.91: Trigger and action control of requirements planning

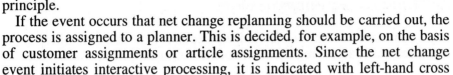

Initially, this holds true for all events from the above applications that necessitate replanning as well as the "scheduled deadline reached" event. A trigger thus reacts when one of these events occurs and activates the next function, in this case, the analysis of whether planning should be performed according to the net change principle or the reoptimization principle.

If the event occurs that net change replanning should be carried out, the process is assigned to a planner. This is decided, for example, on the basis of customer assignments or article assignments. Since the net change event initiates interactive processing, it is indicated with left-hand cross hatching.

Some events are suitable for both automatic and interactive processing, as specified in Table B.I.64 in the discussion on interactive causes within requirements planning. These events are represented by both left- and right-hand cross hatching.

The "gross requirement estimated" event is especially important because it initiates the determination of the inventory level for the part in question. If the inventory level is maintained in a special inventory management system, this event triggers a query to this subsystem. This situation illustrates that triggers can also be used for controlling logical sequences that are performed on several (heterogeneous) subsystems.

In a semi-formal representation using the I/O-T concept, the triggers that initiate the function "analyze whether net change or reoptimization" can be roughly defined by:

EVENT	original requirement	(requirement_object:	IB_ID);
EVENT	bill of materials update	(bill_of_materials_object:	DB_ID);
EVENT	delivery update	(delivery_update_object:	DB_ID);
EVENT	plant disruption	(plant_disruption _object:	DB_ID);
EVENT	planning date	(planning_date_object:	DB_ID);

ACTION   analyze_whether_net_change_or_reoptimization
(requirement object, bill of materials object, delivery update object, plant disruption object, planning date object)

TRIGGER   T1 = ON   original requirement   or
                                             bill of materials update   or
                                             delivery update   or
                                             plant disruption   or
                                             planning date
                   do   analyze_whether_net_change_or_re-
                                             optimization   (requirement_object,
                                             bill_of_materials_object,   delivery_
                                             update_object,
                                             plant_disruption_object,   planning_
                                             date_object).

ACTIVATE T1

ACTIVATE T1 activates—i.e., "turns on"—the trigger. In each case, the functions preceding the events trigger the events associated with the respective identifier, e.g., primary requirements planning is initiated by the function:

RAISE original_requirement (r_id)

This command is an acknowledged requirement update, where r_id identifies the concrete requirement update object (instance).

The action "analyze_whether_net_change_or_reoptimization" can exist with this name in the call for a corresponding module (procedure) or be defined by commands in the ACTION element.

B.I.3.4 Implementation Description for Requirements Planning

The implementation description describes the transformation of design specifications into concrete information technology systems. In reference to the function view, this involves programming the preliminary module design in a specific programming language. The organization view depicts the network topology using concrete network protocols and computer systems. The data view converts the data structures for the relational or network model into database descriptions for concrete database systems, and all these components are interlinked in the control view.

Because of the conceptual scope of this book, only segments of the implementation description will be discussed. Thus, for requirements planning, only data models for bill of materials management will be converted to DB2 and UDS database systems and used to show a bill of materials explosion as an implementation description for a function. Since this database application requires knowledge of the database structure for functional application, the database description will be presented first, followed by the bill of materials explosion in the function view.

B.I.3.4.1 Implementation Description for Requirements Planning: The Data View

As examples of relational and network database systems, some of the requirements planning data models introduced in Section B.I.3.3.3 will be transformed into concrete DB2 (IBM) and UDS (Siemens) database systems.

In the DB2 database system, the R. PART and R. STRUCTURE relations of the **relational model** from Figure B.I.79 result in the PART and STRUCTURE tables in Figure B.I.92.

It is absolutely necessary to indicate the attributes HPNO and LPNO in the STRUCTURE table, since they are required for creating the logical links between the entities of the PART table. The illustrated data structure can be supplemented by attributes.

The UDS **network database** yields the scheme illustrated in Figure B.I.93 (for definitions, see *Siemens, UDS Entwerfen und Definieren 1982*).

In the STRUCTURE record, the definition of the attribute HPNO and LPNO is possible but not absolutely necessary, since the link to the entities of the PART record can be created using the address chain for the system component.

```
CREATE TABLE  PART (PNO CHAR(10) NOT NULL,
              NAME  CHAR(20),
              . . .               );

CREATE TABLE  STRUCTURE (HPNO CHAR(10) NOT NULL,
              LPNO CHAR(10) NOT NULL,
              QUANTITY DECIMAL(3) NOT NULL,
              . . .                   );
```

Fig. B.I.92: Scheme definition in DB2

```
SCHEME NAME IS          PRODUCTION.
*
AREA NAME IS            PART STRUCTURE.
*
*
*
*    ENTITY TYPE    PART
*    .................
RECORD NAME IS          PART
         LOCATION MODE IS CALC USING PNO
              DUPLICATES ARE NOT ALLOWED
         WITHIN PART STRUCTURE
         SEARCH KEY IS NAME USING CALC
              DUPLICATES ARE ALLOWED.
*
01    PNO             PIC X(10).
01    NAME            PIC X(20).
*              . . .
*
*    ENTITY TYPE    STRUCTURE
*    .......................
RECORD NAME IS   STRUCTURE
         WITHIN PART STRUCTURE.
*
01    QUANTITY        PIC S9(3).
*              . . .
*
*    RELATIONSHIP BILL OF MATERIALS (HPART ---> LPART)
*    ..................................................
SET NAME IS             BOM-CHAIN
         ORDER IS NEXT
         OWNER IS NEXT
MEMBER IS STRUCTURE MANDATORY AUTOMATIC
         SET OCCURRENCE SELECTION IS THRU CURRENT OF SET.
*
*    REALATIONSHIP PART UTILIZATION (LPART ---> HPART)
*    .................................................
SET NAME IS             PU-CHAIN
         ORDER IS NEXT
         OWNER IS NEXT
MEMBER IS STRUCTURE MANDATORY AUTOMATIC
         SET OCCURRENCE SELECTION IS THRU CURRENT OF SET.
```

Fig. B.I.93: Scheme definition in UDS

B.I.3.4.2 Implementation Description for Requirements Planning: The Function View

In defining the schemes, a database was designed for each data model, which determined the entity types and their relationships. Afterwards a database must be filled with concrete entities (e.g., part P1, A1 or C1; structure C1-A1, etc.). This insertion of data records will not be analyzed further; instead, a sample application using a bill of materials explosion will be illustrated.

The DB2 database system, like most **relational database management systems**, provides the user with the SQL (Structured Query Language) database query language. In SQL, which has since become the standard query language for relational DBMS (database management systems), complicated queries can be created using a basic structure of three key words:

SELECT   Attribute fields to be displayed
FROM   Relations and/or tables that contain the attributes
WHERE   Condition component indicating selection criteria

The single-level bill of materials for part P1 for the gozinto graph in Figure B.I.16 will serve as an example for a bill of materials explosion. The query is executed with the help of a "join" function in which the PART **and** STRUCTURE tables are indicated as relations that must be searched (see Figure B.I.94). Each entity from the PART table is linked with each relationship from the STRUCTURE table—i.e., 42 possible combinations result from six PART entities and seven STRUCTURE relationships. Of all these combinations, those are selected in which the higher-level part number HPNO in the STRUCTURE table equals P1 and the lower-level part number LPNO corresponds to the part number PNO in the PART table. After the selection is made, the data records are displayed with the attributes PNO, DESCRIPTION and QUANTITY.

The result of the query shown in Figure B.I.94 is illustrated in Figure B.I.95.

```
SELECT  PNO, NAME, QUANTITY
FROM    PART, STRUCTURE
WHERE   HPNO = 'P1'  AND  LPNO = PNO;
```

Fig. B.I.94: Definition of a single-level bill of materials using SQL

PNO	DESIGNATION	QUANTITY
C2	COMPONENT PART 2	2
C1	COMPONENT PART 1	3
A1	ASSEMBLY 1	4

Fig. B.I.95: Result of SQL-Query

The bill of materials explosion for the example of the UDS **network database** is illustrated using an implementation-oriented program flow chart. For this type of database application, UDS provides a data manipulation language in the form of a COBOL-DML. The COBOL-DML is a functional extension of COBOL, which is used as a host language.

The most important data manipulation commands of the COBOL-DML are:

READY:	Begins a transaction or process chain
FINISH:	Ends a database transaction
FIND:	Searches a record and enters the database key in the currency table
GET:	Transfers the current record of the currency table to the application program
FETCH:	Combination of the FIND and GET commands
MODIFY:	Modifies an existing data record in the database
STORE:	Transfers a record from the application program to the DB
ERASE:	Deletes a data record and its set relationships from the DB
CONNECT:	Creates a set relationship in the DB
DISCONNECT:	Deletes a set relationship
KEEP:	Protects a data record from being accessed by other programs
FREE:	Cancels KEEP status

When the program executes, the database management system maintains the database key values for all current records (key value of the record in the database) in a currency table. A distinction is made between the following currency entries:
- Current Record of Record (CRR):
- Current Record of Set (CRS):
- Current Record of Area (CRA):
- Current Record of Rununit (CRU):

The program can use the currency table to track the address chain of the set relationships.

Figure B.I.96 shows the explosion of the structural bill of materials; the required database commands are explained below:

1.   FETCH PART USING PNO
      Searches and displays a part record with the given primary key
2.   FETCH NEXT STRUCTURE WITHIN BOM CHAIN
      Searches and displays the next structural record within the current BOM chain

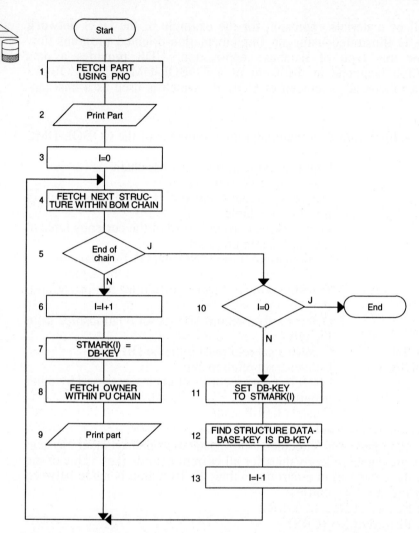

Fig. B.I.96: Program flow chart for the explosion of bill of materials in the network database of UDS

3.   FETCH OWNER WITHIN PU CHAIN
      Searches and displays the record within the current PU chain
4.   FIND STRUCTURE DATABASE-KEY IS DB-KEY
      Searches a structural record with the help of the DATABASE-KEY

Figure B.I.97 shows the composition of the most important currency entries in the structural bill of materials explosion for part P1 from the example shown in Figure B.I.84.

Step in PFC of bill of materials explosion	1	4	6,7,8	4	6,7,8	4	11,12,13	4	11,12,13	4	6,7,8	4	11,12,13	4	6,7,8	4	6,7,8	4	11,12,13	4	6,7,8	4	11,12,13	4	11,12,13	4
Found record type	PART	STRUC-TURE	PART	STRUC-TURE	PART	-	STRUC-TURE	-	STRUC-TURE	STRUC-TURE	PART	-	STRUC-TURE	STRUC-TURE	PART	STRUC-TURE	PART	-	STRUC-TURE	STRUC-TURE	PART	-	STRUC-TURE	-	STRUC-TURE	-
Record content	P1	C2-P1	C2	M1-C2	M1	-	M1-C2	-	C2-P1	C1-P1	C1	-	C1-P1	A1-P1	A1	C1-A1	C1	-	C1-A1	C3-A1	C3	-	C3-A1	-	A1-P1	-
I	0	0	1	1	2	2	1	1	0	0	1	1	0	0	1	1	2	2	1	1	2	-	1	-	0	-
STMARK (I)	0	0	10	10	17	17	10	10	0	0	11	11	0	0	12	12	13	13	12	12	14	-	12	-	0	-
CRR PARTS	1	1	2	2	7	7	7	7	2	3	3	3	3	4	4	3	3	3	3	6	6	-	6	-	6	-
CRR STRUCTURE	0	10	10	17	17	17	17	17	10	11	11	11	11	12	12	13	13	13	13	14	14	-	14	-	12	-
CRS CHAIN	1	10	2	2	7	7	17	7	10	11	3	3	11	12	4	13	3	3	13	14	6	-	14	-	12	-
CRS CHAIN	1	10	2	2	7	7	17	7	10	11	3	3	11	12	4	13	3	3	13	14	6	-	14	-	12	-

Fig. B.I.97: Composition of the currency table (example)

The individual steps in the program flow chart from Figure B.I.96 are explained below:

1. The PART record for which the bill of materials is to be created is retrieved using an index-sequential access (here P1).
2. Print command.
3. I is a variable, in which the bill of materials depth is identified on the basis of the part in question. It is initialized with 0.
4. The STRUCTURE record, which points to the next subordinate part, is retrieved using the CRS entry in the BOM chain.
5. If the end of the chain is reached, the program displays an access error.
6. If a STRUCTURE record is found, I is increased by 1.
7. STMARK is a one-dimensional field. It stores the DATABASE-KEY-Value of the last STRUCTURE record retrieved for each bill of materials depth (I of the gozinto graph). This makes it possible to create a structural bill of materials, i.e., to track a part across all production levels.
8. The subordinate PART record is retrieved using the CRS plant in the PU chain.
9. Print command.
10. If the end of a BOM chain is identified in step 5, i.e., no further STRUCTURE record is present in the chain, a query is made whether I is equal to 0. In this case, the entire gozinto graph is processed.
11. The DATABASE-KEY-Value is set to the last valid STRUCTURE record that was stored in the STMARK (I) field in step 7.
12. Using FIND, the last valid STRUCTURE record is localized via the DATABASE-KEY-Value, which updates the CRS entries of the BOM CHAIN and of the PU CHAIN in the currency table.
13. Variable I is decreased by 1.

B.I.4 Scheduling and Capacity Planning

B.I.4.1 Overview: Scheduling and Capacity Planning

All orders related to the specified primary requirements periods are scheduled in the requirements explosion. Capacity considerations are not taken into account. An order's lead time shift is calculated using the turnaround time assigned to the superordinate order/part and the lead time as it relates to the structural relationship (requirements period of a superordinate part minus turnaround time plus lead time). Rough average values for the assumed durations are thus used for scheduling.
Consequently, within the framework of medium-term scheduling and capacity planning:
-       Time scheduling is fine tuned by specifying start and finish times for the individual operations, with forms of adaptation being taken into consideration
-       Load profiles are created for individual capacity types on the basis of fine-tuned planning data and
-       A capacity adjustment is performed for bottleneck situations or load fluctuations.

"Medium-term capacity planning" means that the capacities themselves remain unchanged. Thus, a distinction is made between medium-term capacity planning and long-term capacity planning (investment planning), in which the capacities are variable.
In the case of scheduling and capacity planning, the order records created during requirements planning must be extended to include data concerning the technological operations to be performed. Moreover, there must be access to information concerning available capacities.
Figure B.I.98 shows the function tree for scheduling and capacity planning. It consists of a basic data management system and supplemental order data taken from requirements planning as well as of the planning

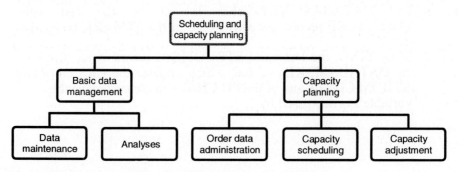

Fig. B.I.98: Function tree for scheduling and capacity planning modules for capacity adjustment and for capacity scheduling without reference to capacity limits. The discussion that follows will conform to this structure. Production Planning is responsible for time management, whereby Process Planning is responsible for basic data management and Production Control, for order-related planning. These tasks can be performed centrally or on the plant level (see Figure B.I.99).

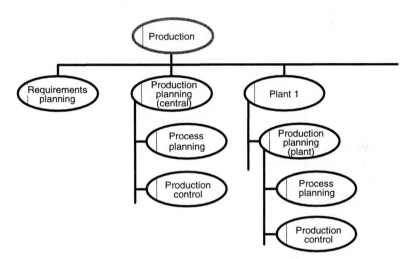

Fig. B.I.99: Organizational chart for scheduling and capacity planning

The rough scheduling and capacity planning process is illustrated in the process chain diagram in Figure B.I.100. The creation of routings based on bills of materials, drawings, and time and technology catalogs is only suggested, since it is treated in detail within the context of the product development process chain. In addition to production protocols, data concerning resources to be utilized are also treated within the framework of basic data management. This process also results in interfaces to other processes, such as fixed asset accounting/investment accounting and to the personnel department. Basic data management is a typical interactive function.

The time management planning function begins by supplementing the order data taken from requirements planning to include descriptive and stipulated technical and organizational values. For the most part, this function can be performed automatically; however, if there are assignment or optimization problems, it too is performed interactively.

Subsequent order scheduling is also primarily an automatic function.

Reconciling capacity peaks and compensating for bottlenecks are functions that lend themselves to interactive decision support.

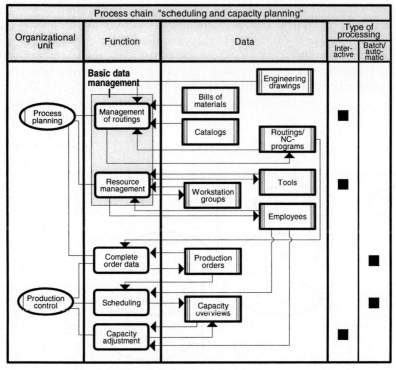

Fig. B.I.100: Process chain diagram for scheduling and capacity planning

B.I.4.2 Requirements Definitions for Scheduling and Capacity Planning

B.I.4.2.1 Basic Data Management

Like bills of materials, basic data for scheduling and capacity planning are key items of information in an industrial enterprise.

The basic data management functions are illustrated in Figure B.I.101.

The routing description characterizes a part from the perspective of Production by representing the technical procedures and resources that are needed for the part. A comprehensive product description—as provided by product models within the framework of the product development process chain—integrates all descriptive views for a part. To this extent, the separate descriptions for bills of materials from the perspective of Materials Management and Control, and for routings from the perspective of Production, merely serve as a didactic aid. The basic data contain the production descriptions without any relationship to an order; however, the order-related production descriptions are subsequently derived from them.

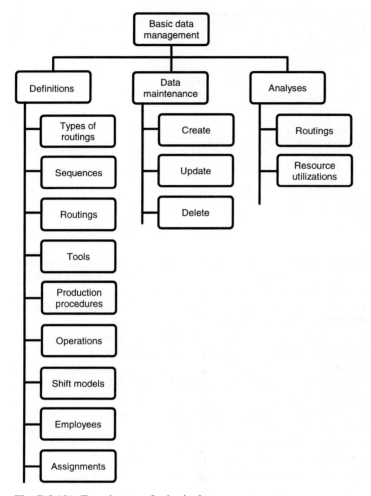

Fig. B.I.101: Function tree for basic data management

B.I.4.2.1.1 Routings and Resources

Routings describe both the technical procedures as well as the necessary resources that are required in the production of a part. The term "routing" is used in a limited sense to designate "header information" in the production protocols, while the necessary activities/operations and the types of resources are described by separate entities. In this sense, the term "routing" serves a unifying function with respect to the operations to be carried out. Since the production processes—and thus the routings—are oriented toward the available resources, a routing can be understood as a link between a resource environment and an in-house part. A resource environment can generally be characterized by a plant, resulting in the data structure shown in Figure B.I.102.

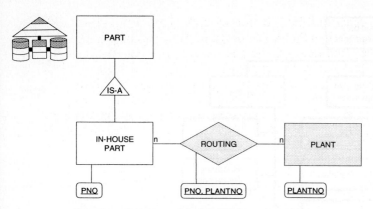

Fig. B.I.102: Plant-related definition of routing

A routing definition must include an indication of the plant in question because it refers to plant-related resource capability. The following discussion, however, begins by defining routings independently of plants. The plant assignment is then created by independent relationships that are not included in the routing identification.

Depending on the application in question, different routings can exist for a part, as indicated by the specializations in Figure B.I.103.

A sequence of operations used for planning or costing purposes, but not necessarily for production, is termed a "scheduling routing." A "trial routing" for a part describes the production of a part that is necessary for testing purposes but is not yet being produced on a regular basis. "Variant routings" provide a link to the problem involving variants that was introduced in the bill of materials description. Supersets of production procedures, from which the process sequences to be used for a specific variant can be selected, can be assigned to a variant operation sequence.

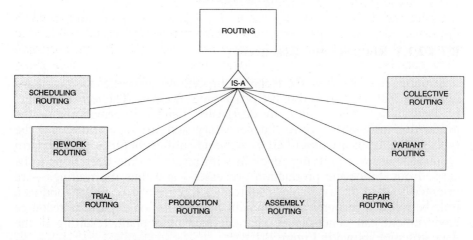

Fig. B.I.103: Specializations of routing

A "collective routing" describes the production of the part components to be used for a specific part. The other types of routings in Figure B.I.103 are self-explanatory. The remainder of the discussion will not make a distinction between the different types of routings.

Basic data management functions can be initiated by releasing new bills of materials, by operation updates in Production (the use of new equipment, tools, etc.), or by organizational changes in the production process (new employee assignments, new labor contracts about working conditions), as illustrated in the rough EPC in Figure B.I.104.

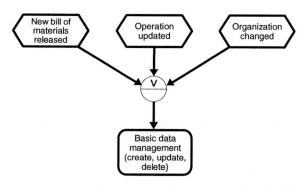

Fig. B.I.104: Event control of basic data management for scheduling and capacity planning

Figure B.I.105 illustrates the ER model for scheduling and capacity planning basic data. Although the data structure seems very technically oriented at first glance, it is actually of great importance with respect to business administration aspects. Thus, it provides important data to both Internal Accounting and Production Planning.

The newly introduced information objects are shaded.

Under the definition introduced in this book, a routing summarizes a sequence of technical process steps that are necessary for the production of a part. A part can be produced according to several different operation sequences (see *Eversheim, Organisation in der Produktionstechnik 1989, Vol. 3, p. 35*). Thus, in Figure B.I.106 the blank is completely manufactured by either the "turning" or "grinding" operation or by the operation sequence of "forging, turning and grinding." This means that several routings could be assigned to one part.

When a routing is selected from several alternatives, the assignment decision is made on the basis of the quantity to be produced, the quality required or timing and cost considerations.

Conversely, parts that require similar production procedures can be produced according to the same routings, although items in their bills of materials can differ. This situation can be encountered frequently in the chemical industry, for example, where the application of different raw materials in the same process sequence produces different products.

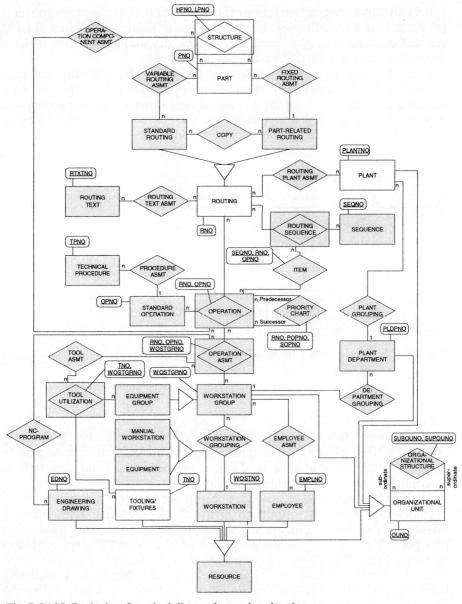

Fig. B.I.105: Basic data for scheduling and capacity planning

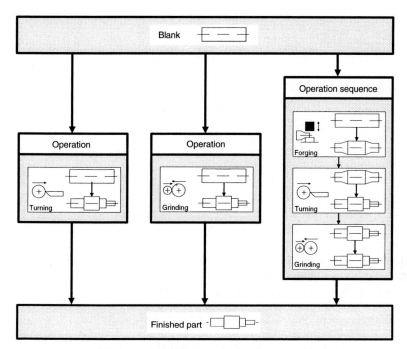

Fig. B.I.106: Manufacturing an axle by alternative operation sequences
(according to *Eversheim, Organisation in der Produktionstechnik, Bd. 3, p. 35*)

Since a routing is managed independently of part references with this data structure, it is designated as a standard routing. If, on the other hand, a 1:n relationship exists between a part and its routings, one routing is unambiguously assigned to a part.

This distinction between standard routings and part-related routings becomes drastically apparent with respect to the number of routings to be managed. Figure B.I.107 clarifies this by first illustrating a 1:n relationship between PART and ROUTING. In this case, introducing a new part P3, which can be manufactured according to the same routing as P2, would lead to the creation of a new routing R4. This routing would be created from routing R3 using a copy function. In an n:m relationship, on the other hand, only an assignment relationship would be created between part P3 and routing R3, as illustrated by the broken line. Since the number of routings to be managed can frequently result in several thousand or even several hundred thousand entities, the decision to employ standard routings or part-oriented routing management can have extremely far-reaching effects. Frequently, the standard routing option is precluded by overly rigid organizational rules such as "when Engineering releases a new part, Process Planning must **create** a routing," although copy functions still make the job easier. In the case of standard routings, on the other hand, organizational rules would dictate that "after a new part is

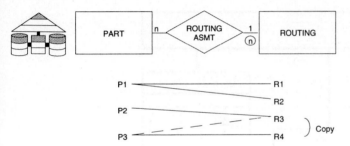

Fig. B.I.107: Impacts of the routing management

released, existing routings must be examined to determine which ones can be **assigned** to the new part." A new routing is created only if no suitable existing one is found.

Figure B.I.105 shows both forms of routing management. It also shows that it is possible to create part-oriented routings by copying standard routings and adapting them to the part. The relationship type COPY thus creates a reference to a new routing copied from several existing routings.

Standard text modules can also be assigned to a routing.

The plant reference in routings discussed above is created by the relationship type ROUTING PLANT ASSIGNMENT. This means that a specific routing can also be valid for several plants and, on the other hand, that routings belonging to one plant can be identified.

The entity type TECHNICAL PROCESS describes basic production processes such as drilling, turning, milling, cutting, welding, forging, etc. Each process is identified by a technical process number TPNO and is described by a number of technical attributes.

As with routings, the individual operations that are valid in a resource environment can be described in the form of standard operations. A standard operation characterizes a specific activity that is performed with a specific technical process, e.g., cutting a 20 mm diameter round bar to length. If such an operation is anticipated within the framework of a specific routing, this standard operation is assigned to a routing via the relationship type OPERATION, which possesses n cardinalities, i.e., several operations are assigned to a routing, and a standard operation can occur in several routings.

Technically necessitated sequential relationships exist between the individual routing operations. In their extreme form, these relationships can be so close that a unique sequence is defined between the operations, but they can also exist in a more flexible form as illustrated in Figure B.I.108.

This form merely stipulates that operations 2, 3 and 4 can begin after operation 1 has ended, but no further sequence is prescribed within these three operations.

In the data model, the predecessor/successor relationships in the priority chart are described by the relationship type PRIORITY CHART.

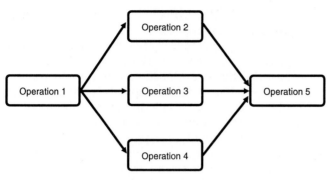

Fig. B.I.108: Priority chart for operations

It is necessary to specify the sequence of operations for concrete part scheduling or costing. This step should occur as late as possible in order to allow as much latitude as possible within Production Planning and Control up until just before execution. The entity type SEQUENCE is introduced to describe different sequences. Its instances are the sequence numbers that can be valid for a routing, i.e., the identification of all sequence options that can be derived from a priority chart. A routing is assigned valid sequence numbers by the relationship ROUTING SEQUENCE. The item position within a sequence that is valid for a routing is assigned to an operation by the relationship type ITEM, whereby the item number is stored as a descriptive attribute.

One specific operation can be performed on different workstation groups. The concept of WORKSTATION GROUP encompasses equipment groups containing equipment that is identical for planning purposes, as well as manual labor and clerical workstations. Thus, capacity analyses can also be carried out for indirect departments. The entity types PLANT, PLANT DEPARTMENT, WORKSTATION GROUP, and WORKSTATION contained in Figure B.I.105 are specializations of the entity type ORGANIZATIONAL UNIT. Likewise, the grouping operations are contained in the general relationship type ORGANIZATIONAL STRUCTURE, which networks organizational units similar to a bill of materials structure. The specialized key attributes are contained in the general key attribute OUNO. In order to represent them more clearly, however, the specialized terms are used.

The relationship type OPERATION ASSIGNMENT links the technically defined operation with the entity type WORKSTATION GROUP. Of the various possibilities for assigning operations to different workstation groups, one frequently stands out because it can perform the operation the most cost effectively. The other assignments are only considered in situations where capacities are limited and are therefore termed "alternative operations." Since many attributes that are used to describe an operation also depend on the assigned workstation group, the relationship type OPERATION ASSIGNMENT is the most important attribute object for standard times, setup times, etc.

Tooling and fixtures are entered in the entity type TOOLING/FIXTURES, whereby each instance is identified by the tool number TNO. In many industries, the importance of tooling and fixtures should not be underestimated—in the event of capacity problems, their significance in bottleneck situations is comparable to that of equipment. In addition to being identified by its own entity types, tooling could, when assigned to fixed workstations, be entered as a part of its definition or wear tools could be entered as outsourced parts within the bill of materials structure. The tools that can be employed for an EQUIPMENT GROUP (specialization of the entity type WORKSTATION GROUP) are represented by the relationship type TOOL UTILIZATION. The assignment to a concrete operation is then created by the relationship type TOOL ASSIGNMENT. A tool can be used both in several equipment groups as well as for several operation assignments. Conversely, several tools can be used in one equipment group, and several tools can also be necessary for one operation.

In the data model, TOOLING/FIXTURES is used as a type concept. Individual instances, i.e., concrete tools, are first analyzed within the framework of Production Control. In practice, tool management systems are frequently used to track tool storage, production, repair and use. Figure B.I.109 illustrates these relationships by showing tool storage, which refers back to the concept of STOCK LOCATION.

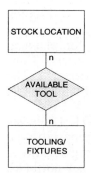

Fig. B.I.109: Illustration of tool storage

The plant employees are characterized by the entity type EMPLOYEE. They are assigned to specific workstation groups by the relationship type EMPLOYEE ASSIGNMENT. This means, for example, that an employee can be used in fill-in and supervisory functions for several workstation groups.

When manufacturing or assembling a part from several components, the components can be required during different operations, as demonstrated in Figure B.I.110.

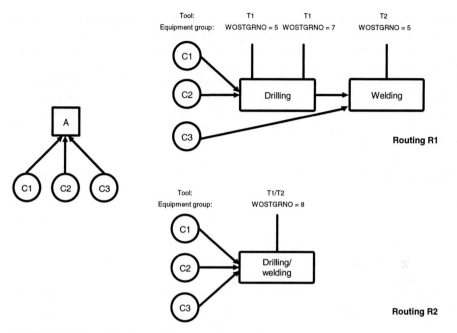

Fig. B.I.110: Example of operation component assignment

Component parts C1, C2 and C3 go into assembly A. In accordance with routing R1, component parts C1 and C2 are used during the first operation, while component part C3 is not required until the second operation. This operation-oriented component assignment concept relates the lead times for requirements planning to the operations, which facilitates more accurate time scheduling.

A second routing R2 exists for manufacturing the part. In this routing, the drilling and welding processes are performed in one operation, and each of the three component parts must be present at the start.

Thus, components that are necessary for manufacturing a part are required in different operations (different routings), and, conversely, several components can be necessary in one operation. The relationship type OPERATION COMPONENT ASSIGNMENT is therefore a relationship type with n cardinalities between the reinterpreted entity types (BILL OF MATERIALS) STRUCTURE and OPERATION.

The individual pieces of equipment are entered in the entity type WORKSTATION. Workstations that are identical for planning purposes are grouped and consolidated into the entity type WORKSTATION GROUP with the identifying attribute WOSTGRNO. A 1:n relationship exists between WORKSTATION GROUP and WORKSTATION. If the grouping is very rigid, it can be formulated as a hierarchical relationship.

Specializations of "workstation" and "workstation group" include "equipment" and "equipment group" as well as "manual workstation" and "manual workstation group."

Tools are entered in the entity type TOOLING/FIXTURES, and each tool is identified by a tool number TNO. The option also exists to treat tools as equipment or to manage wear tools as outsourced parts within the bill of materials structure.

Since it is possible to perform an operation at several workstation groups (see Figure B.I.110) and to perform several operations at one workstation group, the relationship type OPERATION ASSIGNMENT exists between OPERATION and WORKSTATION GROUP, with n cardinalities.

The relationship TOOL UTILIZATION assigns tooling to those equipment groups where it is utilized. The tools necessary for performing a specific operation at an equipment group form a relationship between the relationships TOOL UTILIZATION and OPERATION ASSIGN-MENT, which have been reinterpreted as entity types. Since a tool that is assigned to a specific equipment group can be used for several operations, and conversely, several tools can be required for one operation at an equipment group, the tool assignment possesses n cardinalities.

Figure B.I.111 illustrates the production protocol that can be derived from the example in Figure B.I.110, which shows operations, components, tools and equipment groups within their processing context.

Assembly A, Routing R1

Operation OP 1 (drilling)
    Part C1
    Part C2
    Workstation group 5   <u>or</u>
    Workstation group 7
    Tool T1
Operation OP 2 (welding)
    Part C3
    Workstation group 5
    Tool T2

Fig. B.I.111: Production protocol for Fig. B.I.104

The most significant repositories for descriptive attributes are the ROUTING and the OPERATION ASSIGNMENT, since attributes are assigned to this relationship that refer to the OPERATION and the related WORKSTATION GROUP, while the OPERATION simply possesses a "header function." Important attributes such as "cost rate per time unit," "capacity," etc., are taken from the WORKSTATION GROUP.

The following list shows typical attributes for several information objects.

ENTITY TYPE:	ROUTING
Identification data:	
Routing number:	RNO
Description:	A separate entity type with standard text modules is frequently created for long text descriptions.
Classification data:	
Routing type:	Identifier designating scheduling routings, repair routings, rework routings, etc.
Status data:	Date of last update.
Planning data:	
Necessary raw materials:	If only one starting component (i.e., a blank) is necessary for a part, it can be stored in the routing. Generally, however, the components are entered in the bill of materials.

RELATIONSHIP TYPE/ ENTITY TYPE:	OPERATION ASSIGNMENT
Identification data:	
Routing number:	RNO
Operation number:	OPNO
Workstation group number:	WOSTGRNO
Planning data:	
Setup time:	The (calendar) dates required to set up the workstation for the operation. If this is highly dependent upon which operation was previously performed at the workstation, special tables can be used to record sequence-dependent setup times.
Job setup time:	Number of man hours required for the setup procedure.
Machine time allowance:	The machine time that is necessary to perform an operation (without proportionate setup time).
Run time allowance:	The machine and run times that are necessary to perform an operation.
Transfer time to next operation:	The time that is necessary between the end of one order-related operation and the beginning of the next one. The transfer time consists of the following typical elements: - Evaluation time (inspection) for the job order

- Transport to the next workstation
- Waiting time in the job order queue before the next workstation
- Preparation time, possibly overlapped by the changeover time before the next operation.

If the elements are required separately as a result of specific considerations—e.g., in the case of flexible production—separate attributes must be created. Transport times depend on the locations of the successive workstations. A distance matrix that takes into account different transport modes can be created to determine these times.

Transfer time reduction factor: This factor indicates the percentage by which the transfer time can be reduced if a job is to be handled on a rush basis.

Overlap key: This key indicates whether—and if so, according to which rules—the operation can be performed under flexible production. This decision can be made, for example, on the basis of the quantity involved.

Minimum lead time: Minimum duration of an operation, including overlaps, before the parts should be transported to the following operation. (The same information can also be expressed by a minimum lead quantity.)

The minimum lead time is determined by the capacity of the parts handling container as well as by the production speed of the downstream operation. If the production speed of the second operation is higher, the lead time for the first operation must be configured in such a manner as to prevent waiting times from occurring at the second operation.

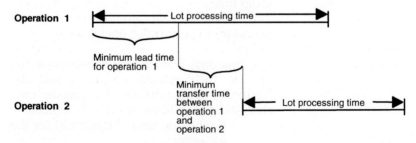

Fig. B.I.112: Illustration of minimum lead time

Splitting key: This key indicates whether—and if so, according to which rules—a production order can be distributed among several pieces of equipment in the same group. Since splitting involves setup times (setup costs) at each piece of equipment, it is advisable only for larger lots.

Splitting factor: If the split-up is to be made on the basis of lot size, the splitting factor is determined by the quotient of the order size and the size of the sublots. The upper limit to the number of sublots is the number of pieces of equipment in the group.

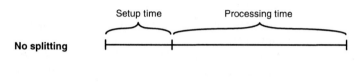

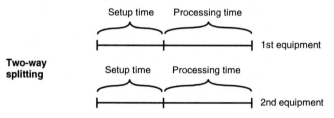

Fig. B.I.113: Splitting

RELATIONSHIP TYPE: ROUTING ASSIGNMENT

Quantity range: If several routings exist for a part—e.g., distinguished by the degree of mechanization of the production method to be employed—a specific production method (shop floor or assembly line production) is assigned on the basis of the quantity to be manufactured, whereby the degree of mechanization generally increases with the order size.

ENTITY TYPE:	WORKSTATION GROUP or EQUIPMENT GROUP
Description:	...
Workstation type:	Identifier
Location:	...
Supervisor:	Personnel ID number of the supervisor responsible for the group.

Planning data:

Number of workdays per week:	...
Number of shifts per workday:	...
Maximum number of shifts per workday:	...
Number of hours per shift:	If this number depends on the shift, a separate field must be provided for each shift.
Maximum number of overtime hours:	...
Utilization factor:	This figure indicates the percentage of time the equipment group is available, taking into account downtime, etc.
Efficiency factor:	Relationship of the standard times to the actual required times. The efficiency factor is used to convert the standard times contained in the routing records into planning values.
Waiting time before equipment group:	This average rate serves as a component in calculating transfer times.
Setup time:	Average setup time at the machine. This information is necessary if the corresponding information is not contained in the routing record.
Capacity adjustment:	Identifier that indicates whether an adjustment is to be performed for the workstation group.
Hourly machine rate:	This figure aids in product costing and process selection.

ENTITY TYPE:	WORKSTATION or EQUIPMENT

Data that refer to the individual machine of an equipment group are entered here.

Acquisition date:	...
Planning dates:	...
Period capacity of equipment in hours:	...

Date of next scheduled
preventive maintenance: ...
Duration of preventive
maintenance: ...
Number of a recently
processed preventive
maintenance order: ...
Depreciation: Acquisition cost, depreciation method.

ENTITY TYPE: TOOL
Purchase date:
Capacity in
utilization hours:

As discussed above, the data structure for the production description exhibits close relationships to neighboring departments, especially Cost and Income Accounting and Personnel. Figure B.I.114 clarifies these interfaces.

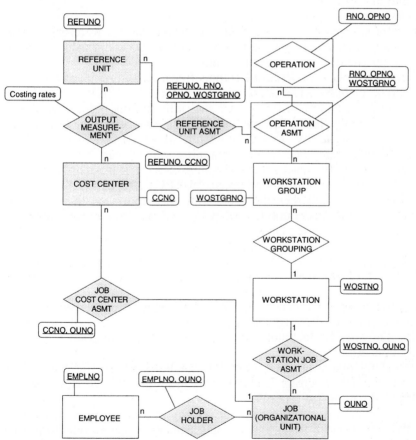

Fig. B.I.114: Interfaces to cost and income accounting and to organization/personnel

The data structure in Figure B.I.105 assigns employees to specific workstation groups.

In a more detailed view of Personnel, an entity type JOB is introduced that indicates the smallest unit of the organizational structure. Employees can be assigned to this organizational unit by the relationship type JOB HOLDER. It is also possible to assign an employee to several organizational units (e.g., job sharing). Conversely, an organizational unit can also be distributed among several employees. The assignment between WORKSTATION and JOB is created by the relationship type WORKSTATION JOB ASSIGNMENT. This relationship assumes that each workstation is clearly assigned to an organizational unit, while an organizational unit can encompass several workstations.

The way in which workstations are structured is also important for internal income accounting. The term "cost center" encompasses an organizational unit from the perspective of Accounting. An important criterion for forming a cost center is the cost accountability of its supervisor. The criteria for grouping specific workstations into a cost center from the perspective of Cost Accounting differ from those for organizational grouping.

Specific reference units (output types) are assigned to the cost centers. These reference units measure their output (income). Reference units include setup, machine hours, repair hours or even potential values such as the maximum heat of an annealing oven.

Detailed cost rates for different outputs (measured in terms of reference units) can be included in an operation assignment.

Thus, cost rates are attributes of the information object OUTPUT MEASUREMENT. The reference units affecting an operation assignment are assigned to it by the relationship type REFERENCE UNIT ASSIGNMENT. Specified values (planning values) can be entered for each reference unit. These specified values can be linked with the cost rates contained in the information object OUTPUT MEASUREMENT.

The links shown between the production description on the one hand and internal income accounting and personnel planning/organization on the other will be discussed later.

B.I.4.2.1.2 An Example

The numerous informational interrelationships introduced in the example in Figures B.I.110 and B.I.111 are further clarified in Figure B.I.115. The specific technical accuracy of this representation is not the primary concern here.

The drilling operation in routing R1 can be performed at equipment group 5 or equipment group 7. Operation 2 in routing R1 (welding) can be performed at equipment group 5.

The combined operation of drilling/welding in routing R2 is performed by equipment group 8 (e.g., a processing center). Since an operation can be performed at several equipment groups (drilling operation in routing

PART

PNO	Name
A	...
C1	...
C2	...
C3	...

WORKSTATION GROUP

WOSTGRNO	Cost center
5	...
7	...
8	...

STRUCTURE

HPNO	LPNO	Quantity
A	C1	...
A	C2	...
A	C3	...

WORKSTATION

WOSTNO	Capacity
5 - 1	...
5 - 2	...
7 - 1	...
8 - 1	...

STANDARD OPERATION

OPNO	Name
1	Drilling
2	Welding
3	Drilling/welding

TOOLING/FIXTURES

TNO	Name
T1	...
T2	...

ROUTING

RNO	Name
R1	...
R2	...

ROUTING ASSIGNMENT

PNO	RNO	Output limit
A	R1	...
A	R2	...

TOOL UTILIZATION

WOSTGRNO	TNO	Phase out date
5	T1	...
5	T2	...
7	T1	...
8	T2	...
8	T1	...

OPERATION COMPONENT ASSIGNMENT

RNO	OPNO	HPNO	LPNO
R1	1	A	C1
R1	1	A	C2
R1	2	A	C3
R2	3	A	C1
R2	3	A	C2
R2	3	A	C3

TOOL ASSIGNMENT

WOSTGRNO	TNO	RNO	OPNO
5	T1	R1	1
7	T1	R1	1
8	T1	R2	3
8	T2	R2	3
5	T2	R1	2

OPERATION ASSIGNMENT

RNO	OPNO	WOSTGRNO	Standard time
R1	1	5	...
R1	1	7	...
R1	2	5	...
R2	3	8	...

OPERATION

RNO	OPNO	Name
R1	1	Drilling
R1	2	Welding
R2	3	Drilling/Welding

Fig. B.I.115: Representation of numerous informational interdependencies of Fig. B.I.110 (example)

R1), and, conversely, several operations can be performed at one equipment group (equipment group 5: drilling and welding in routing R1), the type n cardinalities can clearly be seen for the relationship type between the equipment group and the routing.

The assignment of components to their assembly operations is entered in the information object OPERATION COMPONENT ASSIGNMENT. Of the two tools, tool T1 in routing R1 is used at both equipment group 5 and equipment group 7, while tool T2 is only used at equipment group 5.

As far as the operation assignment for routing R2 is concerned, both tools are necessary for the "drilling/welding" operation.

B.I.4.2.1.3 Analyses

A multitude of analyses can be generated from the data structure developed here. As with bills of materials, these analyses can be created from the "explosion perspective" and from the "application perspective."

The most important analysis from the explosion perspective is the production schedule for a specific part as illustrated in Figure B.I.116. The sources necessary for gathering the data are indicated in the figure and show that almost all data relationships are used.

The application perspective is typically concerned with determining which operations or which parts can be manufactured at a specific equipment group. These questions are of interest if an equipment group goes down, for example.

These questions can be answered by tracking the data structures WORKSTATION GROUP-OPERATION-ASSIGNMENT-OPERATION as well as by continuing the track to ROUTING-PART.

In order, for example, to analyze the effects of a delayed shipment of tools, it is necessary to determine at which equipment groups, or more specifically, for which operations a specific tool type is used.

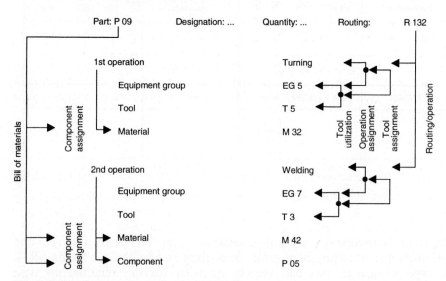

Fig. B.I.116: Content of a production schedule

Figure B.I.117 uses the data structure for the example in Figure B.I.110 to determine which operations can be performed at equipment group 5.

Utilization list for equipment group 5

Operation:	Routing	Standard operation	
	R1	Drilling	(OP 1)
	R1	Welding	(OP 2)

Fig. B.I.117: Equipment group utilization list

B.I.4.2.2 Medium-Term Capacity Planning

In addition to the key for the order header FOUNO, TOUNO, DATE, the entity type (PRODUCTION) ORDER ITEM created during requirements planning was assigned the following identifying characteristics as important attributes: part number PNO and ODATE, as well as the planning variables "order quantity," "turnaround time" and "order status."

In order to be able to perform capacity calculations, the order must be linked to the related workstation groups on the basis of its production protocols. This linking occurs by introducing the technical interrelationships ROUTING, OPERATION and WORKSTATION GROUP. If several assignment options exist (i.e., for operation sequences, workstations), the alternatives are assigned that have been identified as especially appropriate for the order characteristics. If the other options are necessary for subsequent optimization calculations (capacity adjustment, production control), they can be assigned as necessary.

First, the necessary order-related data structure is developed. An order-related deadline is then scheduled without taking into account capacity limits, and capacity loads are derived on the basis of these data.

Finally, a capacity adjustment algorithm is outlined.

Since requirements planning and scheduling are tightly integrated, approaches will be introduced for simultaneous material and time requirements calculations.

B.I.4.2.2.1 Supplementing Production Order Data

In this book, an order—either a customer, purchase, production, quality control or maintenance order—comprises the conceptual structure derived from order header, order items and order subitems (see Figure B.I.118). The order header bundles the items and creates a link between customer, order receiver and time (date order was placed). The order items describe the individual part-oriented outputs, and the order subitems describe individual suboutputs.

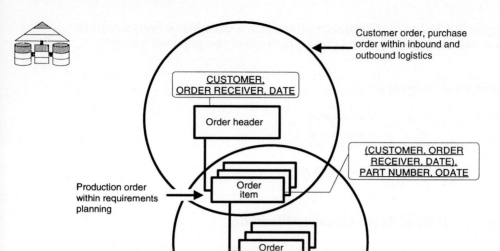

Fig. B.I.118: General order structure with views primarily used by different applications

Based on this fundamental structure, the application-oriented aspects concentrate on different segments. The two higher levels are primarily used for customer and purchase orders, although subitems—e.g., in the form of partial deliveries of an article at different times or to different locations—are generally meaningful.

Part-oriented order items constitute the focus of requirements planning. For purposes of simplification, the more precise term "production order item" is abbreviated to "production order" or simply "order." At the same time, a (*) is substituted for the key taken from the order header (FOUNO, TOUNO, DATE).

A production order is then identified by its part number and its completion date. If the production order is related to a customer order, the corresponding unit is the customer order item. This has already been illustrated in connection with multi-level requirements tracking.

Within the context of requirements planning, a production order contains no subitems. This aspect is introduced in scheduling and capacity planning in the form of operations.

There are two basic options for extending production orders to include production data:

1.   Relationships are used to link the information object ORDER with the production master data. These relationships only possess attributes that are not contained in the master data, since they refer to orders **and** production master data.

2.   All basic data applicable to the order are imported into the order-related structure (redundant).

The following discussion will concentrate on the first of these options. Attributes are, however, imported into the order-related data structures if they must be modified in an order-related manner without affecting the master data area.

The link between the master data structure and the order-related data structure opens many analysis options. For example, in the case of specific master operations it is possible to determine whether concrete orders exist in which these operations are accessed, etc.

Figure B.I.119 illustrates this data structure. Shown on the left side are those basic data created in Figure B.I.105 that are of significance here. On the right side, the order-related data structures are developed.

The point of departure is the (PRODUCTION) ORDER as it was created within requirements planning. The following discussion will identify an order by part number PNO and ODATE omitting the order header key or replacing it with a (*).

The basic data contain several production options for a part, resulting in several routings per part, several plants per routing, several sequences per routing and several workstation groups per operation. Theoretically, these options can also be imported into the order-related data. Figure B.I.119 assumes unambiguous assignment decisions in order to be able to perform concrete capacity calculations. For the data structure, this means that the cardinalities are set at 1. Either fixed decision rules can be invoked on the basis of the order data (e.g., when assigning a routing based on order quantity), or "standard assignments" can be defined from the start in the basic data or determined interactively by the planner.

If the other production options are used in the capacity adjustment in order to define alternative capacity assignments, the corresponding cardinalities must be set to n. For the time being, however, only unambiguous assignments will be analyzed.

The following discussion will briefly explain the data structure in Figure B.I.119.

The <u>routing assignment</u> within the master data structure indicates which routings can be used to manufacture a given part. If there are several possible routings, the selection is generally based on the order quantity. Since the order quantity is fixed within the order-related data structure as a result of materials planning for each order, the routing assignment that corresponds to each order is imported into the order-related data structure, forming the relationship type ORDER ROUTING ASSIGNMENT.

Since several assignments can exist in the order-related area for a specific routing assignment in the master data structure (e.g., because several orders exist for a specific part), the cardinality from the perspective of the master data is n. This relationship can, among other things, specify which orders for a part will be manufactured using a specific routing.

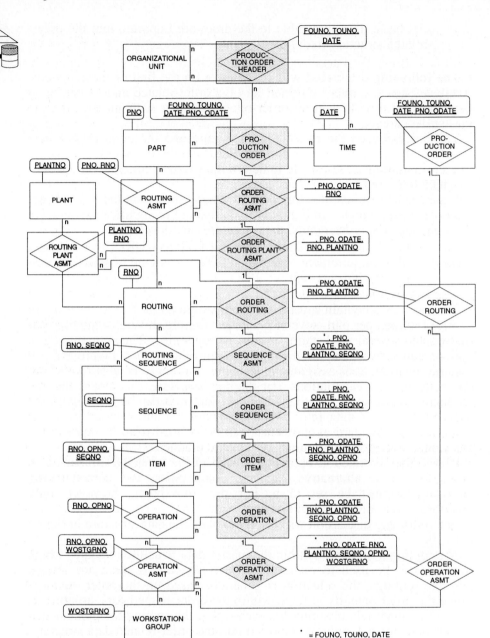

Fig. B.I.119: Order-related data structure for scheduling and capacity planning

Since a part can be manufactured in several plants, the routing is linked to a valid plant by the relationship type ORDER ROUTING-PLANT ASSIGNMENT. The deciding criterion can be either the order quantity or the capacity utilization of the plant.

The information object ORDER ROUTING is a repository for attributes imported from the master routing, which must be modified according to the order. If several operation sequences exist within a routing, one is selected and assigned by the relationship type SEQUENCE ASSIGNMENT. This procedure also assigns the entity type SEQUENCE.

The operations and their items are assigned to the entity type SEQUENCE ASSIGNMENT by the ORDER ITEM. The cardinality n applies here. The reference to the entity type OPERATION is already contained implicitly.

In the assignment for workstation groups, on the other hand, a selection must be made again, whereby cost effectiveness can be a deciding criterion. The assignment is entered in the relationship type ORDER OPERATION ASSIGNMENT.

User-oriented data for scheduling results, e.g., the duration of an operation, can be appended to this relationship type.

An operation assignment for the master data area can occur in several order-related operations.

Fixing the cardinalities at 1 reduces the alternative production options to a single production sequence. This reduced data structure is shown in the right side of Figure B.I.119. The information objects include only the assigned ORDER ROUTING and the ORDER OPERATION ASSIGNMENT, for which all other assignments are known due to the imported external key attribute. The PNO and ODATE contain key characteristics for the ROUTING, and the attributes PNO, ODATE and OPNO provide them for the ORDER OPERATION ASSIGNMENT. Consequently, these properties are underlined twice. The other attributes that are underlined only once are descriptive.

Several additional order-dependent attributes for the entity and relationship types introduced here are:

ORDER:	FOUNO, TOUNO, DATE, PNO, ODATE, (quantity, status, turnaround time), new turnaround time, priority, earliest start (ES), earliest finish (EF), latest finish (LF), latest start (LS), planned start (PS), planned finish (PF), free float time (FF), total float time (TF), actual start (AS), actual finish (AF), etc.
ORDER ROUTING:	*, PNO, ODATE, RNO, PLANTNO, textual information, supplemental texts

ORDER-OPERATION-
ASSIGNMENT:

*,   PNO,   ODATE,   RNO,
PLANTNO,   SEQNO,   OPNO,
WOSTGRNO, setup time, transfer
time,   transfer   time   reduction,
overlap, splitting, specified machine
time, specified run time, minimum
lead time, priority, ES, LF, LS, PS,
TF, FF, SP, FP, etc.

Since the entity type ORDER is taken from requirements planning, some attributes are already known. However, the order turnaround time can be calculated more precisely using operation data than with the time taken from requirements planning. The order turnaround time is equal to the sum of the utilization times and transfer times for its operations.

Figure B.I.120 indicates the components of these times with their major interrelationships.

Additional, new attributes include priority, which is necessary for scheduling, as well as attributes for scheduling results. These include: earliest possible start/finish date (ES, EF), latest permissible start/finish date (LS, LF), total/free float time (TF, FF) and planned start/finish date (PS, PF).

In an order-related routing, text updates are introduced vis-à-vis the master data area. In the order routing assignment, attributes are set up for operation-oriented time scheduling.

The order-related operation information is not explicitly linked with the necessary tools, since this information is not required for scheduling and capacity planning until the order release or production control stage.

Figure B.I.121 shows the sequence of supplemental order data as an EPC. The process is initiated by new order definitions from requirements planning (new orders and updates to existing orders are grouped under "order updates"), updates in the master routing data and production events that necessitate replanning. The further processing sequence relates to an individual order.

Time component	Interrelationships	Lot size	Opera-tion	Operation sequence	Equip-ment group
Equipment setup	Setup time		x	x	x
	Processing time	x			x
Transfer time	Evaluation time	(x)	x		x
	Waiting time for transport		x		
	Transport	(x)		x	
	Waiting time in the job order queue				x
	Preparation time	(x)	x		x

The crosses in brackets merely are to indicate a lesser dependence.

The equipment setup time (ES) is calculated as $ES = \text{setup time} + \dfrac{\text{lot size} * \text{time/unit}}{\text{splitting factor}}$

Fig. B.I.120: Time component interrelationships of an order

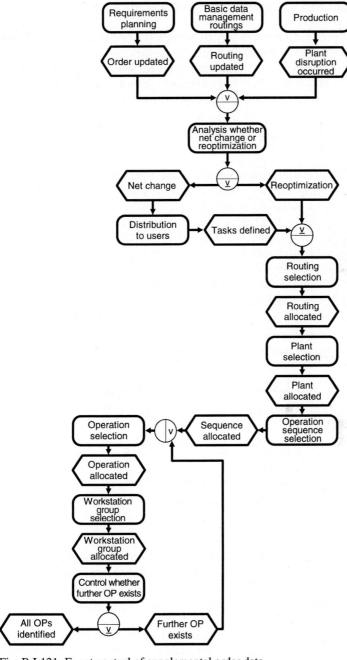

Fig. B.I.121: Event control of supplemental order data

B.I.4.2.2.2 Scheduling without Regard to Capacity Limits

Requirements planning applies global values for order turnaround times in reference to the corresponding part. This process provides detailed order-related time components, which are used for initial order scheduling without regard to possible capacity constraints. Load profiles can then be generated using the relationships to the capacities.

B.I.4.2.2.2.1 Throughput Scheduling

The sum of the transfer times between the operations for an order is frequently significantly greater than the sum of the equipment utilization times (see Figure B.I.122). As a result, the transfer times (including the waiting times) contain a considerable stochastic element. Since transfer times are virtually independent of the order quantity for <u>one</u> individual order, the turnaround time globally assigned to a component can provide sufficiently accurate values for medium-term requirements planning.

For a more accurate time calculation, however, quantity-dependent utilization times are now also available.

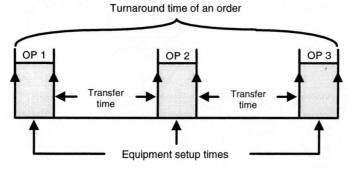

Fig. B.I.122: Turnaround time components of an order

When recalculated to account for splitting, overlapping and order quantity, the turnaround times for all orders are then assigned to the orders as attribute values. When an average order quantity is applied, this computational function also provides the average turnaround times stored in the part record.

Subsequently, a kind of network scheduling time calculation is used to determine the earliest possible and latest permissible start and finish dates for all orders, along with their float times. Processes, sequential relationships and process time values are required as data for the network scheduling calculation.

A process is defined as a time-consuming event with definable start and finish times. Processes thus include orders, i.e., planning orders for primary requirements, customer orders, production orders and purchase orders. Each order definition refers to one part, e.g., the order item in the case of customer and purchase orders. The sequential relationship must be known for all orders, i.e., either the direct successors or the direct predecessors. The direct successors of an order are those orders in which the order being analyzed is included, i.e., from which it was derived.

These data are contained in the requirements tracking relationships for the order being analyzed.

In order to establish the direct order successor, REQUIREMENTS COVERAGE is used to determine the requirements for the same part to be covered by the order, and then REQUIREMENTS DERIVATION is used to determine from which superordinate orders those requirements were derived.

The computed turnaround times are applied as process times.

The variables necessary for network planning are thus available, forward and backward calculations can be performed and float times can be computed using known formulas (see Figure B.I.123), in which $D(i)$ represents the process time.

In addition to forward and backward scheduling, midpoint scheduling— a combination of the two—is also utilized. Midpoint scheduling allocates a specific operation within an order in a predetermined period—e.g., for capacity reasons—using backward calculation to schedule the preceding

Forward calculation:

Earliest start date: $ES(i) = \underset{h \in P(i)}{Max} \{ EF(h) \}$

$\qquad P(i) =$ Number of direct predecessors of process i.
For processes having no predecessor,
default value of $ES(i)$ will be the first period of
the planning period.

Earliest finish date: $EF(i) = ES(i) + D(i)$

Backward calculation:

Latest finish date: $LF(i) = \underset{j \in S(i)}{Min} \{ LS(j) \}$

$\qquad S(i) =$ Number of direct successors of process i.
For processes having no successor, default value
of $LF(i)$ will be the predetermined requirements
period of the relevant customer order or of the
primary requirements.

Latest start time: $\quad LS(i) = LF(i) - D(i)$

Total float time: $\quad TF(i) = LF(i) - EF(i)$

Free float time: $\quad FF(i) = \underset{j \in S(i)}{Min} \{ ES(j) - EF(i) \}$

Fig. B.I.123: Formulas for the network planning

operations and forward calculation to schedule the subsequent operations. All orders for a planning period can be broken down into several disjunct networks.

The end processes of a network are the primary requirements (customer order items or planning orders). The starting processes are typically purchase orders. In extremely customer-oriented planning, in which essentially no lots are formed, each order derived from a customer order or planning order constitutes a network. If, on the other hand, lots are formed, i.e., requirements for different superordinate orders are compiled into one order, a network can relate to several customer order items.

Figure B.I.124 shows the network for the sample requirements statement treated in Figure B.I.59. It is supplemented by the relationships to the two customer orders. Each of these relationships possesses a turnaround time of 0 TU. All orders are linked by sequential relationships so that only **one** network exists. If, on the other hand, no lots were formed, two networks would result. Each order can belong to one and only one network. If the networks are required as a unit for planning purposes, individual entity types can be generated for network identification. Every order is assigned to a network by a 1:n relationship (see Figure B.I.125).

Networks are identified on the basis of a part order on the highest planning level. Then the direct predecessors and successors are determined in sequence and marked by entering the network number. As soon as a network has been completed, the system continues to process the planning level chains until an unmarked order is found. This order is the point of departure for the new network explosion. Afterwards, the stipulated time variables are calculated for each network. This also identifies time-critical orders, i.e., orders with a float time that is less than a given value.

In order-oriented scheduling, subquantity-related float times within the order lot cannot be seen. Thus, for example, the 600 units of C that go directly into P are not required until point in time 2 and are thus less "critical" than the 900 quantity units that go into A at point in time 1. In the example, however, there are no float times greater than 0.

The latest permissible start and finish dates for the orders determined from backward calculation can deviate from the dates calculated within the framework of the requirements explosion if the turnaround time is recalculated, if it is calculated in smaller time units or if splitting is performed.

If time scheduling indicates that the specified delivery date for a customer order cannot be maintained, the turnaround time for the processes (orders) can be reduced by reducing transfer times between operations using the stored reduction factors. Time scheduling must be corrected accordingly.

Time scheduling results in the determination of the earliest possible and latest permissible start and finish dates for all orders.

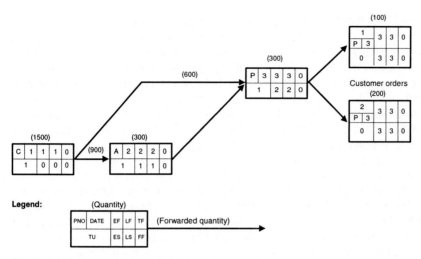

Fig. B.I.124: Network plan of Fig. B.I.59

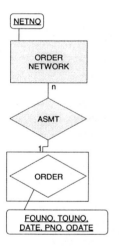

Fig. B.I.125: Order network relationship

The operation-oriented deadlines can be derived from the order-oriented variables. The finish date for the order is equal to the finish date for its final operation. Likewise, the start date for the order is the start for its first operation. The processing deadlines can be determined for the operations by taking transfer times into account. Since the calculated float times relate to orders, they are not transferred unless they are distributed among the operations.

This time scheduling results in attributes ES through LF being occupied by valid deadlines in all orders and related operations.

B.I.4.2.2.2.2 Capacity Overviews

After importing the results from capacity scheduling as attributes of the entity types ORDER and ORDER OPERATION ASSIGNMENT, capacity overviews can be generated to serve as important analysis functions.

The workstation group at which the operation is performed is specified in the ORDER OPERATION ASSIGNMENT. Thus, all the operations (and consequently all the orders) that load a workstation group can be entered for a specified time-slot grid at that workstation group and arranged in sequence, each according to its earliest start date.

Capacity loading is created by the relationship type LOAD as a link between TIME and ORDER OPERATION ASSIGNMENT (see Figure B.I.126). The instance of the entity type TIME is designated the PLANNING PERIOD, which indicates the distribution of the capacity planning time period. The load hours for an operation assignment are assigned to the relationship type as a descriptive attribute. A comprehensive operation can cover several planning periods.

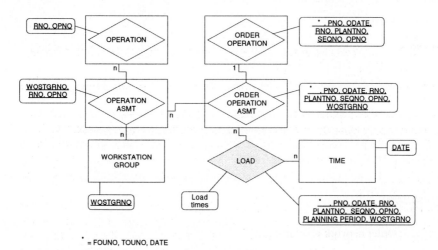

Fig. B.I.126: ERM for generating capacity overviews

Figure B.I.127 shows an example of the load profile for a workstation group. If only a few orders are loaded per period, the individual operations that result in the loading can be indicated directly in the graphical representation. If this is inappropriate, the operations can be listed in tabular form by period, together with their predecessors and successors. This is also indicated in Figure B.I.127.

Depending on the results of time scheduling, operations can be loaded on the basis of their earliest or latest start date. In the profile, these dates

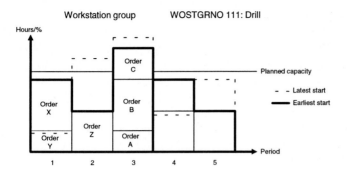

Order operations loaded to WOSTGRNO 111

Order operation	Preceding order operation			Subsequent order operation		
PNO, ODATE, RNO, PLANTNO, SEQNO, OPNO, turnaround time, start date, finish date	Identification	Finish date	Turn-around time	Identification	Start date	Turn-around time

Fig. B.I.127: Load profile of a workstation group (example)

are illustrated by solid overall utilization lines for earliest start and broken overall utilization lines for latest start.

The planned capacities are also indicated, thus immediately revealing capacity overloads, i.e., bottleneck situations.

The table not only shows information about the operations allocated to a given equipment group; it also provides information about material flow by indicating the preceding and subsequent operations. Thus, planners have access to information that can be taken into account during subsequent capacity planning, with consideration being given to bottleneck situations.

Load profiles can be created using different time-slot grids. Since the results of requirements planning generally encompass a medium-term planning period (up to several months or a year), capacity planning can also be geared toward this time period. In this case, the period would be divided into months.

For capacity considerations, it is possible to form only a segment of the planning time period, in which case capacity planning is performed using weekly or daily grids.

The capacity overviews can also be consolidated, e.g., on the plant level, by following the links for the entity type ORGANIZATIONAL UNIT that are specialized for the WORKSTATION GROUP.

Figure B.I.128 illustrates scheduling event control, which is triggered by the completion of order data updates and ends with the alternative events, regardless of whether capacity bottlenecks or capacity outliers occur.

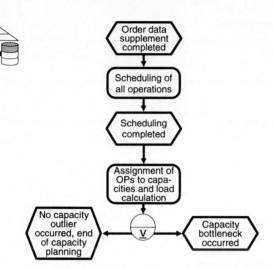

Fig. B.I.128: Scheduling event control and capacity load calculation

B.I.4.2.2.3 Scheduling with Regard to Capacity Effects

If the load profiles indicate that the available capacities at the workstation groups are insufficient, a capacity distribution problem exists.

Large fluctuations in capacity requirements within the planning period indicate that a capacity leveling problem exists.

Bottlenecks and requirement peaks can be eliminated by taking the following measures:

1. Modifying the capacity supply by introducing overtime and additional shifts. Information concerning these options can be assigned to the workstation groups as attribute values.
2. Altering the sequence of operations within the technically feasible options in order to shift critical operations to non-critical time periods.
3. Shifting operations in the same sequence:
    a) To other workstation groups capable of performing the operations (alternate workstation groups). To do this, the operation assignment information that manages an operation's potential workstation groups is entered in the basic data structure.
    b) To other subperiods in which the workstation group is not yet being fully utilized.

In cases 1, 2 and 3a, there is no change to the temporal structure of the order network. (It is assumed that the introduction of overtime and additional shifts is incorporated into the frequency grid.) On the other hand, in the event of a shift as in case 3b, the effect on the sequence of operations and on the overall network interrelationship must be

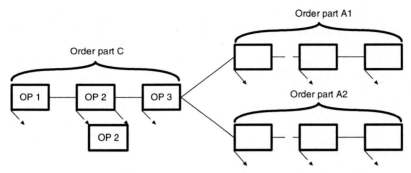

Fig. B.I.129: Impacts by a temporal shift of operations

considered. For example, shifting operation OP 2 in Figure B.I.129 causes subsequent operation OP 3 to be started later, which in turn means that orders for superordinate products A1 and A2, which follow this operation, must also be started later.

If an effort is made to avoid disturbing existing operations timing within an order, delaying operation OP 2 also requires that operation OP 1 begin later.

When shifting the other operations, it is important to observe any capacity ramifications that might arise, i.e., whether avoiding a capacity peak in one operation will result in new bottlenecks or capacity peaks in other operations.

These interrelationships necessitate that all operations be scheduled simultaneously, taking capacity limits into consideration. It is virtually impossible to use exact procedures (e.g., integral linear optimization) in view of the several thousand operations that real manufacturing environments involve. Consequently, theory and practice developed heuristic procedures early on, although they also require significant computation time (see *Brankamp, Terminplanungssystem 1973; Kinzer, Kapazitätsabgleich 1971; VDI, Produktionsplanung II 1974, pp. 125 ff.*).

This problem also largely corresponds to capacity planning within the context of network planning techniques. Heuristic methods are also used here for planning on a realistic scale (see *Gewald/Kasper/Schelle, Netzplantechnik 1972*).

Since the application of heuristic methods has frequently provided unsatisfactory results, attempts are increasingly being made to solve the problem through more interactive processing. To accomplish this objective, load profiles and related operations are displayed to the capacity planner, as shown in Figure B.I.127. Color graphics can improve the display. The planner can access operation-oriented planning data at any time to obtain information concerning production flow as well as capacity utilization for other equipment.

Alternative calculations can be simulated without altering the actual data structure. This is achieved by using the relationship type LOAD and the OPERATION ASSIGNMENTS that were created in the basic data structure and contain all assignment options. The same principle holds true for alternate plant assignments or sequences per routing. Thus, the planning alternatives that were not imported during the derivation of the order-oriented data structure in Figure B.I.119 are reincorporated by accessing the basic data. Only after this planning phase is complete are the fixed assignments re-created.

Despite the interactive planning options that are available, solving a highly diverse planning situation consisting of strongly interdependent integrations remains a problem. Thus, planners are overtaxed in trying to achieve optimum, cost-effective solutions to such assignment problems. Consequently, it can be advisable to combine the use of algorithms with human abilities to assess and synthesize larger interrelationships. In concrete terms, this involves displaying capacity allocation suggestions to planners and allowing them to simulate changes. They can then decide for each trial simulation whether to employ algorithmic support. They can form subproblems, i.e., define only specific network segments for which they can then perform capacity adjustments. This substructuring, which categorizes the overall problem into loosely related subproblems, can reduce planning complexity.

Since the significance of algorithms can increase when they are embedded in the interactive process, the kind of basic capacity leveling algorithm used today in standard software systems will be outlined.

Figures B.I.130,a-c show a structogram from *Kurbel, Software Engineering 1983, pp. 252 ff.*, which in turn shows the procedure proposed by Brankamp (see *Brankamp, Terminplanungssystem 1973, pp. 112 f.*). Figure B.I.130,a shows the framework of the algorithm, in which two subalgorithms are embedded. The subalgorithm in Figure B.I.130,b serves to determine the direction in which orders are to be shifted (present or future), and the subalgorithm in Figure B.I.130,c checks whether the capacities available during the planning period are sufficient for the overall capacity requirement; if this is not the case, the problem cannot be solved (for additional descriptions of this procedure, see *Kurbel, Software Engineering 1983, pp. 252 ff.* and *Brankamp, Terminplanungssystem 1973, pp. 112 f.*).

In addition to combining interactive problem solving with algorithmic support, the use of **expert systems** can represent a new approach to solving the capacity allocation problem. These systems enable the wealth of heuristic allocation rules applied in the real world to be stored, thus allowing the heuristic knowledge of expert production planners, supervisors, etc., to be utilized (see *Steinmann, Einsatzmöglichkeiten von Expertensystemen in integrierten Systemen der Produktionsplanung und - steuerung 1992*).

Many capacity adjustment procedures utilize order priorities. The following list includes typical components that can be incorporated into these kinds of priority figures (see *IBM, CLASS*):
- Latest finish date for the order
- External priority, which is derived from the importance of the customer(s) and the size of the order. This information is

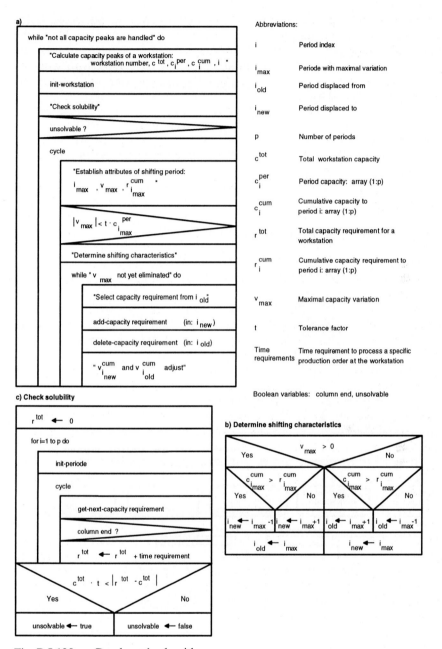

Fig. B.I.130a-c: Brankamp's algorithm

contained in the customer order and can be accessed via the order links. If the order goes into several customer orders, the priority figure must be derived from the most important customer order

- If transfer times have already been reduced during scheduling, the priority figure is increased
- Order float time
- Number of direct superordinate orders (the more superordinate orders an order goes into, the higher its priority figure)
- Value of the order.

$$\text{Priority figure of an order} = \sum_i W_i * P_i$$

P_i = Priority figure of component i for the order

W_i = Weighting figure for component i

Fig. B.I.131: Determination of priority figures

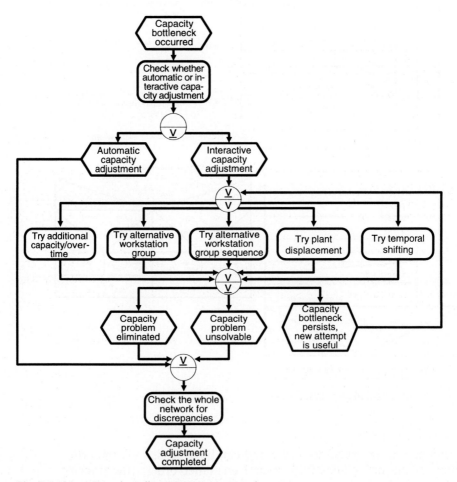

Fig. B.I.132,a: Capacity adjustment event control

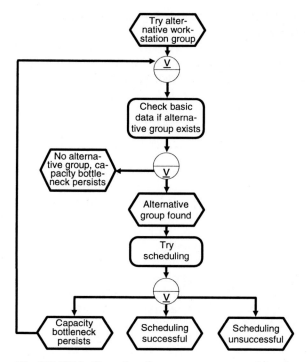

Fig. B.I.132,b: Capacity adjustment event control by alternative workstation groups

The individual components must be evaluated, weighted and added together to form an order priority figure (see Figure B.I.131).

Capacity adjustment event control for interactive processing is shown in greater detail in Figure B.I.132,a. If the adjustment is performed automatically, event control is contained implicitly in the algorithm. The process only shows the rough process logic from the perspective of the user. The first distribution node branches to the adjustment alternatives, which each lead to the same events. A somewhat more detailed process flow for alternative workstation assignments is shown in Figure B.I.132,b.

B.I.4.2.2.4 Integrating Requirements Planning and Scheduling

In accordance with the PPC philosophy of multi-stage planning, materials and scheduling were treated as successive planning stages. This means that the orders defined in materials planning are first determined without their effect on capacity and subsequently serve as the point of departure for capacity planning.

Based on the capacity problems discussed above, the orders created within the framework of materials planning can be rescheduled with respect to time. This procedure also affects materials planning, however, since the planning dates have changed, as have the parameters for inventory assignments and outsourced parts.

For this reason, it is an obvious step to integrate these two planning stages more closely, i.e., to perform capacity planning and requirements planning simultaneously. In order to do this, however, the data structures must conform to a unified design view. Figure B.I.133 combines the data structures for requirements planning, capacity planning and scheduling into an integrated ER model. The entity type PART is the nucleus from which the basic data for bills of materials and routings, as well as order-related information, originate.

The individual data structures for the planning stages are represented graphically, whereby the relationships that extend beyond the individual level-specific data structures indicate the degree of data coupling.

For the sake of simplicity, key attributes are not indicated.

Two new approaches are being taken for simultaneous/quasi-simultaneous planning of materials and capacities. The first approach is Creative Output's OPT system, which attempts to solve the problem using an "innovative" algorithm, while the second approach employs interactive capacity- and materials-management-oriented order scheduling on a case-by-case basis. While the first approach utilizes a planning-period-oriented algorithm that follows explicit optimization criteria in addition to validity criteria, the second approach focuses on validity, i.e., optimization criteria are not formally specified.

The OPT system (see *Goldratt/Cox, The Goal 1984; Fox, OPT 1983*) is more of a planning philosophy than a concrete software product. After what was at first a euphoric discussion, marked disillusionment has set in with respect to its use in actual practice. Several fundamental OPT concepts have been adopted by other standard software systems, which should be briefly mentioned.

OPT is based on the premise of following the bottleneck principle in operation scheduling. This means that those operations that are performed on bottleneck machines are given priority. At the same time, larger lots are formed at bottleneck machines, which keeps changeover times lower than at non-bottleneck machines. Figure B.I.134 shows the rough sequence for this process.

The master data for bills of materials, routings and equipment, as well as inventory levels and primary requirements, are imported from upstream DP systems. The BUILD NET module uses these data to generate the enterprise's order network (see Figure B.I.135). A requirements explosion is also generated for this process.

The SPLIT module divides the network into operations that require bottleneck machines and non-bottleneck-oriented operations. The operations are temporarily assigned to capacities in order to identify bottlenecks. This is both the most important concept of the method as well as its main difficulty. Since the bottlenecks are also influenced by subsequent scheduling and lot formation, they cannot be clearly identified during the process. For this reason, multiple iterations of the entire planning process can be necessary.

The OPT module schedules the "critical" network by reducing it to operations that are prone to becoming bottlenecks. The capacity limits of the machines are analyzed by shifting into the future those operations that can no longer be scheduled for reasons of capacity (forward scheduling).

The result of this step is thus valid (from a capacity standpoint) scheduling of the critical network. At the same time, this module forms lot sizes with reference to production as well as to the transfer from one workstation to the next. Giving preference to smaller lots—for transfer as well as for production—results in production overlap and thus in accelerated turnaround time. At the same time, lots are formed on the basis of operations and not on the basis of orders, which reflects the principle that changeover times and operation costs occur at each equipment group and are not caused by one order across all operations.

Buffer inventories are set up upstream of the bottleneck machines to ensure maximum utilization of the bottleneck machines.

The SERVE program component schedules non-critical operations. In contrast to forward scheduling of critical operations, this process is supported by backward scheduling. This enables the non-critical operations to be scheduled in close temporal proximity to the critical ones in order to tightly integrate the process sequences.

Although several user reports about the system have appeared (see *Smith, Einsatz der OPT-Software 1985*), no process steps that refer to the optimization algorithm have been published.

The second approach—interactive fine-tuning between materials planning and scheduling—conforms to the principle that both the materials situation and the capacity situation must be taken into account when planning a customer or production order. An order is delayed until it is valid from a capacity perspective and the necessary materials are available. This principle is followed by PSI (see *PSI, PIUSS-Bedienerhandbuch 1987*) and Kazmaier (see *Kazmaier, Berücksichtigung der Belastungssituation eines neuen PPS-Systems 1984*). In concrete terms, this means that within the framework of the planning-level-oriented order explosion procedure, every operation is allocated in terms of capacity, and the availability of the necessary components is checked. The order is then accepted and becomes the basis for determining the secondary requirement for subordinate components. However, the capacities required for processing it must be ensured and the necessary materials must be available or covered on schedule by purchase orders. If this is not the case, the order is delayed.

This method has the advantage that only one case-oriented replanning process occurs with relatively few downstream orders being affected. On the other hand, the disadvantage is that scheduling data—especially routings and workstation data—must be available within the framework of requirements planning.

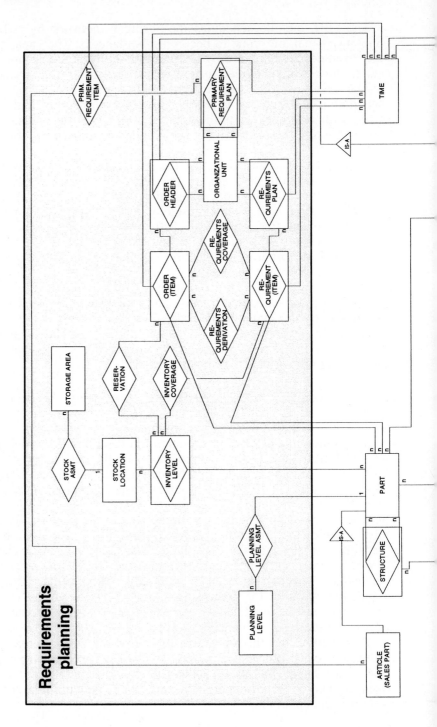

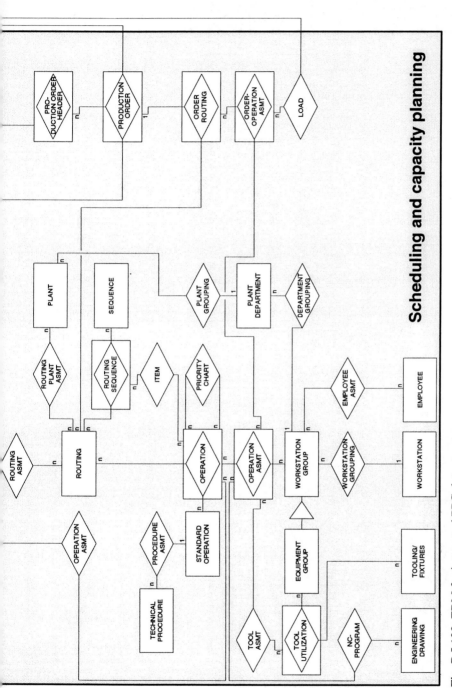

Fig. B.I.133: ERM for integrated PPC-data structure

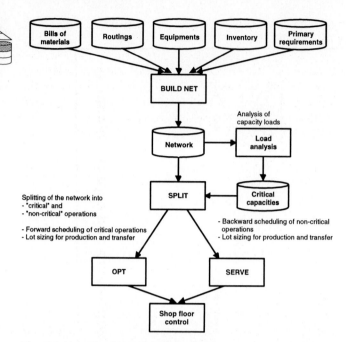

Fig. B.I.134: The OPT-SERVE-system

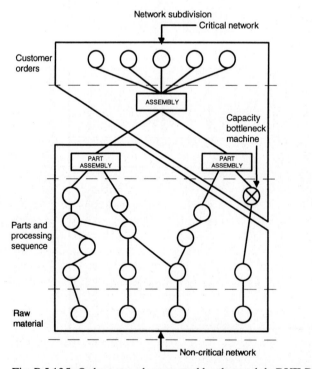

Fig. B.I.135: Order network generated by the module BUILD NET

In order to support the integration of requirements and capacity planning, the data structures between materials planning and scheduling can be interlinked more closely (see *Kazmaier, Berücksichtigung der Belastungssituation eines neuen PPS-Systems 1984*). The result is a kind of object-oriented data view, which is illustrated in Figure B.I.136 using the example introduced in Figure B.I.110. Assembly A consists of component parts C1, C2 and C3. In order to produce assembly A according to routing R1, two operations must be performed. Component parts C1 and C2 are necessary in operation 1 (drilling), which can be performed using tool T1 at equipment group 5 or equipment group 7. Operation 2 (welding) is performed at equipment group 5 using tool T2; additional component part C3 is also added here.

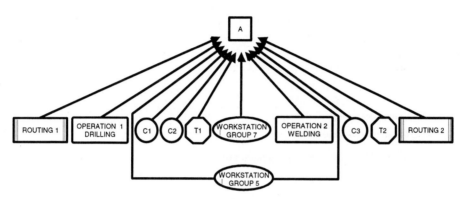

Fig. B.I.136: Object-oriented data view of capacity planning

The figure clarifies this interrelationship by representing parts as well as routings, operations, tools and equipment groups as elements of a "bill of materials" for assembly A. On the descriptive level of the ERM diagram, this means that these elements form **one** entity type, which is designated here as COMPONENT (see Figure B.I.137). Structural relationships are provided within this entity type, as they have already been identified by the bill of materials structure (albeit only within the entity type PART). By stipulating the sequence of the arrows—e.g., by using an item number—the production-oriented interrelationships between the individual components and assembly A can be established, and at the same time, arrows that possess the same starting nodes and terminal nodes can be distinguished from one another. In the example, this convention is used to represent the relationships to the workstation groups.

The previously derived data structure—in which the different entity types PART, ROUTING, OPERATION, etc., were distinguished explicitly (see Figure B.I.105)—is thus formally reduced to a kind of bill of materials structure. If the operations must also be linked with the related routing, or the equipment groups with the operations performed at

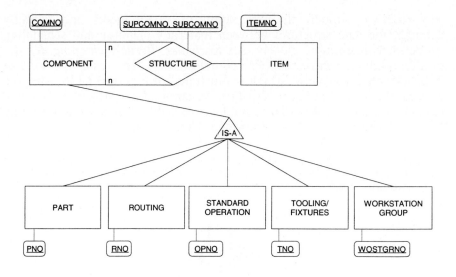

Legend:

SUPCOMNO = superordinate component number

SUBCOMNO = subordinate component number

Fig. B.I.137: ERM for creating an extended bill of materials

them, corresponding structures must be indicated by defining new identifying characteristics, without having to extend the fundamental, inherently simple structure of the n:m relationship within the object type.

In order to be able to better differentiate between them , the component types are distinguished as "specializations."

In the interactive method, planning is performed only quasi-simultaneously, since requirements are only reconciled iteratively for requirements and capacity planning.

The more closely the overall planning philosophy for requirements and capacity planning conforms to the net change principle, and is thus transformed from time-period-oriented planning to case-oriented planning, which means that only limited volumes of data are processed, the more advisable it is to perform requirements and capacity planning as closely together as possible.

For this reason, this procedure is primarily suitable for customer-order-oriented production structures involving only little vertical integration.

The different processes for successive and simultaneous interactive requirements and capacity planning are indicated in Figure B.I.138.

In the first case, the planned load is allotted twice—but according to different criteria (part numbers for requirements planning and workstation groups for capacity planning)—and extensive coordination functions might be necessary between both departments.

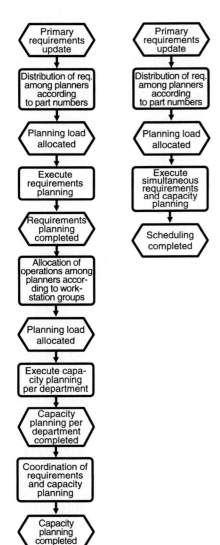

Fig. B.I.138: EPC for successive and simultaneous requirements and capacity planning

In the second case, these coordination functions are not required or are incorporated into the planning process.

B.I.4.2.3 Summarizing and Supplementing the Requirements Definitions for Scheduling and Capacity Planning

The requirements definitions for the ARIS capacity planning components will now be systematically tabulated and supplemented with any descriptive information that may still be missing. The comments will not exhibit the same degree of detail as in requirements planning. On occasion, the relatively high representational level necessitates relatively generalized statements, which would have to be worked out in significantly greater detail, and thus more precisely, in a practical application. This holds true, for example, in the discussion of access tables, which are maintained primarily at the information object level but would have to be broken down into attributes or even attribute instances in a real-world application.

B.I.4.2.3.1 Requirements Definition for Scheduling and Capacity Planning: The Function View

The scheduling and capacity planning functions are shown in the form of a function tree in Figure B.I.139. The distinction between reoptimization and net change planning can be made for various planning functions; as functions, however, each is only globally indicated in the individual planning blocks.

Like requirements planning, capacity planning must also distinguish between period-oriented and case-oriented processing. At first glance, batch processing at periodic intervals would seem to make the most sense here because of the large volume of data involved as a result of the fact that each order now contains five to ten more operations than in requirements planning. This also holds true if comprehensive algorithms (e.g., capacity adjustment) are introduced, which, of course, requires that the planning situation be adequately described in terms of alternative quantities, data situation and secondary conditions.

There will be a large number of alternatives if it is necessary to replan for a comprehensive planning time period. Conversely, case-oriented scheduling should make as few changes as possible to the existing situation, which means that continuously scheduling individual cases can result in relatively large deviations from the overall optimum. This is why it is suggested that both principles be combined, that optimization techniques be employed at predefined intervals for the replanning process incorporating as many alternatives as possible, and that changes be made in net change mode during the time between two planning periods without adversely affecting the planning situation.

Figure B.I.140 analyzes the subfunctions for capacity planning with respect to their processing modes.

Analogously to requirements planning, basic data management lends itself to interactive processing, primarily for reasons of currency and plausibility. If routings are generated from standard routings, iterative modification can also be an important factor.

Within the framework of scheduling without reference to capacity limits, automatic processing is meaningful for both the reoptimization method and the net change method if fixed algorithms (forward and

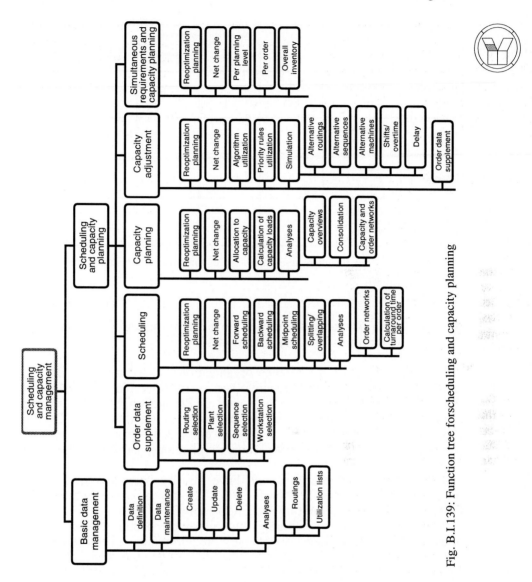

Fig. B.I.139: Function tree for scheduling and capacity planning

backward calculation of the network planning technique) are employed. Load profiles can be generated and consolidated interactively should the need for current analyses arise.

The capacity adjustment is especially suited to interactive decision-making processes. If math-intensive optimization techniques are employed, however, there is a tendency toward automatic processing.

Function	Subfunction	Reasons for interactive processing				Automatic/batch
		Currency	Plausibility	Iterative modification	Interactive decision process	
Basic data management	Create/delete	X	X	X		
	Update	X	X	X		
	Analyses	X				
Scheduling	Reoptimization					X
	Net change					X
Load profile	Reoptimization	X				
	Net change	X				
	Analyses	X				
Capacity adjustment	Reoptimization				X	X
	Net change				X	X
	Analyses	X				

Fig. B.I.140: Reasons for interactive processing of functions of scheduling and capacity planning

B.I.4.2.3.2 Requirements Definition for Scheduling and Capacity Planning: The Organization View

The function-oriented reference organizational chart in Figure B.I.141 shows the organizational units involved in capacity planning. Most of these organizational units can be found in Production. In a centralized organizational structure, capacity planning is assigned to Central Production Control, while in a decentralized structure, capacity planning—at least order-oriented capacity planning—occurs on the plant level.

In Figure B.I.141, the functions have already been assigned to the organizational units (see Section B.I.4.2.3.4.2), revealing the interfaces to Personnel, Internal Accounting and Engineering.

When requirements planning and capacity planning are tightly integrated, the functions of primary requirements planning, rough requirements planning and capacity planning can be performed within the framework of central production logistics. Operative units in which detailed requirements and capacity planning can be carried out can then be formed for subsegments.

This organizational structure leads to the concept of a networked leitstand organization along the lines of the Y model shown in Figure B.I.142, whereby the review functions are performed on the plant level and the operative order control functions on the operative level. This concept will be treated again in the discussion of logistical islands and job control centers (see Section B.IV.3).

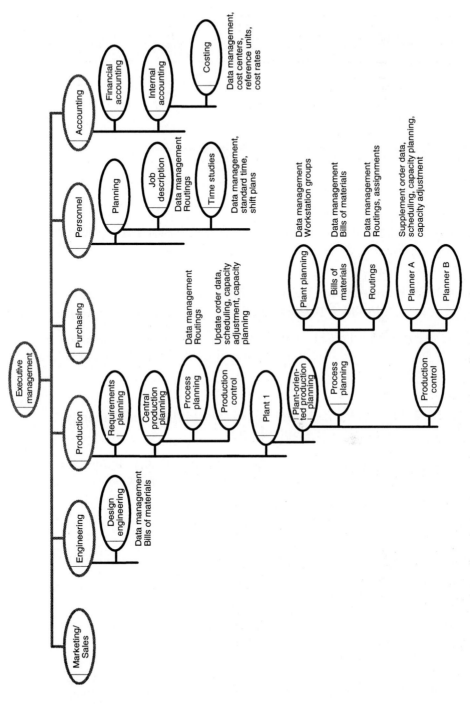

Fig. B.I.141: Allocation of scheduling and capacity planning into the functional reference model of the organization

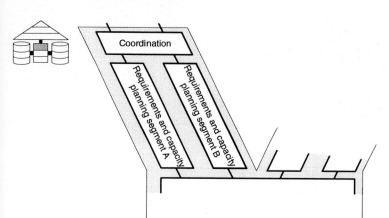

Fig. B.I.142: Networked leitstand organization within simultaneous requirements and capacity planning

B.I.4.2.3.3 Requirements Definition for Scheduling and Capacity Planning: The Data View

The data model created for scheduling and capacity planning has already been discussed briefly in Figures B.I.105 (basic data) and B.I.119 (order-related data).

B.I.4.2.3.4 Requirements Definition for Scheduling and Capacity Planning: The Control View

In keeping with the ARIS structure, all of the dual relationships will first be presented, followed by an overview of all components.

B.I.4.2.3.4.1 Functions - Organization

The assignment of functions to organizational units has already been discussed in the organizational chart shown in Figure B.I.141. This assignment process also results in the options for central and decentral differentiation on the planning levels.

B.I.4.2.3.4.2 Functions - Data

The EPC in Figure B.I.143 summarizes scheduling and capacity planning event control. It shows the major initiating basic data management events as well as the individual planning steps.

The transformation from input data to output data is suggested in the analysis of all ARIS components within the process chain diagram.

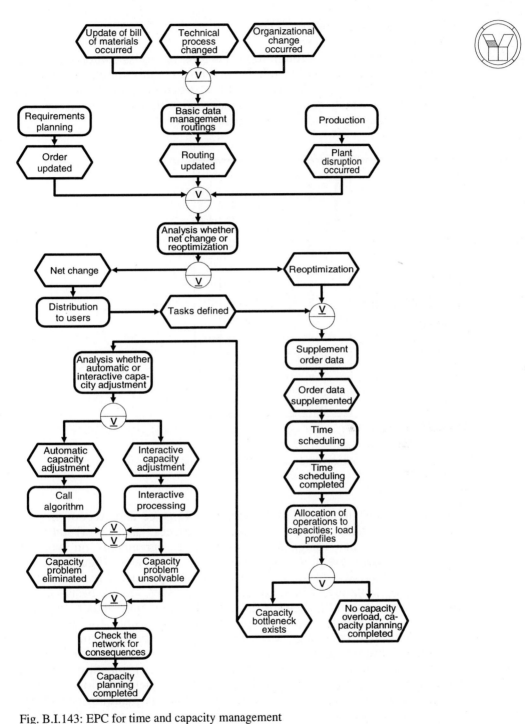

Fig. B.I.143: EPC for time and capacity management

B.I.4.2.3.4.3 Organization - Data

Figure B.I.144 shows a rough representation of access authorizations. In the routings, a distinction is made between the creation of entities and the processing of attributes. At the same time, a distinction is made between trial routings—which belong to Engineering within the context of new design and redesign—and routings/operations for Production.

		Marketing/sales	Engineering	Production	Purchasing	Personnel	Finance and accounting
Routing entities	Trial		C	R		R	R
	Production		R	C		R	R
Routing attributes	Trial		C	C		R	C
	Production		R	C		R	C
Operation	Trial		C	C	R	C	R
	Production		R	R	R	C	R
Workstation			R	C		C	C
Tooling/fixtures			C	C			
Employee			R	C		C	R
Relationships of routing in the broader sense			C	C	R	C	R

Legend: C = Create
                 R = Read

Fig. B.I.144: Access authorization within scheduling and capacity management

Organizational units such as Personnel or Finance and Accounting are authorized to create entities such as "employees" and "workstations." Moreover, they also assign attributes such as agreements on working hours, wage rate groupings (Personnel) and cost rates. Figure B.I.145 shows the allocation of task packages among planners. In contrast to requirements planning, which forms task packages on the basis of part groups, the workstation group is the planning unit under capacity planning. This means that each planner is responsible for a specific production department (e.g., workshop or plant) and performs capacity adjustment optimizations for it. The change in the criterion for defining the task package between requirements and capacity planning impedes simultaneous processing of both departments. In each individual case, a decision must be made as to whether simultaneous planning can utilize both criteria or whether a lead criterion can be introduced for distributing the task packages. Forming production departments according to part groups (production islands) solves this problem in any case.

Production		
Capacity planning		
Planner A	Planner B	
WOSTGRNO 1 - 5	WOSTGRNO 6 - 10	

(row label: Workstation-groups)

Fig. B.I.145: Distribution of work packages according to workstation groups

B.I.4.2.3.4.4 Functions - Organization - Data

The process chain diagram in Figure B.I.146 shows a condensed representation of the interrelationships between all of the ARIS capacity planning components.

B.I.4.3 Design Specifications for Scheduling and Capacity Planning

A detailed analysis of design specifications that takes into account objectives such as modularization, reusability, information hiding, etc., would make much more of a distinction between the design objects on the requirements definition level and thus extend beyond the scope of the representation capability. It is virtually impossible, on the other hand, to obtain additional information by employing a quasi 1:1 import of the design objects into the design specifications. Thus, a representational compromise is sought that contains additional design aspects for the design specification—particularly from the perspective of distribution—but is otherwise closely oriented to the requirements definition.

B.I.4.3.1 Design Specification for Scheduling and Capacity Planning: The Function View

The modules in Figure B.I.147 are derived from the function tree for the requirements definition in Figure B.I.139. For the most part, the main modules, or those submodules that lead to different distribution options within the control view, have been retained. The close proximity to the requirements definition does not result in any new aspects to the subject.

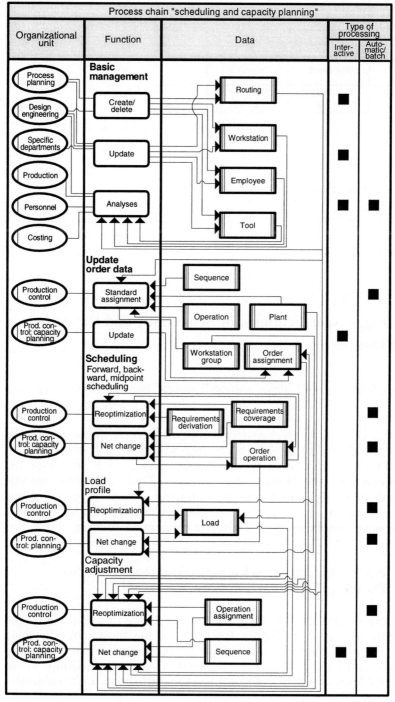

Fig. B.I.146: Process chain diagram ot scheduling and capacity planning

M.1.0 Basic data management
     - M.1.1 Data definition
     - M.1.2 Data maintenance
     - M.1.3 Analyses

M.2.0 Order data supplement
     - M.2.1 Routing selection
     - M.2.2 Plant selection
     - M.2.3 Sequence selection
     - M.2.4 Workstation group selection

M.3.0 Scheduling
     - M.3.1 Time scheduling
     - M.3.2 Analyses

M.4.0 Capacity planning
     - M.4.1 Capacity utilization calculation
     - M.4.2 Capacity analyses

M.5.0 Capacity adjustment
     - M.5.1 Alternative plant
     - M.5.2 Alternative sequence
     - M.5.3 Alternative workstation group
     - M.5.4 Shifts/overtime
     - M.5.5 Delay

M.6.0 Simultaneous requirements and capacity planning
     - M.6.1 Per planning level
     - M.6.2 Per order
     - M.6.3 Overall inventory

Figure B.I.147: Function modules for scheduling and capacity planning

B.I.4.3.2 Design Specification for Scheduling and Capacity Planning: The Organization View

Figure B.I.149 treats the network topology for scheduling and capacity planning within the context of function and data distribution, with a client/server architecture being assumed. The topology has already been discussed within the context of requirements planning.

B.I.4.3.3 Design Specification for Scheduling and Capacity Planning: The Data View

Figures B.I.148,a-c show the relations derived from the ER models for the requirements definition data view. The top of Figure B.I.148,a shows the strong entity types, which are identified by only **one** key attribute. External keys that result from 1:n relationships are imported for the relations R. STANDARD OPERATION and R. WORKSTATION. The lower section shows the relations that are derived from the relationship types whose keys comprise several attributes. Figure B.I.148,b shows the supplements to the basic data for scheduling and capacity planning from the perspective of Accounting and Organization/Personnel. The order-related data are shown in condensed form in Figure B.I.148,c. Only the order routings and order operations are named as independent relations, since their keys can be imported into the ORDER OPERATION relation as external keys, and their descriptions can be imported as attributes by virtue of the 1:n assignments of routings, plants, sequences and workstation groups.

(1) R. ROUTING (RNO, routing type, name, etc.)
(2) R. STANDARD ROUTING (RNO, name, etc.)
(3) R. PART ROUTING (RNO, name, etc.)
(4) R. ROUTING TEXT (RTXTNO, long texts, etc.)
(5) R. PLANT (PLANTNO, location, number of employees, etc.)
(6) R. SEQUENCE (SEQNO, identifier, etc.)
(7) R. TECHNICAL PROCEDURES (TPNO, name)
(8) R. STANDARD OPERATION (OPNO, TPNO, name, etc.)
(9) R. WORKSTATION GROUP (WOSTGRNO, PLOPNO, number of workstations, etc.)
(10) R. WORKSTATION (WOSTNO, WOSTGRNO, CCNO, OUNO, etc.)
(11) R. TOOLING/FIXTURES (TNO, purchase date, etc.)
(12) R. EMPLOYEE (EMPLNO, name, date hired, etc.)
(13) R. RESOURCES (RESNO, resource type, etc.)
(14) R. PLANT DEPARTMENT (PLOPNO, PLANTNO, location, number of employees, etc.)
(15) R. ENGINEERING DRAWING (EDNO, name, etc.)
(16) R. ORGANIZATIONAL UNIT (OUNO, etc.)
(17) R. PART (PNO, part name, etc.)
----
(18) R. VARIABLE ROUTING ASSIGNMENT (RNO, PNO, quantity range,
     etc.)
(19) R. COPY (VRNO, ARNO, date, user, etc.)
(20) R. ROUTING TEXT ASSIGNMENT (RNO, RTXTNO, etc.)
(21) R. ROUTING PLANT ASSIGNMENT (PLANTNO, RNO, quantity range)
(22) R. ROUTING SEQUENCE (RNO, SEQNO, priority, etc.)
(23) R. OPERATION (RNO, OPNO, etc.)
(24) R. PRIORITY CHART (RNO, POPNO, SOPNO, etc.)
(25) R. ITEM (RNO, SEQNO, OPNO, INO, etc.)
(26) R. OPERATION COMPONENT ASSIGNMENT (HPNO, LPNO, RNO, OPNO , etc.)
(27) R. OPERATION ASSIGNMENT (RNO, OPNO, WOSTGRNO, standard time, etc.)
(28) R. TOOL ASSIGNMENT (TNO, WOSTGRNO, RNO, OPNO, etc.)
(29) R. TOOL UTILIZATION (TNO, WOSTGRNO, etc.)
(30) R. EMPLOYEE ASSIGNMENT (WOSTGRNO, EMPLNO, etc.)
(31) R. NC PROGRAM (EDNO, RNO, OPNO, WOSTGRNO, etc.)
(32) R. ORGANIZATIONAL STRUCTURE (SUBOUNO, SUPOUNO, etc.)

Figure B.I.148,a: Scheduling and capacity planning relations from Figure B.I.105 (basic
            data)

(33) R. REFERENCE UNIT (REFUNO, name, etc.)
(34) R. COST CENTER (CCNO, name, etc.)
(35) R. ORGANIZATIONAL UNIT (OUNO, etc.)
----
(36) R. OUTPUT MEASUREMENT (REFUNO, CCNO, name)
(37) R. REFERENCE UNIT ASSIGNMENT (REFUNO, RNO, OPNO, WOSTGRNO, value, etc.)

Figure B.I.148,b: Scheduling and capacity planning relations from Figure B.I.114

(38) R. PRODUCTION ORDER (FOUNO, TOUNO, DATE, PNO, ODATE, quantity, etc.)
(39) R. PRODUCTION ORDER HEADER (FOUNO, TOUNO, DATE, status, etc.)
----
(40) R. ORDER ROUTING (FOUNO, TOUNO, DATE, PNO, ODATE, RNO, PLANTNO, etc.)
(41) R. ORDER OPERATION ASSIGNMENT (FOUNO, TOUNO, DATE, PNO, ODATE, OPNO,
     RNO, PLANTNO, SEQNO, WOSTGRNO, etc.)

Figure B.I.148,c: Order-related relations from Figure B.I.119 for scheduling and capacity
            planning

B.I.4.3.4 Design Specification for Scheduling and Capacity Planning: The Control View

The interaction between all three descriptive views will now be discussed without treating the dual relationships between ARIS components.

In Figure B.I.149, an extended form of the client/server topology previously discussed in requirements planning is used as the basis for scheduling and capacity planning. The individual departments are assigned the relation numbers from Figure B.I.148 as well as the module numbers from Figure B.I.147.

The individual relations can be distributed among the three hierarchical levels of product, central process setup planning and plant-oriented process setup planning. The basic data and the functions linked to them are assigned on the left side to Process Planning, while the order-related data with the modules that affect them are assigned on the right side to Production Control. The relations can be separated by attributes as well as by tuples. Thus, for example, not all attributes that are maintained on the product level are required on the central production setup planning level. This affects certain detailed cost information that is maintained as overlapping master data on the product level, but is primarily available to Accounting.

On the level of plant-oriented production setup planning, the order tuples are classified by the plants that produce the orders. If a distinction is made between central and plant-oriented production setup planning, Central Production Setup Planning can allocate orders to the individual plants, while detailed assignment problems, such as selecting different sequences within the predefined priority chart, are handled decentrally. In Figure B.I.149, for example, both data for tooling/fixtures as well as the priority chart for defining different sequences are maintained on the plant level.

The use of computer workstations within the network topology is particularly advisable with respect to analytical functions (e.g., graphical representations of load profiles) as well as within the framework of the interactive decision-making process for capacity adjustment. Although the data come primarily from central functions and files, segment-related data can be transferred to computer workstations to make them available for more highly interactive applications (simulation).

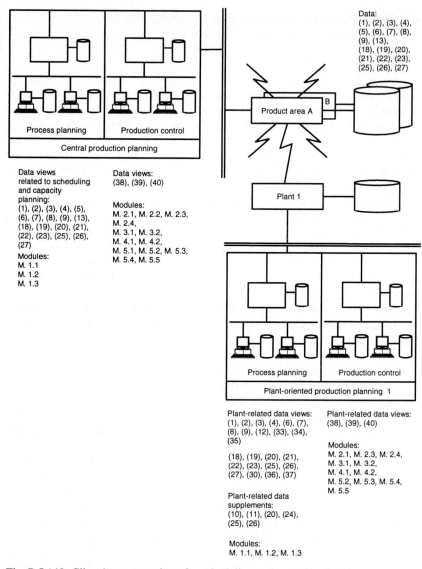

Data:
(1), (2), (3), (4),
(5), (6), (7), (8),
(9), (13),
(18), (19), (20),
(21), (22), (23),
(25), (26), (27)

Product area A   B

Plant 1

Process planning

Production control

Central production planning

Data views
related to scheduling
and capacity
planning:
(1), (2), (3), (4), (5),
(6), (7), (8), (9), (13),
(18), (19), (20), (21),
(22), (23), (25), (26),
(27)
Modules:
M. 1.1
M. 1.2
M. 1.3

Data views:
(38), (39), (40)

Modules:
M. 2.1, M. 2.2, M. 2.3,
M. 2.4,
M. 3.1, M. 3.2,
M. 4.1, M. 4.2,
M. 5.1, M. 5.2, M. 5.3,
M. 5.4, M. 5.5

Process planning   Production control

Plant-oriented production planning 1

Plant-related data views:
(1), (2), (3), (4), (6), (7),
(8), (9), (12), (33), (34),
(35)

(18), (19), (20), (21),
(22), (23), (25), (26),
(27), (30), (36), (37)

Plant-related data
supplements:
(10), (11), (20), (24),
(25), (26)

Modules:
M. 1.1, M. 1.2, M. 1.3

Plant-related data views:
(38), (39), (40)

Modules:
M. 2.1, M. 2.3, M. 2.4,
M. 3.1, M. 3.2,
M. 4.1, M. 4.2,
M. 5.2, M. 5.3, M. 5.4,
M. 5.5

Fig. B.I.149: Client/server topology for scheduling and capacity planning

B.I.4.4 Implementation Description for Scheduling and Capacity Planning

Implementation aspects will not be discussed.

B.I.5 Production (CAM in the Broader Sense)

B.I.5.1 Overview: Production

The planning levels for requirements planning, scheduling and capacity planning are geared toward medium-term time frames with relatively rough period divisions. They result in order definitions and resource assignments, which, however, do not yet have a binding effect on operations. Because planning pertains to a longer time frame, it contains sources of numerous problems, e.g., customer orders can be canceled, requirements forecasts can be revised, capacity data can change, etc.

Order release marks the end of the planning phase and the beginning of the implementation phase. This phase is especially complex within the context of production logistics: During this stage, tracking of the order-related data flow using detailed planning and feedback meets the data flow for technical execution of production, storage, transport, tooling, quality and maintenance control tasks.

Because of the tight integration between short-term production control and technical execution, the entire production department will be treated as **one** section of the book.

The terms used to describe this process are inconsistent. In Figure B.I.150, the term "computer aided manufacturing" (CAM) with the additional designation "in the broader sense" has been selected. This concept encompasses all computer-supported activities associated with production implementation as well as with order release and order control, resource management, resource preparation, maintenance and quality assurance.

Moreover, the term "CAM" is also used for resource-oriented functions, i.e., for the lower right portion of the Y model. Here, "CAM" is used with the additional designation "in the narrower sense."

Order release links the planning phase with the implementation phase.

After performing an availability check to verify the necessary resources from the overall (central) production order inventory, the order release function selects those orders to be processed in a shorter, pending time period and provides them to the decentralized detailed production control system. At the same time, the required resources are reserved and thus linked to the order. The order release accesses the basic data for scheduling and capacity planning as well as resource management data for the individual CAM components. This means that no new data structures have to be created for the availability check. New data structures are not formed until the released order is transferred to Production Control.

Since order release plays an intermediary role between planning and control, it does not completely fall within the definition of CAM. This situation is expressed in Figure B.I.150 by the diagonal division of the function box. In order to avoid redundancy, however, this stage will be discussed in conjunction with the implementation phase.

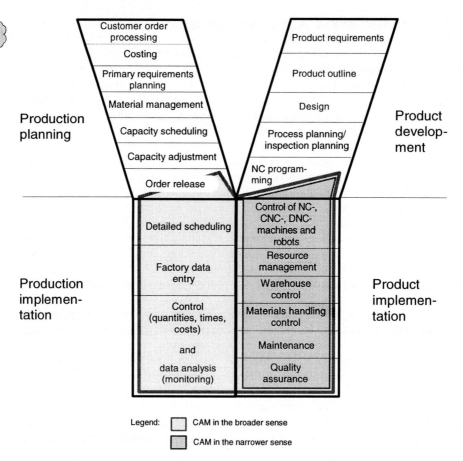

Fig. B.I.150: Definitions of CAM in the broader sense and CAM in the narrower sense

Many approaches are based on the organizational model of Production. In Figure B.I.151, the reference organizational chart is expanded on the planning level to include the organizational units for resource management. Figure B.I.152 shows the planning levels.

An important addition to this organizational chart, as compared to the one for scheduling and capacity planning, is the introduction of plant departments as well as the organizational units Quality Assurance and Tool Management and the explicit introduction of the organizational unit NC Programming as a subclassification of plant-related process planning.

This approach assumes that the plant level is functionally organized in the same manner as the reference model for the enterprise level. The plant level contains the functions Production, Purchasing, Personnel and Internal Accounting, while the functions Marketing/Sales, Engineering and Finance are always centralized, i.e., product-group-oriented.

Figure B.I.151 assigns all resource management functions as well as Quality Assurance and Maintenance to the plant level. Only production is performed in the "plant department" organizational unit. Later, decentralized organizational models, in which resource management, quality assurance and maintenance functions are also assigned to the plant departments, will be compared with this more centralized organizational form. This comparison, however, does not necessarily lead to changes in the organizational structure, since only the above-mentioned functions are assigned to the plant departments; however, they are integrated into the manufacturing process and thus do not result in independent organizational units. Although the plant-oriented organizational units are thinned out, they continue to exist for coordination functions. This decentralized structure is thus primarily revealed by the change in the assignment of functions to organizational units.

The plant departments are subdivided into workstation groups down to the workstation level. In a production environment, "equipment" and "machines" are used as specialized terms for "workstation."

The organizational classification principles for this process can vary. If plant departments are formed according to the operation principle, the term "shop" is used (e.g., milling, welding, etc.). A plant department can also be formed based on a part group that is processed in it, e.g., production and assembly islands. A workstation group constitutes an integrated manufacturing unit that can be formed according to the operation principle (identical automated milling machines within a milling shop) or according to the object principle.

In the latter case, a workstation (machine) group can comprise heterogeneous workstations (machines), e.g., the processing center can comprise an integrated machine tool, a materials handling system and a storage system.

Other organizational units in addition to Production can also be subdivided in this manner, e.g., for plant-related storage and materials handling departments.

Thus, Figure B.I.152 shows the generalized planning levels within a plant. The lowest level (process) is responsible for controlling machines and using actuators and sensors to set speeds, temperatures and directions.

Instead of the planning structure, plant departments could also be subclassified on the basis of function assignments as was done on the plant level in Figure B.I.151.

All the functions belonging to Production are shown in the function tree in Figure B.I.153. Drastically differentiated subfunctions are hidden behind the individual functions shown here. This is true, for example, in the case of the detailed scheduling function, which encompasses the application of different control algorithms. The functions for CAM "in the narrower sense" can also distinguish between differentiated resource management analyses as well as application control.

The process chain diagram in Figure B.I.154 shows the rough sequence of production-related interrelationships.

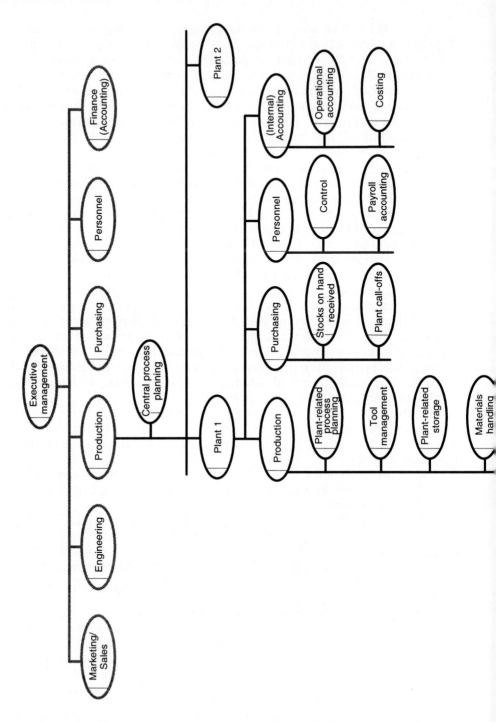

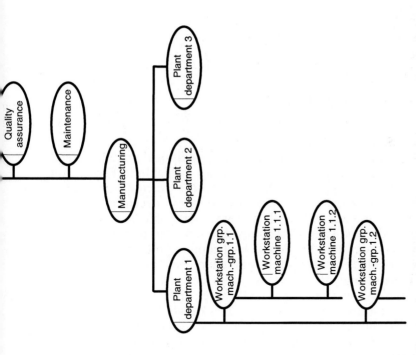

Fig. B.I.151: Manufacturing within the functional reference organizational chart

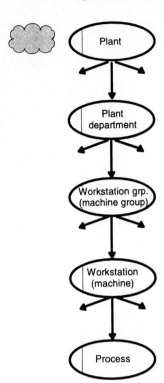

Fig. B.I.152: Planning level model of production

This sequence does not reflect a concrete organizational model; instead, it assumes that all components are transparently available to Production. Thus, the sequence can apply to plant-oriented (i.e., central) production control as well as to plant-department-oriented (i.e., decentral) control. The only thing that matters is that all necessary data objects be available to the user. If Production Control requires differentiated routings that are not assigned to an order until the detailed scheduling process—if need be, in a situation-oriented manner—this procedure requires decentralized routing management and, to a certain extent at least, bill of materials management, which take into account these differentiated analyses. Workstation and employee management is also known from the preceding order-oriented planning steps, but it is also supplemented on the production control level to include differentiated information. The new information consists of differentiated shift models, which not only take into consideration workdays and holidays, but also rules for scheduling breaks.

Both basic data and production orders transferred during order release are maintained interactively.

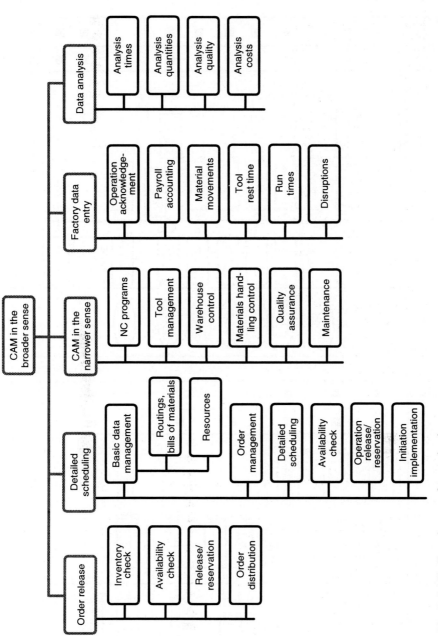

Fig. B.I.153: Function tree for production

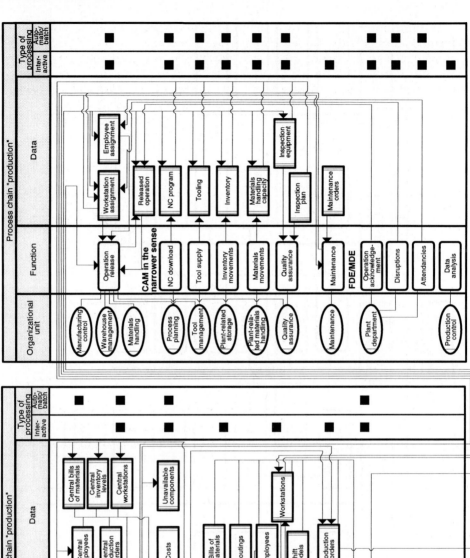

Fig. B.I.154: Process chain diagram "production"

Within the framework of detailed scheduling, operation sequences are formed automatically by algorithms and/or interactively by planners. This stage can take numerous different objectives into consideration. Business administration and, in particular, operations research have developed optimization techniques for this aspect, but space does not allow them to be represented in their entirety. They are, however, unnecessary for the sequence and data interrelationships represented here; instead, they are therefore treated more as a "black box." This optimization step results in concrete workstation and employee assignments. An optimization process that takes into account all resources also assigns the necessary NC programs, tooling, components, materials handling capacities and inspection procedures. In the process chain diagram, this interrelationship is not shown by individual assignment data; instead, it is shown by data flow relationships to the corresponding resources.

After detailed scheduling has been performed, the pending operations are released. An availability check of all resources ensures that the necessary components will be physically available when needed. This step does not employ a planning or scheduling availability check, as was already performed within the framework of both capacity planning and order release; instead, it is geared toward time- and location-oriented physical availability. If the order release function is performed for a specific time period, it can be carried out automatically. It can also be performed interactively for case-oriented situations, but the planner has the option of planning releases selectively in the event components are not available.

Resource management is typically an interactive function. In highly automated systems, however, control signals can be automatically routed from one resource to another. This is why automatic processing is also shown.

The maintenance function can also be analyzed in a differentiated manner. It encompasses not only the planning of preventive maintenance procedures, but also extensive order control and accounting functions. The same holds true for toolmaking. In both cases, independent PPC systems can be analyzed in complete detail, including complete production logistics and production, since these departments can be structured as "factories within a factory."

Feedback messages refer to the start and the finish of released orders. These data can be used for piecework payroll accounting. Employee attendance data can be entered either by automated data capture systems or interactively. Machine run times and downtimes are registered within the framework of machine data entry (MDE) and used to adjust workstation utilization data. In systems with a higher level of automation, the data are entered automatically by intelligent machine controls.

Analyses relating to all resources and controls are provided interactively in a wide variety of forms. For the sake of simplicity, the illustrations do not show these relationships since virtually all data clusters are accessed.

The sequence outlined here is illustrated as a largely sequential process; however, in reality it comprises a series of interconnected control loops.

Figure B.I.155 (from *Zäpfel, Taktisches Produktions-Management 1989, p. 2*) therefore shows the entire production process, i.e., "CAM in the broader sense," as a control loop. The process begins with control variables; as target values in the form of quantities, deadlines and quality characteristics, these variables result from requirements and capacity planning and detailed scheduling and are predefined for Production. The detailed scheduling process converts these initial values into setpoints while making ongoing comparisons with the information from the factory and machine data entry systems. During the production process controlled in the control loop, resource utilization is converted into the desired job results. Setpoints provide the information that initiates resource utilization. Random downtimes such as machine stoppage and material flow interruptions can affect the controlled process. For this reason, the data feedbacks necessitate ongoing review and readjustment. Continuous decentralized adaptation of the production system to downtime events is also a basic element of the fractal factory concept (see *Warnecke, Die fraktale Fabrik 1992*).

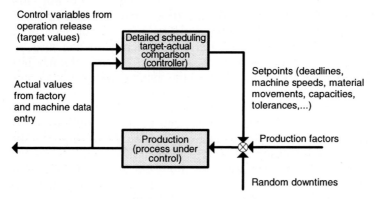

Fig. B.I.155: Control loop for CAM in the broader sense

B.I.5.2 Requirements Definitions for Production

B.I.5.2.1 Order Release

The order release function typically involves determining the production orders to be run for a specific period (release period), transferring them to the next PPC level (detailed scheduling) and ensuring that all necessary resources are available. At the same time, it provides the information necessary for Production. Since the control level can be differentiated on the basis of production-oriented organizational forms (e.g., shops, production islands, processing centers), orders and/or operations can also be differentiated on the basis of these units.

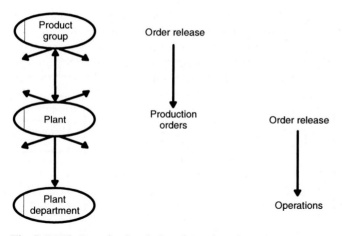

Fig. B.I.156: Organizational chart for order release

This is a two-tier organizational model (see Figure B.I.156). The order release possesses a "central" component in that it makes selections from an existing "central" order. Order control performs this operation on the product group level or on the plant level. If the order inventory is conducted on the product group level, the order inventory check, availability check, release and order distribution are assigned to this level. This process results in released orders that are assigned to plants. On the plant level, orders must be "re-released"—if need be, at shorter intervals—which results in released operations for the individual plant departments. Figure B.I.156 shows both forms. The discussions will tend to conform to the second form, i.e., orders released on the plant level and assigned to plant departments. The released orders/operations are then transferred to decentral department controls.

Figure B.I.157 shows the order release function tree.

Subroutines in the order inventory check, availability check, release and order distribution routines can distinguish between tracking according to either the reoptimization principle or the net change principle. In this context, the reoptimization principle applies if the released orders from the previously processed order release are to be transferred back into the order inventory of the orders to be checked, thus annulling the previously issued release authorization. This procedure is advisable for a periodic analysis, since the overall order release process is controlled on the basis of priorities, and incoming orders can be assigned a higher priority than those released during the most recent planning cycle.

If the functions are applied to an order inventory, they are generally automated; in case-oriented applications, e.g., for handling a rush order, they can be performed interactively. As a result, both processing forms are indicated for these functions. Order release can be triggered at predetermined intervals or on a case-by-case basis, e.g., for an individual rush order.

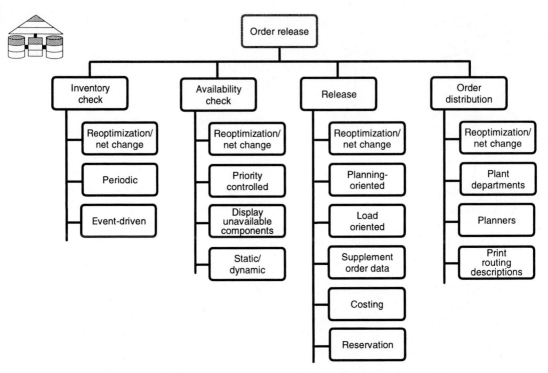

Fig. B.I.157: Order release function tree

Although production flow quantity and time factors have already been taken into account during requirements and capacity planning, the system checks whether the necessary resources (parts, employees, tooling, equipment, NC programs and inspection equipment) are actually available prior to order release. This check illustrates the principle of prudence that is built into the entire planning philosophy: Although theoretically all resources must be present as a result of the preceding planning operations, the system checks whether the resources are, in fact, available before a binding action is initiated.

The planner can also release an order if the results of the availability check turn out to be negative. For example, the planner can initiate a rush order to compensate for unavailable components or arrange for additional overtime if capacities are inadequate—measures that do not yet exist in DP-supported availability checks. This planning release must be identified to allow the measures to be monitored during subsequent production control.

When the orders are released, all orders for a specific period (e.g., a week) whose planned start date falls within this period are examined for releasability. In order to assign resources to the most important order, the orders are sorted according to urgency, which is expressed by order priority.

A distinction must be made between a static release and a dynamic release in connection with the release algorithm. A static order release gears the availability check to the order release date, i.e., an order is released only if the necessary components are physically available on the release date.

Dynamic release, on the other hand, simulates the production process so that orders are also released whose components will not be physically available on the date of the availability check but will be available on the planned start date based on the production simulation. Elements of production control, which involves determining the production sequence and detailed scheduling, are imported into the availability check as a simulation algorithm.

The data necessary for production control are assigned to released orders. As in scheduling and capacity planning, the system either merely creates references to the basic data or data can also be imported (redundant). Alternate routings, sequences and workstation assignments are also provided, which form the basis for production control optimization. Standard assignments can be used for order costing, which provides a basis for comparison with the costing results obtained during the implementation phase.

Separating the operations for released orders according to production control planning departments is the last functional step. Before the implementation functions for the operations are actually initiated, a re-release with an availability check can be performed, this time on the basis of operations.

Generally speaking, the frequency and location-specific assignment for the "order release" function depends on the organizational control hierarchy.

Orders can be released at periodic intervals (e.g., weekly or daily) by checking the orders whose start dates fall within the release period (see the EPC in Figure B.I.158). Case-oriented orders can also be released, e.g., rush orders that must be immediately transferred to Production. Rush orders can bypass capacity planning since capacity checks are performed during order release. Their results, however, must be imported into capacity planning in order to ensure currency. At the same time, actions in Production can also initiate order release.

Orders that are to be analyzed for release are sorted by priority, so that the most important orders can be given priority if resources are limited.

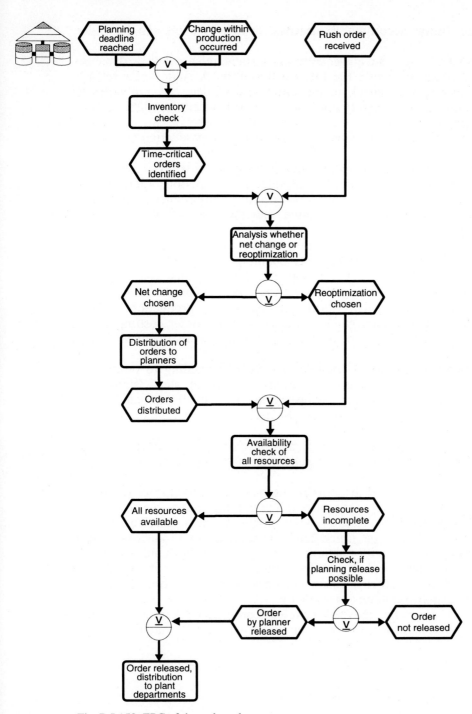

Fig. B.I.158: EPC of the order release process

B.I.5.2.1.1 Static and Dynamic Availability Checks

Figure B.I.159 shows the algorithm for a static availability check for an order in the form of a structogram. A production order can be released if the necessary components and tools are physically available in inventory on the date of the release check and the required equipment groups (including manpower) still exhibit free capacities. Additional resources, such as inspection equipment for quality control or NC programs, can be handled analogously. The potential capacity allocation time remaining in the system is viewed as a measure of resource availability. The potential consumption factor is viewed as a measure of the available inventory. In

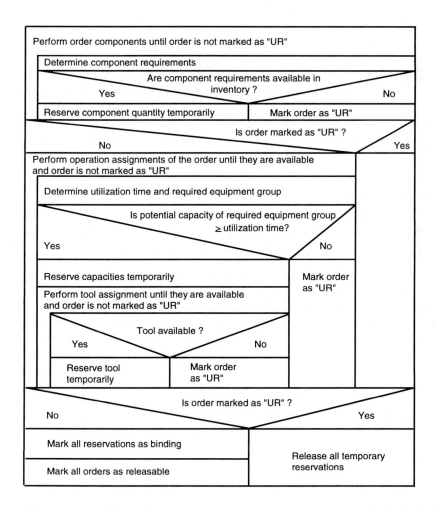

Annotation: "UR" means "unreleasable"

Fig. B.I.159: Structogram for availability check

order to ensure that a resource is not allocated more than once, the resources for a releasable order are reserved.

Reservations were discussed in terms of the gross-net calculation within the framework of requirements planning,. In this context, the components and materials reserved for released orders—but still present in inventory— were not counted as part of the available inventory in the gross-net calculation. These reservations are now created using the bill of materials data within the framework of order release. The RESERVATION is an n:m relation between INVENTORY and PRODUCTION ORDER (see the requirements planning data structure above).

Every reservation entity assigns the necessary quantities of a component to a release order. In a static analysis, only those quantities that are actually available on a reservation date are assigned.

The other resources can be reserved in a similar way, albeit without creating such detailed direct connections. Procedures for tooling, equipment and employee capacity ensure that period capacities are continually reduced by the utilization times required by the orders (or more precisely, by the operations). This process does not treat the time-related effects of process planning or maintain detailed assignments; instead, only the capacity package available on the order release date is continually reduced. Since the OPERATION ASSIGNMENT creates links to equipment groups, manpower and tools for each production order, the allocations from the capacity planning data structure can already be identified.

Only the capacity value (measured in equipment hours, employee hours and tool use hours) per entity of each resource for the period in question is calculated. This value is then deducted from the appropriate account on an ongoing basis using existing ORDER-OPERATION-ASSIGNMENT relationships. The newly calculated available value is then used for a new availability check.

When the resource categories are processed, temporary reservations are first created until it can be determined that all resources are available. Only then can the reservations be considered fixed. If resources are unavailable and the order cannot be released, the temporary reservations are re-released. The designation "releasable" implies that lack of availability will not result in the failure of an order to be released.

Dynamic availability checks simulate the production sequence. Thus, for example, orders are entered as additions to inventory as per their planned completion date and are immediately available for availability checks of superordinate orders. At the same time, equipment group allocations are detailed on the equipment level. Precise time scheduling is also performed for manpower and tool utilization.

Thus, a complete production control procedure is embedded within the simulation process, and the necessary data structures must be available. The simulation procedure can utilize either the system used for concrete production control or—which is advisable if different decentralized control procedures exist—a simplified procedure that only contains the major control components. In any case, however, Production Control must have access to the detailed data structures. Since these structures will not be discussed until the next section, this section will only indicate that they are incorporated into the dynamic order release process.

The allocation-oriented order release can be used in simulating the progress of the order, since the simulation process provides continuous information about inventory and turnaround times.

B.I.5.2.1.2 Order Release and Distribution

During the availability check, the orders to be examined are determined on the basis of whether their start date falls within the release time period. This procedure implicitly conforms to the objective of implementing the deadlines that were planned retrogradely within the framework of requirements and capacity planning. Thus, the order release function supports objectives that are tracked in these planning departments. For requirements planning, these goals include meeting deadlines (through retrograde time scheduling) as well as minimizing setup and storage costs through lot formation; for capacity planning, they include uniform utilization of equipment groups.

Actual order release is then simply a confirmation of the availability check. On the other hand, a scheduler can also release an order even if the availability check was negative. This is a valid procedure in the case of important orders for which the scheduler wants to provide resources by using rush orders or reallocation, for example.

Production Control pursues the following more specialized objectives:
- Minimizing order turnaround time
- Maximizing equipment capacity utilization
- Meeting deadlines
- Minimizing the amount of capital tied up in material inventory.

It is a well-known fact that conflicts can arise between these objectives (see *Gutenberg, Die Produktion 1983, p. 216*).

Since order release represents the interface between planning-oriented functions and production control, it should support not only the objectives of requirements and capacity planning, but also those of production control.

These objectives are pursued via the process of load-oriented order release, which has been a topic of discussion in recent years and has also been implemented in standard PPC software (see *IFA, Fertigungssteuerung 1984; Kettner/Bechte, Belastungsorientierte Auftragsfreigabe 1981; Wiendahl, Betriebsorganisation 1983; Wiendahl, Belastungsorientierte Fertigungssteuerung 1987*). The point of departure for the process is the realization that the shop inventory level is a good indicator of production flow and thus of order turnaround time. A high shop inventory level means waiting times in front of equipment groups and thus highly fluctuating turnaround times, which makes precise scheduling difficult.

During load-oriented order release, therefore, only as many orders (measured in production hours) can be released to Production as it can process within specific scheduling limits that are designed to compensate for unexpected downtime and misjudgments. Figure B.I.160 (from *Wiendahl, Verfahren der Fertigungssteuerung 1984, p. 12*) shows this principle in the form of the familiar funnel model. The funnel's contents indicate the existing orders in Production. Ongoing analysis of production output closes the feedback loop that links newly released orders, existing orders and completed orders.

Order (lot) turnaround time is equal to the average order inventory divided by mean output (measured in production hours per TU). This figure is expressed in the illustration by the level in the funnel.

The relation between funnel input from the order release process and funnel output on the basis of completed hours is set in such a manner as to maintain the desired average turnaround time. In other words, this means that orders will continue to be released until a critical order inventory is exceeded.

Thus, order release is used as a true control instrument. The special algorithm for computing control variables will not be discussed in greater detail here (see *Wiendahl, Belastungsorientierte Fertigungssteuerung 1987; Glaser/Geiger/Rohde, Produktionsplanung und -steuerung 1992, pp. 211 ff.*).

One objective of load-oriented order release is to decrease the cost of tied-up capital by reducing inventory levels in Production. Nevertheless, it

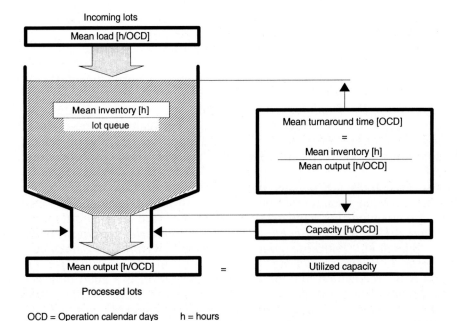

OCD = Operation calendar days   h = hours

Fig. B.I.160: Funnel model of load-oriented order release

must be noted that freeing up capital will only have an earnings impact if it produces actual changes in payment flows. If load-oriented order release only results in shifting the inventory levels to or from the production department, capital will not be freed up. Capital will only truly be freed up if the effect can be transferred to Requirements Planning, and thus to Purchasing.

Figure B.I.161 (from *Bechte, Belastungsorientierte Auftragsfreigabe 1980*) shows the load and performance profiles for an equipment group that is continuously controlled by the release algorithm. The figure also indicates the correlation between turnaround time and other inventory.

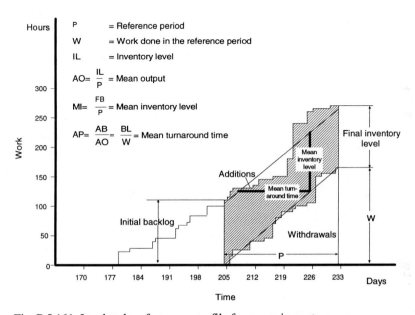

Fig. B.I.161: Load and performance profile for an equipment group

While many publications treat load-oriented order release as an independent production control principle, it is embedded within the order release process here. The reason for this is that the process provides no further information about the type of production control involved, i.e., it does not specify sequences, optimize job sequences, etc. Load-oriented order release has been adopted in several standard PPC systems, and numerous elaborations and reports on the topic have also been published (see *Wiendahl, Anwendung der belastungsorientierten Fertigungssteuerung 1991*).

Business administration has only recently begun to consider this approach and, to some extent, to commence a serious discussion of the subject (see *Adam, Fertigungssteuerung 1987, Hansmann, Produktionssteuerung 1987; Glaser/Geiger/Rohde, Produktionsplanung und -steuerung 1992, pp. 201 ff.*).

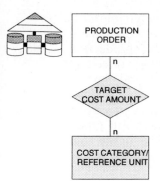

PRODUCTION
ORDER

n

TARGET
COST AMOUNT

n

COST CATEGORY/
REFERENCE UNIT

Fig. B.I.162: Order calculation

Production costing can also be calculated on the basis of order release using the data structure shown in Figure B.I.114. Each order is assigned a target cost value on the basis of cost category and reference unit (see Figure B.I.162).

There are two different options for further processing of order releases:

1.   The released orders are transferred to centralized, i.e., plant-oriented, Production Control, which arranges the operations in optimal sequences and initiates production. Only then are the orders (operations) transferred to the appropriate plant departments and/or their respective workstation groups. In this case, all data structures are available on the central level.

2.   The released orders are transferred to decentralized production departments for further independent processing. The following discussion is based on this option.

In this context, plant departments can be organizational units such as shops, production islands, flexible manufacturing systems or assembly lines.

The plant departments must receive all of the information necessary for implementation so that they are able to function self-sufficiently, i.e., without access to master or order data from the planning level.

The basic production order structure thus expands to the structure shown in Figure B.I.163.

Planning and costing data are assigned to the production order as comparison values for concurrent costing, and data relating to resources and the components in the bill of materials are assigned to the operations. The objects shown in Figure B.I.164 serve as resources for this process.

The planning options for further scheduling can be categorized according to three different scenarios, which in turn determine the mode of data transfer and thus the data structure that will be used:

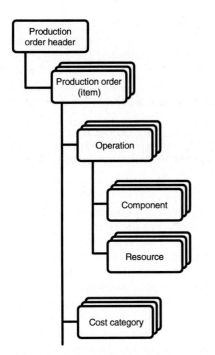

Fig. B.I.163: Extended production order structure

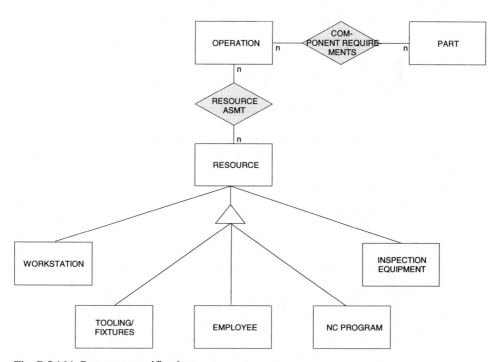

Fig. B.I.164: Resource specifications

1.   Upon order release, the routings defined in the context of capacity planning are transferred to the plant departments in printed (or electronic) form. No additional DP-supported detailed scheduling is performed.

2.   The plant departments perform production control independently and manage the data structures for their own resources.

3.   The plant departments perform production control independently and manage the data structures for their own resources, routings and the information contained in the bills of materials.

Figure B.I.165 shows the data structure for the first scenario. In this case, the existing order definitions are imported, and the plant departments make no further planning-oriented changes. The released orders are specialized from the general object ORDER and assigned to the pertinent plant departments. The plant departments can be identified on the basis of the workstation groups contained in the operation assignments.

The key attributes for the production order header are replaced by an asterisk.

Because an order may pass through several plant departments—e.g., in the case of shop floor production—the department assignment is of the n:m type. Operations to be performed in a plant department are identified via the OPERATION-DEPARTMENT ASSIGNMENT relationship. Detailed routings for both complete orders as well as segments based on plant departments can be generated using these data. In this case, however, total production control has already been performed "centrally."

In the second scenario cited above, the data structures for resources are managed in the plant departments.

The corresponding order-related assignments must then be transferred by Order Release. Order definitions generated during capacity planning are geared toward standard assignments in order to simplify the planning process. These data structures can also be sufficient for the availability check.

All degrees of scheduling latitude are used for detailed planning in order to optimize the production process. Thus, all possible sequence and resource assignments are transferred. Figure B.I.166 is a combination of the basic and order-related data structures for scheduling and capacity planning (see also Figures B.I.105 and B.I.119).

Each of the various types of resources managed by the plant department is represented by an entity type in Figure B.I.166.

The transferred operation assignments contain degrees of latitude for alternative workstation groups, alternative tools, etc.

The priority chart contains the predecessor and successor relationships from which Production Control can determine valid sequences. If necessary, there can also be alternative routings for an order within a plant. The necessary parts are assigned to an operation. This data structure

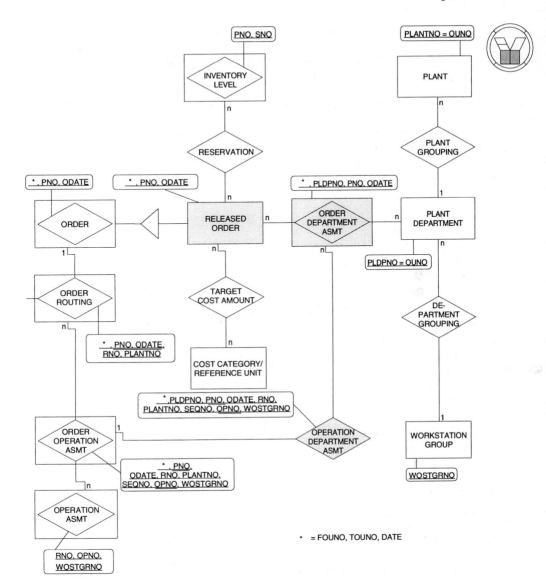

Fig. B.I.165: Data transfer for first scenario: no production control

is derived from the OPERATION COMPONENT ASSIGNMENT. The data structures for costing and reservation are the same as in Figure B.I.165 and are therefore not illustrated.

In the third scenario, all production master data are maintained in the plant departments. Thus, only the released orders (identified by order header, PNO and ODATE) are transferred to them by Order Release. All assignments to routings, sequences, etc., are then made centrally. The

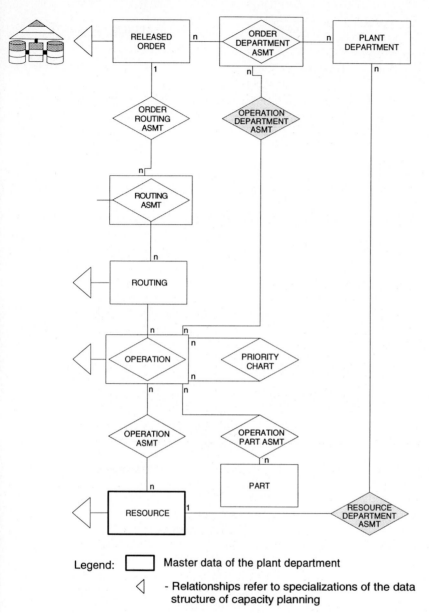

Legend: ▢ Master data of the plant department

◁ - Relationships refer to specializations of the data structure of capacity planning

Fig. B.I.166: Central/decentral data structures

assignments used within the framework of scheduling and capacity planning serve only as planning functions, but they do not affect production control. The plant-department-oriented master data can be interpreted as specializations of Figure B.I.105.

These data structures can be further refined by the plant departments for detailed scheduling.

B.I.5.2.2 Detailed Scheduling

B.I.5.2.2.1 Data Management

In order release, a distinction was made between different degrees of decentralization for Production Control. These degrees influence the basic data structure only if they permit different degrees of latitude in Production Control. Purely location-oriented data assignment, on the other hand, does not influence the fundamental logic of the data. The following discussion is based on a form of production control that can independently assign routings, priority chart sequences and resources. All data structures introduced in scheduling and capacity planning that characterize these degrees of latitude must also be available to Production Control. Although in principle no distinction concerning algorithms and data structures can be made between central (plant-oriented) production control and department-oriented production control, this discussion will be based on the latter scenario. This means that all basic data are specializations of the general data structure in Figure B.I.105. For the sake of clarity, the abbreviation PD (plant department) is assigned to the names of the information objects. Thus, data management for production control comprises the data structures taken from Figure B.I.105, which have been transferred as specializations as represented in the left part of Figure B.I.167. It should be noted that the fundamental structure of the data conforms to that of Figure B.I.105 in this respect, but the contents do not need to conform to the same degree on the entity level. It was already noted that capacity planning occurs on a rougher level and can thus contain consolidated data. Therefore, different priority charts can be generated on the detailed scheduling level than on the medium-term planning level.

Detailed scheduling can use shift models that already show equipment idle times. There can be different reasons for these intervals of time, shown as breaks, such as shifts that were not earmarked for production, lunch and coffee breaks, holidays, plant vacations, as well as times reserved by Planning (preventive maintenance). These reserved times are assigned to a shift as breaks and are linked with the entity type TIME by "from-to" indicators.

In the order release planning stage, the released orders are represented as specializations. For the sake of simplicity, only keys for the newly introduced information objects are listed. The order header key is replaced by a (*).

Assignments to the plant departments must be carefully specified. For example, the imported structural relationships for the parts produced in the plant department transfer one of the components that will be effective within the plant department, i.e., typically single-level bills of materials, since the subordinate components are required outside the plant department.

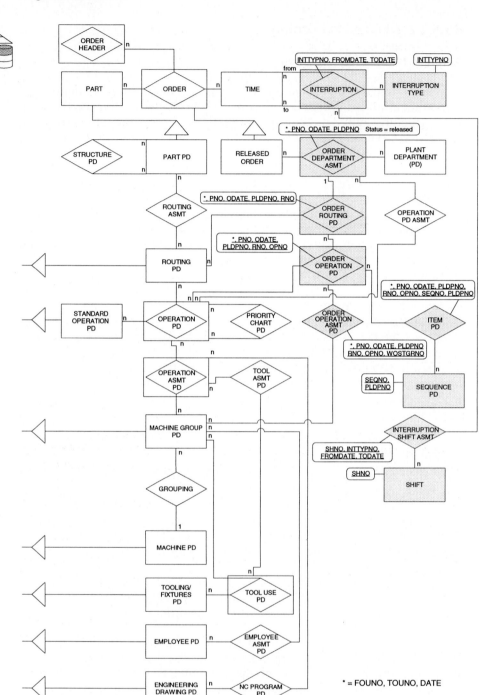

Fig. B.I.167: Data management for detailed scheduling

The order release function has specialized the released orders from the general order pool by assigning the order status "released" and assigning them to plant departments via the relationship type ORDER DEPARTMENT ASSIGNMENT. Thus, the plant department knows the orders that affect it. An order can also be assigned to several plant departments if it cannot be processed completely in one plant department. The plant department number PLDPNO thus serves as an identifier for this assignment relationship.

B.I.5.2.2.2 Information Objects for Detailed Scheduling

Detailed scheduling performs a shorter-term, more differentiated analysis than was the case for scheduling and capacity planning. The length of the planning time period ranges between one shift and several weeks, with the time units being measured in minutes or hours.

Capacity planning is no longer performed on the level of equipment groups, but rather on the level of individual machines.

Theoretically, overall detailed scheduling must simultaneously take into account all degrees of latitude and secondary resource conditions. Approaches based on computer-assisted mathematical modeling can be formulated to satisfy this need (see *Jacob, Produktionsplanung 1986* and *Adam, Produktions-Management 1993*). Since space does not permit a discussion of these types of approaches, however, it will be assumed that heuristic or precise procedures are available for making assignment decisions. Figure B.I.167, for example, expresses the assignment of a routing to an order via the relationship type ORDER ROUTING PD. Likewise, it will be assumed that concrete operations—together with their sequential items—can be assigned to a routing from the priority chart.

The detailed scheduling algorithm assigns the equipment group to operations.

The order-related data structure for the plant department developed thus far closely conforms to the data structure developed within the context of scheduling and capacity planning. Further assignments to machines, tools, employees and NC programs, however, are based on a finer level of scheduling and will thus be newly developed in greater detail.

Detailed scheduling draws up a machine utilization plan that specifies the relevant operation times, and a corresponding equipment assignment is created for each operation.

Detailed operating plans are generated in the same way for the other resources (tools and employees).

While the production order constituted the planning unit on the planning levels up to and including order release, the operation becomes the focus during detailed planning, although it is geared toward different objects due to the large variety of goals and secondary conditions involved. The operations are bundled into new units, which will be termed "sequences." Sequence formation is geared toward the respective reference objects.

The objective of minimizing setup costs

focuses on **equipment** as the reference object. The operations in question are assigned to this reference object in such a way as to keep the setup times as short as possible. This means, for example, that operations for different orders that are similar in terms of setup requirements are combined into new "lots." Operations for orders that are due on a later date can be moved forward in such a way as to increase turnaround times. It has already been shown that lot formation during requirements planning is problematic because changeover costs are incurred for each operation rather than for each production order. Renewed lot formation on the production control level is therefore a logical process. Thus, the "sequence" control unit is formed by combining similar operations.

The objective of minimizing order turnaround times

can involve "splitting" operations in order to perform them simultaneously on different pieces of equipment. These operations can be "combined" with other operations to form sequences.

The objective of maximizing materials utilization

can involve optimally combining parts from different orders into one cutting operation. In a milling operation, for example, different-sized parts from different orders are arranged on a specified metal plate. The planning unit here is the **material**, i.e., the metal plate. These types of nesting problems require access to geometrical data and, consequently, to CAD systems.

The objective of maximizing equipment capacity utilization

again focuses on **equipment** as the planning object. This objective is typical for shop floor production. In order to fully utilize capacities, operations that are not yet due can be moved forward, resulting in higher turnaround times. Physical indications of this objective include large inventories in front of equipment units. Midpoint scheduling can provide a concrete planning strategy in this case by initially scheduling a network operation on a critical machine and then scheduling the preceding operations backwards and the subsequent operations forwards. The control sequence is the sequence of operations on the bottleneck machine. The complexity of sequence planning problems is well-known (see *Seelbach, Ablaufplanung 1975; Dinkelbach, Ablaufplanung in entscheidungstheoretischer Sicht 1976; Adam, Produktions-planung bei Sortenfertigung 1971; Adam, Produktionspolitik 1990; Schmidt, CAM: Algorithmen und Decision Support 1989; Blazewicz/Ecker/Schmidt/Weglarz, Scheduling in Computer and Manufacturing Systems 1993*). In the case of real-world problems, this leads to extremely long computation times. Consequently, real-world applications utilize heuristic procedures that are typically based on operation-oriented priority rules. Newer approaches include genetic algorithms (see *Schmidt, Fertigungs-leitstände - ein Überblick 1992*) and rule-based expert systems (see *Steinmann, Einsatzmöglichkeiten von Expertensystemen in integrierten Systemen der Produktions-planung und -steuerung 1992*).

The following section will first discuss information objects for detailed scheduling and then introduce a simple priority-controlled algorithm.

In addition to pursuing the various goals outlined above, physiological aspects can also play a role in detailed scheduling. For example, labor contracts can call for a particularly demanding operation to be followed by a less strenuous operation. Other factors can include combining setup procedures with maintenance measures. All these considerations lead to combining "order" and "operation" planning units into new units, which are termed "operation sequences" or, simply, "**sequences**." Sequences are essentially created by:

"Acceleration" (combining operations) and
"Splitting" (dividing up the quantities in an operation)

as well as combinations of the two.

Several options will now be illustrated using a simple example (see Figure B.I.168).

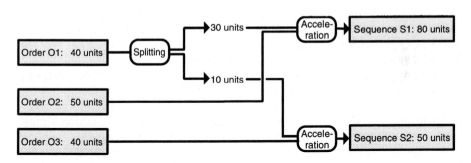

Fig. B.I.168: Acceleration and splitting (example)

There are three orders, each of which contains a "milling" operation. Order O1 is split into two sequences, S1 and S2. Order O2 is assigned to sequence S1 and accelerated with the first suborder O1. Order O3 is accelerated with the second suborder from O1 to form sequence S2.

Figure B.I.169 extends the example to include tool and employee utilization, as well as breaks. These interrelationships are used to design the data structure for Production in Figure B.I.170.

The point of departure for Figure B.I.170 is the OPERATION ASSIGNMENT PD previously developed in Figure B.I.167, which was allotted to a machine <u>group</u> in the earlier example but is now planned with

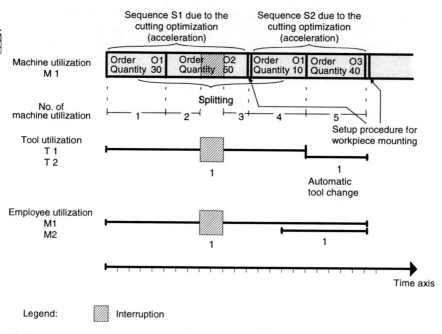

Fig. B.I.169: Example of detailed scheduling (simplified)

reference to more specific resources. The resources are represented by the information objects MACHINE PD, TOOL ASSIGNMENT PD, EMPLOYEE ASSIGNMENT PD and NC ASSIGNMENT PD. For the sake of simplicity, only the most important keys are shown.

Machine utilization is the central relationship. It is the most detailed identifiable order-related control unit. An operation can be split up among several machines, and several utilizations can be assigned to one machine.

Machine utilization is identified further by its start and finish times; thus, time intervals can be identified within the same operation and the same machine assignment. They can, however, be interrupted by shift changes or other events. Figure B.I.169 shows this situation for machine utilization times 2 and 3.

The entity type SEQUENCE is introduced in order to bundle the machine utilization times into the new control unit. This entity type is identified by the sequence number SEQNO. Depending on the production structure, a sequence can encompass:

-    One material unit (e.g., metal sheet, paper roll, glass pane) from which several different parts are manufactured. An optimization algorithm can be used to combine several parts to form a new control unit. Figure B.I.171 shows such a combination as a result of nesting or cutting optimization for a milling process in parts production for the aerospace industry. This type of sequence is termed a "materials sequence."

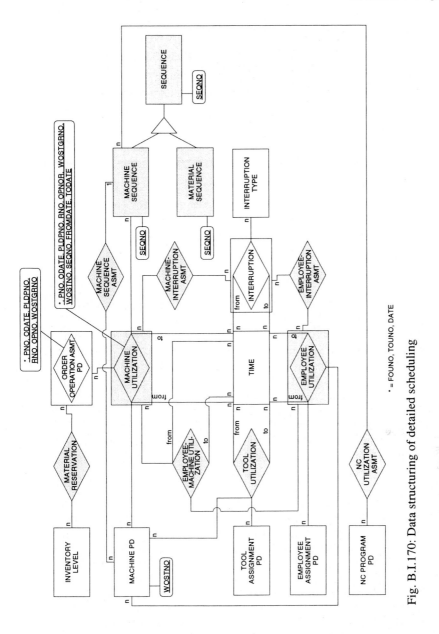

Fig. B.I.170: Data structuring of detailed scheduling

A series of similar operations that can be processed without setup interruptions. This sequence is termed a "machine sequence."

The sequences can be formed from existing operations or, in the case of extremely repetitive production, stored as standard sequences. The following section will first discuss the formation of machine sequences, followed by the special aspects of materials sequences.

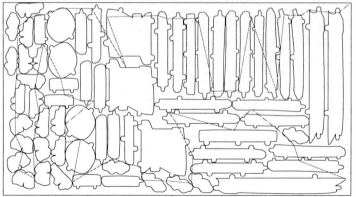

Fig. B.I.171: Example for a cutting optimization sequence
        (Source *Deutsche Airbus*)

The objective of detailed scheduling is to produce a chronological process plan on the level of the individual machines.

The concrete sequence load for a machine is thus the sum total of the machine utilizations assigned to it. Operation-related interruptions are assigned to a machine utilization (MACHINE INTERRUPTION ASSIGNMENT). In addition to machine utilization, detailed scheduling also schedules the resources EMPLOYEE and TOOL. This function also relates to Figure B.I.169. A TOOL UTILIZATION PD is identified by tool, machine, as well as installation-and-removal changeover times. An EMPLOYEE UTILIZATION PD is identified by the employee, by the assigned machine, as well as by the start and finish times at the workstation. Since individual interruptions (breaks) can apply for employees, the employee utilizations are assigned individual interruptions.

A direct relationship to machine utilization can be necessary for calculating incentive pay, e.g., in order to enter differentiated work results. It is possible to identify the involvement of an employee in a machine utilization by using time tracking—but data relating to employee **and** machine utilization cannot be entered. Thus, the relationship type EMPLOYEE MACHINE UTILIZATION is introduced.

An employee can be involved in several utilizations, and vice versa. This relationship provides the data for differentiated incentive pay.

The materials necessary for an operation are identified by tracking the bill of materials structure using the PNO contained in the operation key. Since a machine sequence represents a closed process, the NC program is assigned to it.

The interrelationships shown in Figure B.I.170 refer to machine utilization times. Materials-oriented sequences lead to the data structure in Figure B.I.172.

The term "materials sequence" designates a specific material, e.g., a metal sheet, to which the different (sub)operations are assigned as a

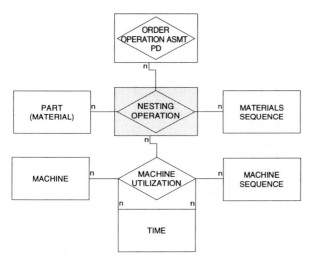

Fig. B.I.172: Materials-oriented sequencing

nesting operation. This nesting operation is then redistributed to a machine as a machine utilization time. Thus, additional, new sequences can be formed from the perspective of the machine.

Because of the relatively complex nature of these interrelationships, the machine utilization times for the examples in Figures B.I.169 and B.I.173 are shown in a table together with the key attribute instances.

Detailed scheduling results in detailed sequence plans for operations and utilization and assignment plans for resources.

The release of sequences for execution initiates a status change in the corresponding objects.

Resource availability requirements can be checked in detail on the basis of the data structure developed here.

Upon release, all resources are locked in, i.e., the processed assignments receive the status "reserved" or "in process."

Order operation assignment PD [1]							Machine	Sequence	Time		Machine utilization	
PLDPNO	PNO	ODATE	RNO	WOST GRNO	OPNO	Total quantity	WOST NO	SEQNO	from	to	Quantity	Remarks
1	O1	10/01	536	MG 4	Milling	40	M1	S1	08.10	08.40	30	Accelerating Splitting
1	O2	11/01	763	MG 4	Milling	50	M1	S1	08.40	09.45	50	
1	O2	11/01	763	MG 4	Milling	50	M1	S1	10.05	10.30	50	
1	O1	10/01	536	MG 4	Milling	40	M1	S2	10.30	10.50	10	Accelerating
1	O3	10/07	542	MG 4	Milling	40	M1	S2	10.50	11.30	40	

Fig. B.I.173: Example of machine utilization times at entity level

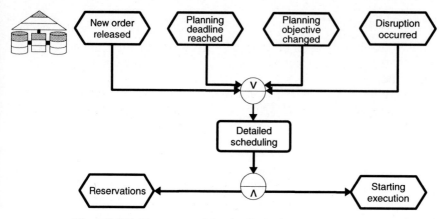

Fig. B.I.174: Event control for detailed scheduling

Figure B.I.174 summarizes rough event control for detailed scheduling. A more detailed analysis can be found in *Dangelmeyer, Ereignis-orientierte Fertigungssteuerung 1992; Klein, Datenintegrität in heterogenen Informationssystemen 1992.*

The more important the influencing factors on the detailed scheduling level when restructuring operations into sequences, the less important order formation during requirements and capacity planning becomes for production control. The more important the optimization options are on the control level, the larger the existing released order must be in order to incorporate as many alternatives as possible.

Thus, it becomes increasingly difficult to synchronize the planning and control levels.

For example, cost objectives are defined within the framework of preliminary costing and forecasting that are oriented toward order formation for requirements and capacity planning. If quantities are recombined on the control level to accommodate cutting optimization, data relating to material cutting enter the system for this unit, and it becomes difficult to sensibly cost it to the original orders within the framework of continuous costing.

Likewise, standard times are formulated from routing information to calculate incentive pay. These times lead to individual orders with individual percentage values for setup time. Forming operation-oriented sequences, however, results in collective setup times for the sequence, which in turn are difficult to compare to the specified values.

A further problem involves introducing flexible working hours, since personnel assignments to equipment and operations cannot be preplanned in any fixed way.

B.I.5.2.2.3 Leitstand Organization

Detailed scheduling is subject to significant stochastic parameters, such as machine downtime, material interruptions, tool failure, planning changes and customer order changes. For this reason, a form of decentralized production control is presented that occurs on the plant department level. In contrast to earlier PPC system concepts and many simultaneous planning approaches in business administration, this approach emphasizes an organizational separation between the planning and control levels. By segmenting the order pool among different plant departments, the control situation within a department is simplified with respect to the overall problem. At the same time, more differentiated degrees of latitude, such as different routings, different sequences within a routing, and alternative machines, can be employed than is possible under a centralized approach. The many degrees of latitude and the stochastic parameters make a closed algorithmic solution difficult. Many business administration modeling approaches, therefore, are more explanatory in nature rather than examples of practical implementations. Heuristic control principles are less precise, but they are more feasible if they are embedded in corresponding DP solutions because the data situation can be kept more current, and they can react more quickly to disruptions.

The electronic leitstands developed in recent years conform to this concept. They are an independent conceptual development designed to support detailed scheduling and are linked to the order release function in a PPC system. The released orders, with their earliest start and latest finish dates, serve as the point of departure. During order release, the order can be assigned operations with their earliest start and latest finish dates, depending on the degree of decentralization. The organizational form proposed here, in which individual routings are maintained on the plant level, does not require this step since the operations are assigned by the detailed scheduling function.

A leitstand imports the order data as "cornerstone" values, autonomously assigns operations to resources, and schedules them within the specified time period. The exact or heuristic algorithms used in this process support the planner, but do not replace him. The electronic leitstand must employ a highly graphical user interface to provide the planner with a fast overview of the control situation so that he can intervene if disruptions occur. This combination of data currency and algorithmic support on the one hand and human knowledge, experience and ability on the other is the advantage of the leitstand organizational structure.

In line with the organizational model developed here, a two-tier leitstand organization is meaningful (see Figure B.I.175).

On the plant level, the orders are imported from the order release function of a PPC system. The plant level handles the leitstand coordination functions, which means that it distributes the orders among the individual plant departments and coordinates the individual leitstands

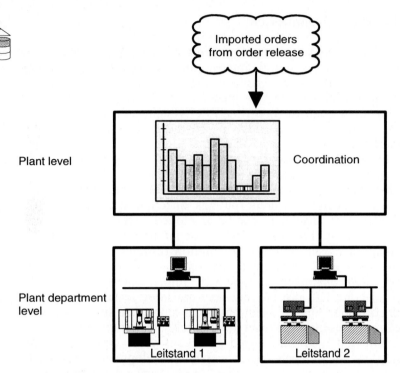

Fig. B.I.175: Two-tier leitstand organization

set up for each plant department. Coordination also encompasses determining the effects that disruptions in one leitstand department will have on other leitstands or analyzing the overall order throughput affecting several leitstand departments. In complex production structures, it is possible for a leitstand organizational structure to consist of more than two tiers.

Figure B.I.176 shows the graphical interface for a leitstand. Its basic design is standard in today's software systems. The individual workstations are represented as rows in the top portion of the screen. Production order operations are scheduled in these rows across a timeline according to Gantt charts. The lower portion shows the orders assigned to the plant departments together with their operations. The orders are allocated to the workstations algorithmically or manually. At the same time, the scheduling table is continually updated via interconnected feedback systems.

The float time between the latest finish date and earliest start date for an order provides the leitstand with individual planning capabilities. As long as these dates are not violated, the leitstand can function autonomously, i.e., without synchronizing with the planning level. Figure B.I.177 shows how the order float times imported from the planning level are assigned to the individual operations as supplemental times to compensate for

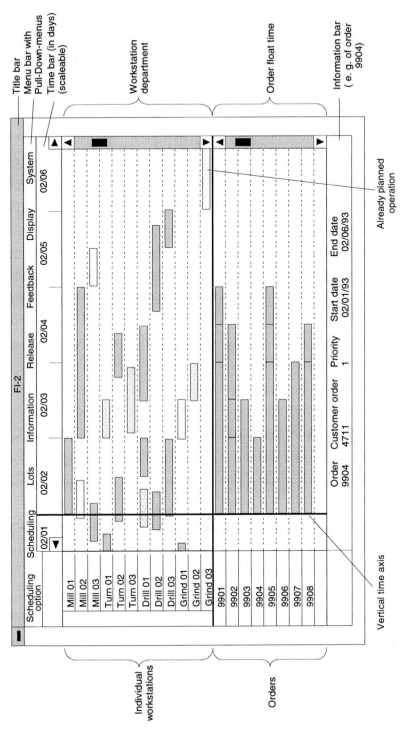

Fig. B.I.176: Graphical scheduling board of a Leitstand system
(Source IDS, *Der Fertigungsleitstand FI-2 1991*)

unforeseeable disruptions within the framework of detailed scheduling. The implementation stage identifies the actual start and finish dates for the operations and can initiate replanning of the outstanding operations. For this reason, the lower portion indicates the actual process; it is assumed that the allocated float times did not have to be used, so that overall throughput could be accelerated.

For a more in-depth discussion of leitstand design, see *Kruppke, Problematik bei der organisatorischen und technischen Integration von Fertigungsleitständen in die Unternehmenspraxis 1991, pp. 269 - 291; Herterich, Objektorientierte Leitstandsmodellierung 1993; Strack, Elektronische Leitstände - Ein Thema für den Mittelstand? 1989; Kurbel, Engpaßorientierte Auftragsterminierung und Kapazitätsdisposition 1989; Haas, Schlanke Fertigungs- und Kapazitätsdisposition 1993* as well as the appropriate user manuals for actual leitstand systems, e.g., *IDS, Der Fertigungsleitstand FI-2 1991; mbp, Factory Tower - Funktionen und Nutzen 1992; SAP, DASS, Der Leitstand im SAP System 1992.*

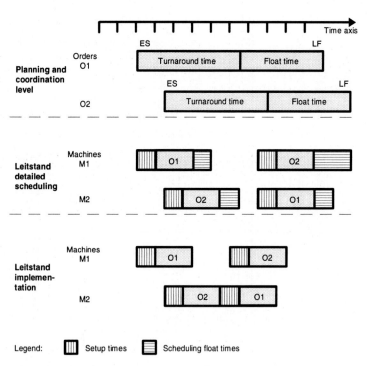

Fig. B.I.177: Utilization of scheduling float times within the Leitstand organization

B.I.5.2.2.4 A Simple Algorithm for Detailed Scheduling

A simple algorithm is introduced to demonstrate the basic algorithmic procedure for detailed scheduling. The related literature provides an overview of algorithms and complex priority rules (see *Glaser, Verfahren zur Fertigungssteuerung in alternativen PPS-Systemen 1991; Schmidt, CAM: Algorithmen und Decision Support 1989; Blazewicz/Ecker/Schmidt/ Weglarz, Scheduling in Computer and Manufacturing Systems 1993*). The algorithm presupposes the assignment of routings and operation sequences within a routing, as discussed in Section B.I.5.2.2.1.

The structogram in Figure B.I.178 shows a rough outline of the detailed scheduling process. The results of capacity scheduling and order release

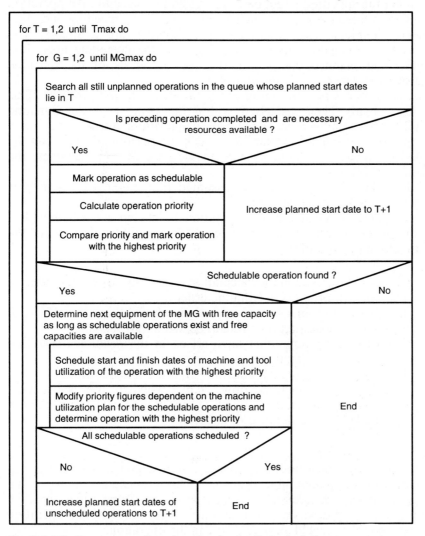

Fig. B.I.178: Structogram of an algorithm for detailed scheduling

are imported and **no** new sequences are formed through acceleration or splitting. The goal of this procedure is simply to distribute the queue from released operations in front of equipment groups, taking into account the permissibility of machines according to priority figures.

The period classification scheme introduced within the framework of order release constitutes the outermost loop of the algorithm. The algorithm begins with $T = 1$ and runs through the last period of the planning period, processing each equipment group. This loop clearly shows that the planning objects are the individual machines, i.e., the ultimate goal is optimum capacity utilization.

For each equipment group, the system first processes all operations in the queue whose planned start dates lie in period T. This procedure ensures that the specified target dates are taken into account. An operation determined in this manner is then checked to see if its preceding operation has been completed and the necessary resources are available. The criterion here is not the effective completion of the preceding operation, but rather the planned completion date on the basis of the machine utilization time generated by the algorithm.

Thus, the process is self-controlling with respect to job progress. This point has already been discussed within the context of the dynamic availability check and is represented here in algorithmic form.

An operation-oriented availability check is performed that can be extended to include components and, in the case of NC machines, the availability of NC programs.

For the sake of simplicity, it is assumed that employee capacity is already contained in machine capacity.

If the capacity is available, the operation is labeled as "schedulable." Next, the operation priority is calculated. This constitutes the core of the heuristic planning algorithm.

Typical factors involved in the calculation of priority figures include:
- The order priority taken from the order
- The processing time for the operation, which allows the effects of the shortest operation time rule to be taken into account
- Delays or float times that have arisen in the deadlines specified during capacity planning
- The extent of completed reductions in order transfer times
- Anticipated production flow; e.g., whether the subsequent operation is to be performed at an equipment group that is overloaded or free in terms of capacity
- Setup times.

If setup times are determined by the operation sequence, an attempt can be made to design a favorable sequence. This procedure requires using corresponding keys to identify similar operations. Setup times must be split up into a fixed time and a variable time determined by the operation sequence, and then created as an attribute in the operation.

A priority figure can be compiled by evaluating and weighting these factors.

Certain factors (production flow, setup times) cannot be identified for all operations at the beginning of the control algorithm; instead, they result from the generation of the machine utilization plan. Consequently, the priorities must be adapted to each corresponding situation during the process.

After all operations in the queue have been processed, the system queries whether a schedulable operation has been found. If this is the case, all machines in the equipment group are processed as long as free capacities are available and schedulable operations exist.

The operation with the highest priority is planned and the machines and tools are scheduled. Afterwards, the priority figures that are contingent on the machine utilization plan are modified if they apply to operations that can be scheduled, but have not yet been taken into account. The operation with the highest priority figure is determined and then scheduled in the next step if machines are free, etc.

If, after this procedure is complete, an operation could not be scheduled, its target start date is increased by one period unit so that it can be reconsidered when the next subperiod is run.

Detailed scheduling results in representable utilization plans for each machine, tool and employee. These plans can then be stored in the previously developed data structure. These results constitute detailed specifications for the implementation phase, which makes the conclusion of detailed scheduling a convenient point for preparing job documents. If this is done during order release, specific deadlines cannot be assigned to the operations. Online management of job documents means that these "documents" are kept electronically, so that detailed scheduling need only update the results.

B.I.5.2.3 CAM in the Narrower Sense

"CAM in the narrower sense" is understood as the computer-supported execution level for the production process. It comprises the systems for computer-controlled machines, tool management, warehouse and materials handling control, quality assurance and maintenance. The systems will be described briefly and embedded within the context of detailed scheduling. The relevant literature on industrial engineering provides a more in-depth description.

B.I.5.2.3.1 NC Machines

An operator can control a machine himself, i.e., he can control workpiece and tool guidance and speed settings; however, this task is increasingly being handled by computers. The programs used in the process are termed "NC (numerical control) programs." An NC program contains the geometric data for tool movements as well as technical instructions for the feed rate, the spindle speed of the individual tool movements and information concerning tool changing, recommended coolants, etc. (see *Eversheim, Organisation in der Produktionstechnik 1989, Vol. 3, p. 58*). Thus, an NC program contains information about the operation to be performed, the machine to be used, the workpiece to be processed and the tool to be employed. Essentially, an NC program is a detailed description of an operation. Since the creation of routings is discussed in conjunction with the product development process, that section will also treat the creation of NC programs due to their close relationship with parts geometry and CAD systems. The close link between parts geometry and the conversion of geometrical information into tool travel data is an important field of integration in CIM and is termed "CAD/CAM coupling."

Process Planning is responsible for creating routings and NC programs. Thus far, the trend has been to categorize Process Planning as a centralized function on the product or plant level. In the case of particularly simple parts, however, a decentralized, machine-oriented form of programming—i.e., (work)shop-oriented programming, or WOP—is discussed (see *Eversheim, Organisation in der Produktionstechnik 1989, Vol. 3, p. 64* and *Bullinger/ Fähnrich/Erzberger, Werkstattorientierte Produktionsunterstützung 1990*).

Decentralization allows the system to react particularly quickly to rush orders.

Shop-oriented programming is being furthered by the trend toward more and more user-friendly graphical support at the machines, which even include the graphical components of a CAD system.

The machines controlled by NC programs are categorized as production, handling, and inspection machines.

Programming for handling devices and robots presents special problems, since "play-back" and "teach-in" programming are possible in addition to programming languages (see *Reitzle, Industrieroboter 1984*).

In **play-back programming**, a robot is moved by manually manipulating its tool holder or gripper. The movement that is performed is stored and converted into a robot control program, which can then be accessed as often as desired.

In **teach-in programming**, a movement is performed by activating switches and keys; this movement is also stored and can be accessed as needed.

In contrast to typical NC programming, the integration of sensor feedback and requests for sensor data constitutes a special feature (see *Spur/Krause, CAD-Technik 1984, pp. 580 ff.*). Robots possess sensory capabilities that allow them to analyze and react to workpiece properties.

Thus, a full range of capabilities can be implemented in robots, from logic functions to techniques involving artificial intelligence (expert systems).

Robot programs, too, can be generated automatically from geometry information about the workpiece to be produced and location data for the parts to be assembled.

NC machines served as the point of departure in the development of computer-supported production systems (see Figure B.I.179). Paper tapes were used to load programs into the production machines (e.g., lathes, milling and drilling machines). The control function itself was hard-wired, which means that control changes were extremely difficult to make. Moreover, the NC program could only be changed by loading a new paper tape.

Computerized numerical control (CNC) machines were developed to allow greater flexibility. CNC machines employ a machine tool equipped

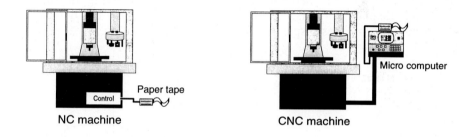

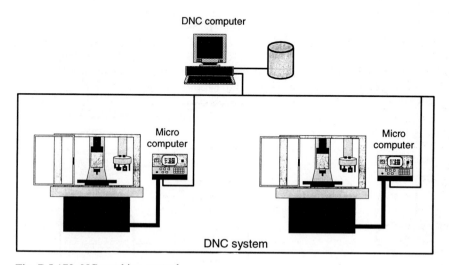

Fig. B.I.179: NC machine control

with a microcomputer that handles the task of numerical control. Programs can be loaded or modified directly at the machine or, as with NC machines, loaded using paper tapes and then kept in storage for processing.

A direct numerical control (DNC) system links several NC or CNC machines to one computer, which manages the control data, i.e., the NC programs (NC program libraries), and distributes them to the individual machines when they are needed. NC programming is also performed on this (central) computer.

In addition to production system control, a DNC computer can also be used for analysis and data entry functions (e.g., for machine statistics). This aspect will be discussed in the section on factory data entry.

Since an NC program directly controls the execution of machine functions, it must be linked to the electronic controls built into the machine. Since these controls are machine-dependent, in that they are either developed by the manufacturer or consist of commercially available controls from various manufacturers, they possess differing instruction sets and display formats. If an NC program is to be developed independently of these specifications, it is first written in a general

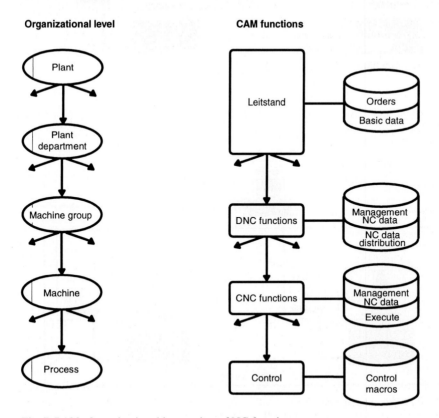

Fig. B.I.180: Organizational integration of NC functions

programming language and then automatically adapted to the existing control properties using postprocessors.

Figure B.I.180 assigns the different NC concepts to the units in the plant organizational chart.

Leitstand functions are located on the plant level for coordination and on the plant department level for production control. The DNC functions for NC program management and NC program distribution are performed on the machine group level. A CNC machine manages its NC programs and provides control functions on the process level.

In a "flat" organizational structure, the plant department and machine group levels can be viewed as one unit. The leitstand, however, remains logically superordinate to the DNC functions for planning purposes, since the loading functions for the NC programs are determined by the leitstand scheduling control function.

A distinction can also be made between different degrees of organization with respect to NC program development. The creation of NC data is closely linked with the organization of process planning and, from a central perspective, can be distributed among the product level, the plant level, the plant department level or even to shop-oriented programming on the CNC machine level.

The essential event for the transfer of an NC program from the DNC computer to the CNC machine is the release of an operation or an operation sequence. Several NC programs can also be released in the case of a sequence of similar operations that can be performed on several different workpieces (see Figure B.I.181).

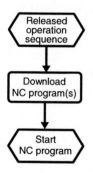

Fig. B.I.181: Transfer of an NC program

In the case of a materials-oriented sequence, the NC program cannot be developed until the nesting optimization step because the sequence determines the optimized geometric position of the part contours and thus the tool travel, e.g., of the milling cutter. This aspect reveals the close link between NC program generation and detailed scheduling.

With respect to the data structure in an NC program, relationships are created to the workpiece (especially its geometry), to the required tool, to the blank or raw material and to the machine tool used.

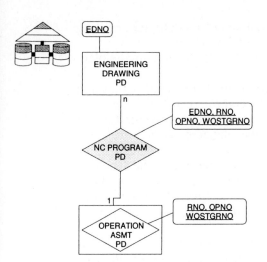

Fig. B.I.182: Data structure of the NC program management

In Figure B.I.182, NC PROGRAM forms a relationship type between the geometric object described by ENGINEERING DRAWING and OPERATION ASSIGNMENT. All additional assignments to the workpiece, tools and materials are entered via the links originating from OPERATION ASSIGNMENT. Since the NC program refers to the master operation assignment, it is also considered to be master data.

Typically an operation is completely described by an NC program, so that NC PROGRAM forms an n:1 relationship between ENGINEERING DRAWING and OPERATION ASSIGNMENT.

Several NC programs can exist for a drawing. They can either describe alternate production procedures or refer to several operations. If several operation sequences are combined in **one** NC program (e.g., for processing centers), the operation-related programs (extended to include tool-changing information) are bundled; however, this does not require a change in the data structure.

This data structure supports the identification of all NC programs for one equipment group, all NC programs that refer to a drawing, or the NC program necessary for a specific operation.

The availability check for an NC program checks the status entry in the NC program in order to determine whether the program has already been generated by Process Planning. As shown in Figure B.I.170, the NC program's link to the machine sequence establishes its link to the order-related data structure. If the NC program is changed in a way that affects the order, e.g., if several operations are bundled in a sequence and controlled by a closed NC sequence, the relationship type NC ASSIGNMENT becomes the repository for this information. Likewise, during material sequence formation, the NC modules are recalculated by indicating the positions specified by the nesting algorithm. Thus, the cardinality value that expresses the relation of the sequence to the relationship type NC ASSIGNMENT is set at n in order to combine several NC modules into a sequence-oriented NC program.

B.I.5.2.3.2 Toolmaking and Tooling Control

As manufacturing becomes increasingly automated, tooling and fixtures are taking on increasing significance. Fixtures hold and secure the material until it is processed at a machine. Tooling and fixtures, together with machines, are the means of production that, according to the German Association of Engineers (VDI), serve as "the means for achieving direct or indirect mechanical or chemical change in form, substance or fabrication status" (see *Eversheim, Organisation in der Produktionstechnik 1989, Vol.. 3, p. 38*).

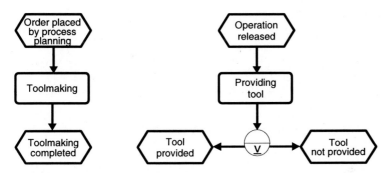

Fig. B.I.183: EPC for toolmaking and tooling control

Individual means of production also constitute specializations of the general entity type PART, whereby they function both as complex parts that exhibit bill of materials items and as simple tools that can be maintained as component parts. This definition of PRODUCTION MEAN and particularly of TOOLING/FIXTURES as subtypes of the entity type PART allows all of the attributes defined for PART to be inherited by further data structures and functions (see Figure B.I.184). In the case of standard means of production, i.e., standard tools and standard machines that are purchased on the open market, these elements include purchasing and storage functions. Many tools, however, are manufactured within an enterprise as special-purpose tools. Their purpose is to ensure the production know-how of the enterprise in terms of quality, cost effectiveness and process innovation. Industrial enterprises frequently establish their own tool- and die-making departments that can be organized as independent organizational units, i.e., as "factories within a factory." This is advisable because toolmaking can involve special working methods. Employees must be more highly qualified, which also requires special pay rates (hourly wage) in contrast to typical production.

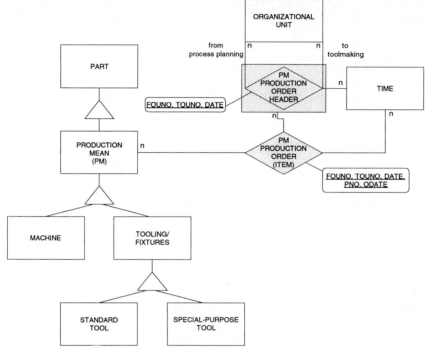

Fig. B.I.184: Data structure for the integration of toolmaking

Cost accounting also assumes special importance since tools are typically included in costing as special direct production costs. Figure B.I.185 shows an organizational chart for toolmaking, which can include individual departments for tool design and production, along with the subdepartments for production planning and manufacturing. There are no independent departments for payroll and cost accounting. Production orders for tools, fixtures and machines that are manufactured in-house also qualify the general entity type PART with the subtype entity. Consequently, the logical data structure shown in Figure B.I.184 constitutes a special instance of the general definition of a production order.

In the order header for the means of production, Process Planning is indicated as the customer and Tool- and Die-Making as the order receiver, and both are shown as organizational units. An order header is identified by customer, order receiver and date. The order items show the relationship to the requirements deadline and to the means of production to be manufactured under the order.

This definition of the means of production order allows all additional planning-related data structures and functions, as they have been discussed thus far, to continue to be used.

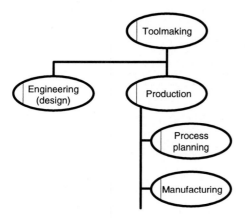

Fig. B.I.185: Organizational chart for toolmaking

B.I.5.2.3.3 Warehouse Control

Automated production processes also require an automated management and supply system for tooling, workpieces and materials. Automated warehousing systems are increasingly being employed to manage individual storage containers or bins as well as to control inventory additions and withdrawals (stock movement). In this connection, optimization routines are performed so that several stock-in and stock-out functions can be performed with the smallest possible number of movements.

Depending on the principles used, a distinction is made between different types of inventories, such as static or active inventories. A leitstand organization similar to the one used for production can be established where the inventory leitstand imports orders from the production leitstand and compiles them into (optimal) stock movements and routes them to warehouse control stations (see Figure B.I.186; see also *Pfohl, Logistiksysteme 1990, p. 141*).

Different strategies can be employed for assigning warehouse locations and for stock-in/stock-out functions (see Figure B.I.188). Figure B.I.189 provides an overview of warehouse control functions.

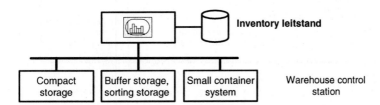

Fig. B.I.186: Inventory leitstand organization

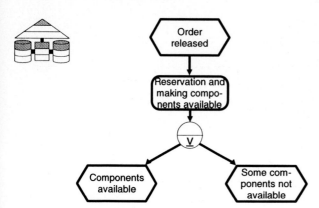

Fig. B.I.187: EPC for warehouse control

Strategy			Brief description	Advantages
Strategies for assigning stock locations	Fixed stock location assignment	Fixed stock location storage	Fixed stock location for each article	Access security in case of loosing full data file
	Random storage within fixed areas	Zoning	Distribution of storage units according to the transfer frequence	Increased transshipping service
		Cross distribution	Distribution of storage units on several aisles	Access security in case of transport device disruption
	Completely random storage	Chaotic storage	Distribution of storage units to random stock locations	Increased storage capacity utilization
Stock-in and stock-out strategies		Fifo	Stock-out transfer of storage units stored first	Avoidance of ageing
		Quantity leveling	Stock-out transfer of complete and opened storage units (adapted to order quantity)	Increased space utilization, less return transfers
		Transport-optimized stock-in and stock-out transfer	Stock-out transfer of storage units with the shortest route	Route minimization
		Lifo	Stock-out transfer of storage units stored last	Avoidance of stock transfers within existing warehouse techniques

Fig. B.I.188: Warehouse management strategies

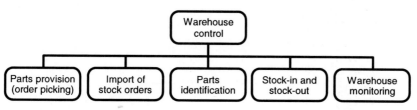

Fig. B.I.189: Warehouse control functions

In connection with the data structure for an inventory system, reference can be made to the data structure introduced in requirements planning: STORAGE AREA, STOCK LOCATION and INVENTORY LEVEL. The entity type STOCK LOCATION, however, must now be interpreted as a real bin or pallet.

Inventory quantities and requirement dates can be transferred from a (superordinate) production control system to a dedicated system. The dedicated system manages the orders and converts them into control instructions on the basis of optimization criteria. Consolidated data involving parts inventory levels, etc., are then returned from the dedicated subsystem to the superordinate PPC system or production leitstand. The use of dedicated systems is advisable because special computers (process control computers) are typically necessary for integrating warehouse control systems.

Figure B.I.190 shows the data structure for an inventory system for all part classes, such as workpieces, tools, end products and outsourced parts.

This figure is not concerned with whether the data relate to a general structure or to a decentralized inventory system. In the latter case, this information would merely have to be supplemented to include the inventory system, e.g., by indicating the key SNO (stock location number), in order to identify the data structure specialization.

When an order is released, reservations are made for the necessary components. These reservations contain as attributes the requirement date, component number and quantity. The entity type RELEASED PRODUCTION ORDER and the relationship type RESERVATION thus form the data interface between order release and the inventory system.

If reservations are reactivated during detailed scheduling on the operation level, the point of reference is the OPERATION ASSIGNMENT instead of the production order (see Figure B.I.170).

The entity types STOCK LOCATION and PART and the relationship type INVENTORY LEVEL are imported from the data structure for requirements planning.

RESERVATION serves as input information for the inventory system; this information is then transformed into concrete stock movements (withdrawal orders).

STOCK MOVEMENT is defined as an n:m relationship type between RESERVATION and the entity type TIME. RESERVATION is interpreted as an entity type and serves the function of an inventory

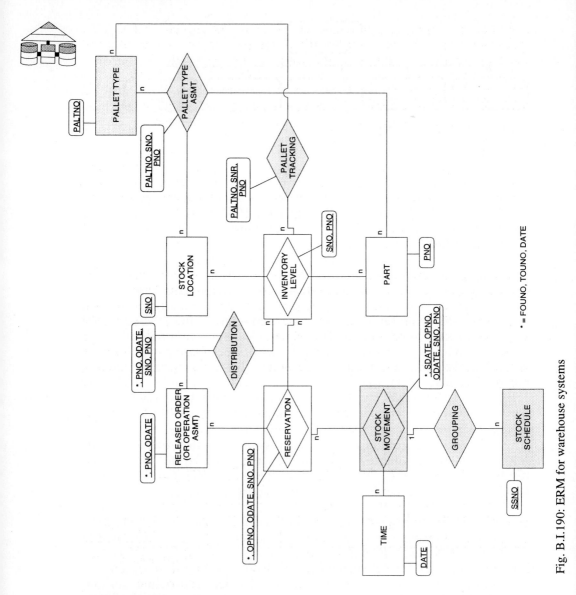

Fig. B.I.190: ERM for warehouse systems

requisition. Stock movements for a period (e.g., a shift) are grouped into a STOCK SCHEDULE. This process also specifies the sequence of the transactions and stores them as an attribute in the stock-movement entity.

Attributes that occur multiple times in a complex key are distinguished by identifying them with the first letter of the original entity type.

In addition to key attributes, a stock movement also contains the subquantity to be taken from a bin.

The entity type PALLET TYPE with the key PALTNO is introduced to manage different pallet types. The relationship type PALLET TYPE ASSIGNMENT is used to assign a specific pallet type to specific stock locations in which the pallet type can be stored and to the parts that can be stored on it. This discussion treats the general case in which several pallet types are stored in one stock location, one pallet type in several stock locations (and for several parts) and one part on several pallet types.

Continuous pallet tracking between INVENTORY LEVEL and PALLET TYPE is supported by the assignment relationship PALLET TRACKING. This relationship makes it possible to determine at any time which inventory (sub)quantities are stored on specific pallet types. If each **individual** pallet must be identified, the special entity type PALLET must be introduced with the corresponding degree of detail for the assignments.

The link type DISTRIBUTION is used to distribute the completed order quantities to different stock locations. As with the reservation assignment, this process initiates stock movements for storing order subquantities.

B.I.5.2.3.4 Materials Handling Control

The automation of materials transport systems is characterized by automated guided vehicle systems (AGVS), electronic suspension tracks and controllable gantries. Here, too, a leitstand organization can be established for coordinating and controlling the systems (see Figure B.I.191; see also *Pfohl, Logistiksysteme 1990, p. 141*).

AGVs can be guided via induction loops that define the materials handling routes. The control system requires positional data for vehicles, place of origin and destination, as well as quantitative data for identifying loads.

Figure B.I.192 shows a function overview for materials handling control.

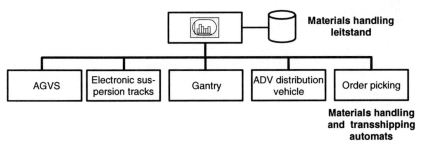

Fig. B.I.191: Materials handling leitstand

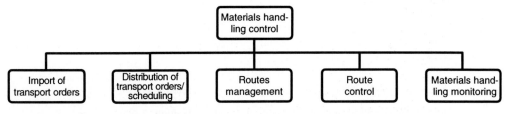

Fig. B.I.192: Materials handling functions

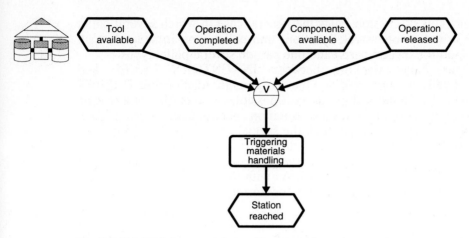

Fig. B.I.193: EPC for materials handling control

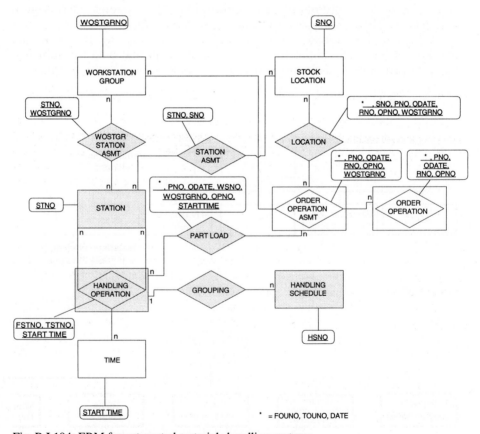

Fig. B.I.194: ERM for automated materials handling systems

Figure B.I.194 shows the data structure.

A general structure is again developed that does not distinguish between materials handling systems or units to be transported (workpieces, tools).

Stations are represented by the entity type STATION with the key attribute station number (STNO). The assignment of WORKSTATION GROUP to STATION forms the n:m relationship WORKSTATION ASSIGNMENT. This relationship can be defined in greater detail depending on the degree of automation (e.g., automatic loading and unloading). The destination station for the necessary workpieces, components and tools can be identified by tracking the OPERATION ASSIGNMENT.

If workpieces are stored in a (buffer) storage system after each operation, the storage location is also identified by the LOCATION relationship between ORDER OPERATION ASSIGNMENT and STOCK LOCATION. Since subquantities of an order operation can exist in different warehouses at different times during materials handling procedures, an n:m relationship exists for LOCATION.

Inventory additions and withdrawals can be initiated by the relationship LOCATION.

A HANDLING OPERATION is defined as an n:m relationship between the departure station and the destination station. Analogously to the bill of materials structure, this relationship is formed within the same entity type STATION. Moreover, HANDLING OPERATION is linked with the entity type TIME. Correspondingly, HANDLING OPERATION is identified by the key F(rom)STNO and T(o)STNO, as well as by the date START TIME.

If one handling operation encompasses several suboperations, an operation can be transported to several storage locations. This means that an n:m relationship for PART LOAD exists between HANDLING OPERATION, which is reinterpreted as an entity type, and ORDER OPERATION ASSIGNMENT. The most important attribute is the transported subquantity.

Several handling operations are grouped hierarchically into a HANDLING SCHEDULE.

If handling operations are initiated immediately after the completion of an operation, the materials handling system can be used as an automatic information signal for an FDE system, in that the initiation of a handling operation is used as a completion message for an operation.

The combination of automated materials handling and storage systems opens up new possibilities for production control. Since it is known that a significant percentage of order turnaround time involves materials handling and idle times, turnaround times can be reduced by streamlining internal logistics.

If the status of an order (operation) is always known, and an automated storage and materials handling system ensures that a specific order can be immediately identified, located, taken from or put into inventory, and transported, then flexible control procedures that react to short-term events can be employed.

The data structure developed here can be refined if handling operations are initiated on the sequence or machine utilization level.

B.I.5.2.3.5 Quality Assurance

Quality is a significant competitive factor and, in many industrial enterprises, is the most important cost element after personnel and material costs.

A large portion of these costs is used for testing and inspection, removing defective parts and rework. Recent Japanese initiatives have led to an increased demand for assuring quality through quality-oriented design and production rather than targeting quality after the fact through expensive inspection and rework procedures. This demand for quality requires tight integration between Quality Assurance and Production, as opposed to viewing them as separate departments. This approach prevents defective parts from being further processed.

Quality assurance measures are performed in all three logistics chains: in inbound logistics by assuring the quality of outsourced components, in outbound logistics by assuring the quality of the product that is delivered to the customer (final inspection), and in production logistics by assuring the quality of the individual production steps. In addition, the product development process—and because of cost concerns, Internal Accounting—are becoming increasingly involved in questions of quality. Because of the integrated nature of quality assurance, enterprise-wide quality philosophies are gaining increasing importance (e.g., Total Quality Management, Total Quality Control).

As defined by ISO, quality is "the totality of features and characteristics of a product or service that bear on its ability to satisfy stated or implied needs."

Quality can relate to processes as well as products. Thus, the concept of quality can apply to organizational procedures, for example. Control of production processes, i.e., the predictable behavior of certain process characteristics, is a prerequisite for quality. ISO 9000 through ISO 9004 provide guidelines for organizing an enterprise-wide quality assurance system.

Figure B.I.195 classifies quality assurance into the subfunctions of quality planning, quality inspection and quality control (see *Westkämper, Integrationspfad Qualität 1991, pp. 68 f.*). Quality planning, i.e., defining the relevant quality characteristics for a product together with their specifications, will be discussed within the context of the product development process chain. Quality inspection comprises planning activities, particularly those involving the creation and management of inspection plans as well as the inspection equipment to be employed. Inspection equipment can range from measuring devices to CNC systems. The actual performance of the quality inspection is controlled by inspection orders, which result in the determination of the actual characteristics.

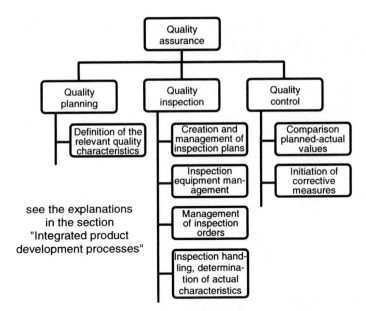

Fig. B.I.195: Function tree for quality assurance

Quality control determines the differences in characteristic instances between specified and actual values and then initiates corrective measures by reworking defective parts, adjusting machine settings and performing maintenance measures.

Computers can be used to support all three major quality assurance functions: this is then termed "computer-aided quality assurance" (CAQ).

A quality inspection is initiated either after completion of an operation that requires a subsequent quality inspection or by taking random samples within the framework of a random sampling schedule (see Figure B.I.196).

If the result of the inspection is unsatisfactory, rework of the defective parts as well as correction of the production process, e.g., machine settings, are initiated. The results of the quality inspection are forwarded to Production Control.

A leitstand organization is also advisable for quality assurance. The quality leitstand manages the inspection plans and inspection orders and initiates the inspection procedures to be performed.

In the past, quality control was frequently required to be totally independent. Consequently, separate organizational departments were created that sometimes exhibited extremely complicated organizational structures (see *Wiendahl, Analyse und Neuordnung der Fabrik 1991, p. 349*). Because of the cited need for tightly integrating quality assurance with the production process, there is a stronger link between planning and control activities and Production Control today. This means that quality leitstand tasks can also be handled by the general production control

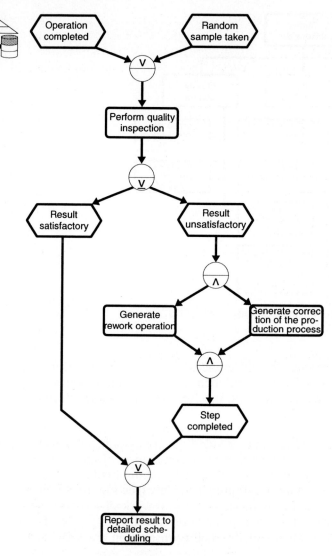

Fig. B.I.196: EPC for quality inspection

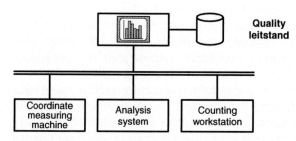

Fig. B.I.197: Quality leitstand

leitstand. The development of the data structure conforms to this close link between quality inspection and production order control. The sample inspection plan shown in Figure B.I.198 provides the point of departure. It consists of a header segment and individual inspection operations, each of which refers to a characteristic.

Inspection plan	Sheet: ....

Object: .... Draw. No.: ....
Processing status: ....
Function: .... Employee: ....
Lot size: ....units Date: ....

Inspection operation no.	Character-istics	Measure	Tolerance about	AQL	Fine tuning of inspection	Inspection: A=altr., B=var.	Amount of inspection	Sampling inspection plan	Inspection equipment no.	Inspection location	Tester/wage bracket	Materials handling: S=Supply G=Go, F=Fetch	Inspection time T [min]	Costs of inspection C [DM]	Inspection instruction	Distribution list for inspection results

Fig. B.I.198: Example of an inspection plan
(according to *Westkämper, Integrationspfad Qualität 1991, p. 99*)

Figure B.I.199 shows a frequently cited relationship between a production routing and an inspection plan. Operations that characterize the inspection plan are incorporated into the routing. Thus, for example, inspection times can be taken into account during detailed scheduling of the operation sequences. From the standpoint of quality assurance, this kind of inspection procedure included in a production routing is assigned to an inspection plan, which can contain several individual inspection procedures.

This data logic is implemented in Figure B.I.200. As with production procedures, standard procedures can be defined for the inspection procedures and can be assigned to different inspection plans. A relationship is created from an inspection procedure to the inspection equipment, which, for example, can be an analytical device or a measuring workstation. An inspection plan is assigned to an operation, whereby an inspection plan can also be used for several different operations.

The data structure shows the parallelism between the representation of inspection plan logic and production schedule logic. This parallelism

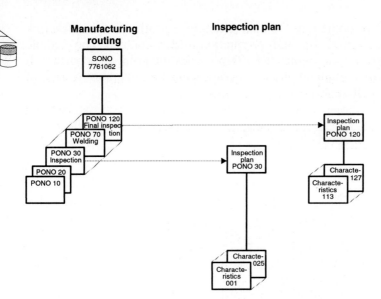

Fig. B.I.199: Relationship between routing and inspection plan
            (according to *Westkämper, Integrationspfad Qualität 1991, p. 113*)

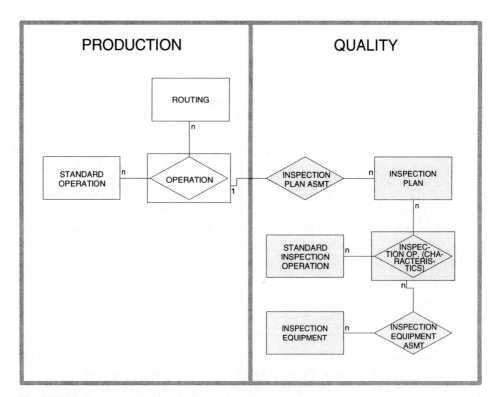

Fig. B.I.200: Data structure for the inspection plan integration

would continue if relationships to additional resources such as employees and NC programs (e.g., for a CNC coordinate inspection machine) were included in the representation. At the same time, redundancies are revealed because the application of an inspection procedure has already been shown as an operation within the production routings.

Figure B.I.201 shows a non-redundant data structure that also exhibits the desired tight link between Quality Assurance and Production.

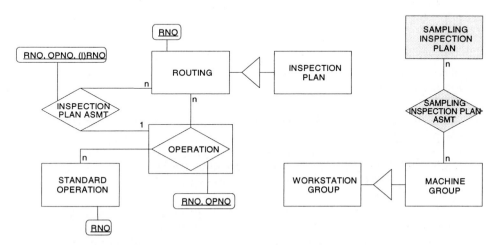

Fig. B.I.201: Integrated data structure of production and quality control

In the example, INSPECTION PLAN is depicted as a specialization of the entity type ROUTING. If a quality inspection is performed after a production operation, the production routing references an inspection plan. This relationship is created via the INSPECTION PLAN ASSIGNMENT. The routing number is preceded by "I" to identify the inspection plan.

The inspection equipment is also contained as specializations in the entity type WORKSTATION. The same holds true for the tools, NC programs and employees that are needed at the inspection equipment. Thus, the data structure shown in Figure B.I.201 makes available all the information created for production basic data management as well as the data structures created for order-related planning. It should be noted, however, that additional attributes that are not necessary for production planning must be maintained for inspection plans.

Because the data structure was embedded in the general data structure, the availability checks did not specifically refer to the availability of particular inspection equipment, since it is contained in the general workstation availability check.

If the individual parts within an order are not subject to a quality inspection, but are monitored instead by the production process itself, this is termed "statistical process control" (SPC). This procedure tracks when specific characteristics fluctuate beyond an acceptable average value, resulting in a systematic process change. The quality control chart provides the typical instrument for monitoring processes. Since the process relates to a specific machine or machine group, it is assigned random sample schedules for statistical process control, according to which the corresponding parts can be inspected. Inspection plans are developed for the inspection itself; these plans are treated in the same manner as above.

B.I.5.2.3.6 Maintenance

Because of the increasing degree of automation in industry, a high percentage of the employees who work in production perform maintenance activities.

Inspections determine the current status, **preventive maintenance** maintains the target status, and **repair** (corrective maintenance) reestablishes the target status. Inspections and preventive maintenance are conducted according to a fixed schedule and involve checking and servicing a machine or a group of machines in order to avoid the need for subsequent repair.

Within the scope of operations research, preventive maintenance policy models have been developed for optimizing preventive maintenance intervals, the size of the maintenance group and combinations of preventative maintenance procedures (see *Bussmann/Mertens, Instandhaltungsplanung 1968; Kistner, Betriebsstörungen 1978; Männel, Anlagenerhaltung 1968; Ordelheide, Instandhaltungsplanung 1973; Scheer, Instandhaltungspolitik 1974*).

Other events that initiate maintenance activities include machine failures as well as QA notices concerning defective production or statistical process control values that are exceeding the control limits. Maintenance measures result in either the release of the machine or in protracted downtime (see Figure B.I.202).

Figure B.I.203 shows the maintenance function tree.

Maintenance exhibits similarities to tool management and quality assurance, i.e., it conforms significantly to the general production functions in an industrial enterprise. Thus, maintenance, like QA, can also be viewed as a "factory within a factory." A specific maintenance function involves planning preventive maintenance measures, which exhibits similarities to inspection procedure planning within the context of quality assurance.

An independent organizational unit can be formed for maintenance; however, as with QA, there is a trend toward integrating maintenance and production. For this reason, a leitstand structure is suitable here as well, as shown in Figure B.I.204. In addition to independent organizational leitstand control, a tightly integrated solution allows individual functions to be shifted to the appropriate "neighboring" leitstands for production and inventory.

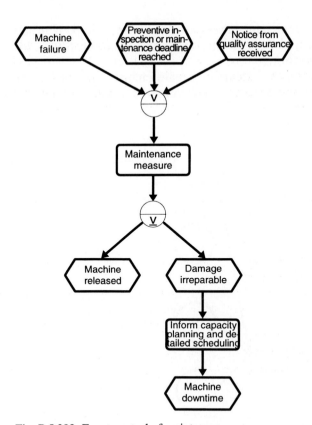

Fig. B.I.202: Event control of maintenance

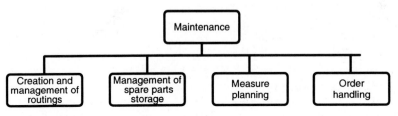

Fig. B.I.203: Function tree for maintenance

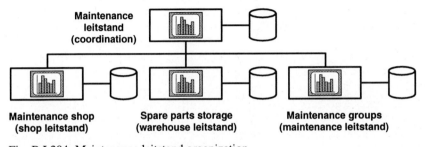

Fig. B.I.204: Maintenance leitstand organization

Planned or unplanned maintenance measures lead to machine downtime. These interruptions have already been discussed in connection with detailed production scheduling.

In the case of frequently occurring maintenance measures, the customary production setup procedures are employed, e.g., routings are created.

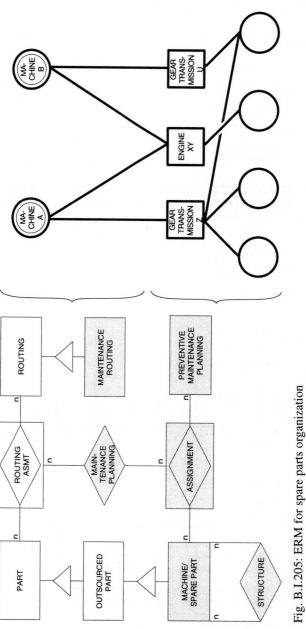

Fig. B.I.205: ERM for spare parts organization

Spare parts are frequently ordered along with the system when it is purchased. The assignment of spare parts to the pertinent machines is treated as a bill of materials structure, as shown in the right side of Figure B.I.205. Instead of describing the entire machine, only the spare parts provided for the machine or those that are deemed important are illustrated. Vendors are increasingly providing these data in electronic form.

A machine is viewed as a specialization of the general entity type PART, whereby the entity type MACHINE is a further specialization of the part class OUTSOURCED PART. Thus, all of the procedures and data structures used within the framework of inbound logistics are available for procurement activities. Preventive maintenance plans are maintained in the entity type MAINTENANCE PLANNING. The specializations of the general entity type ROUTING, which are maintained as maintenance routings, are also available via the relationship to the entity type PART. The maintenance routings to be employed within the framework of a specific preventive maintenance procedure can be categorized more precisely by linking maintenance planning with ROUTING ASSIGN-MENT.

A maintenance order is sent to the maintenance department in the form of an order from an internal organizational unit, e.g., Quality Assurance or Production (see Figure B.I.206).

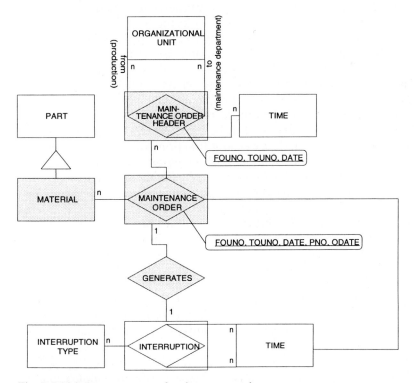

Fig. B.I.206: Data structure of maintenance order

Individual items that contain concrete maintenance measures for specific machines or machine parts can be assigned to this order header.

Thus, the maintenance order is identical to the production order in terms of structure, and all production planning and control measures can be employed.

A maintenance order uses operation assignments to plan the resources to be used for maintenance in the form of maintenance workstations, tools, employees and machines.

At the same time, it blocks the machine undergoing maintenance. Thus, a maintenance measure is a type of interruption, and a maintenance order generates an INTERRUPTION.

Since certain spare parts can be used for different superordinate components or machines, an n:m relationship exists within the entity type MACHINE PART.

Analogously to bill of materials management, utilization lists for specific spare parts can be generated for tracking this data structure, e.g., in order to identify spare parts that are no longer required.

B.I.5.2.4 Factory Data Entry

Time-critical processing functions for both detailed scheduling as well as for CAM systems require up-to-date information about the current situation. For this reason, factory data entry (FDE) was recognized early on as a basis for up-to-date detailed scheduling. But since machine-related data (run times, downtimes) are of interest as well as order-related data, a second data group is identified by the term "machine data entry" (MDE). Time-critical control of other CAM subsystems such as inventory, quality, etc., also require up-to-date feedback regarding the current situation. Today, FDE is therefore understood to be the collection and recording of factory data along with related processing functions for correcting, editing and transferring data (see *Kraemer/Wiechmann, Die Betriebsdatenerfassung als integraler Bestandteil der Fertigungssteuerung und Kostenrechnung 1991*, and *Roschmann, Betriebsdatenerfassung im CIM-Konzept 1990, p. 168*). If target data are provided for the plausibility check of the current data, factory data entry functions are broadened, so that it is more meaningful to speak of "factory data processing." In many practical situations, factory data entry systems have been used without DP support for corresponding functional planning systems. In these cases, FDE systems serve primarily to increase the transparency of operations, but they are unable to respond adequately. With the introduction of DP-supported systems for detailed scheduling and CAM, data entry functions are also largely being handled by these subsystems. Thus, factory data entry involves the use of **special** FDE systems to support the kind of data entry functions that are not yet being performed by corresponding DP-supported subsystems. It also includes the definition of comprehensive

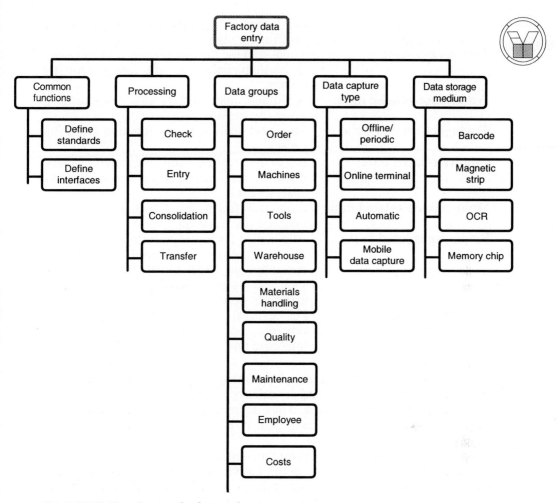

Fig. B.I.207: Function tree for factory data entry

standards for entering different types of data in order to be able to combine them into comprehensive factory information, as well as the definitions for interfaces between the individual subsystems.

Figure B.I.207 shows the function tree for factory data entry regardless of whether it is handled by special FDE systems or by CAM subsystems.

There are several other typical data entry characteristics involving the data groups:

Order-related data: Start and finish of a machine utilization, an operation, quantity produced, idle times.

Machine-related data: Run times, production quantities, downtimes, malfunction times (by duration and cause), waiting times (by causes such

	as disruptions in the materials flow or insufficient manpower).
Tool-related data:	Times and location of use, current additions and withdrawals, tool life, tool failure (by cause).
Warehouse-related data:	Additions and withdrawals, malfunction times (by cause).
Transport-related data:	Transport operations, malfunction times (by cause).
Quality-related data:	Inspection values and measured values, error codes, reasons for scrap, quality analysis data.
Maintenance-related data:	Start and finish for maintenance orders, maintenance duration.
Employee-related data:	Attendance (in, out), performance (quantity and quality produced, materials consumption), types of activities performed such as setup activities, maintenance activities, processing times.
Cost-related data:	Per general data entry operation: cost category, cost center, cost objective, reference unit.

Some data overlap with other departments, e.g., in the case of order-related data that are also used to calculate incentive pay and thus also serve as employee-related data. Thus, factory data entry must ensure that data is entered only once and that it is entered on the basis of a coordinated definition.

As a general rule, factory data that are entered in the system are not only necessary for control purposes in the individual subsystems but also form an "infrastructure" for every time-critical overall control function in the enterprise. This means that data entered in one department also provide the basis for control functions in another department, e.g., machine run times provide critical information for preventive maintenance.

FDE capture devices can be used on different levels (see Figure B.I.208).

Plant-related data capture is typically performed by a central plant office where feedback , some of it in paper form, is collected and entered.

Through online terminal entry, production leitstand functions and the functions of other CAM leitstands can be utilized for data capture on the plant level.

Data capture on the machine group level can employ special FDE terminals that route the consolidated data to the plant department (leitstand) either directly or via concentrators. Special FDE terminals are more rugged and can therefore be used directly in the plant department.

FDE terminals can be used for data capture on the machine level or data can be imported automatically from the microcomputers in a CNC system. Machines that move or that move the worker (forklifts) can employ

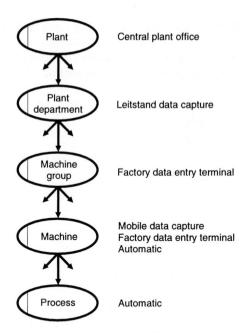

Central plant office

Leitstand data capture

Factory data entry terminal

Mobile data capture
Factory data entry terminal
Automatic

Automatic

Fig. B.I.208: Level model of capture types

mobile data capture systems that use infrared systems to transmit data to central collection nodes.

Data capture on the process level involves transferring data concerning rotation speed, temperature, humidity, etc., directly via sensors and transducers.

Determining the data storage medium to be used to identify an operation for data capture purposes is a significant decision and should apply for the broadest possible range of applications; for instance, assigning the order to the appropriate operation in the case of machine utilization or identifying the part number with the requesting or supplying operation in the case of a stock-in or stock-out operation. Proper identification of an operation is vital for assigning the captured data. For this reason, the FDE system must automatically capture data with the highest possible identification potential on data storage media. Barcoded labels affixed to the workpieces have proved especially effective in this regard. New media include electronic programmable memory chips, in which order data feedback can be performed automatically.

In order to reduce data capture effort as much as possible in non-automated systems, "milestone feedback" can also be used; under this concept, preceding operations are automatically updated on the basis of logical principles. An example of this is the feedback of information concerning the completion of the last operation for an order, which also marks all preceding operations for the order as completed.

In the EPC shown in Figure B.I.209, the initiating events include reaching a periodic data capture deadline, e.g., an hour before the end of a shift or a specific day of the week, an automatic message from a subsystem or receipt of a document (time ticket or material requisition).

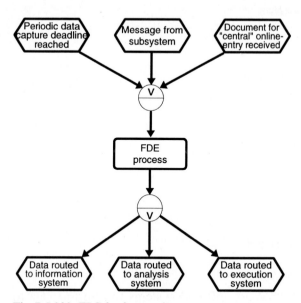

Fig. B.I.209: EPC for factory data entry

The data capture process reviews, adjusts and consolidates the data, then routes information to the factory information system or to a special analysis system in the case of error analysis for an identified machine malfunction or, finally, to other subsystems in order to initiate production or materials handling in those subsystems.

Reference can be made to the data structures previously introduced for detailed production planning as well as for CAM systems with respect to the data structure. The current data feedbacks from the FDE system are always attributes for the information objects contained in the FDE system.

Machine malfunctions are captured by using the term INTERRUPTION. The different types of machine malfunctions are specializations of the entity type INTERRUPTION TYPE (see Figure B.I.210).

Employee-related data refer to the results of an employee's work. These data are captured via the information object EMPLOYEE UTILIZATION, which is similar to a time ticket. A relationship between the entity types EMPLOYEE, EVENT TYPE and TIME is created for employee clock-in/clock-out functions. The clock-in/clock-out processes form different time entry types. Each employee clock-in/clock-out at a special time clock

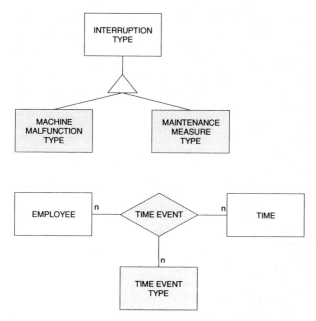

Fig. B.I.210: Extended data structure of factory data entry

system is such an event. This aspect will be discussed in greater detail in the section on personnel logistics.

Material additions and withdrawals can be posted in the part reservation information object introduced previously. All other data types are also captured in a similar manner in the information objects discussed previously.

It should again be noted, however, that a factory data entry system encompasses not only the gathering of data in the individual subsystems, but also can involve processing this data to form a comprehensive, integrated information system of the type characterized by the "glass factory" concept. Another concept that has developed in connection with factory data information systems is FIT—the Factory Integration Tool. In this information system, all current and target values for analysis and control measures are available in transparent form.

B.I.5.2.5 Production Information System - Production Monitoring - Production Controlling

The systems that have been developed for production support are intended not only for planning and control, but also for ongoing enhancement of system performance, i.e., improvement of data, organizational operations, resource utilization and resource inventory. To this end, it is necessary to analyze the available target and current data.

These analyses should not only be made within the individual subsystems; the database must also be expanded into a comprehensive factory information system (see *Wiendahl/Birnkraut, Ganzheitliche Fabrikplanung als Bestandteil des rechnerintegrierten Industriebetriebes 1990, p. 531*). Many production support systems currently on the market are still geared toward operative processing and provide too little analysis and information support. At the least, though, reports are frequently generated from the databases, which is shown in Figure B.I.211 in the form of a rough overview (further information concerning analysis reports can be found in *Hackstein, PPS 1989; SAP, System RM-PPS Funktionsbeschreibung 1993, p. 162*).

Additional reports that are not directly related to these data groups but can be derived from them include period-oriented production statistics for tracking quantity- and quality-oriented data.

Concurrent, up-to-date costing for production orders is particularly important because current order-related machine utilization data from the FDE system are analyzed and totaled in cost objectives (see *Kraemer, Effizientes Kostenmanagement 1993*).

Although these types of reports can even provide for detailed comparisons of target and current data for up-to-date cost accounting, they do not automatically result in a corresponding qualitative analysis. Instead, a great deal of effort has to be expended to generate these reports, as well as the necessary data on which they are based on FDE systems; but

Production orders:	Order reports Control reports of order progress Lists of not yet processed orders
Workstations:	Utilization boards Failure analyses Maintenance analyses Run time reports
Tooling/fixtures:	Tool utilization reports Break analyses
Material/warehouse:	Inventory status reports Inventory movement reports
Quality:	Error statistics Scrap statistics
Employees:	Attendance and absence statistics Time-off analyses Reference time analyses

Fig. B.I.211: Report analyses

then they are hardly ever analyzed due to lack of time on the part of the employees involved in the process and the lack of support tools. For this reason, rule-based DP-supported analysis systems are employed for data analysis (see *Kraemer, Effizientes Kostenmanagement 1993*). On the time-critical level, these types of systems can be used for event-oriented control, e.g., by using an expert system to search for the cause of a machine malfunction or by utilizing the suggestions of an expert system to reschedule an order in the event of an interruption of operations. (see *Steinmann, Expertensysteme in der Fertigungssteuerung 1991*). In the following simple case, a typical rule for this kind of planning support expert system could be (see *Steinmann, Expertensysteme in der Fertigungssteuerung 1991, p. 382*):

IF	a machine is down
AND	it is Lathe 0012
AND	Lathe 0013 possesses free capacities
OR	Lathe 0014 possesses free capacities
OR	Lathe 0015 possesses free capacities
THEN	an alternate machine is available
END	

By continuously applying rules, the expert system can suggest an appropriate alternate machine or even automatically utilize it.

These types of scheduling support systems can be employed directly in the affected subsystems; however, they can also necessitate data from several subsystems so that the system must be designed around an integrated production database.

In addition to supporting event-related responses, support can also be provided for periodic analyses.

An analysis system always follows a symptom-cause-action chain. Symptoms can be negative target/actual deviations from specified production values or even costs. These variables can be entered as both target and actual data. Causes include categories that initiate corresponding deviations. Causes can be eliminated by corresponding operational measures. The interrelationships between symptoms and causes and between causes and corrective measures can be entered in the form of rules. The interrelationships can be either causal or simply empirical in nature. The cardinalities between the three variables are always type n. Figure B.I.212 shows a simple example of a rule-based analysis system.

The rules shown in the free form example illustrate that if manufacturing costs increase in an otherwise normal production situation, the assignment of incorrect wage rates can be a probable cause, which can be remedied by improving employee planning. If there is an increase in tool failure **and** materials usage **and** scrap **and** material costs in an otherwise normal production situation, this can be traced back to defective material; improved inspection of incoming materials can prevent defective materials from being processed. If order turnaround times **and** setup times

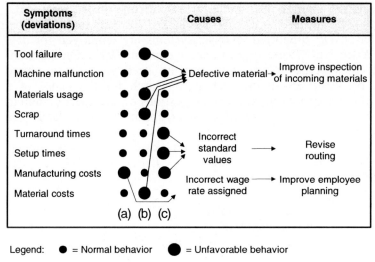

Legend: ● = Normal behavior   ⬤ = Unfavorable behavior

a, b, c = Deviating situations

Fig. B.I.212: Example of a rule-based analysis system

are too long **and** manufacturing costs are too high in an otherwise normal production situation, the cause may be incorrect standard values in the routing, which can be corrected by revising the routing.

Although setting up these types of rules does involve a great deal of effort, this effort should nevertheless be undertaken in order to be able to utilize the comprehensive and sophisticated data that are available from modern factory data entry systems to improve operations.

In this connection, a distinction must be made between a static analysis, as expressed by reference numbers of the type already discussed (for a comprehensive Production reference system, see *Hildebrand/Mertens, PPS Controlling 1992* and *Zell, Simulationsgestützte Fertigungssteuerung 1992*), and a dynamic analysis. Dynamic behavior can be mapped using simulation models. Production operations are simulated in advance on the basis of existing planning, or system behavior can be modeled on the basis of the current data that have been captured for a previous period. These types of simulation models can be used to evaluate alternative control strategies. Computer-supported animation can be employed to provide an especially illustrative simulation, in which the production processes can be depicted quasi-photorealistically (see *Zell, Simulationsgestützte Fertigungssteuerung 1992*). These types of systems are also used to optimize the layout of the factory floor (see Figure B.I.213).

An analysis of the chronological flow of production orders is especially important as well. Generally, comparisons focus on quantity rather than deadlines. For a smooth production flow, however, it can be more important to adhere to deadlines than to concentrate on production quantities.

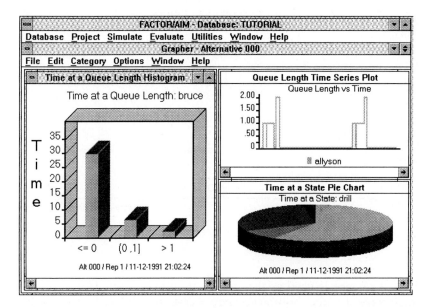

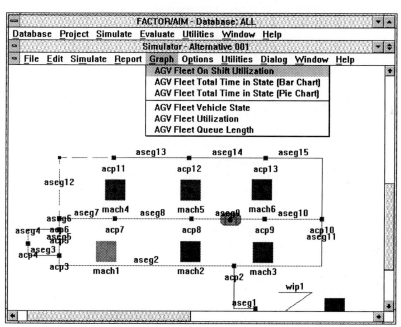

Fig. B.I.213: Animation example in FACTOR

Figure B.I.214 shows the "arrive" and "leave" characteristics of completed operations (orders) for a machine (see *Lorenz, Warteschlangen-modell 1984* and *Wiendahl/Birnkraut, Ganzheitliche Fabrikplanung als Bestandteil des rechnerintegrierten Industriebetriebes 1990, p. 531*).

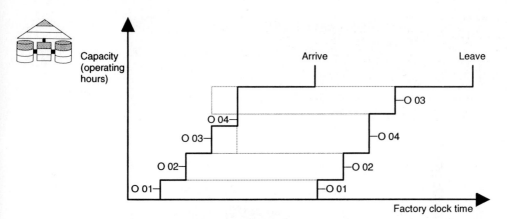

Fig. B.I.214: Arrival and leave characteristics of completed operations

The time of release is used as the arrival of an operation. These arrivals are characterized by the boldfaced step curve on the left side of the illustration; the completed operations are indicated by the step curve on the right. If the operations are performed according to the FIFO (First-In First-Out) principle, the individual orders must fit into the curves. If an order is overtaken by other orders, however, its processing will be delayed, i.e., it is shifted toward the top of the graph.

The illustration shows this clearly by indicating the order numbers in the "arrive" and "leave" curves.

Order O03 arrives before order O04, but is completed after it. Thus, it is moved toward the top as a result of its processing sequence. Typical information that can be extracted on the basis of this data analysis include:

-        Minimum, average and maximum turnaround time
-        Minimum, average and maximum processing time
-        Minimum, average and maximum waiting time.

Standard software systems are already offering this type of analysis for order control.

The analysis objects, period divisions and analysis profiles are geared toward user information requirements and thus significantly toward the user's planning level. Figure B.I.215 shows several typical analysis objects assigned to the tier model for production.

Leitstand systems are not only employed for production control, but also for production analysis. Figure F11 shows the planning table for the FI-2 system, which generates the control dates. Figures F12 through F14 show evaluations of these data.

Figure F12 shows production order behavior in the form of an order network. Each of the orders processed in a plant department is represented by a branch. This illustration clearly shows the branches that are processed

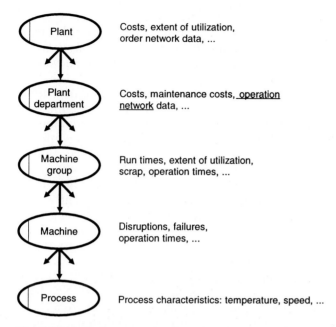

Fig. B.I.215: Assignment of analyses into the tier model

in parallel along with the assembly operations that combine them. While only those order operations that are performed in the plant department are analyzed in a plant department, the entire interrelationship of orders is of interest on the interdepartmental level, i.e., on the plant level, so that disruptions that occur in a plant department can be identified, for example, and tracked across the entire order network.

B.I.5.2.6 Summarizing and Supplementing the Requirements Definitions for Production

In the summary representation of DP systems for production support, the data, function and organizational structure interrelationships between the subsystems are further clarified. The integration requirements are primarily based on order flow, since the object **order** passes through all subsystems. It was these integrated relationships that also brought about the demand for computer integrated manufacturing (CIM). Consequently, Harrington also emphasized the integration of production-oriented DP systems in his 1973 book (see *Harrington, Computer Integrated*

Manufacturing 1973); it was only later that the term "CIM" was expanded to include the integration of all systems, from planning to business administration, in an industrial enterprise (see *Scheer, Schnittstellen zwischen betriebswirtschaftlicher und technischer Datenverarbeitung 1984*).

Due to order flow, the integration of CAM systems is extremely time-critical and thus requires a very close DP link. Implementing this integration, however, is particularly difficult, since the CAM components are intrinsically complex and are consequently offered by different specialized vendors. In order for heterogeneous systems to be able to intercommunicate in real time, it is necessary not only to physically network them, but also to use identical definitions of the terms. In order to ensure this, a transparent architecture is essential. Consequently, this section will present a design for a framework system for CAM integration under the ARIS concept. If all parties involved in implementing a CAM system adhere to this concept, conceptual and technical integration of even heterogeneous partners and systems is possible.

The "HP OpenCAM" concept, developed jointly by Hewlett Packard and the Institut für Wirtschaftsinformatik at the University of Saarland, conforms to this basic principle. In the HP OpenCAM concept, vendors of production control, FDE, QA, NC/DNC and process visualization systems are cooperating with the aim of creating an overall concept on the basis of the ARIS architecture (see *Hoffmann, HP OpenCAM 1993*).

B.I.5.2.6.1 Requirements Definition for Production: The Function View

The function tree shown in Figure B.I.153 has already provided an overview of CAM functions. Individual functions were subsequently substantially refined, particularly those from CAM in the narrower sense. The reasons for interactive processing in CAM systems, shown in Figure B.I.216, reveal the options available for automation. The less need there is for planners to intervene in the process, the greater the possibility for automatic processing. If interactive processing is suggested only for reasons of currency, this indicates that the human being is still acting as a data capture interface; in principle, though, it is possible to establish a direct data link with the sensors in the CAM execution system. Consequently, automation of these functions is also suggested.

The distinction between a time-period-oriented analysis according to the reoptimization principle and a case-oriented analysis according to the net change principle is considered during order release and detailed scheduling.

Order release is a typical period-oriented function that is performed according to the reoptimization principle.

During the analysis of individual orders (rush orders), on the other hand, case-oriented processing according to the net change principle is also meaningful, since the orders should be incorporated into the existing

Function	Subfunction	Reasons for interactive processing				Batch/automatic
		Currency	Plausibility	Iterative modification	Interactive decision process	
Order release	Inventory check R					X
	Availability check R NC		X			X X
	Release/reservation R NC				X	X X
	Order distribution R NC				X	X X
Detailed scheduling	Basic data management	X	X			
	Detailed scheduling R NC				X	X X
	Availability check R NC		X			X X
	Operation release/reservation R NC				X	X X
	Initiation/realization				X	X
CAM in the narrower sense	NC programs	X				X
	Tool management	X	X	X	X	X
	Warehouse control	X				X
	Materials handling	X				X
	Quality assurance	X	X			X
	Maintenance	X	X	X	X	X
Factory data entry	Entry	X	X			X
	Processing		X		X	
Data analysis		X				X

R = Reoptimization; NC = Net change

Fig. B.I.216: Reasons for interactive processing for CAM in the broader sense

planning environment without any significant changes. Interactive processing is meaningful if the availabilities must be obtained from different sources and planners have to check their plausibilities. The release of an order that does not formally satisfy all availability requirements is an interactive decision process. When orders are distributed among different plant departments, conflicts can arise that the planner can solve interactively.

The high degree of detail in the scheduling grid for detailed scheduling, as well as the multiplicity of interruption possibilities, require a high degree of currency. Only under net change processing is it possible for Production and Order Control to react to interruptions in real time. Of course, it is also meaningful to conduct an overall planning inventory at specific periodic intervals using the reoptimization principle. This holds true in particular for reoptimization processes for cutting and sequence optimization. The longer time frame provides more latitude.

The control rules that are being employed can be checked at specific intervals. Business administration literature has developed a number of priority rule techniques for detailed scheduling and analyzed their properties using simulation studies. Hoitsch provides a summary of these priorities, together with relevant bibliographical sources (*Hoitsch, Produktionswirtschaft 1993, p. 274*).

In line with the degree of currency required by detailed scheduling and the high degree of complexity involved in the planning situation, complicated optimization algorithms have thus far enjoyed only little success. Branch and bound algorithms frequently cannot be used for the orders of magnitude that occur in actual practice. Heuristic procedures based on priority rules also require long computation times. For this reason, analogously to the capacity adjustment procedure, a combination of human planning ability and rapid information acquisition using DP systems, as introduced in the leitstand concept, is proposed. This means that current process conditions and resource utilizations are displayed on-screen to the planner (supervisor, job distributor, job planner).

If changes are necessary, the planner can simulate different scheduling alternatives on the basis of the net change principle and allow the system to analyze the different target criteria. Depending on the objective—e.g., minimizing order turnaround times, maximizing equipment utilization, utilizing overall turnaround time for an order bundle, minimizing the capital that is tied up, minimizing changeover costs, etc.—the planner can select the alternative that he finds most appropriate.

Due to the high degree of complexity involved, however, it is virtually impossible for the planner to completely control the situation. For this reason, algorithmic decision support must also be incorporated into the process. Expert systems can also be advisable, since heuristic rules exist in practice that can be analyzed for use on a general scale (see *Krallmann/Huber, Constraint-basierte, heuristische Planung in der industriellen Produktion 1990*).

Behind the individual CAM components, such as tool management and maintenance, lie complex systems that assume the role of "factories within a factory." Consequently, only general assumptions can be made. NC program management can be performed interactively; in the case of an integrated DP solution, an automatic NC download can also be initiated during detailed scheduling. Tool management is a complex system that allows all options for interactive and automatic processing. For reasons of currency, interactive processing can be used for warehouse control, but it can also be performed completely automatically without planner intervention. This also applies to materials handling. Within the framework of quality assurance, analysis functions can be performed interactively, whereby both plausibility and currency concerns can come to bear. An automatic approach is also meaningful in the case of process inspection. As a result of its complex nature, the maintenance function is also suitable for all processing forms.

In the case of factory data entry, all data capture functions should be generated automatically from the CAM subsystems. The processing functions, e.g., consolidating and initiating reactions in the event of target/actual variances, require both plausibility checks and an interactive decision process.

Plausibility checks serve to reduce input errors during data entry. In particular, key attributes such as order number, routing number, operation number, workstation number, employee number, etc., should be imported from automatically generated data media.

On the one hand, data analysis can be viewed as an interactive, case-oriented, analysis function; algorithm-supported monitoring can also be run automatically, with the user simply being notified of outliers.

Overall, the relatively few Xs in the column for iterative modification and interactive decision process suggest that a large percentage of CAM functions can be performed without user intervention. On the other hand, however, many functions involving resource allocation, conflict resolution and time-oriented scheduling require the interactive intervention of a planner.

B.I.5.2.6.2 Requirements Definition for Production: The Organization View

The functional reference model for production organization has already been introduced in Figure B.I.151. The individual organizational units have been further refined and are shown in the upper portion of Figure B.I.217 (the cross-hatching is insignificant for the time being).

The function principle for organizational structuring corresponds to the operation principle on the production level in that production units are formed for similar operations, such as sawing, turning, milling and polishing (see the left side of Figure B.I.218).

This approach frequently presupposes a central production control department—i.e., one that is superordinate to the production departments—since the organization of the materials flow between the individual shops is specifically a matter for production control.

In the discussion of detailed scheduling, a decentralized, i.e., production-department-oriented, organization for detailed scheduling was introduced in the form of the leitstand concept. This concept is taking on increasing importance as a result of new computer-supported forms of production organization, which involve not only decentralization of detailed scheduling, but also decentralization—and thus integration—of all CAM components.

B.I.5.2.6.2.1 Computer-Supported Forms of Organization for Production Flexibility

New forms of organization have been developed by combining different computer-supported production systems. These new forms document the fact that the use of DP systems is having an impact deep within the organizational structure. On the other hand, the benefits of data processing will only come to bear if these systems are used creatively to develop new organizational structures. The objective of all systems is an increased level of functional integration.

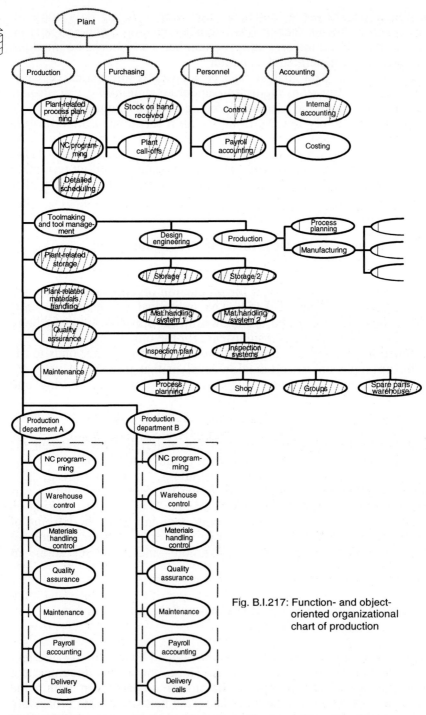

Fig. B.I.217: Function- and object-
oriented organizational
chart of production

Fig. B.I.217: Function- and object-oriented organizational chart of production

The following discussion will introduce several typical organizational forms (see *Hedrich et al., Flexibilität in der Fertigungstechnik 1983*).

Processing Centers

A processing center is a machine that is equipped with NC control and an automatic tool change capability and allows several operations to be performed in one setup run (i.e., in one uninterrupted process). The processing sequence of drilling and milling is a classic example of a processing center application (see *Hedrich et al., Flexibilität in der Fertigungstechnik 1983, p. 33*). Processing centers are employed in small- and medium-scale mass production and can even be economical in the case of small runs of highly complex workpieces. By combining several operations, turnaround times can be significantly reduced compared to a more specialized organizational form.

While a processing center is an individual automated machine that is not linked to other logistical functions, several systems will be interlinked to form more complex systems in the following organizational forms.

Flexible Manufacturing Cells

A flexible manufacturing cell consists of automated machines, a buffer storage system into which workpieces can be placed and from which they can be removed, as well as an automated loading and clamping station. Additional computer-supported functions can include tool failure control, tool wear measurement, variable tool location coding and automated tool life control.

Thus, a flexible manufacturing cell is a unit comprising several NC machine tools that automatically process similar workpieces over an extended period of time. If the supply and removal of workpieces is also automated, flexible manufacturing cells can function autonomously.

Flexible Manufacturing Systems

The flexible manufacturing system (FMS) constitutes a further refinement of flexible manufacturing cells. It consists of the processing system, the material flow system and the information flow system, which are all interlinked. Overall control is performed by a computer that handles workpiece and tool transfer and also supplies production systems with the appropriate control programs (NC programs).

The system owes its flexibility to the fact that different production tasks can be performed without significant changeover costs, since the changeover operations are largely integrated into the production process. The sequence of operations can also be designed flexibly, since materials handling is not bound to the sequence of machine operations. Since the FMS control computer supplies the processing stations with NC programs, the flexible manufacturing system is similar to a DNC system in terms of design. The individual processing stations, in turn, are typically CNC systems, but they can also consist of more extensive processing centers.

Flexible Transfer Lines

The organizational forms that have been developed more with a view to smaller production quantities have also influenced the technology of large-scale production processes, which are generally performed on transfer lines. The objective of a flexible transfer line is to provide quick system changeover and, thus, quick adaptation to changing production orders. At the same time, however, the general characteristics of a transfer line are maintained (adjustable materials flow and precise workpiece transfer within an optimum processing station layout). The flexibility of a transfer line relates to all of its components, i.e., materials handling control, material flow and individual processing stations.

The above-mentioned computer-supported production systems are frequently initially designed as experimental systems and, thus, as island solutions. It is evident, however, that they are increasingly being combined into larger units and consequently necessitate a fundamental decision on the part of the enterprise concerning which organizational forms to use for which range of parts and how the production systems should be interlinked. This decision requires careful layout planning. These factors suggest that the development of forms of production made possible by increased computerization are determining all components of a plant's layout through layout planning (location of production systems, materials flow and information flow) (see *Bullinger/Warnecke/Lentes, Factory of the Future 1985, p. IL*).

Production and Assembly Islands

This organizational form is based on the criterion that production and assembly islands can in effect completely manufacture or assemble assemblies and end products from given starting materials. The necessary equipment is determined on the basis of production flow. Although production and assembly islands can also be set up for manual processing forms (the reason being reduced turnaround times and increased employee motivation), there is a close link to the computer-supported organizational forms cited above. Thus, for example, a production island can be organized in the form of a flexible manufacturing system in that planning and concrete machine control functions, including materials transfer and storage, are performed by a control computer for a specified range of parts.

The most important criterion for a production island is that it be assigned all the resources necessary for production, as well as comprehensive planning and control functions. Figure B.I.218 shows the organizational differences between shop control and production island organization and, above all, illustrates the simplified flow of materials in the case of production islands.

Parts that lend themselves to island production or assembly can be selected on the basis of statistical similarity studies (cluster analysis).

Although the basic principle of the island concept dictates that islands must be as autonomous as possible, there can be relationships between the different islands in which different ranges of parts are manufactured.

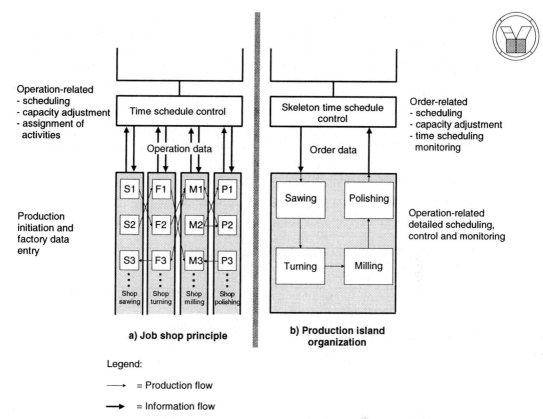

Operation-related
- scheduling
- capacity adjustment
- assignment of
  activities

Time schedule control

Skeleton time schedule control

Order-related
- scheduling
- capacity adjustment
- time scheduling
  monitoring

Operation data

Order data

Production
initiation and
factory data
entry

Operation-related
detailed scheduling,
control and monitoring

a) Job shop principle

**b) Production island
organization**

Legend:

⟶ = Production flow

➡ = Information flow

Fig. B.I.218: Differences between shop control and production island principle
(according to *Ruffing, Integrierte Auftragsabwicklung 1991, p. 67*)

Thus, parts can "leave" the island for individual operations in order to utilize expensive production systems that are installed in only <u>one</u> island. They are then processed further in the original island. In this case, the control system must be able to track the order network across several islands.

B.I.5.2.6.2.2 The Object-Oriented Organizational Model

The formation of organizational units that conform to the concept of production islands supports a holistic decentralized processing form. This form leads to a higher degree of employee motivation by ensuring more autonomy for planning and control and, at the same time, reducing overhead and coordination costs (see *Ruffing, Informations- und Kommunikationssysteme 1991*). Figure B.I.219 is based on *Wiendahl/Brinkraut, Ganzheitliche Fabrikplanung als Bestandteil des rechnerintegrierten Industriebetriebes 1990, p. 531* and shows the layout of a plant organized under the production island principle. In the production departments, the production machines and assembly devices are organized on the basis of the production flow. Order interrelationships can exist between the production islands, allowing an operation to be swapped out from one island to another and then processed further by the first island. An order can also be processed in sequence at several production islands.

The individual plant departments not only have the authority to perform detailed scheduling, but are also responsible for the NC and DNC programming, toolmaking and raw materials management that are necessary for the islands. In a JIT production environment, detailed calls

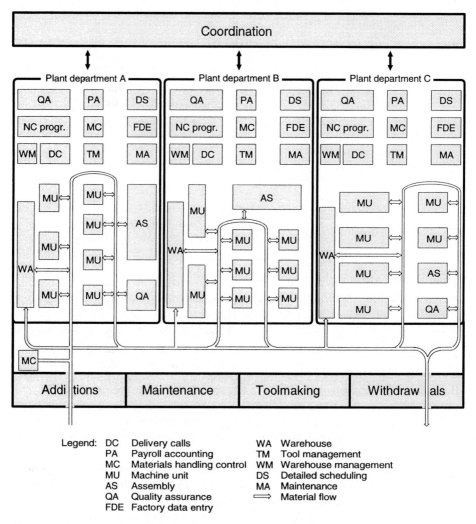

Fig. B.I.219: Object-oriented production organization

can be initiated directly from the island. Moreover, materials handling control within the plant department, quality assurance and simple maintenance—particularly preventive maintenance—can be decentralized. Because they require special qualifications in terms of design engineering and production, toolmaking, shipping, complicated maintenance functions and complicated receiving functions remain on the plant level as centralized functions.

By dividing a plant on the basis of production segments, special pay systems can be introduced for the segments. This shifts personnel management functions to the production departments.

The cross-hatching in the organizational chart in Figure B.I.217 shows the shift in functions from a function-oriented organization to an object-oriented organization. The new responsibilities are indicated by the plant department functions. Functional integration ensures that employees are more qualified, e.g., machine operators can also perform routine maintenance or quality inspections. This functional bundling is shown in the illustration by the broken lines surrounding the functions.

The degree of functional shift is shown in Figure B.I.217 by the hatching in the plant-oriented organizational units, with the degree of hatching indicating the degree to which an organizational unit can be decentralized.

Only skeleton functions remain on the plant level. These functions consist of coordination functions between the plant departments as discussed previously in connection with the leitstand organization, as well as special tasks for which there is no corresponding capability in the individual production departments.

The various organizational models initially have no influence on the derived logical data structures or the general function description. They do have a significant effect on the assignment of data structures and functions, however, as well as on the communication requirements of the design specification.

Further examples of segmented factory organization can be found in *Westkämper, Integrationspfad Qualität 1991, p. 152*; *Scheer, CIM 1990, pp. 49 ff.* and *Wildemann, Werkstattsteuerung 1984*.

Order release to plant departments, order-related planning of "cornerstone" dates and departmental coordination of detailed scheduling activities remain the task of Process Setup Planning on the plant level.

If there is a risk that the "skeleton functions" could develop into "spores" for new indirect departments, each decentralized unit can also be assigned special functions that it then performs for all departments. In this case, the rest of the "central" organizational units can also be shifted to the decentralized organizational units.

Process-oriented CAM organization with concurrent decentralization leads to the Y slice model shown in Figure B.I.220. All CAM functions for each production process are integrated into one slice. A coordination level is then made superordinate to the individual slices.

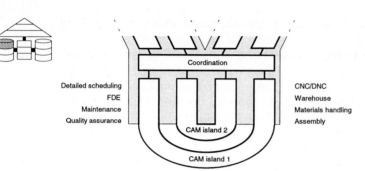

Fig. B.I.220: Y slice model for segmented production units

B.I.5.2.6.3 Requirements Definition for Production: The Data View

The conceptual data model is especially important in the development of an integrated CAM system. The data structures for the individual CAM components are therefore combined into a CAM data model in Figure B.I.221. For the sake of simplicity, the key attributes and the cardinalities are not indicated.

The data structure relates to the segmented production concept shown in Figure B.I.219.

The master data for parts, routings and resources form the central vertical string of data structures. Order processing is illustrated to the right. The point of departure for order processing is the general information object ORDER. For purposes of simplification, the information object for the order header is not shown. Within the framework of order release for the plant, the status attribute is changed to "released." At the same time, an order is assigned to a plant department, by virtue of which the information object ORDER DEPARTMENT ASSIGNMENT becomes the point of departure for all subsequent order-related controls. Making the plant department number the key attribute for all information objects derived from it ensures that the data structures will be divided on the basis of the individual order types and plant departments. By assigning operations within a routing to the plant departments, it is also possible to segment operation sequences among different plant departments within an order.

Orders that are generated within the plant as maintenance, inspection or toolmaking orders are specializations of the general information object ORDER. The departmental assignment ensures that they will be distributed among the "Maintenance," "Quality Assurance" and "Toolmaking" plant departments. Generalizing the three types of orders results in a uniform data structure for detailed scheduling.

Warehouse management is arranged in the upper left part of the diagram. This function is continued in the lower left part with warehouse control. The warehouse structures do not distinguish between different types of inventory (materials, semi-finished products or spare parts). This distinction is made either by the storage area assignment or by parts specializations.

The data structures for materials handling control are indicated in the left center portion of the illustration.

This largely non-redundant data structure utilizes subclassification in order to reveal the high degree of integration that is possible within Production. It also again emphasizes the need for using a uniform CAM logic system in order to integrate the subsystems, which are currently still specialized, with their data and functional redundancies.

Overall, the data structure, with only some 70 information objects, provides a relatively detailed view of the data logic for an integrated CAM system.

B.I.5.2.6.4 Requirements Definition for Production: The Control View

The assignment of functions to organizational units has already been discussed in connection with function- and object-oriented organizational models.

The event-driven concept as illustrated in Figure B.I.222 forms a link between the data view and the function view and, like the integrated data model, reveals the interaction between the various CAM components. Only those constructs that are relevant to other CAM components are transferred from the individual representations.

The availability check during order release requires tightly integrated relationships, since it is geared toward all CAM components. The queries can comprise manual confirmations (telephone or face to face), or they can occur via DP-supported communication, e.g., electronic mail, without the need for the systems to communicate directly with one another. In the case of automated production, however, these queries can be answered directly via a system-to-system coupling. These differences in the design specification, however, are not yet revealed on the requirements definition level.

Detailed control is a second point for collecting integrated relationships. All malfunction messages from the various subsystems are reported, and detailed scheduling checks whether rescheduling is necessary. Lines show the individual malfunctions from the different subsystems. At the same time, FDE feedback from the subsystems is recorded, and the order situation is updated. Upon order release, reservations and requirement messages are transferred to the subsystems.

An operation cannot be released by detailed scheduling until the physical provision of materials and tools has been reported by the successful completion of a stock movement. This initiates handling operations for materials and tools and starts the NC program, i.e., the execution of an operation.

This step results in either a success message or, if at least one component is unavailable, a shortfall message.

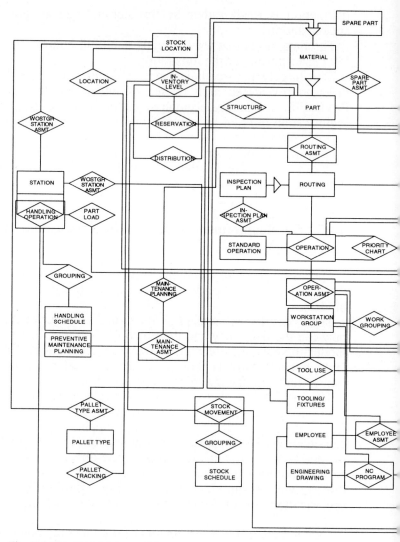

Fig. B.I.221: CAM data model

A handling operation for transfer of the manufactured products to the next processing station is triggered by the release of an operation to deliver required components when tools and components are provisioned and when an operation is completed. The operation is completed by the "station reached" event.

The many logical AND relationships, e.g., when availability checks are initiated, once again reveal the high potential for parallelism between production operations.

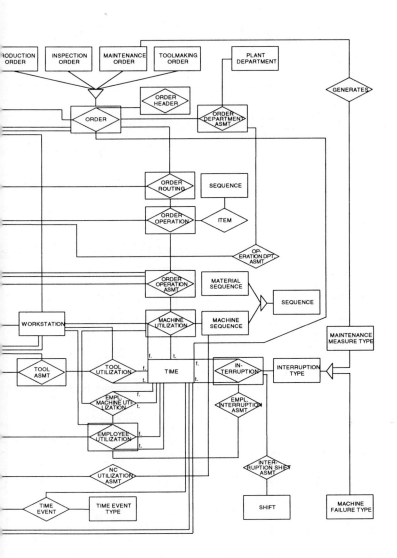

Order processing for Maintenance and Toolmaking is not explicitly represented. Since both departments form "factories within a factory," sequences that are virtually identical to those illustrated in Figure B.I.222 would occur. They can be viewed as specializations of the event control illustrated there.

When a new tool is designed and made, Process Planning issues the appropriate order to initiate the operation (see Figure B.I.183). Provision of a tool is initiated with the release of its operation. This practice can lead to positive results or, in the event of improper scheduling or disruptions, to negative results.

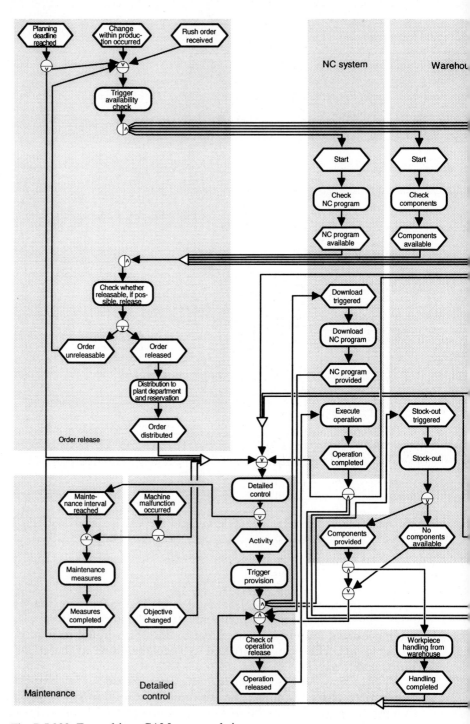

Fig. B.I.222: Event driven CAM process chain

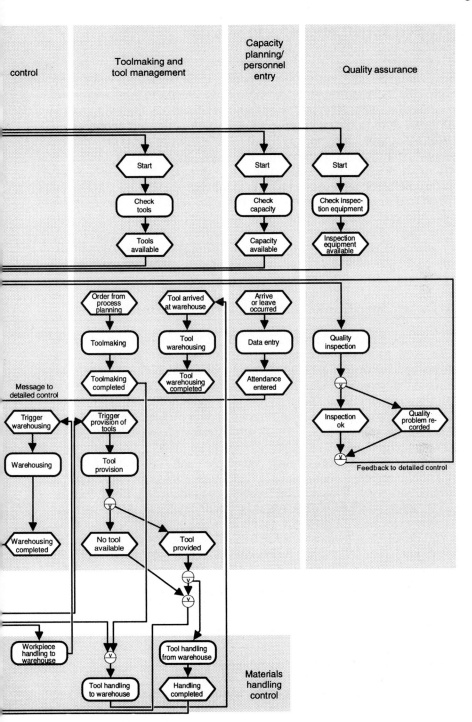

B.I.5.3 Design Specifications for Production

The high degree of production process integration developed in connection with the requirements definition also leads to high demands with respect to the integration of the design specifications. Since a greater degree of detail than in the requirements definition is needed here, design specifications cannot be portrayed in their entirety. The design specification for functions focuses on the high degree of DP function reusability made possible by modularization. Within the framework of the organization, different network topology requirements will be developed for the functional or object-oriented organizational forms examined. In the data view, reference will be made to a summary representation of the relations for the logical data structure that has been developed and to the necessary additions to the relational model. Within the context of control, several basic designs will be expanded into comprehensive concepts.

B.I.5.3.1 Design Specification for Production: The Function View

The function-oriented classification of DP-supported production systems has led to many overlaps. Thus, for example, FDE systems contain functions for operation management that are also contained in the production control leitstand. Quality assurance systems manage inspection plans that are also contained as operations in production control systems. Similar overlaps apply not only with respect to data management, but also with respect to functions. Thus, several subsystems use availability check and order release functions.

The software module reusability principle can be supported in converting the integrated requirements definition for an object-oriented organizational structure. This practice avoids redundant functions both in parallel systems as well as within organizational levels in which similar functions are performed on different levels of consolidation. *Scheer, CIM 1990, p. 160* develops a proposal in this regard that builds on the premise of standardizing the following functions for each planning level in Production (see Figure B.I.223):

- Importing orders from the superordinate planning level
- Combining algorithmic modules for level-specific processing
- Checking availability prior to releasing orders to the next planning level
- Reserving components
- Distributing orders to the downstream planning levels
- Coordinating subordinate planning departments
- Transferring data as feedback from the subsystems of the downstream planning level.

The modules shown in Figure B.I.223 are used for different objects on the individual planning levels (e.g., release of a materials handling order, a production order, an inventory withdrawal order or a quality assurance

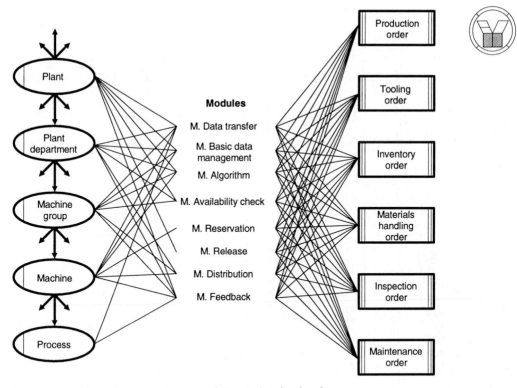

Fig. B.I.223: Reusability of software modules at planning level

order) as well as for one object on different levels of consolidation (e.g., order release on the plant level, release of a bundle of operation sequences within an order on the plant department level, release of a sequence on the machine group level, and the start of an NC program on the machine level).

A good portrayal of nested feedback loops on the individual planning levels can be found in *Ruffing, Integrierte Auftragsabwicklung 1991, p. 84*.

B.I.5.3.2 Design Specification for Production: The Organization View

The appropriate topologies will be derived from the two alternatives presented for a strictly functional and an object-oriented organizational structure. The discussion will then introduce developments aimed at standardizing communications in Production.

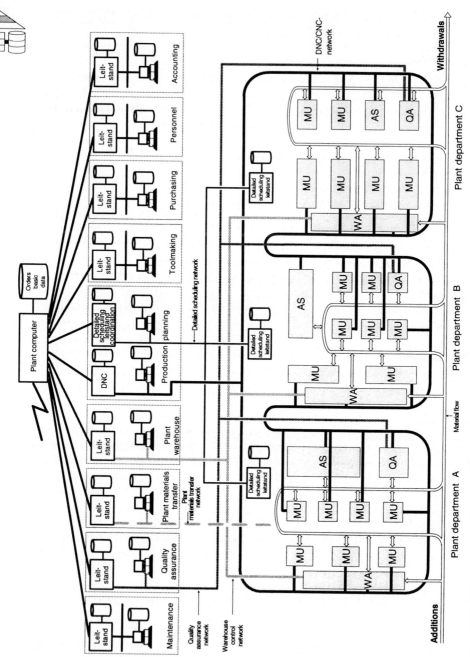

Fig. B.I.224: Network topology within a functional organization

B.I.5.3.2.1 Network Topologies for Functional and Object-Oriented Organizational Models

In designing the communication pathways in a functional organizational structure, the needs that exist **within** the functional organizational units are the dominating factor. For instance, different communication relationships can involve different requirements with respect to network fault tolerance, data transmission volume (network speed) and network response time in the case of interrupt-driven applications in a real-time environment.

This situation leads to the known functional island solution. Each functional island is linked with the superordinate plant computer. This computer handles central communications to the outside world and is thus responsible for sending and receiving messages to and from external partners and the superordinate product level. Figure B.I.224 shows one possible network topology for the functional organizational reference model developed in Figure B.I.219. The central plant functions of Purchasing, Personnel and Accounting have their own communication systems in the form of local area networks (LANs). The networks for the "Toolmaking" and "Maintenance" organizational units are only suggested, since they are "factories within a factory" and a large part of the network structure would be repeated in them. The communication relationships that exist between Quality Assurance, Plant Materials Transfer, Plant Warehouse and Production Planning result in independent networks within Production, which are geared toward the special needs of these subsystems. Two different communication systems exist within Production Planning: The DNC network supplies the connected NC machines with NC programs, while the production control leitstand routes order information to the plant departments and simultaneously transfers order-related feedback within the framework of factory data entry.

The plant warehouses are controlled via a central leitstand, which, in turn, transfers messages to the subsystems via its own communication channels. The measuring systems for Quality Assurance also result in their own network.

Although the situation represented here involving different network concepts in one plant may seem unrealistic at first glance, it actually corresponds to many real-world developments.

The network topologies represented here are defined on the logical level, i.e., even if the same physical network were used for data transmission, no data could be exchanged between the individual subsystems. The only communication relationships between the systems are produced by the superordinate plant computer. In the case of functionally isolated subsystems, the use of different data structures, programming languages, functional definitions, as well as the interplay of all these factors, gives rise to difficulties that must be taken into account.

Figure B.I.225 shows the network topology for the object-oriented organizational model. The plant-oriented skeleton functions are primarily geared to analytical activities, since the planning functions are delegated

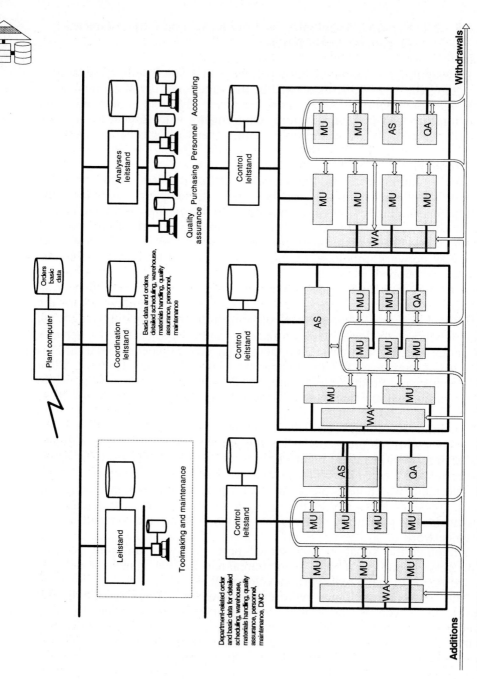

Fig. B.I.225: Network topology within an object-oriented organization

to the decentralized plant departments. The analyses are controlled via analysis leitstands in order to be able to formulate comprehensive conclusions across several departments.

Toolmaking and Maintenance form individual organizational units that are again not shown in their entirety since they can contain production equipment similar to the overall system.

All of the CAM subsystems are distributed among the plant departments. Interdepartmental functions are handled by the coordination leitstand, which distributes orders and receives feedback messages, and thus serves as the central clearinghouse for all data in the plant. The plant computer is the bridgehead to the plant's external relationships. If need be, it can be combined with the coordination leitstand or made into a pure communications center for handling external communications.

In each plant department, all CAM functions are supported by the central control leitstand, which transfers initiation messages to the technical subsystems and their control systems. All communications are processed via a holistic network topology. Different subnetworks for special communication needs (e.g., real time) can be embedded within it. In contrast to Figure B.I.225, however, these subnetworks are then supported by a uniform logical control leitstand. Different I/O devices are incorporated within the individual plant departments in order to process FDE information feedback and to receive operational information. These devices will not be discussed in further detail.

The principal difference between the two network topologies is that in the case of the functional organizational structure, the communication systems are also geared toward the individual functional organizational units, while in the case of the object-oriented organizational structure, the various functions can be coordinated via uniform data structures, functional sequences and event controls; thus, a uniform communication structure can be built that also supports the exchange of data **between** the systems.

B.I.5.3.2.2 Network Standards for Production

The network topologies developed in Figures B.I.224 and B.I.225 for functional and object-oriented organizational structures are only intended to illustrate rough integration requirements. In particular, the topology for the object-oriented organizational form reveals that a close communication relationship must exist between the control leitstand and the various systems for materials transfer, inventory, quality assurance, production, etc. Thus far, proprietary communication services for the individual subcomponents have frequently dominated, which hinders transparent communication. With the increasing demand for integration, in particular the demand resulting from the CIM concept, a trend toward communication **standards** can be seen. These standards range from physical descriptions for PIN configurations to application-oriented file transfer services. Figure B.I.226 shows the communication hierarchies within an enterprise. Large volumes of non-time-critical data in the form of orders and feedback messages must be transferred on the upper communication levels consisting of the plant or plant department, while smaller volumes of data with high currency requirements are exchanged on the lower levels. In this context, time-critical applications are understood to be those with response times of approximately 10 ms. These are speeds that cannot be guaranteed by computers that are geared more toward commercial applications or by their operating systems, e.g., UNIX. For this reason, other operating systems must also be employed (process computers). CAM event-driven control, which was developed in the discussion of the requirements definition for control, also only shows a rough sequence logic, which must be further refined on the process-oriented level, where concrete instructions for actuators and responses to sensor signals are encountered. On the process level, the control systems access the actuators (e.g., valves, temperature switches, etc.) directly and collect sensor data (temperature sensors, tachometers, etc.) in order to control the process in the form of a feedback loop. Thus, a control leitstand can initiate a materials transfer order from one location to another on the basis of the feedback from a completed operation. This materials transfer order is subdivided into subtransfer processes for subroutes by the storage programmable controller, which functions as a "computer" to operate the actuators and sensors of the transport system. A subtransfer is initiated when the preceding subtransfer route is completed. This process must occur without any delays in order to provide a smooth overall materials transfer process between the departure location and the destination.

In contrast to the control leitstand, the process leitstand is more closely connected to the field level of process execution. Thus, it exhibits a close interface to the control systems via the interrupt-controlled operating system. As a cell controller, it can control an entire production cell. The leitstand on the department level, however, can be classified as a continuation of the PPC system and coordination of the individual CAM components and must be assigned to a non-time-critical level.

The right side of Figure B.I.226 shows the terms selected here to describe the planning levels and compares them with other common terms (shown on the left side of the diagram) that apply to the architecture of communication relationships for Production. Typical standard protocols are assigned to the individual network levels, and a rough distinction can be drawn between two groups of protocols: MAP, TOP and TCP/IP, which are geared more toward sales- and engineering-oriented mass data, and MINIMAP and PROFIBUS, which are more suitable for time-critical applications.

Due to the major importance of these protocols, several aspects will now be discussed in greater detail. For a more basic discussion or for further details, see *Tannenbaum, Computer Networks 1988; Kauffels, Klassifizierung der lokalen Netze 1986; Henn, Schnittstellen für die Automatisierungstechnik 1990; Wein, Integration technischer Subsysteme in die Fertigungssteuerung 1991; Suppan-Borowka, Anforderungen an MAP 1986.*

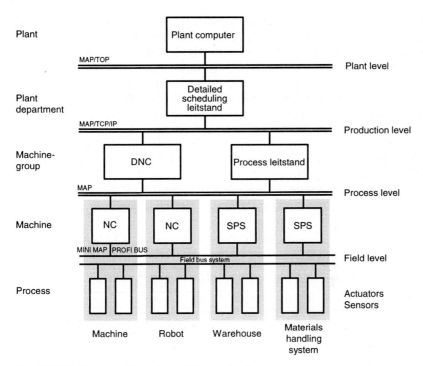

Fig. B.I.226: Network hierarchy within production

For the user, the most important aspects of a network protocol are network access, services and configuration options.

The direct link to different controls, some of which are factory-installed machine components, results in the problem of having to interconnect heterogeneous hardware.

Networks are based on protocol standards. The Manufacturing Automation Protocol (MAP), developed specifically for production applications, represents an important contribution toward standardizing data interchange in production (see *Suppan-Borowka, Anforderungen an MAP 1986, pp. 170 ff.; Suppan-Borowka/Simon, MAP in der automatisierten Fertigung 1986; Schäfer, Technische Grundlagen der lokalen Netze 1986, pp. 14 ff.*).

The integration of material flow control with computer-supported inventory and materials handling systems and automated production devices (NC, CNC, DNC, robotics) and planning-oriented control functions on a leitstand computer necessitates that the various computer-controlled systems be able to intercommunicate. The situation today, however, is still plagued by incompatibilities. Each individual control and computer system uses proprietary codes for displaying drawings, proprietary formats for record structures and files, proprietary security mechanisms and proprietary definitions for controlling peripherals. Some of the systems are partially embedded in comprehensive operating system environments that are also proprietary. If vendors offer proprietary networking designs (e.g., SNA from IBM, DECNET from Digital Equipment, SINET and TRANSDATA from Siemens, DATA HIGHWAY from Allen Bradley, and MOTBUS from Gould), only peripherals manufactured by the network vendor can usually be attached.

Despite the existence of standardization concepts proposed by international organizations (e.g., ISO and IEEE), vendors have shown little interest in developing concrete standards in this field. In the late 1970s, General Motors (GM) therefore took the initiative in developing a network standard for factory automation. To this end, GM formed the "Manufacturing Automation Task Force," which designed the MAP concept for open communication systems between 1980 and 1983. GM

ISO layer	Task	MAP specifications
		Application programs
		C-Calls
		API
Layer 7: Application	User interface	MMS/RS - 511 Filetransfer (FTAM) Network management (NM) Directory services Virtual terminal CASE
Layer 6: Presentation	Adaptation/conversion of formats, coding, etc.	ISO presentation - Service - Protocol
Layer 5: Session	Synchronization and administration of links	ISO connection oriented session - Service - Protocol
Layer 4: Transport	Safe end-to-end link	ISO transport - Service - Protocol
Layer 3: Network	Protocol adaptation between different networks, routing	ISO internet Connectionless
Layer 2: Data link	Error detection, transfer between topologically adjacent knots, media access	LLC type 1 802.4 token-bus
Layer 1: Physical	Coding and bit-serial transmission of packets	Broadband, carrierband, fiber optics ISO token-bus 802

Fig. B.I.227: MAP 3.0 protocol specifications

was then able to use its market position to involve a number of important vendors of communication technology products in the project. There have been several versions of MAP, the most recent being Version 3.0 (see Figure B.I.227). Despite several setbacks, in particular due to high costs, leading vendors of information technology components for production are expected to adopt this standard (i.e., vendors of controls and OEMs that incorporate these controls in their production systems). MAP is based on the ISO/OSI reference model for open systems.

MAP not only regulates data interchange, which was the primary support offered by earlier protocols, it also provides comfortable functional services. Applications that conform to the ISO/OSI specification access these services via the Application Program Interface (API). It provides applications with a C-interface to allow them to interactively communicate with the MAP services.

The heart of MAP, though, is the definition of services on **layer 7**, which are directly accessed by superordinate applications. In addition to the file transfer definition as well as the terminal emulation definition, which are necessary for connecting different devices, the principal function here for production automation is the Manufacturing Message Specification (MMS). This function defines objects that can be accessed by more than 80 services. These objects can be files or variables, for example, and can be accessed by services such as download, upload, verify, start programs, etc. Figure B.I.228 (from *Gora, MAP 1986*) provides an impression of MMS commands for an NC production system.

The basis for the definition for layer 7 is the ISO CASE (Common Application Service Element) protocol.

MAP covers monitoring and design of network configurations as well as monitoring and rectification of error situations. Since errors can occur on all levels, MAP covers layers 3 - 7 within the management concept. Suitable backup services already exist for layers 1 and 2 within the definitions adopted by ISO.

Function	Description
CYCLE START	Starting or closing of the current machine cycle
PART	Identification of single workpieces
AXIS OFFSET	Axis manipulation (e.g. in robot control)
UNITS	Definition which units (inch, meter) are used
EXCHANGE	Manipulation of workpiece pallets
LIFT	Lifting of a special device

Fig. B.I.228: MMS commands

The broadband token bus based on the IEEE 802.4 standard serves as the MAP standard for layer 1. This broadband system has a data transfer rate of 10 MBit/sec. It can transmit large volumes of data over long distances and can transmit parallel data streams. Virtually any medium can be used if it conforms to the ISO DIS 8802/4 interface for data transfer on level 2a (Medium Access Control, MAC).

MAP's high degree of comfort comes at the expense of time-critical applications. MMS messages can last between 20 and 50 ms, which rules out real-time processing. Although anticipated optimizations, particularly by putting protocol services on faster chips, will be able to drastically reduce transfer times, special protocols have since been developed to mitigate the problem until they are available.

Thus, MAP 3.0 has attempted to improve options for real-time applications using two strategies. On the one hand, the option for priority control when accessing the transfer medium, which was not used in Version 2.1, has been incorporated in 3.0 (4 priorities: Access classes 6, 4, 2 and 0). The second strategy involved the implementation of direct access from layer 7 to layer 2 (EPA = Enhanced Performance Architecture and Mini-MAP). Mini-MAP nodes can now communicate with Mini-MAP or EPA nodes in the same segment, while EPA nodes can also communicate with other network segments.

The services between the layers are handled by layer 7 in a simplified form.

Although MAP was a spectacular stride toward LAN standardization, at least in terms of production-related LANs, it nevertheless does not satisfy all requirements for an open network architecture in an industrial enterprise. Consequently, many enterprises have already introduced subnetworks for connecting automated islands. These subnetworks will remain in place for the medium term and must therefore be linked with a general network. This means that MAP must be linked with other network services or network concepts.

Thus, MAP is becoming a backbone network for other dedicated subnetworks. This involves the use of gateways, routers, bridges and broadband components (see *Simon, Kommunikation in der automatisierten Fertigung 1986*).

Gateways connect networks having different protocol structures on higher levels.

Routers are of particular importance within the network concept since they provide a relatively efficient connection. Routers connect subnetworks with layers 1 and 2 even if they are not alike, which are then interlinked via a uniform network protocol on layer 3. This also affords a connection to public networks, e.g., the Datex-P packet-switched network.

Bridges interlink different subnetworks that possess a unified address structure. Broadband components such as branches, equalizers and amplifiers enable the network to be structured and expanded on the physical level.

The Technical Office Protocol (TOP) was developed to support applications that are not oriented toward manufacturing, such as those for production planning or design engineering. TOP is largely compatible with MAP 3.0, thus permitting production- and office-oriented applications to be integrated through the use of MAP/TOP. Instead of the MMS service, TOP 3.0 uses the X.400 mail and messaging protocol developed to support electronic mail.

Since the major effort involved in adapting MAP/TOP has resulted in delays, and the unsuccessful Version 2.1 resulted in setbacks for vendors, other protocols with broad application potential have since been developed. The TCP/IP protocol, for example, was developed under contract from the U.S. Department of Defense and has a much simpler design than MAP.

The Process Field Bus (PROFIBUS) was developed under the support of the German Ministry for Research and Technology (BMFT) to provide real-time support. As in the case of Mini-MAP and EPA, PROFIBUS only takes into account layers 1, 2 and 7 of the ISO/OSI reference model (see *Wein, Integration technischer Subsysteme in die Fertigungssteuerung 1991, p. 301*). Layers 1 and 2 support a token bus architecture. The Field Bus Message Specification (FMS) is used to embed a subset of the FMS protocol on layer 7.

The network hierarchy shown in Figure B.I.226 shows meaningful protocols on the individual CAM planning levels. The rough network topologies shown in Figure B.I.225 contain only the plant level, the production level and the combined process and field levels. Subsystems for real-time applications can be defined more specifically by subclassifying process- and machine-oriented structures.

B.I.5.3.3 Design Specification for Production: The Data View

The data structure developed in Figure B.I.221 has been transferred to the relational model in Figure B.I.229. In the case of order-related relations, the key attributes of the order header are only suggested.

Translating a data structure into the relational concept on the basis of the entity relationship model is particularly problematic in the case of production data (see *Loos, Datenstrukturierung in der Fertigung 1992* and *Loos, Probleme des Datenbankeinsatzes in der Fertigung 1991*).

R. DISTRIBUTION (FOUNO, TOUNO, DATE, PNO, ODATE, SNO, PNO)

R. EMPLOYEE (EMPL, name, hire date)

R. EMPLOYEE ASSIGNMENT (EMPL, WOSTGRNO)

R. EMPLOYEE INTERRUPTION ASSIGNMENT (EMPL, WOSTGRNO, WOSTNO, OPNO, MUT-TO-DATE, MUT-TO-DATE, INTTYPNO, FROM-DATE, TO-DATE)

R. EMPLOYEE UTILIZATION (EMPL, WOSTGRNO, WOSTNO, OPNO, FROM-DATE, TO-DATE)

R. EMPLOYEE-MACHINE UTILIZATION (EMPL, WOSTGRNO, WOSTNO, OPNO, MUT-FROM-DATE, MUT-TO-DATE, FOUNO, TOUNO, DATE, PNO, ODATE, MUT-FROM-DATE, MUT-TO-DATE, MACHSEQNO, WOSTNO, FROM-DATE, TO-DATE)

R. ENGINEERING DRAWING (DNO, creation date)

R. GENERATES (FOUNO, TOUNO, DATE, PNO, ODATE, INTTYPNO)

R. GROUPING (<u>FSTNO</u>, <u>TSTNO</u>, <u>DATE</u>, <u>HSNO</u>)

R. HANDLING OPERATION (<u>FSTNO</u>, <u>TSTNO</u>, <u>DATE</u>, duration)

R. HANDLING SCHEDULE (<u>HSNO</u>)

R. INSPECTION PLAN (<u>RNO</u>)

R. INSPECTION PLAN ASSIGNMENT (<u>RNO</u>, <u>OPNO</u>)

R. INTERRUPTION (<u>INTTYPNO</u>, <u>FROM-DATE</u>, <u>TO-DATE</u>)

R. INTERRUPTION SHIFT ASSIGNMENT (<u>SHINO</u>, <u>INTTYPNO</u>, <u>FROM-DATE</u>, <u>TO-DATE</u>)

R. INTERRUPTION TYPE (<u>INTTYPNO</u>, name of interruption type)

      R. MACHINE MALFUNCTION (<u>INTTYPNO</u>)

      R. MAINTENANCE MEASURE TYPE (<u>INTTYPNO</u>)

R. INVENTORY DISTRIBUTION (<u>SNO</u>, <u>PNO</u>, <u>PTYP</u>, <u>PNO</u>, <u>PTYP</u>, <u>DATE</u>, quantity)

R. INVENTORY LEVEL (<u>SNO</u>, <u>PNO</u>, inventory quantity, safety stock)

R. INVENTORY STATION ASSIGNMENT (<u>SNO</u>, <u>STNO</u>)

R. ITEM (<u>FOUNO</u>, <u>TOUNO</u>, <u>DATE</u>, <u>PNO</u>, <u>ODATE</u>, <u>RNO</u>, <u>OPNO</u>, <u>SEQNO</u>)

R. LOCATION (<u>SNO</u>, <u>FOUNO</u>, <u>TOUNO</u>, <u>DATE</u>, <u>PNO</u>, <u>ODATE</u>, <u>RNO</u>, <u>OPNO</u>, quantity)

R. MACHINE UTILIZATION (<u>FOUNO</u>, <u>TOUNO</u>, <u>DATE</u>, <u>PNO</u>, <u>ODATE</u>, <u>RNO</u>, <u>OPNO</u>, <u>FROM-DATE</u>, <u>TO-DATE</u>, <u>MACHSEQNO</u>, <u>WOSTNO</u>)

R. NC PROGRAM (<u>DNO</u>, <u>RNO</u>, <u>OPNO</u>, <u>WOSTGRNO</u>, programmer)

R. NC SEQUENCE ASSIGNMENT (<u>DNO</u>, <u>RNO</u>, <u>OPNO</u>, <u>WOSTGRNO</u>, <u>MACHSEQNO</u>)

R. OPERATION (<u>RNO</u>, <u>OPNO</u>)

R. OPERATION ASSIGNMENT (<u>RNO</u>, <u>OPNO</u>, <u>WOSTGRNO</u>, cost rate, time)

R. OPERATION DEPARTMENT ASSIGNMENT (<u>PLDPNO</u>, <u>FOUNO</u>, <u>TOUNO</u>, <u>DATE</u>, <u>PNO</u>, <u>ODATE</u>, <u>PLDPNO</u>, <u>OPNO</u>, <u>RNO</u>)

R. ORDER (<u>FOUNO</u>, <u>TOUNO</u>, <u>DATE</u>, <u>PNO</u>, <u>ODATE</u>, RNO, quantity, status)

      R. PRODUCTION ORDER (<u>FOUNO</u>, <u>TOUNO</u>, <u>DATE</u>, <u>PNO</u>, <u>ODATE</u>)

      R. INSPECTION ORDER (<u>FOUNO</u>, <u>TOUNO</u>, <u>DATE</u>, <u>PNO</u>, <u>ODATE</u>)

      R. MAINTENANCE ORDER (<u>FOUNO</u>, <u>TOUNO</u>, <u>DATE</u>, <u>PNO</u>, <u>ODATE</u>)

      R. TOOLMAKING ORDER (<u>FOUNO</u>, <u>TOUNO</u>, <u>DATE</u>, <u>PNO</u>, <u>ODATE</u>)

R. ORDER DEPARTMENT ASSIGNMENT (<u>PLDPNO</u>, <u>FOUNO</u>, <u>TOUNO</u>, <u>DATE</u>, <u>PNO</u>, <u>ODATE</u>)

R. ORDER HEADER (<u>FOUNO</u>, <u>TOUNO</u>, <u>DATE</u>, status)

R. ORDER OPERATION (<u>FOUNO</u>, <u>TOUNO</u>, <u>DATE</u>, <u>PNO</u>, <u>ODATE</u>, <u>RNO</u>, <u>OPNO</u>, <u>WOSTGRNO</u>)

R. PALLET TRACKING (<u>PALTYPNO</u>, <u>SNO</u>, <u>PNO</u>)

R. PALLET TYPE (<u>PALTYPNO</u>, height, width, length)

R. PALLET TYPE ASSIGNMENT (<u>PALTYPNO</u>, <u>SNO</u>, <u>PNO</u>)

R. PART (<u>PNO</u>, name, date of last update)

      R. PRODUCTION MEAN (<u>PNO</u>)

          R. SPARE PART (<u>SPNO</u>, service life)

          R. TOOL (<u>TNO</u>, service life)

          R. WORKSTATION (<u>WOSTNO</u>, purchase date, total machine hours)

R. PART LOAD (<u>FSTNO</u>, <u>TSTNO</u>, <u>DATE</u>, <u>FOUNO</u>, <u>TOUNO</u>, <u>DATE</u>, <u>PNO</u>, <u>ODATE</u>, <u>RNO</u>, <u>OPNO</u>)

R. PLANT DEPARTMENT (<u>PLDPNO</u>, location, manpower)

R. PREVENTIVE MAINTENANCE ASSIGNMENT (<u>MPLNO</u>, <u>WOSTNO</u>)

R. PREVENTIVE MAINTENANCE PLAN ASSIGNMENT (<u>MPLNO</u>, <u>WOSTNO</u>, <u>RNO</u>, <u>PNO</u>)

R. PREVENTIVE MAINTENANCE PLANNING (<u>MPLNO</u>)

R. PRIORITY CHART (<u>RNO</u>, <u>FOPNO</u>, <u>TOPNO</u>)

R. RESERVATION (<u>FOUNO</u>, <u>TOUNO</u>, <u>DATE</u>, <u>OPNO</u>, <u>ODATE</u>, <u>SNO</u>, <u>LTNO</u>, quantity)

R. ROUTING (<u>RNO</u>, name, quantity, status, date of last update)
R. ROUTING ASSIGNMENT (<u>RNO</u>, <u>PNO</u>)
R. SEQUENCE (<u>SEQNO</u>)
R. SEQUENCE (<u>SEQNO</u>)

      R. MATERIAL SEQUENCE (<u>MATSEQNO</u>)
      R. MACHINE SEQUENCE (<u>MACHSEQNO</u>)

R. SHIFT (<u>SHINO</u>, time period)
R. SPARE PART ASSIGNMENT (<u>SPNO</u>, <u>WOSTNO</u>, installation date)
R. STANDARD OPERATION (<u>OPNO</u>, name)
R. STATION (<u>STNO</u>, station type)
R. STOCK LOCATION (<u>SNO</u>, capacity)
R. STOCK MOVEMENT (<u>SNO</u>, <u>PNO</u>, <u>FOUNO</u>, <u>TOUNO</u>, <u>DATE</u>, <u>ODATE</u>, <u>MDATE</u>, <u>SSNO</u>, quantity)
R. STOCK SCHEDULE (<u>SSNO</u>)
R. STRUCTURE (<u>HPNO</u>, <u>LPNO</u>, production coefficient)
R. TIME (<u>DATE</u>)
R. TIME EVENT (<u>EMPL</u>, <u>DATE</u>, <u>TETYPNO</u>)
R. TIME EVENT TYPE (<u>TETYPNO</u>)
R. TOOL ASSIGNMENT (<u>TNO</u>, <u>RNO</u>, <u>OPNO</u>, <u>WOSTGRNO</u>)
R. TOOL USE (<u>TNO</u>, <u>WOSTGRNO</u>)
R. TOOL UTILIZATION (<u>TNO</u>, <u>RNO</u>, <u>OPNO</u>, <u>WOSTGRNO</u>, <u>WOSTNO</u>, <u>FROM-DATE</u>, <u>TO-DATE</u>)
R. WORKSTATION GROUP (<u>WOSTGRNO</u>, location, function)
R. WOSTGR-STATION ASSIGNMENT (<u>WOSTGRNO</u>, <u>STANO</u>, position)

Figure B.I.229: Relational model for the data structure for production

The specialization of the order type into the subtypes of production order, maintenance order and toolmaking order can be taken into account by introducing an attribute for the order type. In the figure, the specialized relations are indented. Since the specializations are disjunct, type-dependent attributes can also be taken into account in the order relations (see *Loos, Probleme des Datenbankeinsatzes in der Fertigung 1991, p. 161*).

If time relationships in the keys are provided by "from/to" attributes in relations, only the start date is necessary in the case of non-overlapping definitions, since this information is sufficient for purposes of identification. If, however, overlaps are possible, e.g., in the case of employee assignments for people who perform supervisory functions on several machine groups simultaneously, both time indicators possess key properties.

Not all logical information in the data structure can be entered directly in the tabular notation for the relational model; rather, this requires formulations within the application program or via special procedures and triggers. This applies, for example, in the case of integrity conditions that ensure time-related restrictions: A simple example is the condition that the completion time for an operation must be $\geq$ the start time. The example shown in Figure B.I.230 from *Loos, Probleme des Datenbankeinsatzes in der Fertigung 1991, p. 159* shows the formation of this contingency that is possible using SQL.

Relation:	R. Order (..., start time, completion time, ...)
Program:	PROCEDURE order check

 if (start time > completion time)
     return (error)
 endif

 return (OK)

Trigger:	CREATE TRIGGER
	AFTER INSERT, UPDATE
	OF order
	EXEC order check

Fig. B.I.230: Time-related integrity condition

Both the ER model and the relational model reduce complex objects into their structural elements. This leads to the flat tabular structure for the relational model. Complicated, nested SQL commands might be necessary in order to reassemble an object from this structure. To avoid this, the NF^2 (Non First Normal Form) models can be used to transfer the substructures as repetitive groups into the superordinate relation that represents the complex object. This can be accomplished if relationships within the data structure pertain only to the overall object and not to its substructural elements as well. If, however, the data structure for the object also overlaps the other objects within the substructures, an object-oriented data model must be employed (see *Budde et al., Objektorientierter Entwurf von Informationssystemen 1992*).

Further problems in the design specification for the data view will only be enumerated. On the process-oriented production level, these include necessary fault tolerance, which can be provided by hardware solutions, e.g., data mirroring. At the same time, however, it also requires appropriate support from the database system. Real-time applications impose conditions on the maximum response time of the database system. The network architecture developed here requires that the data be distributed. Typically, this distribution will not be disjunct; instead, the hierarchically subordinate data can be subsets of the superordinate databases.

Special data media are used for data capture within the framework of factory data entry and processing. The design specification for the data view must also specify a particular type of data medium (OCR or barcoded labels, magnetic stripes or chips).

B.I.5.3.4 Design Specification for Production: The Control View

Space does not allow for a systematic, detailed analysis of all relationships between ARIS components on the design specification level. Some aspects, e.g., the distribution of data and functions among nodes of the computer system, have already been mentioned. In addition to the usual criteria used to make the distribution between host systems, processing workstations and presentation workstations within a client/server architecture, Production also requires the properties of "time-criticalness" and connectivity with the production process control level.

The trigger definition for implementing an event-driven application environment is also extremely important. The EPC developed here can provide the initial impetus for this process, but it would still have to be developed in greater detail to provide a real-world representation (see *Klein, Datenintegrität in heterogenen Informationssystemen 1991*).

In many real-world situation, the integrated CAM solution that is suggested and developed here cannot be implemented without further modifications. Thus, there are currently no standard applications available that completely conform to this concept. Many users have already implemented partial solutions, which makes an integrated solution difficult due to the cost and effort already invested.

The Interface Management System (INMAS) developed within the framework of the ESPRIT project "CIDAM" (CIM System with Distributed Database and Configurable Modules) constitutes a concept for integrating heterogeneous applications. INMAS is now available in prototype form and has already been employed in the first pilot applications. The basic principle (see Figure B.I.231) involves linking the individual subsystems via an intermediate interface management system rather than using dual couplings. Thus, the number of coupling modules increases by only $2 \cdot n$ rather than by $n \cdot (n-1)$, where n is the number of

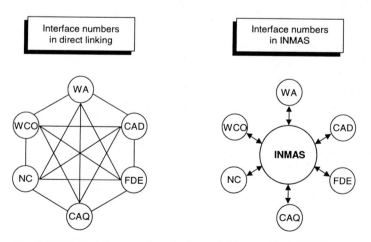

Fig. B.I.231: Interface numbers in direct linking and in INMAS

subsystems to be linked. Figure B.I.232 is a schematic representation of the INMAS coupling operation (see *Herterich, Datenmanagement in der Fertigung 1991; Heß/Scheer, Kopplung von CIM-Komponenten - ein europäisches Projekt 1991; Heß/Hoffmann/Houy/Jung/Scheer, INMAS - ein Tool zur Datenintegration über eine neutrale Schnittstelle 1992*). An application that initiates a data modification that is also of interest for other subsystems sends a trigger to the INMAS system along with the data modification. The INMAS system processes the data modification and transforms it into a neutral data structure for the overall system that it manages. This "neutral" data structure can conform to an integrated database design for the overall system, as developed for Production in Figure B.I.221. Moreover, INMAS knows which other subsystems are affected by the data modification and thus converts the data to the formats required by the target systems and activates a trigger to transfer them to a gateway following a renewed transformation.

The subsystem interrelationships are formulated into rules, which, together with the neutral data structure created in INMAS, can serve as the point of departure for an integrated overall solution.

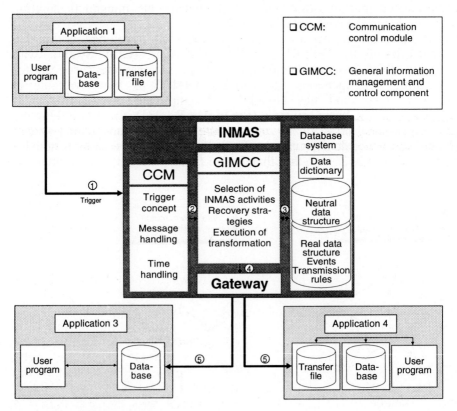

Fig. B.I.232: INMAS operations

B.I.5.4 Implementation Description for Production

Since the transition between the design specification and the implementation description is often fluid, some implementation-related aspects have already been discussed in previous sections. Further aspects concerning the implementation of programs, networks, databases and the interrelationships between them will therefore not be discussed in any greater detail.

B.I.6 Application Systems for Production Logistics

Up to now, no functionally integrated, process-oriented standard software packages have been available for production logistics.

The PPC systems that have been available for over 20 years focus on basic data management for bills of materials and routings as well as for requirements and capacity planning. Dedicated systems are being offered for the individual CAM functions, some of which systems integrators have bundled into overall concepts (e.g., the HP OpenCAM concept; see *Hoffmann, HP OpenCAM - Offene Strukturen mit der ARIS-Architektur 1993*).

Production control systems based on the leitstand concept encompass functions for detailed scheduling, production coordination, resource management and coordination of the interfaces to the other CAM systems.

New designs that conform more closely to integration- and process-oriented principles are on the horizon, however.

B.I.6.1 Change in Emphasis between Planning and Control

The traditional PPC concept conforms to a tier-oriented approach. This means that results from one tier serve as the input for planning and control activities on the next tier. It has already been shown that the tiers for primary requirements planning, requirements planning, scheduling and capacity planning, order release, detailed scheduling, CAM in the narrower sense, FDE and analysis not only contain unilateral relationships, but also encompass reverse information and planning flows.

Standard software packages that support production logistics conform to the profile shown in Figure B.I.233,a, which is based on the experiences of the author and has been confirmed in discussions with many users. This profile displays three characteristic tendencies:

1.   There is only very limited support for input variables for the primary requirement, which are very important for the requirements and capacity planning levels. However, this function forms a filter to intercept market disturbances that result in order changes that affect production logistics.

2.   There is insufficient support for production-oriented control. This is because the development of standard software, with its top-down approach, has come to a standstill; consequently, production-oriented systems never materialized. Moreover, changes in information technology have made it necessary to continually revise the systems, which has also halted further development. Because of this lack of support for production, interruptions are never really stabilized; instead, they simply lead to continuous replanning within the context of requirements planning.

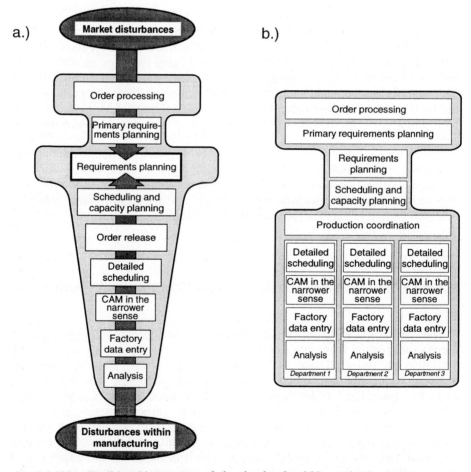

Fig. B.I.233,a: Traditional importance of planning levels within production logistics
Fig. B.I.233,b: Today's importance of planning levels within production logistics

3.   The technical functions for CAM in the narrower sense are rarely supported by PPC since the systems are oriented more toward business aspects and thus build on DP platforms geared toward those departments. CAM systems, however, require their own computer structures (process control computers, real-time-capable business systems) due to their close connection to the process level. Thus, application software for production logistics would have had to have been developed across different information technology platforms.

Future PPC systems must therefore conform to the profile shown in Figure B.I.233,b.

The discussion of DP-supported production systems has revealed new trends in organizational structuring that result in more pronounced segmentation, along with networking.

The stronger emphasis on decentralized units—and thus on the problems of control—will reverse the importance of the individual PPC functions. The limited support for rough planning has led to a lack of results for requirements and capacity planning, thus necessitating ongoing planning adaptation.

Consequently, support for rough planning should be increased by employing forecasting, simulation and optimization techniques. A stronger rough planning process incorporates functions from medium-term requirements and capacity planning. Moreover, these planning levels are thinned out by shifting functions to the control level. The focus of PPC systems thus shifts from medium-term planning to longer-term rough planning and shorter-term control.

A significant reason for making the control level more independent is that it contains its own control objects. In the case of planning functions, the planning unit is the order that relates to a **part**. Lots are also defined for these functions. Aside from the fact that lot formation is losing importance as a consequence of JIT, it should be noted that lots are formed by weighing changeover costs and storage costs. Changeover costs, however, do not relate to the order unit "part"; instead, they relate to the operation level, since this is where the assignment is made to equipment groups.

In addition to changeover costs for bundling operations, other criteria can also be decisive in terms of control. For example, it can be meaningful to optimize the cutting process by combining operations from several different orders to improve material utilization. This means that detailed planning can combine the orders (lots) formed in the context of requirements planning into new planning units to facilitate better material utilization. In addition to material utilization, technical conditions can also result in replanning—e.g., combining different volume dimensions for charging furnaces, combining parts on the basis of similar pressure requirements in a press capacity allocation or balancing the complexity of operations in the case of manual processing. Further criteria for combining orders include utilizing materials transfer units, cost-effective stock withdrawal operations, etc. All these criteria result in more emphasis being placed on control as an independent decision-making and optimization level.

The shift in emphasis from planning-related processes to implementation-related processes can also be attributed to the trend toward greater simplification in industry, which is characterized by the "lean production" principle.

Placing greater emphasis on the control level allows the implementation and development strategies involved in DP-supported production logistics systems to shift from a top-down approach to a bottom-up strategy. The first step toward realizing this goal involves supporting Production with leitstand concepts embedded in integrated CAM systems. This means that the basic data for bills of materials and routings will be maintained in different ways—separately for the individual segments, yet synchronized by the coordination functions. The basic data necessary for the planning levels are then consolidated from the differentiated basic data on the control level. As a result, a PPC system can be built from the bottom up. Current leitstand systems thus serve as the point of departure for integrated DP systems for production logistics.

The concept of decentralization plus networking is treated in greater detail in the discussion of integrated logistics systems, i.e., systems that include inbound and outbound logistics.

B.I.6.2 Parameters and Scenarios

The production logistics concept discussed above can be differentiated on the basis of the different production structures that exist at manufacturing companies.

Examples of special needs in different industries have already been suggested (e.g., variant handling or requirements statements), but not in a thorough, systematic manner. Consequently, this section will discuss important parameters in designing production logistics systems.

Some industries face problems that are insignificant to other industries. For example, material cutting problems are prevalent in the glass and paper processing industries, while they are not of primary importance in mechanical engineering. The problem of managing large numbers of variants poses special needs in the furniture industry, while this problem is virtually unknown in the case of series production in other industries.

When a production logistics system is developed, it is therefore necessary to specify which functions are independent of special production structures and which have to be specially designed on the basis of the type of user involved.

These special features can be taken into account by gearing the application software toward specific industries, types of production and organizational forms of production. Moreover, specialized software that addresses the above-mentioned problems (e.g., cutting optimization, variant management) is currently on the market.

If the individual systems are too specialized, however, there is a risk that island solutions will be created that are difficult to link with other programs, thus making it even more difficult to implement the holistic solution emphasized here. Nor would it appear to be advisable to develop overall solutions for individual industries merely in response to needs in **one** problem area, when many aspects of these solutions would differ only insignificantly from those for other industries. For this reason, the following discussion will develop a system for categorizing parameters pertinent to PPC systems that illustrates typical differences in the needs of specific industries.

Consequently, only a global classification will be made of the numerous criteria cited in the literature for describing the problem structure. Typical characteristics for industrial enterprises, as they are discussed in the literature, include (see *Kittel, PPS im Klein- und Mittelbetrieb 1982, p. 97; Glaser/Geiger/Rohde, Produktionsplanung und -steuerung 1992, p. 277*):

- Number of products
- Product structure
- Degree of product standardization
- Type of order explosion
- Type of planning
- Proportion of outsourced parts
- Type of production
- Type of production process
- Degree of vertical integration

A different form of classification (see *Hoitsch, Produktionswirtschaft 1993, p. 12; Große-Oetringhaus, Fertigungstypologie 1974; Riebel, Industrielle Erzeugungsverfahren 1963; Schäfer, Der Industriebetrieb 1969; Hansmann, Industrielles Management 1996*) makes distinctions on the basis of the following criteria:

- Product and production program types (output types)
- Production factor types (input types)
- Production process types (throughput types).

This again shows the large variety of problem structures. As a result, the differences will be reduced to three basic types that are based on the degree of manufacturing repetition during a planning period. Subsequently, typical scenarios for problem structuring in PPC systems will be presented that each contain a combination of different classification criteria.

Based on the criterion of the number of identical production processes, a distinction can be made between:

1.   One-off production
      In the case of one-off and order-oriented production, basic product types are modified in accordance with customer requirements. This type of production requires a high degree of flexibility and thus primarily involves shop production.
2.   Series production
      Products are (primarily) manufactured for stock (inventory), whereby production is organized according to the repetitive production principle, i.e., production groups are arranged on the basis of the production process. Job lot production can be classed between one-off and series production; job lot production frequently takes the form of shop production.
3.   Mass production
      This form of production employs an assembly line structure to manufacture for stock.

In a **one-off production** environment, problems arise for PPC systems in the following areas:
-    Basic data management
-    Quotation phase
-    Rough planning phase
-    Detailed scheduling and implementation

During the quotation phase, customer inquiries and bidding specifications must be used to provide information concerning delivery dates and anticipated costs as quickly as possible. Since only incomplete information is available at this stage, it must be possible to access similar prior orders. This necessitates appropriate search algorithms for identifying similar orders or parts. At the same time, however, the user must be able to employ an easy-to-use copy function to access the data for customer-specific modifications without inflating master data management or the management of active orders and parts.

Within the context of rough planning, the task is to obtain information about production times and costs early on, e.g., in the case of a customer order that has been accepted even though not all details have been specified. Short delivery times can result in the need for issuing outside purchase orders—or production orders in the case of critical in-house parts—before the bill of materials structure has been completely defined.

All this leads to an ongoing revision process for an accepted customer order. A highly flexible DP system is essential for incorporating data that are incomplete or that will only be completed over the course of time into requirements and capacity planning. This is particularly true in the case of functions for trial- or simulation-oriented planning.

Network planning techniques can be used for scheduling, whereby the network plan can be revised as the degree of detail in the customer order increases. The transition from the rough planning phase to the structure of a PPC system poses a special problem, which will be discussed further below.

After specifying the primary requirements and the bill of materials definition, detailed planning and scheduling must ensure that the relationship between the production order and the customer (i.e., the customer order) can be established at all times. This information is necessary, for example, if the customer makes changes to his order, wants information concerning the status (time or quantity) of the order, or customer-specific information has to be maintained in connection with costing. These factors make multi-level requirements tracking an absolute necessity; however, this requirement has led to the situation where many PPC systems developed for the Anglo-American market are difficult to implement in the German mechanical engineering industry, with its very strong orientation toward specific customer needs.

Determining the optimal series size (lot size) presents a typical problem in the case of **series production**. Because of the increasing degree of flexibility offered by automated manufacturing systems, however, this is becoming less of a problem. Nonetheless, an important aspect comprises the implementation of new organizational forms such as production islands, flexible manufacturing systems, processing centers, etc. Overall, series manufacturers are the typical users of traditional production planning and control systems.

Mass production involves continuously manufacturing a product in large quantities. Inventories of finished products are generally maintained to compensate for fluctuations in requirements. Given the high volume involved here, inbound and outbound logistics are of particular importance. For this reason, inventory control systems for both outsourced parts and finished products are employed to compensate for fluctuations in market demand.

Classifying problems on the basis of the degree of production repetition reveals important differences in the needs involved in selecting a PPC system; however, this approach is inadequate for a complete description. Figures B.I.234,a - e (from *Scheer, Neue PPS-Architekturen 1986, p. 7*) thus introduce several typical problem scenarios for PPC systems that also incorporate such additional factors as production parts, number of outsourced parts, etc.

At the same time, the illustrations take into account their suitability for different industries.

The degree of cross-hatching indicates the extent to which current PPC philosophy supports the individual scenarios.

Figures B.I.234,a and B.I.234,b show two extreme **initial scenarios**. Figure B.I.234,a shows a **raw-materials-oriented production structure** that manufactures a large variety of end products from only a few raw materials. This form applies, for example, to the ceramics industry, to the paper-making industry, to the chemical industry and to much of the food

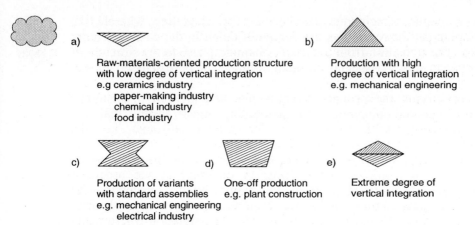

Fig. B.I.234,a-e: Scenarios for PPC-systems

industry, where end products can often differ only in terms of their packaging or size. These types of production structures focus on material flow tracking and assembly line cycling—and thus on optimizing the production sequence in terms of changeover costs. The degree of vertical integration is generally not very significant, and the individual operations are integrated in a closed assembly process (in extreme cases, in a single production system).

Figure B.I.234,b, on the other hand, shows the dominant production structure in the manufacturing industry, e.g., in mechanical engineering. A number of manufacturing and assembly processes combine a large number of materials and outsourced parts into complicated products. A pressing problem in this regard concerns managing product composition and standard operating procedures in the form of bills of materials and routings, as well as determining production orders via requirements explosion techniques. Further structures can be combined from the basic types shown in Figures B.I.234,a and B.I.234,b, as indicated in Figures B.I.234,c-e.

Pronounced customer-orientation is typical of many German industrial enterprises and necessitates a large number of product variants and, frequently, very specific one-off production requirements. Figure B.I.234,c illustrates such a case where parts are initially combined into standard assemblies, and a wide variety of end products are then manufactured in the form of variants.

Figure B.I.234,d illustrates the nature of one-off production, without emphasizing the assembly level. Figure B.I.234,e indicates an extreme degree of vertical integration, where many different intermediate products are first manufactured from raw materials and then assembled into complex units.

The traditional philosophy of PPC systems primarily supports the form of production shown in Figure B.I.234,b, while the other structures can only be covered incompletely.

Industry-specific derivatives of general application systems together with modern DP techniques for CUSTOMIZATION are increasingly expanding the range of applications. In the case of the chemical industry, for example, a modern system for production logistics is being developed under the ESPRIT project "CAPISCE" (see *Loos, Planungshierarchien für die dezentrale Auftragsabwicklung in der Prozeßindustrie 1993*; the following discussions are based on these publications).

Process conversion processes are the main concern in the chemical industry. Depending on the type of project output, a distinction can be made between continuous and noncontinuous production. Continuous production is marked by a uniform flow of materials in special system configurations. Continuous processes are typical of the raw materials industry, e.g., petroleum refining. Noncontinuous production, on the other hand, involves utilizing a technical process to produce a defined quantity of a material. Such a quantity is termed a "lot," a "charge" or a "batch" and, in terms of production planning and control, is similar to a production lot in the context of discrete production. In order to be able to respond flexibly to market demands, the process industry is beginning to show a tendency toward noncontinuous production, i.e., "batch production."

The following criteria help clarify the different requirements for noncontinuous process-oriented production (see *Hofmann, PPS - nichts für die chemische Industrie? 1992*):

- While in mechanical engineering many raw materials typically lead to a broadly differentiated bill of materials structure, in the process industry a large number of product variants are manufactured from a few raw materials on the basis of flat structures. The process industry is more raw-materials-intensive than discrete production. Consequently, adjusted average balance sheet totals indicate inventories of 63.5% for the process industry as opposed to 50.4% for mechanical engineering (see *Siegwart/Raas, CIM orientiertes Rechnungswesen 1991*).
- The process industry places particular demands on the management of materials and material structures (interlinked production, cyclical materials dependencies, variable and substitutable quantity relationships).
- While in discrete production, routings can be used to document the production process relatively well, processes are generally subject to significant fluctuations, which must by taken into account by Production Planning. Thus, recipes in the process industry must frequently indicate spreads for process parameters, whose actual values depend on factors such as raw materials quality, weather conditions or reaction speed, and exhibit non-linear characteristics.
- Environmental restrictions have to be taken into account not only during product development, but also during production planning. Thus, it can be necessary to take peak and average emissions levels into account or to permit emissions only under certain weather conditions.

- Not only is the effort and expense involved in setting up production systems product-dependent, the product sequence is also frequently of key importance as well. This situation leads to "campaign production," in which the product sequence is designed to keep setup costs as low as possible (e.g., producing white before black). If these sequence formations span several successive production systems, this situation is termed "multi-stage campaign production" (see *Overfeld, Produktionsplanung bei mehrstufiger Kampagnenfertigung 1990*).

Because of these different needs, the CIM concept cannot be applied directly to the chemical industry. Figure B.I.235 uses the Y model to show the information systems for Production in process industries; these systems are termed "Computer Integrated Processing" (CIP). The representation of business-oriented systems (left side of the Y model) deviates only slightly from that of the CIM concept. This is because in principle the concepts for the process industry are identical from the perspective of business administration. This is reflected in the largely uniform functionality of the systems, which are primarily adapted to the individual needs of the process industry through internal modifications (see *Hofmann, PPS - nichts für die chemische Industrie? 1992; Luber, How to Identify a True Process Industry Solution 1992*). In contrast, there are marked deviations in the case of the technology-oriented systems. The

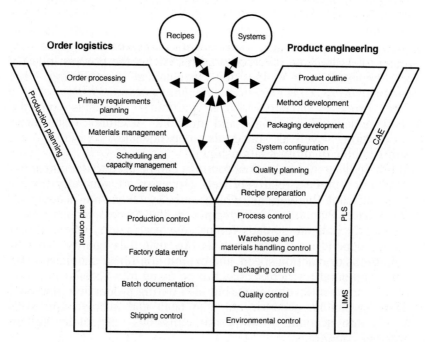

Fig. B.I.235: Information systems for the production in process industry (CIP)

master data for CIP, which are termed "systems" and "recipes," also deviate from those of discrete production.

The plant constitutes the highest level in the production system hierarchy. A plant can contain several system complexes (see *NAMUR Empfehlung NE33 1992; ISA-dS88.01, Batch Control Systems 1992*), and a system complex can be divided into several physically or logically related systems. A system is defined as a production unit that can perform an entire procedure. It consists of several subsystems, each of which can be controlled independently and are thus particularly important in terms of order control. Different subsystems within a system can be combined into a train, e.g., if they are interlinked by piping, or if subsystems are always used in this configuration. Train groupings can change flexibly over time. System components, e.g., vessels and agitators, are the components of a subsystem to which a function relates. Several system components that can perform a function together can be combined into a production unit. Control modules are appurtenances such as valves or pumps that are assembled into a system component, and their interaction ensures the functionality of the system component.

Recipes describe the manufacturing process for a product and are therefore comparable to routings in discrete production. Moreover, recipes contain all necessary starting materials as well as the intermediate and end products that are produced and thus exhibit characteristics of bills of materials. Recipes can be broken down into different components (see *Uhlig, Erstellen von Ablaufsteuerungen für Chargenprozesse mit wechselnden Rezepturen 1987; Kersting, Betriebsleitsysteme zur Rezeptverwaltung und Produktionsdatenverarbeitung 1991*) (see Figure B.I.236).

A recipe segment describes a procedure, e.g., hydrogenation. An operation is the smallest independent executable unit within a recipe and is performed on a subsystem. An operation comprises different functions. If functions are performed automatically, they can be assigned programming codes in the form of control phases. In addition to this hierarchical structure, it is also possible to differentiate between implementation conditions affecting recipes. A procedure describes the general approach for manufacturing a specific material (see Figure B.I.237). It can be subdivided into individual procedural segments analogous to the recipe structure in Figure B.I.236. Procedures are used to generate general recipes, which include information concerning raw materials, intermediate products, products and volumetric ratios as well as the general requirements for the necessary production systems. General recipes consist of general procedures and basic chemical engineering operations. They are further classified into master recipes, which include information concerning the actual systems to be used. Thus, the existing subsystems and control modules are known and basic functions and control phases can be created. While up until now the recipe types have exhibited the nature of master data, control recipes are generated for production orders and always relate to concrete batches. They contain deadlines, quantities and quality data relating to the planned production order as well as the actual values of completed orders.

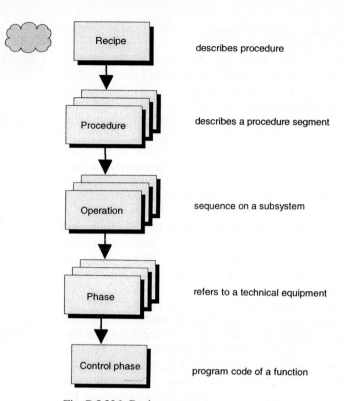

Fig. B.I.236: Recipe structure

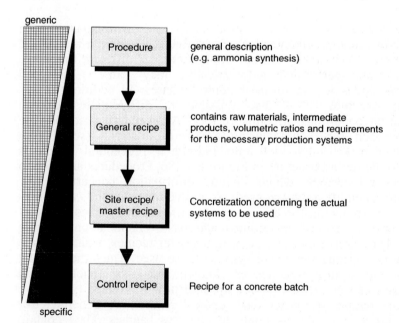

Fig. B.I.237: Recipe types

B.I.6.3 Special Forms

B.I.6.3.1 KANBAN

In the 1980s and 1990s, the introduction of the Japanese principle of KANBAN met with an almost euphoric response. It finally appeared possible to markedly simplify the production structure in contrast to complicated DP systems (see *Wildemann, Werkstattsteuerung 1984*). The KANBAN principle involves "minimum-inventory-oriented" production planning in that an upstream production level always generates new production orders when it "realizes" that its assigned inventory level of finished products has declined below the minimum level. This principle introduces a simplified organizational structure in which predetermined production quantities are manufactured and stored in materials transfer containers (KANBAN containers). Each KANBAN container is assigned an order card (KANBAN is the Japanese word for "card") that contains the order quantity and other information. The planning process is begun by transferring this card (similar to the "shuttle card" technique). KANBAN is generally organized on the basis of the fetch principle, i.e., the order specifications to the final production level determine the further pull of the production quantities into the production process.

In contrast to requirements planning on the basis of exploding primary requirements, KANBAN is a minimum-inventory-level system, while requirement-driven planning, strictly speaking, is a zero-inventory system, since orders are only processed when a specific requirement exists and not when a minimum level has been reached. Nevertheless, KANBAN was discussed as a synonym for inventory reduction because an acceleration of the production flow had been anticipated. Moreover, the KANBAN discussion has led to an increased involvement with questions of changeover and, in individual cases, has resulted in organizational improvements in changeover operations. In addition to the internal application of the KANBAN principle, this procedure also lends itself to interplant supply movement. Particularly impressive is the Japanese example involving automobile manufacturers and suppliers, who can organize their deliveries according to a strict hourly schedule (see below the JIT concepts for external logistics).

In the meantime, however, concrete implementations have shown that KANBAN, for various reasons, cannot be used as a comprehensive control system in German industry. On the one hand, it requires the kind of tight integration between manufacturers and suppliers for interplant applications that does not exist in Germany, and in-house it requires highly stable production quantities and highly reliable quality. Nevertheless, the control principle for production subdepartments has also met with success in Germany, and it does not conflict with DP-supported production planning and control or with the MRP planning principle previously described.

KANBAN approaches can also be supported by DP systems in that the releases are issued via electronic messages, which provides a higher degree of information availability with respect to inventory levels and order progress than manual processing.

B.I.6.3.2 Progress Numbers

For the assembly-oriented series and mass production that typifies the automotive industry, the concept of progress numbers marks a further step in the development of DP-supported planning systems (see *ACTIS, FORS 1993*). A progress number is a cumulative value that can refer to different characteristic variables. If the progress number refers to planning variables, it is termed a "target progress number." Likewise, values that have actually been achieved are referred to as "actual progress numbers." Figure B.I.238 shows a typical progress number as both target and actual values. The broken line representing the target value indicates the cumulative planned production quantity for a part; the solid line, the actual quantity produced as an actual progress number.

Other information can be derived by comparing target and actual progress numbers. If the solid line lies above the broken line, production is running ahead of schedule. This situation can be expressed either in terms of quantity units (by the vertical distance) or in terms of time units (by the horizontal distance). In Figure B.I.238, the arrows express this situation relative to the present point in time.

A logistic concept that is driven by progress numbers uses a multitude of reference units for which progress numbers can be calculated. These include, for example:

<u>Target</u>	<u>Actual</u>
Release progress number	Shipping progress number
Production planning progress number	Assembly progress number

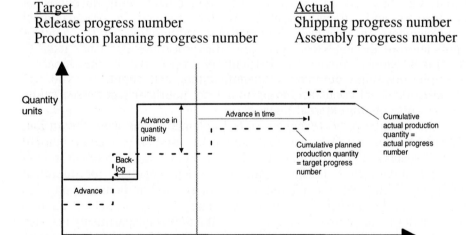

Fig. B.I.238: Progress numbers diagram

Inventory figures can be determined from the difference between the progress numbers for inventory additions and withdrawals.

This concept requires a high degree of customer-orientation. Thus, the total number of customer orders serves as the point of departure, whereby established delivery dates provide the basis for chronological assignments. This **order progress number**, which is a target value, can be compared with the **shipping progress number**, the corresponding actual value.

The progress number concept is in widespread use in the automotive industry, where planned order figures are additionally compared with effective releases as additional progress numbers. The system can encompass the entire production logistics chain down to the level of operation-specific production tracking. The difference between target and actual values and their interpretation as advance or backlog items (expressed either in time or quantity units) enables comprehensive enterprise-wide control. In particular, changes and their ramifications can be easily seen. The progress number concept, therefore, represents an effective supplement to current PPC methods. This method employs standard requirements explosions for determining target progress numbers, e.g., for component requirements.

This concept is also gaining in significance as a result of the proliferation of intercompany data exchange. Thus, in the automotive industry, manufacturers and suppliers exchange progress numbers for deliveries, orders and releases (see *Scheer, CIM 1990, pp. 98 ff.; Meyer, Informationssysteme 1987*).

B.I.6.4 Standard Software for Production Logistics

Figures B.I.239,a-c show several promising new standard software systems for production planning and control and technical CAM applications.

Due to the high development costs involved in comprehensive PPC systems—50 to 200 man years are not uncommon—standard software packages frequently represent the only option for implementing a system.

The charts shown here indicate the functions provided by the various standard software systems, which reveals the importance of the various options available on the market for implementing integrated systems.
The three levels for evaluating the functions are:
Functions unavailable   (-)
Basic functions available   (x)
Full functions available   (xx)
These levels give a rough impression of system performance; however, this representation should not be construed as the only criterion for choosing a system. This would necessitate a more thorough catalog of production-specific and DP-specific requirements.

PPC systems

Trade mark / Function	SAP R/3 resp. R/2	TRITON	PSK 2000	PIUSS-O
Basic data	XX	XX	X	XX
Order processing	XX	XX	XX	XX
Accounts receivable	X	X	X	-
Primary requirements planning	XX	X	X	X
Requirements planning	XX	X	X	X
Purchasing	XX	XX	XX	X
Accounts payable	X	X	X	-
Capacity planning	XX	X	X	XX
Adjustment	X	X	-	X
Order release	XX	X	X	XX
Detailed scheduling	X	X	X	X
Factory data entry	X	X	X	X
Load-oriented order release	XX	-	X	XX
KANBAN	-	-	-	-
JIT	XX	XX	-	XX
MRP II	XX	XX	XX	XX
Progress numbers	XX	-	-	-
Leitstand	XX	X	X	XX

Fig. B.I.239,a: System performance of selected PPC systems

Leitstand systems

Trade mark / Function	FI-2/ RI-2	DASS	AHP	Factory Tower
Basic data	XX	-	XX	XX
Order processing	XX	X	XX	XX
Primary requirements planning	-	-	-	-
Requirements planning	X	-	X	X
Purchasing	X	-	-	-
Capacity planning	XX	XX	XX	XX
Adjustment	XX	XX	XX	XX
Order release	XX	XX	XX	XX
Detailed scheduling	XX	XX	X	XX
Factory data entry	XX	XX	XX	X
Factory data analysis	XX	X	X	XX

Fig. B.I.239,b: System performance of selected leitstand systems

Dedicated CAM-Systems

System	Producer	System function	Modules
FIT	A&B Systems	Factory data entry	Factory data entry Machine data entry DNC Time data entry Quality data entry
SysQua	eas	Quality assurance	Receivings Manufacturing Withdrawals Inspection equipment management FMEA
unc8500i	mbp datentechnik	NC programming	Run time calculation Post processor output Resource management (opt.) Data import from CAD PPC, Leitstand, Tool management
APROL	PLT	Process visualization and control	Resource image design Operating interface design Control, monitoring and operation of processes

Fig. B.I.239,c: Functions of dedicated CAM systems

The integration of holistic logistics processes requires, for example, that all functions be able to access specific data and that the individual functions be able to interact. Thus, all modern systems employ database systems for supporting data integration.

Functional interaction—e.g., in the case of a net change operation for customer order processing where all subsequent order processing functions through to production control are initiated—is already available. As a result, some systems employ trigger concepts for controlling related function sequences.

Detailed market studies—which, however, quickly become outdated due to rapid innovation in the industry—can regularly be found in computer magazines such as Computer Week or in publications from consulting firms (see *Ploenzke, PPS Studie 1989* and *Ploenzke, Fertigungsleitstand-Report 1992*).

B.II Inbound and Outbound Logistics

Inbound and outbound logistics encompass the planning and scheduling activities that accompany the flow of goods between an enterprise and its external associates, i.e., its suppliers and customers. The term "goods" relates to the production factors to be employed. In addition to physical goods, however, the term "goods" also encompasses services and financial resources. Moreover, employee recruitment is also encompassed under inbound logistics.

Although business administration has traditionally treated inbound and outbound logistics as separate concepts, this section will discuss them in the same context. This approach takes into account the fact that many functions and processes in inbound and outbound logistics mirror—and are thus similar to—one another.

The following examples illustrate the similarity between inbound and outbound logistics, which is a result of mirror-image relationships, data overlaps, functional overlaps and functional interchange:

> The exchange of goods between two enterprises is handled by the interaction between the purchasing and sales functions of both parties. Thus, both logistics systems process the same objects: Inquiries, orders, complaints, invoices, etc.

> New logistics concepts associated with the increased cooperation between customers and suppliers are leading to an exchange of functions between the parties, e.g., the customer's incoming inspection is replaced by the supplier's final inspection.

> In materials transfer planning, the aim is to combine purchasing and shipping activities, e.g., delivery to a customer is coupled with a delivery of goods from a supplier located near the customer.

> Generating a "pro forma invoice" when an order is created constitutes invoicing from the standpoint of the supplier. Thus, purchasing also involves invoicing in the same way that sales transactions do.

> Industrial enterprises not only cost their in-house parts, they also seek to determine supplier production costs in order to be able to use this information when negotiating terms. Thus, both systems feature a costing function.

> Many customers are also suppliers; a strict separation of their data would result in redundancy. The general entity type BUSINESS ASSOCIATE, however, can be assigned the same attributes (e.g., address) and the same functions (e.g., address management) to avoid redundancy.

Businesses are increasingly employing merchandise management systems that allow an article to be tracked from planning to ordering, receiving and storage through to sale and shipping. Purchasing and sales activities are linked in a process chain via the common object ARTICLE.

In order to be able to discuss the special terminology and processes of these subsystems, the two logistics systems will be treated one after another within the context of the requirements definition, whereby the discussion of outbound logistics will make reference to the parallel processes for inbound logistics, which will have already been discussed. In the summary of the requirements definition as well as in the discussion of design specifications, inbound and outbound logistics will be treated simultaneously. This will allow a high degree of reusability of the functional modules and data structures on the design specification level, for example.

B.II.1 Overview: Inbound and Outbound Logistics

Figure B.II.01 shows the function trees for inbound and outbound logistics. The functions are arranged on the basis of their sequence within the respective process, revealing a mirror-image parallelism. The information objects processed by both process chains are indicated in the middle of the diagram. They represent general object types for the specialized information objects processed by both process chains. Thus, for example, the term "external business associates" is used as a superordinate concept for both suppliers and customers.

The input and output relationships of the process chains to data clusters are indicated in the process chain diagrams shown in Figures B.II.02,a and b, which reveal that many functions can be performed either interactively or automatically. If, for example, detailed supplier- and terms-related data are available for a purchasing requisition for materials, a programmed decision rule can automatically initiate the ordering process. If, on the other hand, there is a need for a special material for which the terms first have to be determined, interactive processing is necessary.

Data can be exchanged with external parties by mail, fax or electronic data interchange (EDI).

Both logistics chains pass through virtually all of the organizational units in the organizational chart shown in Figure B.II.03. In the case of materials sourcing, essentially every department in every organizational unit can initiate requirements.

The organizational unit "Standardization," which decides which materials are to be included in basic data management and determines the necessary specifications for them, reports to "Engineering."

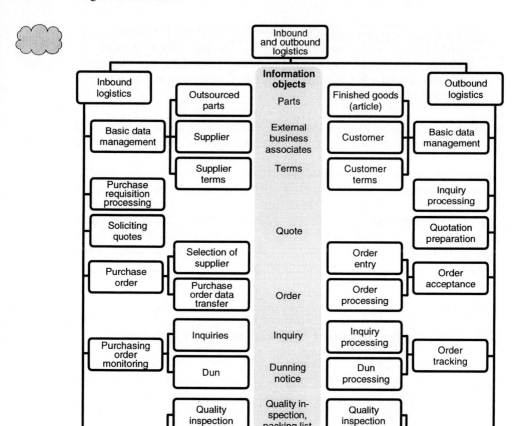

Fig. B.II.01: Function tree for inbound and outbound logistics

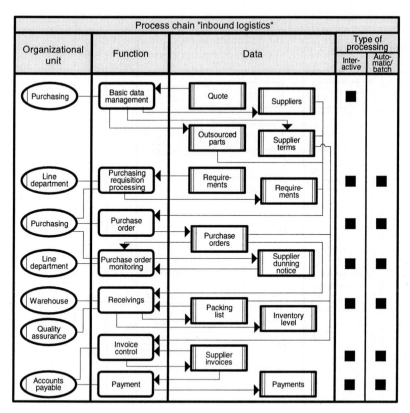

Fig. B.II.02,a: Process chain diagram for inbound logistics

Production, together with its organizational unit "Requirements Planning," forms an important interface to inbound logistics. This is where the net requirements for outsourced parts are determined as the point of departure for purchasing decisions within the framework of the gross-net calculation. While inbound logistics more or less follows requirements planning, outbound logistics—by generating customer orders—serves as the source of the primary requirements and in effect initiates requirements planning.

The goods receiving function is assigned to the organizational unit "Warehouse."

Purchasing performs materials planning, supplier management, purchase order writing and dunning. In a functional division of labor structure, these functions could be assigned to independent organizational units. In the case of functionally integrated processing, on the other hand, the functions are combined and organizational units are structured according to the object principle, i.e., on the basis of certain classes of materials. The organizational chart shows both options.

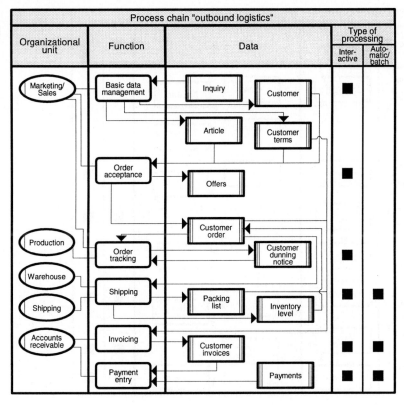

Fig. B.II.02,b: Process chain diagram for outbound logistics

If the purchasing warehouse reports to the purchasing department, the receiving inspection is an organizational unit within the purchasing department.

The finance and accounting department is involved through the organizational unit "Invoice Control." Invoice control is an essential integration function of inbound logistics because this is where data from the entire process—i.e., ordering, receiving and supplier management—flow together.

Figure B.II.03 also shows the special forms of personnel recruitment as well as investment and capital acquisition.

Personnel recruitment is handled in the personnel department, while investment acquisition is handled both in Engineering as well as in Finance and Accounting through the links to financing and invoice control. Capital acquisition is a function of Finance and Accounting.

Outbound logistics is mainly handled in Sales/Marketing. In a strictly functional structure, organizational units can be formed for quotations, order acceptance and order tracking. In a functionally integrated solution, however, the sales groups are organized according to the object principle and perform all three of these functions for a defined group of articles.

Design Engineering is incorporated into outbound logistics if customer-order-oriented changes to a product have to be performed. In a customer-

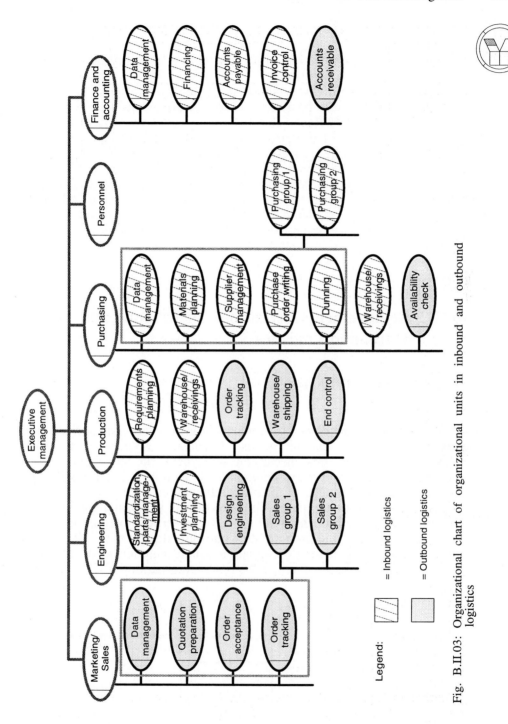

Fig. B.II.03: Organizational chart of organizational units in inbound and outbound logistics

oriented production environment, the production departments are linked to order tracking.

Purchasing can be involved so it can supply availability information in response to customer inquiries.

The link to Accounting is established via Accounts Receivable.

Both logistics chains possess intensive relationships to Finance and Accounting. Accounts Receivable and Accounts Payable have access to most of the data from the logistics chains and assign account codes early in the order handling process, e.g., as part of inbound logistics in conjunction with the purchasing requisition or as part of outbound logistics at the time an order is accepted. Postings are not made until later when invoices are received or issued. In addition, account coding for internal accounting, i.e., the indication of cost category, cost center or cost objective, can already be performed at the start of the respective process chain.

B.II.2 Requirements Definitions for Inbound and Outbound Logistics

B.II.2.1 Inbound Logistics

The resources handled by inbound logistics are categorized into materials, services, capital goods, financial resources and human resources. However, this discussion will focus on the acquisition of materials. The process representation and Section B.II.2.1.6 will treat some of the special aspects of the other inbound resources.

The importance of the purchasing function is increasing for industrial enterprises as a result of the trend toward less vertical integration and the resulting increase in the proportion of outsourced parts within the overall range of parts. This leads to a situation where materials costs constitute the greatest expense in many industrial enterprises. It also means that

	BEFORE	AFTER	
OUTSOURCED MATERIALS	50 %	49 %	2% REDUCTION IN THE COST OF MATERIALS
WAGES etc.	40 %	40 %	
EARNINGS	10 %	11 %	10 % INCREASE IN EARNINGS

Fig. B.II.04: Cost structure before and after reduction in the cost of materials

efforts to improve efficiency in this area can have a substantial impact on the success of the enterprise, even if the proportion of the savings is relatively small. Figure B.II.04 uses a typical cost structure in the manufacturing industry to illustrate how a 2 % reduction in the cost of materials leads to a 10 % increase in earnings.

The high proportion of outsourced materials leads to a high inventory value, and thus to correspondingly high interest expense.

High inventory levels have also been known to conceal problems in planning, inventory management and requirements forecasting (see Figure B.II.05,a, which is based on a rock and water metaphor, with the "peaks" representing problems in the system, and the water level representing the inventory level).

High inventory levels are criticized in conjunction with high interest rates. Reducing the inventory levels, however, reveals the problems in the planning functions (see Figure B.II.05,b).

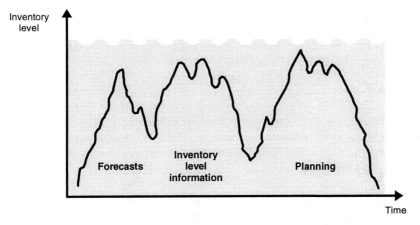

Fig. B.II.05,a: Concealment of problems by high inventory levels

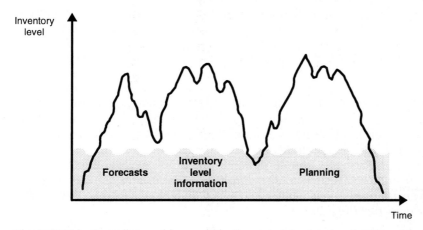

Fig. B.II.05,b: Revealing problems within the materials planning functions by reducing the inventory levels

One approach, therefore, involves linking the purchasing function more closely with Production and thus manufacturing on a virtually "inventory-free" basis. At the same time, however, it is essential to maintain the high degree of flexibility within Production that market conditions are increasingly demanding. Terms such as "Kanban" and "just-in-time production" are used to discuss logistics chains that not only necessitate a chronologically streamlined organizational structure within the enterprise, but also encourage intercompany cooperation. The current cooperation among automobile manufacturers and their suppliers, for example, represents initial attempts at implementing these methods (see *Scheer, CIM 1990, pp. 98 ff.; Mertens, Zwischenbetriebliche Integration 1985; Wildemann, Werkstattsteuerung 1984*).

A further problem within the purchasing department results from the increasing degree of automation within Production, as described in the section on CAM. Automated production systems require strict adherence to materials quality standards. There are real-world examples where minor deficiencies in quality in relatively low-value materials have brought complex production systems to a standstill, resulting in high downtime costs. For this reason, quality assurance and the chronological streamlining of purchasing processes are becoming more and more important.

Non-redundant processing of the process chain for planning, order processing, collections, receiving, invoice control and accounts payable requires an integrated data structure. Thus, the following discussions will focus on the design of this data structure. After a representation of the basic data, the data structure will follow the functions of order processing, receiving and invoice control.

Traditional business administration theory focuses on the decision-oriented concerns of determining order quantities and maintaining an optimum safety stock. Given the existing deterministic and stochastic data situations, optimization models are developed that take into account costs relating to order quantities, shortfalls and inventory. Standard references for this business-administration-oriented perspective to materials management include: *Grochla, Materialwirtschaft 1992; Hartmann, Materialwirtschaft - Organisation, Planung, Durchführung, Kontrolle 1992; Oeldorf/Olfert, Materialwirtschaft 1995; Schneeweiß, Lagerhaltungssysteme 1981; Glaser/Geiger/Rohde, Produktionsplanung und -steuerung 1992, pp. 136 ff.; Tempelmeier, Material-Logistik 1992.* These approaches represent only one aspect of DP systems for inbound logistics. This discussion tends to be dominated by organizational procedures for controlling the numerous processes, while taking into account the high volume involved.

Figure B.II.06 shows a more detailed functional overview than the one shown in Figure B.II.01 (see also *Rauh, Die Gestaltung der individuellen Datenverarbeitung am Beispiel des Einkaufs 1992; Witt, Beschaffungscontrolling 1992*).

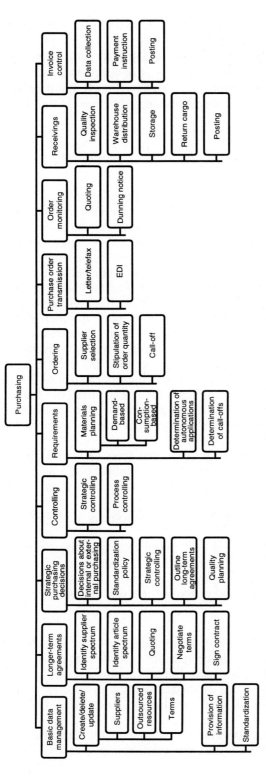

Fig. B.II.06: Function tree for inbound logistics

B.II.2.1.1 Basic Data Management

Basic data are the master data for outsourced resources and their suppliers. The master data are filled in on the basis of supplier quotes that have been obtained or other documents from Purchasing. Related master data from Accounting are also incorporated, together with their relationships to Purchasing.

B.II.2.1.1.1 Data on Goods and Suppliers

Within the context of production logistics, parts purchased from external suppliers were incorporated into bill of materials management and termed "outsourced parts." This term will now be expanded into "outsourced resources" in order to include other types of resources as well (see Figure B.II.07). On the basis of Figure B.II.07, the outsourced resources can be categorized into materials (raw materials, supplies, consumables and outsourced components), services, capital goods, as well as financial resources and labor. For the sake of simplicity, these resources are identified by the previously introduced key part number PNO. Materials and capital goods have already been introduced as specializations of the entity type PART. The other types of resources, particularly services and financial resources, can also be described as specializations of the entity type PART and thus incorporated into bill of materials relationships and "part applications." The use of human resources, on the other hand, was described within the context of operations, but it also belongs to the performance description in the broadest sense.

The typical attributes of the specialized entity type OUTSOURCED RESOURCE have already been discussed in connection with the introduction of the general entity type PART; only a few of these attributes are therefore listed here:

-    Purchasing code, quantity unit, weight, supplier's part number, name, width/diameter
-    Materials-planning data such as estimated quantity, reorder inventory level, safety stock, minimum order quantity, maximum order quantity, planner, planning method, lot sizing key, forecasting model selection key, fixed lot costs and storage cost rate.

A classification (see Figure B.II.08) is advisable in order for Design Engineering to be able to handle a large number of different outsourced parts or in order to be able to deal with unsolicited supplier quotes.

This classification forms a new bill of materials logic in addition to the one previously introduced for design, production and sales bills of materials.

For this reason, the classification can be entered in the familiar data structure for the entity type PART and the relationship STRUCTURE.

This merely necessitates generating a new view. To this end, PART entities are formed for the individual classification instances, and the assignment arrows are converted into STRUCTURE relationships.

An actual material can be described by further characteristics, in addition to its categorization into a class.

Figure B.II.07 shows this function using the entity type MATERIAL CHARACTERISTIC, which results in an n:m assignment to the entity type MATERIAL. This data structure is also employed in the discussion of the product development process, particularly in the case of computer-aided design (CAD). The use of classification systems within the context of CAD is an important factor in increasing efficiency, which leads to a high degree of parts reusability.

The n cardinalities indicate that a material can be found under different characteristics, and, conversely, that one characteristic usually occurs in several different materials. The branch of industry associated with the outsourced resource can also constitute an important characteristic, e.g., in order to determine new suppliers for an outsourced resource (for additional examples of classifications, see *Grochla, Materialwirtschaft 1992, pp. 36 ff.; SAP, System RM-PPS Funktionsbeschreibung 1993, p. 86*).

If, for example, a pine log is needed with a specific diameter, length or grade, it is relatively easy to locate the appropriate material by accessing the corresponding material class and then searching the individual characteristic instances.

In addition to materials, suppliers constitute a second group of master data. The entity type SUPPLIER is a specialization of the entity type BUSINESS ASSOCIATE and is categorized into in-house organizational units that form their own company code, outside industrial, trading and service companies, banks and manpower as suppliers of labor. Since including personnel procurement along with the other resources in an overall analysis would result in unwieldy formulations—despite the similarities—the analysis of manpower as a supplier is only suggested. In addition to the supplier number SUPNO, typical attributes for the entity type SUPPLIER include the supplier's name and address, the country code, the cumulative order value, information concerning reliability in terms of deadlines and quality and general rebate class rules.

It is advisable to include potential suppliers as well as suppliers with whom concrete business relationships have already been established. It is also possible to formulate characteristics for suppliers. A qualitative evaluation of suppliers, for example, can include characteristics such as price history, quality capability, supplier reliability and engineering potential (see *Herzog, QS-Komponenten in Beschaffung und Materialfluß 1992*). Other characteristics can include industry, nationality, company size, etc. The following special evaluations can be performed for supplier groups on the basis of these characteristics:

- Number of inquiries per period
- Purchase obligations received per period.

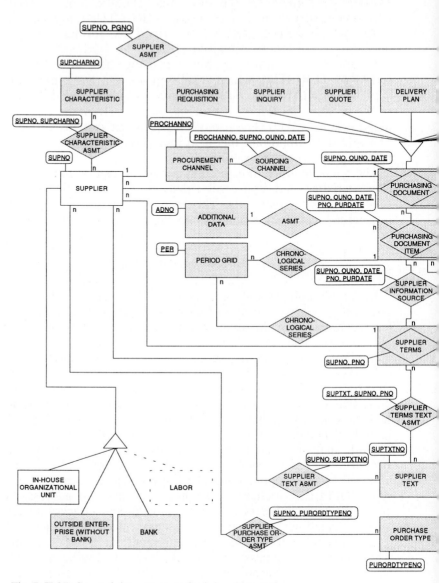

Fig. B.II.07: General data structure for inbound logistics

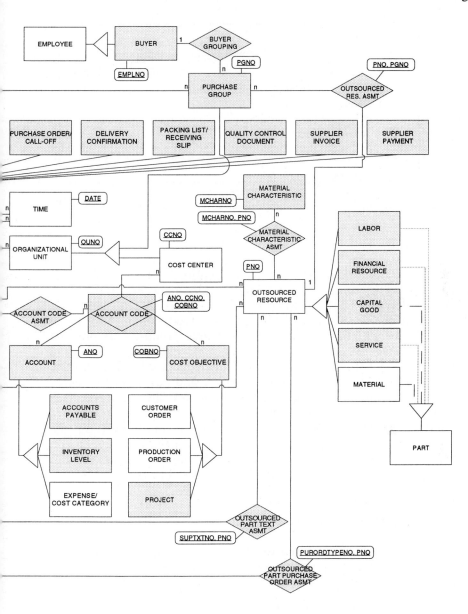

Legend: — — —   already introduced specialization of PART
....   possible further specializations

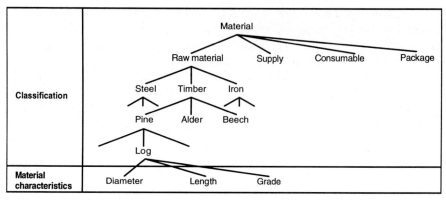

Fig. B.II.08: Material classification

This grouping is denoted via the entity type SUPPLIER CHARACTERISTIC with an n:m relationship between SUPPLIER CHARACTERISTIC ASSIGNMENT and the entity type SUPPLIER.

Depending on the organizational principle involved, certain buyers can be responsible for supplier or outsourced resource groups. This practice can ensure that one specific buyer represents the enterprise vis-à-vis a supplier or that the necessary specialized knowledge concerning specific outsourced resources is available. Each supplier and outsourced resource is assigned to a purchase group, which comprises several buyers (as specializations of the entity type EMPLOYEE).

The entity type PURCHASE ORDER TYPE is introduced for the different types of purchase orders (cash, rental agreement, loan agreement, leasing agreement, delivery schedule, call-off agreement) and linked with the entity types OUTSOURCED RESOURCE and SUPPLIER.

B.II.2.1.1.2 Documents and Terms

A number of documents are used to exchange information between the parties involved in preparing and processing a purchase. These documents are also termed "purchasing documents" and accompany the purchasing process from notification of the need to solicit quotes, ordering, delivery plan, delivery confirmation and packing list all the way to quality control and invoicing. The contents of these documents relate to one another and portions of them are frequently identical. Since they reflect the entire purchasing process, they could be viewed as the development of one individual document whose status changes. Because of the chronological nature of the process and the changing parties involved, however, this is not entirely apparent, so that the different terms cited above are also firmly established in the organizational structure. Thus, the beaurocratic aspects of purchasing procedures will be critically discussed here in light of the attempt to streamline and simplify the process (see the "just-in-time" organizational structure discussed later).

The following discussion will take both situations into account by introducing the individual documents as data objects and, at the same time, emphasizing their content-related and structural similarities using the generalized analysis shown in Figure B.II.07. The documents serve not only to accompany an actual purchasing process, but also as the source of data for Accounting as well as for updating master data and agreed terms.

In Figure B.II.07, the generalized entity type PURCHASING DOCUMENT is introduced as a representative document. It is identified by information concerning its date of issue and the "supplier" as well as of one other party, e.g., one of the organizational units "Purchasing," "Warehouse," "QA," or "Accounts Payable." One of the internal organizational units can also be the previously introduced purchasing group. If different procurement channels exist, such as direct sourcing from the manufacturer or via distribution channels, this is expressed by the assignment to the entity type SOURCING CHANNEL.

The document header is followed by document items that relate to the purchased outsourced resource and the delivery date. In the case of complicated outsourced resources, additional data, e.g., texts, can be assigned to a purchasing document item via the entity type ADDITIONAL DATA.

The individual document items enable chronological developments in supplier information to be tracked. To this end, the entity type PERIOD GRID is introduced, whose instances are period identifiers, so that attributes of interest such as the prices or quality ratings of a supplier are available in the form of a chronological series via the relationship type CHRONOLOGICAL SERIES. This can be important in the case of purchase negotiations, for example.

The data structure serves not only to determine all of a supplier's quotes for an outsourced resource, but the current quotes from several suppliers as well. Conversely, analyses concerning one supplier's pricing for several different resources can be generated as well.

If not all individual documents have to be stored over an extended period of time, extracts can be maintained in the information object SUPPLIER TERMS. These extracts are strictly defined information that is updated by purchasing documents, e.g., quotes, and designed as quasi master data between OUTSOURCED RESOURCE and SUPPLIER. Current data from the accepted quote are transferred to this relationship type, as well as additional information that relates to the links between the supplier and the outsourced resources, such as:

- accepted price schedules, transport costs, supplier capacity, delivery time with calculated standard deviation, quality data from receiving inspections with different statistical parameters, name of contact at the supplier, total order quantity for the previous year (per supplier and part), quantity ordered for the current period, etc.
- In the case of loan agreements, typical information includes installment payments, repayment periods, collateral, etc.

Terms also include inspection plans that are used for receiving inspections. Due to the tighter integration between suppliers and customers, receiving inspections are increasingly being shifted to the supplier's final inspection. Here, too, corresponding terms are then agreed upon. Likewise, specific delivery schedules and blanket order agreements can be stipulated. These issues will be discussed later.

In order to track the origin of this information, e.g., which quote items will be used to fill the terms, the relationship type SUPPLIER INFORMATION SOURCE is introduced between the reinterpreted entity types SUPPLIER TERMS and PURCHASING DOCUMENT ITEM.

Moreover, a history of chronological series relationships can be maintained for supplier terms.

B.II.2.1.1.3 Texts

Standard text modules are formulated for writing orders. These modules relate to suppliers, e.g., to a supplier's address and general terms of sale and delivery. Text modules can, however, also exist for outsourced resources, e.g., in the form of part descriptions, material specifications, etc. Text modules such as terms of sale and delivery, supplier inspection procedures, etc., relate to the link between SUPPLIER and OUTSOURCED RESOURCE, as characterized by the relationship type SUPPLIER TERMS.

Since only some of the texts depend on the concrete instances of the three entity types, they are combined into their own entity type SUPPLIER TEXT and assigned to the three entity types via links. Thus, the initially anonymous text modules can be assigned parameters from the corresponding entity attributes. For example, a text module could read:

"Terms: ...weeks...%"

The actual discount rate and the number of weeks can be taken from the agreed terms. Thus, transferring a concrete percentage rate into the order is simply a matter of using a relationship to create a reference from the entity type SUPPLIER TERMS to the text module.

The entity type SUPPLIER TEXT is first introduced in Figure B.II.07. Each text module is identified by a text module number (SUPTXTNO). Relationships lead from the SUPPLIER TEXT to each of the three entity types SUPPLIER, OUTSOURCED RESOURCE and SUPPLIER TERMS.

B.II.2.1.1.4 Account Coding

During the entire purchasing process, data become available that can be used for internal and external accounting. This holds true particularly in the case of account coding, i.e., the allocation of the business transaction to accounts in the financial accounting system or to "cost categories," "cost centers" and "cost objectives" in the internal accounting system.

Since Financial Accounting and Internal Accounting are independent departments that will be discussed in greater detail later, only a few basic processes will be mentioned here that are particularly useful for illustrating the link between Purchasing and the value level.

In the case of financial accounting accounts, a distinction can be made between personal accounts, inventory accounts and expense accounts. The personal accounts accessed by the purchasing process are the accounts payable accounts. A 1:1 relationship can exist between the accounts payable account and the entity type SUPPLIER, i.e., an account payable is identical to a supplier.

In a purchasing process, the account payable involved is clear from the beginning on the basis of the "supplier inquiry" or "supplier quote" purchasing documents.

An inventory account is addressed if warehoused outsourced resources are purchased that are initially capitalized as inventory. This holds true not only for materials, but also for capital goods that are subsequently entered in the fixed asset accounting system.

When non-warehousable materials are received, they are immediately assigned to an expense account as consumed goods. Agreements can be reached to ensure a close correspondence between the allocation of cost categories and the expense definition, thus eliminating the need to maintain independent cost category definitions.

Information concerning inventory and expense accounts is taken from the items in the purchasing documents. This information, too, is available early in the purchasing process, usually when the goods are ordered, at the latest. **Posting** to inventory and expense accounts, on the other hand, does not occur until the incoming goods are received.

The cost center that is debited with a purchase can also be identified in advance on the basis of the purchasing documents. Frequently, the cost center is identical to the organizational unit requesting the purchase, so that this allocation is already known when a purchase is requested. This interrelationship also applies, for example, when employees are hired, with their costs being allocated to a cost center.

Cost objectives can be customer orders, production orders or investment projects. This information is already available in the initial documents such as purchase requests.

The relationship type ACCOUNT CODE combines information concerning accounts, cost centers and cost objectives. A relationship to the PURCHASING DOCUMENT ITEM is created as a reinterpreted entity type. This means that several account code allocations can be initiated from a document item. For example, an account code allocation among several cost centers can be derived from an invoice item that refers to a specific quantity of an outsourced resource if this outsourced resource is apportioned among several consuming units according to a specified known account code allocation. This situation is termed "multiple account code allocation."

B.II.2.1.2 Purchasing Process

The following discussion will develop the functional process of inbound logistics, which is oriented primarily toward the procurement of physical goods. The basic process is illustrated in the event-driven process chain shown in Figure B.II.09. The illustration shows that the above-mentioned

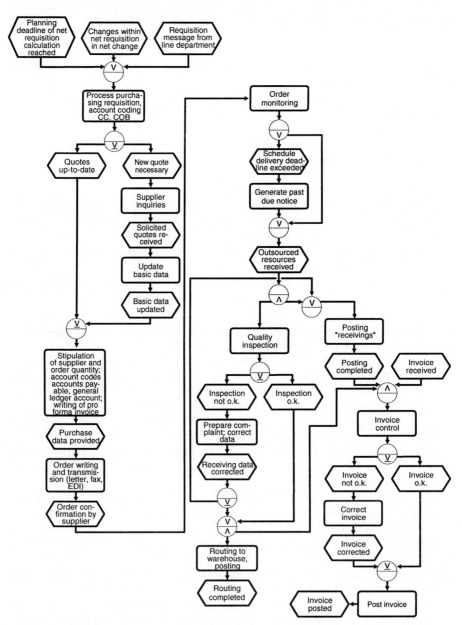

Fig. B.II.09: Event-driven process chain for inbound logistics

purchasing documents represent events that initiate processing steps. Posting procedures can be performed in parallel with operative processing steps; in the case of adjustments, loops to an adjusting entry are also necessary. Invoice Control requires that both the bookkeeping functions from Receiving and feedback from QA have been completed.

B.II.2.1.2.1 Requirements and Purchasing Requisitions

Within the context of requirements planning for the PPC system, gross requirements for outsourced parts were derived as secondary requirements from the production order records for superordinate parts. Net requirements were then determined from the gross requirement by subtracting inventory levels, and order requisitions were derived using lot sizing techniques, with the order costs being used as "fixed lot" costs. An order requisition is thus an entity of the entity type ORDER introduced in the context of requirements planning.

Essentially, however, it is not necessary for purchase orders to be created for outsourced parts within the framework of requirements planning, since, unlike parts on higher planning levels, they cannot be further exploded. Thus, it would be possible to stop after determining the gross requirement and not determine the order requisitions until the purchasing stage. However, in order for Production Planning to gain an initial overview of outsourcing on the basis of the production program for the overall planning period, it is advisable to perform a net requirements analysis for outsourced parts up to provisional order requisitions. Then the order deadlines can be taken into account during simultaneous requirements and capacity planning in order to identify time-critical purchase orders.

Just as it is possible to recombine the orders formed in the context of requirements planning in the course of time management and detailed scheduling, the suggested orders from requirements planning can be reoptimized within the framework of purchasing. In this case, for example, orders from the same supplier are bundled into consolidated orders or new purchase order quantities are formed on the basis of new order requisitions received in addition to the quantities already included in requirements planning.

Figure B.II.10 clarifies this interface to Requirements Planning by introducing the results from Requirements Planning as DEMAND-BASED PURCHASING REQUISITION. This is a relationship type between REQUIREMENTS PLANNING (the organizational unit that determines the requirements), PURCHASING (the addressee for the requirement) and TIME. The header information object thus characterizes the planning calculation, to which the part-related requisition items later refer.

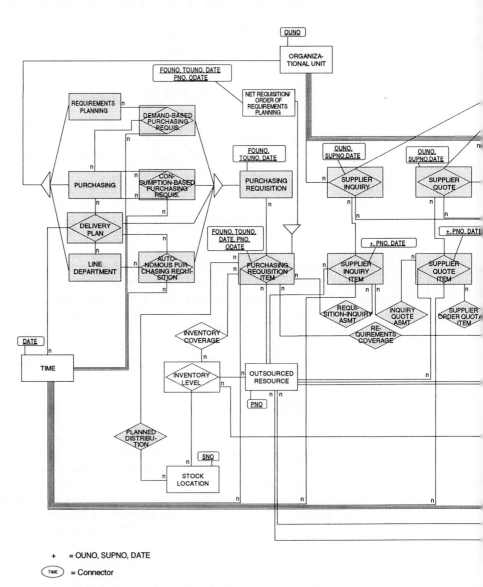

Fig. B.II.10: Detailed data structure for purchase order handling

CONSUMPTION-BASED PURCHASING REQUISITION occur in addition to these demand-based requisitions. The consumption-based requirements are determined statistically by the purchasing departments using forecasting procedures and formally indicate the demand scheduler and the demand receiver. This relationship type also bundles the part-

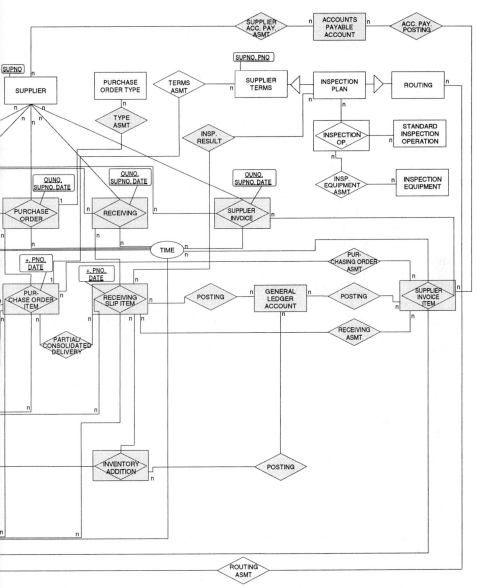

related requisitions. In making this determination, the same statistical procedures can be used, as in determining the consumption-based in-house parts, i.e., exponential smoothing, the Box-Jenkins method, etc., as well as those used in requirements forecasting for end products. Without going into the properties of these methods in detail, relatively simple—i.e., formally oriented and thus automatically applicable—forecasting methods are appropriate (see *Mertens, Prognoserechnung 1981; Scheer, Absatzprognosen 1983*) due to the number of types of materials to be analyzed as well as their sometimes relatively low value. Delivery schedules can exist for certain outsourced resources; longer-term purchasing requisitions can be stipulated in these delivery schedules. The delivery schedules are maintained by line departments and are directed to Purchasing.

In addition to the requisition types discussed thus far, line departments can also autonomously direct purchasing requisitions to Purchasing, e.g., for equipment and capital goods. The requisitions from one department are bundled in the information object AUTONOMOUS PURCHASING REQUISITION.

The four requisition types are generalized into the entity type PURCHASING REQUISITION since their respective processes do not differ significantly. This entity type is also assigned the keys FOUNO, TOUNO and the purchasing requisition date ("F" stands for "FROM," "T" for "TO"). It bundles the requisition items that establish the reference to the entity type OUTSOURCED RESOURCE and to the resource delivery date. For demand-based outsourced parts, the purchasing requisition items are identical to the net requirement created during requirements planning or to the order if lots have already been formed. Because of its importance, it is indicated as an "is-a" relationship.

Since some PURCHASING REQUISITION ITEMS are gross values, they are linked via the INVENTORY COVERAGE relationship with the INVENTORY LEVEL, so that the net requisitions can be calculated.

Regardless of its source, the purchasing requisition is the point of departure for further purchase order processing.

With the definition of a purchasing requisition, it is also possible to know the subsequent stock location, either if the stock location is defined via a demand-based derivation from the initiating order or by a line department in the case of a consumption-based requisition or an autonomous requisition. This assignment is subsequently used for stocking the delivered materials and is the basis for posting the increase in inventory. If a requisition has to be distributed among several stock locations, an n:m assignment exists, as indicated for the relationship type PLANNED DISTRIBUTION. A 1:n assignment is also conceivable if apportionment to several stock locations does not appear to be advisable.

Before placing a purchase order, quotes are solicited from one or more suppliers. The supplier inquiry forms a relationship type between the entity types inquiring ORGANIZATIONAL UNIT, SUPPLIER and TIME, whereby the items reference the OUTSOURCED RESOURCE and the desired delivery date. For purposes of simplification, an asterisk is substituted for the key document header items. Since inquiries can be made to several suppliers for one requisition item, and an inquiry can also relate to several requisition items if several purchasing requisitions exist for the same outsourced resource, an n:m relationship exists for REQUISITION INQUIRY ASSIGNMENT.

Supplier quotes are submitted in response to the inquiries. Suppliers frequently submit unsolicited quotes as well. If a quote activates a supplier or outsourced part for the first time, it initiates the introduction of a corresponding entity.

The purchasing department is responsible for decisions concerning the acceptance of a supplier. There is frequently a position in the engineering department that is responsible for decisions concerning acceptance of outsourced resources. This function is often called "Standardization."

The supplier's quote number is an important non-key attribute. Each quote item relates to the quote, the outsourced resource and the delivery date. Those attributes that relate to this combination are entered in the quote item. These include price information, rebate terms, delivery times, order quantity, supplier's part numbers, etc. They are also used to update the supplier's terms.

Several, e.g. revised, quotes pertaining to a single supplier inquiry can be submitted from the same supplier; this results in a 1:n assignment between the items from the SUPPLIER INQUIRY and the SUPPLIER QUOTE.

B.II.2.1.2.2 Selecting Suppliers and Determining Quantities to be Ordered

On the one hand, the actual stipulation of the quantities to be ordered takes into account the optimization criteria discussed in connection with lot sizing approaches (EOQ, adapted EOQ, unit period adjustment and the Wagner-Whitin algorithm) within the framework of requirements planning for in-house parts or, on the other hand, restrictions that can result from supplier capacity, specific transport resource limitations, etc. Business administration literature contains numerous approaches to these types of optimization problems (see *Schneeweiß, Lagerhaltungssysteme 1981; Glaser/Geiger/Rohde, Produktionsplanung und -steuerung 1992, pp. 136 ff.; Tempelmeier, Material-Logistik 1992*).

One particular problem related to purchasing involves rebate rates that are based on the quantity ordered. In reality, extremely diverse rebate systems are customary. They relate not only to a quantity-specific rebate scale for an individual material sourced from a supplier, but also to the overall volume of business with a supplier during a given period, to specific part groups, etc. Sometimes, the agreed terms for rebate policies are so complex that they cannot be understood by Invoice Control and thus are virtually meaningless. In the data structure developed in Figure B.II.07, the entity type SUPPLIER TERMS permits a variety of rebate policies.

It is possible to either solicit new quotes for a purchasing requisition or to use existing terms.

Using the PURCHASING REQUISITION, the outsourced resource is first compiled via the part numbers in the items and the potential suppliers via the relationship type SUPPLIER TERMS. When selecting a supplier, different alternatives can be reviewed interactively, whereby accessing the quote items incorporates not only the currently applicable values, but also allows trend forecasts to be derived on the basis of the quote history. This decision process is geared toward pricing, delivery time, quality and deadline reliability scores, rebate scaling and any quantity quotas that apply for individual suppliers. The order items (purchase order items) that result from these decisions are subsequently combined into purchase orders.

The PURCHASE ORDER ITEM is a relationship between PURCHASE ORDER, OUTSOURCED RESOURCE and TIME. The PURCHASE ORDER is an n:m relationship between ORGANIZATIONAL UNIT, SUPPLIER and TIME. A relationship is created from the PURCHASE ORDER ITEM to SUPPLIER TERMS or to SUPPLIER QUOTE ITEM.

Since the interrelationship between purchase order and purchasing requisition cannot necessarily be created via the links to inquiries and quotes, it is explicitly incorporated as requirements coverage.

A purchasing requisition can be covered by several purchase order items (different, successive orders) and, conversely, a purchase order item (in the case of lot bundling) can cover several requisitions. This situation is expressed by the relationship type REQUIREMENTS COVERAGE.

On the basis of the relationship REQUIREMENT INITIATION set up by Requirements Planning, the (demand-based) order initiator can be determined from the PURCHASE ORDER ITEM for demand-based purchasing requisitions. This is necessary, for example, for tracking the effects of delivery delays.

Status attributes in the entity types ORDER and PURCHASE ORDER ITEM provide identifiers that indicate whether a purchase order is still outstanding, a partial delivery has been made or the purchase order has been completed.

Account codes can be allocated—as explained in connection with Figure B.II.07—at any time during the entire process.

The power of this data structure can be demonstrated through its ability to provide information. All purchase orders that exist for a SUPPLIER entity can be accessed from that entity. Moreover, all purchase order items for the purchase orders are accessible and thus all materials presently being sourced from the supplier.

From any given SUPPLIER TERMS entity, it is possible to access all purchase order items that have presently been agreed to under specific terms, as well as all purchase orders.

The purchase order items created to cover a purchasing requisition can be accessed from its PURCHASING REQUISITION entity.

From the entity PURCHASE ORDER ITEM, it is possible to access the requisitions that initiated it. In the case of demand-based outsourced parts, requirements connection relationships can be used to access all initiating orders on higher planning levels, through to the customer order.

A date can be used to access all purchase orders and purchase order items initiated on this date.

Queries from Accounting, such as those concerning outstanding orders for a cost center, a cost objective or a general ledger account, can be answered.

By using the links to the data structures shown in Figure B.II.07, further inquiries can be formed, for example, on the basis of a material or supplier class.

Thus, this data structure also provides the basis for a procurement information system.

B.II.2.1.2.3 Data Transfer

Linking the supplier inquiries and purchase orders with the text modules shown in Figure B.II.07 can initiate automatic transfer of the data to the supplier. The text modules can be accessed via the suppliers or via outsourced resource keys. At the same time, the relationships TERMS TEXT ASSIGNMENT are accessible via SUPPLIER TERMS. Figure B.II.11 shows a sample purchase order.

In addition to conventional mail, data can be transferred via fax or directly using electronic data interchange (EDI), e.g., by using the EDIFACT standard (see the discussions below on JIT).

Purchase order no. 101

IWi Institut für Wirtschaftsinformatik, Im Stadtwald, 66123 Saarbrücken

Schreibwaren GmbH

D-66125 Saarbrücken

IWi

Delivery terms:	08/21/93	**Payment terms:**

Insurance by you at our expense

Please send order confirmation.

Within 14 days 3,0 % cash discount
Within 20 days 2,0 % cash discount
Within 30 days net payment

Accounts payable account no. 1001

Purchasing: Be

ITEM material	Delivery	Quantity	Price per	Total
1 10000	date	unit	unit	price US $
Your part no.: 111	10/01/93	200 units	1,10	220,00
Ball pen				
Material: St52				
Packed in lots of 10				

Packing list with 3 copies
Inspection according to inspection plan 4711
Delivery to CIM-Center, SITZ Burbach

Total excl. VAT US $ 220,00
==================================

Order supplement
==============
- Delivery deadline: Mon 2-4 pm, Tue-Fri 8 -12 am
- Shipping regulation: shipment as agreed

Fig. B.II.11: Example of order writing

B.II.2.1.2.4 Purchase Order Control

Outstanding purchase orders are checked at regular intervals to see if the scheduled delivery deadline has been exceeded. More precisely, the purchase order items must be checked, since the delivery deadlines refer to individual items. If a supplier has exceeded a deadline, i.e., if Receiving has not confirmed receipt of the order, the system automatically generates a notice of past due delivery on the basis of standard texts stored in the system. The past due notice is a relationship between the purchase order item and the past due date; however, it is not expressly entered in the data structure since it essentially only has to be printed. Only the serial number of the past due notice and the date of the notice are entered in the status field of the purchase order item.

B.II.2.1.2.5 Receiving

As an organizational unit, Receiving is responsible for accepting the goods delivered by suppliers, inspecting them for quality and quantity—or arranging for inspections to be made by special departments (Quality Control)—and either for putting them in buffer inventory until the results of the inspection are available or for routing them to either the warehouse department or directly to the requisitioning organizational unit.

Consequently, incoming goods can have the following status:
- Goods received
- Goods routed to Quality Control
- Goods released for transport
- Goods in transport
- Goods in inventory

The status is noted on the "receiving slip."

Generally, goods sent by a supplier are accompanied by a packing list, which provides the basis for data entry or for receiving inspections.

The packing list and the receiving slip are thus represented as **one** information object.

Figure B.II.12 shows the receiving slip for the example in Figure B.II.11 (for further examples, see *SAP, System RM-MAT 1993, p. 82*).

As the illustration shows, many data relate to the purchase order and can be transferred from there. RECEIVING is therefore linked with the information object PURCHASE ORDER. A receiving slip encompasses several outsourced items. Analogously to the purchase order, the

---

RECEIVING SLIP   No. 501   Date 10/01/93

Company name: IWi

Purchase order no.: 101   **INVENTORY MATERIAL**

Supplier	: 2000	Mat no.	: 10000
	Schreibwaren GmbH		Ball pens
RS no.	:	Purchasing : Be
		Phone	: 0681/302-3106

| Delivery date | : 10/01/93 | Order quantity: | 200 units |
| Disct. days | : 0 | Delivered quantity: | 200 units |

Fig. B.II.12: Example of a receiving slip

RECEIVING (SLIP) contains header information and is a link between SUPPLIER, internal ORGANIZATIONAL UNIT and TIME. Correspondingly, the RECEIVING SLIP ITEM is a relationship between RECEIVING (SLIP), OUTSOURCED RESOURCE and delivery time. In the case of partial deliveries, a purchase order item can encompass several receiving slip items. Conversely, however, a receiving slip item can encompass several purchase order items in the case of a consolidated delivery if several purchase orders were issued. This situation leads to the n:m relationship PARTIAL/CONSOLIDATED DELIVERY between PURCHASE ORDER ITEM and RECEIVING SLIP ITEM.

The receiving slip defines an entire consignment sourced from the supplier and can thus serve to identify materials that were delivered at the same time. This can be important in the case of delivery-related quality concerns.

If delivery schedules (releases) are arranged with a supplier, they are specializations of the PURCHASING REQUISITION. A delivery schedule initially encompasses the blanket contract with the supplier as well as one delivery schedule item for each of the individually scheduled material shipments.

Outstanding deliveries can be seen at any time via the PARTIAL/CONSOLIDATED DELIVERY relationship to the derived purchase orders.

Random samples or complete inspections can be performed for each receiving item and the results analyzed on the basis of an inspection plan drawn up with the supplier. Until the result is known, the goods are quarantined in Receiving and held from further processing. The INSPECTION PLAN is a specialization of the previously introduced entity type SUPPLIER TERMS. At the same time, INSPECTION PLAN is a specialization of the entity type ROUTING and is linked with the entity type OUTSOURCED RESOURCE via the ROUTING ASSIGNMENT as a specialization of PART. An n:m relationship exists between INSPECTION PLAN and RECEIVING SLIP ITEM if different samples are picked from a receiving slip item that will provide inspection results. On the basis of the inspection result, the goods can either be returned or transferred to the warehouse department or the requisitioning line department.

The planned assigned stock location is known via the informational relationship between PLANNED DISTRIBUTION and STOCK LOCATION introduced previously in the context of the purchase order requisition via the relationship between RECEIVING SLIP ITEM, PURCHASE ORDER ITEM and REQUIREMENTS COVERAGE. New events can cause a deviation, however, so that a new relationship INVENTORY ADDITION to the inventory level is created instead of the planned one. An n:m relationship exists between INVENTORY LEVEL and RECEIVING SLIP ITEM, since the quantity received can be distributed among several stock locations. This relationship triggers the increase in inventory posting.

After the receiving notice has been entered, not only is the quantity-related increase in inventory posted, but value postings are also initiated for financial and cost accounting.

In the case of warehoused outsourced resources, the delivered goods are entered in an inventory account. Figure B.II.13 shows the individual entries for the example shown here. The outsourced resource has a standard price of $ 1.00 per quantity unit. 200 quantity units have been ordered at a price of $ 1.10, which also leads to the receipt of 200 quantity units. 200 quantity units are posted to the inventory account as an addition at the standard price, and the difference between the order price and the standard price is posted to the price variance account. At the same time, $ 200 is posted as a credit to the GR/IR (goods received, invoice received) clearing account. When the invoice is later received and the price actually invoiced by the supplier is identified, the price variance account and the clearing account will again be addressed.

The data structure in Figure B.II.10 uses the n:m relationship of POSTING to take into account the fact that a receiving slip item initiates postings to different general ledger accounts, and, on the other hand, the fact that a general ledger account can be affected by several receiving slip items. At the same time, reference is made to the account code allocation previously discussed in the context of the purchase order. If the inventory value accounts are differentiated and maintained on the stock location level, the posting is made on the inventory addition level. Figure B.II.10 shows both cases.

Similarly, consumable materials can be posted to consumable accounts and the corresponding cost center or, in the case of cost-objective-oriented orders, directly to the cost objective.

Posting of receivings

Inventory account	Price variance account
(200 • 1 =) 200	(200 ⋆ 0,1 =) 20

Clearing account
RG/IR

(200• 1 =) 200

Standard price: 1 $/unit
Order: 200 units at 1,10 $/unit
Receivings: 200 units

Fig. B.II.13: Example of posting of receivings

B.II.2.1.2.6 Invoice Control

Following the purchasing requisitions, the purchase order, and receipt of the goods, receipt of the invoice is the fourth event that leads to new data structures. Here, too, there are close overlaps with the previous data structures.

A SUPPLIER INVOICE is an n:m relationship between SUPPLIER, internal ORGANIZATIONAL UNIT (as the invoice receiver) and TIME. The invoice number of the original document sent by the supplier can be assigned to it as an important attribute. An invoice consists of several invoice items that each relate to an OUTSOURCED RESOURCE (material) and a delivery date. Attributes of an invoice item include quantity delivered, unit price, extension, discount information and terms.

If a purchase order exists for the invoice, many of the data in the invoice are identical to those in the purchase order and therefore do not need to be re-entered. Thus, only one relationship type, PURCHASE ORDER ASSIGNMENT, is introduced between SUPPLIER INVOICE ITEM and the corresponding PURCHASE ORDER ITEM. If the ordered quantity has been delivered, a receiving slip item document is created within the context of the receiving inspection. This allows information to be accessed concerning the actual materials and grades delivered. To do this, INVOICE ITEM is linked with RECEIVING SLIP ITEM.

These links provide both the purchase order dates and the receiving dates for a purchase order item. The invoice reviewer is able to determine if the quantities delivered coincide with the invoiced quantities and if the order price agrees with the invoice price. By accessing data from the receiving quality inspection, it is also possible to check the quality conformity of the invoiced goods. These checks can be performed largely automatically by programs. Only in special cases (e.g., invoices that cannot be assigned to a purchase order) are manual invoice processing and data input necessary. Thus, invoice data entry is largely automated.

Upon successful completion of the invoice review, the invoice amounts are released for payment. Incorrect invoice items must be transferred to the line departments for further handling, and payment is withheld. At the same time, postings are automatically made to accounts payable. A sample invoice and the postings it initiates are shown in Figures B.II.14,a and b and relate to the example introduced in the discussion of receiving procedures. Thus, the GR/IR clearing account is cleared (this clearing account indicates whether invoices were issued although no goods were received or whether goods were received without an invoice). At the same time, the input tax accounts payable, the accounts payable debit account and the price variance account are also affected.

This interrelationship is again represented in the data structure by n:m relationships for the postings between SUPPLIER INVOICE ITEM and GENERAL LEDGER ACCOUNT as well as ACCOUNTS PAYABLE ACCOUNT. The information concerning the account code allocations can be taken from the documents.

Invoice no. 4911

Schreibwaren GmbH, Straße, 66123 Saarbrücken

I W i
Institut für Wirtschaftsinformatik
Im Stadtwald

D-66123 Saarbrücken

Your order no.:   101

Insurance by us at your expense

Payment terms:

Within 14 days 3,0 % cash discount
Within 20 days 2,0 % cash discount
Within 30 days net payment

Accounts payable account no 1001

Purchasing: Be

ITEM material	Delivery	Quantity	Price per	Total price
1 111	date	unit	unit	US $
Your part No.: 10 000	10/01/93	200 units	1,10	210,00
Ball pen				
Material: St52				
Packed in lots at 10				

VAT (15%)   31,05

Total incl. VAT US $ 241,50
==================================

Fig. B.II.14,a: Supplier invoice

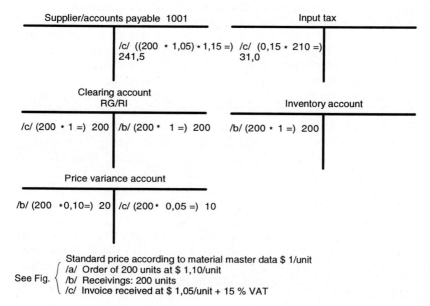

Postings of invoice control

Supplier/accounts payable 1001   Input tax

/c/ ((200 * 1,05) * 1,15 =) /c/ (0,15 * 210 =)
241,5   31,0

Clearing account
RG/RI   Inventory account

/c/ (200 * 1 =) 200   /b/ (200 *   1 =) 200   /b/ (200 * 1 =) 200

Price variance account

/b/ (200 *0,10=) 20   /c/ (200 * 0,05 =) 10

Standard price according to material master data $ 1/unit
/a/ Order of 200 units at $ 1,10/unit
See Fig.   /b/ Receivings: 200 units
/c/ Invoice received at $ 1,05/unit + 15 % VAT

Fig. B.II.14,b: Example of postings of invoice control

The accounts payable account is linked with the entity type SUPPLIER via an n:m relationship. This means that several accounts can be maintained for one supplier and a single account for several suppliers (e.g., different plants belonging to a group).

If the postings are not performed until the "goods received" and "invoice received" events, the obligations entered into as a result of purchase orders are not revealed in the accounting system. However, these "obligations" can be determined statistically from the outstanding orders. Since the accounts payable data already exist when the purchase order is issued, however, it is already possible to make the postings at this time— but these postings must be marked as "tentative" and must not be included when the accounts are reconciled.

B.II.2.1.2.7 Payment Procedures

Initiating and posting the payment concludes the purchasing process. This function is performed by Accounts Payable, since it is solely an accounting function. Since assignment problems occur that can only be solved from the standpoint of several payment processes, case-oriented processing is terminated. The system tracks the outstanding invoices (in the form of "ledgerless accounting") and checks their due dates while taking into account cash discount terms. This process generates a suggested payment list that the user can process interactively. This list must specify which payments are the most urgent and from which banks the payments are to be made. Simulation postings can be used to support the decision process. The amounts approved for payment are then processed on the basis of the payment terms agreed with the supplier.

The basic posting record for the payment reads:

Credit accounts payable account, debit payment account (e.g., bank, cashier, etc.)

Data media can be generated automatically and then sent to banks under electronic funds transfer (EFT) procedures.

Figure B.II.15 shows the data structure for payment procedures. The point of departure here is the previously introduced data structure for the supplier's invoice. Only the outstanding invoices, as a subset of all invoices, are relevant. The payment to a supplier on a specific date can comprise several payment items that relate to different forms of remittances (EFT, check, bill of exchange, etc.).

A payment item can relate to one or more outstanding invoice items. On the other hand, a single invoice item might only be settled through several payments (e.g., payments on advance).

Each payment item initiates posting operations that update both the affected financial accounts (bank, check, etc.) and the accounts payable account.

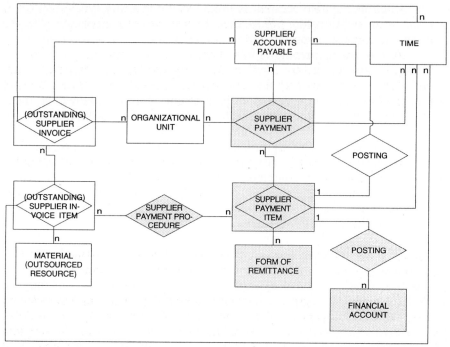

Fig. B.II.15: Data structure for payment procedures

B.II.2.1.2.8 Potential for Simplifying the Purchasing Process

The data model shown in Figure B.II.10 illustrates the high degree of complexity involved in the purchasing process. It is characterized by numerous n:m relationships between the individual document types. These n:m relationships result from continuously splitting the various processes and combining them with others. At the same time, the multitude of document types only adds to the complexity.
This complexity is attributable to:

- Alternatives with respect to the assignment of suppliers to a purchasing procedure. These alternatives result in obtaining alternative inquiries and quotes for a purchase order inquiry and the need to manage their assignments.
- Alternatives with respect to combining different purchasing requisitions into one order quantity in order to utilize the advantages of greater order size.
- Alternatives with respect to combining purchasing requisitions for different products in order to take advantage of the effect of consolidated purchase orders to a supplier in order to gain favorable terms.

-     Latitude in distributing an order quantity among different stock locations, which in turn makes it necessary to manage the planned assignment relationships.
-     Allowing supplier flexibility with respect to combining partial and consolidated deliveries that deviate from the quantities ordered. This practice, in turn, necessitates the management of assignments between purchase orders and deliveries.
-     Uncertainties with respect to the supplier's conformance with quality requirements, which make it necessary to manage quality inspections and their results.
-     Involvement of different organizational units in the processes on the basis of a functional organizational structure, which results in the use of different organizational elements, terminology and document types, even though the differences between them are only minimal.

Experts are increasing their critical analyses of the causes of purchasing complexity and are attempting to eliminate them by restructuring the process.

The complexity caused by the many alternatives and bundling effects can be reduced by separating the long-term structure of the purchasing process from its operative execution. Instead of coupling supplier selection and price negotiation with each purchasing process, this approach necessitates that these items be specified in longer-term blanket contracts under whose terms the individual operative purchasing processes are then handled. Likewise, "optimal" order quantities can also be determined on a longer-term basis for sourcing operations.

This means that information concerning the terms and the supplier already exists when the purchase is requisitioned, as illustrated in Figure B.II.16 using a 1:n relationship between the reinterpreted entity type SUPPLIER DOCUMENT and the information objects SUPPLIER TERMS and SUPPLIER.

A second simplification option involves handling requisitions as a holistic process rather than mixing them. This makes it possible to assign the requisitions specified by a cost center (or by an organizational unit in general) to a stock location right from the beginning. Moreover, it also enables the allocation of an unambiguous account code (eliminating the need for multiple coding), which leads to a 1:n relationship between the information object SUPPLIER DOCUMENT ITEM and both STOCK LOCATION and ACCOUNT.

Another way to reduce complexity is to organizationally standardize supplier and account payable definitions, thus eliminating the assignment relationships between these two concepts.

If the supplier's terms specify that the ordered goods be delivered in the quality and quantity stipulated in the agreements, the assignment relationships for partial and consolidated deliveries as well as for quality assurance can be eliminated.

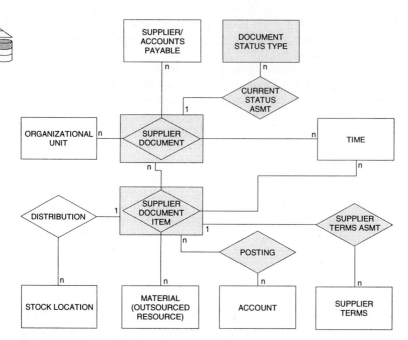

Fig. B.II.16: Simplified data structure for the purchasing process

If these conditions are ensured, the purchasing requisition will coincide with the goods received. Thus, only the status of the purchasing requisition defined at the beginning of the process chain changes as it passes through the ordering and receiving procedures. Figure B.II.16 expresses this principle by introducing the entity type DOCUMENT STATUS TYPE. The relationship type CURRENT STATUS ASSIGNMENT indicates the current status of the process. This again creates a 1:n relationship type.

The simplicity of the data structure in Figure B.II.16 as compared to the one shown in Figure B.II.10 is obvious. It is made even more evident in that the remaining relationship types are all 1:n, so that no relations have to be defined for them on the relational model level. Instead, only external key fields must be maintained in the SUPPLIER DOCUMENT ITEM relation.

JIT-based purchasing models not only meet the above-mentioned conditions for simplifying the purchasing process, they also surpass them in many instances. JIT distinguishes between agreed terms and operative processes. The customer provides information about planned releases under the negotiated blanket schedule. Operative handling of these releases takes place in a hierarchically structured form in response to information conditions (see Fig. B.II.17). In the case of short-term immediate release, only the part number, quantity and, if relevant, current delivery date need to be transferred. All the other information required by the supplier for delivery are known to the supplier on the basis of the

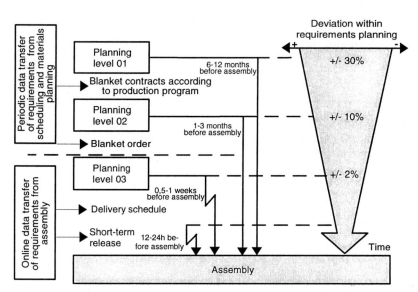

Fig. B.II.17: Planning levels within JIT
    (according to *Wildemann, Just-In-Time - Informationsflußgestaltung 1990*)

agreed terms. Moreover, the supplier no longer needs to issue invoices; instead, the customer can initiate a credit memo on the basis of the information pertaining to the released quantities and the agreed terms. Thus, the customer's invoice control is replaced by the supplier's credit memo control.

Agreements concerning quality inspections eliminate the need for incoming inspection.

JIT manufacturing makes it unnecessary to store the ordered quantities because the delivered parts are processed, e.g., assembled, immediately. Figure B.II.18 shows the JIT process in the form of an EPC.

The hatched events represent the links to the supplier's outbound logistics.

The simplification options illustrated here do not lend themselves to all outsourced resources. For example, complex parts such as capital goods require a more complicated purchasing process. These different requirements can be handled differently by segmenting the purchasing process on the basis of the sourcing properties of outsourced resources. A process can then be defined for each purchasing segment, which creates a situation similar to the one previously discussed in the context of segmenting the production control functions, where different part segments were supported by their own production and planning processes via leitstand concepts. This concept can be applied to the purchasing process by gearing purchasing leitstands to the specific problems involved and installing one for each purchasing segment. Figure Abb. B.II.19 illustrates such a concept. Since relationships also exist between the

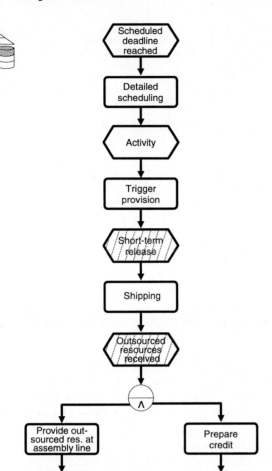

Fig. B.II.18: EPC for JIT releases

individual purchasing segments, a coordination level is introduced, which makes it possible to support comprehensive functions, e.g., blacklisting a supplier for all purchasing segments. The coordination level can also be responsible for longer-term purchasing agreements, e.g., in order to exploit the synergy effects between the individual purchasing segments during negotiations with a supplier. An additional planning level can be introduced for long-term planning and negotiating activities, which would be responsible for several planning-related coordination leitstands.

The JIT segments are supported by a special JIT leitstand. If this JIT leitstand is current enough for releases to be made from production control, e.g., from an assembly system, a close relationship to the CAM system results. In the discussion of decentralized CAM systems, Figure

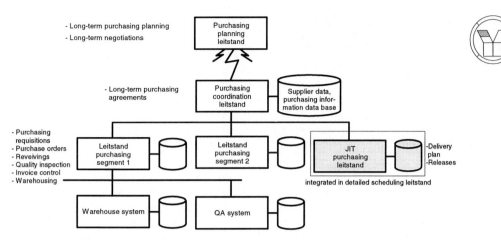

Fig. B.II.19: Purchasing leitstand

B.I.219 shifted the release functions to the decentralized production control systems. Thus, the purchasing leitstand is a part of the detailed scheduling leitstand.

B.II.2.1.2.9 Analyses

The data structure developed here for basic data and the purchasing process offers a multitude of options for data analysis in the sense of a purchasing information system. The analyses can support strategic purchasing decisions (see Figure B.II.06) and provide data for purchasing controlling. The purchasing process is the subject of many activity-based costing case studies (see *Witt, Beschaffungscontrolling 1992; Wäscher, Prozeßorientiertes Gemeinkosten-Management im Material- und Logistik-Bereich eines Maschinenbauunternehmens 1991; Glaser, Prozeßkostenrechnung 1992; Horváth/Mayer, Prozesskostenrechnung 1989*). Typical cost drivers that can be provided by the database include the number of purchasing processes per period; the number of blanket contracts that have been entered into or must be managed; the number of purchasing variants maintained in the system, etc.

Since the objectives and methods of analysis in a purchasing information system are virtually identical to the structures of other executive information systems (EIS), they will not be discussed in any further detail; instead, reference will be made to discussions of production information systems, marketing information system and EIS.

B.II.2.1.3 Special Purchasing Processes

The purchasing process has been described primarily on the basis of the procurement of physical consumable goods; however, the procurement of services also follows this pattern as well. As a rule, services are expensed immediately, but they can, when associated with a capital project or extensive repairs, be capitalized in a fixed asset account. Many services involve simplified processes, i.e., a reduced number of purchasing documents or fewer alternatives to manage.

The procurement of capital projects is typically a comprehensive process that fully utilizes the options shown in Figures B.II.07 and B.II.10. Within the framework of capital goods procurement, new suppliers can be created and new terms generated. The individual document items can contain comprehensive textual descriptions, which are permitted by the entity type ADDITIONAL DATA in the data structure shown in Figure B.II.07. At the same time, a bill of materials structure can also be created for procurements of capital goods. In particular, this bill of materials structure also contains spare parts with their relationships to major assemblies and to the capital goods in question.

The procurement of financial resources also differs from the purchasing process developed here primarily through the use of different terminology. As in the case of services and capital goods, no storage functions are necessary; instead, the financial accounting system maintains financial resources in inventory accounts similar to capital goods. The individual instances of types of credit facilities form the individual entities of the general entity type OUTSOURCED RESOURCE. They can be assigned specific characteristics for purposes of classification. A loan agreement is understood as a relationship between the monetary supplier (e.g., a bank), the requisitioning organizational unit within the enterprise (e.g., Finance) and time. Each of the individual items in the contract references different credit facilities that can be utilized within the framework of a financing operation. The individual types of financing can be distinguished by different maturity periods or collateral requirements. Comprehensive additional data or texts covering terms and agreements can be assigned to the individual items.

If financial resources are used to finance specific projects, the relationships between the source and application of the funds can also be maintained in the data structure.

Personnel procurement can also be interpreted as a special procurement process. As was already shown in Figure B.II.07, the labor to be procured is a specialization of the general concept of outsourced resources, and employees are a specialization of the general concept of supplier. Correspondingly, the classification systems for employees and labor can be adopted. It is important to note that both the labor, as the resource to be procured, and the provider can be characterized by the same personnel characteristics. The analogies in this regard will not be discussed in further detail, since the problems of the provision and employment of personnel are of a different nature and will be discussed in the section concerning the structure of labor.

B.II.2.2 Outbound Logistics

Outbound logistics accompanies the logistics chain from issuance of the quote, acceptance of the order, control of the order, shipping and invoicing all the way to transferring the data to the financial accounting system. Outbound logistics dovetails with the PPC system for the logistics chain via order control and with inbound logistics via order-related purchasing processes.

The mirror-image parallelism that exists between the functions and data structures for inbound and outbound logistics has already been suggested and will be emphasized in the following discussion. In order to reduce redundancy in the representations, explicit reference will be made to the corresponding discussions of inbound logistics. On the other hand, several new discussions concerning outbound logistics can also apply to inbound logistics. In order to distinguish between inbound and outbound logistics, the same terms will be used, but they will be preceded either by a C (customer) or an S (supplier).

An interplant view reveals that the data maintained by a manufacturer concerning delivery terms are identical to his customer's data concerning purchasing terms, at least to the extent that they relate to the same reference unit (combination of article and customer or supplier). Likewise, a manufacturer's purchase orders are identical to customer orders at the corresponding supplier.

The redundancies revealed by interplant analysis necessitate that future logistics chains extend beyond customer and supplier information systems.

Depending on the type of order involved, individual activities in the order acceptance, shipping and invoicing order chain can be emphasized differently and, in some cases, can even be eliminated. The process structures for several order types are illustrated in Figure B.II.20. (These order types can also lead to different processes within the context of inbound logistics, although this was not discussed in detail in that section.)

In the case of a **deadline order**, order acceptance, shipping and delivery do not occur simultaneously, which results in distinct, independent subfunctions.

In the case of a **cash sale**, the invoice is issued when the order is accepted, and shipping is replaced by direct hand-over of the order to the customer. The three subfunctions thus occur simultaneously.

In the case of a **branch office order**, the branch office's order is entered at the plant and the shipping documents are generated, but no invoice is issued.

In the case of a **replenishment of consignment stock** for a customer, the order is only entered and shipped, as in the case of a branch office order.

In the case of a **withdrawal** from **consignment stock**, the customer's order is entered; however, since shipping is unnecessary, the process corresponds to that of a cash sale, i.e., the three subfunctions occur simultaneously.

Order types	Order acceptance	Shipping	Invoicing
Deadline order	X	X	X
Cash sale	X		
Branch office order	X	X	
Replenishment of consignment stock	X	X	
Withdrawal from consignment stock	X		
Drop-shipment order	X		X
Released order with set fixed delivery schedule		X	X

Fig. B.II.20: Process structure for several order types

In the case of a **drop-shipment order**, i.e., an order for which delivery is not made by the plant itself but is transferred to an external supplier instead, the order is only accepted and invoiced; shipping is performed by the third party.

In the case of **release orders** with set delivery schedules, order acceptance can be omitted since it is initiated under the terms of the contract. Only the shipping and invoicing functions are performed.

In addition to the above-cited order types, there are additional operations such as sample orders, pick-up of loaned goods, pick-up of returned goods, etc., which, however, will not be discussed individually.

B.II.2.2.1 Basic Data Management

The basic data encompass master data for salable parts (articles), customers, customer texts, salespeople and classifications. Since there is a close relationship with the quote data as a source for updating master data, these transaction data will also be discussed.

The data structure for basic data as developed in Figure B.II.21 largely mirrors the data structure for purchasing as shown in Figure B.II.07.

B.II.2.2.1.1 Data on Articles and Customers

The entity type ARTICLE describes salable parts, i.e., end products, independent assemblies, spare parts, services and packaging. Thus, it describes a subset of the entity type PART. Significant attributes of the entity type ARTICLE have already been introduced along with the entity type PART. In addition to the imported part number PNO, the following attributes are also significant:

-       Article name, pricing information, costing information, inventory level, part introduction date.

Customers are represented by the entity type CUSTOMER, which is closely related to the entity type ACCOUNT RECEIVABLE in the accounts receivable accounting system (similar to inbound logistics in the case of SUPPLIER and ACCOUNT PAYABLE). Customers can be outside companies or organizational units of the enterprise itself (e.g., branch offices). In addition to the customer identification number CNO, significant attributes include:

-       Name, address, assigned branch, customer employee, total order amount for previous year, order amount for current year, target order amount for current year, outstanding accounts receivable, credit limit and general customer-related agreements.

The entity type CUSTOMER ORDER TYPE describes the different order types shown in Figure B.II.20.

Corresponding relationships are created for specific assignments between CUSTOMER ORDER TYPE and CUSTOMER or ARTICLE. Since each order type can be assigned to several customers or articles, and, conversely, a customer or article can appear in several order types, the order assignment relationships between CUSTOMER or ARTICLE and CUSTOMER ORDER TYPE possess type n cardinalities.

Classifications for articles and customers are introduced analogously to inbound logistics for materials and suppliers. These classifications not only support quote preparation, order processing and organizational assignment of operations to departments, they also represent components of a marketing information system.

A rough representation of the organizational structure for outbound logistics has already been provided in Figure B.II.03. In line with the process-oriented approach used here, a sales group is responsible for data management, quote preparation, order acceptance and order tracking functions. Different criteria can be used to form organizational units. The left side of Figure B.II.22 shows a hierarchical organizational structure for sales that conforms to a regional market structure. The relationship to a product-group-oriented structure (segment or product group) is of the n:m type, i.e., branch offices can be responsible for several segments. One or several sales groups that focus on customers and/or article groups can be assigned to the regional sales units. A sales group, in turn, comprises sales representatives (clerks and associates), which are specializations of the entity type EMPLOYEE.

A further structural criterion can be the sales channel (direct sales, large accounts, distributors) that generate different processes.

In the data structure shown in Figure B.II.21, the general entity type ORGANIZATIONAL UNIT represents all organizational structures. At the same time, the SALES GROUP is indicated as a specialization. The sales groups are assigned their respective articles, customers and sales channels via relationship types. These assignments are viewed as mutually

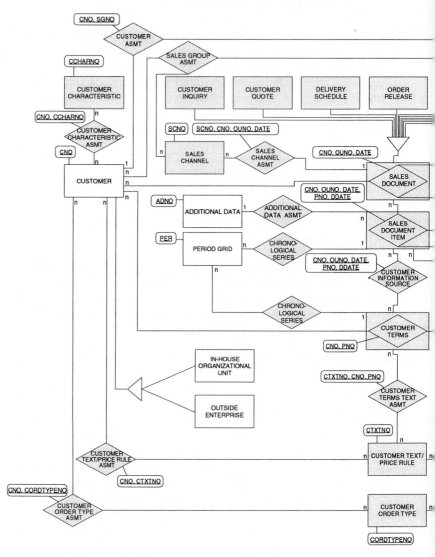

Fig. B.II.21: General data structure for outbound logistics

independent. However, it would also be conceivable to assign certain combinations of articles, customers and sales channels to sales departments that are defined by the characteristic properties of articles and customers (see Figure B.II.23) (see also the definition for "sales department" in *SAP, SD-Grundfunktionen-Stammdaten 1992, pp. 1-6*).

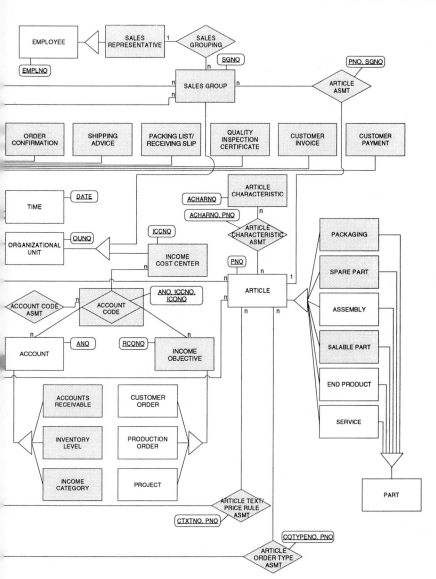

Each sales operation is represented by a sales document and identified, among other things, by the organizational unit that performs it. Further identifying attributes include the customer number (CNO) and date. Each document can be assigned to a specific sales channel.

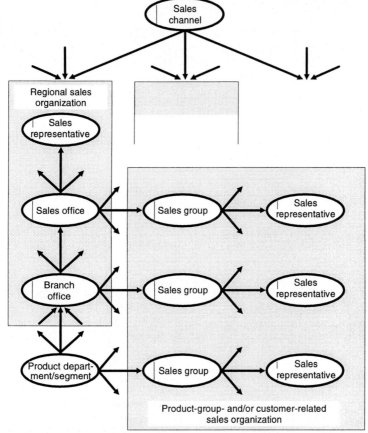

Fig. B.II.22: Organizational structures of inbound logistics

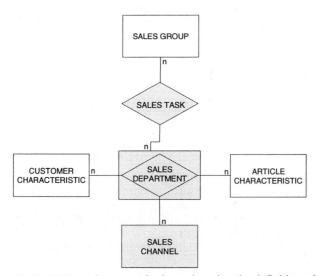

Fig. B.II.23: Assignment of sales tasks using the definition of sales departments

B.II.2.2.1.2 Documents and Terms

As in the case of inbound logistics, different types of documents accompany the outbound logistics process from the quotation phase through shipping. These documents are shown in Figure B.II.21 as specializations of the general entity type SALES DOCUMENT. Sales documents are assigned article-related document items. They also receive the delivery date as an additional key attribute. A document item can be further subdivided into "partitions" if, for example, partial deliveries of an item are scheduled at different locations (see *SAP, SD-Verkauf 1992, pp. 2-3*). This subdivision will not be discussed in any greater detail here. Instead, relationships are created to additional data (texts) and to a period grid for forming chronological series, as in the case of inbound logistics.

The master data entered in the relationship type CUSTOMER TERMS are the terms, which are continually updated. The attribute values for the terms come from the document items and are assigned to the entity CUSTOMER TERMS via the relationship type CUSTOMER INFORMATION SOURCE .

Typical attributes that relate to the combination of CUSTOMER and ARTICLE include price scales taken from current quotes, quality guarantees, established delivery times and blanket order agreements for delivery releases, quantities of a specific article delivered to a customer, number of customer complaints relating to a specific product, article number used by the customer, etc.

As in the case of purchasing, the attribute values that relate to the CUSTOMER/ARTICLE combination are largely handled during the creation and documentation of requested or unsolicited quotes.

Chronological series are created via a link to the entity type PERIOD GRID in order to chronologically track the development of the terms. By creating dual relationship types to the entity type TIME, it is also possible to represent term validities on a "from-to" basis.

B.II.2.2.1.3 Texts and Price Rules

Comprehensive word processing functions are necessary in connection with quote and order processing. Text modules are represented by the entity type CUSTOMER TEXT. The assignment of article-, customer- and terms-related text modules is represented by the appropriate relationship types.

This also reveals the inverse equivalence to the corresponding data structures for inbound logistics.

In contrast, price rules and price modules supplement the inbound logistics structure and are also entered in the entity type CUSTOMER TEXT. They are linked to the customer's terms during the pricing process via complex computational rules.

B.II.2.2.1.4 Account Coding

Analogously to inbound logistics, during the sales process, information becomes available concerning the account coding that relates to the business transaction, i.e., its assignment to accounts in the external accounting system and to the categories of income (cost) categories, cost center and income (cost) objective.

The most important personal account is the accounts receivable account, which can exist in either a 1:1 relationship or an n:m relationship to the entity type CUSTOMER.

B.II.2.2.2 Sales Process

The sales process also exhibits an inverse similarity to inbound logistics. It comprises the following levels:
-           Inquiry processing and quote preparation
-           Order acceptance and tracking
-           Shipping
-           Invoicing

The individual functions, in turn, are closely linked with the accounting systems. Internal accounting is involved in connection with pricing (costing) in the context of quote preparation, account coding information becomes available during all phases, and postings are performed in connection with shipping or invoicing.

Figure B.II.24 shows this general process in the form of an EPC, which will serve as the basis for the following discussions.

As in the case of inbound logistics, the most important events that initiate processing are represented by the documents introduced in the context of basic data management.

Figure B.II.25 develops the data structure for the sales process, which relates to standard articles (including variants). Data structures that deviate from this example, i.e., one-off production orders for which the article descriptions do not exist until they are processed, are handled separately.

B.II.2.2.2.1 Inquiry Processing and Quote Preparation

Order processing begins with a customer inquiry, which subsequently leads to quote preparation. Important business administration control functions can also be performed during this phase. For instance, customers can be referred to alternative products that are available at a better price than the originally requested article. Data concerning inventory levels and price components must be available for this purpose. This is not a problem in the case of defined article structures, since inventory levels and price elements (as part of the article texts) are available via the entity type

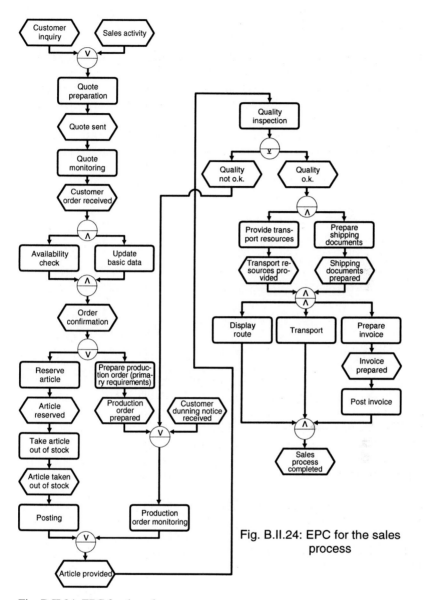

Fig. B.II.24: EPC for the sales process

Fig. B.II.24: EPC for the sales process

ARTICLE. Well-planned control during the quotation phase can prevent the need for complicated production processes if, for example, it is possible to convince a customer to use a standard article instead of a special production item he originally requested (see *Mertens/Steppan, Die Ausdehnung des CIM-Gedankens in den Vertrieb 1990*). A more detailed analysis of pricing/costing will be provided within the context of internal accounting. Figure B.II.25 introduces the data structures for customer inquiries and customer quotes, whereby a 1:n assignment exists between both items since a customer inquiry can lead to several (updated) quotes.

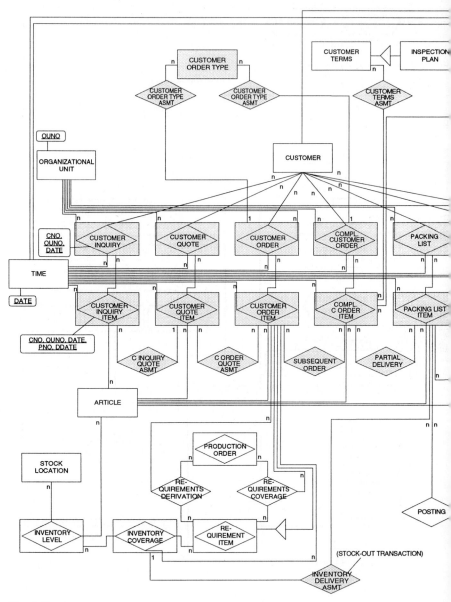

Fig. B.II.25: Detailed data structure for the sales process

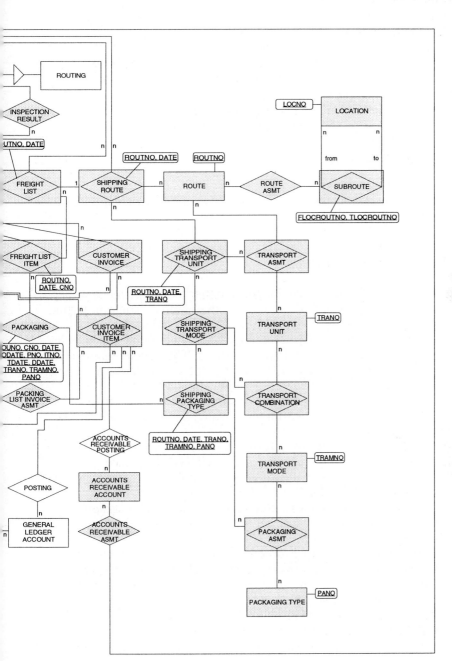

ROUTING

INSPECTION RESULT

UTNO, DATE

LOCNO | LOCATION

n | n

from | to

FREIGHT LIST — 1 — SHIPPING ROUTE — ROUTE — ROUTE ASMT — SUBROUTE

ROUTNO, DATE | ROUTNO

FLOCROUTNO, TLOCROUTNO

FREIGHT LIST ITEM | CUSTOMER INVOICE | SHIPPING TRANSPORT UNIT | TRANSPORT ASMT

ROUTNO, DATE, CNO

ROUTNO, DATE, TRANO

PACKAGING | CUSTOMER INVOICE ITEM | SHIPPING TRANSPORT MODE | TRANSPORT UNIT | TRANO

OUNO, CNO, DATE, ODATE, PNO, ITNO, TDATE, DDATE, TRANO, TRAMNO, PANO

PACKING LIST INVOICE ASMT | SHIPPING PACKAGING TYPE | TRANSPORT COMBINATION

ROUTNO, DATE, TRANO, TRAMNO, PANO

ACCOUNTS RECEIVABLE POSTING

POSTING | ACCOUNTS RECEIVABLE ACCOUNT | TRANSPORT MODE | TRAMNO

GENERAL LEDGER ACCOUNT | ACCOUNTS RECEIVABLE ASMT | PACKAGING ASMT

PACKAGING TYPE | PANO

B.II.2.2.2.2 Order Acceptance and Control

Standard articles also include variants. The comprehensive data structure for the bill of materials definition that is necessary for variant management is not employed here; instead, reference is made to the representations used in the context of requirements planning.

The individual substeps for order acceptance and control are:
-        Article identification
-        Order creation with assignment of terms
-        Reservation
-        Order tracking.

Depending on whether standard or one-off production is involved, these steps are of different significance.

B.II.2.2.2.2.1 Standard Articles

Frequently, customers do not provide the supplier's exact article number when placing an order; instead, they describe the ordered article in terms of technical specifications, or, in the case of telephone orders, by means of a verbal description. The salesperson must then determine the article number by "paging" through the PART entities. The article number is used to create the ORDER entity or, in the case of a request for a quote, the QUOTE entity.

Prior to acceptance of the order, the system employs the customer's credit limit to check his creditworthiness, which is an attribute of the entity type CUSTOMER.

The CUSTOMER ORDER, too, forms a relationship type between ORGANIZATIONAL UNIT, TIME and CUSTOMER (see Figure B.II.25) and is correspondingly identified via customer number, OUNO and date. CUSTOMER ORDER ITEM is a relationship between the CUSTOMER ORDER, ARTICLE and delivery date. The assignment between orders and the quotes they are based on is created by an n:m relationship on the item level.

If customers reference previous orders when reordering articles, it is advisable to keep completed customer orders available for an extended period of time. Moreover, a time-slot grid assignment can be used to perform statistical time comparisons.

Past customer orders receive their own relationship types, which parallel the previously introduced order structures. It is advisable to separate active and past customer orders, since the attributes for completed orders can be different. These data can also serve as the basis for a sales information system.

The creation of a customer order item also specifies order-related terms such as:

Prices, rebates, quality guarantees including inspection plans, as well as the assignment to a set delivery schedule in the case of release orders.

If it is necessary to access existing agreements relating to terms, they are linked by assignment relationships.

Both completed customer orders and the entity type for active customer orders are linked with the previously introduced entity type CUSTOMER ORDER TYPE. This makes it possible to maintain the assignment of an order to a drop-shipment order, normal delivery order, branch office order, consignment stock order, etc.

The assignment of the terms for an order also specifies its priority for production planning and control purposes. This identifier is entered as an attribute and provides the initial interface to production logistics. Further interfaces result from reservation functions and order tracking.

If the customer wants immediate delivery, the system checks whether the corresponding quantities are available in inventory. If there is free stock on hand, the quantities necessary to fill the customer order are reserved. The INVENTORY LEVEL, INVENTORY COVERAGE, ORDER, REQUIREMENT, REQUIREMENTS DERIVATION and REQUIREMENTS COVERAGE entity and relationship types are imported from the data structure for multi-level requirements tracking and are used to represent these interrelationships.

First, the system checks whether free (i.e., anonymously scheduled) requirements exist for the article on the desired date. If this is the case, they are assigned to the customer order item. This is done by creating the corresponding (customer-order-related) requirements derivation relationships. An anonymously scheduled primary requirement is continuously identified by concrete customer orders (see Figure B.II.26). If inventory assignments to the anonymous requirement exist, they are also reserved by linking them to the CUSTOMER ORDER ITEM.

If the assignable inventory quantities are insufficient to fill the order, existing production orders for the free requirements are assigned via REQUIREMENTS COVERAGE relationships.

If the existing anonymous requirements are insufficient for covering the customer order, a new primary requirement is created (in the form of a net

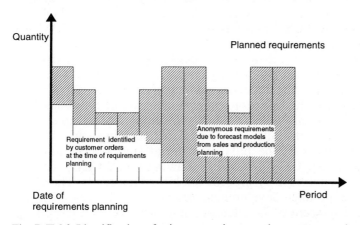

Fig. B.II.26: Identification of primary requirements by customer orders

change operation). In this case, the system must check the availability of capacities and materials (see "Planning the Sales and Production Program"). Relationships to the customer order item are also created for this new (primary) requirement.

Customer inquiries concerning the production status of the customer order are available at all times and across all levels of production on the basis of the requirements derivation and requirements coverage relationships geared toward the customer order item. Conversely, the effects of any delays in production on actual customer orders can also be tracked via these relationships.

The customer order definition also makes it possible to assign account codes such as the account receivable number and the article group number for the product inventory account and thus to specify assignments to article clarifications for direct costing.

B.II.2.2.2.2.2 One-Off Production and Project Management

The unique aspect of a one-off production order is that the bill of materials structure for the article is not developed until the order processing stage. A one-off production order (e.g., in the case of plant engineering or special machines) typically contains extremely comprehensive engineering specifications. Despite this comprehensiveness, it is possible to maintain the basic order structure shown in Figure B.II.25. In the case of one-off production, the entity type CUSTOMER ORDER describes a single complex machine. The order header creates the relationship to the customer, and the relationship type ORDER ITEM initially contains only one instance in the form of the project to be created. The corresponding project is not defined as an article until the individual customer order itself is defined, i.e., a very specific entity ARTICLE is created for a customer order, which, in turn, is a component of the general entity type PART.

The texts and comprehensive terms that belong to the order are entered in the previously introduced entity and relationship types CUSTOMER TERMS, CUSTOMER TEXT and CUSTOMER-TERMS-CUSTOMER-TEXT ASSIGNMENT.

At the beginning of the specification process for the customer order, the bill of materials structure can be virtually empty, i.e., it need only consist of the entity introduced for the customer-specific article. During the design phase, standard components or components developed in-house are increasingly linked with this order, gradually resulting in a complete bill of materials. Since it constitutes the basis for planning, this bill of materials is a component of the bills of materials introduced thus far. Existing information, such as engineering drawings (i.e., CAD), can be accessed in order to continuously process the bill of materials. The close relationships to the product development process will be discussed in greater detail in that section. In addition, prior orders whose bills of materials are documented can be employed for developing the specifications via the SUBSEQUENT ORDER relationship to COMPLETED CUSTOMER ORDER.

The similarity relationships between the current one-off customer order and the completed one-off customer order are also type n:m, since several completed customer orders can provide information for a one-off customer order, and, conversely, a completed one-off customer order displays similarities to several current one-off customer orders.

Bills of materials are drafted in a "top-down" manner, i.e., the most important assemblies are first roughly defined and then continually refined during the further course of the design process.

In order to be able to obtain time- and capacity-oriented overviews early in the process, a network plan can be created from the bill of materials information. The similarities between bills of materials and network plans have already been discussed in the context of capacity planning.

Standard bills of materials can provide an additional source of information if they are defined for articles in such a way that they already cover certain basic versions. An assignment relationship can create the link from a one-off customer order to the standard structures. This link, i.e., the product composition that is valid for the current one-off customer order, is then transferred into the planning bills of materials via copy functions. Analogously, this information acquisition process is also performed for transferring information from the completed one-off customer order.

The overlap between order definition and production planning and control is multifaceted. For example, time-critical components and materials can be produced and procured in advance even though their superordinate assemblies have not yet been completely defined. Planning consistency is maintained by continuously updating the bill of materials via net change functions and by changes that are made in requirements- and order-related data.

The same functions for requirements and capacity planning result with respect to the current status of the bill of materials as in the case of standard articles, so that the data structure need not be modified following transfer of the bill of materials. The interrelationship between production orders and the customer order is ensured via customer-order-oriented requirements tracking.

Project engineering is a special form of one-off production in which a general contractor assumes responsibility for a complex project without actually being involved in its execution.

The data structure that is necessary for this scenario also largely corresponds to the previously introduced logic (see Figures B.II.27 and B.II.28).

The project order, too, constitutes an n:m relationship between the entity types ORGANIZATIONAL UNIT, TIME and CUSTOMER. A project order defines a project, which, in turn, consists of operations. Each operation is defined as an instance of the entity type PART.

The project operations are logically incorporated into predecessor/successor relationships by assignment relationships. These

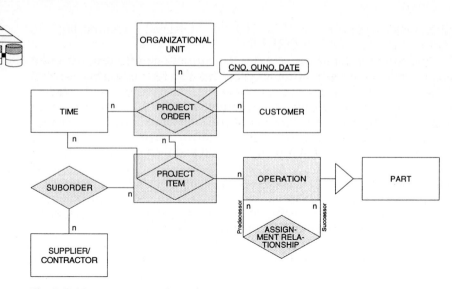

Fig. B.II.27: Data structure for project management

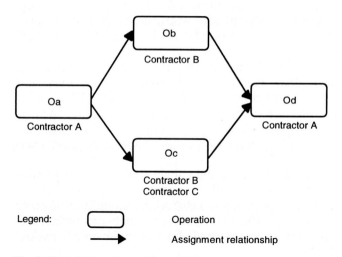

Fig. B.II.28: Network chart for project management

relationships can be represented in the same form as the parts composition for a bill of materials. Each operation (subproject) can be assigned several contractors that perform the operation, and a contractor can be assigned several subprojects. Project control support through the network planning technique, which contains scheduling and capacity calculations, will not be discussed in further detail (see *Scheer, Projektsteuerung 1978; Gewald/Kasper/Schelle, Netzplantechnik 1972*). The content of the control process largely corresponds to that of the product development process and can be pursued in greater detail there.

B.II.2.2.2.3 Shipping

The data structure for shipping exhibits similarities to the data structure for receiving. The discussion of route planning and transport presented here could also apply to inbound logistics if the customer handles purchase order transport himself or combines it with shipping.

Prior to shipping an order, it is frequently necessary to perform quality inspections that have been prenegotiated with the customer. These inspections are included in the terms, which were entered at the time the order was accepted. The final inspection can be defined as a part of quality control in Production, where it is treated as a subcategory of CAM, or it can be an independent function of the shipping department. In the latter case, it belongs to Sales, which uses the data structures for INSPECTION PLAN and INSPECTION RESULT.

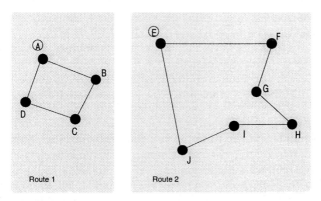

Fig. B.II.29: Example of transport routes

If specific shipments are made regularly, special techniques can be employed to optimize routes (see *Falk/Spieck/Mertens, Teilintelligente Agenten in Lager- und Transportlogistik 1993* and *Ohse, Transportprobleme 1992*).

A route consists of several subroutes, as illustrated in Figure B.II.29. Each subroute links two locations and is identified by the place of departure and the destination. A subroute can occur in several routes. A customer is assigned to a location. The optimized routes are combined in the entity type ROUTE and identified by the route number ROUTNO. They are master data, i.e., the routes identified as optimal are only reoptimized at longer intervals.

The units used for transport, such as rail, tandem trucks, etc., are combined in the entity type TRANSPORT UNIT and identified by the transport unit number TRANO.

The entity type ROUTE is assigned all possible transport units via the TRANSPORT ASSIGNMENT. This is an n:m assignment since a route can be traveled by several different transport units, and, conversely, a transport unit can be used for several itineraries.

A transport unit can comprise several TRANSPORT MODES, which results in an additional classification level. A transport mode can be a freight car or a container, for example, and is identified by the transport mode number TRAMNO. Valid combinations of transport modes and transport units are entered via the relationship type TRANSPORT COMBINATION.

At the smallest classification level, the individual types of packaging constitute containers, pallets, etc. An n:m relationship PACKAGING TYPE ASSIGNMENT exists between PACKAGING TYPE and TRANSPORT MODE. It specifies that certain packaging units can only be transported using certain transport modes, and, conversely, certain transport modes can only handle certain packaging units.

The data structure represented thus far has the character of master data. At the same time, the transport resources TRANSPORT UNIT, TRANSPORT MODE and PACKAGING TYPE can be defined as specializations of the general entity type RESOURCE or EQUIPMENT.

The master data will now be linked with the concrete order consignments that result from order processing.

For purposes of distinction, the order-related shipping data is preceded by the word "shipping." Decisions concerning the selection of transport combinations are associated with the assignments, and optimization models can also be employed in this regard.

Orders pending shipment are initiated via shipping advice lists generated on the basis of the agreed delivery dates, and a packing list is issued for each customer affected by the shipment. A PACKING LIST is a relationship between ORGANIZATIONAL UNIT, CUSTOMER and TIME. The cardinalities are type n, since a customer can receive several packing lists over a period of time, and, on the other hand, several packing lists can be issued on the same date. A packing list item that includes the delivery date is created for each article. A packing list can contain several items if several articles are shipped at the same time.

A PARTIAL DELIVERY is a relationship between CUSTOMER ORDER ITEM and PACKING LIST ITEM and is type n:m, since a customer order item can be satisfied in several delivery items, but, in the case of consolidated deliveries, a packing list item can also result from several order items.

The inventory level must be reduced with each packing list item that is taken from inventory. This situation is created by the relationship INVENTORY DELIVERY ASSIGNMENT or STOCK-OUT TRANSACTION between the reserved inventory amount (INVENTORY COVERAGE) and PACKING LIST ITEM. If a packing list item is taken from several stock locations, several stock-out transactions can occur. An inventory level can also be reduced by several stock-out transactions, resulting in an n:m relationship. In addition to quantity-oriented inventory postings, value-oriented postings must also be performed. The POSTING forms a link between the general ledger account and the packing list item.

The general ledger account is identified by the account code previously assigned during order entry.

The freight load is represented by a freight list and encompasses the individual deliveries relating to the concrete transport unit. Each FREIGHT LIST ITEM relates to a customer and encompasses all deliveries to the customer for a given route; these deliveries can also stem from several orders. The freight list is assigned the individual packing list items via the relationship type PACKAGING.

The assignment of individual packing list items to packaging units such as containers, pallets, etc., is created via the n:m relationship PACKAGING. A packing list item can go into several packaging units, and a packaging unit can encompass several packing list items. The relationship PACKAGING thus represents the elementary assignment. The implicit relationships to PACKAGING TYPE, TRANSPORT MODE, TRANSPORT UNIT and TRANSPORT ASSIGNMENT thus facilitate transport tracking of each packing list item.

The data structure shown here consists largely of assignment relationships. If a customer order is shipped in accordance with the entered order items, the packing list data are largely identical to the order data. Thus, the potential for simplification in this regard is similar to that for inbound logistics.

B.II.2.2.2.4 Invoicing

The invoice is typically generated on the basis of the packing list. This ensures that the customer will be billed for only those goods that Shipping has actually processed. In special cases, an invoice may be necessary before the packing list has been generated if it has to accompany the goods along with the packing list (e.g., in the case of export deliveries). In this case, the order serves as the source of the data.

The following discussion will assume the normal scenario, where the packing list provides the basis for generating the invoice. The CUSTOMER INVOICE is an n:m relationship between ORGANIZATIONAL UNIT, CUSTOMER and TIME. The individual invoice items result from assignment to the articles and to the delivery time. An n:m relationship exists between the PACKING LIST ITEM and the INVOICE ITEM. An n:m relationship is also conceivable with respect to the assignment to CUSTOMER ORDER ITEM; however, this has already been implicitly entered via the packing list assignment. If a consolidated delivery is made for a part as a result of several different orders, or a partial delivery occurs so that one order item results in several invoice items, this situation is represented by an n:m relationship.

Complex procedures can occur in connection with invoicing as a result of currency conversions, customs regulations, etc.

Invoices provide the basis for the accounts receivable accounting system. One or more accounts receivable accounts can be created for each customer, or vice versa, resulting in an n:m relationship. The objective, however, is frequently a 1:1 relationship in order to make "customer" and "accounts receivable" identical. Since the departure of the goods is entered in the shipping account, and thus in the general ledger accounting system, as well as in the accounts receivable account, postings occur in both systems. Similarly to accounts payable, the value-oriented warehouse debit postings can be entered with clearing prices and then reconciled with the actual prices by means of a clearing account.

B.II.2.2.2.5 Payment Procedures

As in the case of the purchasing process, payment procedures also mark the completion of the sales process, whereby the processes in both departments are inversely related to one another. Customer payments can be made by mail (check) or through a bank (electronic funds transfer). If necessary, the accounts receivable clerk must then make the assignments between the amounts and the entries to be reconciled. A payment item can relate to several entries to be reconciled, and an outstanding entry can be reconciled by several partial payments. The assignment decisions between payment items and the invoice items to be reconciled can be largely automated by employing priority rules, e.g., on the basis of due dates. Despite this option, however, this function must generally be designed for interactive processing.

Figure B.II.30 shows the data structure for payment procedures.

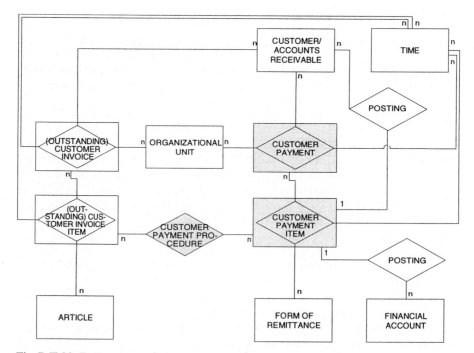

Fig. B.II.30: Data structure for payment procedures

As subsets of customer invoices, the outstanding customer invoices are linked to the process shown in Figure B.II.25.

A customer payment made on a specific date can encompass different payment types (electronic funds transfers, cash, checks, etc.) as payment items.

The application of a (sub)amount to outstanding order items is represented by the CUSTOMER PAYMENT PROCEDURE.

Payment initiates the corresponding postings

Credit financial account, debit account receivable.

B.II.2.2.2.6 Potential for Simplifying the Sales Process

As in the case of inbound logistics, there is also significant potential for simplifying the outbound logistics process, with both the causes of the complexity and the possible actions for eliminating it being similar for the two functions. The continuous splitting and combining of the process is the major cause of its complexity. The changing status of the process is characterized by different types of documents that are each defined and processed by different organizational units. The need for managing the assignment relationships between the types of documents is a significant cause of the inflated data structure shown in Figure B.II.25.

Here, too, the process can be simplified by separating long-term sales activities from operative execution. Price negotiations are then not an object of each individual sales process; instead they are conducted at longer intervals. This at least reduces the number of quotes relating to concrete sales processes, since the quotation phase numbers among the long-term sales processes and is thus separate from the operative processes. In the case of stabile delivery scheduling, it is also possible to make a concrete assignment of the delivery quantities from one or at least only a few stock locations. Moreover, it is possible to consolidate the concepts of "customer" and "accounts receivable" as well, so that only one entity type is necessary for both. If there is a long-term agreement on customer terms, the final inspection can be directly linked with the end phase of production control, since a tight production assignment to known delivery agreements makes it possible to assure quality characteristics during the production phase. Consequently, inspection sample size and frequency can at least be reduced for the final sales inspection, if not eliminated entirely.

A disciplined sales process also ensures that the customer order results in a shipping process that coincides with the order, without being distorted by consolidated and partial deliveries. All this results in a simplified data structure for sales processing, which is shown in Figure B.II.31 as an analogy to Figure B.II.16 for inbound logistics.

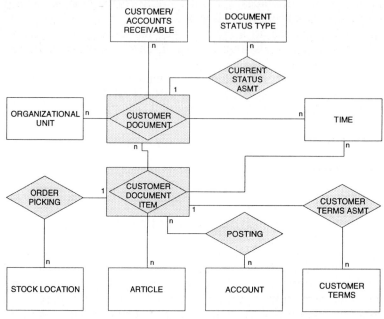

Fig. B.II.31: Simplified data structure for the sales process

Using JIT links to the customer in order to integrate the sales process provides even further possibilities for simplification. The event-driven process chain shown in Figure B.II.32 is incorporated into the JIT process for inbound logistics shown in Figure B.II.17 via the hatched events "customer release" and "received by customer."

As in the case of inbound logistics, different factors must be taken into account in outbound logistics, since not all products conform to a uniform process. For this reason, a segmented sales process is suggested here as well, and a sales leitstand concept is outlined for this process in Figure B.II.33. Simplified sales processes can thus be developed for the different article segments, whereby a leitstand tailored to a specific sales segment performs sales activities from inquiry processing to transport coordination and invoicing. This leitstand is assigned the CAM systems responsible for performing warehousing, quality assurance and materials handling control.

The sales process can be integrated with the detailed production scheduling leitstand for the JIT process if the logical link to the customer is timed to be current enough for customer releases to directly affect the supplier's production, and if the articles can be delivered directly to the customer from Final Assembly without having to couple the logistics process with warehousing functions. As in the case of the JIT purchasing process, functions from other departments (Purchasing or Sales) are shifted to time-critical production control functions. In order to exploit synergy effects vis-à-vis the customer, for example, coordination of the different purchasing processes is handled by a coordination leitstand, which can also reconcile conflicts in the event of contending capacity demands. Long-term planning activities can also be performed by an additional superordinate planning leitstand.

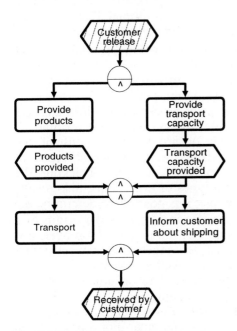

Fig. B.II.32: EPC of the JIT sales process

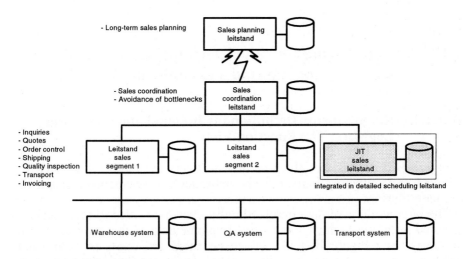

Fig. B.II.33: Sales leitstand concept

B.II.2.2.2.7 Analyses

The data structure developed here can be used for medium- and short-term analyses in the sense of a sales information system. In particular, analyses can be performed by different customer groups, article groups, sales regions, etc. Due to their links with the accounting system, these analyses are not only quantity-oriented, but value-oriented as well. The tight integration between operative processes and the accounting system is particularly important in the case of urgent information requirements. For a discussion of the special conditions relating to a sales information system for durable assets (capital investments), see *Spang, Informationsmodellierung im Investitionsgütermarketing 1993.*

The link between master data and the sales processes provides answers to a multitude of questions. For example, the system can determine all sales activities for a specific customer or article. The status of the individual sales activities, as characterized by the different types of documents, can be determined and analyzed as well. Tracking the document flow, i.e., linking the different types of documents, also results in interesting analysis options. For example, it is possible to determine the orders and invoices that result from specific inquiries or the origin of a delivery on the basis of the order, the quote or the inquiry. Moreover, it is also possible to perform up-to-date analyses concerning new customer inquiries, active quotes and orders received as well as revenues.

Analyses concerning orders involving incomplete documents and lists of "hot" customers and articles can also be meaningful.

During the sales process, the transparent information system ensures ongoing information availability vis-à-vis the customer. For more detailed analysis options, see *SAP, SD-Verkauf 1992, Chapter 9 Informationen, Analyse, Auswertungen.*

B.II.2.3 Summarizing and Supplementing the Requirements Definitions for Inbound and Outbound Logistics

B.II.2.3.1 Requirements Definition for Inbound and Outbound Logistics: The Function View

Figure B.II.01 has already provided an overview of the functions for inbound and outbound logistics. The subsequent refinements will not be discussed further.

The large volume of data involved in Purchasing has led to time-period-oriented solutions, which have been implemented in the form of batch processes (see Figure B.II.34). However, there are limits to automated batch processing as a result of the manual data input that is necessary in

Function	Subfunction	Reasons for interactive processing				Batch/ automatic
		Currency	Plausibility	Iterative modification	Interactive decision process	
Inbound logistics Basic data management		X	X			
Requirements processing			X	X		
Quote obtaining	Soliciting			X		X
	Processing	X	X	X		
Ordering	Supplier selection				X	(X)
	Order quantity determination				X	(X)
	Order quantity data transfer					X
Order monitoring	Inquiries	(X)	(X)			X
	Dunning	(X)				X
Receivings	Transport planning				X	
	Data entry					X
	Quality inspection	X	X			
	Distribution				X	(X)
	Posting	X	X			X
Invoice control	Entry					X
	Inspection		X			X
	Posting		(X)			X
Outbound logistics Basic data management		X	X			
Preparation of inquiries and quotes			X	X		
Order acceptance	Entry (identification of articles)	(X)	(X)	(X)		X
	Costing			X	X	
	Reservation				X	
Order control	Deadline monitoring	X				X
	Query processing	X	X			
	Dunning processing	X	X			
Shipping	Quality inspection	X	X			
	Order picking				X	
	Route optimization				X	X
	Posting					X
Invoicing	Entry		X			X
	Writing					X
	Data transfer					X
	Posting					X

Fig. B.II.34: Processing forms of inbound and outbound logistics

the case of inconsistencies (e.g., variances between ordered and delivered amounts). Moreover, time-critical, case-oriented processing is necessary for rush orders, as well as in situations that require immediate reaction to disruptions (i.e., if quality deficiencies are discovered in time-critical materials).

Important criteria for interactive applications within the context of inbound logistics include currency and plausibility checks.

Supplier selection, order quantity determination, transport planning and goods distribution are interactive decision processes, which can be quite complex due to the numerous qualitative parameters involved. This complexity necessitates the use of expert systems, as well as model-based operations research approaches, for processing heuristic and empirical rules (see *Krallmann, Expertensysteme für CIM 1986*).

Iterative variations are possible in processing requirements, in obtaining quotes—by varying texts in exceptional situations—as well as in determining requirements on the basis of forecast suggestions and in analyzing suppliers' quotes. Plausibility checks accompany data entry, review and posting processes, which all access master data. Questions of currency relate primarily to data input functions.

Many functions can be automated, i.e., they can be processed by means of programmed decision-making rules—even with case-oriented processing. As a result, many of the reasons for interactive processing are shown in parentheses, since they apply only in exceptional cases.

Consolidation effects can also be exploited in the case of non-time-critical operations in order to handle the processes more efficiently in batch mode, e.g., in the case of postings. Moreover, data transfer to and from suppliers is increasingly being automated by using electronic data interchange.

Outbound logistics is extremely event-driven. It encompasses decision processes within the framework of order acceptance (reservation) and shipping optimization. Within the framework of order acceptance, it is possible to transfer information from past orders to current orders and to identify similar orders for purposes of data transfer. Past orders can be interactively modified for this purpose. In the case of customer-oriented production, costing is an important interactive function.

Reservation involves assigning inventory quantities to a rush customer order. It is also possible to reschedule on the basis of customer order priorities. Depending on the complexity of the procedures involved, interactive support can range from plausibility checks to iterative modification of an initial solution, or even to an interactive decision process in the case of differing options for assigning inventory quantities.

Rush orders are inserted into the existing production program. This leads not only to the assignment of new inventory quantities, but also to quantity- and/or time-related changes in production orders. The results of scheduling simulations can influence the decision to accept or refuse the order.

Within the framework of order control, the user can continually perform an interactive check to see if the order deadline is being maintained. Customer inquiries in this regard can be answered on the basis of up-to-date information.

Shipping advices are generated within the context of shipping and are geared toward order due dates. Since this function necessitates that the entire database be analyzed, batch processing is the most appropriate mode. In the case of rush orders, however, individual orders can also be processed on a case-by-case basis.

Extensive mathematical procedures can be employed for optimizing routes, which makes this process a typical batch function as well.

Packaging optimization, i.e., optimally combining delivery quantities into specific packaging units, is a similar issue (see *Isermann, Generierung von Stapelplänen 1984*).

Generating packing lists is essentially a batch function, since it can be performed after the goods have been withdrawn from inventory. If the objective is case-oriented processing, however, each stock-out function that is performed can initiate an action to generate a packing list. The most significant reason for using interactive processing in this case would be currency.

The need to set up plausibility checks for invoicing and accounts receivable accounting makes interactive processing necessary in exceptional situations. The most significant procedures, however, are performed automatically in a batch-oriented solution due to the tight data integration with previous functions.

B.II.2.3.2 Requirements Definition for Inbound and Outbound Logistics: The Organization View

Figure B.II.03 has already shown inbound and outbound logistics arranged in a functional reference organizational chart. Figure B.II.19 illustrates a leitstand concept for inbound logistics, and B.II.33 illustrates a concept for outbound logistics. Figure B.II.35 combines these concepts with the production leitstand concept and arranges them in the planning level model for Purchasing, Sales and Production. Consequently, the process-oriented organizational view, on the one hand, as well as networked decentralization as an organizational principle, on the other, are pursued.

The sales representative primarily performs order entry functions, for which he can be linked to the sales leitstands in a sales office either offline or online. The sales leitstand in a sales office provides the operative process for order entry as well as for reservation of inventory quantities that are maintained on the level of the sales department or even on the level of superordinate organizational units. In addition to order entry, quote preparation is also performed on the sales office level.

The sales coordination leitstand is capable of accessing information across several individual sales leitstands, which gives it the power to solve allocation problems in the event of conflicting reservations.

The operative functions for quote processing, order entry and reservation are also performed on the branch office level. The coordination leitstand on this level coordinates not only the operative sales leitstands for the branch office, but also the coordination leitstands for the sales office, which makes it possible to handle conflicting reservations between sales offices. The coordination leitstand for the branch office is also the link to the shipping actions performed by the production plants.

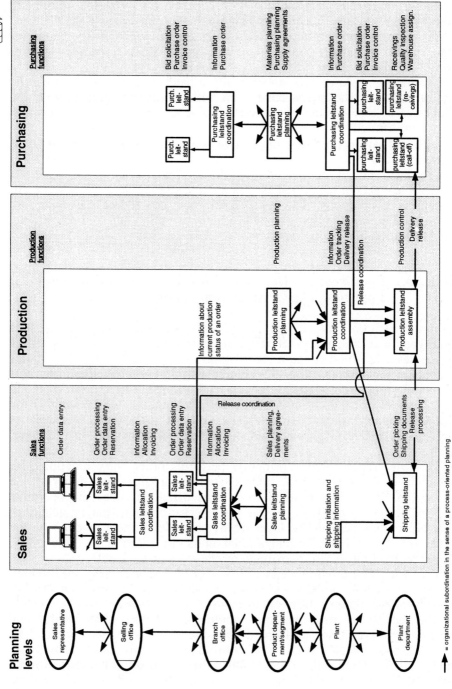

Fig. B.II.35: Networked leitstand organization for inbound and outbound logistics

Thus, the leitstand is capable of accessing information from the subordinate organizational sales units as well as via the link to the shipping leitstand for the plants. If shipping activities are integrated into the concept of the plant production leitstands, the coordination leitstand also has access to the production leitstand responsible for shipping activities.

Since plants can be responsible for several product groups, shipping leitstands can be linked with several branch sales offices that are also responsible for different product groups. The same holds true in the case of the production coordination leitstand, which can be accessed by several branch offices.

The branch office leitstands are subordinate to planning leitstands for sales planning as well as for formulating long-term delivery agreements with customers on the product group level. Because of the n:m relationship between branch office and product group, a sales planning leitstand can access several branch office coordination leitstands; likewise, a branch office coordination leitstand can be supported by several planning leitstands.

The operative purchasing functions are located on the plant level, where purchasing leitstands are set up for individual materials segments for purposes of bid solicitation, purchase order execution and invoice control. They are configured via coordination leitstands for comprehensive information distribution as well as in order to combine optimal order amounts from different order segments for the same suppliers. The purchasing coordination leitstand is also superordinate to a special release leitstand as well as to special receiving leitstands. These leitstands are located on the plant department level, since they are typically set up in a different location than administrative order processing and are assigned to the plant departments. If order releases are performed directly from the production assembly leitstands, the release/purchasing leitstand is integrated with the production assembly leitstand. Figure B.II.35 shows both options.

A planning leitstand for purchasing is provided on the product group level for the long-term functions of materials planning, purchasing planning and negotiating supply agreements.

If assembly control initiates releases directly to suppliers and if customer releases also go directly to assembly control, JIT chains for inbound and outbound logistics converge in the assembly control leitstand.

Although Figure B.II.35 shows only the major organizational links, it nonetheless illustrates the high degree of networking between Sales, Production and Purchasing. The organizational concepts provide the point of departure for forming the network topology within the framework of the design specification.

B.II.2.3.3 Requirements Definition for Inbound and Outbound Logistics: The Data View

The data structures for inbound logistics have been shown in Figures B.II.07 and B.II.10, those for outbound logistics in Figures B.II.21 and B.II.25. They have been separated on the basis of the different logistics chains but developed with a similar graphical arrangement of the information objects. A generalized data structure for external logistics can be easily derived on the basis of these representations. There is no difference between many of the terms for the closely related accounting and requirements planning departments anyway. Important generalized terms are shown in Figure B.II.36.

The area of electronic purchasing and sales data interchange has been the subject of strong standardization efforts across all descriptive levels, i.e., requirements definition, design specification and implementation description, whereby the design specification and implementation description levels are (still) the primary focus. The standardization efforts initially came from large corporations that had already defined their proprietary standards (e.g., Siemens), subsequently developed into national industry standards (VDA standards for the German automotive industry, SEDAS for retailing) and international industry standards (AIAG = Automotive Industry Action Group; ODETTE = Organisation for Data Exchange by Teletransmission in Europe (with the focus on the automotive industry)), and ultimately culminated in the international interindustry standard EDIFACT (Electronic Data Interchange for Administration, Commerce and Transport), which also encompasses industry-specific subsets (e.g., EDIFICE for the electronics industry and CEFIC for the chemical industry).

The types of documents to be exchanged, as well as their structures, must be defined on the requirements definition level. It is impossible to avoid errors unless the exchanged data can be interpreted in the same way by both partners. This patently obvious requirement, however, demands a higher degree of harmonization than merely controlling the syntactical structure of the technical DP formats used to transfer the data.

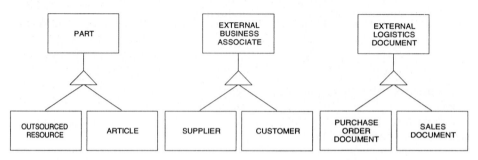

Fig. B.II.36: Generalized terms from inbound and outbound logistics

Figure B.II.37 shows several typical document types that lend themselves to data interchange.

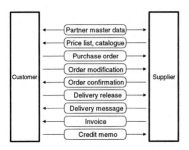

Fig. B.II.37: Data suitable for electronic data interchange (EDI)

Two options exist for harmonizing the logical data structures (see Figure B.II.38). Since the trend is increasingly moving away from point-to-point links between two partners, harmonization can occur in a first step via a standard definition so that each partner only needs to create the logical rules for converting his individual data structure into the standard, and vice versa. This process can result in losses of information if one of the data structures is more powerful than the other. This can be avoided if all of the partners use the same (standard) data structure in their own applications.

In EDI, the data access rights of the individual partners are handled simply by means of a mailbox link, i.e., one partner sends a message to the other's mailbox file; however, one partner does not have direct access to the other's data.

Under this concept, master data such as article definitions and agreed terms, can be exchanged and stored by both partners (redundantly), so that only identifying information such as article numbers and planning data (quantities and deadlines) need to be transferred when orders are placed, since the article name, delivery location, price, etc., are already known.

A direct link to the planning systems, which would allow a supplier to access a customer's inventory levels and use this data to schedule shipments, requires broader access rights. This issue is being discussed under the buzzword "direct data link." Since in this case one partner directly accesses the individual data definition, this definition must be known to him. In the case of contact between several partners, this situation leads to bilateral links again and runs counter to standardization efforts—as long as not all the partners are using a standardized data definition (see *Hübner, Electronic Commerce 1993*).

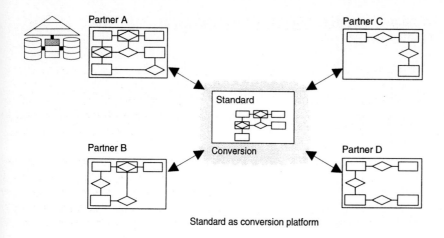

Standard as conversion platform

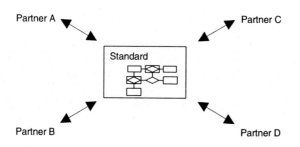

Common (standard) data structure

Fig. B.II.38: EDI's logical data structures

B.II.2.3.4 Requirements Definition for Inbound and Outbound Logistics: The Control View

Relationships between functions and organizational structure have already been treated in rough form in the discussion of the integrated leitstand concept (see Figure B.II.35). By describing the process before and after the introduction of JIT principles, it is possible to illustrate the shifts in functions (receiving inspection to end inspection) and the elimination of functions (invoicing and invoice control).

B.II.3 Design Specifications for Inbound and Outbound Logistics

The design specifications will be discussed primarily with respect to modern logistics concepts such as JIT that use electronic data interchange, as this involves aspects that differ from the ordinary transformation rules between requirements definitions and design specifications.

B.II.3.1 Design Specification for Inbound and Outbound Logistics: The Function View

In a common-module concept, the similarities between inbound and outbound logistics that were discussed on the requirements definition level result in a high degree of reusability. Swapping functions between partners does not lead to savings in terms of software development, however, since one party assumes both roles (customer and supplier). On the other hand, eliminating functions (invoicing, invoice control) has an effect on reducing the number of modules involved.

B.II.3.2 Design Specification for Inbound and Outbound Logistics: The Organization View

The internal network topology for the networked purchasing, sales and production leitstand organization developed in Figure B.II.35 can be developed analogously to the concepts for both production as well as requirements and capacity planning.

The communication relationships that result from intercompany data exchange can be implemented via direct network connections or via independent information services. In the first case involving a point-to-point connection, the logical link of the requirements definition conforms to the network topology (portrayals of the various public and private network services that can be employed will not be taken into account for the time being). Thus, the link must be established and controlled for each data transfer that occurs. However, this involves significant expense and effort on the part of customers and suppliers, since they communicate with a number of external partners. As an alternative, it is possible to introduce neutral or enterprise-related clearing points that collect messages, convert them into different formats and route them to the receiver on a non-real-

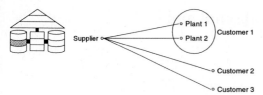

Logical link or physical-topological point-to-point connection

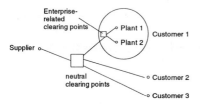

Physical topology about information markets with the same logical connections

Fig. B.II.39: EDI's communication topologies

time basis (see Figure B.II.39). Thus, senders can handle messages to several receivers, and receivers can handle messages from several senders in one session (see *Hubmann, Einsatz neuer Informations- und Kommunikationstechniken in der Beschaffung 1992; Hubmann, Elektronisierung von Beschaffungsmärkten und Beschaffungshierarchien 1989; ACTIS, DFÜ-Box Leistungsbeschreibung 1993*).

Mercedes Benz, for example, replaced its 12 plant-related EDI nodes with 4 enterprise-related clearing nodes. Neutral clearing services are being offered by value-added network providers (IBM, AT&T, General Electric Information Service).

In the case of a direct data link between customer and supplier application systems, a "step backward" to the first form is necessary unless the clearing points keep data that are of mutual interest up-to-date and accessible.

Data transfer between partners can be handled via PTT services or value added network services (VANS). In this case, the data can be received by a special communications computer, converted and routed to the different processing computers on the recipient's end. Figure B.II.40 shows an example of this type of implementation. In this situation, a UNIX workstation can be used as the communications computer and connected to the processing computers via a LAN. Available transmission networks include the long-distance dial-up network, a packet-switched network, ISDN and VANS. The choice between network services with different transfer speeds (e. g., packet-switched at 9,600 bps and ISDN at 64,000

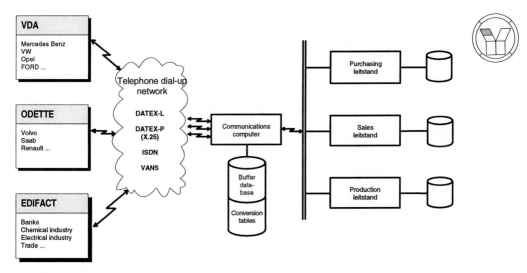

Fig. B.II.40: Communication sequence

bps) should be made on the basis of the volume of data to be transferred and the maximum transfer time that can be tolerated.

The left side of Figure B.II.40 shows typical users of the various standard formats (see *ACTIS, DFÜ-Box 1992*). If these kinds of communication relationships exist at both ends, it is also possible to directly couple the users' applications.

B.II.3.3 Design Specification for Inbound and Outbound Logistics: The Data View

The relational model for external logistics can be derived directly from the ER model developed here.

Separate message structure standards are defined for the EDI standards on the design specification level; these new standards conform more to a traditional data concept, as represented for EDIFACT in Figure B.II.41 (see *Hermes, Syntax-Regeln für den elektronischen Datenaustausch 1988*).

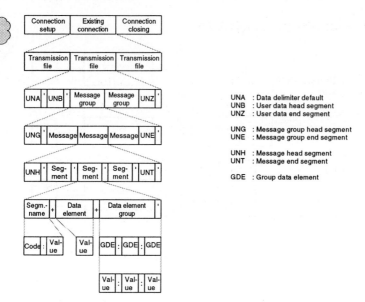

Fig. B.II.41: Structure of an EDIFACT message

B.II.3.4 Design Specification for Inbound and Outbound Logistics: The Control View

The EPCs developed for the JIT process in the context of the requirements definition serve as the point of departure for determining the events for the triggers that (automatically) initiate the EDI message exchange.

B.II.4 Implementation Description for Inbound and Outbound Logistics

The EDI standards also provide assistance on the implementation level by offering file-transfer protocols for specific networks, rules for data compression, restart, reversal or security services for passwords. The user-friendly ODETTE file-transfer protocol (OFTP) is compatible with packet-switched networks and is thus particularly cost-effective.

By using the protocols, a virtually automatic data interchange process is possible.

B.III Human Resource Logistics

Although there has been a trend toward replacing the term "personnel" with "human resources" in order to stress the value of employees as organizational investments (see *Holley/Jennings, Personnel Management: Functions and Issues 1983, p. 7*), this book will use both terms synonymously. Human resource management, with its administrative, planning and control functions, will be treated as a separate logistics problem, although broadening the definition of "outsourced resource" to include labor would allow it to be treated as part of inbound logistics. Since human resource management possesses farther-reaching links to general enterprise management, however, it will be treated individually.

B.III.1 Overview: Human Resource Logistics

The functions of human resource logistics in industry involve retaining and developing the human resources of an industrial enterprise (see *Kupsch/Marr, Personalwirtschaft 1991, p. 778*). Human resources are used in all functional departments of an industrial enterprise that deal with the production and handling of commercial goods.

A formal classification of human resource management can distinguish between (see *Hentschel, Personaldatenbank 1976, pp. 3 ff.*):
- Administrative functions
- Planning-related functions
- Informational/statistical functions
- Financial functions
- Legal functions.

The core functions include (see *Heinrich/Pils, Betriebsinformatik im Personalbereich 1983, p. 39*):
- Determining human resource requirements
- Recruiting human resources
- Placing human resources
- Retaining human resources
- Developing human resources
- Dismissing human resources.

Figure B.III.01 shows a functional system derived from March and Simon's "incentive/contribution" theory (see *Kupsch/Marr, Personalwirtschaft 1991, p. 778*).

"Contributions" in this sense are understood to be the work output that the employee contributes to the industrial enterprise in return for material

Contribution-related functions	Business-related functions
1. Human resource requirements planning	1. Renumeration planning
2. Human resource recruitment, human resource placement and dismissal	2. Training and career planning
3. Job structuring	3. Design of the official management concept, executive management training

Fig. B.III.01: Functions of human resource management according to March and Simon

and non-material "incentives" from the organization. W. Mülder (see *Mülder, Organisatorische Implementierung von computergestützten Personalinformationssystemen 1984, pp. 65 f.*) developed a 49-point function catalog for human resource management, which includes the following administrative function groups:

- Payroll accounting, creating in-house personnel statistics, handling messages and information to different recipients, managing personnel data, organizing social facilities and services, monitoring deadlines and control functions.

Planning-related functions include:

- Obtaining information concerning employees and jobs; creating special, non-periodic reports and statistics; human resource placement and job evaluations; human resource recruitment and development; as well as medium- and long-term human resource planning.

Business-related human resource management functions primarily involve planning and scheduling activities.

Thus far, however, the practical application of information technology in human resource logistics has primarily related to administrative functions, in particular personnel data management and routine payroll accounting. These functions are not explicitly cited in the list of functions presented above or in the function profile derived from the incentive/contribution concept.

Both mass data management in the human resource department as well as routine payroll accounting are of major significance in an industrial enterprise, however. Moreover, these functions generate data that are also used for planning-related functions.

For this reason, the following discussion will make a distinction between basic data management, personnel accounting (which is primarily concerned with administrative functions) and personnel planning (which combines planning- and scheduling-related functions).

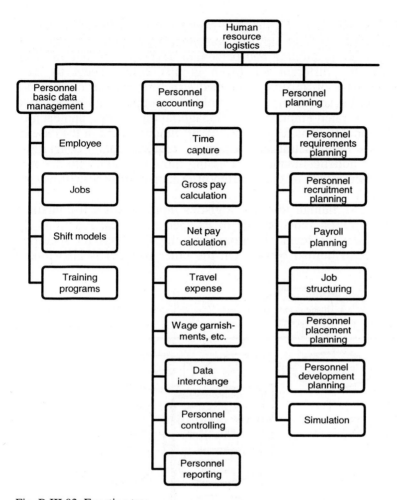

Fig. B.III.02: Function tree

The function tree shown in Figure B.III.02 provides an overview of the subfunctions for these three fields of activity. The structure of the following discussion largely conforms to this functional division, although such individual aspects as travel expense accounting are only briefly mentioned.

The organizational structure for human resource management can distinguish between central (i.e., interplant), administrative and planning-related functions, as well as control and personnel data capture functions on the plant level. Short-term personnel control has already been discussed in the context of production, which also required the use of basic data (shift models and employee information). The central human resource department can be organized either on an object- or function-oriented basis. In the case of a function-oriented organizational structure, organizational units are set up for personnel management, personnel planning, personnel accounting and personnel development that are each responsible for the different employee groups with respect to their function. In the case of an object-oriented structure, on the other hand, organizational units are formed for employee groups, such as salaried employees, hourly-rated employees or managerial employees, and each of these organizational units is responsible for all functions. As in the case of other business administration aspects, requirements concerning specialization or holistic function processing must be taken into account when weighing the merits of these different organizational structures (see Figure B.III.03).

On the one hand, human resource logistics represents a self-contained business administration function due to its special clerical functions for observing a variety of legal situations and the fact that its specified "object" consists of human beings. On the other hand, it is also linked

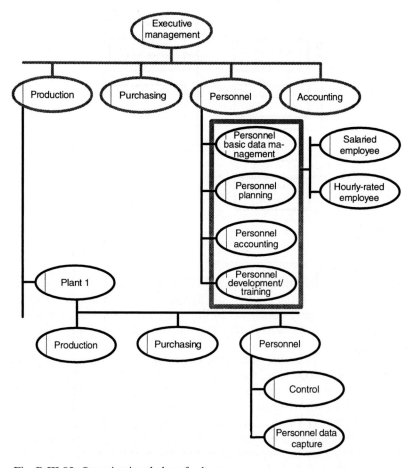

Fig. B.III.03: Organizational chart for human resource management

with other departments. The process chain diagram shown in Figure B.III.04 illustrates this situation. Calculating gross pay involves combining basic data from Human Resources as well as feedback from Production concerning personnel placement and attendance.

Because of the large volume of data involved, those types of planning functions that are performed on a periodic basis can be processed automatically in batch mode. The same holds true in the case of accounting functions for calculating gross and net pay. In a case-oriented analysis, e.g., in order to provide an individual employee with information if he or she suspects discrepancies, interactive processing can also be meaningful. As in the case of general inbound logistics, relationships exist between the enterprise and the outside world, e.g., information from the job market is brought into the enterprise during the hiring process, and

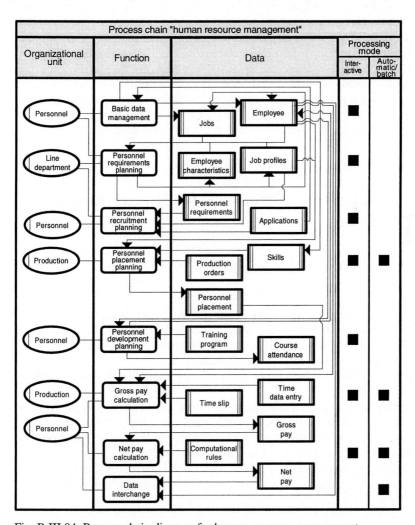

Fig. B.III.04: Process chain diagram for human resource management

relationships to external partners exist with respect to legally mandated exchange of statistical data and to banks via electronic salary deposits.

The data clusters for basic data management encompass both employee data and, as organizational units, the jobs to which employees are assigned. Within the framework of human resource requirements planning, characteristics are defined that allow both jobs and activities to be defined. Activity profiles constitute the qualitative requirements necessary for human resource recruitment, and the necessary number of employees determines the quantitative requirements.

In the case of human resource placement planning, the short-term personnel requirement is derived from production orders and must be reconciled with the required activities and the available manpower capacities. Human resource development planning assigns training programs to the individual employees; this leads to concrete course selections for the employees. The calculation of gross pay reveals relationships to Production in terms of short-term personnel placement planning and performance data entry. Gross pay is routed further to the net pay calculation function as an employee entitlement; in the net pay calculation function, tax and social security tax computation rules are used to determine net pay. The wide variety of statistical data that government regulations require to be supplied to the social security system are primarily taken from the data clusters for net pay and employees.

B.III.2 Requirements Definitions for Human Resource Logistics

B.III.2.1 Basic Data Management

The data structure for basic data is shown in Figure B.III.05. Since it is needed by both accounting- and planning-related functions, it is treated in a separate section of the book. It will subsequently be extended to include planning- and accounting-related basic data.

Several events that initiate basic data management functions are shown in Figure B.III.06.

The employee data constitute the core basic data. They can be used to generate and manage hirings, dismissals and reassignments. Legal regulations alone require that approximately 50 attributes be managed for each employee. Depending on the power and flexibility offered by the personnel information system involved, up to 400 attributes can be entered (see *Mülder, Organisatorische Implementierung von Personalinforma-tionssystemen 1984, p. 68*).

Closely linked with the personnel data are the jobs that exist as a result of an enterprise's organizational structure.

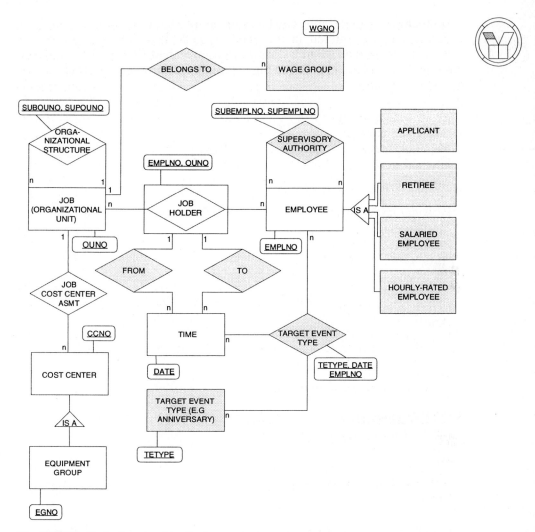

Fig. B.III.05: Basic data structure for human resource management

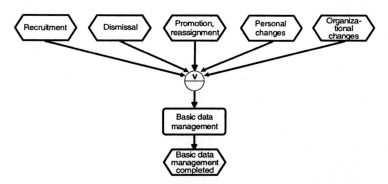

Fig. B.III.06: EPC for basic data management of human resource management

Both employees and jobs can be grouped into larger units.

Employees are entered in the entity type **EMPLOYEE**, regardless of their position in the hierarchy. Employees are identified by the employee number EMPLNO. The following enumeration provides a summary of possible attributes:

Identifying attributes:
Employee number
Name, address
Place of birth
Sex

Personal information:
Marital status
First name of spouse
Number of children
Religion

Hiring information:
Date
Previous employer

Qualifications:
Education and vocational training
Title
Foreign languages
Level of legal responsibility

Placement:
Positions and how long held
Department

Evaluations:
Date of last evaluation
Evaluation results
Date of next evaluation
Performance ratings

Payroll information:
Contract wage rate
Shift differential
Overtime pay
Mileage rate
Income tax class
Tax-free allowance
Cumulative tax withheld
Tax office

Social security information
Vacation entitlement

Banking information:
Account number
Bank

More detailed representations involving different classification criteria for the data groups can be found in: *Mertens/Griese, Integrierte Informationssysteme II 1993; Domsch, Systemgestützte Personalarbeit 1990, pp. 39 ff.; SAP, System RP 1990, pp. 41 ff.; SAP, System R/3, Die Personalwirtschaft der SAP 1992, pp. 3 ff.*

If specific data groups (e.g., qualification- and skill-related data) are logically linked with other data groups within the framework of human resource planning, e.g., in the context of a profile analysis involving the requirements profile for a job, these data can be taken from the entity type EMPLOYEE and used independently. This aspect will be discussed in greater detail in the discussion of the data structure for human resource planning. The overview is intended to provide an initial impression of the variety of data involved.

Employees can be grouped into subsets for differentiating between specific accounting functions and data structure links.

Figure B.III.05 thus formulates specializations of the employee groups APPLICANT, RETIREE, SALARIED EMPLOYEE and HOURLY-RATED EMPLOYEE. This is similar to the specializations PURCHASING AGENT, SALES REPRESENTATIVE, etc., introduced earlier. For the sake of simplicity, the exact assignment of structural relationships to these subsets will not always be represented. Instead, the entity type EMPLOYEE will be used as a general reference.

Depending on the collective bargaining agreements, different wage groups exist (e.g., for light jobs, trainees, etc.). Each JOB is unambiguously assigned to a wage group.

The workstations in an enterprise constitute the entity type JOB, which is identified by the organizational unit number OUNO.

The organizational structure of the enterprise is formed on the basis of the jobs and is represented in the form of a detailed organizational chart. In this sense, the term "job" is synonymous with the smallest organizational unit. While the job definition also—and precisely—encompasses the non-supervisory level, the organizational view of an organizational chart frequently only depicts the upper levels in the hierarchy.

An organizational chart is thus a job plan, i.e., a combination of all the jobs that exist in the enterprise. It usually forms a "tree," i.e., a job can have several directly subordinate jobs, but only one directly superordinate job. This situation is represented by the relationship type ORGANIZATIONAL STRUCTURE as a 1:n relationship with the key superordinate and subordinate organizational unit number (SUBOUNO, SUPOUNO).

Several jobs can be combined into a cost center. This can be identical to the entity type WORKSTATION GROUP in the production department.

The assignment of an employee to a job is represented by the relationship JOB HOLDER, which is identified by combining the attributes employee number (EMPLNO) and organizational unit number (OUNO). The relationship type forms an n:m relationship, since a job can be held by several employees (e.g., part time employment) and one employee can hold several jobs.

Frequently, for example, two departments can report to the same employee without being structurally linked within the organization.

The history of a job holder is expressed by the chronological relationships "from" and "to" for the job holder. This relationship makes it possible to track which jobs a specific employee has held and which different employees have held a specific job during a given period of time. A job assignment sequence is identified by a combination of the employee number (EMPLNO), the organizational unit number (OUNO) and the chronological period, expressed by the beginning and end of the assignment (FROM ... TO ...). In contrast to the current job holder assignment, which can contain a multitude of agreement information, only the attributes necessary for chronological analyses are entered in past job holder assignments.

Generally, the organizational structure also specifies the chain of command among the employees. However, a disciplinary and task-oriented separation can sometimes exist, e.g., if an employee is assigned to a specific department in terms of organizational structure, but belongs to another department in terms of the tasks performed. This situation leads to a "multi-track" organization as characterized by Taylor's function master system in its extreme form. In terms of the data structure, this means that deviations in the hierarchy expressed by the organizational structure are expressed by a special relationship type SUPERVISORY AUTHORITY. This is an n:m relationship type since an employee can have several subordinates and a subordinate can have several superiors. A supervisory authority is indicated by the combination of the subordinate employee number (SUBEMPLNO) and the superordinate employee number (SUPEMPLNO).

B.III.2.2 Human Resource Accounting

Because of the high volume of data involved, the need for computational adaptations that results from frequent legal and regulatory changes, coupled with the sensitivity in terms of factual and chronological accuracy, personnel accounting is a central application function in DP-supported human resource management. Its complexity should not be underestimated, since both different forms of data capture and different accounting procedures must be taken into account.

Human resource accounting is subdivided into gross pay calculation and net pay calculation. Gross pay calculation involves establishing the gross pay on the basis of performance- or time-related criteria. Numerous labor-contract- and enterprise-oriented characteristics come to bear in this regard.

The function of net pay calculation therefore involves determining employee take-home pay from the gross pay, taking into account mandatory and voluntary contributions and taxes.

Within the context of data interchange, data must be transferred to different public offices (labor offices, social security). At the same time, the payment can be handled through data media exchange.

B.III.2.2.1 Time and Performance Data Capture for Calculating Gross Pay

Depending on the type of pay involved, gross pay can be calculated on the basis of attendance (hourly wage) or on the basis of performance data (incentive pay) (see Figure B.III.07). Attendance times are also used for plausibility checks with respect to performance data. The company calendar includes all workdays, taking into account holidays, vacations, etc. Daily work schedules are entered in daily schedule models, with

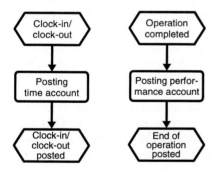

Fig. B.III.07: EPC for attendance and performance data entry

breaks being taken into account. "Running" a daily schedule model through the plant calendar results in a shift schedule, which formulates the standard times for employees. These times can be modified for each employee on an individual basis by taking into account employee-related factors such as vacations, etc. Shift models have already been used in the context of production control (see Figure B.I.221), and "clock-in" and "clock-out" functions have already been mentioned in connection with factory data entry (see Figure B.I.210).

A time account is set up for each period and employee, and the standard times are entered into it. The actual times are cross-posted by entering "clock-in" and "clock-out" events (see Figure B.III.08).

Time account

Actual				Planned		
Day				**Day**		
1	8,15 am	:	17,05 pm	1	8 am	: 17 pm
2	8 am	:	16,59 pm	2	8 am	: 17 pm
3				3	Time off	
4				4	8 am	: 17 pm
5				5	8 am	: 15 pm

Fig. B.III.08: Example of a time account

If the standard values for specific personnel groups are identical, they do not need to be entered into each employee-related time account. Instead, it is more practical to assign the shift schedules formed for each employee group as standard values.

The information can be entered via a separate time data entry system or within the framework of an integrated factory data entry system. In the case of a decentralized data entry system, master data (employee number and name, if necessary) can form the basis for plausibility checks and can be shifted from the central employee database to the decentralized system.

An additional performance account is maintained for hourly-rated employees, which are represented separately in the data structure in the form of an "is-a" relationship to the entity type EMPLOYEE. This account is continuously credited with performance data taken from time slips.

A "time slip" is issued for each operation an employee performs and contains the quantities produced, classified by quality category. This slip provides the data for calculating the wage value of the operation for value-oriented payroll accounting on the basis of the following formula:

Wage = Number of Pieces * Standard Time * Wage Rate per Time Unit

In the case of paper-based order control, time slips can be created as components of the order documentation. After the effective performance values are entered and checked by the supervisor, the data are entered (see Figure B.III.10).

In a DP-integrated solution, payroll data entry is combined with order-related data entry. This means that after an operation is completed, performance data are automatically posted for each employee involved (on the basis of the EMPLOYEE UTILIZATION information introduced in the context of production (see Figure B.I.170)).

In this case, the time slip is not an independent data medium; instead, it should be interpreted as a component of the order-related data. Time- and

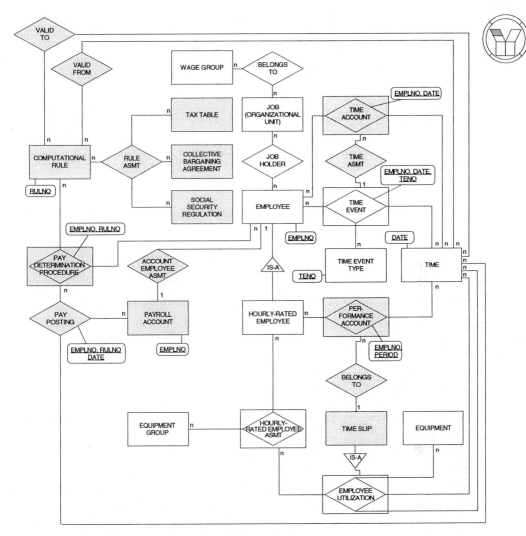

Fig. B.III.09: Data structure for personnel accounting

performance-related data entry is consequently not a component of a personnel system, which is merely responsible for analyzing the data (see *SAP, System RP 1990, pp. 64 ff.*; *SAP, System R/3, Die Personalwirtschaft 1992, pp. 4-9*). In the data structure, the close interaction between FDE and performance data entry is represented by an "is-a" relationship between EMPLOYEE UTILIZATION and TIME SLIP.

Since a time slip entitles an employee to pay, the employee can control the payment date depending on when he submits it. Thus, for example, an employee can hold back time slips to save for a large purchase or a vacation. If a time slip is used as feedback for order-related data, this effect must be taken into account. The savings effect must be prevented

Example of a time slip

Unit	Order number	Order ext.	Alt.	Assembly
2	126271	30000		2533
Unit	Order number	Order ext.	O. No.	Alt.	Tool number

		ID-Number	ZF
SIDE WALL	H .650	68 720 02B	
Description	Part key	T-E	St.-Item	AB

130/ 28/ 159	RST37-2		1	13
Measures	Material		Plant	Work-station

025   MILLING   343120

LENGTH PROD., WIDTH WITH 0.2 MM TOLERANCE
2 UNITS IN ONE PROCESS

Time (min)	8	Time (min)	12,0	Time (hrs)	0,54

PAY: 419278

Right panel:

Supervisor		Controller	
Finished date			
Name			Empl. no.

2	126271	30000	2533	6872002
Unit	Order	Ext.	Assembly	ID number/ITEM

025	8	12,0	0,54	
Op	Setup time	Turnar. time	Tot. st. time (hrs)	Z
Plan.workstation	Act. workstation		Pay type	

343120			
Plan. material	Act. material no.	Ch.	

Plan. quantity	Q	Act. quantity	Q	Kt
Pay month	Time taken (hrs)	Z	Unit corr.	TAS

Date of withdrawal

Thickness	Width	Length	Weight/unit

PAY: 419278

Fig. B.III.10: Time slip

from adversely affecting the currency of concurrent costing and the database for control activities. This difficulty can be avoided by entering the accounting period desired by the employee in such a way that it will be independent of the actual occurrence of the performance data.

The data for calculating gross pay are not only transferred to net pay calculation, but are also used to support cost accounting for determining direct labor costs on the basis of cost center and cost objective. If the cost objective is included on the time slip (or is accessible via the EMPLOYEE UTILIZATION relationship to the order- and requirements-related information), direct labor costs can be added directly to the cost objective.

If the cost center is entered on the time slip, direct labor costs can be apportioned directly among the cost centers within the framework of the object analysis sheet. In the case of an entry system that differentiates only on the basis of cost category, the usual procedures for cost allocation on the basis of reference units are used.

The values from the time and performance accounts, together with the additional employee-related data, are processed within the context of net pay calculation using computational rules (see Figure B.III.11).

B.III.2.2.2 Net Pay Calculation

Because of the legally mandated rules for computing net pay, this calculation is an application that is predestined for standard software.

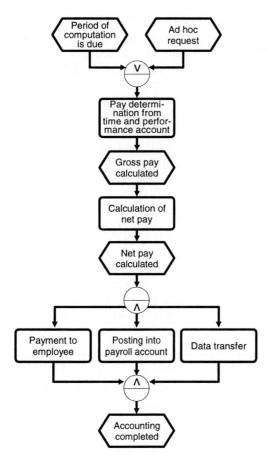

Fig. B.III.11: EPC for payroll accounting

Since laws change extremely often, these programs involve significant maintenance expense.

Net pay is typically calculated on a periodic basis (e.g., at the end of the month); however, both data maintenance and the gross pay calculation are typically performed on an ongoing basis. It can also be meaningful to keep the net pay calculation updated in order to be able to provide current information to employees at any time.

In the computation itself, computational rules are taken from tax tables, collective bargaining agreements, social security rules, etc., and entered in the entity type COMPUTATIONAL RULES. Each computational rule is assigned information from the tax tables, collective bargaining agreements and social security regulations. If only parameters of the tax tables change, it is unnecessary to adapt any computational rules. If, on the other hand, the linking operators or their parameters change, new rules must be entered in the system. Time-related validity information must be taken into account for both the tax information entered in the tables as well as for the computational rules involved. In the case of collective bargaining agreements, for example, tentative solutions can be reached that are later changed (with retroactive effects in some cases), so that different rules can overlap chronologically, which can also be balanced off against one another.

Figure B.III.09 illustrates this situation using VALID FROM and VALID TO chronological relationships.

The PAY DETERMINATION PROCEDURE for the individual employee assigns data to the rules that relate to the employee's social and personal situation (number of children, marital status, etc.) as well as to personal obligations, such as wage garnishments, regular savings deposits, etc. Bonuses, overtime pay, incentive data, etc., are entered via the link to the employee data. All data concerning the time and performance accounts can be reached via the PAY DETERMINATION PROCEDURE relationship to EMPLOYEE.

The net pay calculated on the basis of the pay determination procedure is posted to the employee's payroll account in a posting record. The entity type PAY DETERMINATION PROCEDURE documents the payroll accounting, which each employee receives in paper form for his or her

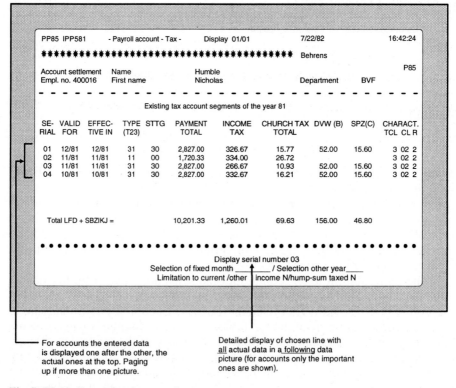

Fig. B.III.12: Example of a payroll account

records or which is available through interactive access to his or her payroll account (with the appropriate data privacy precautions).

An example of a payroll account with pay postings is shown in Figure B.III.12, which is taken from the IPAS system (see *ADV-ORGA, IPAS 1984*).

The link between performance data and order data from Production creates the information for the cost objectives (production orders, customer orders), as well as for additional data necessary for calculating incentive pay. Thus, the number of employees involved in an incentive pay group can be taken from the number of employee utilizations recorded in the detailed scheduling data.

B.III.2.2.3 Data Interchange

In most modern economies, pay and payroll accounting are strictly regulated by federal and state laws and regulations. In Germany, for instance, there are more than a hundred laws and regulations that require employers to document personnel-related data and provide them to external agencies (see *Mülder, Organisatorische Implementierung von Personalinformationssystemen 1984, p. 64*). Under these laws and regulations, data have to be reported to the social security insurance providers by transferring them on data media (tape, diskette) to the local general health insurance fund office, which serves as a central clearinghouse and which subsequently distributes them to the Federal Bureau of Statistics, the individual health insurance funds, old-age pension and unemployment insurance carriers. In Germany, all personnel accounting systems provide these types of data links.

Payments to employees, too, are increasingly being made using electronic funds transfer.

The information necessary for data interchange is either entered in the entity type EMPLOYEE as attributes or it results from the payroll calculation. Consequently, the temporary data structures necessary for the transfer operation are not shown in Figure B.III.09.

B.III.2.3 Human Resource Planning

In addition to administrative and accounting-related functions, human resource management also deals with planning-related functions such as human resource recruitment, control and development. In addition to the use of planning models for structured functions, support must also be provided for ad hoc decisions and unstructured problems. This is the purpose of a personnel information system. It consists of databases, model bases and method bases. There are several common abbreviations for "personnel information system," such as PESIS, PDI (personnel data information system), PDATIS (personnel data information system) or PERSIS.

Vatteroth,   Standard-Software   für   die   computergestützte Personalplanung 1993 provides an overview of standard software systems that support human resource planning.

The most important functions of human resource planning are:
- Human resource requirements planning
- Human resource recruitment
- Human resource placement
- Human resource development.

The process of human resource requirements planning determines how many employees with which qualifications will be needed for which jobs during the upcoming planning periods. This process results in the job assignment plan.

Human resource recruitment determines how suitable applicants should be addressed and manages the applications received.

Human resource placement planning tries to fill each job in such a manner as to provide the characteristics needed for the respective activity (requirements profile). At the same time, an effort is made to match each employee's characteristics (skill profile) to the job requirements without any significant over- or under-qualification.

Human resource development planning provides employees with skills and knowledge they may lack through appropriate training and prepares suitable employees for positions of greater responsibility.

The data structure shown in Figure B.III.13 illustrates these functions; its development will be elaborated in the following discussion.

B.III.2.3.1 Human Resource Requirements Planning

The types of activities required in an enterprise are entered in the entity type ACTIVITY. Each instance describes a complex function that frequently corresponds to a particular professional or vocational profile, e.g., secretary, typist, mechanic, clerk, design engineer, etc.

Each organizational job is assigned to such an activity, whereby the same activity is typically performed by several job positions.

The use of the term "activity" for the defined content of the complex function assigned to an employee is ambiguous. In the RP and HR systems from SAP, for example, it is termed "job," which this book has already associated with the workstation defined in the organizational chart. (The SAP system therefore uses the term "position" in this regard, see *SAP, System RP 1990, pp. 114 ff.*)

The enterprise's organizational units submit personnel requirements messages to decentralized or centralized human resource departments at

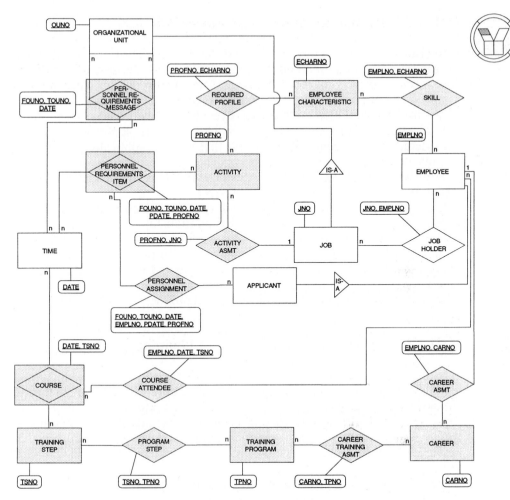

Fig. B.III.13: ERM for human resource planning

specific times. A personnel requirements message can include needs that encompass requirements for different activities.

Taking into account the known new staff for each activity and the anticipated staff that will be leaving results in the net requirement per activity type. Since the requirement is also specified on the basis of hiring periods, the PERSONNEL REQUIREMENTS ITEM is a relationship type between PERSONNEL REQUIREMENTS MESSAGE, ACTIVITY and TIME.

Both statistical procedures and requirements messages from line departments can be used to determine the gross requirement.

B.III.2.3.2 Human Resource Recruitment Planning

Recruiting activities are performed on the basis of the determined human resource requirements and can encompass the use of classified advertisements, employment agencies, etc. Incoming applications are assigned to the corresponding requirements. At the same time, the applicants are included in the employee file (linked as a subset via a specialization relationship). It is possible that one applicant might be considered for different activities and that several applications might be submitted for the same requirement. This practice results in the n:m relationship type PERSONNEL ASSIGNMENT between PERSONNEL REQUIREMENTS ITEM and APPLICANT.

If an applicant is assigned to a job during the selection process, this is expressed by the existing JOB HOLDER relationship.

During the selection process, the applicant takes tests, fills out application forms and submits documents, which provide information on his or her knowledge and skills. The requirements for the activity are then compared to the skills of the applicant. This process is also of fundamental importance for human resource placement planning.

B.III.2.3.3 Human Resource Placement Planning

In order to have access to decision-making criteria when selecting a suitable applicant for an activity or in connection with general planning for assigning employees to workstations, the activities and the employees must be described in greater detail. Catalogs of characteristics developed in the context of human resource management can be meaningful in this regard, e.g., the "Geneva model" (see *Kupsch/Marr, Personalwirtschaft 1991, pp. 820 f.*).

Typical characteristics for white-collar employees include:
- Specialized knowledge or physical dexterity
- Sense of responsibility for
  -- job performance, safety and the health of others
  -- workflow
- Physical strength
- Concentration
- Attentiveness
- Manners and verbal skills
- Personal time management skills
- Leadership ability
- Response to environmental influences

Skills and knowledge can also be entered as characteristics, such as:
- Education and professional training
- Job experience
- Continuing education

As well as such psychological characteristics as:
- Learning ability
- Practicality
- Memory
- Responsiveness
- Aptitude for individual work, etc.

A comprehensive catalog of characteristics has been developed by the Forschungsinstitut für Rationalisierung at the RWTH in Aachen, Germany (see *FIR, Vergleich von Arbeitsplatzanforderungen und Personalfähigkeitsdaten 1975*).

The different characteristics are combined in the entity type EMPLOYYEE CHARACTERISTIC, and a characteristic that is necessary for a specific activity is defined in the relationship type REQUIREMENT (as an n:m relationship between EMPLOYEE CHARACTERISTIC and ACTIVITY). These requirements thus constitute workstation descriptions for the workstations (jobs) associated with an activity.

Employee instances for a specific characteristic are entered in the relationship type SKILL.

As shown in Figure B.III.14, profile comparisons can be created for personnel decisions (see *Zülch, Profilmethode bei der Personaleinsatzplanung 1976, p. 227*).

For other forms of representation, see *Kupsch/Marr, Personalwirtschaft 1991, pp. 798 f.*

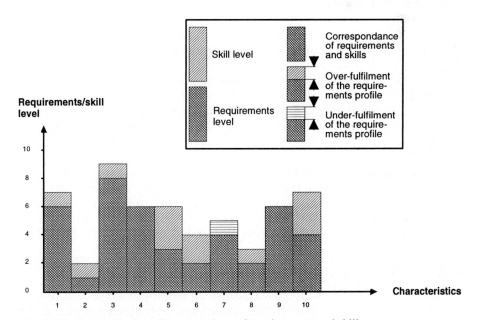

Fig. B.III.14: Graphical profile comparison of requirements and skills

The requirements for the workstation (job) and the skills of the employee are compared with one another for identical characteristics and for those that are reasonably easy to evaluate. Since it is virtually impossible for an applicant to meet all the requirements, ranges must be defined to mark upper and lower tolerance levels.

Business administration theory has discussed the problem of human resource assignment in great detail and has developed many mathematical models that require the assignment of requirements- and skills-related values to express the suitability of employees for certain workstations (see *Domsch, Simultane Personal- und Investitionsplanung im Produktionsbereich 1970, Adam, Produktionsplanung 1993, pp. 511 ff.*).

In addition to human resource assignment, short-term scheduling is also a function of human resource placement. As it relates to the control of hourly-rated employees, this problem has already been discussed in connection with production control. Categorized according to type and quantity, manpower capacity is a subtype of the entity type RESOURCE, which is relevant for availability checks and scheduling.

Human resource schedules can be represented graphically in the form of scheduling tables (Gantt charts). This is the reason why human resource control for hourly-rated employees has already been included in the production leitstand concept. But the leitstand concept can also provide support for workstation assignments and scheduling in non-production contexts. This aspect will be discussed in detail with respect to the product development process chain, in particular in connection with computer-aided design. The concept of a general personnel leitstand will be discussed in conjunction with the summary of requirements definitions for human resource logistics.

B.III.2.3.4 Human Resource Development Planning

In terms of career planning, human resource development planning encompasses promotion activities and thus the specification of promotion criteria, in addition to training and continuing education. Potential careers (e.g., the career ladder of marketing assistant, product manager, product group manager, marketing manager) are entered in the entity type CAREER.

A career is assigned specific training programs that a candidate must complete. The individual training programs, in turn, contain individual training steps, e.g., courses, internships, job rotations, etc. The assignments between the entity types CAREER and TRAINING PROGRAM and between TRAINING PROGRAM and TRAINING STEP are each type n:m.

A COURSE is an n:m relationship between TIME and the TRAINING STEP in question. The assigned participants are entered via the relationship COURSE ATTENDEE. Since an employee can attend several courses during the same time frame, and several employees can attend one course, an n:m relationship exists.

The assignment of employees to specific careers is continually updated by conducting evaluations. The relationship CAREER ASSIGNMENT provides support for the personnel department in selecting suitable training candidates. In general, an individual employee is assigned only one career, but an individual career can be assigned several employees.

B.III.2.4 Summarizing and Supplementing the Requirements Definitions for Human Resource Logistics

B.III.2.4.1 Requirements Definition for Human Resource Logistics: The Function View

The processing modes for human resource logistics will be analyzed as a supplement to the functional description.

Primarily because of the need to maintain currency and plausibility, basic data management functions are viewed as being suitable for interactive treatment (see Figure B.III.15).

Time- and performance-related data entry also lends itself to interactive processing as a result of plausibility control, whereby both independent data entry systems and general factory data entry systems can provide integrated solutions. Both pay calculation and data interchange are typically period-oriented automated functions for mass data processing, performed in batch mode. However, an interactive solution can also be meaningful for information purposes in the case of updated payroll accounts.

Function	Subfunction	Reasons for interactive processing				Automatic/ batch
		Currency	Plausibility	Iterative modification	Interactive decision process	
Basic data management	Hiring/Dismissal	X	X			
	Reassignments	X				
	Schedule control	X				
Personnel accounting	Time data entry	X	X			
	Performance data entry		X			
	Gross pay	(X)	(X)			X
	Net pay	(X)				X
	Data interchange					X
Personnel planning	Requirements					X
	Recruitment	X				
	Placement - Profile comparison - Assignment				X X	(X)
	Development - Course planning - Career planning		X	X		

Fig. B.III.15: Types of processing of subfunctions within human resource management

Profile comparisons and the solution of personnel assignment problems can constitute interactive decision processes in connection with human resource planning functions. In the case of complex computation-intensive assignment problems, however, batch solutions can also be employed. Within the framework of human resource development, interactive solutions can be used for administering training courses and for planning promotions.

B.III.2.4.2 Requirements Definition for Human Resource Logistics: The Organization View

As in the case of the other logistics processes, it is possible to consider similar decentralization solutions for human resource logistics.

If the functions are bundled on the basis of processes and simultaneously incorporated with coordination and planning functions, a three-tier organizational model results, as shown in the form of a leitstand concept in Figure B.III.16.

A combined leitstand is provided for planning and accounting functions, so that simulation calculations can be performed together with accounting functions. In parallel to this, an accounting leitstand is formed for routine operative personnel accounting. Several leitstands can be set up in the case of an object-oriented separation of processing on the basis of employee groups.

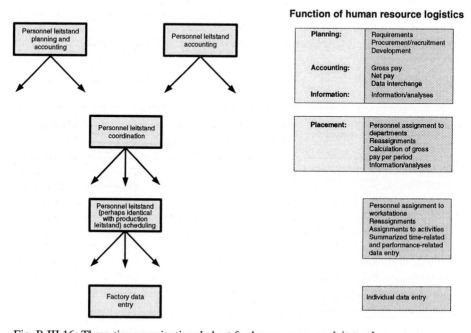

Fig. B.III.16: Three-tier organizational chart for human resource leitstand

Workstation-oriented assignments are provided on the lowest level for human resource placement planning. In Production, these can be processed together with the other resource control functions in a production leitstand or, in the case of Product Development, in an engineering leitstand.

A coordination leitstand is set up for bundling planning leitstands in the case of interdepartmental operations such as relocations or management evaluations. Time- and performance-related data entry is performed by FDE systems and summarized in the planning leitstand.

Gross pay calculation can be performed on the coordination level (if need be, in temporary form) or on the level of the special accounting leitstand.

B.III.2.4.3 Requirements Definition for Human Resource Logistics: The Data View

The three data structures that have been developed will not be tabulated (see Figures B.III.05, B.III.10 and B.III.13).

B.III.2.4.4 Requirements Definition for Human Resource Logistics: The Control View

Several links between the analysis views have already been discussed, e.g., the assignment of functions to the organizational model for human resource logistics within the framework of the leitstand concept or event control for basic data management or personnel accounting.

Ensuring data privacy is particularly important in connection with human resource logistics, i.e., the link between the organizational and the data model via access authorization. These links can be defined in the form of authorization tables.

Highly detailed authorization distinctions can be necessary here. They can be geared toward attribute types (e.g., a supervisor is authorized to access data concerning his subordinates' vacation schedules, but not the results of their evaluations), toward entity groups (e.g., a department manager is only authorized to access data concerning employees within his or her department) or toward combinations of attributes and entities. The attribute instance can also control access authorization (e.g., a system user is only authorized to access data concerning employees under the age of 30). Care should be taken to ensure that it is impossible for someone to cleverly combine valid access authorizations in order to obtain unauthorized information, e.g., to identify an individual through a selection involving combinations of general characteristics, even though access to identifying characteristics is not allowed.

B.III.3 Design Specifications for Human Resource Logistics

In contrast to the other operational applications, the high rate of change in accounting procedures and different access authorizations have been particularly emphasized.

In order to increase processing flexibility, the RP and HR systems from SAP, therefore, define accounting procedures in decision tables that are outside the programming code, so that changes can be performed without the need for making changes to the processing program. These are then called by a payroll accounting driver that contains general process control functions and general payroll accounting modules and are interpreted for the concrete payroll accounting process (see *SAP, System RP 1990, pp. 73 ff.*).

Triggers can be defined on the design specification level for formulating access authorizations. These triggers contain access conditions and attach themselves to a (query) transaction when it is called. This makes it possible to check the authorization of the user placing the query to access the query object (see *Reuter, Maßnahmen zur Wahrung von Sicherheits- und Integritätsbedingungen 1987*).

B.III.4 Implementation Description for Human Resource Logistics

Problems of implementation will not be discussed in any further detail.

B.IV Overall Concepts for Logistics

The following discussion will introduce several approaches that take into account all logistics components: Production, inbound, outbound and human resource logistics.

These approaches include integrated planning of medium-term sales, production and purchasing plans, the MRP II concept and the job control center with networked segmentation.

Various standard software systems are already beginning to feature approaches that cover the integrated logistics chain.

B.IV.1 Integrated Planning of Sales, Production and Purchasing Programs (Primary Requirements Planning)

The primary requirement serves as the point of departure for production logistics, and all logistics aspects must be taken into account in determining it.

Only primary requirement **management** was discussed in the context of requirements planning. The objective of **specifying** the primary requirement, however, involves determining the most cost-effective sales, purchasing and production programs in light of capacity, material, personnel and financial limitations. Rough planning functions will be suggested within the sequential planning approaches as a solution to this problem, which the functions seek to achieve by employing simulations of different production programs. Business administration theory has developed numerous model-based approaches that are based in particular on linear optimization (see *Kilger, Optimale Produktions- und Absatzplanung 1973; Jacob, Produktionsplanung 1986*).

Although these model-based approaches have met with resistance in actual practice, the following discussion will show how these types of optimization methods can be combined with concepts for DP-supported production planning and control systems.

Primary requirements planning occurs on a rougher level than the logistics planning functions. This is due to the longer planning time frame involved. Moreover, only critical variables and resources are of interest, not the overall problem.

The following section will first outline the data structure that must be provided for a consolidated planning process, followed by a treatment of the link between rough and detailed planning within the context of sequential planning systems. Finally, these aspects will be used as a basis for developing a concept for linking sequential planning with simulations and optimization calculations.

B.IV.1.1 Data Consolidation

Since rough planning is a consolidated planning approach, the data structure is extended to include consolidated planning units (see Figure B.IV.01).

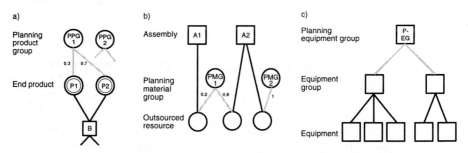

Fig. B.IV.01,a: Extended bill of materials to include planning product groups
Fig. B.IV.01,b: Extended bill of materials structure to include planning material groups
Fig. B.IV.01,c: Consolidation of equipment groups

A planning product group unit encompasses a bundle of end products. A product group unit represents a conglomeration of different articles, but the group itself does not necessarily have to be a product *per se*. The "production coefficients" indicate the (anticipated) percentage of the product in the product group. For example, the planning product group "passenger car" consists of 30% type A and 70% type B.

Significant bottleneck resources that must be taken into account during rough planning include machine and manpower capacities, the materials to be used and financial resources. Manpower capacities will not be treated separately, but will be taken into account in connection with equipment capacities; however, it would also be a simple matter to plan them on an independent basis, analogously to equipment capacities. Consolidated units are also selected in terms of capacities and outsourced resources. Thus, equipment groups are combined into rougher planning equipment groups and outsourced resources into planning material groups. The planning material groups are also defined by an extended bill of materials structure.

Both planning product groups and planning material groups are specializations of the entity type PART.

For the sake of clarity, the new relationships introduced for rough planning are represented by broken lines.

The consolidated planning units are thus introduced into the new data structure without modification; however, providing the data groups—i.e., the capacity requirement and the materials requirement—that relate to these consolidated variables is another matter entirely. These data groups could be algorithmically calculated from the detailed data structures on the planning date, making a separate data structure unnecessary, but this approach is extremely computation-intensive. An ad hoc simulation, however, would require that the necessary data be available. For this reason, a separate data structure is developed for the consolidated data.

Figure B.IV.02 shows the consolidated planning product, planning material and planning equipment groups as specializations.

New key names are introduced for the sake of clarity.

The further data structure will be developed using the example shown in Figure B.IV.03.

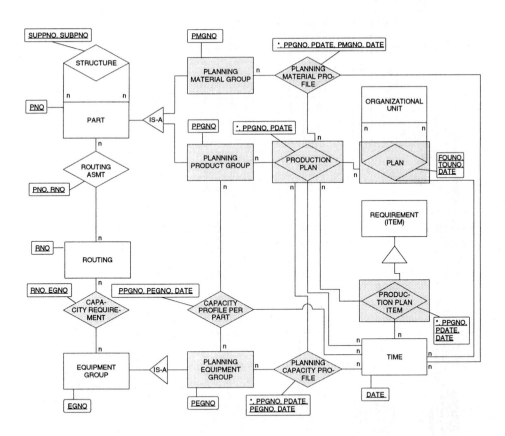

Fig. B.IV.02: Consolidated data structure for planning

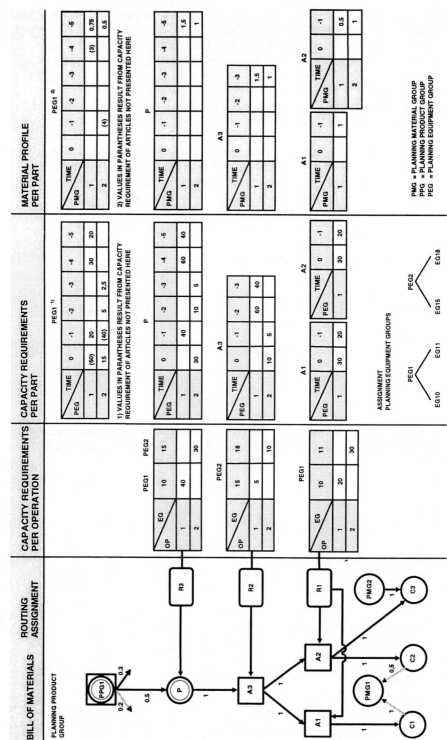

Fig. B.IV.03: Example of the sales and production program

The example shows only **one** planning product group, PPG1. Moreover, only **one** end product (article) P is tracked across two assembly levels. The materials are combined into two planning material groups, PMG1 and PMG2.

The routings (R), operations (OP) and equipment groups (EG) previously discussed in the context of production logistics serve as the point of departure for capacity data. The data structure shown in the example has been slightly simplified.

A capacity requirement matrix is generated for each routing from the basic data. Because of the n:m relationship between ROUTING and PART, a routing can be valid for several in-house parts (R1 for assemblies A1 and A2).

The CAPACITY REQUIREMENT (see Figure B.IV.02) is a relationship between ROUTING and EQUIPMENT GROUP, since several capacity requirements can exist for a routing (at different equipment groups as a result of multiple operations within the routing), and several requirements resulting from different routings can exist for each equipment group. An element of the capacity matrix shown in Figure B.IV.03 thus corresponds to an instance of CAPACITY REQUIREMENT in Figure B.IV.02. For the sake of simplicity, an n:1 relationship is assumed between equipment groups and operations, so that the equipment group can identify a capacity requirement within a routing. The operation number OPNO is thus a descriptive attribute along with the capacity requirement coefficient. If different equipment group assignments are technically conceivable for each operation (alternative operations), the first priority is to specify an unambiguous assignment that is meaningful in terms of planning.

In addition to the capacity requirement, other variables such as lead times and transfer times can be entered for each operation (equipment group). These capacity data are transferred from the basic data for all active routings.

Thus, the capacity requirements for all in-house parts are entered via the ROUTING ASSIGNMENT.

The next stage involves generating capacity profiles for each part and relating the capacities to the consolidated planning equipment groups.

A capacity profile for each part contains the capacity requirements (expressed in hours) for a part unit in relation to the chronological production flow across all semi-finished products and production levels. The capacity profile for each part is a relationship between TIME, the PLANNING PRODUCT GROUP to which the capacity analysis relates, and the PLANNING EQUIPMENT GROUP. The entity type PLANNING PRODUCT GROUP is treated as a specialization of PART and contains the planning product groups. The general key attribute for all part groups is the part number PNO; for the sake of clarity, the keys PPGNO and PMGNO are used to distinguish the subsets.

The example assumes that each operation will be completed within a time period. On the other hand, it is assumed that only one operation in a routing can be performed within a time period. Transfer times are included within a time period. Thus, the turnaround time for a part corresponds to the number of operations it requires.

The period 0 is used as a chronological point of reference for completion of production.

Since the capacity profiles relate to parts, separate data structures exist for A1 and A2. When generating the capacity profile for A3, the capacity requirements for subordinate assemblies A1 and A2 are transferred, taking into account the chronological relationship to the beginning of routing 2, as well as the capacity requirement for assembly A3 itself. Since equipment groups 15 and 18, which are combined into planning equipment group 2, are addressed in routing 2—although only planning equipment group 1 was addressed in the case of subordinate assemblies— only two planning equipment groups affect the capacity profile for A3.

Analogously, the capacity requirement is transferred to product P.

A weighting factor is determined to reflect the percentage of the planned product group unit represented by product P. When the profiles are transferred to the planning product group, the capacity loads are multiplied by the weighting factor. A factor of 0.5 means that product P constitutes only 50% of the planning product group, and the other 50% is made up of additional products (weighted at 0.2 and 0.3). These capacity profiles are calculated analogously, multiplied by their percentage values and added to the profile for the planning product group. In the example, the capacity requirements resulting from other end products are contained in parentheses.

Thus, the capacity profile for a planning product group unit indicates the number of capacity units that occur for each planning equipment group in the time period relating to completion time 0.

These data only have to be generated once, after which they are available for planning calculations.

If the basic data (e.g., bills of materials or routings) change, all superordinate cumulative capacity profiles must be changed as well, while the subordinate data situations based on the bill of materials structures remain unchanged.

The process for generating material profiles is similar to that for capacity profiles. The data structure for MATERIAL PROFILE is a relationship between TIME, the assigned PLANNING PRODUCT GROUP and PLANNING MATERIAL GROUP, and it is identified by the key PMGNO, PPGNO, DATE.

The initial data for the material profile can be taken directly from the bill of materials structure.

The example assumes that each material is used in the first operation. This means that the material requirement occurs in period -1 for assemblies A1 and A2.

The materials are consolidated into planning material groups with proportionate coefficients, which can represent percentage values, being taken into account.

Under this procedure, a coefficient within the matrix indicates how many units of the planning material group are required to manufacture a part during a specific period.

Since the example shows the direct use of material only in the case of assemblies A1 and A2, these quantities are transferred to the superordinate assemblies during the remainder of the process by taking into account the chronological flow and the quantity relationships characterized by the bill of materials structure. In transferring material requirements to the planning product group, their weighting factors are taken into account. In this example, material requirements resulting from other end products are again shown in parentheses.

Profiles for additional resources can be generated in a similar manner (e.g., financial resources, human resource qualifications, etc.).

B.IV.1.2 Linking Rough and Detailed Planning in Sequential Planning Systems

The data structure developed in Figure B.IV.02 is available for planning purposes. For example, by multiplying the resource profiles that relate to the planning product group by the planned production quantities, it is possible to immediately generate resource overviews.

Several planning processes that are either created over the course of time or that represent various simulation alternatives exist for each planning product group. The data structure shown in Figure B.IV.02 is extended in order to include these data.

The individual planning processes form the PLANNING PROCESS relationship between the planning organizational unit, the affected organizational unit and TIME. Under this definition, the term "planning" is located on the level of header information for orders or requirements. Specific logistics processes or plant names can be indicated as concrete organizational units. PRODUCTION PLAN relates to a planning product group within a planning process. The individual planning quantities for each planning product group are entered in the relationship type PRODUCTION PLAN ITEM by indicating the planning quantity for a specific production plan, a specific planning product group (PPGNO) and period (date). PRODUCTION PLAN ITEM is a relationship type between PRODUCTION PLAN and the entity type TIME. PRODUCTION PLAN ITEM, together with the primary requirement released for execution, is a specialization of the entity type REQUIREMENT (ITEM), which is also indicated by the "is-a" relationship. Via the link to the entity type REQUIREMENT (ITEM), it is possible to use the requirement links created in the requirements explosion in order to retain the origin of requirements from specific planning processes.

Figure B.IV.04 shows a production plan with two items, which contain a planning requirement of 10 and 5 quantity units in periods 7 and 6, respectively.

The planning capacity profile results from multiplying the requirements quantities by the capacity profiles for the product group and then totaling the mathematical products. The interrelationship with the relationship type CAPACITY PROFILE PER PART (planning product group) is used. The PLANNING CAPACITY PROFILE is a relationship between PRODUCTION PLAN, PLANNING EQUIPMENT GROUP and TIME. In the example, it should be noted that the requirements are assigned to the completion periods, which means that the capacity requirements must be calculated retrogradely from that point.

The PLANNING MATERIAL PROFILE relationship type results analogously and is a relationship between PLANNING MATERIAL GROUP, PRODUCTION PLAN and TIME.

Thus, starting from one date, it is possible to identify the different planning approaches together with their effects on capacity and materials requirements. Moreover, requirement profiles can be created for each

PRODUCTION PLAN FOR PPG 1   } **PRODUCTION PLAN**

REQUIREMENT TIME 7   10 UNITS } **PRODUCTION PLAN ITEM**
REQUIREMENT TIME 6   5 UNITS

PLANNING CAPACITY PROFILE PER
PLANNING PRODUCT GROUP PPG 1

PERIOD	1	2	3	4	5	6	7
PEGNO = 1	100	350	300	0	100	500	600
PEGNO = 2			12.5	50	250	475	150

PLANNING MATERIAL PROFILE PER
PLANNING PRODUCT GROUP PPG 1

PERIOD	1	2	3	4	5	6	7
PMGNO = 1	3.75	22.5	30	0	0	0	0
PMGNO = 2	2.5	5	0	0	20	40	0

Fig. B.IV.04: Example of a production plan

planning material group by adding up totals across different planning product groups.

In addition to analytically determining the capacity profile for each product group from the capacity requirements of the routings throughout the entire bill of materials structure, global estimates can also be employed. For example, this would be the case for one-off manufacturers if the anticipated loads are estimated globally for an anticipated customer order in the rough planning phase.

The result of rough planning is a production plan that has been tailored to the affected resources and is subsequently incorporated into the production planning and control system in the form of a primary requirement. The requirements for the subordinate assemblies and materials are derived from this plan.

Both the requirement status and the order status are continuously updated by feedback from the factory data entry system. These updates can also be transferred into the planning capacity and planning material profiles. Each (quantity-related) feedback from a completed production order is converted into a capacity feedback via the assigned capacity requirement matrix of the routing and deducted from the planning capacity profile for the corresponding planning equipment group and the corresponding periods.

If the values from the production plan are based on customer orders (firm or anticipated), a feedback can also be assigned to a customer-order-oriented requirement for the production plan by using multi-level requirements tracking. This informational relationship is important if the planning capacity profile for each product group is based on estimated values that, for example, were formulated for an anticipated customer order. In this case, it must be ensured that the entire planned resources from rough planning are also deducted from rough planning upon completion of a concrete order. If, for example, a capacity requirement of 300 units of a specific type of capacity was initially estimated for an order, but 200 units were actually sufficient, the 300 quantity units created in rough planning must be deducted despite the feedback of only 200 units.

For this reason, special status "quasi" customer orders can be defined for assumed forecast values in order to ensure uniformity between rough planning and concrete detailed planning via the customer-order-oriented requirements explosion.

The capacity overviews developed in the example are shown in tabular form. However, the use of graphics can also be meaningful in this regard, as has already been demonstrated within the framework of time management for capacity profiles. At the same time, the different types of origins (capacity requirement from firmly accepted orders, anticipated orders as well as anonymously estimated requirements) can be represented by different colors in the display.

B.IV.1.3 Linking Simultaneous Rough Planning Models with Sequential Planning Systems

During primary requirements planning, complicated validity conditions must be taken into account for capacity, manpower and material, as well as cost and income effects.

In the case of capacity- and/or cost-related product integration, the optimal production program can be determined only by using a simultaneous approach.

Business administration theory has developed model-based approaches on the basis of linear optimization. This discussion will illustrate how these approaches can be incorporated into the sequential planning system that has been developed here and in which form they can be linked with the database that has been developed.

Within the context of capacity planning, production order operations are assigned to capacities. In order to precisely enter the interdependencies between sales and production planning, the production variable would have to be defined on the basis of operations within an optimization model as follows:

x_{tzysi}, where:

t = time
z = in-house production part
y = routing
s = operation
i = machine type.

The model suggested here is represented in greater detail in *Scheer, Produktionsplanung 1976, pp. 29 ff.*

x_{tzysi} indicates how many quantity units of part z are manufactured in period t using routing y involving operation s at machine type i.

This formulation allows the model to be used to determine the routing for each part and the machine assignment for each operation.

The variable $r_{tz'}$ is defined for the purchasing department, where z' denotes outsourced parts. It indicates how many quantity units of outsourced part z' have to be ordered in period t.

The variable v_{tz^+} is defined for the sales department, where z^+ represents end products. It indicates how many quantity units of end product z^+ are to be sold in period t.

The following aspects are defined as secondary condition types:

Minimum sales conditions for existing firmly accepted customer orders and **maximum sales conditions** for the sales ceilings determined on the basis of forecasts. Respectively, they indicate the minimum number of quantity units of an end product that has to be sold during a period and the maximum number that can be sold.

Capacity conditions ensure that the number of hours scheduled does not exceed the production hours that are available for each machine group.

Inventory and operation continuity conditions ensure that the production flow is maintained between periods (by taking turnaround times into account) and between production levels. To this end, inventory level variables must be introduced for each part, operation and period.

The data necessary for this type of detailed model—such as prices, costs, initial inventory and production coefficients—have been defined in the data structures introduced previously and can thus be taken directly from a database.

At the same time, a special program (matrix generator) can be used to generate the model structure for the pending planning problem directly from the database by defining only specific parameters such as period division, capacity and sales limits. Production variables are created only for parts/operations for which a requirement exists, i.e., that go into end products for which sales conditions have been stipulated.

The PART ROUTING ASSIGNMENT shows which alternative routings must be defined for a part, and the EQUIPMENT GROUP ASSIGNMENT shows which alternative machine assignments must be defined for an operation.

An approximate calculation of the model variables for real-world problem scenarios reveals, however, that the approximation far exceeds the order of magnitude that has thus far been able to be calculated. For approximately 40,000 active parts records, which include 100 end products, 10,000 in-house parts and 30,000 outsourced parts, 2 routings for each production part and 5 operations for each routing, which can each be executed on two equipment groups, the result per subperiod is approximately 200,000 production variables and approximately 150,000 purchasing, inventory and sales variables as well as 120,000 secondary conditions. Given 26 subperiods for each planning time period, these values increase accordingly on a multiplicative scale.

For this reason, in real-world production planning models the production variables are not chosen on the basis of the operations to be performed, but rather on the basis of the higher-level assemblies, products or even product groups to be manufactured, so that the principle of rough planning is adopted.

Only in industries with a very low number of end products and few production levels are the production variables of LP planning models related to operations. The petroleum industry belongs in this category, for example.

The consolidated production variable is thus x_{tG}, where t is the time index and G is the index for assembly, end product or product group.

In contrast to the variables x_{tzysi}, the consolidation in this case is already evident.

This radically reduces the number of variables.

Since quantity-related continuity conditions between the operations, which constitute the bulk of the secondary conditions, are eliminated, the number of secondary conditions associated with the model is sharply reduced.

Frequently, secondary capacity conditions are not related to equipment groups (where **cost- and function-equivalent** equipment is combined), but rather to shops in which equipment with only **fundamentally** similar functions is combined. While NC drilling machines and standard drilling machines belong to different machine groups, they are included in the same planning equipment group for drilling machines. This reduces the number of secondary capacity conditions.

Two problems result from model consolidation: First, the results of the models change. Second, the data also have to reflect the higher degree of consolidation.

Before these problems are discussed in greater detail, Figure B.IV.05 will introduce a consolidated sales and production planning model (see *Scheer, Produktionsplanung 1976, pp. 56 ff.*). The approach of the model will be self-explanatory for the experienced reader. The inexperienced reader can follow the explanations without detailed knowledge of the model.

Simultaneous model for sales and production planning

Where:

t	Time
G	Part group $G \in S = S^+ \cup \overline{S}$
G^+	End product group $G^+ \in S^+$
$\overline{G}$	Assembly $\overline{G} \in \overline{S}$
I	Machine group or shop

Variables:

x_{tG}	**Production variable:**	Units of part group G that are completed in period t
L_{tG}	**Inventory variable:**	Inventory level for part group G at the end of period t
v_{tG}	**Sales variable:**	Units of part group G sold in period t

Data:

L^+_{0G}	Initial inventory for part group G
I_G	Storage cost rate for part group G
k_G	Variable unit costs for part group G
P_{tG^+}	Selling price for part group G^+
$A^+_{tG^+}$	Lower sales limit for part group G^+ in period t

A_{tG^+} Upper sales limit for part group G^+ in period t

$f_{G,t-t',l}$ Capacity requirement of capacity type I for a unit of part group G that is completed in period t taking into account turnaround times in period t'. The coefficients $f_{G,t-t',l}$ are a function of only the difference t-t', not of the values themselves, whereby the difference indicates the number of lead times (a part group that is supposed to be completed in t can be assigned to several periods t' ≤ t capacity in shop I).

T_{tl} Available capacity of capacity type I in period t

T_{0l} $= \sum_z L^+_{0z} \cdot f_{zl}$; type I capacity "tied up" in initial inventory amounts; where f_{zl} is the total capacity requirement for capacity type I for part z.

L^+_{0z} Initial inventory for part z

$b_{\overline{G}G'',t'-t}$ Quantity of assembly $\overline{G}$ necessary in t for a unit of the superordinate part group G" with completion date t' (where t' ≥ t). To calculate $b_{\overline{G}G'',t'-t}$, only the difference t'-t is important. This formulation makes it possible to take into account the fact that assembly $\overline{G}$ can go into a specific part group G" in different subperiods due to the turnaround times (lead times).

Support variables for model formulation α $= \begin{cases} 1, \text{ if } t = 1 \\ 0, \text{ otherwise} \end{cases}$

Global variables:

$P_{t'l} = \sum_G \sum_{t=t'}^{T} f_{G,t-t',l} \cdot x_{tG}$

$1 \le t' \le T$

Capacity requirement for capacity type I in period t'. This results from the capacity requirements for all product groups completed from t' to the end of the planning period with the throughput times being taken into account in the calculation.

$P_{0l} = \sum_G \sum_{t'=-\infty}^{t'=0} \sum_{t=1}^{T} f_{G,t-t',l} \cdot x_{tG}$

Capacity requirement that exists on the basis of the through-put times for period 1 (and thus prior to the beginning of the planning period).

$EB_T = \sum_G L_{TG} \cdot k_G$

Inventory at the end of the planning time period.

THE MODEL

Target functions:

$$\sum_{t'=1}^{t} \left[\sum_{G^+}(P_{tG^+} \cdot v_{tG^+}) - \sum_G (k_G \cdot x_{tG} + l_G \cdot L_{tG}) \right] + EB_T \rightarrow \max.$$

Secondary conditions:

Sales conditions

- *Upper sales limit*

  $v_{tG^+} \le A_{tG^+}$ for all t and G^+

- *Lower sales limit*

  $v_{tG^+} \ge A^+_{tG^+}$ for all t and G^+

Secondary capacity conditions

$$\sum_{t'=0}^{t} P_{t'l} \leq \sum_{t'=0}^{t} T_{t'l} \qquad \text{for all l and } t=0, 1, 2, ..., T$$

Inventory continuity conditions

-     *End product groups*

$$L_{tG^+} - (1 - \alpha) \cdot L_{t-lG^+} - x_{tG^+} + v_{tG^+} = \alpha \cdot L^+_{OG^+} \quad \text{for all t and } G^+$$

-     *Assemblies*

$$L_{t\bar{G}} - (1 - \alpha) \cdot L_{t-1, \bar{G}} - x_{t\bar{G}} + \sum_{G''} \sum_{t'=t} b_{\bar{G}G''}^{t'-t} \cdot x_{t'G''} = \alpha \cdot L^+_{0\bar{G}}$$

Fig.: B.IV.05: Consolidated sales and production planning model

Since, in contrast to an operation-oriented formulation, only the number of quantity units for an assembly or product group to be produced is defined as a production variable, the model can determine neither the routing according to which nor the machine group on which the planning groups are to be produced.

Accordingly, standard routings and standard equipment assignments must be specified in the model formulation. This holds true not only for the assemblies and product groups defined as variables, but also for all subordinate parts for which no variables have been defined. The applied routings and machines are included in the calculation of the capacity profile and of the variable costs relating to the group.

While each operation is performed at only **one** machine group, and thus the related variable also possesses a coefficient > 0 in only **one** secondary capacity condition, the variable x_{Gt} typically possesses coefficients > 0 in several secondary capacity conditions. The LP matrix of production planning models, in which the variables are defined on the basis of products and product groups, therefore also possess a higher assignment density than models with operation-related variables.

Not only the data necessary for the simultaneous model can be generated from the data structure, but also the model itself, i.e., the definition of the variables (columns in the LP matrix) and secondary conditions (rows in the LP matrix), as well as the assignment of the coefficients to columns and rows in the LP matrix.

This type of model-generating program, in combination with the data-generating program, has the advantage that it is possible to quickly calculate several planning processes distinguished on the basis of degree of consolidation, the type of capacity cumulation and the method used in taking initial inventory into account.

Figure B.IV.06 summarizes the planning principle developed here. It shows how optimization and sequential planning procedures can be combined.

Program-controlled generation of the data and the model structure from a database significantly simplifies maintenance of these types of models.

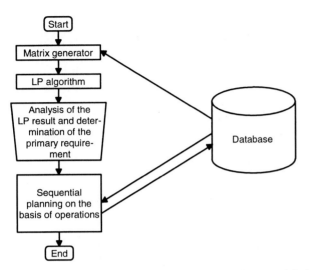

Fig. B.IV.06: Combination of optimization and sequential planning procedures

Since the data and the model are created from scratch from the database for each run, cost-intensive model maintenance is unnecessary. It is largely ensured through maintenance of the database itself. Since the database has to be updated for the planning functions anyway, the **additional** costs that arise for model calculations are kept within limits. Moreover, the data provided by the data generator can also be used for other business functions (e.g., special computations for cost accounting).

A disadvantage of the proposed concept is that it is not yet being offered in standard PPC programs. However, problem-independent LP matrix generators are being offered on the market (see *Scheer, EDV-orientierte Betriebswirtschaftslehre 1990, pp. 154 ff.*).

The strict approach to structuring the problem and the data that has been developed here shows that it is also possible to create standard programs for LP modeling of rough planning that need only be externally supplied with rules concerning the type of consolidation to be used, etc. These types of programs could strongly foster the use of optimization models for simultaneous sales and program planning.

B.IV.2 MRP II

The MRP II concept (MRP = Material Requirement Planning, MRP II = Management Resources Planning) developed by Oliver Wight embeds the planning and control problem within the context of the logistics chain. It

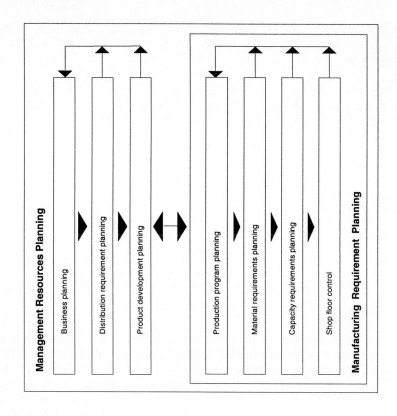

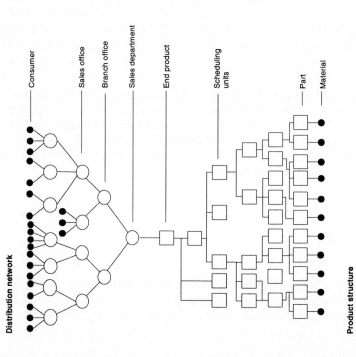

Fig. B.IV.07: MRP II concept

also takes into account the idea of hierarchical planning, beginning with strategic planning by generating master schedules and ending with the production plan. (see Figure B.IV.07, from *Gesellschaft für Fertigungssteuerung und Materialwirtschaft e.V., MRPS 1987*).

This concept conforms to the long-standing situation in Germany, for example, and is covered by the concept developed here (e.g., *Scheer, Computergestützte Produktionsplanung und -steuerung 1983*).

B.IV.3 Job Control Center with Networked Segmentation

The job control center (i.e., central order planning and control) represents an organizational approach whose objective is to bundle all the logistics aspects of a customer order (see *Keller, Informationsmanagement in objektorientierten Organisationsstrukturen 1993*).

The fundamental idea of this concept is to institutionalize an interdepartmental analysis of order handling functions. The organizational form was initially developed for one-off manufacturing environments, but today, with terms such as "central logistics unit," it is also common in the context of series production and in the process industries. By setting up a central coordination unit for all jobs involved in order handling, harmonization problems, which are the cause of long turnaround times and insufficient capacity utilization, can be reduced. The job control unit functions as an interface between Sales, Production and Purchasing with the objective of harmonizing customer needs as well as production and purchasing requirements with respect to quantities, deadlines and capacities. This solution is designed to provide a neutral organizational unit where conflicting objectives due to department-specific attitudes can be taken into account; this includes Sales' need, for instance, to guarantee short delivery times and to meet individual customer demands, Production's desire for high, uniform capacity utilization, and Purchasing's preference for high order quantities with long lead times (see *Gerlach, Zentrale Auftragsabwicklung in Produktionsunternehmen, 1983, p. 135*)

Part C: Integrated Product Development Processes

Because product lifecycles are becoming increasingly shorter—and new products have to be brought to market more quickly as a result—the importance of product development in industry is taking on increasingly greater significance. Moreover, product development time is becoming a significant competitive factor as well. In many industries (e.g., electronics), "time to market" constitutes the primary factor governing a company's success: Only the company that brings a product to market first can take advantage of higher market prices and thus quickly recoup development costs; this company gains the most important customers and defines the industry standards. The company that brings its product to market after the competition is forced to sell it at a lower price—making it more difficult to cover development costs—and to spend more to attract customers.

Product development is increasingly becoming the center of the decision-making process in industry, where important parameters concerning the company's logistics chain procedures and cost situation are specified.

These examples illustrate just a few reasons for the intense discussion that is presently being conducted regarding the role of the product development process within the organizational structure. But the concepts developed here cannot be implemented without the support of integrated information systems, which again reveals the close link between organizational structure and information technology.

C.I Overview: The Product Development Process

The product development process constitutes the right branch of the Y model shown in Figure C.I.01.

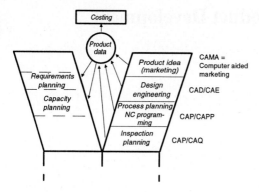

Fig: C.I.01: Incorporation of the product development into the Y model

The figure illustrates that product development can be described from various perspectives. Marketing, for example, defines the product requirements in a product concept and is primarily interested in how the product affects the customer's purchasing decision. Design Engineering develops the technical properties of the product and defines it using topological and geometrical data. Production creates routings to plan the steps necessary to manufacture the product. Quality Assurance describes a product on the basis of the testing procedures and inspection plans that are necessary to ensure quality-related properties.

All descriptions created during product development are termed "product data." Within the context of requirements planning, the product data form the foundation for the requirements explosion in the form of bills of materials as well as for capacity planning in the form of routings. At the same time, they also provide the basis for product costing. This reveals the central importance of the product development process as a source of data.

The terms used in Figure C.I.01 relate to the manufacturing industry. In process-oriented manufacturing, including the chemical, food, alcohol and tobacco industries, the process sequence is largely analogous (see the earlier Y model for the process industry). Instead of Design Engineering, however, the process industry speaks of Research and Development; routings are termed "manufacturing procedures," which together with the product composition (bill of materials) are called "recipes." Packaging design is also important and can employ CAD techniques.

In order to reflect the importance of product development as a center for data definition and decision making, the entire product lifecycle will be analyzed in order to allow design decisions to take into account factors that influence subsequent development and exploitation stages within the lifecycle. Effects on subsequent phases in the process are included in the analysis as the consequence of empirical evidence that the costs involved in correcting mistakes in a product are all the higher the later the mistakes are discovered (see *Bullinger, Forschungs- und Entwicklungsmanagement in der deutschen Industrie 1992, p. 25*). These effects are expressed by

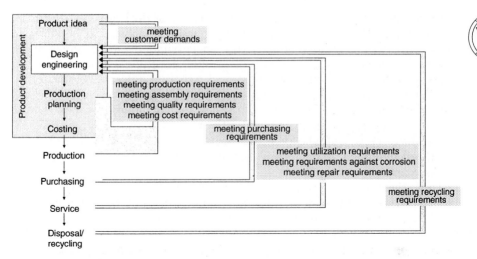

Fig: C.I.02: Impacts of the product life cycle on product development

"suitability requirements," as shown in Figure C.I.02 (see *Grabowski, Entwerfen in Konstruktionsräumen zur Unterstützung der Teamarbeit 1992, p. 132; Rude, Rechnerunterstützte Gestaltsfindung auf der Basis integrierter Produktmodelle 1991, p. 74*).

In this context, design engineering is at the heart of product development activities. It has to take into account the effects that planning decisions will have on production, for example, by creating only workpiece geometries that do not lead to collisions with the tools during processing or by requiring only those tolerances that can be maintained with the available tooling and equipment.

Design Engineering must also define the quality requirements in such a way that they can subsequently be incorporated into the system in the form of inspections.

The costs of the product to be developed can be influenced by cost-effective design requirements with respect to materials and production procedures. The number of potential suppliers is determined by the material requirements that are specified.

Design Engineering influences the serviceability of the part by specifying materials, stability and robustness. At the same time, the use of modular structures determines the product's suitability for repair.

A product's materials, material identification options and ease of disassembly determine its recyclability.

In order to keep pace with the demand for shorter product development times, companies are attempting to perform the individual phases concurrently. In this respect, the objective is to reduce transfer times between the individual departments involved as well as to avoid the need for corrective and rework cycles. Terms used to describe this trend include "simultaneous engineering," "concurrent engineering" and "simultaneous product development."

Both aspects—taking into account the effects of decisions on all phases of the lifecycle as well as the strong parallelism that exists between networking and development activities—necessitate drastic changes in the current organizational structure of the product development process.

Figure C.I.03 shows the organizational structure currently embraced in the form of a largely sequential product development process that involves numerous different departments. The transfer and break-in times for the process are proportionately long. The figure also shows how the different descriptive views of the various organizational units involved have produced independent databases that are scattered on various application systems and hardware platforms.

Thus, the product geometry description is maintained in CAD system databases, and bills of materials and routings constitute components of production planning and control systems. This situation alone reveals the narrow view that is taken with respect to data organization. Since production planning and control is involved with planning products that have already been completely defined, the bills of materials and routings are not entered until Design Engineering releases the product. Bills of materials and routings for products that have not yet been completely developed do not exist in the PPC database. This means that product costing activities that require bills of materials and routings cannot be performed until a later time, i.e., after product development has been completed. Although it is widely known that a large proportion of product costs is determined by Design Engineering ("make or buy" decisions, selection or assignment of tools and equipment by stipulating design specifications, stipulating materials through design specifications, etc.), costing cannot be employed in support of decision processes. A much more common approach currently involves incorporating a costly, time-consuming modification cycle to correct products that have been identified as too expensive.

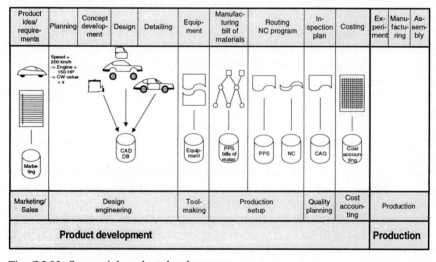

Fig: C.I.03: Sequential product development process

In the simultaneous product development process shown in Figure C.I.04, all descriptive aspects of products, from the initial raw idea to the fully developed detailed description, are entered at the same time. In this way, the structural descriptions for the bill of materials, the production description in the form of routings, etc., are created virtually concurrently with the geometric description. While in the initial phase, a routing need only contain the assignment of a part to a specific plant, which provides a certain specification of the technology and cost situation involved, the concrete definition of routings, operations, sequences, equipment assignments, tool utilization, etc., is determined subsequently as the detailing process progresses.

This type of simultaneous product development (see Figure C.I.04) necessitates that all organizational units involved in the process be continuously informed of the product development status. This requirement means that descriptive data must reside in a uniform product description database instead of being scattered on different systems that, in addition to their physical separation, also relate to different phases of the product development process. Since external parties can also be involved in the development process, e.g., component and tooling suppliers, data and processes must be organized on an intercompany basis as well.

The process chain diagram shown in Figure C.I.05 shows the variety of the data clusters that occur and the extent to which they interact with one another.

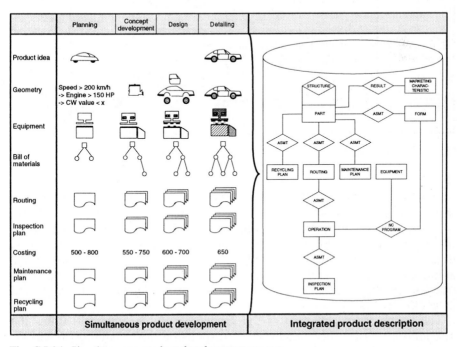

Fig: C.I.04: Simultaneous product development process

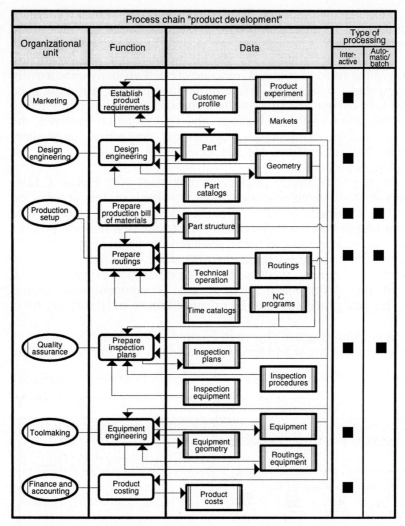

Fig: C.I.05: Process chain diagram for product development

The figure illustrates the highly interactive nature of the process, which results because the definition of bills of materials, routings, etc., allows the user degrees of latitude that he can employ in interactive decision-making processes or by iteratively modifying initial solutions. At the same time, there is a trend toward deriving data, e.g., bills of materials, automatically from the description of the parts geometry. The same holds true for routings, in that expert systems are used to generate routings and inspection plans.

The rough process shown in the process chain diagram illustrates the distribution of organizational responsibilities among various organizational units. As shown in Figure C.I.06 in the form of an

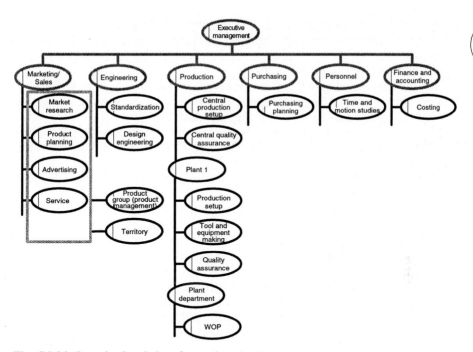

Fig: C.I.06: Organizational chart for product development

organizational chart, these units relate to virtually all major departments of the functional reference organizational chart for the industrial enterprise.

The marketing department provides initial new product concepts that result from market research, customer complaints or directly from ideas originating from the product management staff itself. The marketing department can be organized in such a manner as to provide a division of labor on the basis of the functions of market research, product planning and advertising, or it can also combine these functions in other organizational forms that are geared toward product groups (product management) or territories.

The standardization unit of the engineering department defines the parts definitions that are valid for the enterprise; at the same time, Design Engineering also reports to Engineering.

Within the production department, a central production setup planning unit lays down general guidelines for routing preparation, NC programming and quality planning on an enterprise-wide level.

In a semi-decentralized organizational structure, routings are maintained on the plant level and assigned toolmaking activities.

In a decentralized production organization, the product descriptions, i.e., routings, inspection plans and, in particular, NC programs, required for Production are created in plant departments (e.g., production islands). This is suggested in Figure C.I.06 by the WOP ((work)shop-oriented programming) concept.

This type of decentralized organizational structure is primarily meaningful for simple parts ranges, so that a mixture of the three organizational forms (centralized, semi-decentralized and decentralized) can be encountered in actual practice.

The purchasing department is involved in the product development process through its contact to suppliers and can play an important role by providing suggestions for outsourcing new parts.

Responsibility for time and motion studies and new work-related organizational activities can be governed in the human resource department.

The finance and accounting department is responsible for product costing.

Each of the various organizational units that are indicated can provide ideas for developing or modifying new products. In the event-driven process chain shown in Figure C.I.07, these functions are therefore indicated as sources of product (modification) proposals. As a result of such a proposal, a rough design is first created, which is then reviewed by the various descriptive views involved to see if it meets the "suitability requirements." If this evaluation is positive, the development process can continue; if not, the proposal is corrected. After the final detailed development step, the product development process is complete, provided it passes an overall evaluation.

The process represented in the form of an event-driven process chain characterizes the fundamental nesting effect and the options for concurrent development. If the overall development process is subdivided into many smaller, individual steps, according to which the other views are evaluated, a different form of status tracking is necessary to ensure that a department will not perform a subsequent design or development activity unless the prior activities have been completed. At the same time, it must be ensured that corrections in one department are immediately available in all other departments. Support for simultaneous product development requires both a unified product description (database) and a networked process structure with appropriate status tracking. Consequently, the following discussions will focus on both of these aspects.

The representation that follows assumes a highly integrated process for supporting simultaneous product development. For didactic reasons, however, the individual functions involved in the development process, e.g., marketing, design engineering, process planning, quality planning, tool planning, costing and recycling planning will be treated separately on the requirements definition level, but they will then be discussed together in the summary and on the design specification level.

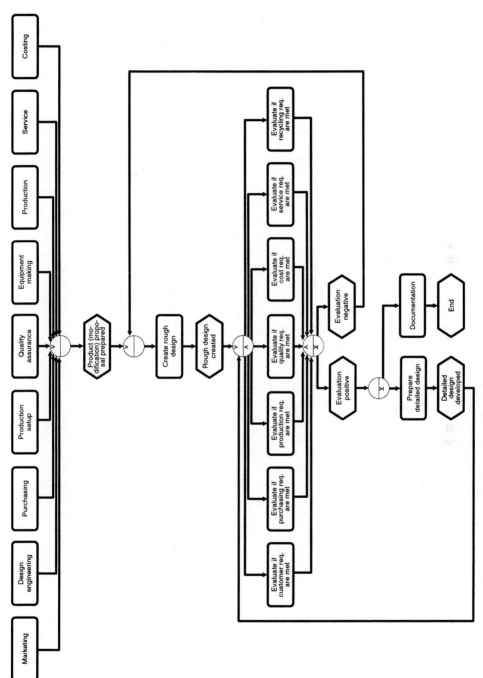

Fig: C.I.07: Event-driven process chain for product development

C.II Requirements Definitions for Product Development

C.II.1 Marketing

According to the new definition in business administration theory, "marketing" is understood to be the act of gearing all company functions toward market demands (see *Backhaus, Investitionsgütermarketing 1993, p. 1936* and *Meffert, Konsumgütermarketing 1993, p. 2242*). According to E. Gutenberg, the tools to be used to this end include sales techniques, pricing policies, advertising and product design (see *Gutenberg, Der Absatz 1984, p. 11*). A closer analysis reveals that the product itself is the point of reference for these activities, at least with respect to pricing policies, advertising and product design. Thus, it would appear to be justifiable to treat marketing as an element of the product development process. Moreover, new demands such as environmentally-oriented marketing are becoming part of the product development process, as well.

In the business administration literature, the central significance of product policy within the context of marketing also comes to bear by way of a differentiated analysis of product properties. If a product is initially characterized as a "combination of physical, symbolic and service-related components" (see *Kupsch/Marr, Personalwirtschaft 1991, p. 674*) that evoke certain buyer expectations or satisfy certain buyer needs, the properties that meet these needs can be differentiated and described on the basis of form, packaging, name, technical quality, lifecycle, safety and additional benefits in the form of warranties or customer service.

In order to determine and track these properties and parameters, information concerning their effects on the buyer must be collected. Market research is used for this purpose. The data from market research are then managed in marketing information systems (see *Zentes, Marketing-Informationssysteme 1993, p. 2706*).

Transferring goods to customers is differentiated here as an independent function and has already been treated in the discussion of logistics—in particular, in the context of outbound logistics. Figure C.II.01 shows the most important function categories.

While the outbound logistics processes are well-structured, this is not entirely the case for design functions in the context of marketing. Thus, a marketing information system can only provide data, models and methods that the user can employ for decision support. The more this type of system is used, however, the more research and decision processes evolve out of this process that contribute to a more effective structuring of the problem area (see *Spang, Informationsmodellierung im Investitionsgütermarketing 1993*).

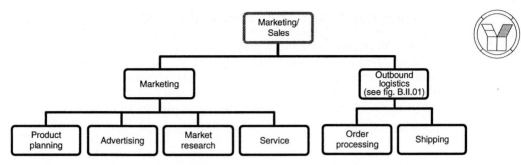

Fig. C.II.01: Functions of marketing/sales

C.II.1.1 Basic Data Management: Marketing Information Systems (MAIS)

The operative applications of order processing as well as of sales and production program planning are structured. One of the implications of this is that problems frequently occur in identical or similar form, so that the data structure and procedures that are used to solve them can be tailored to reflect these recurring concerns.

On the other hand, many decisions concerning product policy are poorly structured, making standard problem solving methods impossible. In this context, the decision maker must be provided with a tool that provides support in making unstructured and ad hoc decisions. Typical concerns of marketing information systems include:

Specifying product-related pricing and advertising strategies, analyzing market segments, examining different product ideas in order to gear product properties in a certain direction, etc.

The user should be linked to the marketing information system components—i.e., database, method base and model base—via a uniform interface (see Figure C.II.02, from *Scheer, Interaktive Methodenbanken 1984, pp. 105 ff.*, and the literature cited there).

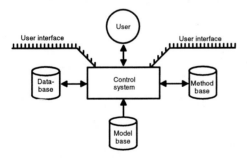

Fig. C.II.02: Components of a marketing information system

The terms "method base" and "model base" are not identical. A method is understood to be a procedure for solving a class of problems, while a model is understood to be the representation of a real system (see *Alpar, Interaktive Methodenauswahl 1980, pp. 40 ff.*). Under this definition, a method base can contain statistical and mathematical procedures for problem solving, while the actual structures for real-world problems are stored in a model base. This means, for example, that the equation for a forecasting model (i.e., type of chronological series incorporated, their linkage and the individual equation setups) forms a model, but the regression analysis is contained in the method base in the form of a statistical procedure. Simple analytical support tools such as report generators, graphical output options, etc., can also be part of a method base. Thus, the boundaries between model bases and method bases are fluid.

Decision support systems typically feature man-machine interaction, which is necessary because neither the "human" information processing system nor the "computer" information processing system is capable of efficiently solving poorly structured decision problems by itself. Figure C.II.03 compares the expertise necessary in the areas of application, methods and computer use. Expertise in the area of application is the primary concern, followed by a knowledge of the methods to be used. DP knowledge ranks last (see *Mertens/Bodendorf, Methodenbanken 1979, p. 540*).

On the one hand, the data in the marketing information system comprise in-house data that are extended to include marketing perspectives and are made available from the operative systems for order handling or from in-house studies, and, on the other hand, external data provided by market research institutes.

Since marketing primarily analyzes the effects of product properties on customers, customer and product characteristics are entered in the database together with their links.

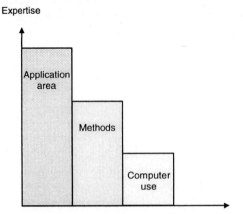

Fig. C.II.03: Expertise required for decision support systems

The discussion will first center on in-house data.

The use of order data for marketing analyses has already been mentioned within the context of outbound logistics in the discussion of classification systems for articles and customers. That classification system can be organized in greater detail in order to take into account the requirements of a differentiated market segment calculation in which the company's success is classified according to individual customers and product segments (see *Köhler, Strategische Marketingplanung 1981*).

A classification system was also necessary for outsourced parts in the context of inbound logistics. In the product development process, these parts descriptions are extended to include additional views. The parts characteristics to be included from the marketing perspective constitute properties that enable the product to satisfy the customer's needs. In the consumer goods industry, these properties can include shape, taste, color and affordability; in the capital goods industry, examples include ease of maintenance or robustness. From the marketing perspective, then, each part—specifically, each article—can be described using instances of these properties. The various characteristic catalogs from logistics and product development are shown in Figure C.II.04 as specializations of the general entity type PART CHARACTERISTIC. This does not mean, however, that the classification systems are completely different; rather, it is precisely the relationships **between** the characteristic catalogs that are important for taking into account the decision-related interdependencies addressed between the development views. New characteristics for categorizing customers can also be defined from the perspective of marketing. In the case of consumers, these can include size of household, income level, etc. This characteristic catalog is shown in Figure C.II.05 as a specialization of the general entity type CUSTOMER CHARACTERISTIC.

Figure C.II.06 shows the data model for internal marketing data. Although marketing characteristics are included to represent characteristic

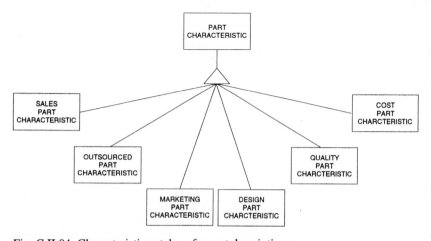

Fig. C.II.04: Characteristic catalogs for part descriptions

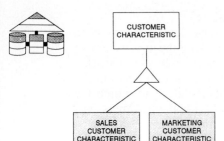

Fig. C.II.05: Characteristic catalogs for customer descriptions

catalogs, the other catalogs can also be relevant. The currently valid instances are always assigned to the (marketing) characteristic assignment relationships.

Marketing data are typically maintained in the form of chronological series in order to reveal chronological developments. A chronological series is identified by its source (e.g., product test or operative application system) as well as by its article- and customer-related characteristics. The individual elements of the chronological series are identified by an additional period index as a time-related instance. Analytical values are then assigned to them as attributes. A chronological series can, for example, be formed for product XY and the product characteristic "advertising expenses," or for customer X and the customer characteristic "sales region."

Thus, a chronological series element represents the elementary unit for analyses.

Individual data from advertising campaigns, such as prices, quantities sold or the individual orders received, must be consolidated for a period value. In the case of time-related variables, e.g., prices, either average values have to be formed for the periods or a reference point has to be defined within the period. The period unit that is chosen should be as small as possible in order to facilitate detailed analyses (for the sake of consistency, the key for the entity type TIME will continue to be referred to as DATE). On the other hand, the classification must be chosen in such a manner that many of the incorporated characteristics can be measured using the same dimension. For example, problems arise if one characteristic is expressed in two-month values, and another in three-month values.

With the data structure shown in Figure C.II.06, it is already possible to perform differentiated segmentation analyses.

The data structure also allows individual key attributes to be omitted. For example, advertising expenses can only be defined on the ARTICLE and PERIOD levels. In this case, customer classification is eliminated for the chronological series. It can also be meaningful to forego any subdivision on the basis of individual customers from the very beginning

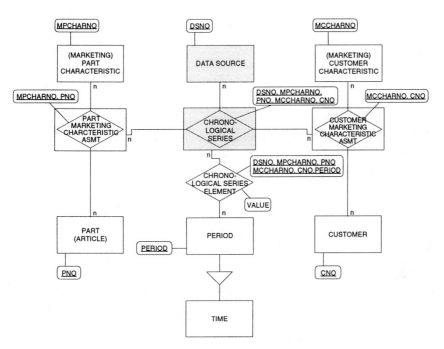

Fig. C.II.06: Data structure for internal data sources

and to define the chronological series on the level of customer characteristics.

In addition to the data from the enterprise itself, data that are regularly sourced from external data suppliers can also be stored in the marketing database (see Figure C.II.07). Of particular importance in the consumer goods industry are such sources as:

- Retailer panel data (source: market research institutes),
- Consumer panel data (source: market research institutes) and
- Advertising data (source: market research institutes and publishers).

Since a set characteristic structure is defined for these data, the characteristic types are differentiated and represented as specializations of the marketing characteristics. In contrast to the in-house data structure, which reflects the enterprise's own customers, the households and retail outlets surveyed in the panel studies are analyzed.

SOCIAL CHARACTERISTIC serve as special characteristic types for characterizing households, while BUSINESS TYPE and ORGANIZATIONAL FORM describe the retail outlets. REGION and SIZE OF CITY are common to both reference objects.

In the case of a retailer panel, the staff of the market research institute forms a sample of representative stores and visits them at regular intervals. Sales are tabulated on the basis of value and quantity, purchases, inventory levels and distribution for each article. Thus, data are collected

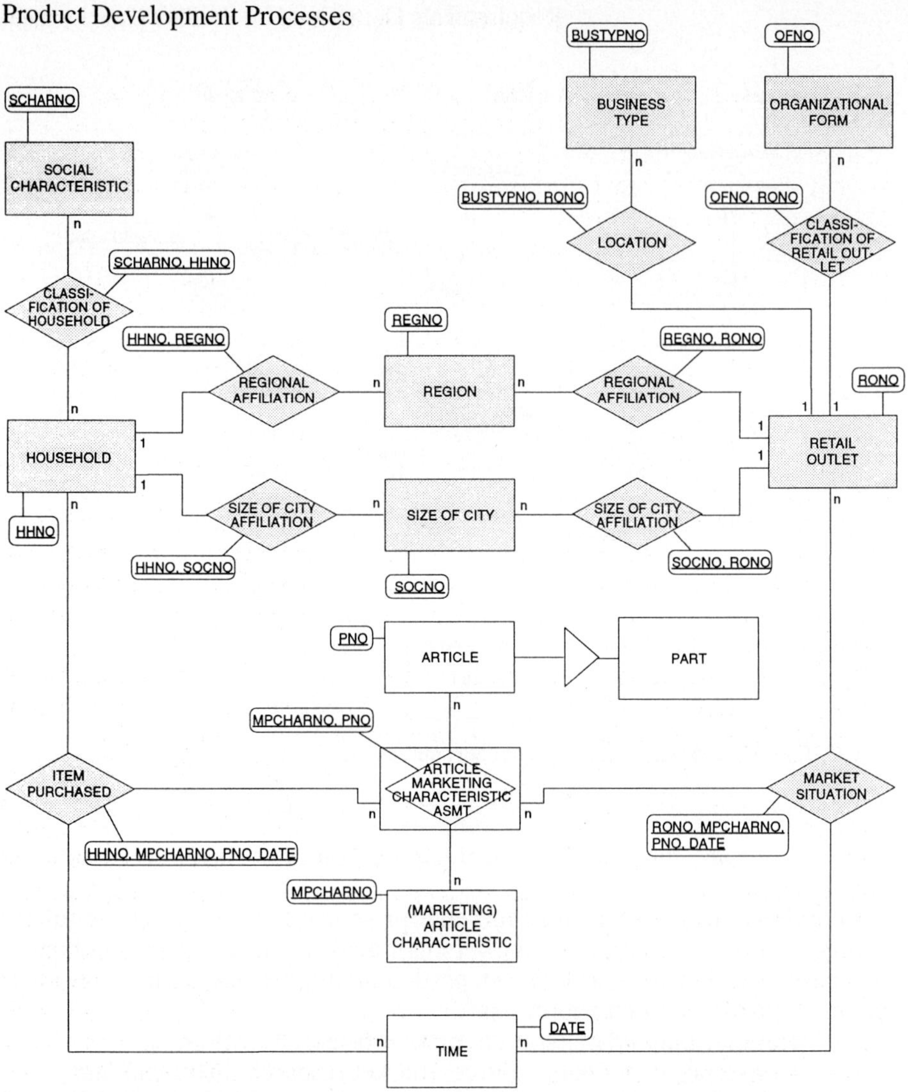

Fig. C.II.07: Data structure for external marketing sources

both for the business's purchases from producers and for its sales to end users.

In the case of a consumer panel, selected consumers keep "purchasing diaries."

While external suppliers need to provide data at regular intervals in the form of consolidated mathematical tables, it is increasingly becoming possible to access this information directly in the form of raw data. To some extent, these institutes also perform data storage and management functions, making it possible to directly access the data online as they are needed. These organizational forms, however, do not have any influence on the logic of the data structure.

In contrast to the consolidated mathematical tables, storing the data in raw form has the advantage that special questions that crop up within the marketing department can be resolved immediately, and the selection criteria can be combined to reflect the situation, e.g., in order to analyze a short-term marketing campaign.

The use of scanners (automatic point-of-sale data capture systems) facilitates more precise and faster data input for retailer panels (see *Simon/Kucher/Sebastian, Scanner-Daten 1982*). Direct links between retail outlets and market research institutes make it possible to route the collected data electronically, eliminating the need for intermediate manual logs.

The individual retail outlets are classified on the basis of organizational form (e.g., cooperatives, normal chains, independent grocer associations, etc.) and represented by the entity type ORGANIZATIONAL FORM. At the same time, the entity type BUSINESS TYPE is formed for different types of operations (self-service department stores, hypermarkets, discounters, etc.). In addition to regional affiliation (REGION), the size of the city in which the retail outlet is located is also a significant descriptive characteristic.

The raw data from the retailer panel are thus a combination of ARTICLE CHARACTERISTIC (e.g., inventory level, quantity purchased, etc.), ARTICLE, RETAIL OUTLET and reference period (TIME).

The external data can contain information relating to in-house articles as well as to competition products, thus also allowing market share analyses to be performed. The ARTICLE entity type is linked with the PART entity type via an "is-a" relationship, so that logical relationships also exist to the in-house data. The same holds true if further segmentation characteristics are linked with the in-house data.

In the case of a household panel, a household log is kept by a representative sample of households in which each purchase is noted on the basis of location, time, article, quantity and price. The market research institute provides this information to the subscribers at regular intervals or makes them available for online access (e.g., in the INMARKT system from G+I, Nuremberg).

A household is initially classified into household groups on the basis of specific social characteristics such as household size, income or social status. Moreover, the characteristics introduced in the retail outlet description, such as REGION and SIZE OF CITY, can be linked with HOUSEHOLD via location relationships. The household maintains records on individual items purchased that are taken from the household logs. Each individual ITEM PURCHASED is described largely by the purchased article, the purchase date and the logged article characteristics (price, quantity, etc.).

In the data structure presented here, cross analyses between the individual data groups can be performed via the links to identical segmentations such as REGION, SIZE OF CITY, ARTICLE and TIME, as well as via identical characteristic definitions. For example, it is widely known that price information from household panel data is more precise than price data from retailer panels. On the other hand, more precise market share information can be obtained from the retailer panels. In the case of marketing analyses that compare price and market share developments, a uniform user interface is used to access data from different data sources.

In addition to household and retailer panel information, it is also possible to enter additional data, e.g., data that relate to advertising expenses and advertising contacts, broken down on the basis of such media as television, radio, magazines and newspapers, as well as to attitude and recall values, into a marketing database.

The data structure developed here applies to enterprises in the consumer goods industry. For enterprises in the capital goods industry, information concerning sales markets, in particular their demographic and political structures, is of primary relevance. At the same time, differentiated contract relationships, installations of competing products and sales representative contacts can be managed as well (see *Heinzelbecker, Marketinginformationssysteme 1985; Brombacher/Scheer, Marketingin-formationssysteme 1985; Spang, Informationsmodellierung im Investitionsgütermarketing 1993*).

C.II.1.2 Decision Support

A decision support system (DSS) provides marketing managers with an interactive man-machine interface for solving poorly structured sales decisions (see *Brombacher, Marketing-Management-Entscheidungsunter-stützungssystem 1987, p. 33*). A DSS is generally geared toward special decision problems—e.g., product policies such as setting up an advertising budget, specifying product prices or optimizing special campaigns—and is closely linked with the information needs of the decision maker. Thus, decision support systems are largely user-specific solutions. Suitable instruments for finding these solutions are provided in model and method bases.

Criteria for characterizing decision support systems include:
1. High degree of interaction
2. Flexible modeling capability for end users
3. Short DSS start-up time, so that it can be embedded in the human decision-making process
4. The model must be able to be largely developed by the user himself, in order to ensure that he accepts it and the results are correctly interpreted
5. Fast information availability takes precedence over mathematically exact optimization.

Special DSS programming environments are being offered for model formulation and method support (e.g., IFPS, FCS, EXPRESS, SAS, MARK^{2}MAN). They also provide data management systems in which the data structure that has been introduced can be stored and analyzed by means of easy queries. Many of the systems initially developed for mainframe environments are now available in PC versions (e.g., SPSS/PC, PCSAS, etc.) or were developed for PC platforms right from the start (MARK^{2}MAN).

The wealth of methods that are being offered can be evaluated on the basis of the following criteria:
- Documentation quality
- Support for data security and privacy
- Selection aids
- Interpretation aids.

In addition to a thorough explanation of the system, the method documentation should also include information on how to perform the DP functions, as well as an on-screen tutorial. The possibility of circumventing the anonymity of personal data by cleverly combining methods must be eliminated by a good data privacy mechanism. In order to provide support for complex mathematical methods, automatic support functions must ensure that the methodological premises and their orientation toward specific problem structures are secured. It is particularly convenient for the user to have the option of formulating a problem verbally and using a text retrieval system to provide suggestions for selecting methods (see *Alpar, Interaktive Methodenauswahl 1980, pp. 40 ff.*).

Users can also be guided interactively using problem-related menu control. Care should be taken, however, to ensure that no cumbersome guidance is necessary for expert users.

Support in interpreting results is just as important as support in selecting methods. The user must be prevented from misinterpreting information, e.g., when using potentially misleading correlations.

Figure C.II.08 shows the architecture for a decision support system.

An extraction routine is used to transfer DSS data structures from the databases for operative applications to the DSS database. The user can then generate analyses directly from these databases. For farther-reaching analyses, particularly those involving the use of methods, the data are converted, and the results are either displayed on screen or written back to the database to be re-analyzed by report generators. A distinction is made between a "chauffeur system," in which the user accesses information with the support of an expert who is familiar with the manipulation of the system, and direct user access.

Because of the definition of a DSS as a system in which the user possesses a relatively close relationship to the application models, there is a trend toward direct user access (see *Keen/Morton, Decision Support Systems 1978; Sprague/Carlson, Effective Decision Support Systems*

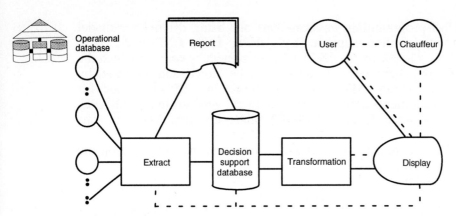

Fig. C.II.08: Architecture for a decision support system

1982; Thome, Datenverarbeitung im Marketing 1981; Röske/Gansera, Strategisches Marketing 1981; Heinzelbecker, Marketingin-formationssysteme 1981; Rieger, Vergleich ausgewählter EIS-Generatoren 1990; Spang, Informationsmodellierung im Investitionsgütermarketing 1993).

The inclusion of interpretations in the results from method bases and support for process selection demonstrates problem structures that lend themselves to the introduction of expert systems. Since expert systems are suitable for unstructured decision-making situations, they can constitute a very worthwhile application in the context of marketing (see *Alpar, Expert Systems 1986*).

The XSEL system (see *McDermott, XSEL 1982, pp. 325 ff.*) supports computer configuration for marketing purposes, which therefore results in a close relationship to the order acceptance problem.

The PROMOTOR system (see *Horwitt, Exploring Expert Systems 1985*) provides support in analyzing short-term campaigns on the basis of both Nielsen and in-house data. The EXPRESS decision support system is incorporated here, so that the interlinking of expert systems and decision support systems can also be seen in concrete prototypes.

The Institute for Consumer and Behavioral Research at the University of the Saarland is conducting a comprehensive study involving the computer-supported analysis, evaluation and development of advertising activities—in particular, print media (see *Kroeber-Riel;Weinberg, Konsumentenverhalten 1996; Kroeber-Riel, Computer-Aided-Advertising-Systems 1993; Esch/Kroeber-Riel, Expertensysteme für die Werbung 1993; Esch, Expertensystem zur Beurteilung von Anzeigenwerbung 1990; Neibecker, Werbewirkungsanalyse mit Expertensystemen 1990*).

Moreover, expert systems can also be used for long-term marketing planning and computer-supported training of sales staff, as well as for analyzing changes in market share through the use of retailer panels (see

Alpar, Expert Systems 1986). An example of a simple rule would be:
-       If a product's market share was not stabile <u>and</u>
        it moved in the same direction as sales support <u>and</u>
        the price was stabile
-       <u>then</u> the market share was influenced by sales support.

Or, to use an example from advertising budgeting (media plan):
-       If the product is an article of clothing <u>and</u>
        the product has a high price <u>and</u>
        the product is a leisure article
-       <u>then</u> select tennis (0.8) and golf (0.7) magazines.

In the COMPLETE management game (see *Stender, Expertensysteme im Marketing 1986*), expert systems are used for decision support by analyzing the output of the simulation model, e.g.,:

-       If the market share for each product amounts to 10 or more points
        relative to the next competitor for at least two quarters <u>and</u>
        revenue per share for both quarters is increasing
-       <u>then</u> expand to region III

or

-       If the average price for a product steadily declines for two
        successive periods
-       <u>then</u> reduce the markup by one half.

These examples are only intended to demonstrate the fundamental applicability of expert systems. But the interlinking of database systems, method bases, decision support systems and expert systems can be expected to develop into a marketing information system, although caution against euphoria would be advisable (see *Zentes, Marketing-Informationssysteme 1993, p. 2707*).

The marketing information system developed here provides the foundation for the marketing-oriented development and evaluation of product ideas. Market niches for new products can be recognized, target audiences identified and product concepts developed by using differentiated analyses and by formulating product characteristics. For a description of methodologies for forecasting the success of new product launches using marketing information and decision support systems, see *Gaul/Baier, Marktforschung und Marketing Management 1994, pp. 220 ff.*
The close interrelationship between the technical design of the product and the way it is shown in advertising literature is apparent, as is the relationship between product costs, pricing and market positioning. Thus,

C.II.2 Design Engineering

The design process involves the creation of technical product specifications. Guideline 2223 of the Society of German Engineers (VDI) defines this more precisely as follows:

"The design process consists primarily of the predominantly creative intellectual conceptualization of technical products utilizing knowledge and experience, and endeavors to find optimal solutions; it involves the determination of the functional and structural characteristics of the product and the generation of definitive production documentation."

VDI Guideline 2210 distinguishes between new designs, modifications, variants and designs based on fixed principles.

The product idea from Marketing serves as the point of departure for the design process. It is defined on the basis of functional requirements and is topologically and geometrically refined by Design Engineering.

According to the traditional approach based on a division of labor, the design process can be categorized into the following phases:

1. Planning (specifying requirements, defining the development order)
2. Concept development (analyzing requirements, developing alternative solutions, evaluating the solutions)
3. Realization (concretizing the solution concept, rendering the design to scale, producing models, evaluating the solutions)
4. Detailing (representing the component parts, evaluating the solutions).

The first stage puts the marketing idea into concrete terms. For an example of a detailed requirement list, see *Gröner, Entwicklungsbegleitende Vorkalkulation 1991, p. 16.*

The fourth stage serves as the transition to process planning in that the production documentation is generated.

The levels are interwoven on the basis of the results of the respective evaluations and can be repeated in cycles.

The most important activities within the context of design engineering include:

- Gathering information from existing files and data sources
- Preparing computations on the stresses to be guaranteed and the specified tolerances to be maintained
- Preparing drawings
- Evaluating the designs in terms of technical and economic aspects.

Typically, the design engineer works in a function-oriented manner, i.e., beginning with the terms of reference, functional elements are selected and combined in order to develop a solution. During the concept development phase, which involves creating a functional plan and a schematic diagram, approximately 70 % of the documents are generated in graphical form (see *Spur/Krause, CAD-Technik, 1984, p. 257*). During the realization phase, this number increases to 95 %, and in the detailing phase, it amounts to 65 %. This reveals the importance of computer-supported graphics generation. Thus, computers were first introduced to support drafting activities (Computer Aided Drafting). CAD (Computer Aided Design), however, encompasses such additional functions as automatic sizing, as well as the organization and retrieval of design results, which extends far beyond the concept of computer aided drafting. Extensive computations (finite element method, load simulations, etc.) can also be classified under the concept of CAE (Computer Aided Engineering).

In particular, the objective of CAE is to optimize the design solution using simulations and analysis techniques, i.e., to also provide decision support during the design process.

In a holistic view of computer support during the design process, however, it is impractical to separate the terms CAD and CAE. Thus, the term CAD, introduced in 1959 by D. T. Ross of MIT, is today increasingly being understood in a comprehensive sense that also encompasses CAE (see *Grabowski/Langlotz/Rude, 25 Jahre CAD in Deutschland 1993, p. 135*). CAD should support the design engineer "in all his activities."

In the context of design engineering, the previously mentioned trends toward using organizational measures to shorten development times is expressed by such terms as "simultaneous engineering" (SE) and "concurrent engineering" (CE). These terms are sometimes used synonymously (see *Ochs, Methoden zur Verkürzung der Produktentstehungszeit 1992*) or with the distinction that CE involves several design engineers solving a design problem as a team—whereby the focus is on problems of task division, distribution and coordination—while SE involves performing activities in parallel that have traditionally been performed sequentially (see *Grabowski, Entwerfen in Konstruktionsräumen zur Unterstützung der Teamarbeit 1992, p. 127*). Although this parallelization initially related to product and tooling development, it has been expanded today to include all activities involved in the development process. This situation is reflected in the definition that "simultaneous engineering is a strategy for achieving the most simultaneous possible coordinated interaction between all functional departments that influence the product lifecyle, with the ultimate goal of shortening innovation cycles" (see *Ochs, Methoden zur Verkürzung der Produktentstehungszeit 1992*).

Up until now, however, there have been no DP systems that support the entire **design process** as defined in VDI Guideline 2223, so that the problems concerning the more far-reaching coordination functions of various DP systems within the framework of the **simultaneous development process** have not been solved. Modern CAD systems concentrate more on the employment of the functions within the design process, i.e., on the "realization" and "detailing" phases.

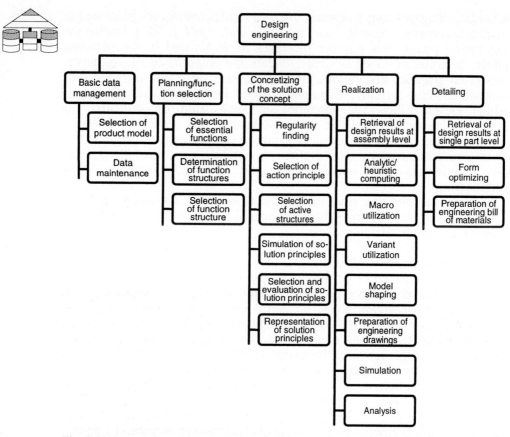

Fig. C.II.09: Function tree for design engineering

At the core of each DP design application is the internal computer representation of the product model. Since this addresses the description of logical data structures, it will be treated as part of the requirements definition description. The product model must capable of accommodating all relevant product properties in a structured fashion. It will be discussed in the section on basic data management.

Flow problems involved in the design process will be discussed in the section entitled "Design Process." Figure C.II.09 provides an overview of design functions (see *Mattheis, Vorgehensmodell einer prozeßorientierten Informations- und Organisationsstrategie 1993*).

C.II.2.1 Basic Data Management: Product Models

The perspective changes during the individual phases of the design process (planning, concept development, realization, detailing).

Planning primarily involves describing functional requirements, which are assigned basic solution principles during concept development. The focus here is on physical variables, effects and influencing elements. In the "realization" and "detailing" phases, then, the actual form of the product is designed, i.e., parts topology and geometry are specified and the technical properties (dimensions, tolerances, material grades) are described. Realization builds on the solution principle and concretizes it via the parts definition, materials assignment and production procedures. This results in three views: Functions, solution principles and form.

C.II.2.1.1 Integrated Product Models for Design

In order to satisfy the conditions for simultaneous processing, all descriptive views must be entered in an integrated product model (see *Grabowski, Entwerfen in Konstruktionsräumen zur Unterstützung der Teamarbeit 1992, p. 137; Rude, Rechnerunterstützte Gestaltsfindung auf der Basis integrierter Produktmodelle 1991*). Only in this way is it possible to ensure that the interrelationships between the views will be entered and supported during search operations. A part can then be retrieved on the basis of functional descriptions, solution principles or topological and geometric properties. Before resorting to new design, therefore, this comfortable function can be employed to support a search for existing parts, or to transfer properties (e.g., costs) to a new, similar part. An integrated product model is extremely complex and can therefore only be outlined here.

Figure C.II.10 shows the interrelationship between function, solution principle and form using the example of automobile development (see *Bock, Simultane Produktentwicklung 1993*). The development project "automobile" is described by the (requirement) functions of "produce speed," "produce power" and "overcome wind resistance." In this connection, a function can also be hierarchically divided into subfunctions (see DIN 40150). In Figure C.II.11—in which the integrated product model is developed—this is shown by the relationship type FUNCTIONAL STRUCTURE.

Solution principles can be assigned to a function (regardless of the level of the functional structure), e.g., the different engine types "diesel engine" and "gasoline engine" are assigned to the function "produce speed." Hierarchical classifications can also exist for the solution principles. Solution principles constitute the link between the functions and the parts view, i.e., the form.

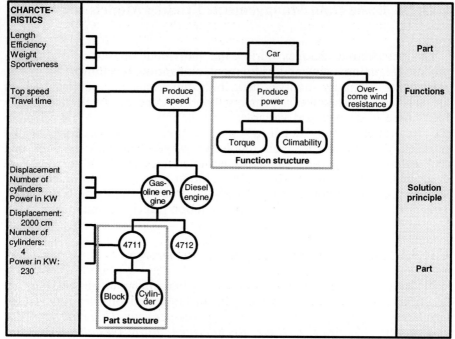

Fig. C.II.10: Interrelationships between functions, principles, form and specific characteristics

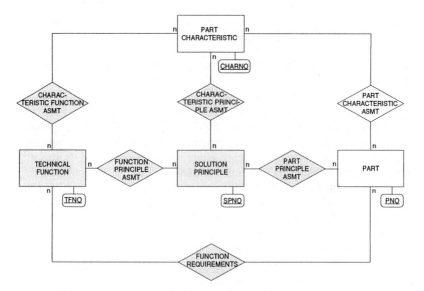

Fig. C.II.11: Rough integrated product model of design engineering

The actual engine models 4711 and 4712 can be assigned as parts to the solution principle "diesel engine." Representation of the parts structure as a bill of materials is already familiar. The assignment of production methods can also be tracked via routings.

Each of the three views of **functions, solution principles** and **form** can be described by (specific) characteristics.

Part characteristics have already been discussed from the perspective of Sales, Purchasing and Marketing. The definition will now be extended to include design-related characteristics. Figure C.II.11 expressly introduces only <u>one</u> characteristic entity type in order to emphasize the fact that the part characterization affects all aspects of the system in the sense of simultaneous engineering.

A structure can also be defined between the characteristics, e.g., in the form of a tree, as shown in Figure C.II.12 for the gasoline engine. One path in the tree thus represents a characteristic description for a concrete part (see the path shown in Figure C.II.12).

The option of representing the characteristics in a hierarchical fashion has not been adopted in this data structure. Each characteristic is thus an

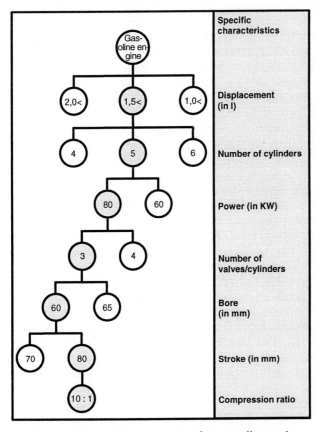

Fig. C.II.12: Characteristics structure for a gasoline engine

element of the entity type CHARACTERISTIC, which is the point of origin for relationship types to the three views.

The search operations and inter-view comparisons must then be supported by analytical logic.

Comprehensive analyses can be performed using the data structure developed here. Starting with functions, for example, it is possible to identify solution principles, which can then be directly assigned or accessed via characteristic descriptions. Part descriptions, in turn, are accessible from the solution principles, and can be identified via direct assignment relationships or via common characteristic descriptions.

C.II.2.1.2 Topological/Geometrical Product Models

Various concepts have been developed for the topological/geometrical representation of parts, which is a prerequisite for CAD application in the realization and detailing phases. Since these concepts are a prerequisite for a discussion of their DP ramifications and form the premise for new developments in database development, they will be briefly discussed.

The internal computer representation (ICR) of solids builds on topological/geometrical product models that have to be flexible enough to be able to allow various views and manipulations to be generated from the ICR. The topology describes the composition of a solid, i.e., type, number and proximity relationships of the descriptive elements (see *Ruf, Featurebasierte Integration von CAD/CAM-Systemen 1991, p. 56*). Thus, the surfaces shown in Figure C.II.13, which are characterized by edges and points, are topologically equivalent. Consequently, additional geometrical data must be taken into account, such as location of the points on the basis of coordinates or characterization of the edges as straight or curved.

The models can be evaluated in terms of their degree of ambiguity. A model is ambiguous if it is identical for **more than one** real-world object. For example, several object representations can be generated from the polyhedron shown in Figure C.II.14,a (from *Eberlein, CAD-Datenbanksysteme 1984, p. 60* and *Ruf, Featurebasierte Integration von CAD/CAM-Systemen 1991, p. 51*).

Thus, the wire-frame model, which depicts objects using lines and points, is an ambiguous product model that is primarily suited for two-dimensional geometries. Although three-dimensional representations can be generated using wire-frame models, they are generally ambiguous, as demonstrated in Figure C.II.14,a. Moreover, sectional views and shadings cannot be generated automatically.

Figure C.II.14,b shows the ER model for the wire-frame model. A solid can consist of several (n) edges; an edge is delimited by two points; a point can delimit several edges.

The point set model, the boundary representation (BREP) model, the constructive solid geometry (CSG) model and the translation/rotation of

a)   b)

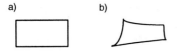

Fig. C.II.13:Topological equivalent objects

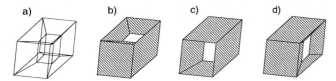

Fig. C.II.14,a: Different representations from an object model

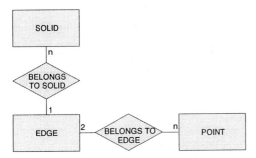

Fig. C.II.14,b: ERM for the wire-frame model

form features will be briefly discussed as examples of unambiguous product models (see *Eberlein, CAD-Datenbanksysteme 1984, p. 56* and *Ruf, Featurebasierte Integration von CAD/CAM-Systemen 1991, pp. 52 ff.* and the literature cited there).

In the case of the point set model (see Figures C.II.15,a and b), the geometric object is rasterized into a quantity of cubes. The process is performed hierarchically to save storage space. Beginning on the upper level, a decision is made in the case of each cube as to whether it lies completely inside or completely outside the solid to be described, and it is then characterized accordingly. In the case of cubes that only partially overlap the solid, the analysis is continued on the next lowest level of the hierarchy. The process ends when a sufficiently precise approximation has been achieved. The point set model provides fundamental insights into the representation of geometrical solids, but does not actually enjoy widespread application.

The BREP model is particularly suited to deriving manufacturing information, e.g., contour lines for NC milling operations.

It represents a solid by indicating the surfaces that delimit it as an "envelope." The surfaces are described by the edges that surround them,

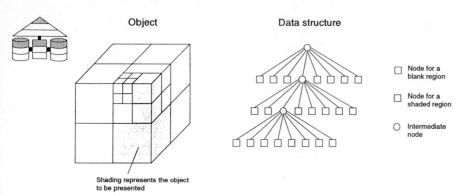

Fig. C.II.15,a: Object representation by a point set model

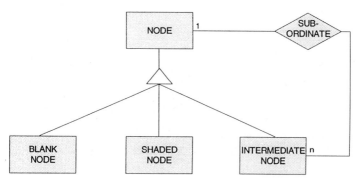

Fig. C.II.15,b: ERM for the point set model

which, in turn, are described by the points that delimit them.

Figure C.II.16,a shows an example, and Figure C.II.16,b, the corresponding ER model.

When working with a BREP model, topological correctness can be verified using the Euler formula:

$$B + P - E = 2 + R - 2 * H$$

B = Number of boundary surfaces
P = Number of points
E = Number of edges
R = Number of rings in surfaces
H = Number of holes in the solid

The geometrical properties are indicted on the left side of the ER model shown in Figure C.II.16,b, and are maintained either as attributes of the topology information objects or as independent information objects (see *Ruf, Featurebasierte Integration von CAD/CAM-Systemen 1991, p. 66* and *Eberlein, CAD-Datenbanksysteme 1984, p. 74*). Solid objects can be spheres, cylinders, polyhedrons, cubes, etc.

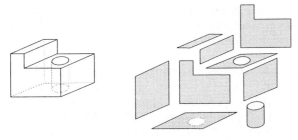

Fig. C.II.16,a: Boundary representation model (BREP)

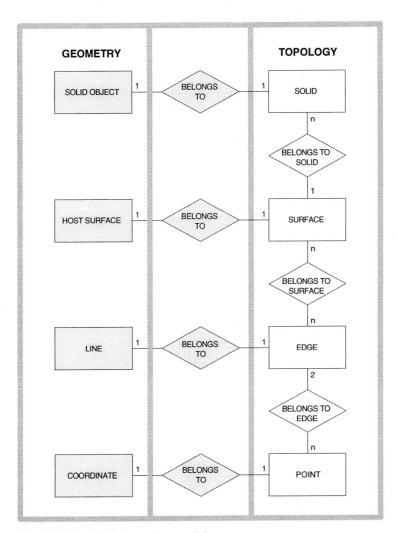

Fig. C.II.16,b: ERM for surface model

The geometry of a host surface can be characterized more precisely as a cylindrical surface, a spherical surface, a flat surface, etc. An edge is characterized as straight, curved, elliptical, etc. Points are characterized by x, y and z coordinates.

In the case of a CSG model, an object is constructed sequentially by adding and removing "material." Standard solids such as spheres, cones and cylinders can be used for these operations. Thus, an object is formed by way of set-related operations such as average, combine and difference. The construction of an object from solid elements can be represented by a binary tree, whereby two instances (nodes) form the next higher instance using logical operations. The geometrical position of a solid element is described by a transformation matrix.

Figure C.II.17,a shows a solid using two different options for CSG representation (see *Ruf, Featurebasierte Integration von CAD/CAM-Systemen 1991, p. 59*). Figure C.II.17,b shows the ER model for the CSG model. Since mathematical operations are part of topological representations, the model is procedural.

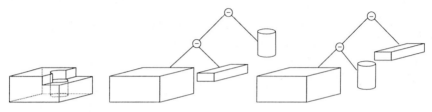

Fig. C.II.17,a: Representation options of a solid in the CSG model

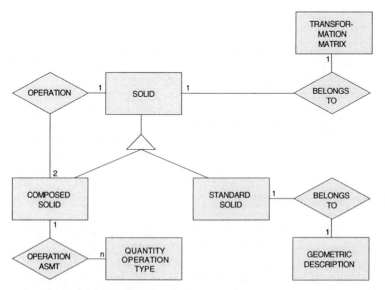

Fig. C.II.17,b: ERM for the CSG product model

CSG models lend themselves particularly well to calculations and simulations.

In addition to 2-D and 3-D systems, "2 1/2-D" systems also exist. In this case, a 2-D view is described and stored, and a 3-D view is then generated from it using a mathematical operation (rotation and translation) (see Figure C.II.18).

The various types of models can be combined (hybrid models), for example, by employing a BREP model or by using translation to describe basic solids and then using CSG operations to link them (see *Ruf, Featurebasierte Integration von CAD/CAM-Systemen 1991, p. 62*).

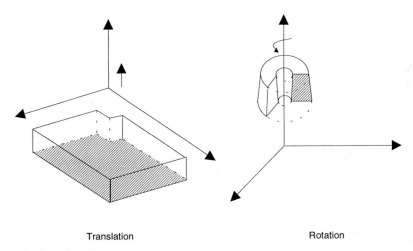

Translation   Rotation

Fig. C.II.18: 2 ½ D representation

As the name implies, topological/geometrical models involve only geometric concepts, e.g., solids, points, edges, polyhedrons, coordinates, etc. However, there is a need to extend the data model to include additional, content-related information (see *Grabowski, Entwerfen in Konstruktionsräumen zur Unterstützung der Teamarbeit 1992, p. 137*). This need is being satisfied through the employment of "feature" concepts. A feature consists of a form element description and additional semantics. This results in a production-oriented parts description, since it transfers the geometrical terms into manufacturing terms such as groove, pocket, thread, stage, recess, etc. The process of identifying these geometric objects is termed "feature analysis." A feature can be represented as an object (in the sense of object-oriented design) that is assigned a functional description. Recent CAD systems that embrace this principle thus give preference to object-oriented representations. Figure C.II.19 shows the interrelationship between the topological/geometrical term SOLID and the term FEATURE in the form of an n:m relationship. The data structure would have to be refined in a more precise analysis of the feature concept,

Fig. C.II.19: Combination of geometric objects with feature objects

for example, by breaking features down (compound features into basic features) and defining links between features and views of features (see *Ruf, Featurebasierte Integration von CAD/CAM Systemen 1991, p. 239*).

C.II.2.1.3 Relationships between Geometry Management and Bill of Materials Management

During the design process, the design engineer develops the composition of a part from components and materials, thus effectively specifying the single-level bill of materials for the part to be developed. This structure becomes particularly clear in the case of assembly installation or exploded drawings.

Figures C.II.20,a and C.II.20,b show the composition of the simple example of a ball bearing from several components, as entered in a single-level bill of materials.

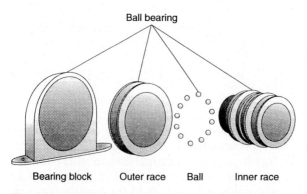

Fig. C.II.20,a: Exploded drawing of a ball bearing

Fig. C.II.20,b: Bill of materials structure of a ball bearing

This provides the link between the bill of materials structure created thus far for production planning and the geometry-oriented data for product representation. Design engineering conforms to a more function-oriented view, so that the design bill of materials can be distinguished from the production bill of materials, which conforms to the logic of the production process. For the sake of simplicity, a 1:1 relationship is used between the part from the materials planning perspective and its geometrical representation as a solid.

Figure C.II.21 shows this interrelationship in the data model. Upon closer examination, it can be seen that this interrelationship applies primarily to in-house parts, i.e., a subset of the entity type PART. Geometry data can also be managed for outsourced parts, for example, in order to have access to more precise information in the event of defects, etc. To achieve this, suppliers are increasingly providing data for spare and outsourced parts.

Because of the interrelationships between part and solid, the bill of materials data structure can be generated largely from topological and geometrical data, although only the structural information is entered, i.e., the composition of a superordinate part from its components (solids), together with the production coefficients. Additional planning-related data such as costs, turnaround times, etc., must be supplied by Production Setup Planning, the organizational unit responsible for bill of materials management.

Fig. C.II.21: ERM to link bill of materials data with geometry data

C.II.2.1.4 CAD Interface Standards

It is frequently necessary for data to be exchanged between different CAD systems. Within Design Engineering, CAD systems can be employed for various applications (electronics, mechanics) or used for transcompany data interchange between producers and suppliers. If 1:n, or worse yet n:m, relationships are possible between the elements in the different data models—as opposed to 1:1 relationships—direct data interchange between different CAD systems becomes extremely problematic. For this reason, standard interfaces are being developed to provide a "standard format" into which data from CAD models can be converted and then reconverted into a different system format (see *Sorgatz/Hochfeld, Austausch produktdefinierender Daten 1985*). Well-known interfaces include the IGES (Initial Graphics Exchange

Specification) format, which was published as an ANSI standard in 1981, the French SET (Standard d'Exchange et de Transfert) system or the free-form VDA-FS surface interface developed by the Association of German Automotive Manufacturers (VDA) and the proposed international standard STEP (Standard for the Exchange of Product Model Data) (see *Grabowski/Glatz, Schnittstellen 1986*).

The CAD systems are not directly coupled; instead, the data are converted into the interface and then transferred to the receiving system; however, information can be lost during this process. Figure C.II.22 illustrates the basic problem involved by showing the data model relationships between the VDA-FS interface and the STRIM 100 CAD system (see *Rausch/de Marne, VDA-Flächenschnittstelle 1985*). A wide variety of logical relationships exist between the data model elements,

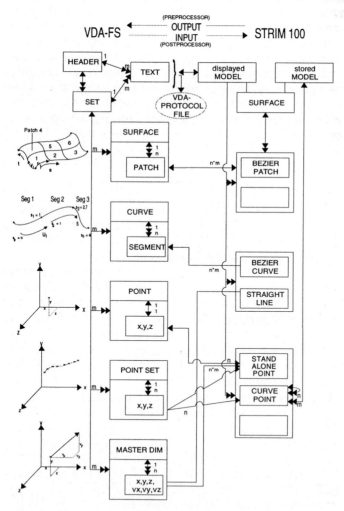

Fig. C.II.22: Data exchange between VDA-FS and STRIM 100

e.g., the "master dimension" element is represented by an isolated point in the VDA-FS model and by an isolated line in the STRIM 100 model. The lack of uniformity in the data models is the reason why significant information loss can occur when using a standard interface for conversions. For this reason, some of the transferred data must be manually post-processed at the terminal.

The VDA free-form interface developed by the Association of German Automotive Manufacturers primarily serves to provide an interchange of surface data needed for producing tooling for body components (see *Encarnãçao, CAD-Handbuch 1984, p. 53*).

The STEP approach involves the development of an international standard for product data interchange. The project, begun in 1984, is being undertaken by an international task force of the ISO (The International Organization for Standardization). A methodical procedure is being developed that is analogous to a software lifecyle and leads from a technical description (concept phase) to the design specification (specification and validation phase) and finally to implementation. Within the framework of the requirements definition, both the IDEF 1x (I-CAM Definition Method No. 1 Extended) method supported by the U.S. government and the NIAM (Nijssen Analysis Method) are being used for modeling, which both bear similarities to the ER model approach. A function-oriented requirements definition serves as the point of departure for creating the data model. The IDEF 0 method, which is based on SADT, is used to describe the functions and the data flow. The development of the EXPRESS language constitutes an independent approach that also contains elements of object-oriented design (see *Anderl, STEP - Grundlagen, Entwurfsprinzipien und Aufbau 1992*; *Grabowski/Anderl/Schilli/Schmitt, STEP - Entwicklung einer Schnittstelle zum Produktdatenaustausch 1989*; *Grabowski/Anderl/Schmitt, Das Produktmodellkonzept von STEP 1989*).

The scope of STEP now not only extends beyond a standard for product data interchange, it is also being developed into a general product data model that encompasses all characteristics of a product across all phases of its lifecycle, i.e., from production, utilization and operation views to recycling. Consequently, this approach will also be discussed again in the summary data analysis for the product development process.

C.II.2.2 Design Process

During the design process, the design engineer accesses a library of standard geometric elements (circles, lines, spheres, cubes, etc.).

In addition, the system also maintains a library of standard parts, including actual standardized parts, which can also be copied into a drawing. Of particular importance, however, is the use of in-house drawings, e.g., for customer-order-oriented production.

When approaching any design problem, the design engineer must ascertain whether an identical or similar part has previously been designed, which would allow the corresponding drawing, bill of materials description, etc., to be used. The avoidance of redundant work is one of the major reasons for the cost-efficiency provided by CAD systems. Thus, they are more widely used for redesign than for new design (see *Anselstetter, Nutzeffekte der Datenverarbeitung 1986, p. 83*). The ease with which searches for similar parts can be performed is an important feature to consider when evaluating the quality of computer support for design procedures. It is essential that the design engineer be able to use DP support to access bill of materials data for similarity searches directly from the workstation. To perform the similarity search, a classification system can be established for the entire parts range (e.g., the Aachener-Opitz key, see *Opitz, Klassifizierungssystem 1966*). Similarities between parts can be determined by using statistical procedures such as cluster analysis. If comprehensive textual information is necessary to describe a part, text retrieval systems can also be employed.

The design process can be carried out using the traditional sequential phase approach or the more modern parallel approach, in which the phases overlap and task packages are distributed among several workgroups.

C.II.2.2.1 Phase-Oriented Design Process

The event-driven process chain shown in Figure C.II.23 illustrates a phase-oriented design process, as portrayed in numerous publications and specified in VDI Guideline 2222 (see *VDI, VDI-Richtlinie 2222, Blatt 1, Konstruktionsmethodik 1977, pp. 3 f.; Beitz/Birkhofer/Pahl, Konstruktionsmethodik in der Praxis 1992, p. 392; Gröner, Entwicklungsbegleitende Vorkalkulation 1991, p. 170*).

This process is characterized by complete processing of large segments; once the results from a given segment have been released, that segment initiates the next segment. If a result cannot be released for technical or economic reasons, the system must "jump" back to a previous phase, which leads to significant delays.

C.II.2.2.2 Distributed Design

The design process can be shortened by overlapping the design phases instead of performing them sequentially (see *Ochs, Methoden zur Verkürzung der Produktentstehungszeit 1992, p. 18; Schmelzer, Steigerung der Effektivität und Effizienz durch Verkürzung von Entwicklungszeiten 1990, p. 45*).

The system must ensure that the results achieved during an overlapping phase are immediately passed on if they affect other phases (see Figure C.II.24).

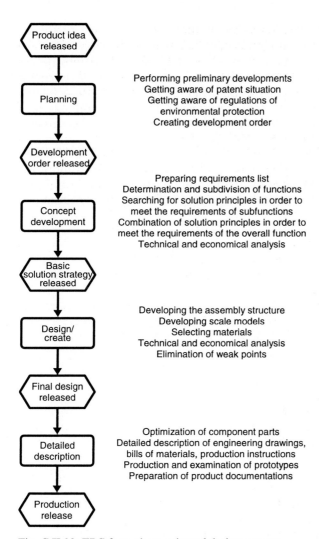

Performing preliminary developments
Getting aware of patent situation
Getting aware of regulations of
environmental protection
Creating development order

Preparing requirements list
Determination and subdivision of functions
Searching for solution principles in order to
meet the requirements of subfunctions
Combination of solution principles in order to
meet the requirements of the overall function
Technical and economical analysis

Developing the assembly structure
Developing scale models
Selecting materials
Technical and economical analysis
Elimination of weak points

Optimization of component parts
Detailed description of engineering drawings,
bills of materials, production instructions
Production and examination of prototypes
Preparation of product documentations

Fig. C.II.23: EPC for a phase-oriented design process

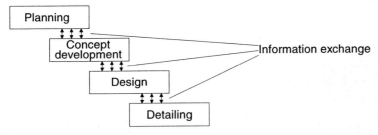

Fig. C.II.24: Overlapped design process

Parallel processing is also possible within an individual phase by distributing the design task among several design workstations within a team (see Figure C.II.25). The design object can be divided into design rooms for this purpose (see *Grabowski, Entwerfen in Konstruktionsräumen zur Unterstützung der Teamarbeit 1992, p. 137*), which each select the product model objects that are processed by the design engineer (see Figure C.II.26, from *Grabowski, Entwerfen in Konstruktionsräumen zur Unterstützung der Teamarbeit 1992, p. 156*).

Harmonization problems also result here, and the transaction principle is employed to coordinate them. A design transaction constitutes the transformation of the product model from one consistent state into a new consistent state. It contains several design steps. Through reservation and

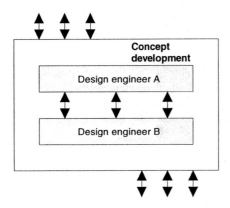

Fig. C.II.25: Designing in teams

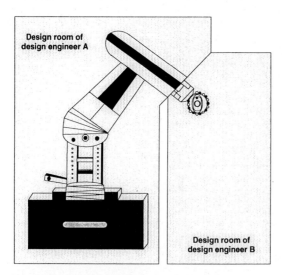

Fig. C.II.26: Design rooms of a design object

release of the design room, the design engineer can prevent others from accessing a particular aspect of the product model while it is being processed; at the same time, interface problems between the design rooms are taken into account by the mutual exchange of information (see Figure C.II.27, from *Grabowski, Entwerfen in Konstruktionsräumen zur Unterstützung der Teamarbeit 1992, p. 154*). This organizational model will later provide the basis for creating the DP prerequisites for the cooperative use of CAD systems.

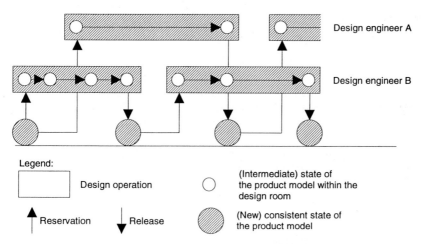

Fig. C.II.27: Strategy of design transactions for design rooms

The design process can be divided into a number of design transactions that can be performed sequentially, in parallel or iteratively. The complexity involved in planning and controlling design orders is thus similar to that for production orders, and similar methods and tools can be used in order to ensure scheduled times and costs. The network planning technique is a suitable method for controlling complex design projects (see *Ochs, Methoden zur Verkürzung der Produktentstehungszeit 1992, p. 40*; *Dorbandt et al., Ausgewählte Projektbeispiele zur Reduzierung der Entwicklungszeit 1990, pp. 176 ff.*), whereby graphical leitstands can also be employed for DP support (see *IDS, Produktbeschreibung Engineering Leitstand EI-2 1993*). The concept of distributed design can also be effectively supported by networked leitstands.

Figure C.II.28 shows the organizational structure of the design leitstand. A leitstand for controlling the individual CAD workstations is set up for each design function and categorized on the basis of part or function groups. The CAD workstation level corresponds to the "machine level" in production leitstands. The individual design steps (design transactions) correspond to the operations in production control. In contrast to production control, however, computer-supported design control is not very widespread, although the analogy between the problems involved

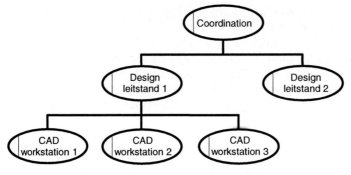

Fig. C.II.28: Organizational chart for distributed design

would make the potential transfer of the solutions seem feasible. The contrast between expensive, highly sophisticated CAD workstations and insufficient control quality, however, will eventually necessitate the adoption of these concepts.

Since this problem relates to the entire development process, the approach will be discussed again in the summary section.

C.II.3 Process Planning (CAP)

A routing describes the transformation of a workpiece from its raw state to its finished state. The point of departure can be a single material or, in the case of assembly-oriented activities, in-house assemblies or component parts. The routing contains the description of the raw part, defines the sequence of operations for manufacturing the part, assigns machines and production support materials to the operations, and includes information on standard times and wage groups.

Figure C.II.29 graphically illustrates the basic process of routing preparation together with its results (see *Eversheim, Organisation in der Produktionstechnik 1989, Vol. 3, p. 15*).

The initial basis for routing preparation consists of geometric and technical information relating to both the raw part and the finished part. The geometric information is taken from the drawings created in Design Engineering. At the same time, these drawings can also contain technical data, e.g., data relating to material properties, tolerances, surface properties, etc. To some extent, the preparation of the technical information is also a function of process planning itself. Moreover, design bills of materials constitute important job documents, as well.

Design bills of materials have to be modified with respect to their suitability for manufacture and assembly.

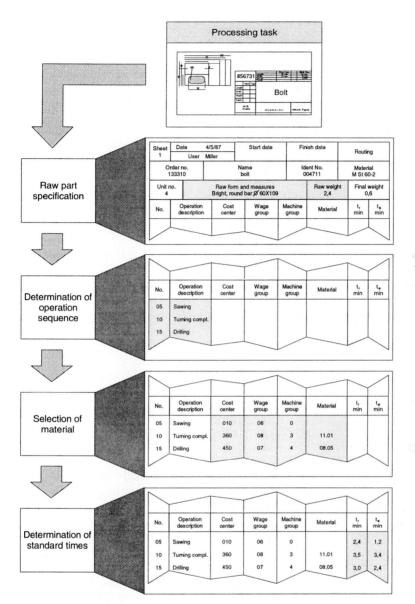

Fig. C.II.29: Routing preparation process
(according to *Eversheim, Organisation in der Produktionstechnik 1989, Bd. 3, p. 15*)

Process planning functions are shown in Figure C.II.30 in the form of a function tree. A separate department on the plant level is responsible for process planning. Figure C.II.31 shows an organizational structure for a series manufacturing environment (see *Eversheim, Organisation in der Produktionstechnik 1989, Vol. 3, p. 23*). The organizational chart is

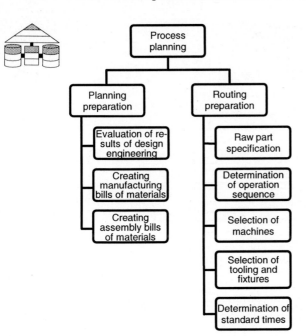

Fig. C.II.30: Function tree for process planning

structured on the basis of different criteria such as technologies (chip-forming, non-chip-forming), stages (production, assembly), as well as objects (parts and equipment). Additional segmentation options are assigned to the organizational units to permit more far-reaching structuring.

Process planning is increasingly being performed with computer support, leading to such terms as "computer aided planning" (CAP) and "computer aided process planning" (CAPP).

In computer aided process planning, a distinction must be made as to whether the routing is being created for conventional production or for computer-controlled production systems (NC machines). In the latter case, the routing is replaced by or supplemented with NC programs. NC programming is employed not only for processing machines, but also in a modified form for robot systems and measuring machines. The creation of inspection programs for measuring machines will be discussed in greater detail in the section entitled "Quality Planning." The long-term goal of CAPP is to generate routings automatically from a product description database. In addition, there are also interesting "human-centered" concepts that are based on rigorous decentralization of routing preparation within the shop (WOP). The following discussion will first treat the data logic for process planning, followed by an explanation of the various processes involved in routing preparation.

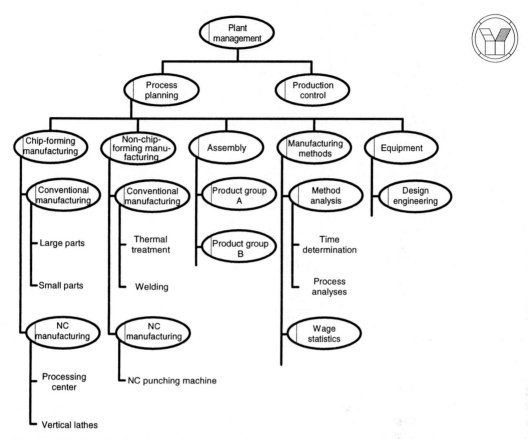

Fig. C.II.31: Organizational chart for process planning

C.II.3.1 Basic Data Management

The data structures for production bills of materials and routings, including the assignment of machines and production support aids, have already been discussed in the sections on requirements planning, capacity planning and CAM. Consequently, only additions and relationships to design engineering data need to be treated. In conventional manufacturing, the same type of routing used within the context of capacity planning is prepared. In addition to the data for design engineering, i.e., drawings and bills of materials, numerous other production data sources are also accessed (see Figure C.II.32, from *Wievelhove, Arbeitsplanerstellung für Varianten 1976*).

All indicated documents relating to routings, parts, equipment groups and tooling have already been defined as entity types in the previously discussed data structures and therefore do not need to be reintroduced.

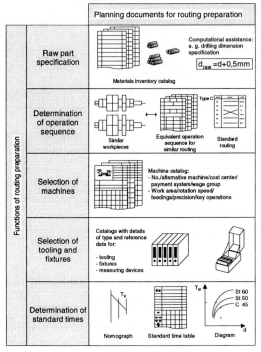

Fig. C.II.32: Planning documents for routing preparation

Only the documents necessary for determining the standard times need to be added. This necessitates a more precise specification of the procedure used for process planning (e.g., REFA or a predefined time system as per MTM).

Nomographs, standard time tables and diagrams are all used to determine standard times. This information, too, can be stored electronically, with typical forms of storage including microfilm or paper-based documents.

This extension of the data structure is only suggested. The relationship type STANDARD TIME ELEMENT creates an n:m relationship between WORKSTATION GROUP and TECHNICAL PROCEDURE (see Figure C.II.33). Depending on the degree of differentiation, this must be extended to include relationships to TOOLING/FIXTURES and OUTSOURCED PART.

While in the case of a conventional production system, machine control is initiated by human beings using the information from production documents (routings and drawings), in the case of computer-controlled production systems these functions are initiated by programs. Thus, the programs handle the functions of the information objects "routing" and "drawing" as well as those of the machine operator, who converts this information into concrete control actions. Consequently, an NC program

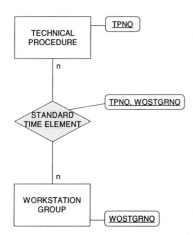

Fig. C.II.33: ERM for the document administration within process planning for conventional processing

is a detailed routing that performs instruction functions that extend beyond mere informational functions.

The database necessary for NC programming is similar to the one for manual process planning. The initial information includes geometric contour data necessary for the path of a tool, technical data such as clamping or cutting values, tooling data, operating data and materials data. Figure C.II.34 (from *Eversheim, Organisation in der Produktionstechnik 1989, Vol. 3, p. 15*) shows the structure of an NC program.

The NC program consists of instructions in accordance with the geometrical and technical descriptions of the raw part, production part and tool. Geometric data are taken from the data structure of the CAD system. Machining speed and materials properties, among other things, are described in the technical description. The final portion contains the actual control instructions.

Many of the descriptive data have already been entered in the previously developed data structure. This is particularly true in the case of the geometric data that are already contained in the product model. Automatic transfer of these data is one of the primary requirements of the CIM principle and is termed the "CAD/CAM chain" or the "CAD/CAP/CAM chain."

Figure C.II.35 shows the milling path with reference to the midpoint of the milling cutter for the outer contour of a sheet steel part. The example refers to the same production procedure as the nesting operation that was discussed in the section on detailed scheduling. The circles represent the positioning of the milling cutter at "critical" points and indicate whether the milling cutter is making contact with the part at undesirable locations.

The NC PROGRAM object has already been introduced in the section on CAM as an information object of the data structure, i.e., more precisely as a relationship type between the drawing and the operation assignment.

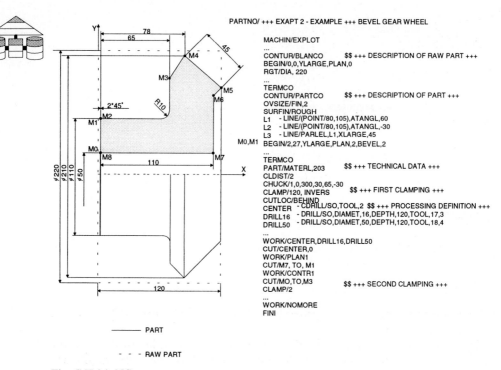

```
PARTNO/ +++ EXAPT 2 - EXAMPLE +++ BEVEL GEAR WHEEL

MACHIN/EXPLOT
...
CONTUR/BLANCO          $$ +++ DESCRIPTION OF RAW PART +++
BEGIN/0,0,YLARGE,PLAN,0
RGT/DIA, 220
...
TERMCO
CONTUR/PARTCO          $$ +++ DESCRIPTION OF PART +++
OVSIZE/FIN,2
SURFIN/ROUGH
L1    - LINE/(POINT/80,105),ATANGL,60
L2    - LINE/(POINT/80,105),ATANGL,-30
L3    - LINE/PARLEL,L1,XLARGE,45
BEGIN/2,27,YLARGE,PLAN,2,BEVEL,2
...
TERMCO
PART/MATERL,203        $$ +++ TECHNICAL DATA +++
CLDIST/2
CHUCK/1,0,300,30,65,-30
CLAMP/120, INVERS      $$ +++ FIRST CLAMPING +++
CUTLOC/BEHIND
CENTER   - CDRILL/SO,TOOL,2 $$ +++ PROCESSING DEFINITION +++
DRILL16  - DRILL/SO,DIAMET,16,DEPTH,120,TOOL,17,3
DRILL50  - DRILL/SO,DIAMET,50,DEPTH,120,TOOL,18,4
...
WORK/CENTER,DRILL16,DRILL50
CUT/CENTER,0
WORK/PLAN1
CUT/M7, TO, M1
WORK/CONTR1
CUT/M0,TO,M3
CLAMP/2                $$ +++ SECOND CLAMPING +++
...
WORK/NOMORE
FINI
```

———— PART

- - - RAW PART

Fig. C.II.34: NC program structure

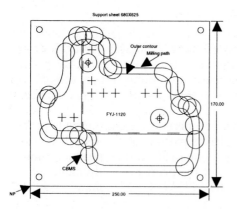

Fig. C.II.35: Computer-based circuit-board contour and milling path specification using the CADAM system

The data generated during the design process are highly relevant for process planning, necessitating a close link between the product models. Figure C.II.36 shows the logical links between design engineering and process planning activities in the form of an association matrix (see *Ochs, Methoden zur Verkürzung der Produktentstehungszeit 1992, p. 94*).

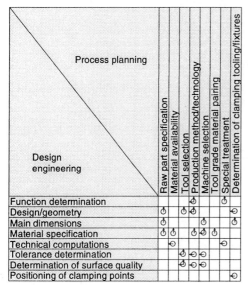

Process planning → / Design engineering ↓	Raw part specification	Material availability	Tool selection	Production method/technology	Machine selection	Tool grade material pairing	Special treatment	Determination of clamping tooling/fixtures
Function determination				↱			↱	
Design/geometry	↱	↱	↱		↱		↱	
Main dimensions	↱	↱		↱			↱	
Material specification	↱	↱		↱	↱	↱		
Technical computations		↱				↱		
Tolerance determination			↱	↱	↱			
Determination of surface quality			↱	↱	↱			
Positioning of clamping points								↱

Legend:
↲ : Bidirectional association
↤ : Unidirectional association

Fig. C.II.36: Links between design engineering and process planning activities

The concrete data interrelationships between CAD and CAP are determined by the data requirements for production with respect to geometry, production procedures and the information content of the CAD system (see *Diedenhoven, Informationsgehalt von CAD-Daten 1985*). Thus, not all geometric information is relevant for Production (e.g., shading).

Figure C.II.37 (from *Diedenhoven, Informationsgehalt von CAD-Daten 1985, p. 59*) shows the production results to be achieved by a workpiece using different options for milling control, expressed by the number of axes to be controlled. The example demonstrates greater or less significant variations from the specified shape. In the case of a 5-axis control concept, which permits any desired tool position to be controlled, the only variations are those caused by the finite expansion of the tool. The more complex the control options, the more the CAD system requires a complete geometric description.

Since each production process is essentially solids-oriented, 3-D CAD systems are necessary to completely transfer the geometric data. Even in the case of production processes involving flat sheet steel parts, for which a two-dimensional drawing would seem sufficient at first glance, the third dimension—the thickness of the workpiece—must be known. For this reason, missing geometric information for NC control frequently has to be (interactively) supplemented when using 2-D systems.

In 3-D systems, wire-frame models, surface models and CSG models lend themselves to data utilization in the above order. In particular, collision tests, which prevent undesired contact between the tool and the workpiece, can only be performed satisfactorily using CSG models.

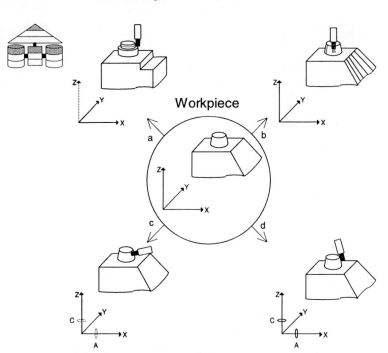

Fig. C.II.37: Production results to be achieved using different options for milling control

Although it would seem obvious that direct transfer of geometric data to the NC programming reduces data redundancy, it is by no means the case in all systems. The reason for this is that vendors of CAD programs do not always offer programs for computer-aided manufacturing, and vice versa. There are, however, signs of strong efforts toward standardization, which will eventually simplify direct data transfer.

Standard CAD interfaces are also important in this connection (e.g., IGES), as they can serve as an "intermediate format" for a common preprocessor.

The geometric data transferred from CAD are extended to include engineering data that are either taken from an existing routing or entered interactively. A machine-independent program code is then generated from this information (e.g., in the EXAPT or APT NC languages). As soon as the equipment involved has been specified, the program is adapted to the specific properties of the equipment as well as of the tools and materials to be used, which produces an equipment-oriented program. Adaptation of the machine-independent NC program to the formats for controlling a specific piece of equipment can be performed automatically or using postprocessors. Typically, however, the NC programmer has to input supplemental data interactively.

Figure C.II.38 shows the logical process for creating this type of CAD/CAM-integrated NC program.

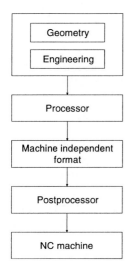

Fig. C.II.38: Data flow for creating a CAD/CAM-integrated NC program

The long-term goal of CAPP is virtually automatic generation of routings from the parts descriptions that come from CAD systems. It is easy to automate process planning in the case of those functions that can be defined in an algorithm. On the other hand, functions that involve making decisions based primarily on heuristic knowledge are more difficult to automate. The automatability of functions is expressed in the order of determining the sequence of operations, selecting the machine, the tooling and fixtures and the standard times (see *Eversheim, Organisation in der Produktionstechnik 1989, Vol. 3, p. 122*). Because of the connection between algorithmic and formal methods on the one hand and heuristic knowledge on the other, knowledge-based systems seem promising. Under this concept, rules are entered into a knowledge base that employ an inference component for parts description to generate and assign the technologies and activities necessary for production (see *Heinz, Beispiel einer CAD-CAPP-Kopplung für die wissensbasierte Arbeitsplanerstellung 1992, p. 196*).

This type of approach places high demands on the part description. Technological descriptions are anticipated that go beyond purely topological and geometrical descriptions and conform to the concept of defining "form features." This means that the geometric elements (circles, points) contained in the CAD systems must be extended to include their definitions (e.g., thread). This situation leads to a common product model for CAD and CAP. Incorporating process plan generation into the design process also makes it possible to use computations and simulations to obtain information concerning process duration and costs.

C.II.3.2 Process Planning Process

The process of generating a routing conforms to the previously cited phases leading from selection of the raw part to determination of the standard times. The functions that cannot be automated are performed interactively, whereby valuable support can be provided by the basic data for production.

Via the search for similar parts in the parts database, it is possible to determine the basic process sequence by accessing their routings, which then only need to be modified. Standard routings can be maintained that are typical for parts families and serve as the point of departure for preparing a specific routing. Thus, bill of materials management and routing management constitute important information functions for preparing routings.

In selecting the materials to be used, a materials catalog can be accessed in which such properties as strength, surface type, castability, weldability, yield points, etc., have been entered.

Equipment group data can be accessed to specify the machine to be used. Likewise, tool properties are taken from the tool data.

Figure C.II.39 shows the routing preparation process in the form of a Nassi/Shneiderman diagram.

In the case of simple parts or individual rush orders, NC programming can be performed directly at the machine by inputting the NC program directly into the CNC system. Newer CNC systems already employ easy-to-use graphical user interfaces, so that shop-oriented programming offers advantages for utilizing the organizational advantages of decentralization, acceleration of special cases and simplification of processes.

Enter basic data		
Load material and machine data		
Display overview - Screen -		
Enter and balance of all job cycles		
	- Operation -	
	Entry of key - Job procedure -	
	Entry of key - Factory data -	
	Determination of cutting data	
	Computing and adjusting of rotation speed	
	Cutting performance check	
	Determination of main and auxiliary turnaround times	
	Display results - Screen -	
	Display overview - Screen -	

Fig. C.II.39: Structogram for routing preparation

C.II.4 Quality Assurance

Quality assurance is incorporated into the product development process in several different ways.

Quality planning transforms the product requirements from Marketing into concrete quality characteristics and specifies permissible deviations in these characteristics.

Quality inspection determines the extent to which the manufactured products conform to the quality requirements. To do this, inspection plans must be created that—analogous to routings in the context of production—control the actual execution of quality inspections. Inspection plan preparation can be viewed analogously to routing preparation, and will thus not be discussed in any great detail (see *Eversheim, Organisation in der Produktionstechnik 1989, Vol. 3, pp. 96 ff.*). Results from Design Engineering and Process Planning serve as the basis for determining the following aspects on the basis of defect catalogs, random sample plans, inspection equipment catalogs, organizational instructions and workstation classifications:

- Characteristics to be inspected (e.g., length, angle, flatness, etc.)
- Inspection scope
- Inspection equipment
- Inspection documents
- Inspection time
- Inspection location.

Quality assurance involves all departments within the enterprise under the concept of "Total Quality Management" (TQM), i.e., it does not simply focus on the quality of products (see *Nedeß, Wissensbasierte FMEA-Erstellung zur Unterstützung der Simultanen Produktentwicklung 1992*). Thus, quality assurance is viewed as an enterprise-wide function that involves all employees within the enterprise. An additional basic principle states that **preventing** defects must take precedence over **discovering** and **eliminating** defects. This means that design decisions in the context of design engineering and decisions concerning the production process in the context of process planing must be made in such a way as to result in as few potential sources of errors as possible.

In this connection, an important method for preventive quality assurance is the failure mode and effects analysis (FMEA), which is termed the "design FMEA" in the context of design engineering and the "process FMEA" in the context of process planning. The FMEA constitutes a systematic procedure for identifying all potential failures, effects of failures, causes of failures, the probability that failures will occur and be discovered, as well as the planning and control of failure prevention actions (see *Hahn, Computergestütztes Qualitätsinformationssystem 1992, p. 169; Nedeß, Wissensbasierte FMEA-Erstellung zur Unterstützung der Simultanen Produktentwicklung 1992*).

If there is a close link between the FMEA on the one hand and CAD and CAP on the other, design and process weaknesses can be identified in advance and eliminated. At the same time, extending the instances of the "dimensions" and "tolerances" characteristics that are specified in the CAD systems to include relevant inspection data (inspection equipment, inspection intervals) can lead to a close coupling of data models that supports the principle of a uniform product description.

The application of the FMEA can be effectively supported through the use of expert systems (see *Nedeß, Wissensbasierte FMEA-Erstellung zur Unterstützung der Simultanen Produktentwicklung 1992; Bock/Kube, Weiterentwicklung der Leitstandkonzepte 1993*).

At the same time, analogously to routing generation, this approach can be tracked up to automatic inspection plan generation. The data model for inspection planning has already been developed in the discussion of quality assurance problems within the framework of CAM.

C.II.5 Planning Tooling and Fixtures

Design engineering and process planning also specify requirements concerning the tooling and fixtures to be used. Tooling consists of tools and dies, which are devices that directly effect form changes in a material and are thus defined on the basis of the geometric requirements of a part. In the case of press tooling, the part geometry is virtually a mirror image of that of the tooling. For this reason, an obvious solution is to transfer the workpiece geometry directly from its CAD system to the CAD system for toolmaking.

The interrelationship between workpieces and fixtures is similar, although not so close. Fixtures hold a material in position at the machine and are thus also influenced by its geometry.

The design and manufacture of tooling and fixtures is generally performed in a separate department (e.g., Equipment Making), which fulfills the same functions as an industrial enterprise itself and is thus termed a "factory within a factory." Since this means that no special features result with respect to design, planning and control, equipment making will not be discussed in any greater detail.

C.II.6 Development-Concurrent Costing

The costs of a product also constitute significant properties that must be covered by a product model. Costs not only support business-related decisions, e.g., pricing; they should also guide all decisions during the development phases as well. According to a much-cited statistic, 70% of the costs involved in a product are defined during the development phase, since this is where the important cost-determining product characteristics are specified, e.g., volume, surface quality, weight, degree of complexity, extent of in-house production or outsourced development, selection of production and testing procedures, etc. This assertion that design decisions account for a higher proportion of product costs is not yet meaningful in terms of decision content, however. Even more important is the fact that degrees of latitude exist when making design decisions that lead to different cost ramifications for roughly identical technical results. This is attributable to the fact that form-related decisions are made possible during the development process in that alternative solution principles exist for a specific function, various types of parts can be used to implement a specific solution principle or alternative production procedures are available for manufacturing a specific part. The alternative between in-house production and outsourced materials and services also has significant cost ramifications. In this connection, the assumption is made that rough decisions that are made early in the development process, and thus determine the initial product profile, have the most influence on subsequent product costs (see Figure C.II.40) (see *Scheer, Konstruktionsbegleitende Kalkulation in CIM-Systemen 1985*).

On the other hand, knowledge concerning product costs is inversely proportionate to cost affectability. In the early stages of a product concept, only very vague cost ideas exist, which increase with the degree of detail.

Within the framework of internal accounting, business administration theory has developed finely honed methods for calculating total product manufacturing costs (product costing). However, these methods assume that the structure of these products has been described by bills of materials, and that routings have specified their production sequence as well as the machines and support tools to be used. Nevertheless, this is the case only after the design, process planning and inspection planning phases have been completed.

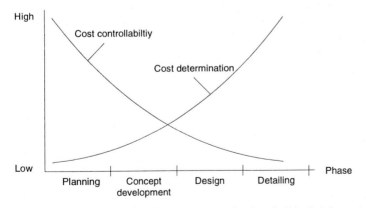

Fig. C.II.40: Cost controllability and determination during development

The value analysis, which is used to examine existing products in terms of cost and function structure, should also be viewed critically, however, as it leads to subsequent product changes, which are associated with additional costs.

As there is a disproportionate relationship between the demand for cost information for decision support during the development process and the amount of information provided by business-related procedures, separate procedures have developed within the field of engineering for providing at least rough guiding principles for design-related decisions.

In actual practice, this situation has led to the "costing" function being performed by various organizational departments (see Figure C.II.41): Technical Business Administration, which reports to Engineering, performs cost analyses during the product development process, while Product Costing, which is responsible for parts that are already in production, reports to Finance and Accounting.

Costing within the scope of Technical Business Administration does not relate solely to in-house parts, but also encompasses costing for outsourced parts in order to provide the company with its own ideas concerning permissible costs and price ceilings for use during purchasing negotiations. Precisely this issue is of major importance in the automotive industry during price negotiations with suppliers.

The difference between development-concurrent costing and production-oriented costing is illustrated in Figure C.II.42. Design Engineering (which is used here to represent the entire development process) oversees the technical parameters for determining functions, solution principles and components. Business Accounting manages cost categories, cost centers and reference units. At first glance, the term "reference unit" can create a link to the technical parameters, while the technical parameters are geared explicitly toward design decisions.

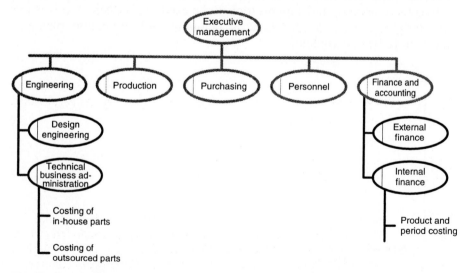

Fig. C.II.41: Organizational chart to integrate costing

Examples of parameters include form, weight, time requirement, production requirements such as material grade, surface quality or production processes (see *Gröner, Entwicklungsbegleitende Vorkalkulation 1991, p. 173*); reference units for business-related costing include dimension variables related to cost causality, which are needed within the framework of cost center accounting to assign cost categories to the appropriate causative cost centers; these same dimensional variables are also needed for measuring cost center output. The costing rates used for business-related costing are geared toward these reference units for measuring output. Thus, in the most detailed case, they relate to the individual production procedures of a cost center. The technical parameters, on the other hand, relate to product properties, such as a part's surface quality, from which can be derived requirements for production procedures. To this extent, the analysis of technical parameters occurs upstream of the business-related view.

A further difference to the business-related view is that during the development process, the object of analysis changes from function to solution principle to part, while business-related costing is geared strictly toward the part.

The variable "product characteristic" was introduced in the context of rough product model development for design engineering and has already been introduced to encompass technical descriptions (see Figure C.II.11). These characteristics are also suitable as parameters for cost determination within the development process and can be extended to include additional properties.

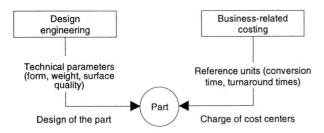

Fig. C.II.42: Views of design engineering and business administration on the calculation object

C.II.6.1 Data Management

The previously-developed concept of an integrated product model for design will be extended to include the view of development-concurrent costing. To do this, the entity type CHARACTERISTIC is extended to include technical parameters. Thus, the terms "technical function," "solution principle" and "part" are assigned decision parameters via

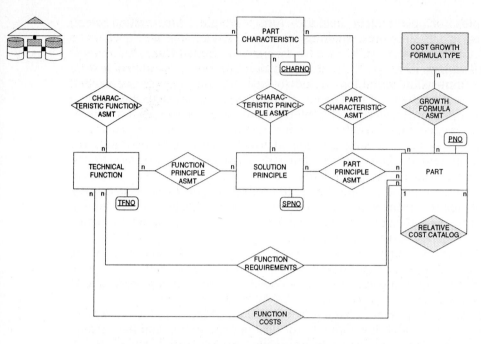

Fig. C.II.43: Data model for development-concurrent costing

assignment relationships. Approaches that are widespread within design engineering, but which are only observed in a cursory manner by business administration, include cost growth interrelationships (sometimes termed "cost growth laws," see *Ehrlenspiel, Kostengünstig Konstruieren 1985, pp. 274 f.* or *Gröner, Entwicklungsbegleitende Vorkalkulation 1991, p. 170*) and relative cost catalogs (see *Eberle/Heil, Relativkosten-Informationen für die Konstruktion 1992, p. 782*).

A cost similarity relationship is understood to be the relationship between the costs of similar products that differ only in terms of a few properties. For example, parts that have the same structure can differ in weight or length. If the relationship of costs to these properties is entered on the basis of a formula, these properties can be used for costing purposes. An entity type is created in Figure C.II.43 for the various types of cost growth formulas and is linked to the parts to which this formula type applies. The parts-specific parameters are entered in the relationship type GROWTH FORMULA ASSIGNMENT.

Relative cost catalogs indicate the cost relationship between two parts. When dealing with a specific solution variant, the part that is considered to be most cost-effective is selected as a reference object and a mathematical relation is set up between this part and the other part that is also being considered as a problem solution. Relative cost catalogs are defined in the data structure as a 1:n relationship type (see *Gröner, Entwicklungsbegleitende Vorkalkulation 1991, p. 177*).

A further supplement to the data structure involves the introduction of function costs. They are calculated from the parts costs used to achieve a function (see Figure C.II.44, from *Gröner, Entwicklungsbegleitende Vorkalkulation 1991, p. 52*). The percentage breakdown of the parts costs on the basis of different functions is a questionable business procedure that is nonetheless widespread in value analysis. The example in Figure C.II.44 shows the function costs for a transmission, which consists of several components. The costs per component are entered as dollar amounts next to the "component" column; the costs per function, in the final column. FUNCTION COSTS form a relationship type between the entity types PART and TECHNICAL FUNCTION.

Filling in the data structure on the entity level necessitates comprehensive procedures such as regression analyses for determining cost growth interrelationships, value analyses for determining function costs or price and cost comparisons in the case of relative cost catalogs. If these data are available, cost studies can be performed during all development phases for cost-optimized product development.

Figure C.II.43 does not illustrate the traditional business administration costing function, since it will not be developed until Part D.

Production cost components	Component	US-$	Percentage of function	Function		Costs per function
	Gears	50	100%	F 1	Increase torque	50
	Shafts	70	50%	F 2	Control torque	35
			50%			
	Bearings	120	100%	F 3	Pivot	275
	Cases	200	60%			
			40%	F 4	Seal	100
	Caps, sealings	20	100%			
	Pipes	30	100%	F 5	Lubricate	30

Fig. C.II.44: Function costing

C.II.6.2 Development-Concurrent Costing Process

The methods cited here can be used during all development phases, in accordance with the information that is available. Consequently, the most suitable method must be selected prior to performing any calculations. Criteria for this include the available initial data, permissible computation effort and expense, and the desired precision of the result. An expert system can be used to support the selection process (see *Scheer/Bock/Bock, Konstruktionsbegleitende Kalkulation im CIM-System aus betriebswirtschaftlicher Sicht 1989*).

During the planning phase, the functional requirements are available in the form of initial information and are expressed by a requirements list. Using these characteristic descriptions, the parts database can be searched for similar parts. If a nearly identical part is found, the existing cost data can be imported from business-related preliminary costing and actual cost analysis. If there are general similarities to the part, but there are differences in height, size or weight, the cost growth formula associated with the part can be applied.

During the concept development phase, the basic components are assigned via the solution principles on the basis of function costs and relative cost catalogs.

During the subsequent phases, increasingly detailed descriptions evolve for topology and geometry.

Thus, detailed interrelationships can also be established between parameters and costs in the form of rules. These rules go beyond the simple formulas used for cost growth relationships, but they are based on the same principle. Moreover, decision aids can also be entered in the rules, as shown in the example in Figure C.II.45 (see *Scheer/Bock/Bock, Expertensystem zur konstruktionsbegleitenden Kalkulation 1990*).

IF
>   the shaft has to meet high quality
>
> **and**
>
>   C 35 is selected as material
>
> **and**
>
>   the material 40 Mn 4 is cheaper
>   than material C 35

THEN
>   prefer the utilization of material 40 Mn 4

Fig. C.II.45: Example of a rule for cost optimization

During the detailing and process planning phases, the data necessary for business-related costing are developed, together with the bills of materials and routings, so that the costing process becomes traditional business-oriented preliminary costing.

Development-concurrent costing is taking on particularly topical significance with respect to "target costing." According to the traditional definition provided by business administration theory, the product price is (at least partly) determined on the basis of costing; target costing, in contrast, involves specifying the product price in advance and then using appropriate product development solutions to gear the costs to the "target" price.

The current discussion is rooted in a paper by Sakurai published in 1989 (see *Sakurai, Target Costing 1989*). However, similar thoughts had also been voiced earlier in the U.S. as well as in Germany (see *Franz, Target Costing 1993*).

The fundamental principle involved in target costing is directly related to the principle of development-concurrent costing. Thus, explicit reference is made to the decreasing importance of standard cost accounting (which has already been discontinued by some Japanese enterprises) and the increasing influence that design engineers are exercising on cost development.

As no cost goal is operational for the entire product for the purpose of controlling the many design engineers involved in a project, the target costs are split up among individual functions. This corresponds to the concept of function costs introduced in the context of the database. An estimation of the importance of the function to the consumer is viewed as the criterion for splitting up the target costs. While this method is theoretically open to criticism, it does lead to interesting consequences.

Overall, it is definitely clear that the development process is taking on increasing significance as the business-related decision center in an industrial enterprise.

C.II.7 Planning Disposal and Recycling

Product Development must also meet the challenge of designing products that lend themselves to proper disposal and efficient recycling (see *Nüttgens/Scheer, Integrierte Entsorgungssicherung als Bestandteil des betrieblichen Informationsmanagements 1993*). VDI Guideline 2243 "Designing Recyclable Technical Products" includes the following suggestions:

-       Use recyclable and reusable materials
-       Use recycled materials
-       Employ modular design for easy disassembly, easy accessibility and non-destructive disassembly
-       Select production procedures that employ supplies and consumables that can be recycled, reused and disposed of using environmentally sound procedures.

These conditions can, for example, be included in the rule structure of an expert system for design consulting, as in the case of the other "suitability requirements."

In terms of the product description, incorporating disposal and recycling management means that in addition to the production bill of materials, a disposal and recycling bill of materials must also be maintained. In Figure C.II.46, the retrograde production flow is indicated by the direction of the

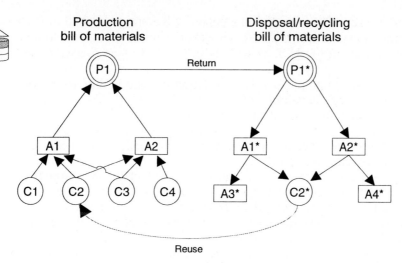

Fig. C.II.46: Manufacturing and disposal/recycling bill of materials

arrows, which flow from top to bottom. For the sake of clarity, the parts to be recovered (old parts) are marked with an asterisk.

The disassembly process can conform to a different teardown process than in the case of assembly. Thus, assemblies A1[*] and A2[*] are not torn down into their original components; instead, only part C2[*] is disassembled. The other components form the "residual assemblies" A3[*] and A4[*], which can be the object of additional recovery procedures. The interrelationship between finished (new) product P1 and product P1[*], which is pending disposal and/or recycling, is represented by a line in the gozinto graph. The production coefficient indicates the proportion with which a finished product has to be treated as a disassembly object. In Germany, for example, this case will take an increased significance as a result of pending amendments to waste control legislation under which automobile manufacturers, computer manufacturers, etc., will have to accept their products back from the last owner. In the bill of materials, reusability is indicated by the broken line. Here, the product coefficient will be > 1, i.e., indicating that more than one unit of recycled part C2[*] is necessary in order to replace a like-new unit C2.

The familiar data model for describing bills of materials does not need to be modified by incorporating the recycling and disposal problem. Used part categories are defined as independent entities, since they are described and planned separately. The relationships between new part categories and part categories designed for recycling can be represented by structural relationships (analogously to the relationship between P1 and P1[*]). Thus, two new bill of materials views can be created along with the general disassembly logic and the "new-used" analysis; these views are treated analogously to the previously introduced production, sales and design views as specializations of the relationship type STRUCTURE (see Figure C.II.47).

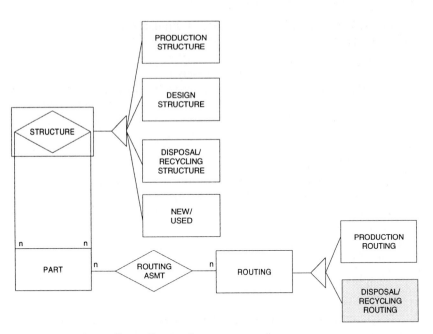

Fig. C.II.47: Disposal/recycling routing

The return and reuse of products produces cycles in the bill of materials structure. These cycles pose no difficulties for the logical data model for bill of materials descriptions, but they do for the requirements planning algorithms.

The routings for the disassembly and overhaul of parts are shown in Figure C.II.47 as specializations of the general information object "routing."

C.II.8 Summarizing and Supplementing the Requirements Definitions for Product Development

The close content- and time-related cross-linkage between the development process phases has already been illustrated during the discussion of these phases. The simultaneous engineering principle builds on this interaction in order to reduce development times and is also the subject of the analysis associated with decision-related interdependencies and cost efficiency. It is precisely in connection with this cost efficiency aspect that it becomes apparent that the use of DP technology for supporting an individual phase does not have the anticipated effect. Thus, for example, a CAD system cannot be evaluated on the basis of the rationalization effect (time reduction, minimizing design errors) at the design engineering workstation alone; instead, it must be evaluated on the basis of the effect to be achieved with respect to materials management and control (increasing the reusability of parts by utilizing classification systems in design engineering reduces the parts range and thus the planning effort within materials management and control), toolmaking (automatic transfer of parts geometry to tool design) and NC programming (automatic transfer of geometry to the NC program), as suggested in Figure C.II.48.

Consequently, the following discussion will treat the entire development process as an entity that necessitates a uniform functional view, a uniform organizational and data model, as well as a uniform process sequence. Linguistic constraints prevent the simultaneity of the functions from always being expressed; however, there can be no doubt with respect to the fundamental principle of maximum networking and parallelism.

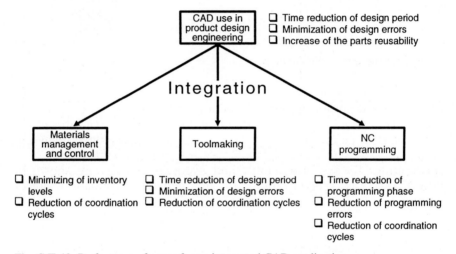

Fig. C.II.48: Performance factors for an integrated CAD application

C.II.8.1 Requirements Definition for Product Development: The Function View

The uniform function tree for simultaneous product development initially results from the combination of all function descriptions treated thus far, from marketing to disposal and recycling. These elements are then supplemented by those functions that were unavailable prior to simultaneous processing, e.g., simulation studies, in which a design change immediately generates a routing, calculates the cost effects involved and uses the results to review the design alternatives.

On the other hand, coordination functions that occur between the individual development phases in the case of a sequential procedure are eliminated.

The development process is predestined for highly interactive processing, with a concurrent trend toward automating functions. This can be expressed in such a way that the actual creative functions are processed interactively, while the subsequent derivative functions are automated. Figure C.II.49 shows the processing modes involved. Basic data management is not included, since the need for currency necessitates interactive processing. Tendencies toward automation are indicated by arrows.

Function	Subfunction	Reasons for interactive processing				Automatic/batch
		Currency	Plausibility	Iterative modification	Interactive decision process	
Marketing	Periodical evaluation					X
	Ad hoc examination	X			X	
Design engineering	Design			X	X	
	Computation					X
Process planning	Model maintenance				X	
	Procedure selection				X ———→ X	
	Sequencing				X ———→ X	
	Time calculation					X
Quality assurance	Model maintenance				X	
	Inspect. plan generation				X ———→ X	
	FMEA				X	
Tool and fixture making	Design				X	
	Process planning				X ———→ X	
Costing	Model maintenance				X	
	Application				X ———→ X	
Disposal/recycling planning					X	

Fig. C.II.49: Processing modes of product development

An interactive decision process is meaningful for setting up models and preparing results. Data preparation and queries incorporating plausibility checks are performed interactively. Batch solutions are indicated only in the case of more extensive data preparation functions and for queries to external databases, for which an interactive solution is not available, as well as in the case of extremely computation-intensive model calculations.

Design engineering is especially oriented toward interactive processing. In all design steps, initial solutions can be interactively modified and decisions interactively supported. Alternatives are evaluated from both a technical and economical standpoint in order to reach an "optimal" solution. Long computation times for performing mathematical operations or for constructing complicated three-dimensional models can necessitate batch processing. Such processes are started interactively and then run as background processes on the CAD workstation.

Decisions involving the selection of production processes and sequences also make process planning suitable for an interactive decision process. Efforts aimed at automatically generating the routing from topological and geometrical data are resulting in a trend toward automation, which has already been achieved in the case of mathematical time calculations. Model maintenance, e.g., maintaining the rules in an expert system for generating routings, remains an interactive function.

The same situation exists in the case of inspection plan preparation as in process planning. Maintenance of models for automatically generating inspection plans remains an interactive function, while inspection plan generation itself is processed automatically. Moreover, performing the FMEA is an interactive decision process.

As a "factory within a factory," tool and fixture making contains all the functions of the development process, although they are only indicated in truncated form.

In the case of costing, too, there is a tendency toward moving from an interactive decision process for selecting processes and varying parameters to an automated costing process. However, model maintenance remains interactive here, as well.

Planning disposal and recycling bears a close relationship to the creative processes involved in design engineering and cannot be automated. The situation for design engineering also applies to the subsequent steps of process planning, inspection planning, etc.

Consequently, it is apparent that basic data management, design decisions and model maintenance—e.g., the rules in expert systems—are stabile interactive functions, while the applications (e.g., creation of process plans) are increasingly being automated.

These validations and evaluations that run automatically in the background of the design process are an important precondition for incorporating the "suitability requirements" into computer-supported design engineering.

C.II.8.2 Requirements Definition for Product Development: The Organization View

Simultaneous product development necessitates changes in the organizational structure. In a traditional function-oriented organizational structure, as shown in Figure C.I.06, responsibilities are distributed among many organizational departments. In networked processing, this type of organizational structure leads to increased coordination effort. At the same time, the numerous exchanges between the different areas of responsibility retard the process and lead to a duplication of effort. For this reason, an organizational structure that encompasses the entire development process is more suitable. Figure C.II.50 shows three alternatives for achieving this. In alternative a), the functional departments involved in product development are assigned to a main organizational department. Within this main department, the individual departments continue to operate on a functional basis; however, the coordination problems that occur between the departments can be resolved more easily than in a purely functional structure.

In alternative b), the product line is segmented. This means that independent development departments are formed for product groups. Within these groups, development teams are established for further subsegments. The teams then collectively solve the different problems that arise. There are thus no organizational units *per se* that are responsible for the individual functions. Instead, individual specialists can handle several of these functions.

The incorporation of the marketing function into the development process eliminates the classical segregation between technical and business-related functions. The same holds true for the incorporation of

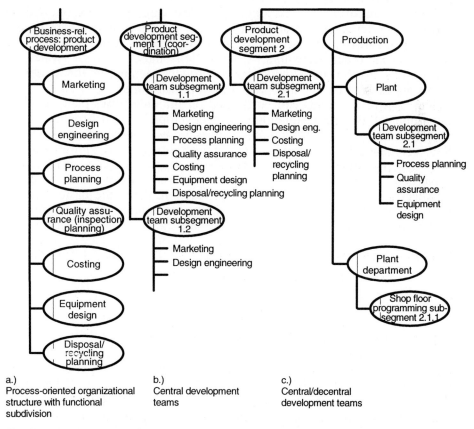

a.)
Process-oriented organizational structure with functional subdivision

b.)
Central development teams

c.)
Central/decentral development teams

Fig. C.II.50: Process-oriented organizational charts for simultaneous product development

preliminary costing, which is a function of Finance and Accounting, into the development process.

The two alternatives discussed thus far assume a centralized product development process. If the plants and plant departments responsible for production are also incorporated, the organizational model can be structured on the basis of alternative c). On the enterprise level, the marketing, design, costing and disposal/recycling planning functions, which are not directly linked to production, are performed in development teams according to b). The production-related functions such as process planning, quality assurance and equipment design are performed by development teams on the plant level. If decentralized WOP-type NC programming exists in plant departments, process planning functions are further decentralized.

Thus, the product development process is distributed among two or three different organizational units. Despite this distribution, the coordination and communication requirements for this structure are significantly less complex than those for the purely functional initial situation (see Figure C.II.09), thus allowing the objectives of integrated simultaneous product development to be achieved.

Process control of the development process can again be supported by leitstand concepts. A coordination leitstand for development (see Figure C.II.51) controls the entire development process and monitors the development order networks. Control leitstands, each of which is responsible for the subnetworks for its product segment or for its design room, are assigned to the individual development teams.

The control leitstands can be located on the enterprise, plant or plant department level. In a situation where development and production are closely intermeshed, programming operations can be tracked within the programming leitstand for (work)shop-oriented programming. Tracking the order networks from design to production is particularly important where there is close interaction between design engineering, equipment making and production. Since the basic data for bills of materials and routings, which are important in terms of requirements and capacity planning, are also created during the

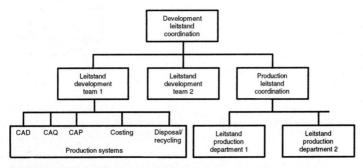

Fig. C.II.51: Development leitstand concept

development process, the development leitstands communicate with the logistics leitstands.

In taking into account the concept of networked decentralization, the Y model then becomes the Y shell model shown in Figure C.II.52 (see *Scheer, Neue Architekturen für PPS-Systeme 1992*).

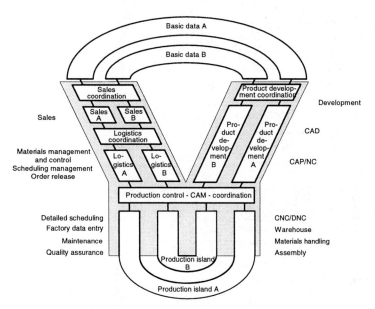

Fig. C.II.52: Y model in the concept of networked decentralization

C.II.8.3 Requirements Definition for Product Development: The Data View

The integrated view of the product development process necessitates an integrated description of all data relating to the product. Figure C.II.53 shows the data clusters that are associated with the description of a product. The ER models developed for the data clusters can be combined accordingly. The central element is the entity type PART, from which the various descriptive views originate. Several data clusters can be bundled using the generalization operation (see Figure C.II.54). Thus, bill of materials structures are maintained on the basis of the views for design engineering, production, service, disposal/recycling and sales. The same holds true for the term "routing," which occurs as a production routing, inspection routing, repair routing and disassembly routing.

The concept for this type of integrated product model has far-reaching effects on the architecture of the application systems used in an industrial enterprise. Currently, the data clusters are distributed among various

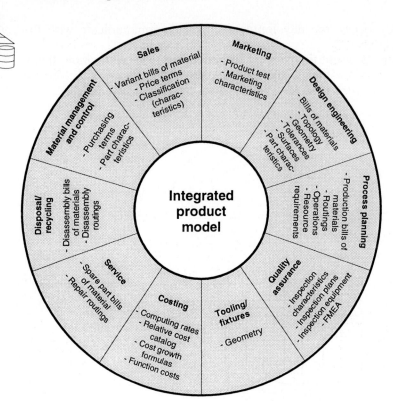

Fig. C.II.53: Data cluster for the integrated product model

systems and contribute significantly to the importance of those systems. For example, PPC systems "own" the data clusters "production bills of materials" and "production routings." If these data management functions were removed from the PPC systems and transferred to a uniform product description database, the importance of the PPC systems would be limited to the functions of requirements and capacity planning, thus sharply reducing their current importance as the data processing backbone in an industrial enterprise.

Only an integrated view of the product model can ensure that changes in one partial model will automatically be recognized, together with its consequences for other partial models.

New CAD systems are being developed that show signs of moving toward this type of view. Thus, their internal computer models already extend beyond merely representing the geometry (see *Rude, Rechnerunterstützte Gestaltfindung auf der Basis eines integrierten Produktmodells 1991, p. 44*). The term "engineering database," which denotes an integrated product description, is heading in this direction. However, these approaches are not as far-reaching as the one shown in Figure C.II.53, which contains all the data groups for a part over its entire lifecycle and from all technical and business-related standpoints.

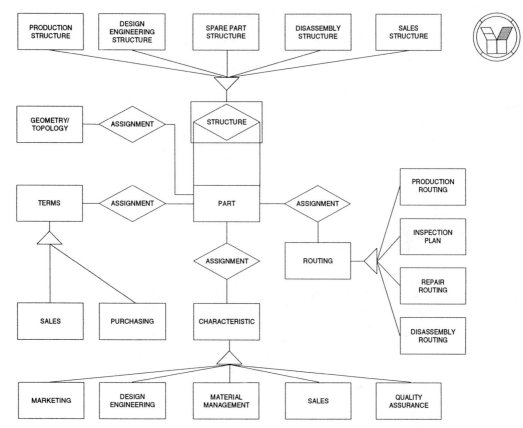

Fig. C.II.54: Integrated product data

The standardization efforts aimed at supporting product data interchange are increasingly conforming to a more comprehensive product description. Thus, the STEP approach constitutes a far-reaching description of the data clusters associated with a product.

C.II.8.4 Requirements Definition for Product Development: The Control View

In the analysis of the relationships between the function and organization views, the individual activities in the product development process are assigned to the organizational units in the sense of simultaneous product development.

The most significant feature of simultaneous product development is that it more strongly parallels the development process than does a phase-oriented sequential process (see Figure C.II.55).

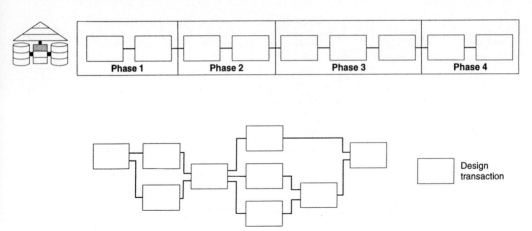

Fig. C.II.55: Sequential and networked development process

The design room concept, in combination with the definition of design transactions, ensures the integrity of the data during parallel processing. Figure C.II.56 shows a rough event-driven process chain for this process. First, a development order is distributed among the various development teams involved. During the course of the team project, individual team members initiate transactions. However, the logical preceding transaction must be complete before a transaction can begin. The transaction begins by reserving a design room, which is subsequently released after the transaction is complete. Several design activities can be performed within the transaction. After a design activity has been completed, transactions are called in order to validate the design activity on the basis of its "suitability" in terms of production, quality and costs. If the validation check is negative, the design activity is reprocessed. If it is successful, the next design activity can begin. If the design activities within a design transaction are self-contained, the design room is released and the "end" information routed to the other members of the development team. The user can then begin a new transaction or end the current interactive session.

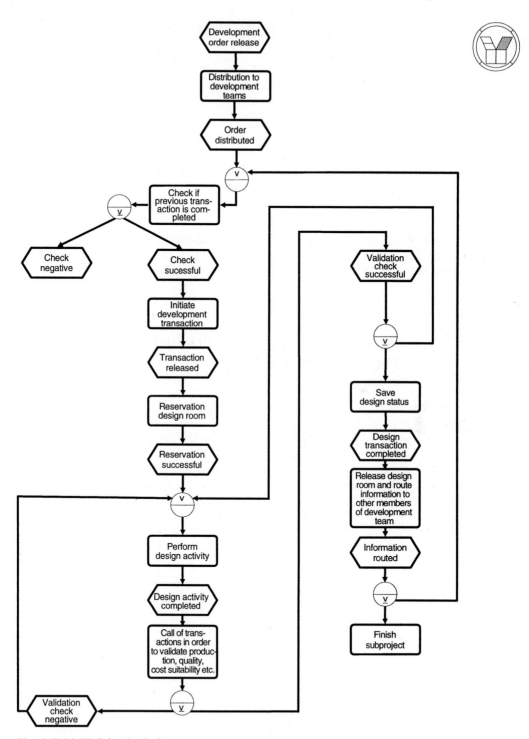

Fig. C.II.56: EPC for the design process

C.III Design Specifications for Product Development

The models developed for the requirements definition will now be transformed into DP interfaces for the design specification.

C.III.1 Design Specification for Product Development: The Function View

Distributed design requires detailed modularization of the application systems in order to take into account the links to the other development functions following completion of a substep or a design transaction.

C.III.2 Design Specification for Product Development: The Organization View

The organizational concepts developed for simultaneous product development are expressed in the network topologies.

All information affecting the product model must be accessible from the perspective of a workstation within the development group. Moreover, external data sources, e.g., from market research institutes, must be available for the marketing view, in addition to supplier and customer data for product data exchange (see Figure C.III.01,a).

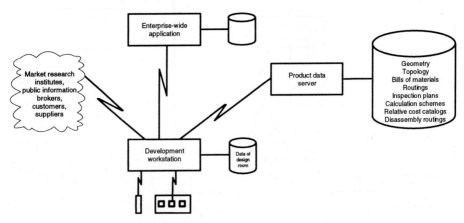

Fig. C.III.01,a: Universal development workstation

CAD applications utilize special tools such as graphics tablets, light pens and mice. Standard components are displayed on the graphics tablet and can be copied into a current drawing.

A high-resolution monitor is essential for displaying drawings. In order to improve system response times, technical functions for screen control and, increasingly, application functions themselves are being shifted to the CAD workstation.

CAD lends itself particularly well to the use of workstation computers. Because CAD applications are extremely computation-intensive, their special hardware requirements led early on to high-performance computers designed specifically for graphics operations, and the workstation computer itself is beginning to handle more and more of the processing functions. This applies to image editing functions as well as to support for the design process itself. There is a trend toward using a file server to manage geometrical and bill of materials information, while employing a processing server to handle all CAD-related functions. The main reasons for shifting the processing functions to workstation computers is to take advantage of their higher graphics resolution, ease of use and support for decentralized organizational activities. So far as hardware solutions are concerned, the ability to attach various plotters and input devices (light pens, mice, graphics menus) is particularly significant.

Many CAD systems are also available in microcomputer (e.g. PC) versions (e.g., AUTO-CAD). Their functionality is increasingly catching up to that of mainframe systems, and they too can be connected to servers via standard interfaces (file transfer, terminal emulation).

If the development process continues to be segmented on a function-oriented basis within a development organization (see the process-oriented organizational model shown in Figure C.II.50), the result is the network topology shown in Figure C.III.01,b.

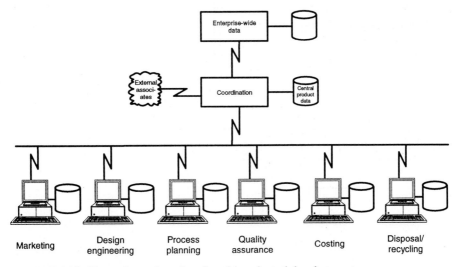

Fig. C.III.01,b: Network topology in a function-oriented development process

The individual functions have their own processing computers with their own databases. Coordination between the individual functions is maintained via a coordination level, which also manages the inter-functional data for the entire development process. Communications with external partners is also handled via the coordination level, which is also linked to the enterprise level in order to provide the development process with access to other enterprise-wide data.

In an organizational structure based on the development-team principle, the development functions are segmented and performed concurrently by different teams (see Figure C.III.01,c). A coordination level is established to coordinate the development teams; it monitors the entire product development order network and maintains the global data. The subnetwork for each development team's segment is managed by a development leitstand. Hybrid workstations can exist within the team at

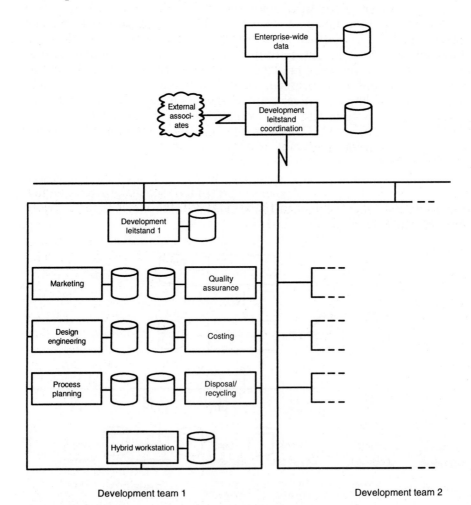

Fig. C.III.01,c: Network topology for development teams

which several functions in the development process can be performed, and, on the other hand, specialized workstations can be set up for design engineering, marketing, etc. Thus, specialized information can be used and functions can be integrated directly at the workstation. In each case, the system ensures that each workstation has access to the results of the work at the other workstations. Only the specific data segment for the design room assigned to a given workstation is made available in workstation-oriented systems.

The concept developed for simultaneous product development involving a universal development workstation can be supported by a blackboard architecture, if it is simultaneously coordinated on the design specification level (see *Ochs, Methoden zur Verkürzung der Produktentstehungszeit 1992, p. 88*). The job results of the individual developers are posted to the blackboard, which corresponds to the coordination level, thus informing it of the current status of the overall project. With each new piece of information that the blackboard receives, it can decide whether another subsystem has to be accessed in order to respond to the completed activity or to another event from a subprocess.

C.III.3 Design Specification for Product Development: The Data View

The design specification for data involves transforming the product model into the relational model and specifying standards for product data exchange.

The process of transforming the product model, which has been defined with the support of the ER model approach, into the relational model conforms to the usual rules. Figure C.III.02 shows the relations for a simple example, a segment from a 2-D surface model. In the example, the knowledge is employed that an edge is delimited by exactly two end points, which are included in the relation R. EDGE by way of the two attributes Point1 and Point2. At the same time, it uses the information that an edge can belong to only one surface; thus, the surface number is included in the relation R. EDGE as an attribute, which creates the relationship between edge and surface. Thus, in contrast to the general formulation as previously represented in the form of an ER model, the relationship types between EDGE and SURFACE and between EDGE and POINT are eliminated.

Similar considerations for applying additional information can be used for specific types of solids, such as cubes, etc. Thus, for example, the BREP model for representing a cube uses the information that an edge delimits two surfaces; consequently the two attributes for edge identification can be assigned to the surfaces, and the relationship type between EDGE and SURFACE can be eliminated.

Example: Representation of a surface using edges and points
(a segment from a 2-D surface model)

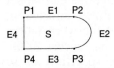

R. SURFACE	SURFACE NUMBER	Description		
	S	Board		

R.POINT	POINT NUMBER	Type	Coordinates X	Y
	P1	End point	0	2
	P2	End point	3	2
	P3	End point	3	0
	P4	End point	0	0

R.EDGE	EDGE NUMBER	Type	Surface
	E1	Line	S
	E2	Arc	S
	E3	Line	S
	E4	Line	S

Fig. C.III.02: Representation of a surface by edges and points in the surface model

Despite these consideration, which do in fact lead to a simplified representation, the relational model for depicting geometric information should be viewed critically. If, for example, the relations of the cube shown in Figure C.III.03 are queried as follows: "Search all cubes that contain one corner located at the source coordinate," this leads to the complex SQL query shown in Figure C.III.03 (see *Lockemann, Weiterentwicklung relationaler Datenbanken 1992, pp. 3-4*).

Even the query "search all topological information for the cube with the identification number 'Q1'" results in significant query effort.

The reason why the query process is so complex lies in the fact that the relational model splits up information about an object into simpler (flat) tables. Then, if the system again searches for the entire object, it has to recombine all the parts from the individual tables using a complicated query logic. Consequently, it is viewed critically as a means of representing product information (see *Dittrich, Nachrelationale Datenbanktechnologie 1990; Härder, Grenzen und Erweiterungsmöglichkeiten relationaler Datenbanksysteme 1989*).

In contrast to other applications, e.g., traditional PPC applications, CAD applications are characterized by the following special aspects:

-     Although the data structures are highly complex, only a few similar data objects occur. In classical PPC applications, on the

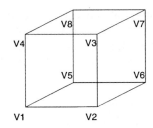

Boundary representation
model (BREP) of a cube

CUBE (cube_Id, weight, material)
SURFACE (surface_Id, cubes_Id, unevenness, light reflectance)   Relational model of
EDGE (edge_Id, surface1, surface2, point1, point2)   a cube
POINT (point_Id, x_coord, y_coord, z_coord)

```
select cube_Id
from   SURFACE
where surface_Id in
   (select  Surface1
    from    EDGE
    where  POINT1 in
       (select   point_Id
        from     POINT
        where   x_coord=0 and  y_coord=0and   z_coord=0)
   or       point2 in
       (select   point_Id
        from     POINT
        where   x_coord=0 and  y_coord=0and   z_coord=0)
   union
   (select  surface2
    from    EDGE
    where  point1 in
       (select   point_Id
        from     POINT
        where   x_coord=0 and  y_coord=0and   z_coord=0)
   or       point2 in
       (select   point_Id
        from     POINT
        where   x_coord=0 and  y_coord=0and   z_coord=0))
```

```
select cube-Id, surface_Id,
       edge_Id, point_Id
from   SURFACE, EDGE, POINT
where cube_Id='Q1´
and    surface_Id=surface1
or     surface_Id=surface2
and    point_Id=point1
or     point_Id=point2
```

Search all cubes that contain one corner located at the
source coordinate

Search all topological
information for the
cube "C1"

Fig. C.III.03: Transition of the BREP model of a cube into the relational model using SQL
queries

other hand, the data structures are simpler, but they necessitate management of numerous identical entities.

-   When drawings are created, different draft versions are produced that must be managed to reflect their historical generation. In classical PPC applications, on the other hand, chronological tracking of the change history of databases is unimportant.

-   The transactions within a design process can involve exceptionally long time frames (e.g., a drawing can take several days to draft). In PPC systems, on the other hand, a transaction that transfers a database from one consistent state to another takes only a matter of seconds.

- When geometric data are created, a variety of complicated consistency conditions, which are derived from design procedures and by maintaining a sequence of processing procedures, have to be taken into account. In contrast, the consistency conditions in PPC systems are considerably simpler.

There are two options for taking the special aspects of CAD more strongly into account—either standard data models can be expanded or new data models can be developed. The first option offers the advantage of facilitating integration with existing database applications. However, there are also disadvantages that have to be considered as well (e.g., performance). The specific problems can be taken into account more adequately in developing dedicated data models and new database systems that build on them. However, this also leads to the use of dedicated database systems that are very difficult to link with existing applications.

A solution to this problem (see *Fischer, Datenbank-Management in CAD/CAM Systemen, n.d.; Dittrich, Datenbankunterstützung für den ingenieurwissenschaftlichen Entwurf 1985*) can be provided by defining a common database core that can be expanded for the various applications by using software modules. In concrete terms, this means that in a relational database system for managing CAD data, special functions are provided for expanding features that ensure data integrity as well as for providing special treatment for transactions in CAD applications.

The object-oriented data model (OODM) has been cited as being suitable for managing geometric data (see *Dittrich, Nachrelationale Datenbanktechnologie 1990, p. 4*). An object-oriented data model uses precisely one data model structure to represent a real-world object, i.e., it does not break it down into several data model structures (relations) as is the case with the relational model. This procedure produces complex objects that can be broken down into subobjects. Objects are also allowed to overlap, which is shown schematically in Figure C.III.04 using the ER model approach. Objects can also be assigned behavioral properties, which are frequently defined in an object-oriented programming language. This results in interrelationships to object-oriented programming. Object-oriented database systems, which are based on the principle of object-oriented data modeling, are currently available as initial approaches. The Pro Engineer system is an example of an object-oriented CAD system (see *Parametric Technologies Cooperation, Pro Engineer 1989*).

An approach that does not quite satisfy all demands of object-oriented data modeling involves easing the restrictions of the relational model and using so-called NF^2 models to represent geometries. In an NF^2 data model, relations can be nested within one another. The data definition for this type of approach is based on the AIM-P prototype developed at the IBM Science Center in Heidelberg (see *Lockemann, Weiterentwicklung relationaler Datenbanken 1991, p. 10*), as shown in Figure C.III.05. The left side of the figure shows the definition of the database scheme; the right side shows the two queries cited above relating to cubes in which one corner is located at the source coordinate and to the search for all

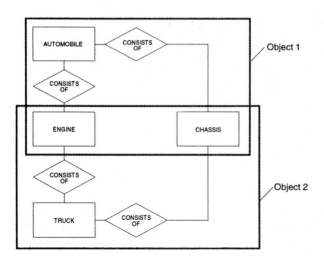

Fig. C.III.04: Object-oriented data model

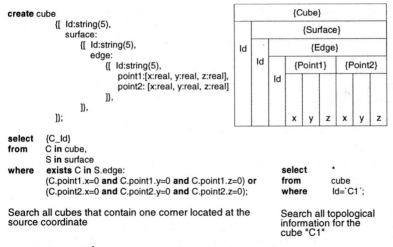

```
create cube
         {[ Id:string(5),
            surface:
                {[ Id:string(5),
                   edge:
                       {[ Id:string(5),
                          point1:[x:real, y:real, z:real],
                          point2: [x:real, y:real, z:real]
                          ]},
                   ]},
            ]};
```

```
select   {C_Id}
from     C in cube,
         S in surface
where    exists C in S.edge:
         (C.point1.x=0 and C.point1.y=0 and C.point1.z=0) or
         (C.point2.x=0 and C.point2.y=0 and C.point2.z=0);
```

```
select    *
from      cube
where     Id=`C1´;
```

Search all cubes that contain one corner located at the source coordinate

Search all topological information for the cube "C1"

Fig. C.III.05: NF^2 representation of a cube using queries

topological information relating to a given cube. The difference in the simplicity of the query structure as compared to the one shown in Figure C.III.03 is apparent.

In addition to using data models on the level of the design specification to adequately represent product models, the exchange of data between different CAD systems also constitutes a significant problem.

Conversion of a drawing from CAD system A into the standard format is handled by a preprocessor residing in the source system; the subsequent conversion from the standard format into the drawing format of the target CAD system is handled by a postprocessor (see Figure C.III.06).

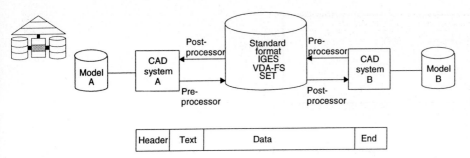

Fig. C.III.06: CAD interfaces

In order for two CAD systems to communicate with one another, the corresponding post- and preprocessors must be provided for each direction. A precise record architecture must be agreed on for this purpose. In the case of the IGES system, for example, this record consists of 80 ASCII characters. Each record consists of: Start, Global Directory Entry, Parameter Data and Terminate. IGES was initially developed for two-dimensional data models and later expanded to include three-dimensional wire-frame models. It is impossible to exchange CSG models.

While the first standards for CAD data exchange concentrated primarily on DP-oriented agreements relating to the file and transfer architectures, STEP provides an approach that encompasses all software development phases and all aspects of product description.

Figure C.III.07 shows an example of the three descriptive levels (from *Grabowski et al., STEP 1989, p. 71*).

STEP not only serves as a data exchange **between** different CAD systems, it also supports data interchange with CAM, CAQ and PPC systems.

The product data model developed on the requirements level is transformed into the design specification using mapping rules (the logical layer in Figure C.III.07). This reference model can be used directly for software development by adapting it to different implementation requirements.

A STEP-specific format is defined during the implementation phase. Due to the object-oriented influences, functions, e.g., integrity rules, can also be defined using the EXPRESS specification language.

In addition to application-independent definitions, application-oriented partial models also exist, e.g., for shipbuilding, mechanical engineering, construction and electronics. The success of STEP will depend to a large degree on the extent to which application software developers embrace this standard.

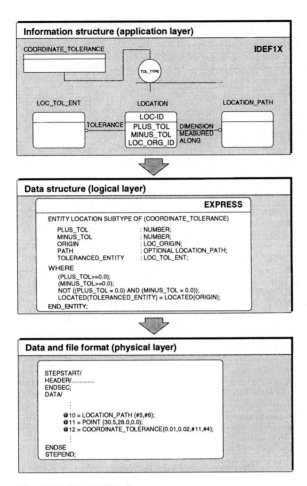

Fig. C.III.07: STEP's layer concept

C.III.4 Design Specification for Product Development: The Control View

The design specification for the control view must satisfy the requirements of a distributed system architecture. With the definition of design rooms and design transactions, the requirements definition provides a solid foundation for the DP-oriented transformation into distributed system constructs. Since product data from several views are managed, it will initially be impossible to maintain them under a unified database system. Instead, they will have to be managed in segments by several database systems. A user transaction, however, can use data from several of these databases, so that transactions that conform to the local security concepts can run on the network nodes. In order to ensure global data integrity, database systems are used that support the two-phase commit protocol (see *Date, An Introduction to Database Systems 1990; Reuter, Maßnahmen zur Wahrung von Sicherheits- und Integritätsbedingungen 1987*).

The two-phase commit protocol is always important in situations where a transaction interacts with several database servers, each of which manages a specific segment of a total database.

The two-phase commit protocol ensures the global integrity of distributed systems. A global transaction must issue a single, system-wide COMMIT (or ROLLBACK) command. This function is handled by the coordinator node, which ensures that all of the database systems involved in the transaction execute the commit (or rollback) in the same manner.

A two-phase commit protocol functions as follows (see Figure C.III.08, from *Reuter, Verteilte Datenbanksysteme 1988*):

The coordinator node sends a "prepare to commit" message to all affected systems and activates a time-out mechanism. Each database system involved then makes its commit decision. Subsequently, the feedback from the commit result is sent to the coordinator node. As soon as the coordinator has received all feedbacks, the second phase begins. If all "commits" are confirmed, a global commit decision occurs; if at least one participant has sent a negative feedback or has not answered within the time-out specification, the decision is "ROLLBACK." The coordinator node enters its decision into its log file and informs all affected

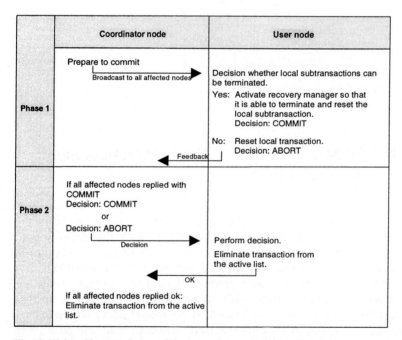

Fig. C.III.08: Characteristics of the two-phase commit protocol

participants of its decision. The participants must perform the commit or rollback as instructed, locally and then notify the coordinator that the instruction has been executed.

C.IV Implementation Description for Product Development

Several implementation-related problems have already been addressed within the context of the design specification. They will not be discussed in any further detail.

Part D: Information and Coordination Processes

Concurrent information and coordination processes are essential for gearing the operative processes of logistics and product development to the overall objectives of the enterprise. In order to provide insight into the economic success of the enterprise, the end results from the operative applications are measured in monetary units. The information systems for financial accounting and for cost and income accounting provide differentiated analytical concepts for these values, upon which Controlling can then build.

Information Management provides the resources for information systems, and itself possesses coordination functions for the operative systems. The coordination functions involve specifying the degree of integration of the application systems and utilizing synergy effects between decentralized information systems. To do this, it is necessary to develop a consistent strategy for establishing fundamental information processing "cornerstones"; in actual practice, this strategy is also termed the "master plan" (see *Waidelich, Informationsmanagement in der Automobilindustrie 1993*).

D.I Accounting (Value-Oriented Information and Coordination Processes)

D.I.1 Overview: Accounting

The logistics and product development processes are located on the operative level of the pyramid diagram shown in Figure A.I.01. They are dominated by quantitative variables such as quantities, times and technical descriptions. The business transactions handled in them, however, contain a value component as well, which is represented by concepts such as "prices," "costs," "expenses," "income," etc. Business administration accounting and analysis systems document, organize and consolidate this value-oriented information and provide it for corporate control and external auditing. This process is shown in Figure A.I.01 by the horizontal arrow.

Business administration literature typically treats these value-oriented systems under the concept of "accounting," which is subdivided into financial accounting, cost and income accounting, Controlling and decision support. However, it is becoming increasingly difficult to make a clear distinction between these individual areas. For example, the financial accounting system is linked with the cost and income accounting system via an integrated operation processing concept. Planning considerations are addressed in both financial accounting, in the form of forecast financial statements, as well as in cost and income accounting, in the form of cost forecasts, and are thus not solely limited to concerns of Controlling and corporate planning. For didactic purposes, however, the following discussions will retain the three-tier structure despite these overlaps. Moreover, the structure also largely corresponds to the data flow, as it can be derived from an operative process.

Financial accounting systematically records all business transactions that effect a change in an enterprise's assets or capital. Data from the financial accounting system can be used to provide insight into a company's assets and liabilities at any given time. Consequently, outside sources of capital and tax authorities are information recipients as well; this is why financial accounting is also termed "external accounting." In contrast, the function of cost and income accounting involves supplying an enterprise's decision-makers with value-oriented decision-support documents for Controlling and corporate planning. Appropriately, this aspect of the accounting department is termed "internal accounting."

The "document" serves as the basis for the value-related documentation. A document portrays a business transaction in such a way that a third party can use the information in the document to reconstruct and understand the transaction at any time. Documents must be entered into the system in a thorough, systematic and up-to-date manner.

The value-oriented links between operative processes have already been discussed in the various sections concerning the individual processes. For example, the postings for the accompanying accounts payable accounting process were illustrated in the discussion of the inbound logistics process; those for accounts receivable accounting in the case of outbound logistics; and the incorporation of human resource accounting in the case of human resource logistics. Documents such as purchase orders, receiving slips, invoices, etc., were treated as the sources of data for the posting operations. The various applications result in many different kinds of documents. In order to standardize these documents within the financial accounting system, all these document types refer back to the general term "document." A "document" can have a schematic structure—e.g., the document header and document items—in which format the individual documents are transferred. However, this means that the business transactions have to be maintained redundantly, i.e., in the documents that represent them on the operative level and subsequently in the standardized form of the document that represents the process. This issue, which is particularly relevant in terms of data representation, will be discussed in detail in the development of the data structures for financial accounting.

Figure D.I.01 shows the rough information flow for the value-oriented systems in the form of a process chain diagram.

Financial accounting is divided into the general ledger accounting system, from which the annual financial statements (balance sheet and income statement) are generated, and subsidiary accounting systems, which are used for certain quantity-intensive business processes or for those that are combined with special clerical activities. However, the data in the subsidiary accounting systems are reconciled with the data in the general ledger accounting system in order to keep them current. Typical subsidiary accounting systems include accounts payable accounting, accounts receivable accounting, inventory accounting, human resource accounting and fixed asset accounting. The subsidiary accounting systems exhibit a very close relationship to their corresponding operative processes.

Internal accounting uses the data from the cost and income accounting system to build on the data from financial accounting. However, periodic accruals and deferrals are made here, as are content-related transformations and supplements that are necessary for cost accounting. At the same time, income accounting uses quantity-related data from Production and Sales.

Within the framework of cost center accounting, cost categories are assigned to organizational units called "cost centers." Cost center accounting produces costing rates for the output of the cost centers. These are entered in object analysis sheets and provided to the cost objective accounting system. Period costing determines the income or loss of the individual cost objectives (e.g., products), while product costing serves, for example, to calculate the lowest limit for prices.

The data from subsidiary accounting systems and from cost and income accounting are essential for effective value-oriented decision and control systems. Both payment dates as well as forecasts based on order data with respect to anticipated receipts and disbursements provide the basis for cash management and medium-term financial planning. Cost and income accounting is essential for effective Controlling of the individual business processes as well as on an enterprise-wide level. Executive information systems (EIS) provide support for the information needs of corporate management in the form of comprehensive consolidation and analysis options from the value-oriented databases.

The process chain diagram shown in Figure D.I.01 uses accounting terminology (accounts, cost categories, cost centers, etc.) to illustrate the interaction of the value-oriented data both with one another as well as with upstream operative systems, which are dominated by terms such as "orders," "bills of materials," etc.

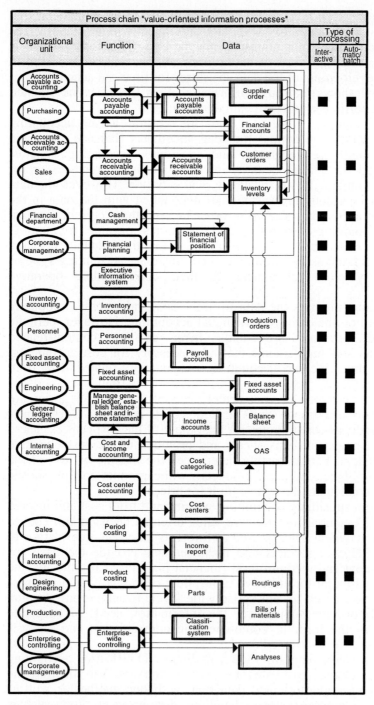

Fig. D.I.01: Process chain diagram „value-oriented information processes"

Both processing modes, i.e., batch and interactive, are indicated for all functions. This means that while the desire is for as much automation as possible in processing mass operations, individual cases resulting from particularly high value or a lack of information can be processed interactively by the user.

Although the long tradition and organizational independence of the accounting system has led to its own terminology, which has only encouraged redundant data organization, the following discussion will

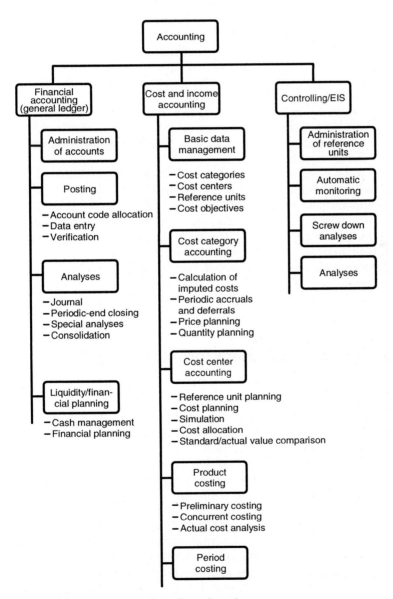

Fig. D.I.02: Function tree for value-oriented processes

pursue a concept of integrating functions and data that involves a low level of redundancy.

Modern DP systems (e.g., the SAP RF (R/2) and FI (R/3) systems) also pursue this objective. Business administration textbooks, however, are still frequently based on traditional descriptions of an organizational structure that has evolved from paper-based organizational concepts, e.g., discussions frequently center on general and subsidiary **ledgers** or on day, petty cash and bank **books** (see *Heinen/Kupsch, Rechnungslegung 1991, p. 1349*).

The organizational responsibilities for the subsidiary accounting systems are either located in specially established departments or have already migrated to integrated processing in the operative systems. Thus, the process chain diagrams contain both the special organizational units for subsidiary accounting as well as the organizational units of the functions responsible for operative processing.

Thus, a general trend exists toward tightly linking cost and income accounting with the operative systems, as well, e.g., Sales is the "user" of period costing (income accounting) or Design Engineering or Production are "users" of product costing.

As a result, it is generally difficult to allocate the functions of an integrated accounting system to a dedicated organizational unit.

As an organizational unit, Accounting is increasingly assuming responsibility for defining methods and developing general accounting principles. More and more, however, the users of the accounting system are the employees involved in the operative processes.

Figure D.I.02 provides an overview of the functions involved in the value-oriented processes.

D.I.2 Requirements Definitions for Accounting

The full utilization of data integration leads to a shift in data entry functions from the organizational department "Accounting" to the "upstream" departments: The data entered during operative processing of a business transaction are automatically transferred to the financial accounting and internal accounting systems. If there is a high degree of integration between logistics and the accounting system, this process can be so comprehensive that only <u>one</u> common document is maintained, which means that the data from a business transaction only have to be stored once. If, however, the accounting system requires its own document, it should be used for both internal <u>and</u> external accounting, and the data should be transferred largely automatically from logistics.

While the organizational procedure of financial accounting has changed drastically owing to the use of electronic data processing, its high degree of standardization has left little latitude for revising its content. Although this latitude does exist in the case of cost accounting, since it can orient itself more toward the business-related objectives inherent in a decision support tool; the existing "classical" procedures, i.e., those oriented toward manual processes, have been retained here as well (for more on this criticism, see *Mertens/Hansen/Rackelmann, Selektionsentscheidungen im Rechnungswesen 1977, p. 77*). In the meantime, however, extensions have become evident, e.g., in the development of activity-based costing and in the accounting information systems. The use of databases that allow unconsolidated cost information to be managed is opening up new approaches that could resolve considerable disputes concerning business administration methods. This objective can be achieved by developing a "basic accounting" system, i.e., a database for cost accounting that is based on the various periodic routine analyses and special ad hoc calculations (see *Sinzig, Rechnungswesen 1989*).

Financial accounting is primarily concerned with recording business transactions between the enterprise and the outside world, i.e., supply, sales and capital markets as well as government. Cost accounting, on the other hand, primarily deals with business transactions that occur in connection with the operational combination process within the enterprise. Despite this difference, interrelationships exist between both systems, primarily as a result of the fact that certain business transactions (e.g., payroll) have to be handled as expenses in financial accounting and as costs in cost accounting. Moreover, financial accounting uses results from the analyses performed by cost accounting, e.g., in valuing semi-finished products.

Common data usage as well as the mutual further use of subresults thus form the umbrella over the various accounting systems. This situation is specifically taken into account in the discussion of requirements definitions.

D.I.2.1 Financial Accounting

The function of Financial Accounting is to represent the relationships between the enterprise and the outside world and to record all business transactions that change the company's assets.

Due to the large number of business transactions to be processed and because their structure is specified by the legal stipulations of the commercial and tax codes, financial accounting has traditionally been an intensive field of application for electronic data processing.

D.I.2.1.1 Basic Data Management

The structure of financial accounting, as specified by the concepts of account and posting record, was embraced early on and used in demonstrations by early supporters of data-oriented design procedures (see *Ortner/Wedekind, Datenbank für die Kostenrechnung 1977*).

W. E. McCarthy (see *McCarthy, Accounting Models 1979*) developed a detailed ER model approach for the American environment.

In the discussion of the data structure, the master accounts data and their relationships will first be portrayed, with the transaction data for posting procedures then being developed.

D.I.2.1.1.1 Accounts

Figure D.I.03 focuses on the entity type ACCOUNT with the key attribute ACNO and the major descriptive attributes "name," "balance forward," "total debits," "total credits," "period balance" and "total balance." Except for the balance forward, the transaction values can be maintained in a defined period grid (e.g., over 16 periods) (see Figure D.I.04 for the "raw materials consumption" account from *SAP, Das Finanzwesen der SAP 1992, pp. 3-12*).

The accounts are classified in a chart of accounts that is structured on the basis of business-related criteria. For example, the Standard Chart of Accounts for Industrial Enterprises (IKR), published in 1971 by the Business Administration Committee of the Federation of German Industries (BDI), conforms to the financial statement classification principle, in that account categories 0 through 4 record the balance sheet and account categories 5 though 7 the income statement. Accounts for cost and income accounting are recorded only in category 9.

A tighter integration between financial accounting and cost and income accounting is provided by the Joint Standard Accounting System (GKR), which was also developed by the BDI (see Figure D.I.05, from *Heinen/Kupsch, Rechnungslegung 1991, p. 1351*). This system provides accounts for cost and income accounting in categories 4 through 8 and also serves as the basis for the standard chart of accounts provided in the FI system from SAP (see *SAP, Das Finanzwesen der SAP 1992, pp. 2-15*). Non-operating expenses and closing accounts are irrelevant for cost and income accounting; accounts for imputed cost categories are also defined in the financial accounting system.

The standard chart of accounts provides a transcompany organizational structure for the entire accounting system. Despite this, it can be modified for the specific needs of individual industries. The number of charts of accounts defined for an enterprise should be kept as low as possible, however, which means that they should be defined on the highest corporate level. In Figure D.I.03, the highest organizational unit is the "client," which is a quasi-representation of the corporate group level, which is superordinate to the separate legal entities that constitute the

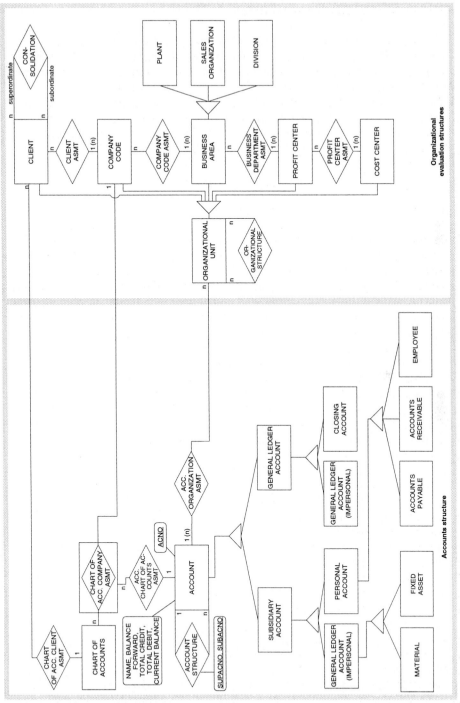

Fig. D.I.03: Account structures and organizational evaluation structures

subsidiaries and affiliates, which have their own discrete accounting systems (company codes).

Several charts of accounts can be defined for a corporate group, which are then assigned to the subsidiary level (company codes). The standard charts of accounts provide for up to 10 account groups for each account category and up to 10 account types for each account group.

The balance of each subordinate account is transferred to the respective superordinate account, resulting in ongoing consolidation. If different closing accounts are formed, e.g., in accordance with commercial and tax code requirements, an account can go into several superordinate accounts. The relationship type ACCOUNT STRUCTURE in Figure D.I.03 thus provides for an n:m cardinality within the entity type ACCOUNT. The clearing relationships are identified by the superordinate and subordinate account numbers (SUPACNO, SUBACNO).

Financial accounting distinguishes between the general ledger accounting system and subsidiary accounting systems. The general ledger accounting system is employed for drawing up the financial statements, while subsidiary accounting systems can also handle operative clerical functions. In subsidiary accounting systems, the individual business transactions are entered, processed and stored in detail. In the general ledger accounting system, the monthly debits and credits are maintained only for the entire account group. For example, the subsidiary accounting

---

⊐ Account balance display: "raw materials consumption": others xx: local currency(1) K1 l h ▲ ▼

Account Goto Options Environment System ?

Account 400 000 Comp. code 0001 Year 1992		Business	* Currency *	Display in US $
Period	Debit	Credit	area	Balance	Account balance
Forward					0.00
1	16,234.50	0.00		16,234.50	16,234.50
2	3,307.89	0.00		3,307.89	19,542.39
4	447,259.59	16,641.35		430,618.24	1,664,452.62
5	340,931.92	15,038.11		325,893.81	1,990,346.43
6	1,050,823.69	150,133.68		900,690.01	2,891,036.44
7	5,031.58	2,081.14		2,950.44	2,893,986.88
8	0.00	0.00		0.00	2,893,986.88
⋮	⋮	⋮		⋮	⋮
⋮	⋮	⋮		⋮	⋮
ooo	5,836,263.66	2,942,276.78		2,893,986.88	2,893,986.88

OK

| F3=Return | F2=Items | F16=Other currency... | F10=Other business area... | ... |

Fig. D.I.04: Account "raw materials consumption" with a 16-period grid of the monthly debits and credits

system for accounts receivable maintains the individual accounts receivable for the customers, as opposed to the general account "accounts receivable" in the general ledger accounting system. By updating the monthly debits and credits in the general ledger accounting system in parallel with the posting in the subsidiary accounting systems, it is possible to ensure the currency and constant reconcilability of the general ledger and subsidiary accounting systems.

The general ledger accounting system also maintains the accounts that are not included in the subsidiary accounting systems on the business transaction level and provides the final accounts. Many business transactions affect both subsidiary accounting accounts as well as general ledger accounts, e.g., payment of an account receivable (bank account and value-added tax in general ledger accounting, account receivable account in subsidiary accounting). The allocation of accounts on the basis of the classification principles of general ledger and subsidiary accounting is represented in Figure D.I.03 by "is-a" relationships. This allocation represents a classification system that parallels the concept of a standard chart of accounts.

An additional structural principle of accounting involves the establishment of accounting-oriented organizational units, as shown on the right side of Figure D.I.03. Since all terms are specializations of the general term "organizational unit," specialized key identifiers are not indicated.

In the SAP FI system, the highest level, the client, is the user of the standard software system, for whom all central processing rules are defined. This could be a corporate group, for example. (see *SAP, Das Finanzwesen der SAP 1992, pp. 1 ff.*) It is possible for several clients that were defined from a technical perspective to be consolidated into a superordinate client (from a business administration standpoint). This is expressed by the relationship type CONSOLIDATION.

A company code represents a separate legal entity that produces its own financial statements (a company).

From the perspective of the Controlling and reporting systems, a company can be subdivided into additional organizational units such as divisions, profit centers and cost centers.

An account can relate to a specific organizational unit, e.g., accounts receivable can be maintained for each sales organization or materials accounts for each plant.

In Figure D.I.03, this situation is reflected by the assignment relationship between ACCOUNT and the generalized term ORGANIZATIONAL UNIT. In a hierarchical organizational structure, assignment of the account to the lowest possible organizational unit also specifies the assignments to the superordinate units, so that, for example, given a 1:n relationship between COMPANY CODE and PLANT, the company code is specified with the plant identifier. The assignments between organizational units become problematic with an n:m relationship, e.g., if a plant maintains materials for different companies. In this case, relationships must be created to both organizational units. In

	Category 0	Category 1	Category 2	Category 3	Category 4	Category 5	Category 6	Category 7	Category 8	Category 9
		Accounting code of annual closing of accounts			Accounting code of cost and income accounting					Accounting code of annual closing
External accounting (chart of accounts)	Fixed asset and long-term capital	Capital, current assets, short-term payables	Non-operating costs and income	Raw materials, operating supplies, purchasing	Cost category	Clearing accounts	Cost center accounting	Cost objectives	Income accounts	Closing accounts
Internal accounting (controlling)	Fixed asset and long-term capital	Capital, current assets, short-term payables	Non-operating costs and income	Materials, inventory levels	Primary cost categories	Secondary cost categories	Order cost categories	Inventory of semi-finished and end products	Income/ changes in stock/ capitalized services	Closing of accounts
	Project costs accounting/ order costing (capital investment)				Cost center accounting				Financial statement	
					Order and product costing					

Joint standard accounting system

Standard chart of accounts of the FI system of SAP

Fig. D.I.05: Joint standard accounting system of BDI and standard chart of accounts of the SAP FI system

Figure D.I.03, the variable formulations of the "many-to-many" relationship are shown in parentheses.

In actual practice, the depiction of the organizational model for an enterprise poses immense problems if it contains "many-to-many" relationships but the standard software package permits only 1:n relationships.

Likewise, inter-divisional or inter-company-code business transactions (central payment clearing procedures, deliveries between companies within a corporate group) are difficult to handle, as well.

D.I.2.1.1.2 Entries and Documents

After the account, the posting record constitutes the second fundamental concept in financial accounting. It represents a business transaction and assigns it to an account in the financial accounting system.

In the operative systems for logistics, business transactions are entered via receiving slips, invoices, etc. However, these documents are geared toward the respective applications and therefore possess different structures. In the case of a generalized view, however, they can be reduced to a uniform structure. Essentially, they consist of header information, which describes the business transaction, and items, in which the reference objects involved (materials, invoice items) are recorded. Thus, Figure D.I.06 illustrates the generalization of the individual document types into ORIGINAL DOCUMENT and ORIGINAL DOCUMENT ITEM. This conceptual unification is essential for transforming the original documents into a DOCUMENT from the perspective of accounting. The "document" serves as a kind of mask that is overlaid on the various original documents and filters out the information that is relevant for accounting. The option of generalizing the original documents enables the data to be transferred to the DOCUMENT and DOCUMENT ITEM grid. In order to nevertheless be able to include the individual items of information that exist for each type of business transaction without disturbing the general structure of header and item information, different document types are introduced in the form of the entity type DOCUMENT TYPE. It is obvious not to wait until the context of the accounting system to generalize the documents in order to characterize business transactions, but rather to do so on the original document level, so that each business transaction can be identified in the same document formula. In Figure D.I.06, this need is indicated by the heavy border around the data structure to be unified.

Currently, however, modern DP systems only automatically fill in the documents using data from the logistics systems, but maintain the separate data structures. However, both internal and external accounting build upon this central document management system (see Figure D.I.07), while logistics (still) possesses its own database.

However, unified management of business transactions between logistics and accounting necessitates a high demand for system integration that is similar to the concept of unified product data management.

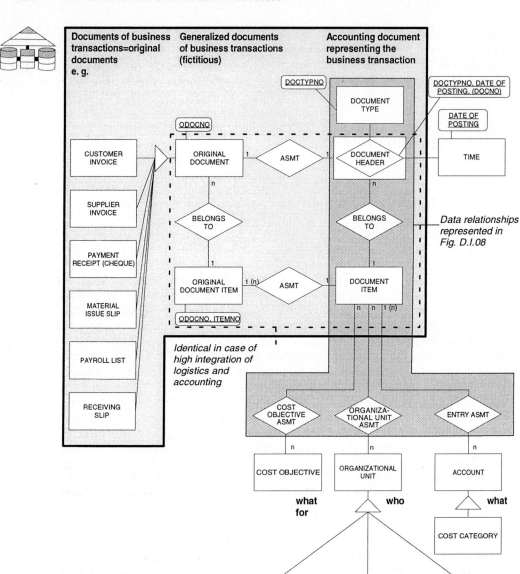

Simplified representation for logistics:

Fig. D.I.06: Document data structure for accounting

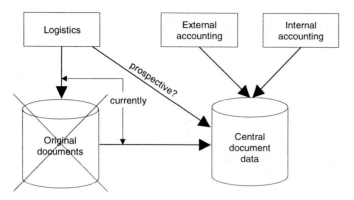

Fig. D.I.07: Document accesses

Integrated systems have already reached the point where a change in data relating to a business transaction in logistics also results in a change in the document file in the accounting system, thus synchronizing the data.

Figure D.I.08 shows a basic document structure, as is also reflected by the data structure. The document header is identified by the information relating to the document type and date. In accordance with generally accepted accounting principles, however, the documents are numbered sequentially. The document items are then identified by an additional item number. A typical attribute of the document header is the company code (assuming that the transaction is processed within the company code).

The document items provide the individual amounts, which in the example can be taken from the original supplier invoice document.

The entries are posted by assigning the document line items to the accounts in the financial accounting system. At the same time, the organizational unit (a department in this example) and the cost center (FF1OOO) are assigned.

In the data structure shown in Figure D.I.06, this interrelationship is created by assignment relationships. The representation of the entry as an assignment relationship between account and document item in parallel to the assignments of the internal accounting system illustrates the neutral significance of the document data. The example shown in Figure D.I.08 is presented in expanded form in Figure D.I.09 using screens from the FI system (see *SAP, Das Finanzwesen der SAP 1992, pp. 3-16*). The lower screen provides a detailed description of a document item, while the upper screen displays consolidated information. The individual entries, including the descriptive data in the document header record, can be accessed from each associated account. Thus, all closed accounts, including those closed in the past, can be accessed at any time and in any desired form, and they represent purely analytical functions.

Document journals can also be included among these analyses and can be generated for any desired time frame, even retrogradely, on the basis of the unconsolidated entries.

Document header

Document type: Supplier invoice for consumable material
Document number: 1 400 000 176   Date: 4/15/92
Company code: 1

Document items

Item	Business area	Account no.	Cost center	Name	US $
1	-	850,000	-	MODPROD Ltd.	115.00
2	1	400,000	FF1000	Raw material consumption	100.00
3	-	154,000	-	VAT	15.00

Assignments of financial accounting

Fig. D.I.08: Basic document structure

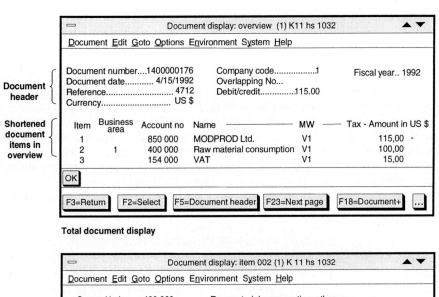

Document header

Document number....1400000176   Company code.................1   Fiscal year.. 1992
Document date............ 4/15/1992   Overlapping No...
Reference............................ 4712   Debit/credit...............115.00
Currency.............................. US $

Shortened document items in overview

Item	Business area	Account no	Name	MW	Tax - Amount in US $
1		850 000	MODPROD Ltd.	V1	115,00 -
2	1	400 000	Raw material consumption	V1	100,00
3		154 000	VAT	V1	15,00

OK

F3=Return   F2=Select   F5=Document header   F23=Next page   F18=Document+   ...

Total document display

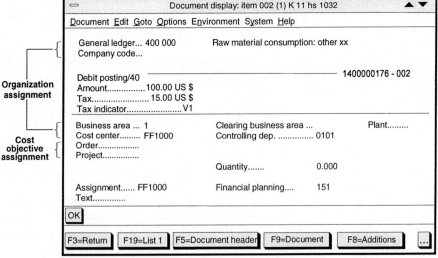

Document display: item 002 (1) K 11 hs 1032

Document Edit Goto Options Environment System Help

Organization assignment

General ledger... 400 000   Raw material consumption: other xx
Company code...

Debit posting/40 ——————————————————— 1400000176 - 002
Amount................100.00 US $
Tax........................ 15.00 US $
Tax indicator...................... V1

Cost objective assignment

Business area ... 1   Clearing business area ...   Plant.........
Cost center......... FF1000   Controlling dep. 0101
Order.................
Project...............

Quantity.......   0.000

Assignment...... FF1000   Financial planning....   151
Text.............

OK

F3=Return   F19=List 1   F5=Document header   F9=Document   F8=Additions   ...

Document item display

Fig. D.I.09: Document representation of the SAP FI system (modified by the author)

Figure D.I.09 illustrates the relationships to the data structure in Figure D.I.06. They correspond to the darkly shaded area of Figure D.I.06.

Multiple views, in a manner of speaking, are geared toward the document via the assignment relationships. The "general ledger" principle in the U.S. accounting system conforms to a similar concept.

The relationships to accounting have already been demonstrated in the discussion of logistics processes; however, that discussion did not introduce separate documents for accounting, in order to avoid getting too far ahead of the discussion. Instead, the entries were derived directly from the lines of the "original document items" in that discussion. This "abbreviation" of the interrelationship is shown in the lower portion of Figure D.I.06. It more or less corresponds to the case described above, where a uniform document management system exists between logistics and Accounting.

D.I.2.1.2 Posting Procedures

An important function of general ledger accounting involves preparing final statements of account in the form of balance sheets and income statements. To do this, numerous regulations have to be taken into consideration in valuing fixed and current assets. These procedures are the central focus of business administration research and theory as it relates to external accounting, while the problem of organizing the processing procedure for the multitude of business transactions in financial accounting is given less attention and is viewed simply as an introduction to business administration theory.

The general ledger accounting system also serves as the basis for consolidating the financial statements within a corporate group. Here, too, complicated legal and business-related situations have to be taken into account, particularly in cases where foreign companies are being consolidated. However, this discussion will not study these problems in any further depth (see *Küting/Weber, Die Bilanzanalyse 1994*).

The posting procedures for financial accounting can essentially be performed on the basis of the data structure developed thus far. However, it is common practice to split off particularly time-consuming or complicated elements into independent subsidiary accounting systems, to handle the high-volume processes at that level, and to transfer only the consolidated totals into the general ledger accounting system. While, for example, an account is maintained for each employee, customer, material, etc. in the subsidiary accounting system, an account exists only for a **category** (i.e., for accounts receivable, accounts payable, payroll expense, material expense) in the general ledger accounting system.

At the same time, individual document types can be defined if subsidiary accounting systems are established, and these document types can go into more detail on the types of business transactions involved. This is expressed in Figure D.I.06 by the entity type DOCUMENT TYPE.

The basic structures of the document header and document item remain unaffected by this classification system.

Due to the high volumes involved, the accounts payable and accounts receivable accounting systems, in particular in the form of "ledgerless accounting," are split off and termed "sub-ledger accounting systems." At the same time, in addition to supplying data to the general ledger accounting system, the sub-ledger accounting systems also handle their own functions such as collections and payment procedures.

Independent business functions are also performed in the other subsidiary accounting systems, in addition to accounting functions in the narrower sense.

The fixed asset accounting system, for example, determines imputed depreciation for cost accounting. Moreover, there are also close links to the maintenance planning and PPC systems.

The payroll accounting system performs payroll accounting as a largely independent function.

The materials accounting system determines value-oriented materials consumption for cost accounting and is closely related to materials planning.

The trend toward shifting data entry functions to upstream departments is continuing (see Figure D.I.10, from *Scheer, EDV-orientierte Betriebswirtschaftslehre 1990, p. 245*). This not only means that data from subsidiary accounting systems are automatically transferred to the general ledger accounting system, but in addition that the subsidiary accounting systems also automatically receive data from the operative processes. Thus, for example, system run times, personnel performance data and materials consumption are all updated by information from the factory data entry system. These data are automatically routed to the fixed asset accounting system, to the gross pay calculation system and—to determine quantity-related consumption—to the materials accounting system. These interfaces to financial accounting have already been suggested in the discussion of operative systems for production, inbound, outbound and human resource logistics.

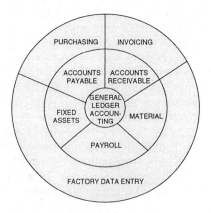

Fig. D.I.10: Financial accounting and upstream departments

Accounts payable accounting has already been addressed in connection with ordering functions, and was illustrated using a typical posting process comprising order procedures, receiving goods and invoices, and payment procedures. The transfer of invoice data to the general ledger and accounts payable accounts was also discussed. This interface will now be discussed in greater detail. The standard posting record for an invoice received in the accounts payable department (without taking into account value-added tax) reads:

Debit receiving, credit accounts payable account

An example has already been shown in Figure D.I.09. The definition of an account payable is similar to that of a supplier. Consequently, both could be maintained in the entity type SUPPLIER. However, an n:m relationship between the entity type ACCOUNTS PAYABLE and the entity type SUPPLIER would also be conceivable if, for example, a supplier has several distribution warehouses with independent accounts or if only one account is maintained for central payment procedures in the case of a corporate group consisting of several companies.

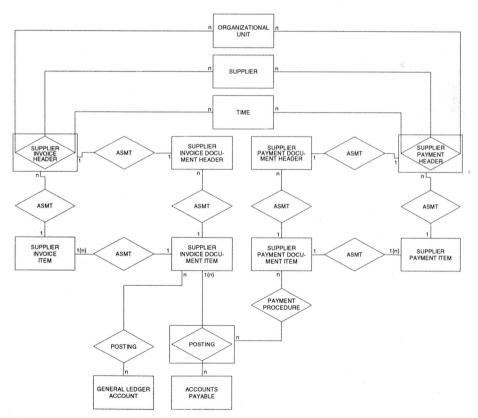

Fig. D.I.11: Data structure for supplier payment procedure

In the discussion of postings in the context of logistics, a simplified approach was chosen that involved deriving the entries directly from the original documents without having to interpose the documents from the financial accounting system. Figure D.I.11 therefore shows the more detailed case in which the original documents "invoice" and "payment" are each assigned document representations in the accounts payable accounting system, and the assignment relationships for payment procedures originate from these document representations. In this case, the payment procedure relates to entry in the account payable account, which performs the assignment of the amount and the accounts payable account number.

The structure of the accounts receivable accounting system mirrors that of the accounts payable system. Upon partial or complete delivery of a customer order, the invoice is written after the packing list is created, with the process referring back to the terms of supply.

The relevant document for accounting is determined on the basis of the original document "invoice," analogously to the procedure for accounts payable accounting. The total amount of the invoice then leads to the standard posting record:

Debit a customer's accounts receivable account, credit goods sold

Figure D.I.12 shows a representation of the process under the FI system (see *SAP, Das Finanzwesen der SAP 1992, pp. 6-9 and 6-10*).

In the accounts receivable accounting system, the account receivable can either be interpreted as a component of the entity type CUSTOMER or a separate entity type can be introduced.

The major business transactions in the context of accounts receivable accounting include invoices, credit memos, cancellations, adjustments and payments.

In the case of payments, assignments are created to the outstanding invoice items (refer to payment procedures in the context of outbound logistics).

These decisions can be made interactively or, with the support of priority rules, can also be performed virtually automatically. In the case of large payments, it is advisable for the user to work directly at the terminal in order, for example, to be able to check discounts that the customer has deducted. However, it is conceivable that decision-support tools, even expert systems, will allow the process to be automated even further.

Interfaces to the inventory accounting system have already been discussed in the context of factory data entry by entering additions and withdrawals as well as with respect to the procurement of materials. In the inventory accounting system, an account is created for each type of material, to which value-related additions and withdrawals are posted. Different valuation approaches (LIFO, HIFO, rolling average prices, planning prices with variance factors) can be applied depending upon the accounting rules and cost accounting procedures in question. If the

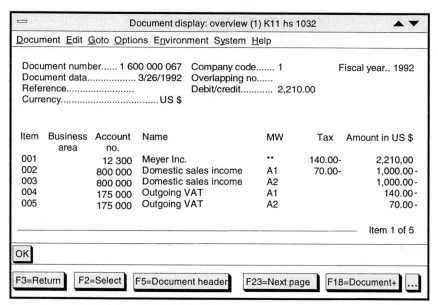

Accounts receivable accounting: posting document

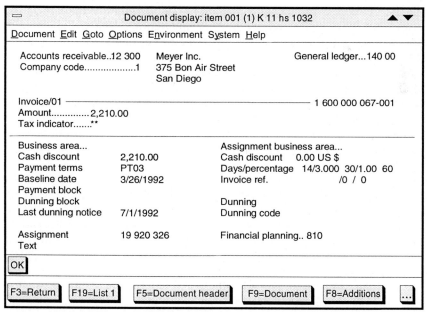

Accounts receivable accounting: document item

Fig. D.I.12: Accounts receivable posting

quantity-related additions are entered on the basis of the receiving slip, but the value-related additions are not precisely known until the invoice is received, the system must work with price variances, as illustrated previously in the example for the purchasing department.

The inventory accounting system identifies materials expenses and provides cost accounting with the basis for valuing finished and semi-finished products. The valued inventories, in turn, are then used in the financial accounting system to produce the financial statements.

The data structure corresponds to the general structure developed in Figure D.I.06, whereby the "original documents" include receiving and materials issue slips as well as invoices for goods received.

For the most part, the account types involved include "materials," "invoice received," "goods received" and "price variance."

Payroll accounting has already been discussed in the context of human resource logistics.

A payroll account is maintained for each employee. After the payroll accounting has been closed, a posting record is executed for each employee as follows:

Debit employee payroll account, credit bank, tax

Within the general data structure, therefore, the original document is the gross and net pay generated by payroll accounting, which leads to a document in the payroll accounting system and thus to the corresponding posting.

On the one hand, the fixed asset accounting system provides inventory values for the inventory accounts in account category 0 of the balance sheet; on the other hand, it provides depreciation and maintenance expense for category 4 accounts. An account is created in the fixed asset accounting system for each piece of equipment. This account is then linked with, or is identical to, the entity type EQUIPMENT in the PPC system.

In the fixed asset accounting system, maintenance and depreciation expenses are determined and entered for each piece of equipment. This discussion will not treat business-related questions concerning precise depreciation tracking in any further detail. The section on factory data entry, however, provides precise records relating to run times and other burdens, thus providing support for a fairly exact consumption-based depreciation policy.

The "original document" is a business-related depreciation form or a posting form for maintenance expenses.

In the case of DP-supported maintenance planning, maintenance orders are maintained electronically, so that the data that have been fed back are automatically transferred into the documents for the maintenance accounting system.

D.I.2.2 Cost and Income Accounting

The cost and income accounting system is a value-oriented documentation, planning, control and monitoring system for supporting corporate management (see *Heinen/Dietel, Kostenrechnung 1991, p. 1162*). In an industrial enterprise, cost and income accounting is particularly concerned with the enterprise's production process. Since management is the recipient of the information, the degree of detail in the data definition and the accounting procedures is geared toward the information needs of these managers. Although this involves a different target group than in the case of the financial accounting system, where the recipients of the information are outside sources of capital and government authorities, close information relationships nonetheless exist between both systems. These relationships become even closer the more flexibly the financial accounting database is configured, i.e., the more flexibility and detail are provided for data entry and analysis in the document database.

"Costs" are understood to be the consumption of financial resources necessary for producing the output, while "income" represents the increase in financial resources produced by the output (which generates income). Thus, costs occur through the use of production resources to generate output, where output is essentially understood to mean manufactured products. The comparison of costs and output (income) yields the operating profit or loss.

A multitude of (complicated) procedures have been developed within the framework of cost and income accounting. Thus, an attempt will be made to distinguish between a goal-neutral basic accounting system and the analyses that build upon it. This structure, which dates back to Schmalenbach, has been embraced by practitioners of business information systems, since it correlates well with a database-oriented concept (see *Ortner/Wedekind, Datenbank für die Kostenrechnung 1977; Mertens/Pfuhl, Computereinsatz im Rechnungswesen 1981; Riebel, Einzelkosten- und Deckungsbeitragsrechnung 1994; Sinzig, Rechnungswesen 1989*). This principle will be followed, while at the same time emphasizing its close link to financial accounting and the operative process of output generation.

Cost category accounting is largely contained within the financial accounting system. Cost center accounting, too, can be viewed as an element of the basic accounting system, even though it also contains analyses in the form of planning and variance calculations. Costing and profitability will be discussed as the important analyses. Costing has already been addressed in the context of (concurrent) order costing within the framework of order release and factory data entry as well as in the case of development-concurrent costing. The fact that the costing function is reused in multiple applications is the reason why it is being developed now in a neutral context rather than having been discussed in individual application interrelationships earlier.

Cost and income accounting has been criticized in recent years due to the high expense and effort it involves and because of its fairly low information potential. This has already been suggested in the discussion of development-concurrent costing. The concepts of target costing and activity-based costing have taken cognizance of this criticism and are revealing new, equally controversial further developments.

The multitude of procedures can be further distinguished on the basis of the valuation principles for the factor sets employed for a given procedure.

In **actual cost accounting**, only the effectively incurred costs are recorded and allocated. Actual cost accounting in and of itself is not suitable for Controlling purposes, since it lacks comparison costs. Thus, modern cost accounting systems determine budgeted and standard costs in addition to actual costs.

In **normalized cost accounting**, actual cost rates that fluctuate over time are replaced by constant normalized cost rates (frequently average values).

In **standard cost accounting**, detailed budgeted costs are determined independently of the actual costs from past periods. Reference units such as machine hours, square feet, etc., are formed for the cost centers and enable costs to be budgeted according to the costs-by-cause principle. The concept of including fixed as well as proportionate costs in the budgeted reference units is termed "full-cost-based standard cost accounting." If only the proportionate costs are included in the cost rates, the concept is termed "flexible standard cost accounting based on marginal costs."

After presenting the basic terms involved in cost and income accounting from the data view, the discussion will treat the classical sequence of the cost accounting levels, i.e., cost category, cost center and cost objective. Subsequently, approaches will be demonstrated for incorporating activity-based costing.

Differing valuation rates have virtually no effect on the basic representation pursued here. The discussion of the individual cost accounting procedures will also be kept as brief as possible. Reference is made to the broad selection of business administration literature that addresses this subject (see *Kilger, Einführung in die Kostenrechnung 1987; Kilger/Vikas, Flexible Plankostenrechnung und Deckungsbeitragsrechnung 1993; Haberstock, Kostenrechnung I 1987; Haberstock, Kostenrechnung II 1986; Jacob, Industriebetriebslehre 1990; Vormbaum, Grundlagen des Rechnungswesens 1977; Heinen/Dietel, Kostenrechnung 1991*).

D.I.2.2.1 Basic Data Management

The development of numerous cost accounting procedures as well as the organizational independence of cost accounting have led to an autonomous data organization, although it is closely linked with the financial accounting system and the operative logistics systems. This means that many cost accounting systems redundantly manage information from the processes under their own control. Figure D.I.13 shows this logical process.

Cost accounting receives data from financial accounting and directly from the goods and financial processes. Data from the financial accounting system, in turn, come from the operative processes or, if no operative operations are involved, entered independently in the financial accounting system. Likewise, data can be entered in the cost accounting system without reference to financial accounting (e.g., in the case of imputed costs).

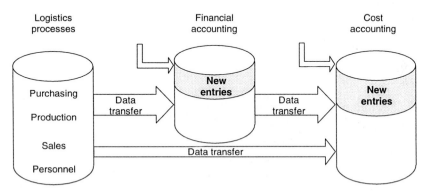

Fig. D.I.13: Logical data flow within accounting

Multiple data transfer practices inevitably lead to a higher degree of data redundancy, which has already been suggested. This data redundancy becomes all the more troublesome the more the cost accounting system is viewed as a decision support system designed to provide answers to numerous ad hoc questions, thus requiring an up-to-date database. Moreover, an application-independent data organization for "basic accounting" necessitates a low degree of data consolidation. Due to the high volume of data involved, however, these needs cannot be satisfied by an independent (redundant) form of data management for cost accounting.

Since the data entry functions for the financial accounting system are increasingly permeating the upstream operative processes, the cost accounting database is beginning to merge with the upstream systems, as well. In concrete terms, this means that the operative systems collect data that are relevant for cost accounting (e.g., a factory data entry system captures payroll data, material withdrawals and production times in the form of current information) and immediately assign them the appropriate coding for the financial and cost accounting systems. Thus, Figure D.I.13 indicates only the logical data flow. However, the data should not be physically transferred to the downstream system; instead, the system should be given access to the data.

The basis for this type of basic accounting system consist of the document file, in which all business transactions are recorded on a value-

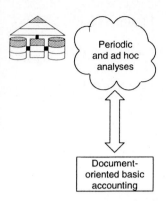

Fig. D.I.14: Basic accounting

oriented basis. This file is supplemented by cost-accounting information and is available for periodic ad hoc analyses (see Figure D.I.14).

The most important concepts in cost accounting are "cost and income categories," "cost centers" and "reference units," as indicators of the output of cost centers, and "cost objectives." Cost accounting procedures are geared toward these concepts. Since cost accounting does not "generate" any operational processes itself, but instead only duplicates them on a computational level, some of the concepts coincide with previously introduced entity types, so that only a cost accounting "view" of existing data structures needs to be defined.

In the discussion on data structure design, therefore, reference will be made to the parallels to previously introduced entity and relationship types.

D.I.2.2.1.1 Cost and Income Categories

The cost categories are defined in category 4 of the Joint Standard Accounting System (GKR); the income categories, in category 8. The cost and income categories are directly linked to the account structure of the financial accounting system.

Costs constitute the value-based input of production factors required to produce output. As such, they can be classified in cost categories on the basis of the type of production factor that is either consumed or utilized. The exact classification of the cost categories is plant- and industry-dependent. Figure D.I.15 shows a segment from a detailed representation (from *Kilger, Einführung in die Kostenrechnung 1987, pp. 71 f.*). As is clear from the breakdown, the cost categories have already been defined as accounts in the financial accounting system, including its specialized accounting systems.

Thus, the materials accounting system maintains accounts for input materials as well as for fuels, the payroll accounting system maintains

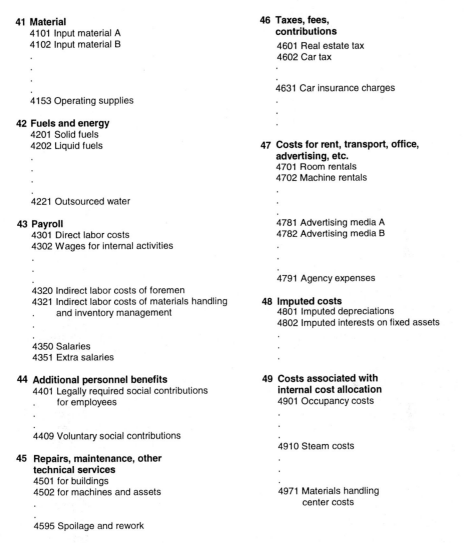

41 Material
4101 Input material A
4102 Input material B
.
.
.
4153 Operating supplies

42 Fuels and energy
4201 Solid fuels
4202 Liquid fuels
.
.
.
.
4221 Outsourced water

43 Payroll
4301 Direct labor costs
4302 Wages for internal activities
.
.
4320 Indirect labor costs of foremen
4321 Indirect labor costs of materials handling
.   and inventory management
.
4350 Salaries
4351 Extra salaries

44 Additional personnel benefits
4401 Legally required social contributions
.   for employees
.
4409 Voluntary social contributions

45 Repairs, maintenance, other technical services
4501 for buildings
4502 for machines and assets
.
4595 Spoilage and rework

46 Taxes, fees, contributions
4601 Real estate tax
4602 Car tax
.
4631 Car insurance charges
.
.
.

47 Costs for rent, transport, office, advertising, etc.
4701 Room rentals
4702 Machine rentals
.
.
4781 Advertising media A
4782 Advertising media B
.
.
4791 Agency expenses

48 Imputed costs
4801 Imputed depreciations
4802 Imputed interests on fixed assets
.
.

49 Costs associated with internal cost allocation
4901 Occupancy costs
.
.
.
4910 Steam costs
.
.
4971 Materials handling center costs

Fig. D.I.15: Cost category classification of the category 4 of the joint standard accounting system

payroll accounts, the fixed asset accounting system maintains accounts for repairs and maintenance, etc.

Figure D.I.16 shows the data structure for cost and income categories.

The entity types COST CATEGORY and INCOME CATEGORY are subtypes of the entity type ACCOUNT.

"Dummy" accounts are created for those types of costs that are not included in the financial accounting system because they cannot be assigned business transactions with external associates. This holds true, for example, in the case of imputed costs or costs associated with internal cost allocation.

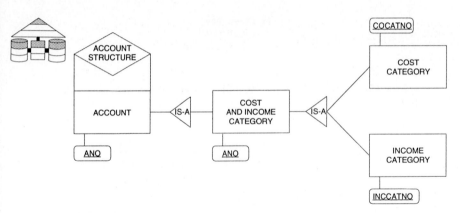

Fig. D.I.16: Cost and income categories as specializations

Important descriptive attributes for a cost category include:

Designation:	Name
Output relationship:	variable, fixed, hybrid
Type of output relationship:	according to number of products, production time, lot size, process, intensity, etc.
Schedulability:	as needed, monthly, semi-annually, etc.
Liquidity impact:	due and payable during the accounting period, not due and payable during the accounting period
Recorded as:	direct costs, indirect overhead costs, overhead costs
Quality of data:	measured, calculated, estimated
Significance for cost control:	relevant, less relevant

The quantity and value fields, e.g., actual, standard and budgeted cost variations, will be discussed below.

Income categories are defined analogously to cost categories and are necessary for period costing (short-term profitability analysis). These types of income categories can, for example, be classified according to product groups. Corresponding accounts can be created in the financial accounting system in this regard, as well.

For purposes of distinction, the separate key attributes COSCATNO and INCCATNO are introduced for the subtypes.

However, the specialized key attributes COSANO and INCCATNO are identical with the key attribute ACNO.

Via the "is-a" relationship between COST CATEGORY and INCOME CATEGORY, the cost and income categories are structured via the relationship type ACCOUNT STRUCTURE. Thus, cost categories can be consolidated into cost category groups, or income accounts into income category groups.

All business transactions are available to the cost accounting system via the document assignments of the financial accounting system.

D.I.2.2.1.2 Cost Centers

Cost centers are operational subdepartments, for which the incurred costs are recorded separately in order to control them and form cost rates.

Auxiliary cost centers provide their output to other cost centers. They can be consolidated into auxiliary cost center departments. The costs of the primary cost center, to which the costs of the auxiliary cost centers are transferred, are charged directly to the products. The primary cost centers, in turn, can be consolidated into primary cost center departments (see Figure D.I.17).

Primary cost
center departments

Primary cost
centers

Auxiliary cost
center departments

Auxiliary cost
centers

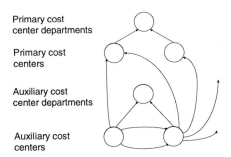

Fig. D.I.17: Consolidation of cost centers

The following principles should be taken into account when an enterprise is classified into cost centers. (see *Kilger, Einführung in die Kostenrechnung 1987, p. 154*; *Heinen/Dietel, Kostenrechnung 1991, p. 1189*):

- Cost centers are independent areas of responsibility under the direction of a cost center manager, typically a supervisor or department head.
- Uniform parameters (reference units) must be defined in order to identify the causes of the costs.
- It must be possible to assign cost category documents to cost centers that caused the costs, without allocation difficulties.

The entity type COST CENTER is created for the cost centers; it is identified by the cost center number CCNO (see Figure D.I.18). It has already been introduced in connection with the discussion of interfaces

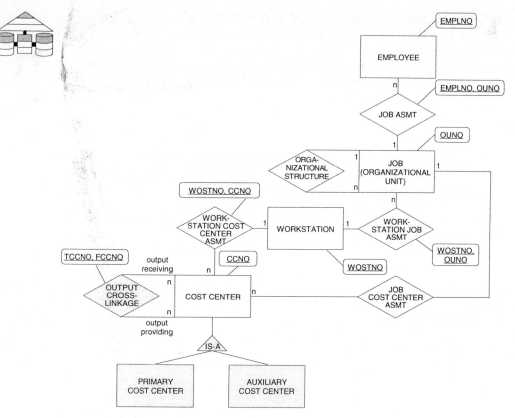

Fig. D.I.18: ERM for cost centers

between Production and Accounting/Organization/Human Resources (see Figure B.I.114).

In particular, the need to assign unambiguous responsibility provides a close relationship between cost center classification and the general corporate structure, as was introduced through the formation of organizational units. This situation is expressed by the relationship of the COST CENTER to the entity types WORKSTATION and organizational JOB. In this context, it is possible to adopt the cost center hierarchy for consolidation accounting (i.e., the formation of primary cost center departments from primary cost centers; the formation of auxiliary cost center departments from auxiliary cost centers). If viewed in uniform terms, the organizational structure will coincide with the cost center classification, and the entity types and key terms will be identical.

Internal cost allocation forms a particular structural relationship between the cost centers. This is expressed in the illustration by the n:m relationship type OUTPUT CROSS-LINKAGE within the entity type COST CENTER. It reflects the accounting relationships, particularly those between auxiliary cost centers.

D.I.2.2.1.3 Reference Variables/Cost Drivers

Output constitutes a significant cost parameter. In a single-product enterprise, output can be specified by the quantity of products produced. If several products are produced, output indicators must be created in order to allocate the variable costs on the basis of cause. Relevant reference units can be production times, setup times, throughput weights, surface areas machined, volume values, energy consumption or directly measurable costs such as labor and materials costs. Since the reference units describe the output of a cost center, they are also termed "output categories." The entity type REFERENCE UNIT is identified by the reference unit number REFUNO (see Figure D.I.19).

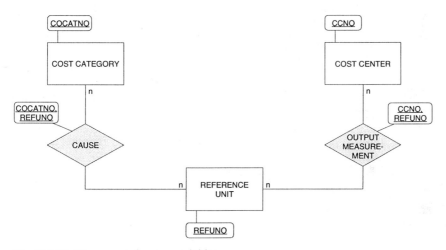

Fig. D.I.19: Views on reference variables

Significant descriptive attributes include:
- Name
- Dimension in which a reference unit is measured
- How it is determined

Typical dimensional units include kilograms per quantity unit, meters per quantity unit, square meters per quantity unit.

The reference units can be analyzed from two different views.

On the one hand, in cost center accounting they serve to allocate the cost categories fairly among the causative cost centers. On the other hand, they also serve as the basis for formulating internal cost allocation rates. In this regard, they function as a dimensional value for the different output categories associated with a cost center.

In the data structure in Figure D.I.19, these views are expressed by the relationship types CAUSE and OUTPUT MEASUREMENT.

The causal relationship indicates which reference units can fundamentally be employed for which cost categories for performing the causative allocation. At the same time, several reference units can be used for each cost category, as indicated in the example shown in Figure D.I.20.

Relationship type CAUSE

Cost category 432
Causative allocation   66,6% according to reference unit machine hours
                       33,4% according to reference unit room size

Cost category 562
Causative allocation   50% according to reference unit production hours
                       25% according to reference unit machine hours
                       25% according to reference unit labor costs

Fig. D.I.20: Example of the causative allocation of cost catergories

The reference unit "machine hours" occurs in the case of the two cost categories shown in the example, No. 432 and No. 562; on the other hand, each of the cost categories is allocated on the basis of several reference units. Thus, the relationship type CAUSE is type n:m.

The relationship type OUTPUT MEASUREMENT is also type n:m. A cost center can produce several output categories, for which internal allocation prices (cost rates) are determined. Figure D.I.21 uses a simple example to show this.

The repair shop produces output in the form of mechanic's hours (which corresponds to the reference unit "production hours") as well as in the form of machine use, which thus yields machine hours as reference units.

The cost center "energy" produces output in the form of types of energy produced, i.e., steam and electricity; it is further assumed that maintenance activities or special repairs performed by the energy cost center are allocated separately as mechanic's hours. Thus, an n:m relationship also exists here.

Relationship OUTPUT MEASUREMENT

Cost center REPAIR SHOP

Output category: Mechanic' s hour, cost rate, ...
(reference unit)   Machine hour, cost rate, ...

Cost center ENERGY

Output category: Steam, cost rate, ...
                       Electricity, cost rate, ...
                       Mechanic' s hour, cost rate, ...

Fig. D.I.21: Example of output categories of cost centers

Significant attributes of the relationship type OUTPUT MEASUREMENT include:
- Output value
- Type of output
- Date of last measurement
- Cost rate.

It is not only necessary to detail the reference units for allocating costs to cost centers or for formulating cost rates, but also primarily to provide detailed cost planning with subsequent cost control as well as to formulate differentiated performance figures.

D.I.2.2.1.4 Cost Objectives

Cost objectives are units that generate costs that can be computed; as such, they enter into the decision-making process. Costs can be related on a per unit basis or on the basis of a specific time frame. The most familiar cost objective is the end product, for which the product costing process determines costs per quantity unit and the short-term profitability analysis determines costs per time unit.

In addition to the end product, all intermediate products (assemblies) can also be cost objectives. However, other categories such as sales regions, individual customers or customer groups, individual orders or order groups can also serve as cost objectives if costs are compared to income in making business-related decisions (e.g., withdrawing from a sales region, determining customer priority). Cost centers can also be cost objectives if they function as profit centers.

A cost objective can be identical to one of the concepts introduced in the context of logistics, e.g., article, customer, order, project, or it can be a

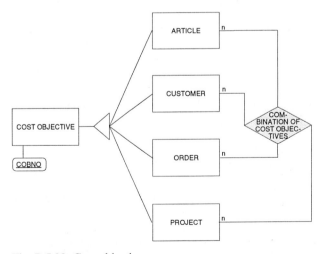

Fig. D.I.22: Cost objectives

combination of these factors. Figure D.I.22 shows this interrelationship. In this case, COST OBJECTIVE forms a relationship between these categories.

When these factors combine, the same data structures can be used as those that were treated in the corresponding subsections. For ad hoc calculations, the cost objectives are first defined on the basis of the combination of different entity types during interactive processing.

In the further discussion, the term COST OBJECTIVE will be identified by the key cost objective number (COBNO). In simplified conceptual terms, it can be equated to the end product. In this case, the key attribute COBNO would be identical with the part number PNO.

D.I.2.2.2 Cost and Income Accounting Process

Cost and income accounting is divided into the subareas of cost category accounting, cost center accounting and cost objective accounting.

Cost and income category accounting records the total costs and income for a specific accounting period (e.g., a month) and classifies them into cost and income categories. In this procedure, it distinguishes between direct costs, which are directly charged to operational output units, and overhead costs, which in **cost center accounting** are first assigned to operational subdepartments and then assigned to the operational output units using cost rates.

Cost center accounting determines the costs of in-house outputs and assigns them to the primary cost centers.

Cost objective accounting records the manufacturing and in-house costs for the order and production units in the context of costing or product costing. In addition, it also incorporates the short-term profitability analysis as a function of period costing.

The short-term profitability analysis (operating profit or loss) determines an enterprise's monthly profit or loss and states the contributions of individual product types and groups to the profit or loss.

D.I.2.2.2.1 Cost and Income Category Accounting

Cost and income category accounting does not actually deserve to be called "accounting," since it is more of a recording and accrual/deferral function.

In an integrated data organization, an account from the general ledger accounting system is assigned to a cost and income category. Thus, the cost category or income category is known every time a posting is made.

Separate accounts are set up for cost categories that are not contained in financial accounting (e.g., imputed costs, costs for in-house orders) in order to keep the system uniform. The assignment of COST/INCOME CATEGORY to ACCOUNT eliminates a further assignment between the individual entries and COST/INCOME CATEGORY.

Costs that can be directly assigned to cost objectives are termed "direct costs"; the rest are termed "overhead costs." The most important direct cost categories are material costs and direct labor costs.

Overhead costs can be further classified as variable and fixed costs. This classification can be performed for each cost category, i.e., by the accounting system or by using mathematical total cost breakdown methods.

If the cost categories are assigned by virtue of the account definition, the cost and income accounting results more or less as a byproduct of financial accounting (see *Plattner/Kagermann, Einbettung eines Systems der Plankostenrechnung in ein EDV-Gesamtkonzept 1991, p. 140*). Its data structure has thus already been developed on the right side of Figure D.I.06. Furthermore, the account codes for the document items have also been assigned to cost objectives and cost centers.

All that has to be done in cost category accounting is to make period-related accruals and deferrals, perform plausibility checks and adjust valuations relative to financial accounting (in the case of imputed valuation-related non-operating costs), enter additional costs (imputed additional costs) and perform further preparatory functions for downstream cost accounting activities.

Because of the many kinds of types and dimensions involved, however, only some of the values of the reference units can be entered via documents from financial accounting. Instead, the original documents must be directly available in the case of quantity- and time-related data. This will be discussed in greater detail within the context of cost center accounting.

D.I.2.2.2.2 Cost Center Accounting

Cost center accounting assigns all of the unposted overhead costs to those cost centers in which they were incurred on the basis of the costs-by-cause principle.

A second function involves cost and income planning as well as variance analysis.

D.I.2.2.2.2.1 Overhead Cost Allocation

The most important support tool for overhead cost allocation is the object analysis sheet, whose structure is shown in Figure D.I.23. An analysis of this sheet is useful with respect to the data structure shown in Figure D.I.24.

Direct costs are shown above the actual cost center accounting. They can be used as reference units for determining the material and production overhead cost rates.

The primary cost centers (final cost centers) relate to purchasing and materials, production, administration and sales. They supply the bulk of

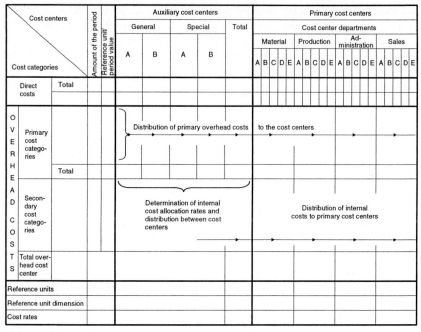

Fig. D.I.23: Structure of the object analysis sheet

their outputs directly to the market. Auxiliary cost centers, on the other hand, supply their outputs to other cost centers. Although this structure is subject to criticism (see *Heinen/Dietel, Kostenrechnung 1991, p. 1193*), it should be retained.

Typical auxiliary cost centers include energy and transportation as well as support areas such as maintenance, metalworking and woodworking.

Overhead costs can be subdivided into primary and secondary cost categories. Primary costs are costs that are incurred from "outside," i.e., for which the enterprise is invoiced. Secondary costs relate to outputs that are obtained from units within the plant.

This distinction is maintained during cost center accounting. The differentiation of overhead costs on the basis of "directly posted costs," "distributed primary costs" and "allocated secondary costs" simplifies more accurate cost control and variance analysis.

The data structures will now be developed in Figure D.I.24 on the basis of these three cost categories.

The object analysis sheet element, which is shown as a relationship type between COST CATEGORY, COST CENTER, CAUSE and TIME, constitutes the core of the data structure. It is assigned **consolidated** cost attributes for the specified analysis period.

The link to the entity type TIME signifies that the calculations can be performed for different periods (e.g., months). REFERENCE UNIT is linked with the information object CAUSE when the overhead costs are

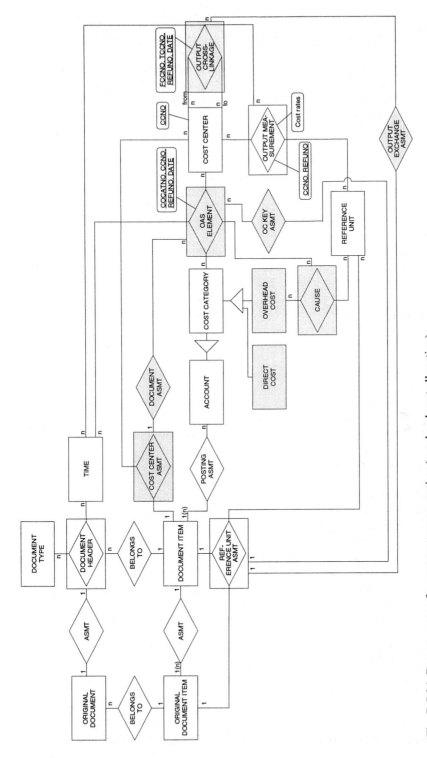

Fig. D.I.24: Data structure for cost center accounting (overhead cost allocation)

distributed. If a cost amount is assigned to a cost center without indication of a reference unit, e.g., in the case of a direct posting when the document is created, the reference unit number will not be indicated. The same holds true if several reference units are combined to form totals for each cost category within a cost center. The document items that are relevant for the analysis period and that have been posted directly to cost centers **and** cost categories are linked with the OBJECT ANALYSIS SHEET ELEMENT via the DOCUMENT ASSIGNMENT. The value consolidated for the period is used as an attribute in the object analysis sheet element.

The (primary) overhead costs that are recorded solely on the basis of cost category are distributed to the cost centers via reference units. To do this, it is necessary to provide the period values of the reference units. The documents from financial accounting are insufficient for this purpose, however, and a wide variety of original documents must be accessed for quantity- and time-related data.

Analogously to the assignment of account codes for cost category, cost center and cost objective, these reference units can be assigned at the time the original documents are created, i.e., it is not necessary to wait until the periodic cost center accounting is performed. For this purpose, the REFERENCE UNIT ASSIGNMENT creates a link to the entity type DOCUMENT ITEM as well as to the ORIGINAL DOCUMENT ITEM, which represents numerous data sources such as orders, FDE feedbacks, production plans, etc.

The documents that are relevant for the accounting period for each overhead cost category, cost center and reference period are recorded via the relationship type OC KEY ASSIGNMENT. The primary overhead costs that have not been posted directly can now be distributed among the cost centers on a causative basis via the reference unit values and recorded in the OBJECT ANALYSIS SHEET ELEMENT as attributes.

The most algorithmically demanding computation relates to determination of the secondary costs, which result when the costs of the auxiliary cost centers are passed on to the primary cost centers. If a hierarchical structure exists for output relationships between auxiliary cost centers, a relatively simple accounting procedure can be applied, e.g., the step-ladder method. However, if there is a mutual cross-linkage of outputs between the auxiliary cost centers, the result will be a system of linear equations that must be solved using more time-consuming procedures.

The basic structure for the output cross-linkage between output-receiving and output-providing cost centers has already been introduced in Figure D.I.18. It will now be refined to include the identification of the output category (reference unit) in question via OUTPUT MEASUREMENT and the reference to the analysis period.

An element of the OUTPUT CROSS-LINKAGE is thus identified by the key attributes of receiving cost center number (TCCNO), providing cost center number (FCCNO), reference unit number (REFUNO) and time (DATE).

Documents that are relevant to the period are assigned via the relationship type OUTPUT EXCHANGE ASSIGNMENT.

These types of original document line items can, for example, be feedbacks from Production concerning hours worked, machine run times as well as measured energy consumption values.

Internal cost allocation procedures are then used to determine prices for the outputs on the basis of the existing value-related primary costs of the cost centers and the output relationships. Subsequently, the outputs received by a cost center are valued and allocated to the corresponding object analysis sheet element as secondary costs.

After the costs from the auxiliary cost centers have been assigned to the primary cost centers, cost rates are formulated by dividing the total costs of the cost center by the value of the reference unit for the cost center. Depending on the cost accounting method being used (absorption costing, marginal costing), this amount is calculated for the total costs or only for the variable costs of the cost center.

If the cost rates are not further differentiated on the basis of individual reference units (output types), they are assigned to the cost centers as attribute values or, in the case of costing that relates to several reference units, they are assigned to the relationship type OUTPUT MEASUREMENT. The cost rates are necessary for cost objective accounting.

An example of this assignment relationship has already been provided in Figure B.I.114, where the document item PRODUCTION ORDER OPERATION was linked with OUTPUT MEASUREMENT in order to enter the differentiated cost rates that relate, for example, to the reference units "setup times" and "machine hours" for an operation.

D.I.2.2.2.2.2 Cost Planning and Analysis

Cost center accounting is employed for controlling the cost efficiency of organizational units (cost centers).

Cost accounting systems, therefore, first determine planned costs for each cost category in a cost center. These planned costs build on specified output plannings for which standard costs are determined after completion of a planning period (e.g., a month) on the basis of actual output and are then compared with the actual costs. The variances resulting from this comparison are analyzed and categorized into variance causes.

In flexible standard cost accounting based on marginal costs, upon which the following discussion will be based, only consumption variances can occur in the cost centers. Output variances are eliminated by the transition from planned output to actual output. Price variations do not occur because both the actual costs and the standard costs use the same cost rates for materials, labor, etc. Since the data structure developed here is largely independent of the cost accounting method, Figure D.I.24 remains the basis for the analysis.

Only the attribute groups for the entity and relationship types are formulated differently on the basis of the cost accounting method being used. In the case of flexible standard cost accounting based on marginal

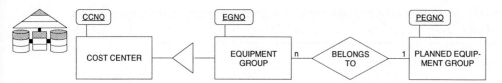

Fig. D.I.25: ERM for output accounting for each cost center

costs, for example, the following value groups are recorded for each cost category and cost center:
- Variable planned costs
- Fixed planned costs
- Variable standard costs
- Fixed standard costs
- Actual costs
- Consumption variance.

This attribute group then has to be included in the relationship type OBJECT ANALYSIS SHEET ELEMENT. Cost planning and analysis is an analytical function that builds on the data structure developed here.

The basic process will be explained on the basis of three typical analysis-oriented screens. In the first step, output accounting is performed for each cost center. The point of departure for this process is the production plan, from which the output—which is measured on the basis of various reference variables—is derived. The data structure for production planning has already been developed in Figure B.IV.02. The loads in machine hours for the planned equipment groups and the actual equipment groups result from the capacity profiles. These planned values can either be imported directly for cost planning or transformed into different reference units via the appropriate internal charge factors. The data relationship shown in Figure D.I.25 is created by the link between the entity type COST CENTER to the terms used in conjunction with planning, i.e., "equipment group" and "planned equipment group."

The entity types created for planning purposes, i.e., PRODUCTION PLAN, etc., can be accessed via the entity type PLANNED EQUIPMENT GROUP.

Figure D.I.26 (from *SAP, System RK 1986, pp. 5.2.2.2.1-2*) shows the output planning screen for a cost center.

By using planned cost rates, costs are planned by assigning values to the output data for the individual cost center cost categories, distinguished on the basis of fixed and variable costs. Figure D.I.27 (from *SAP, System RK 1986, pp. 5.2.2.2.2-2*) again shows this as a screen.

Planning procedures are analogous to the cost allocation procedures shown for actual costs, i.e., the primary costs of the cost centers are first planned. In a second step, the internal outputs are allocated, whereby the

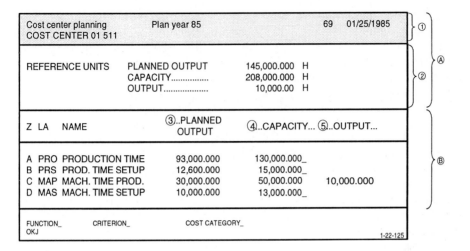

| Cost center planning | Plan year 85 | | | 69 01/25/1985 | ① |
| COST CENTER 01 511 | | | | | |

REFERENCE UNITS	PLANNED OUTPUT	145,000.000 H	②
	CAPACITY...............	208,000.000 H	
	OUTPUT..................	10,000.00 H	

Z LA	NAME	③..PLANNED OUTPUT	④..CAPACITY...	⑤..OUTPUT...	
A PRO	PRODUCTION TIME	93,000.000	130,000.000_		
B PRS	PROD. TIME SETUP	12,600.000	15,000.000_		
C MAP	MACH. TIME PROD.	30,000.000	50,000.000	10,000.000	
D MAS	MACH. TIME SETUP	10,000.000	13,000.000_		

| FUNCTION_ | CRITERION_ | COST CATEGORY_ | |
| OKJ | | | 1-22-125 |

Legend:

Ⓐ Header
  ① Identifying characteristics
  ② Cost center-related planning data generated by the entire range of output categories
Ⓑ Items: Description of the planning data per output category
  ③ Planned activity in the dimension that is specified in the reference unit master file
  ④ Planned capacity for the reference unit in the dimension that is specified in the reference unit master file
  ⑤ Description of the planned activity in an alternative dimension, e. g. hrs --> units

Fig. D.I.26: Output planning screen for a cost center

| Cost center planning | Plan year 85 | 64 01/25/1985 | ① |
| COST CENTER 01 511 | Manuf. dpt. A1 | | |

OUTPUT RELATED COSTS	PLANNED OUTPUT	93,000,000 H	Ⓐ
REFERENCE UNIT PRODUCTION TIME.	CAPACITY...............	0,000 H	②
KEY..............................FEP	OUTPUT..................	0,00 H	

Z	OAS	COST CAT.	NAME	..PLANNED COSTS FIX	...PLANNED COSTS VAR.	E
A	010	420000	Direct labor costs	936,000.00	324,000.00	V
B		421000	Indirect labor costs	18,900.00	12,420.00	F
C	030	434000	Pay scale vacation bonus	95,490.00	33,642.00	F
D		435000	Pay scale yearly output	286,470.00	100,926.00	F
E	210	400000	Raw material	132,000.00	336,000.00	V
F	220	403000	Operating supplies	4,650.00	4,650.00	V
G		404000	Operating supplies	0.00	4,185.00 A	V
H	250	452000	Maint. mach. + equipment	3,240.00	8,400.00	F

| FUNCTION_ | CRITERION_ | _ | |
| OKJ | | | 1-22-125 |

Legend:

Ⓐ Header
  ① Cost center-related data
  ② Cost center and output-related data
Ⓑ Items

Fig. D.I.27: Cost planning screen for a cost center

computation technique is analogous to actual cost allocation. This procedure results in planned allocation rates for each cost center and output category that can be compared to the actual cost allocation rates from internal cost allocation, as cited above. The secondary planned costs can be shown separately for each cost center.

The actual outputs are determined after the end of the planning period. They form the basis for calculating the standard costs by valuing them on the basis of the internal transfer prices (planning prices).

Since the actual costs are also determined at the same time, variances between standard and actual values can be analyzed in cost center reports. Separate analyses can be performed for fixed and variable costs as well as on the basis of different variance causes (price, process, consumption, output), depending on the cost accounting method being employed. A cost center report is shown in Figure D.I.28 (from *SAP, System RK 1986, pp. 5.4.2.1-3*).

Cost reports can be generated not only for each cost center, but also for each cost category for all cost centers. In tracking variances, the individual cost categories can first be examined within a cost center report; then the cost categories can be examined on the basis of their origin (primary costs, secondary costs), on the basis of the type of output relationship involved and, in case of a more detailed analysis, on the basis of the data sources, including accounting documents or original logistics documents.

Cost center standard/actual value comparison in US $ (10**0)					Date: 1/31/90	
85 01 00511 N					Line 16/080	
Manuf. dpt. A1						
Z OAS CE/AT		Name	Nominal 2 2	Actual 2 2	VAR (ABS)	VAR (%)
A	010 *	Wages	104,748	116,645	11,897	11
B	020 *	Salaries	8,333	12,450	4,117	49
C	030 *	Other pers. costs	45,233	51,638	6,405	14
D	050 **	Personnel costs	158,314	180,733	22,419	14
E	210 *	Raw materials	30,401	47,684	17,283	57
F	220 *	Operating supplies	2,431	3,239	807	33
G	230 **	Material costs	32,833	50,923	18,090	55
H	240 *	Energy				
I	250 *	Maintenance	1,123	395	728 -	65 -
J	255 *	Other mach. costs	2,273		2,273 -	
K	258 **	Machinery's costs	3,396	395	3,001 -	88 -
L	260 *	Imputed depreciation	5,243	5,243		
M	265 *	Imputed interests	653	653		
N	266 **	Imputed depreciation/interests	5,895	5,895		
O	268 *	Other imputed costs				
P	280 *	Other external costs		256	256	
OKJ						2-21-201

Fig. D.I.28: Example of a cost center report

D.I.2.2.2.3 Cost Objective Accounting

Cost objective accounting involves calculating the costs of the cost objectives. Product costing calculates the costs per unit; period costing calculates them per period. Among other things, determining the costs aids in calculating contribution margins by subtracting the calculated variable cost prices from income. Although numerous variables are conceivable as cost objectives, e.g., customer groups, sales representatives, regions, etc., this analysis will focus on products.

The discussion of product costing will be conducted in somewhat greater detail, while the discussion of period costing will be more general. Since cost objective accounting is a supplement to the types of cost accounting discussed thus far, the data structure will not be significantly expanded.

D.I.2.2.2.3.1 Product Costing

Product costing enjoys a long tradition in business administration that stems not only from the cost price costing that is needed for making business-related decisions, but also from the requirement that cost prices be determined for government contracts.

Depending on individual needs, a distinction can be made between preliminary costing, intermediate costing and actual cost analysis (see *Heinen/Dietel, Kostenrechnung 1991, p. 1197*). Preliminary costing relates to determining the costs before production begins, e.g., deciding whether a customer order should be accepted. Intermediate, or concurrent, costing relates to products that are already in production and that have long turnaround times, and actual cost analysis relates to products that have been completed.

In contrast to the development-concurrent costing discussed in the context of the product development process, where cost information was derived from the geometrical/topological and technical properties of a product, business-related product costing requires that the product data be available in the form of bills of materials and routings.

The same costing method is used in all three approaches; only the valuations are different (full or marginal costs, planned, standard or actual cost analysis rates). Consequently, the following discussion, which uses an example from standard costing, possesses general validity.

Since it is based on planned values and planned quantities, standard costing calls for differentiated standard costing.

In the example, only variable costs will be incorporated for the purpose of calculating the contribution margin in making a comparison with the price. Figure D.I.29 shows the product structure for the example.

Product P consists of part C and outsourced part M1 (material). Part C is manufactured from material M2. A packaging operation turns end product P into salable product S. The packaging material is indicated as outsourced material PM.

The discussion will first illustrate how the production costs for a part are determined from operation data, reference units and cost rates. Then, the overall business-related costing scheme will be discussed. The basis for the costing is provided by the data structure shown in Figure D.I.30, which is a combination of data from bills of materials, routings and operations as

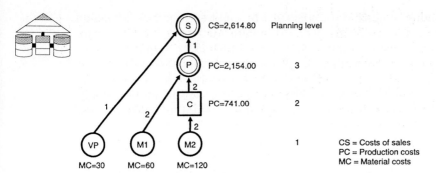

Fig. D.I.29: Product structure for the costing example

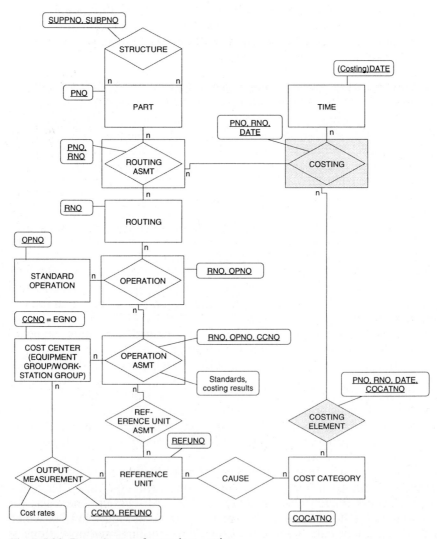

Fig. D.I.30: Data structure for product costing

well as of segments of the cost data structure. The data structure shown here is somewhat more simplified than the data model for production as developed in the context of requirements and capacity planning.

The cost rates determined by cost center accounting for each cost center and reference unit are assigned as attributes to the relationship type OUTPUT MEASUREMENT. The reference units valid for an operation, e.g., setup times, machine run times, are allocated via the relationship type REFERENCE UNIT ASSIGNMENT. The standard values (planned values) are also assigned to this information object as attributes. It should be noted that the cost centers are equated to the equipment groups.

The routing for part C, together with the operation and operation assignment information, is shown as a table in Figure D.I.31,a. The planned values for each reference unit (setup time, production time, machine time) are attributes of the relationship type REFERENCE UNIT ASSIGNMENT. They relate to a (standard) lot size of 10 units.

The variable cost rates for cost centers (equipment groups) 5 and 7, as taken from the information object OUTPUT MEASUREMENT, are shown in Figure D.I.31,b.

The detailed calculation of the production costs for part C is produced by linking both tables, as shown in Figure D.I.31,c.

Routing R1 for part C					
		Standard values (planned values)			
Operation no.	Operation assignment	Setup time	Production time	Machine time	Lot size
1	EG 5	20	-	30	10
2	EG 7	80	20	12	10

Routing R2 for product P					
		Standard values (planned values)			
Operation no.	Operation assignment	Setup time	Production time	Machine time	Lot size
1	EG 4	-	50	16	10

Fig. D.I.31,a: Routing and operation data from the information objects ROUTING, OPERATION, OPERRATION ASSIGNMENT

Cost center/ equipment group	Cost rates per reference unit		
	Setup time	Production time	Machine time
EG 4	-	4.00	8.00
EG 5	1.00	-	4.00
EG 7	1.50	3.00	5.00

Fig. D.I.31,b: Cost rates for cost center and reference units from the information object OUTPUT MEASUREMENT

Calculation formula production costs for part C								
L I N E	Oper- ation no.	Cost center (EG)	Reference unit			Cost rates	Value of reference unit per unit	Costs per unit
			No.	Name	Dimension			
1	1	EG 5	1	Machine minutes	US $/min.	4.00	30	120.00
2	1	EG 5	2	Setup minutes	US $/min	1.00	2	2.00
3	2	EG 7	1	Production minutes	US $/min.	3.00	20	60.00
4	2	EG 7	2	Machine minutes	US $/min.	5.00	12	60.00
5	2	EG 7	3	Setup minutes	US $/min.	1.50	8	12.00
6	Production costs (1-5)							254.00

Calculation formula for product P								
L I N E	Oper- ation no.	Cost center (EG)	Reference unit			Cost rates	Value of reference unit per unit	Costs per unit
			No.	Name	Dimension			
1	1	EG 4	1	Machine minutes	US $/min.	8.00	16	128.00
2	1	EG 4	2	Production minutes	US $/ min.	4.00	50	200.00
3	Production costs (1-2)							328.00

Fig. D.I.31,c: Calculation formula for production costs by linking the tables D.I.31,a and D.I.31,b

The production costs for the other parts can be calculated analogously to this procedure.

Single-level costing can be performed for product manufacturing costs by assigning manufacturing cost values to production costs, direct material costs and intermediate output costs in the form of semi-finished products that go into a product, and then adding up all these costs.

If an overall product structure, i.e., a bill of materials, is costed, the costing process proceeds on the basis of the planning stages, and the costs for each part are transferred to the directly superordinate parts.

Figure D.I.32 shows costing for the bill of materials shown in the example in Figure D.I.29. The parts from planning level 1 are the outsourced materials, for which costs of 30 (PM), 60 (M1) and 120 (M2) monetary units are given.

The costs can be calculated in either consolidated or unconsolidated form for each part. In the case of consolidated calculation, the manufacturing costs for the semi-finished products are transferred in a lump sum as semi-finished product costs, and only the costs incurred for

Line	Planning level	Part no.	Routing no.	Consolidated calculation						Unconsolidated calculation				
				Mate-rial	MOC (50%)	Pro-duc-tion	POC (50%)	Semi-prod-ucts	Produc-tion costs	Mate-rial	MOC (50%)	Prod-uction	POC (50%)	Produc-tion costs
1	2	E	R 1	240	120	254	127	-	741.00	240	120	254	127	741
2	3	P	R 2	120	60	328	164	1,482	2,154.00	600	300	836	418	2,154
3	Management overhead costs 10 % to production costs								215.40					
4	Sales overhead costs 10 % to production costs								215.40					
5	Packaging material								30.00					
6	Cost of sales								2,614.80					
7	Sales price								3,500.00					
8	Contribution margin								885.20					

Fig. D.I.32: Costing process

the part itself are differentiated on the basis of materials and production costs, with additional overhead rates also being applied.

In the case of an unconsolidated calculation, the costs for the in-house intermediate products are also differentiated on the basis of materials and production costs and then transferred. In this calculation, the cost structures are then visible all the way to the end product level. Figure D.I.32 shows both forms of calculation.

Manufacturing costs are calculated for parts C and P, as are management, sales and packaging costs for part P or S, whereby supplemental rates apply for the first two costs, and direct costs are incurred for the packaging costs via the bill of materials relationship to packaging part PM.

The costs relating to the parts are assigned to the part entities as attributes.

If several costing operations are performed over time and stored for comparison purposes, the costing calculation can be identified via the costing date, and the costing elements can be recorded via the information object COSTING ELEMENT.

The apportionment of costs to cost elements corresponds to a cost category classification (materials costs, production costs, setup costs, etc.). As a result, the relationship type COST ELEMENT is linked with the entity type COST CATEGORY (see Figure D.I.30). The cost categories can either be read directly from the reference unit (e.g., setup times lead to the cost category of "setup costs") or identified by the known relationship type CAUSE.

If several routings exist for each part, a costing process will always relate to a specific routing, and its results must be assigned to the individual routings as attribute values. In the case of an n:m assignment between routing and parts, they are assigned to the relationship type ROUTING ASSIGNMENT. Frequently, however, such cases also specify a routing that is particularly meaningful in terms of costing as a standard routing so that parts-related costing information is created here, as well.

The classification of costs into the elements "materials costs" and "production costs," as well on the basis of direct and overhead costs, can

```
PRODUCT COSTING DISPLAY                    PLANNED COSTING (consolidated)

MATERIAL          288500              Hydrocylinder, double-acting
COMPANY CODE/PLANT 1   1   C.DATE  08/01/89  VS: 0  STUE: 1  OP.: 1  MARK: J  FREE:

COST ELEMENT            US $   AMOUNT    COST ELEMENT     US $ AMOUNT
Raw materials          V       1,300.00       Setup costs  F        0.00
Special raw materials  V           0.00       Setup costs  V        0.00
Operating supplies     V         800.00  Manuf. personnel  F    4,857.00
Outsourced materials   V           0.00  Manuf. personnel  V    1,647.69
Material overhead costs F          0.00   Manuf. machine   F        0.00
Material overhead costs V         162.00   Manuf. machine  V        0.00
Semi-finished products F      14,394.88  Manuf. overhead costs  F   577.57
Semi-finished products V      11,768.75  Manuf. overhead costs  V   470.35
MAT.-credit memos      V           0.00
                                          Outsourced labor  V       0.00
Other costs            F           0.00   Planned spoilage  F       0.00
Other costs            V           0.00   Planned spoilage  V       0.00

HK: 35,978.24          / 200.00       ST I 179.89       / 1     PRICE UNIT
FCODE aZ  MARK M/J/B  J  CO-ART VK  PLANNED/ACTUAL  P
OK a       PF: 2=Pickup  3=Return  13=Posting  16=HF Overview....            3-64102
```

```
PRODUCT COSTING DISPLAY                    PLANNED COSTING (unconsolidated)

MATERIAL          00288500            Hydrocylinder, double-acting
COMPANY CODE/PLANT 1   1   C.DATE  12/29/89  VS: 0  STUE: 1  OP.: 1  MARK: J  FREE:

COST ELEMENT            US $   AMOUNT    COST ELEMENT     US $ AMOUNT
Raw materials          V       6,960.00       Setup costs  F    3,296.54
Special raw materials  V           0.00       Setup costs  V      626.53
Operating supplies     V         800.00  Manuf. personnel  F    5,715.01
Outsourced materials   V           0.00  Manuf. personnel  V    3,496.12
Material overhead costs F          0.00   Manuf. machine   F   10,581.16
Material overhead costs V         696.00   Manuf. machine  V    2,796.34
Semi-finished products F           0.00  Manuf. overhead costs  F   573.25
Semi-finished products V           0.00  Manuf. overhead costs  V   437.29
MAT.- credit memos     V           0.00
                                          Outsourced labor  V       0.00
Other costs            F           0.00   Planned spoilage  F       0.00
Other costs            V           0.00   Planned spoilage  V       0.00
Non-allocated costs    F           0.00

HK: 35,978.24          / 200.00       ST I 179.89       / 1     PRICE UNIT
FCODE AU  MARK M/J/B  J  KR-TYPE VK  PLANNED/ACTUAL  P
OK _       PF: 3=Return  14=Consolidated  15=Unconsolidated  16=HF Overview....     1-64102
```

Fig. D.I.33: Product costing with differentiated cost elements in consolidated (above) and unconsolidated (below) form

thus be differentiated; e.g., the RK system from SAP allows up to 25 cost elements to be used. Figure D.I.33 shows examples of costing schemes on the basis of consolidated and unconsolidated calculations involving detailed cost elements (see *SAP, System RK 1990, p. 147*). Variable and fixed costs are used for individual cost categories (cost elements) (V, F). The method of calculation in the example corresponds to the procedure that was demonstrated on the basis of the simplified example.

Costing once again reveals the close link between cost accounting and the other planning and scheduling departments, in particular to the data structure of PPC systems. The close data link has led to the implementation of simple costing algorithms in many PPC systems; these algorithms are particularly suited to online costing. Since, however, value-related variables are also necessary for differentiated cost rates per each cost center and reference unit, the basic data from Production alone are insufficient for performing meaningful costing analyses. Instead, the databases for cost accounting and PPC must be set up in conformance with the same level of business administration quality in order to be able to effectively support the costing process.

In the case of batch-oriented costing runs, it is customary to transfer the basic data from Production to the data structure of the cost accounting system before performing an overall planning costing process for the entire parts range. This option, however, becomes virtually unmanageable if complicated parts structures are involved, e.g., as is common in the automotive industry or in mechanical engineering.

The redundancy that occurs in the powerful databases is compelling program developers to build the costing process upon a database that is designed to integrate cost accounting and technical production. This is an imperative requirement for supporting interactive costing in order, for example, to be able to immediately determine cost ramifications in the case of changes in materials prices or part design.

D.I.2.2.2.3.2 Period Costing

Product costing is the most essential source of data for period costing (also termed "operating income accounting" or "short-term profitability analysis"). It can appear in a variety of forms. Thus, a distinction is made between the "period accounting" method and the "cost of sales" method, and additionally between actual, standard and normalized costs.

Period costing serves functions of income planning and control. It can relate to such various cost objectives as individual articles, article groups, individual customers, customer groups, sales regions, sales representatives, etc. Thus, it is impossible to provide all conceivable reports in the form of standard analyses. Instead, a database must be made available from which analyses can be generated for different forms of data consolidation, whenever possible in interactive form. A comfortable period costing process thus paves the way for a cost information system, which, in addition to a database, also contains method and model bases.

In order to perform variance analyses within the control function of period costing, it must be possible to access data down to the original document level. This also necessitates the existence of a high degree of data integration with the adjacent areas of invoicing (Sales), inventory management and in-process, in-house order inventory (PPC system).

Since this principle has already been followed in designing the integrated data structure for accounting, the data structure for period costing does not need to be extended further. It is a purely analytical function.

Without going into detail on the special aspects of the individual methods (see the pertinent literature on cost accounting for a more in-depth discussion), this discussion will treat the major sources of data that are necessary for the accounting process.

To do this, the typical formulas for calculating earnings will be analyzed, and reference will be made to the origin of the data for the individual mathematical terms. A short-term profitability analysis on the basis of **period accounting** (see Formula (1) shown in Figure D.I.34) yields profits by adding the valued changes in inventory of finished and semi-finished products to the periodic income and then subtracting the total costs for the period. The article price is multiplied by unit sales to yield article-specific products, which are totaled to determine income. These data can be taken from the invoicing system.

Changes in inventory are calculated by multiplying the manufacturing costs by the difference between the quantity produced and the quantity

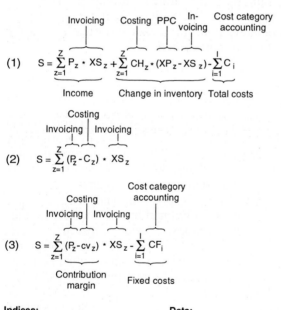

Fig. D.I.34: Formulas for short-term profitability analysis

sold, and then adding the mathematical products for all manufactured products.

Manufacturing costs are taken from product costing, production quantities are derived from PPC system feedback (FDE), and the quantities sold are again taken from the invoicing system.

Total costs are determined by adding the total costs from cost category accounting, classified on the basis of cost category.

While the first two terms in Formula (1) are classified according to article, the costs are differentiated on the basis of cost category. Thus, article-related costs cannot be compared to article-related income, which severely limits the meaningfulness of period costing on the basis of full costs. Despite its simplicity (most of the information can be supplied from financial accounting and it does not necessitate a sophisticated cost accounting system), it is therefore very rarely recommended.

In the **cost-of-sales method**, costs and income relate to the quantities sold during a given period. Costs and income are differentiated on a per-cost-objective basis when they are determined and are then compared. The cost-of-sales method distinguishes between full cost and marginal cost methods. In the first case (see Formula (2) in Figure D.I.34), therefore, the cost prices are subtracted from the product price in the parenthetical expression. The selling prices and quantities sold are again obtained from the invoicing system; the cost prices are determined within the costing framework.

While changes in inventories of finished and semi-finished products have to be recorded for period accounting, this is typically unnecessary in the cost-of-sales method. In order to be able to reconcile the short-term profitability analysis with the other departments, as well as to enable more accurate comparisons of standard and actual values, inventory maintenance is also suggested for the cost-of-sales method. This is then termed "closed period accounting" (see *Kilger, Einführung in die Kostenrechnung 1987, p. 431*).

In cost-of-sales accounting on the basis of marginal costs (contribution margin costing), only the variable unit costs are subtracted from the selling price (see Formula (3) in Figure D.I.34). An appropriately configured cost accounting system is necessary in order to provide the variable unit costs. The fixed costs are recorded on the basis of cost categories and subtracted globally.

The formulas shown in Figure D.I.34 merely serve as examples. In real-world analyses, an extremely wide variety of market segments can be used for predictive profitability analyses or for Controlling. Figure D.I.35 (from *SAP, System RK 1986, pp. 7.4-3*) shows an example of period accounting from the RK system.

Profitability analysis	SECTOR WASPA				
Date 01/28/86	ARTGR ARGRA				
Line 1/036	ARTCAT ARTCAT01				

Z	NAME	Stage	Description	ACTUAL 1 12	PLANNED 1 12	VAR 1 12	%VAR ** **
A	010	*	Gross sales	9,610,000	9,439,000	171,000 -	2
B	020	*	Sales deduction		3,000	3,000	
C	022	*	Sec. sales	951,200	1,002,80^	51,600	5 -
E	030	**	Net sales	8,658,800	8,433,20	225,600 -	3
F	040	*	Material prop.	115,200	142,00	26,800	19 -
G	042	*	Production prop.	5,546,800	4,000,00	1,546800 -	39
I	050	**	Contrib. marg. I	2,996,800	4,291,20	1,294,400	30 -
J	060	*	Prod. costs fixed	1,533,200	1,505,00	28,200 -	2
K	062	*	Mgmt. + sales	1,406,800	1,200,00	206,800 -	17
M	070	*	Contrib. marg. II	56,800	1,586,200	1,529,400	96 -
O	110	*	Sales	40,000	43,000	3,000	7 -
P	120	**	Sales/unit	279,523	263,536	15,987 -	6
OK J							1-82-320

Fig. D.I.35: Example of period costing

D.I.2.2.2.4 Activity-Based Costing

The high degree of differentiation offered by cost accounting—which, in turn, involves enormous effort—has been sharply criticized in recent years. The primary criticism has focused on the global apportionment of the overhead costs to cost objectives in performing the costing. This is particularly true because direct production costs are decreasing more and more as a result of production streamlining, while the overhead costs for process setup planning and purchasing are increasing.

Activity-based costing (ABC), originally developed in the U.S. (see *Cooper, You Need a New Cost System When ... 1989*), has particularly fueled this discussion. However, ABC is primarily a response to the simple labor overhead costing method that is widespread in the U.S., and the criticism is irrelevant with respect to the well-developed flexible standard cost accounting system based on marginal costs that is used in Germany, for example. In particular, it should be noted that cost center accounting is unknown in the U.S.; consequently, the reference unit system developed for cost planning for the purpose of causative overhead cost allocation is not known there either.

To this extent, criticism should distinguish between the original ABC method and the German version of activity-based costing, which incorporates important elements of cost center accounting (see *Franz, Prozeßkostenmanagement 1993*).

Activity-based costing is a topic of intense—albeit in part overly imprecise—discussion. Thus, terms such as "subprocess" and "activity" are used inconsistently or synonymously, as are "activity" and "primary process" (see *Kloock, Prozeßkostenrechnung als Rückschritt und Fortschritt der Kostenrechnung 1992, p. 189*). The use of the term "cost driver" to denote a reference unit also contributes to the confusion. It would be helpful if the topic were discussed on a precise plane of descriptive language, e.g., in the context of data modeling, in order to allow the actual differences to be identified.

The criticism of activity-based costing from the standpoint of a business administration view is oriented primarily toward the breach of the costs-by-cause principle, since fixed overhead costs are also allocated (see *Glaser, Prozeßkostenrechnung 1992; Kloock, Prozeßkostenrechnung als Rückschritt und Fortschritt der Kostenrechnung 1992*).

This business administration criticism will not be pursued further; instead, this discussion will make several observations from the perspective of information structuring that will illustrate the differences and interrelationships between the form of cost accounting initially described here and activity-based costing. This analysis will focus on costing, in particular.

Figure D.I.36 shows the information basis for production costing as the initial basis for a classical flexible standard cost accounting system based on marginal costs. Product P comprises the two parts C1 and C2. Within the context of cost center accounting, cost rates are determined for defined reference units (setup and production times in this example) per cost center.

In calculating the production costs, these rates are multiplied by the number of times they are used by the cost objective, i.e., the parts in this example.

The number of times they are used is individually recorded via the cost objective production process recorded in the routing. The process description is not maintained in the cost accounting system; instead, it is

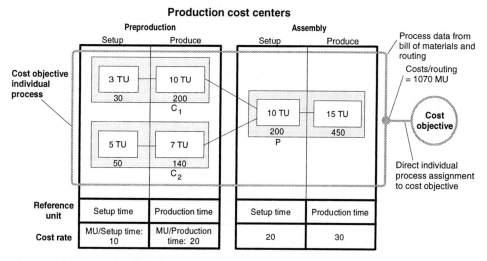

Fig. D.I.36: Information basis for production costs costing

taken from the description of the PPC system. This costing procedure has already been described in detail in Figure D.I.31.

Production has access to a detailed description of its processes in the form of routings and bills of materials, while these types of descriptions are unavailable to indirect departments. However, differentiated reference units can also be formulated for these departments; these reference units represent the activities performed in them. These include the reference unit "number of purchase orders" for Purchasing, "number of invoices reviewed" for Administration, and "number of shipping orders" for Sales (see *Kilger/Vikas, Flexible Plankostenrechnung und Deckungsbeitrags-rechnung 1993*). Although these reference units can be utilized for cost-center-oriented planning, the interrelationship with the individual cost objective is unknown for costing, and the utilization of these activities can only be applied **globally**. Consequently, aggregated cost rates are formed, e.g., on the basis of production costs.

Activity (process) descriptions will now also be introduced for administrative departments within the framework of activity-based costing. In contrast to Production, however, individual "administration activities" are not created for each individual cost objective; instead, **typical** subactivities are defined for each cost center, which are then combined into primary activity types that extend beyond the individual cost centers (see Figure D.I.37). Analogously to Production, a subactivity corresponds to an operation, and a primary process corresponds to a routing.

Cost rates can be determined for each subactivity (costs per typical purchase order, costs per typical invoice); by means of subactivity contributions, costs can also be determined per reference unit for a typical

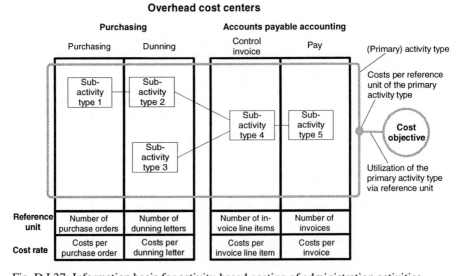

Fig. D.I.37: Information basis for activity-based costing of administration activities

primary activity, e.g., costs for a typical purchase order, by specifying proportional values.

The causative assignment of the utilization of the activity category can only be as good as the accuracy with which the primary activity reference unit is applied and the value of the utilization is determined. A direct assignment of a primary activity unit to a cost objective unit, as applies in the case of production costs, is not feasible.

The main differences between activity-based costing for Administration and Production are that:

- Production has access to cost-objective-specific process descriptions in the form of routings and bills of materials, while this is not the case for Administration. Consequently, the activity-based costing process itself must make these descriptions. Because of the effort involved, this occurs only on the category level.

- In Production, there is a direct assignment between process (routing) and cost objective, while in Administration it has to be coded via reference units.

Despite these differences, administration-oriented activity-based costing can be returned to the structure of classical cost center and cost objective accounting. Thus, the data structure shown in Figure D.I.30 need not be changed in any fundamental way. Approaches for developing an independent data structure for activity-based costing are based more on adopting the different terminology than on actual contentual differences (see *Berkau, Datenstrukturen für die Prozeßkostenrechnung 1993*).

Business-oriented reasoning processes also support this view that classical cost accounting and activity-based costing are structurally identical (see *Kloock, Prozeßkostenrechnung als Rückschritt und Fortschritt der Kostenrechnung 1992*).

The interrelationship between describing the process on the basis of event-driven process chains and the description needed for activity-based costing is apparent. A complete ARIS-based problem description of application systems thus also provides fundamentals for differentiated cost analysis. Using workflow management concepts, an effort is also being made to control administrative activities (processes) individually, analogously to production processes. In doing so, similar data structures can be created as in the case of data for bills of materials and routings in Production, thus leading to the merger of the cost accounting processes in Administration and in Production.

D.I.2.3 Controlling/EIS

The information provided by external, cost and income accounting serves as an important foundation for Controlling and for executive information systems. The major aspect of Controlling is its coordination function. Generally speaking, Controlling is responsible for coordinating the planning and control of operational subdepartments for the purpose of achieving the corporate objectives. Under this definition (see *Küpper, Anforderungen der Kostenrechnung an moderne Unternehmensstrukturen 1992, p. 140*), Controlling has an interdepartmental function. The coordination function becomes all the more important the greater the degree of decentralization of the organizational structure. However, this only holds true if the enterprise is based on a functional organizational structure. In the process-oriented classification pursued here, the primary integration function lies **within** the process chains, while only loose links exist **between** them. This is the reason why Controlling functions have already been discussed within the process chains, i.e., Controlling within the context of logistics, research and development, and accounting.

The ability to accomplish the coordination function depends on the availability of the necessary information. The data supplied by external, cost and income accounting lead to an information overload that cannot be adequately analyzed within the process chains or on the level of corporate management. For example, as early as 1958, Aghte reported that the owner of a metalworking factory received 13,000 items of data per month, of which he could only assimilate and process 50 (see *Kraemer, Entwicklungspotentiale der EDV-gestützten Kostenauswertung 1993, p. 41*; *Aghte, Die Abweichungen in der Plankostenrechnung 1959, p. 102*). More recent studies have also provided similar findings (see *Mertens/Griese, Integrierte Informationsverarbeitung II 1993, p. 52*). This voluminous amount of data leads to a situation in which the information provided by accounting cannot be analyzed to its full potential. Instead, the bulk of the effort is invested in preparing the information rather than in using it as a decision-support tool for management.

Controlling, therefore, has to provide the information filters to supply the information in a recipient-specific, decision-relevant, succinct and adaptable fashion (see *Reichmann/Fritz/Nölken, EIS-gestütztes Controlling 1993, p. 465*).

At the core of this type of Controlling environment is an appropriately designed reference system. For example, such a system can be tailored to the size of the Controlling departments, the information objects to be entered (value-related variables or quantity- and time-related technical variables) and the chronological reference (short-term, medium-term or long-term). Since department-oriented Controlling is increasingly becoming the responsibility of the business process owner, this discussion will focus on interdepartmental Controlling.

Despite the various proposals supporting reference systems, the receiver-oriented nature of Controlling necessitates that the process be designed on an enterprise-specific basis. Consequently, information processing primarily develops **tools** with which consolidations or graphical presentations can be prepared from the operative systems in accordance with the information needs of corporate management. Terms such as "EIS" or "ESS" are significant in this connection. An EIS (Executive Information System) is understood to be a management information system that provides corporate management with real-time goal- and decision-related information for strategic corporate control (see *Reichmann/Fritz/Nölken, EIS-gestütztes Controlling 1993, p. 477*). If this type of system also offers method-based decision support, as is the case in decision support systems (DSS), which run the gamut from statistical analyses to optimization calculations, the EIS becomes an ESS (Executive Support System) (see *Back-Hock, Executive-Information-Systems 1990, p. 190*).

Merely providing a toolbox of solutions for Controlling problems is insufficient, however. Instead, typical analytical strategies for solving Controlling problems can be "prefabricated" in support of the process of determining causes on the basis of the occurrence of negative symptoms (e.g., high cost variances in a department) and deriving suggestions for corrective solutions on the basis of this determination. This process of inferring causes from symptoms and then subsequently adopting therapies exists in connection with all Controlling functions, which means that it can be generalized. These types of interrelationships exist in the form of empirical knowledge. Knowledge can be represented by rules and can express complicated interrelationships between symptoms, causes and suggested therapies. For example, the simultaneous occurrence of high cost overruns in two departments can be explained on the basis of a common cause, e.g., their mutual dependence on raw materials prices. For this reason, the application of knowledge-based systems for variance analysis was discussed early on (see *Mertens, Expertisesysteme als Variante der Expertensysteme zur Führungsinformation 1989, p. 844*). Since then, developers have gained experience with industrial applications (see *Kraemer, Effizientes Kostenmanagement 1993*). These types of systems provide a "prefabricated" analysis strategy as well as options for inputting individual knowledge and experience in a structured fashion. At the same time, they offer user-friendly graphical support for succinctly presenting exceptional situations in a form of an exception reporting system. Ongoing, virtually automated monitoring of the important key figures (reference system) can reveal outliers, which can then be analyzed in detail down to the level of individual cases (drill-down navigation).

D.I.2.4 Summarizing and Supplementing the Requirements Definitions for Accounting

D.I.2.4.1 Requirements Definition for Accounting: The Function View

Value-oriented accounting system functions are analyzed in Figure D.I.38 with respect to their processing modes.

Although financial accounting is characterized by high-volume processes that frequently occur in bundled form, it is nonetheless highly oriented toward interactive processing. The reason for this is the high degree of integration at the workstation that can be achieved through uniform processing. Operations such as account code allocation, data entry, review and posting procedures can all be processed in a case-oriented manner.

An enterprise frequently encounters similar business transactions in bundled form, e.g., if all EFT payments to a bank are then processed as a bundle of payment documents. The advantage of this type of uniform processing is that certain data, e.g., the bank account number, can be retained and automatically used for all of the individual entries and thus does not need to be re-entered each time. These types of bundled transactions can be automatically transferred from upstream DP processes.

Processing automatically transferred transaction bundles in batch mode would seem the obvious solution. Only if inconsistencies occur (e.g., between total debits and total credits) do certain transactions have to be segregated and processed interactively.

Basic account data management is performed interactively for reasons of currency and in order to allow the plausibility check to be carried out with the master data from the operative systems.

The posting process, consisting of account code allocation, data entry, data verification and posting, is performed interactively due to the required direct plausibility check as well as for reasons of currency. Here, too, the process conforms to the principle of exception control in that unproblematic high-volume operations are processed automatically and only special and individual cases are processed interactively.

Because recurrent analyses such as journals and financial statements are so processing-intensive, they can be processed in batch mode; however, they can also be initiated interactively for reasons of currency. Financial statements, too, can also be created within the context of an iterative modification in that the ramifications of financial statement policy objectives can be studied within the framework of valuation latitude.

Similarly, numerous special analyses can be incorporated into an iteration process.

Cash management and financial planning constitute interactive decision-making processes. The strict period-oriented structuring of cost and income accounting procedures as well as period-oriented (annual)

Function		Subfunction	Reasons for interactive processing				Automatic/ batch
			Currency	Plausibility	Iterative modification	Interactive decision process	
Financial accounting	Basic data management	Account maintenance	X	X			
	Posting	Account code allocation		X			(X)
		Entry		X			(X)
		Verification		X			(X)
		Posting	X				X
	Analyses	Journal					X
		Period-end closing			(X)		X
		Special analyses	X		(X)		
		Consolidation					X
	Liquidity/financial planning	Cash management				X	
		Financial planning				X	
Cost and income accounting	Basic data management			X			
	Cost category accounting						X
	Cost center accounting	Planning				X	
		Internal allocation					X
		Variance analysis				X	
	Product costing	Preliminary costing				X	
		Standard costing					X
		Concurrent costing	X				
		Actual cost analysis		X			X
	Period costing		X				X
	Controlling	Updating reference system	X				
		Monitoring					X
		Screw down analyses				X	

Fig. D.I.38: Processing modes of value-oriented accounting systems

accounting—the only form that is possible with manual processing—influenced the development of first-generation DP systems in the direction of time-period-oriented batch systems.

The advent of interactive processing sparked a heated debate with respect to the advantages of this form of application. The course of this discussion can be seen from the published conference proceedings of the "Cost Accounting and DP" workshops in Saarbrücken, Germany (see *Kilger/Scheer, Rechnungswesen und EDV 1980 - 1986; Scheer, Rechnungswesen und EDV 1987 - 1993*), in particular the contributions by Plattner, Plaut and Scheer.

In the meantime, however, more recent developments in interactive applications have met with a positive response.

Analysis of the reasons for choosing interactive control of individual processing functions dictates that "mass processes," e.g., cost transfer from upstream departments (cost category accounting), internal cost and income allocation, standard costing for the total production program, actual cost analysis for completed order inventory, and period-oriented profitability analysis, be retained as batch functions.

However, the more cost accounting develops into a decision support system, the more period-oriented routine analyses are being supplemented or even replaced by ad hoc analytical functions. In this case, even processing functions that were previously developed as batch solutions are increasingly being handled interactively, e.g., in order to simulatively find the correct decision through iterative modification of an initial result.

As in other applications, master data maintenance (cost categories, cost centers, reference units) lends itself to interactive processing due to the need for currency and plausibility checks.

In an interactive solution, the planning functions also enable support to be provided for plausibility considerations. At the same time, however, it is also possible to simulate alternatives.

In customer-order-oriented manufacturing, preliminary costing is typically an interactive function that is incorporated into the order acceptance process. Moreover, it also provides support for price negotiations and can function as an interactive decision support system when examining alternatives.

Updating the Controlling reference system is an interactive function.

Automatic monitoring of variances between standard and actual values for the purpose of identifying exceptional situations should be handled in batch mode in order to protect the user against information overload. The subsequent analysis down to the individual case level is a typical interactive function, whereby the analysis path evolves out of the subresults in the form of an interactive decision-making process.

D.I.2.4.2 Requirements Definition for Accounting: The Organization View

User-oriented accounting is increasingly conforming to the organizational forms of logistics. In a decentralized logistics environment,

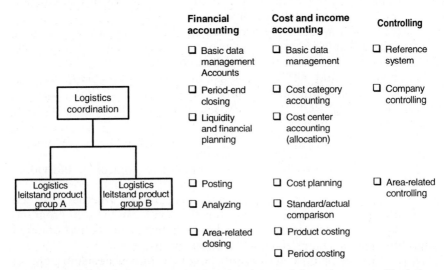

Fig. D.I.39: Integration of accounting functions into the leitstand concept of logistics

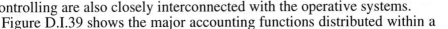

which is structured according to product groups on a process-oriented basis, the subsidiary accounting systems (accounts payable, accounts receivable) are integrated into the logistics leitstands. The master data for accounts payable and accounts receivable are maintained on the coordination level on an inter-product-group basis. The applications for decision-related cost and income accounting as well as departmental Controlling are also closely interconnected with the operative systems.

Figure D.I.39 shows the major accounting functions distributed within a leitstand organizational structure for logistics.

D.I.2.4.3 Requirements Definition for Accounting: The Data View

The most important data-related problem lies in integrating the value-oriented systems with the operative systems. Accounting terminology makes it tempting to define accounting terms (account, document, posting record, account payable, account receivable, cost category, cost center, cost objective, reference unit) as independent information objects, although they are often identical among themselves or with objects in the operative systems. As a result, particular emphasis has been placed on developing a data structure that is as non-redundant as possible and on referencing the correspondence between such terms as customer and account receivable, supplier and account payable, business transaction and document, account and cost category, etc. A further problem results from the heterogeneity and variability of the situations to be processed, e.g., a cost objective can be an order, a customer, a part, a region, etc.

In order to prevent independent systems from being developed to process these subtypes, the data structure has to be created in as generalized a fashion as possible. The same holds true with respect to cost accounting procedures. In this connection, it was emphasized in the discussion of activity-based accounting that, if the data structures for routings are viewed from a generalized perspective, they do not differ significantly different from cost accounting approaches for production processes.

By more strongly emphasizing decision support and up-to-date controls, cost accounting is shifting directions and migrating toward a cost information system. This principle has already been taken into account in the development of the database by depicting the concepts in as procedure-neutral a fashion as possible, as characterized by the concept of general accounting.

D.I.2.4.4 Requirements Definition for Accounting: The Control View

Since the subsidiary accounting systems are intertwined with logistics processes, they are already contained in the EPCs for the logistics chains. The other accounting processes are not as strongly characterized by structured process chains as the operative logistics systems. Instead, analysis paths evolve interactively from ad hoc situations. Figure D.I.40 thus shows only events that initiate fundamental accounting processes.

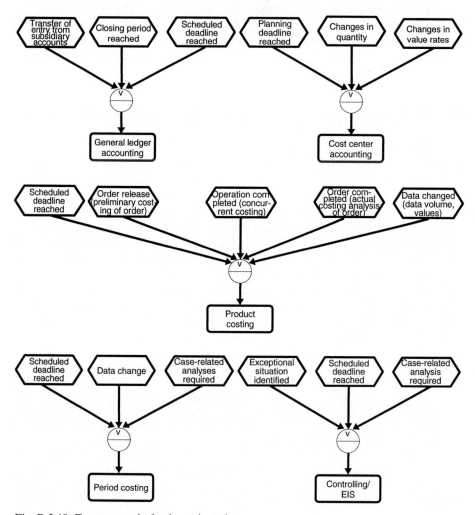

Fig. D.I.40: Event control of value-oriented processes

D.I.3 Design Specifications for Accounting

In adapting the requirements definitions to information technology interfaces, the functional analysis primarily requires a high degree of modularization in order to support the principle of software reusability. At the same time, this is also the only way to support a minimal degree of process structuring.

The costing module, for example, should be kept general enough so that it can process such varied costing objects as customer orders, production orders, maintenance orders, purchase orders, etc.

Figure D.I.41 shows an overview of user transactions for financial accounting (see *SAP, System RF 1983, p.3-1-1*).

User transactions
TB01 - Posting document without account maintenance
TB02 - Modify document
TB03 - Display document
TB04 - Account maintenance
TB05 - Posting and clearing
TB06 - Adding recurring document
TB07 - Modify recurring document
TB08 - Modify accounts payable line item/accounts receivable line item
TB09 - Document entry
TB10 - Display accounts payable line items
TB11 - Change accounts payable line items
TB12 - Display line items general ledger accounts
TB13 - Change line items general ledger accounts
TB14 - Display accounts receivable line items
TB15 - Change accounts receivable line items
TB16 - Display total
TB21 - Control total
TB30 - Posting payment by note
TB31 - Posting bank discount
TB32 - Maintain special transactions
TB33 - Statistical entry
TM19 - Database list display
TM20 - Database list display

Fig. D.I.41: User transactions for financial accounting

Monitoring and analysis functions within the context of Controlling can be effectively supported through the use of expert systems (see *Kraemer, Effizientes Kostenmanagement 1993*).

The implementation of organizational models necessitates reconciliation between interdepartmental data management and coordination with decentralized processing and analysis functions. The leitstand organization derived from this thus leads to a network concept with an interdepartmental data server and department-oriented process and analysis clients.

Blackboard architectures are suitable for a process-oriented analysis in which processes are analyzed in terms of cost across several cost center departments (see *Berkau, Datenstrukturen für die Prozeßkostenrechnung 1993*), and in which the subprocesses are (centrally) coordinated via a common information repository (blackboard) (see Figure D.I.42).

The expansion of cost accounting into a cost information system necessitates a flexible database, such as those that can be provided by modern relational databases (see *Sinzig, Die Bedeutung relationaler Datenbanken 1992*).

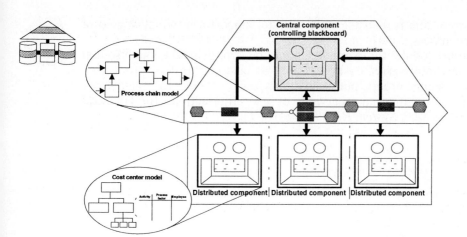

Fig. D.I.42: Concept of a distributed controlling information system

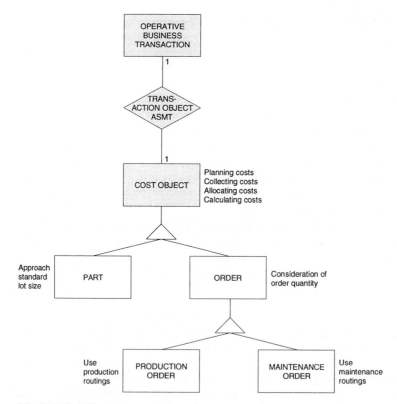

Fig. D.I.43: Object representation of cost accounting

Financial accounting recognized the possibility of generalizing accounting functions early on by choosing a level of abstraction for its description on which all processes can be represented by using the "account" and "posting record" constructs.

Cost accounting, on the other hand, is more heterogeneous. Nevertheless, its functions can also be traced back to the essential elements of planning costs, collecting costs, allocating costs and calculating costs. In an object-oriented approach, these general functions would be further specialized on the basis of the categorization of the cost objects (see Figure D.I.43).

In a consistent analysis of this principle, a cost object can be attached to each business transaction within the operative systems, with this object then performing all cost-relevant functions for the process.

D.II Information Management

D.II.1 Overview: Information Management

In addition to the value-oriented information and coordination processes, management of the "information" resource constitutes the second process for providing the operative applications with information support. In contrast to the value-oriented systems, however, information management does not input data from the operative processes and interpret them from its own perspective; instead, information management provides only information processing instruments for supporting the operative processes. The term "instruments" will initially be discussed in a broader context, followed by a more precise analysis.

"Information management" is short for "information resource management," a concept that was developed in the U.S. (see *Horton, Information Resource Management 1985*). This principle is based on the premise that information can be viewed as a factor of production (resource) that, like other production resources, can be planned, procured and controlled on a cost-efficient basis. Although the term can be interpreted in various ways (see *Österle/Brenner/Hilbers, Unternehmensführung und Informationssystem, Stuttgart 1992, pp. 28 - 30; Heinrich/Burgholzer, Informationsmanagement 1996, p. 21; Krcmar/Elgers, Teams und Informationsmanagement 1993, p. 676; Wollnik, Ein Referenzmodell des Informationsmanagements 1988, p. 40*), the most important functions of information management involve strategically configuring the technical components of an information system, developing application systems, and providing for the cost-efficient operation of the information system. This is achieved, for example, by planning, controlling and monitoring all information processes (see *Waidelich, Informationsmanagement in der Automobilindustrie 1993*) or by providing the right information to the right recipient at the right time in the right format. The function tree shown in Figure D.II.01 conforms to Wollnik's approach and classifies information management functions into the management of:
- The information infrastructure
- Information systems
- Information application and utilization.

Accordingly, Wollnik defines information management as planning, organizing and controlling the employment of information, the individual information systems, and the infrastructures for information processing and communication within an organization (see *Wollnik, Ein Referenzmodell des Informations-Managements 1988, p. 39*).

Although Wollnik's approach provides a rough grid rather than a detailed description of information management functions, the important functions can easily be classified on the basis of this scheme, as shown in the function tree. The most significant function of strategic infrastructure

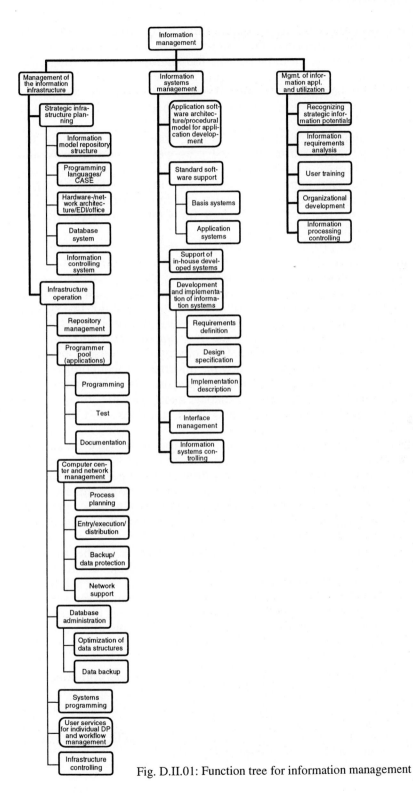

Fig. D.II.01: Function tree for information management

planning involves specifying the basic architecture, which serves as the basis for describing information systems. This is expressed by the definition of the information model as the foundation for a repository. An information model describes the constructs and their relationships, which are used to describe an information system; a repository stores the (application) information system that was described on the basis of these structures.

Moreover, strategic infrastructure planning must also determine the programming languages and tools (CASE), as well as the hardware and network architecture—including the concepts for intercompany data interchange and internal communications within the framework of office management—to be used by the enterprise and must specify the strategy for database system use and the concept for Controlling cost-efficient utilization of information processing.

Because of the problems involved in delineating between the Controlling function and the information systems, the relationship between the two areas has been a topic of frequent discussion. Both involve coordination functions for the operative applications. With respect to applications, however, information management should be viewed more in the context of a support system, while Controlling tends to function as a coordination system (see *Reichmann/Fritz/Nölken, EIS-gestütztes Controlling 1993, p. 474*). One obvious relationship between both functions is that Controlling relies on information technology—and thus on information management—in supporting its information and coordination functions; information management, on the other hand, necessitates cost-efficient control, and thus requires a Controlling function.

In addition to strategic configuration of the **infrastructure**, managing the regular operation of the system is an additional relevant concern. In accordance with the cited functions or subfunctions, operation involves managing repositories, controlling the application programmers, who work together in a programmer pool, and controlling both a computer center and the internal and external communication network, a subject that will take on increasing significance in the future.

Providing ongoing support for the database systems in the form of optimizing the data structures and performing data backups are functions of database administration. Systems programming is responsible for performing functions that relate to the operating system. User services provides ongoing advice, training and resource acquisition for individual data processing areas and workflow management. A Controlling function ensures cost-efficient implementation and utilization of the information infrastructure.

Information systems management involves a strategic component in that it specifies the application software architecture. Specifying the procedural model according to which application systems are developed is a strategic function as well.

Both the use of standard software as well as application systems developed in-house necessitates ongoing support.

Conforming to the ARIS concept, application systems will be developed and introduced in the familiar phases of the requirements definition, the design specification and the implementation description.

The management of the interfaces between different application systems is handled by an interface manager.

An application systems Controlling function should also be provided to ensure cost-efficient control of the development and use of application software.

The management of the **application** and employment of **information** also involves a strategic component with respect to recognizing far-reaching information potential.

The information requirements analysis determines the meaningful information needs of concrete workstations. User training is an important prerequisite for adequately utilizing the information systems that have been developed. Only an organization that is geared toward information technology and its many possibilities can fully exploit the strategic potential of information processing. The Controlling function is also responsible for the cost-efficient use of the information systems that have been introduced.

In the early days of information processing, functions were primarily performed by a central organizational unit; however, information management today is increasingly becoming a general management function and is moving into the individual application departments. Viewed in these terms, information management is a part of every management function, in the same manner as human resource management and Controlling, for example. The decentralization of information management primarily affects management of the ways in which information is applied and used, the development of application systems (at least with respect to the requirements definition) and the department-oriented Controlling of information processing.

On the other hand, strategic management of the infrastructure and of the application software architecture, including the procedural model, is a very comprehensive function that is assigned to a central information management department (see the organizational model shown in Figure D.II.02).

The development and support of interdepartmental application systems is also a centralized function. If client/server architectures are introduced, the focus of a central computer center will, at most, be on data management, including data backup functions. On the other hand, the central responsibility for the operation of the internal/external communication network will grow.

The organizational model assigns the operative business processes of logistics and product development their own areas of responsibility with respect to information management. Since a significant function of decentralized information management involves the subject-specific description of the demands placed on the application systems, these functions have already been treated in the context of their respective business processes. The following discussion, therefore, will focus on the

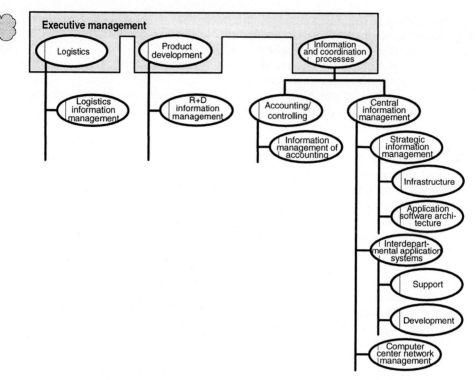

Fig. D.II.02: Organizational chart for information management

coordination function of information management, especially through specification of the general strategic conditions for information application. The information management process will be described using the same approach employed in the case of the application systems, i.e., on the basis of the ARIS concept.

Because of the central importance of the information model and its close affinity to the method of representation used here, the analysis will focus on its role as the basis for the repository as well as on the procedural model for developing application systems that is derived from it.

The ARIS architecture indicates the views and descriptive levels that can be used to describe an information system. If application systems are developed according to this concept, the descriptive structures developed in ARIS, e.g., functional models, organizational models, data models and control models, occur on all descriptive levels, i.e., the requirements definition, the design specification and the implementation description (see Figure D.II.03).

As they are descriptions of application systems, these models are also the subject of information management, which is responsible for storing and maintaining them. To do this, a database must be provided whose logic lends itself to the inclusion of the structures used for model

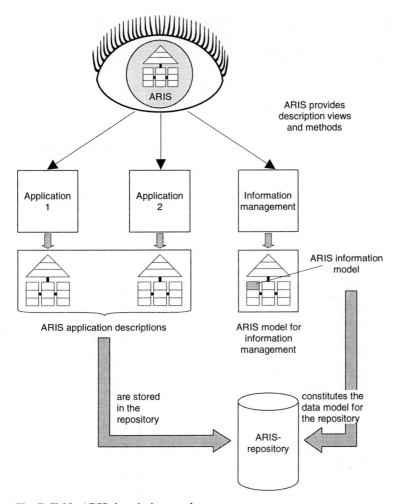

Fig. D.II.03: ARIS description results

descriptions as the data objects. The description of these data structures is termed the "information model" and constitutes the data model for the repository. This perspective thus provides information management with the data view of the ARIS models. It asks which object types are contained in the ARIS models and what their relationships to one another are (see Figure D.II.03). The other requirements definitions consist of the functional model shown in Figure D.II.01 and the organizational model shown in Figure D.II.02. Correspondingly, the design specifications and implementation levels of information management are then described by the DP support tools used to control information management. In the case of technical DP repository administration, for example, this can be a repository manager (see *Dürmeyer, Informationsmodell AD/Cycle 1993, p. 147*).

In the context of basic data management, the following discussion will outline the information model structure that is necessary for the descriptive models shown within the framework of this book and will then treat the procedure for application development projects based on the ARIS concept. The process chain diagram shown in Figure D.II.04 illustrates these information management functions.

Application development encompasses the description of the organization of a given project, on the one hand, as well as the project-oriented procedural model derived from the general procedural model. The descriptions created during handling of the project will be indicated

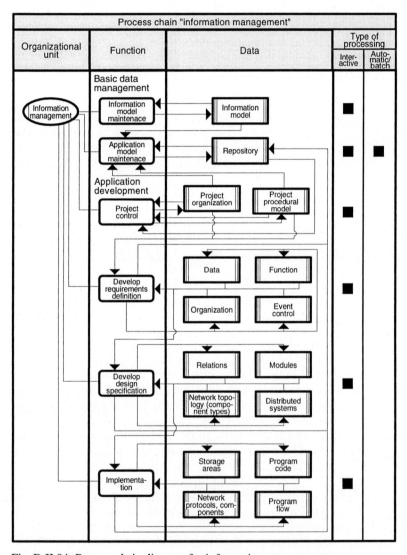

Fig. D.II.04: Process chain diagram for information management

on the levels of the requirements definition, the design specification and the implementation description for the individual ARIS views. Each subsequent descriptive level always uses the description resulting from the preceding descriptive level, with the results being put into the repository. At the same time, the project-oriented procedural model is updated following completion of a data model by changing the status of the "create data model" function from "in process" to "completed."

D.II.2 Requirements Definitions for Information Management

D.II.2.1 Basic Data Management (ARIS Information Model)

Basic data management relates to the strategic function of "stipulating the information model as the foundation for a repository" taken from the function tree for information management shown in Figure D.II.01. Analogously to basic data management as discussed in the context of the previous areas, the objects to be described in the analysis are identified and represented together with their relationships using the entity relationship model.

Figure D.II.05 shows these levels of an information system. The lowest level is the level of individual objects, as expressed by the objects "Customer Miller," "Processing of customer order 1234" or concrete "Workstation WS75." In the description of information systems, however, the individual cases are not analyzed; instead, they are combined into classes or object types. The company's individual customers then form the object type CUSTOMER, the processing of individual orders forms ORDER PROCESSING, and the individual workstations that are used form the type concept WORKSTATION. In this book, functional models, organizational models and data models—together with their links—were created on this level.

Information management has to manage these application-oriented object types. To do this, it forms classes of similar object types. The application-oriented object type "customer," for example, is generalized together with the object types supplier, employee, order, etc., into the term "information object," since each object type belongs to the class "attribute object." Likewise, the term "order processing" is combined with other terms such as "production" or "sales" into the class of "functions." The term "workstation," together with similar terms such as "file server" or "terminal" forms the term "component type."

Since this descriptive level is superordinate to the application-relationship level, it is termed a "metalevel."

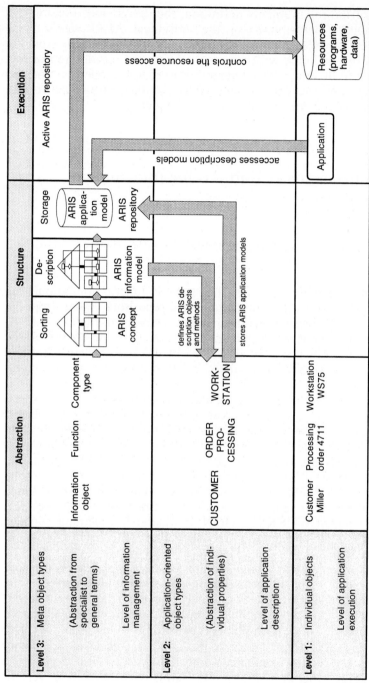

Fig. D.II.05: ARIS metalevel

The levels shown in Figure D.II.05 form a bottom-up abstraction process, whereby the terms on each subordinate level are always elements of the terms on the superordinate level.

At this point, the objects on the metalevel are not imported from the application level in an unorganized fashion, but rather structured according to the ARIS concept. The derivative sequence shown in Figure D.II.05 under the heading "Structure" first describes the ARIS structure for the terms in the information model on the metalevel. The dual relationship between the information model and the application description level is expressed by the arrow leading from the information model to the application description level, since the information model contains the constructs that are used to describe the applications and thus provides the methodological framework. Since, on the other hand, the information model is the data model for the repository, the results of the application modeling process are transferred to the repository. If this repository is active, i.e., if it is directly linked with the physical components of the application system, their physical execution can be controlled via the models. This interrelationship is shown in Figure D.II.05 under the heading "Execution." When a concrete application (e.g., order entry) is executed, it accesses the application descriptions, e.g., the structure for the information objects CUSTOMER and ARTICLE, and transfers them to the database system, which, in turn, accesses the locations of the storage units stored in the repository and provides their types with the necessary physical data for the application.

This kind of active role performed by a repository necessitates a close link between the application modeling level and the application systems as well as the general resource layer of the information systems. These types of concepts are not only of theoretical interest, but also form the architecture for practical development strategies. Figure D.II.06 (from *IBM, CIM-Unternehmen 1990, p. 42*) shows the architecture of IBM's CIM concept, in which the approach just described can be seen to be the guiding principle for the future development of CIM application systems.

The physical data are allocated to both a central data storage unit as well as to individual decentralized functions. Applications then access the data via the model definitions contained in the repository and from there to the centrally or decentrally stored data.

In the following discussion, the basic data for information management, i.e., the information model, will be represented on the basis of the ARIS views and descriptive levels. Not all the descriptive objects on the application level that are used in this book will be transferred to the information model (for a more detailed analysis of the ARIS information model, see *Scheer, Architektur integrierter Informationssysteme 1992*).

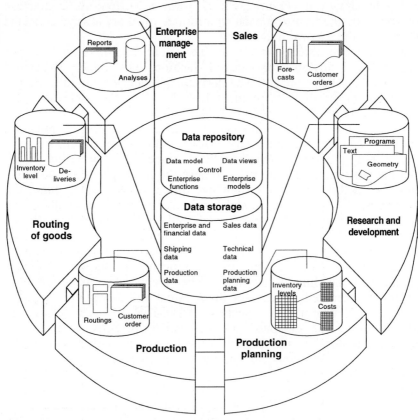

Fig. D.II.06: Repository controlled reference model for CIM
(from *IBM, CIM-Unternehmen 1990, p. 42*)

D.II.2.1.1 Functions

In the requirements definition description for application functions, the individual functions were represented by a function tree. In the representation of this structure, the first step is to identify the information object FUNCTION, which encompasses such instances as order acceptance, invoicing, etc. The F. STRUCTURE represented by the function tree forms a 1:n relationship within the information object FUNCTION. This data structure constitutes the focus of the requirements definition description for the function view within the ARIS information model shown in Figure D.II.07. If the functions are internetworked among one another, the structural relationship becomes a "many-to-many" cardinality.

Primary functions support business processes, whereby a business process can be incorporated by several functions and, conversely, a function can be incorporated into different business processes. Each

638

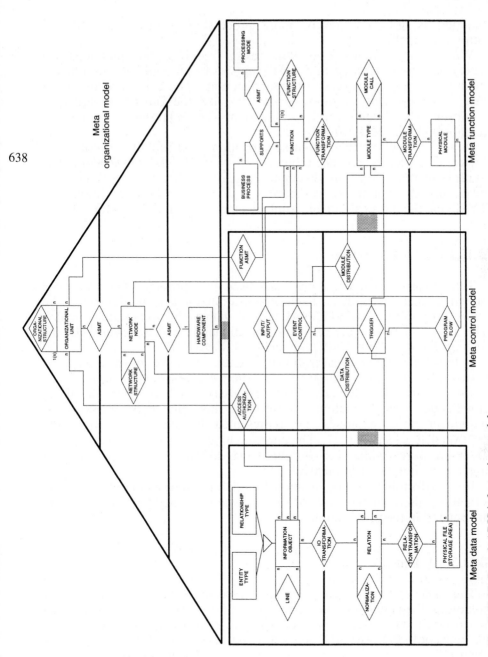

Fig. D.II.07: Rough ARIS information model

function is assigned one or more processing modes (interactive or automatic/batch).

Within the framework of the design specification, functions are categorized into modules. In order to support the principle of reusability, a module can go into several different functions. The call-up relationships that exist between the modules—which, like the functional structure, conform to a hierarchical logical system—are represented by the 1:n relationship type MODULE CALL.

A module type on the design specification level initially describes the logical function. It can be implemented using several physical module implementations, e.g., in different languages. On the implementation level, an n:m relationship is therefore also assumed between MODULE TYPE and the physical module implementation (PHYSICAL MODULE).

D.II.2.1.2 Organization

The organizational chart has been used to represent subject-oriented organizational descriptions. Each organizational unit is an element of the entity type ORGANIZATIONAL UNIT within the information model. The hierarchical structure of the organizational units is represented by the relationship type ORGANIZATIONAL STRUCTURE.

In transforming the organizational structures into design specifications, network nodes are assigned to the organizational units. This transformation has already been discussed in particular detail in connection with production control. The links that exist between the individual network nodes are represented by the relationship type NETWORK STRUCTURE. The concrete hardware components that exist at a network node are assigned via a 1:n relationship on the implementation description level.

By transforming the organizational model into physical communication structures, the resource level of the hardware and network infrastructure are entered in the information model.

D.II.2.1.3 Data

The data structures were developed especially intensively within the context of the application models. The central concepts in this connection are the entity type and the relationship type, and both are generalized into the concept INFORMATION OBJECT. Instances of this INFORMATION OBJECT entity type include, for example, such application-oriented entity and relationship types as CUSTOMER, ARTICLE, ORDER, ACCOUNT, COST CENTER, etc. The lines in the entity-relationship model, which link information objects with one another, are represented by the relationship type LINE. The significant descriptive attributes of this LINE relationship type are its cardinalities.

In transforming the information objects into relations for the design specification, several relations can arise from one information object or, in the case of a relational representation that has been bundled according to performance criteria, several information objects can be combined into one relation (e.g., in the case of the NF^2). The normalization process for the relational model describes how relations are split up in order to satisfy specific normalization criteria. The occurrence of relations as a result of the normalization process is represented by the relationship type NORMALIZATION.

In the implementation description, the relations are combined into physical files and allocated to physical storage areas.

D.II.2.1.4 Control

The requirements definitions for the applications control view encompasses all the dual relationships in the ARIS views as well as an overall view of them. Event control is particularly emphasized as a link between the data and the function views.

The link between the organization view and the function view is entered in the information model via the relationship type FUNCTION ASSIGNMENT. This relationship type describes the allocation of functions within an organizational level model, as discussed in detail within the context of logistics. Since several functions can be assigned to one organizational unit and one function can be performed by several organizational units, the cardinalities for the function assignment are type n.

The relationship between organizational structure and the data model can be represented by access authorizations. This aspect specifies which organizational units can access which information objects with which authorization rights (read, modify, write, delete). This relationship type also has type n cardinalities.

The links between the data view and the function view are represented by the relationship type INPUT/OUTPUT, which indicates which information objects are processed by a function and which information objects are changed by a function. In a more detailed analysis, this relationship should be constructed on the attribute level; however, for the sake of simplicity, this discussion will define the information object in broad terms, together with the attributes assigned to it.

Event control is portrayed using event-driven process chains and represented through the relationship type EVENT CONTROL. It is linked with information objects that represent events, i.e., that initiate functions by generating a new instance or by status changes.

In the case of the interrelationships between the design specification organization (network topology), the design specification data (relations) and the design specification functions (module types), the design specification for control leads to the concepts of distributed databases and distributed data processing. These distribution options are expressed by the relationship types DATA DISTRIBUTION and MODULE DISTRIBUTION.

On the design specification level, event control is represented by the trigger principle. A trigger consists of the elements "event," "condition" and "action." Events are derived from the subject-specific description of event control. Conditions typically relate to data, which creates a relationship to the relations in the data view. The actions to be performed are module calls, indicated by a corresponding link to the term "module type."

On the implementation description level, the combination of physical information system structures is represented by the relationship type PROGRAM EXECUTION, which links the triggers, as initiating actions, with the physical data storage units and the physical program modules.

The definition of the information model is a purely strategic function of information management. In their refined form (see *Scheer, Architektur integrierter Informationssysteme 1992*), which contains approximately three hundred metainformation objects, both the ARIS information model outlined here as well as the application-oriented models for the corresponding application areas developed in this book can serve as a reference model for information management.

The information model forms the requirements definition description for the data view of information management. If information management is viewed as an application, the information objects developed in Figure D.II.07 are themselves instances of the entity type INFORMATION OBJECT represented on the requirements definition level for the data view. This means that the metamodel from the information management view constitutes the application level for the data view.

D.II.2.2 Project Process (Application Development)

D.II.2.2.1 General ARIS Procedural Model

Figure D.II.08 shows a more detailed representation of a typical project organization for development of a system. Corporate management is represented in the reference group in order to ensure that the project will be structured on the basis of corporate objectives. The project manager is responsible for operative project handling and coordinates the subprojects. The subprojects, in turn, are managed by subproject managers. By providing as much overlap as possible between project personnel from line departments and from information management in the subprojects and the coordination meetings between the subprojects, support is provided for the coordination process during operative project development.

The organizational structure shown in Figure D.II.08 is a part of the ARIS organization view of information management. However, since this

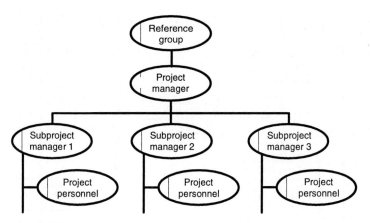

Fig. D.II.08: Project organization for information systems

information is stored in the repository, it is also entered in the information model on the metalevel (see Figure D.II.10).

The processes within information management relate to the operation and development of information systems. Regular operation is geared toward the application logic represented in the information systems. Consequently, the processes have already been handled within the individual process chains. These processes are structured, i.e., they largely follow a set process scheme, e.g., the program process for order processing. In the case of batch processing, information management is responsible for execution control. In the case of interactive processing, on the other hand, the application processes lie within the user's realm of responsibility, and information management is only responsible for providing the resources.

The process of creating information systems exhibits the nature of a project. A project is a time-consuming event with a definable start and finish. The procedure for creating information systems conforms to the procedural model for information management derived from the architecture model. If the ARIS model is followed, the procedural model is geared toward the constructs that are specified to be developed there. With its defined views and analysis levels, the ARIS procedural model thus specifies the project results to be developed. However, it contains degrees of latitude with respect to the sequence and the bundling of activities. Figure D.II.09 shows the ARIS procedural model in the form of an event-driven process chain. Following a rough analysis of the weaknesses inherent in the existing information system using a process chain analysis, a rough target concept is represented in the form of process chains. This rough analysis has already been treated in the section entitled "Overview." Subject-related subprojects are defined on the basis of the rough analysis; target concepts are worked out in detail for these subprojects in the subsequent processing steps. To do this, requirements definitions, design specifications and implementation descriptions are

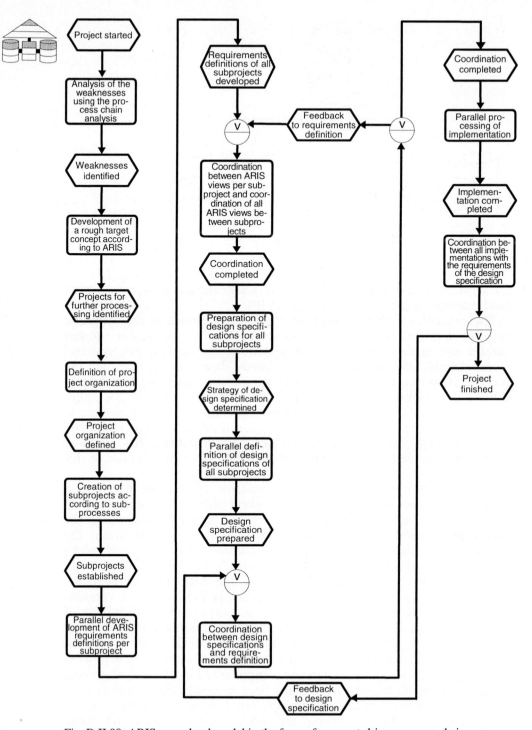

Fig. D.II.09: ARIS procedural model in the form of an event-driven process chain

worked out. The models for the individual views are handled simultaneously within the individual levels.

Following completion of the design specification and implementation description phases, conformity with the requirements from the superordinate phases is verified. In the event of variances, it is necessary to return to the coordination level of the previous development phase.

The procedural model shown in Figure D.II.09 is merely a rough guiding principle. Within each individual development step, in turn, detailed procedural models can be developed, e.g., by first developing rough concepts and then fine-tuning them into detailed concepts.

With the ARIS information model, the logical grid was developed for recording the project results. The models put into the repository must remain identifiable with respect to when they were created and who was responsible for creating them. Consequently, in keeping with the project development view, the information model is extended to include the project structure shown in Figure D.II.10. A project begins with the project order, which an organizational unit, e.g., corporate management or the owner of a business process, submits to Information Management. A staff member is assigned to the project as the project manager, whereby over the course of time, several project managers can be assigned to the project. The overall project can be classified into several subject-specific subprojects, to which staff members are assigned as a project group. The individual ARIS models are created for the subprojects, and each of these models represents a relationship between an ARIS model type (function, organization, data and control), time and the subproject. The link with the

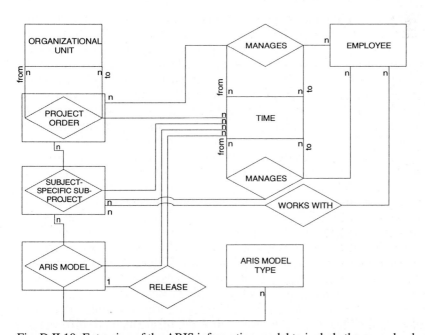

Fig. D.II.10: Extension of the ARIS information model to include the procedural model

entity type TIME is necessary in order to distinguish between different versions of the same model. After a model has been released, it is transferred to the repository, and thus incorporated as an instance into the data structure of the information model. Thus, the relationship type ARIS MODEL shown in Figure D.II.10 represents a cluster of one of the fields in the ARIS "house" shown in Figure D.II.07.

D.II.2.2.2 Detailed Procedural Model for Developing an Enterprise-Wide Data Model (EDM)

The ARIS procedural model is initially a general concept that can be further refined for individual projects for developing the ARIS views. Thus, the project development functions can be described in a more differentiated manner, which will be explored in greater depth using an example relating to the data view. The projects for developing functional and organizational models, as well as their subsequent transformation, will not be discussed in any further detail, since many of the basic principles can be adopted despite the differences in subject matter.

First, project processing will be detailed, followed by a discussion of the different procedures (top-down and bottom-up), and, finally, several observations will be made about the degree of consolidation.

D.II.2.2.2.1 Project Process

An enterprise-wide data model (EDM) necessitates special coordinating functions, since it is a significant part of a master plan for information management. The EDM can incorporate ongoing and planned development projects, and interfaces or overlaps between them can be discussed. Nor does the application of standard software eliminate the need for development of a company's own EDM, since it is impossible to determine the suitability of the standard software until a comparison can be made between the company's own data requirements and the data structures offered by the standard software. If there is an early strategic focus on a standard software system, however, the enterprise-specific model will be strongly influenced by standard software's model. It will then serve as a reference model, from which deviations can only be made in special cases. In addition to reference models provided by standard software systems, neutral, industry-oriented reference models can also be useful in the development of an EDM (see *Bürli et al., Vorgehen beim Aufbau von CIM-Datenmodellen 1992; Scheer/Brombacher, Klare Regeln und Abgrenzungen erforderlich - Wege zum Unternehmensdatenmodell 1993; Endl/Fritz, Rezepte gegen Datenchaos 1993*).

Figure D.II.11 shows a proposal for the project organization of an enterprise data model. In an initial information meeting, corporate management, the heads of important line departments and information management are introduced to the benefits and methodology involved in

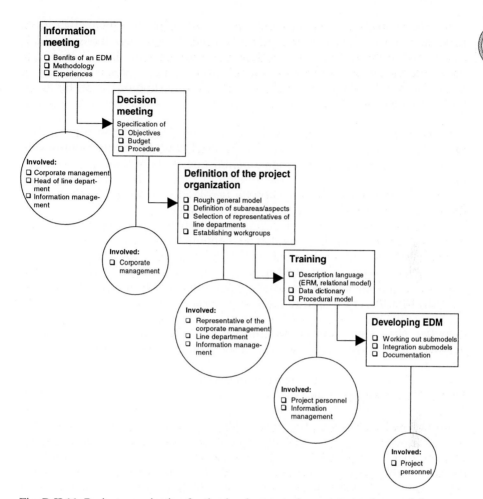

Fig. D.II.11: Project organization for the development of an enterprise data model

setting up an enterprise data model. Afterwards, corporate management specifies the budget and the fundamental procedure to be employed in pursuing the project. The involvement of corporate management in this phase of the project is extremely important. Interdepartmental coordination is necessary in setting up an enterprise data model. Typically this will only be successful if corporate management documents a high priority for the project. The specification of a general budget is important in order to ensure speedy creation of the data model and to avoid being caught up in discussions of individual questions. At the same time, this also serves to concretize the degree of detail involved in the project.

The next step specifies the subsequent project organization procedures. Thus, for example, a rough general model is first created, which serves as the point of departure of the further detailed subarea models. To do this, it is necessary to define the corresponding workgroups. In addition to the workgroups for working out submodels, a coordination panel has to be formed that watches over the interrelationships between the submodels right from the very beginning. Representatives from corporate management should also sit on this panel, which serves as a power promoter. Workgroups involved in specifying the submodels, on the other hand, are primarily made up of representatives from the affected line departments.

In the next step, the staff involved must be identified and trained. For example, the descriptive language to be used, e.g., the entity-relationship model, has to be taught, and fundamental questions of data management, data dictionaries, as well as the modeling tools to be used have to be discussed. Employees who are directly involved with working out the data models, above all, participate in these educational activities.

In the fifth step, the project groups work out the submodels, which are then coordinated with one another and integrated into an overall model. Documentation of the individual steps is particularly important.

The development of an enterprise data model takes place in individual steps. In accordance with the selected procedure (bottom-up, top-down or hybrid), first the entity and relationship types are identified, together with their key attributes.

In the next step, further descriptive attributes are added. The more detailed the design, the fewer descriptive attributes remain to be identified.

In the third step, content-related integrity conditions are defined after the information objects and the descriptive attributes have been identified. These items can relate to the information objects (e.g., specifying existential dependencies), referential integrity, the assignment of attributes to domains, as well as cardinality relationships. Cardinality relationships indicate that a specification has been made as to whether specific content-related conditions must exist, dependent on the number of instances of a relationship type that occurs. It is possible to specify, for example, that a fixed route assignment for deliveries has to exist for customers who sign at least five contracts per year, while this may not be the case for occasional customers.

A proposed enterprise data model must be reviewed for accuracy, completeness and consistency (see *Lockemann/ Radermacher, Konzepte, Methoden und Modelle zur Datenmodellierung 1990, p. 12*). However, there are only limited formal support tools available for performing this verification. It is particularly easy to introduce inconsistencies when indicating detailed degrees of complexity (min, max notation) for relationship types (see *Knolmayer/Myrach, Anforderungen an Tools 1990, p. 100*). Moreover, semantically superfluous relationships can also exist.

Prototypes that permit data model evaluations to be performed can be used to validate the model, i.e., to check it for conformance with the intentions of its designer.

The project duration—and thus the project effort and expense—for creating an enterprise data model depends primarily on the required degree of detail. In principle, setting up a strategic enterprise data model can take just a few days. On the other hand, preparing a detailed data model (level 2) can involve several man-months to several man-years. In particular, the expense and effort are necessary for identifying the information objects as well as for defining the names of information objects and attributes. This necessitates costly clarification and coordination phases with the different departments involved (see *Brombacher/Hars/Scheer, Informationsmodellierung 1993*).

D.II.2.2.2.2 Top-Down or Bottom-Up Procedure

The fundamental procedures in this process are the top-down approach, which involves refining an existing data structure in a step-by-step fashion, and the bottom-up approach, in which consolidations and generalizations are performed on the basis of real, existing data structures. What is common to both procedures is that, during the course of development, data models are created on different levels of consolidation and thus in different sizes.

This book has used both procedures in designing data structures. The distinction between the two types of procedures becomes particularly clear with respect to the generalization/specialization operation. Generalization involves generalizing detailed terms, and is therefore frequently used if the data structures are consolidated within the information pyramid. Within the context of cost accounting, for example, the terms introduced on the operative level, e.g., CUSTOMER, ARTICLE, ORDER, etc., are generalized into the term COST OBJECTIVE. The same holds true for the special account relationships introduced in the subsidiary accounting systems, i.e., ACCOUNT RECEIVABLE, ACCOUNT PAYABLE, INVENTORY LEVEL, etc., which are generalized into the term ACCOUNT during the transition to the general view of financial accounting.

In the top-down analysis, the process of specialization is used to split up general terms into more detailed terms. An example of this is the breakdown of the term PART into the subtypes of ARTICLE, OUTSOURCED PART and IN-HOUSE PART.

In a top-down approach, the developer has more latitude and is more likely to come up with new concepts than in the case of the bottom-up approach, in which the existing solution is documented after the fact.

The discussion will begin by demonstrating the **top-down approach**.

The point of departure is the typical business administration definition of an enterprise as a system that acquires production factors (resources) from supply markets, combines them during production in order to generate output, and sells them on sales markets.

In Figure D.II.12,a, the four entity types BUSINESS ASSOCIATE, OUTPUT, RESOURCE and TIME are derived from this definition. Relationships exist between them in the form of EXTERNAL ORDER and INTERNAL ORDER. External orders relate to outputs that are provided to business associates or are acquired from business associates.

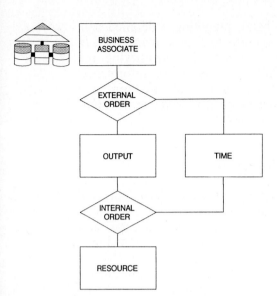

Fig. D.II.12,a: Fundamental information objects of an EDM (1st stage)

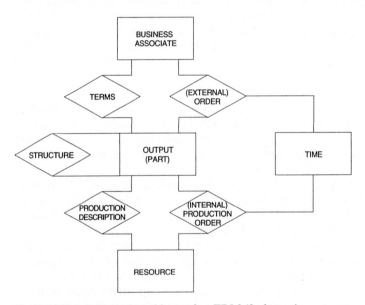

Fig. D.II.12,b: Information objects of an EDM (2nd stage)

Internal orders form a relationship between the outputs generated in-house and the resources necessary for output generation.

This basic EDM will now be refined step by step. The interaction of outputs, as described by the bill of materials, is shown in Figure D.II.12,b by the relationship type STRUCTURE. Interrelationships between OUTPUTS and BUSINESS ASSOCIATE that function as master data are

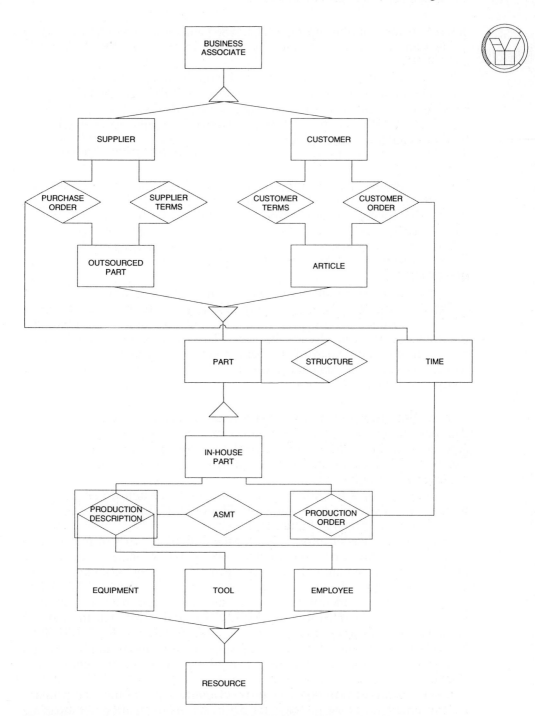

Fig. D.II.12,c: Using the operation „specialization" for differentating the data structure
(3rd stage)

entered in the relationship type TERMS. Generating an output by using production factors is represented by the relationship type PRODUCTION DESCRIPTION.

The data structure is split up in Figure D.II.12,c by applying the "specialization" operation. The entity type BUSINESS ASSOCIATE is broken down into SUPPLIER and CUSTOMER. The entity type OUTPUT (PART) is split up into outsourced outputs (OUTSOURCED PART), salable outputs (ARTICLE) and in-house outputs (IN-HOUSE PART). RESOURCE is split up into EQUIPMENT, TOOL and EMPLOYEE.

Along with the specialization of the entity types, the relationship types are also differentiated. Thus, the relationship TERMS is split up into SUPPLIER-related relationships, and OUTSOURCED PART into CUSTOMER- and ARTICLE-related relationships. External orders are differentiated analogously into purchase orders and customer orders.

The PRODUCTION DESCRIPTION relates to the various RESOURCES.

A production description is assigned to the production order.

The data structure shown in Figure D.II.12,c resides on an even higher level of abstraction. Despite this, however, important informational interrelationships can already be seen. This is true, for example, with respect to the parallelism of the data structures in purchasing and sales, which arises from the specialization of BUSINESS ASSOCIATES and the entity type PART.

In the **bottom-up procedure**, existing documentation such as forms and data descriptions are analyzed in terms of their entity types, relationship types and attributes. Moreover, interrelationships that are not documented can be ascertained by the line departments involved by employing the "interview technique."

An example of a bottom-up procedure can be demonstrated using the form "materials requisition" shown in Figure D.II.13,a and the ER model derived from it, shown in Figure D.II.13,b.

In addition to header information for the individual types of materials to be withdrawn, the form contains the corresponding names and quantity information. It is apparent that a number of primary key attributes of other entity types are shown. In an initial analysis, the MATERIALS REQUISITION is identified as a relationship type between STOCK LOCATION, the requisitioning EMPLOYEE and TIME via the date of issue of the materials requisition. The MATERIALS REQUISITION ITEM is then introduced via a relationship to the material number (which corresponds to the part number as a primary key for the entity type PART).

The inclusion of primary keys of other entity types allows the primary keys to function as external keys for the materials requisition. At the same time, this means that a cardinality of 1 has to exist from the standpoint of the information object MATERIALS REQUISITION. If this data structure is subsequently transformed into the relational model, this means that the

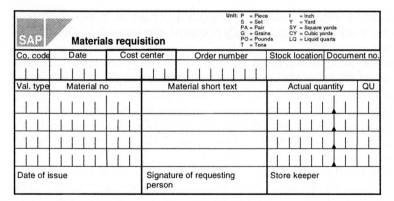

Fig. D.II.13,a: Form of a materials requisition

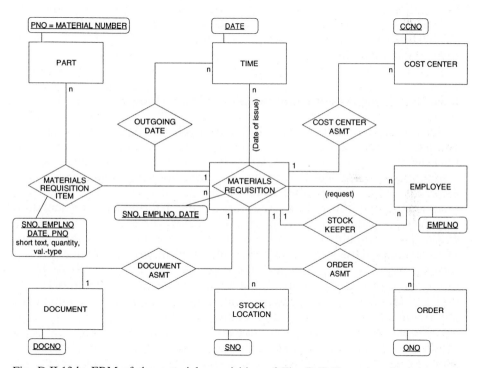

Fig. D.II.13,b: ERM of the materials requisition of Fig. D.II.13,a using the bottom-up
procedure

1:n relationships do not form their own relationships; instead the primary
keys for the entity types are transferred to the relationship type
MATERIALS REQUISITION as external keys.

Virtually all descriptive attributes of the materials requisition or
materials requisition item are external keys (i.e., primary keys of other
entity types), which are assigned via relationship types. Only in the case of

a rough concept in which the entity types still represent complex objects—which, in turn, represent nested subentity types—do numerous descriptive attributes exist.

The example is also intended to show that there can be different approaches to identifying the entity and relationship types. For example, the materials requisition could also have been introduced with the primary key "document number." In this case, all links and additional attributes would have had to have been created as relationship types to the other entity types. Since the document number is typically not assigned by the issuer, however, it is designed according to the origin principle.

In transforming the initial data, ambiguities such as homonyms and synonyms must be identified and eliminated. Here, too, aids such as the KWIC (keyword in context) list can be helpful. Compound terms (e.g., stock location) are split up into their term elements (stock and location) and combined. All terms in which "stock" or "location" occur are then interrelated and can be checked for inconsistencies or redundancies (see *Mayr/Dittrich/Lockemann, Datenbankentwurf 1987, pp. 512 ff.*; *Hars, Referenzdatenmodelle 1994*).

D.II.2.2.2.3 Degrees of Consolidation in Data Models

Depending on their scope, different levels of data models can be defined. A strategic data model combines the most important entity and relationship types that express only fundamental, industry-specific differences. Figure D.II.14 (from *Biethahn/Rohrig, Datenmanagement 1990, p. 743*) shows the data model for an insurance company. Graphically, the illustration conforms to the ER model representation introduced by Bachman (see *Bachman, A CASE for Reverse Engineering 1988*). The cardinality of the relationship types is expressed by the number of arrowheads. **One** arrowhead represents a cardinality of 1, **two** express a cardinality of n. For example, a policy can contain several contracts (accident or property insurance), but a contract always relates to only one policy. This type of strategic data model typically encompasses approximately 20 to 30 entity and relationship types.

Different structures within an industry can be entered on the next level of detail. Differentiated manufacturing structures (one-off production, series production) can be taken into account for industrial enterprises, for example. This type of detail model typically encompasses 200 to 500 entity and relationship types. The enterprise data model for industrial enterprises developed in this book can be positioned on this level. The model would then have to be expanded for an enterprise-specific analysis.

Enterprise-specific adaptations involve a high level of terminology specialization. For example, the introduction of the term PURCHASE ORDER ITEM provided only for the differentiation made on the basis of the material numbers and delivery date to which the item refers. However, it is also conceivable that a purchase order item would have to be differentiated on the basis of different delivery locations, which

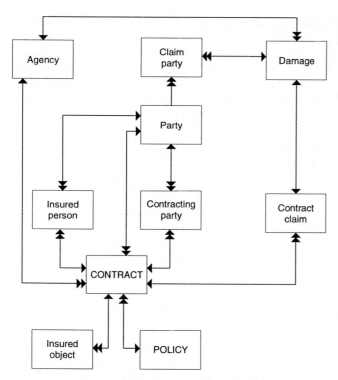

Fig. D.II.14: Data model for an insurance company

consequently results in an additional subitem. However, this increased granularity can be easily introduced by a link to the term STOCK LOCATION.

This type of enterprise-specific enterprise data model can easily encompass 300 to 1,500 entity and relationship types.

D.II.2.3 Workflow Management

The information management functions of resource provision and systems development relate not only to well-structured applications, as emphasized in this book, but also to more poorly structured processes, as discussed under the buzzword of "office automation."

Office automation initially focused on the office workstation, whose DP support requirements were analyzed independently of the application environment. In the meantime, however, this automation-oriented perspective has given way to a procedure-oriented view of office work, which is being discussed under the buzzword "workflow management."

Under the workflow concept, office processes should be organized using all available DP support tools.

These support tools include communications services such as electronic mail, desktop tools such as spreadsheets, multimedia techniques, as well as the classical operative DP systems. Since this general view extends beyond individual applications, the implementation of workflow systems is an important function in a comprehensive information management concept.

The following instructional example should help to clarify the workflow principle (see *Götzer, Moderne Systeme für die Bürokommunikation 1993, pp. 46 f.*):

> "*An insurance company receives correspondence from a policyholder. This letter is scanned in the mail room, assigned to the appropriate clerk on the basis of the policyholder number (using the data from the central operative systems) and then sent to him or her over the local area network (LAN) via electronic mail. The clerk opens the "mailbox" on his or her desktop and finds, among other things, this policyholder letter. Using the insurance number indicated in the letter, the clerk can view both the corresponding data record from the operative system as well as any previous correspondence found in the electronic department filing system, **all in one operation**. For example, if the policyholder is complaining about an insufficient payment, the clerk can call up a spreadsheet and verify the calculations. He or she can then automatically import the result into a word-processing program. At the same time, he or she can use an interface to access the necessary policyholder data, such as name, address, etc., from the operative system. The response letter is then printed at the workstation. No copy is printed out for the clerk; instead, it is automatically stored in the electronic filing system. Then the clerk transfers the data to accounting and initiates the supplemental payment.*"

An important property of workflow management is that the user is given a high degree of process control capability: His own intervention determines the control flow.

This principle has been emphasized throughout this book in that all applications have been analyzed with respect to their potential for interactive intervention. The procedure-oriented organizational analysis of the applications by event-driven process chains is a perspective that is recommended for workflow analyses (see *Karl, Prozeßorientierte Vorgangsbearbeitung 1993*). An important extension can therefore be provided simply by including communications services and workstation-oriented administration services in the information models developed here.

D.II.2.3.1 Characteristics of Office Activities

Figure D.II.15 (from *Picot/Reichwald, Bürokommunikation 1987, p. 30*) shows a much-cited structure of office activities that has been developed on the basis of German and American empirical studies.

The figure illustrates that only 31 % of all activities are performed on an individual basis and 7 % are strictly administrative activities. In contrast, approximately 2/3 of the activities are associated with communications. Consequently, the use of support techniques is geared primarily toward this aspect, which is underscored by the term "office communications." Figure D.II.15 relates to the office activities of upper and middle management. This group typically has to handle individual cases and poorly structured problems more frequently than does the clerical level. As soon as the content-related functions for an office, e.g., processing an order, are formalized with respect to the data structure, these structures do not differ from the structures developed in the process chains.

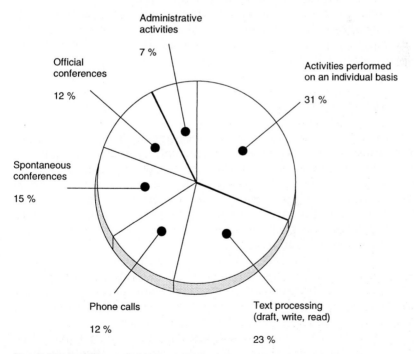

Fig. D.II.15: Office activities structure
(Upper and middle management)

The most important technologies involved in office communications are (see *Picot/Reichwald, Bürokommunikation 1987, p. 19*):
- Telex
- Fax
- Videotex
- Electronic mail
- Computer conferencing
- Telephone conferencing
- Videoconferencing.

Moreover, if the functions that typically involve office work that is performed directly by secretarial, clerical and management are included, the following would also have to be added:
- Word processing
- Text module assembly
- Spreadsheets
- Graphics
- Image processing
- Personal resource management (e.g., appointment calendar),
- Document management and archiving (multimedia).

This list could easily be extended to include other functions.

An important instrument for supporting the various communications and data processing forms is the multifunctional workstation system, which serves as a central vehicle for accessing the various services.

The following discussion will treat electronic mail as a typical example of a communications activity and personal resource management as a typical example of processing an unstructured task, thereby avoiding overlaps with previously discussed areas.

D.II.2.3.2 Message Exchange

Electronically supported systems for message exchange are termed **electronic message systems** or **electronic mail systems**. The partners involved in the exchange can be human beings or application systems. Consequently, these systems possess a high degree of similarity to process event control and the trigger concepts derived from it. Thus, the data structure developed in Figure D.II.16 represents a refinement of the data structure for events and triggers previously introduced with respect to the information model (see Figure D.II.07).

Figure D.II.16 shows message exchange between employees, who are identified on the basis of a personnel number. The term "employee" is to be understood in its broad sense, since the data structure does not distinguish between partners who, although they do not belong to the same organization, have access to identical technical resources.

Different message types can be distinguished, e.g., mail messages, EDI transmissions, drawings, text files, etc., which are each identified by a message type number MESTYPNO. A message is identified by the

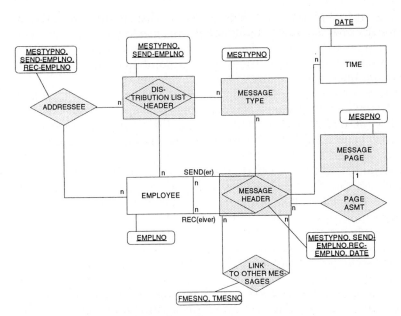

Fig. D.II.16: ERM for electronic mail

message number, the date, and the sender and receiver. This message header does not contain any content-related information; this is stored in the message pages, which additionally contain a page numberMESPNO. In this connection, it is also possible to form an additional hierarchy, e.g., by dividing the pages into blocks.

Thus, this discussion relates to the metalevel of the information model, since it uses only application-independent terminology. Consequently, the terms can also be tracked on the subordinate levels for application type and application instance.

The metaterm MESSAGE HEADER is an abstraction of the application-oriented terms order confirmation, collections and purchase order, which, in turn, are abstractions of the instances "order confirmation for operation 23" or "dunning letter for operation 86," etc.

Relationships can exist between messages; e.g., a message can be a response to a previous letter. But content-related relationships, e.g., the exchange of letters relating to a specific subject between different partners, can be represented by the relationship type LINK TO OTHER MESSAGES. For the sake of simplicity, the complex key for the message header is abbreviated to a simple key attribute MESNO. Thus, a linking entity is created by the two key attributes "sender" and "receiver" (shown here as FMESNO and TMESNO).

If the recipients of specific message types are specified from the start, they can be represented in distribution lists. A distribution list, as header information, is a relationship type between the message type and the sender. For example, the creator of a monthly sales report can define the regular circle of recipients and then create a distribution list that is identified by the message type number and his personnel number. The individual recipients then constitute items in the distribution list header. They are correspondingly identified by the combined three items of message type number, sender number and receiver number.

The exchange of messages between different DP systems necessitates appropriate standards. A general standard for data interchange between different DP systems has been provided by the ISO/OSI protocol system; however, it has been formulated for the lower layers only—standards still need to be developed for the individual applications with respect to the application-oriented layers—in particular, layer 7. In 1984, the CCITT launched the proposal for the X.400 ff mail and messaging protocol (see *Racke/Effelsberg, X.400-Empfehlungen 1986*). The eight proposals form a standard for application layer 7 of the ISO reference model for implementing electronic mail functions in heterogeneous computer networks. Without going into the technical details (see the bibliography for additional sources), Figure D.II.17 shows the fields in the message header, as defined in the X.400 protocol (see *Schumann, Bürokommunikationssysteme 1987, p. 97*). The checked items are explicitly contained in the data structure shown in Figure D.II.16. The other fields can easily be introduced as extensions or consolidations. For additional information on standardization efforts, see. *Schumann, Bürokommunikationssysteme 1987, p. 108*; *Götzer, Bürokommunikation 1993, pp. 444 f.* This results in overlaps with respect to the standard protocols previously discussed for networks (e.g., MAP/TOP) and for electronic data interchange (EDI). This situation once again emphasizes the link between office functions and application-oriented systems.

X - Sender
  - Person responsible for message
X - Primary receiver
  - Extended receiver class
  - Receiver of a copy of the message
  - Subject
  - Message as reply to
  - Reply request
  - Address chain for the form/message
X - Link to other messages (no.)
X - Indication of priority
  - Duration of message validity
  - Message to be deleted or no longer valid
  - Protection level of the message
  - Encoded text
X - Multi-part text

Fig. D.II.17: Fields in the message header of the X.400 protocol

D.II.2.3.3 Personal Resource Management

In addition to communications, management of personal resources is another important office application. This is understood to include the management of appointment calendars on the one hand and the management of personal notes that are created or used to process individual case-oriented activities.

The data structure is shown in Figure D.II.18. The term "document" is introduced for the information units. This term should be interpreted in a very broad sense. A document can include an appointment calendar, a graphic, a text, a sketch, etc. A document type is identified by the document type number DOCTYPNO. A special document consists of a header and individual items, which are termed "document pages" here. The document header, then, is a relationship between the employee who creates the document, the document type and time.

A keyword index is generated in order to simplify search procedures within the documents. The keywords, or descriptors, are represented by the entity type KEYWORD, whereby a keyword is identified by the keyword number KEYNO. The keyword index is an assignment between

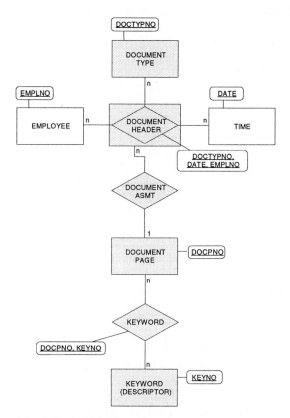

Fig. D.II.18: ERM for personal resource management

the document pages and the keywords. Each instance indicates which keyword is contained on which document page, whereby an n:m relationship is typically the case. The search support that has merely been suggested here can be supported by comfortable retrieval systems with automatic text analysis and indexing functions. This allows the user to easily relocate the documents he created by searching for a specific keyword.

Via access to the entity type TIME, it is also possible to access documents defined on the basis of time.

Special analysis operators (triggers) can automatically generate reminder notices if a given date has been reached.

D.II.2.4 Summarizing and Supplementing the Requirements Definitions for Information Management

It has been seen that information management offers important contributions in shaping interdepartmental information and coordination systems. The first step involves the definition of an information architecture, from which the information model is derived. The information model, in turn, serves as the basis for the repository that forms the foundation on which the procedural model for information systems development is built. Information management provides additional coordinating support in defining an enterprise model. This model serves as a kind of general framework concept for specifying the important information concepts from the different views of the information architecture. All of the department-oriented detailed information systems that have been described are structured along the lines of this information architecture. Figure D.II.19 shows a rough enterprise model (EM) based on the views of the ARIS architecture, together with the process-oriented application view for industrial enterprises pursued in this book. Only the requirements definition levels are included from the enterprise model.

The primary functions for the seven business processes treated in this book are shown in the function view. The process-oriented organizational chart is shown in the organization view. On the one hand, the data view encompasses the information model, which simultaneously represents the metalevel of the application architecture. On the other hand, the data model for the application architecture is represented by a rough enterprise data model (EDM).

The control view encompasses the seven event-driven process chains. The interrelationship between the three logistics chains is established by the control flow from acceptance of the customer order to generation of the primary requirements and, building on this foundation, the production planning chain from which the purchasing chain is initiated via the requirements derivation. The logistics and product development processes

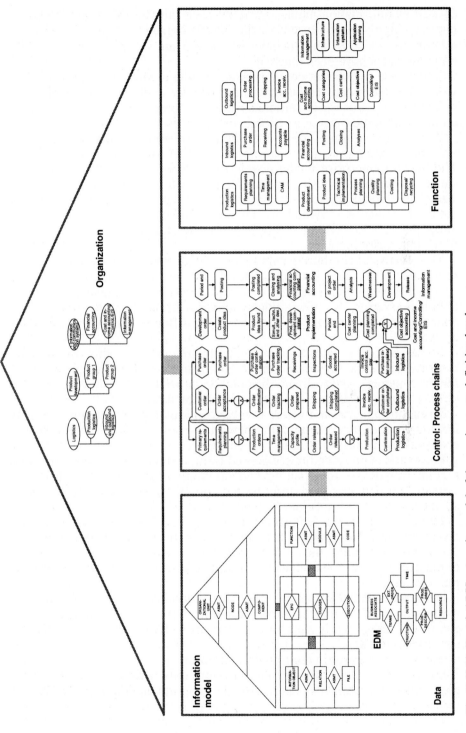

Fig. D.II.19: Rough ARIS enterprise model of the requirements definition level

as well as information management are each initiated by orders. Because they are highly period-oriented, the value-oriented systems for financial accounting and cost and income accounting are initiated when specific planning dates have been reached.

In the case of product costing, however, the diagram indicates that the value-oriented processes become more heavily event-controlled when an order costing process is initiated following order release, or following completion in the form of an actual cost analysis.

The enterprise model developed here is so abstract that it still offers little information potential as a reference model for practical applications. The general enterprise model developed in this book, on the other hand, can indeed provide fresh impetus for practical developments. Since the size of the model precludes a comprehensive representation in print form, the entire model is provided in a DP-supported navigation tool in order to allow the user to navigate freely between the individual views and levels of the enterprise model.

The process of combining submodels into an overall model does involve problems. The data structures developed by different users in the submodels have to be analyzed with respect to terminological conformity. In concrete terms, this means that synonyms (different names for the same concept) and homonyms (the same name for different concepts) have to be identified.

These problems are not exceedingly relevant to this discussion, however, since the integration interrelationships—and thus the problem of identical names—have already been taken into account within the context of developing the process-oriented information model.

The high expense and effort involved in creating an enterprise model has to be offset by corresponding benefit factors. An initial benefit factor always consists of documenting the enterprise.

Because it is presented in condensed form, an enterprise model serves as a solid foundation for training and orienting new employees. There is virtually no better way to describe the complex interrelationships within an enterprise in such succinct fashion.

The creation of an enterprise model is the fundamental basis for designing new information systems. It has been shown that only by carefully designing the enterprise model can all the integration requirements of a comprehensive information system be properly taken into account.

Proponents of the argument against an individual enterprise model can maintain that it is impossible to implement this type of model if the enterprise subsequently opts to use standard software. Many application structures are already specified in standard software and thus have to be used by the purchaser in their predefined form.

Enterprise models are intended to not only reveal the established processes of an enterprise, but to also aid in optimizing those processes.

D.II.2.4.1 Requirements Definition for Information Management: The Function View

The primary functions of managing basic data and handling IS projects are highly conducive to interactive processing. On the one hand, there is a need to ensure the currency of the descriptive data with respect to changes in the actual information objects; on the other hand, reference models can also be used to support the model creation process (see Figure D.II.20).

Function	Reasons for interactive processing				Automatic/ batch
	Currency	Plausibility	Iterative modification	Interactive decision process	
Management of information models	X		X	X	
System development	X		X	X	

Fig. D.II.20: Processing modes of information management

D.II.2.4.2 Requirements Definition for Information Management: The Organization View

The organizational structure developed for IS projects—with its hierarchical levels of "overall project manager" and "subproject manager"—leads to the leitstand organization shown in Figure D.II.21. This organizational structure bears a striking similarity to the form previously proposed for product development. The support tools for modeling and software engineering, as well as for customizing standard software, are shown as the production level below the subproject control leitstands. Feedback can be automatically generated from these tools, analogously to the CAD production systems for the product development leitstands or to the machine level for production leitstands.

The leitstand organization can utilize the same time-management tools previously cited in the graphical Gantt charts (see color plates). The

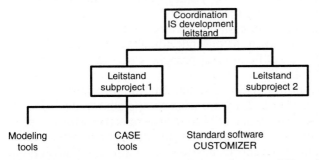

Fig. D.II.21: Leitstand organization for development of IS projects

coordination level then has to track the entire project process, while each of the subproject leitstands controls scheduling and resource planning for its respective problem segments.

D.II.2.4.3 Requirements Definition for Information Management: The Data View

With the two different aspect of the information model, a subject-oriented data model for information management and the enterprise data model as a general framework for detailed, subject-related data modeling, the data view has already been treated in detail.

D.II.2.4.4 Requirements Definition for Information Management: The Control View

Basic data management and control of IS development projects have already been discussed in the context of event-driven process control for information management. Since the routine processes of operating the information system—e.g., computer center control or data backup—are not specific enough to the industrial enterprise that is the focus of this book, they will not be discussed in any greater detail.

D.II.3 Design Specifications for Information Management

DP systems can also support information management functions. The analysis systems that could be used for Controlling functions will not be treated in this connection—e.g., neither those that record resource utilization by users and programs nor DP-supported operation of computer centers. In accordance with the focus of this book, the discussion will instead emphasize support of basic data management for the information system, i.e., the design of the information model and the repository, as well as support during application systems development.

The discussion will not conform to the individual ARIS views; instead, it will follow a holistic classification approach, since certain types of systems are to be analyzed.

Support functions for setting up and maintaining the information model are difficult to separate from the software used to operate a repository. If, for example, the repository software is geared toward a fixed information model from the start, only very little latitude is available with respect to its design. The situation is different if a repository allows configurable information structuring, e.g., as is the case with the MSP (Manager

Software Products) system. A repository manager is a software system for operating a repository (see *Dürmeyer, Informationsmodell AD/Cycle 1993*).

A distinction must be made between different groups of tools for supporting software development. The first group encompasses tools that support the creation of requirements definitions. They frequently offer graphically oriented design procedures that, in the case of a rule-based approach, can also contain organizational knowledge in the form of reference models or can support process optimization via simulation options. This group also includes such systems as the ARIS family of products (IDS Prof. Scheer GmbH), CIM-KSA (see *Scholz-Reiter, CIM-Informations- und Kommunikationssysteme 1990*), as well as special systems developed within the framework of workflow management for analyzing office process structures (see *Niemeier, Analyse- und Gestaltungsmethoden für den Bürobereich 1991*).

A second group of tools has been developed with the aim of allowing the entire software development process to be performed with computer support. These fall under the buzzword "ICASE" (Integrated Computer Aided Software Engineering) (see *Schwyrz, ICASE, 1993, pp. 737 f.*). Their primary emphasis is on transforming results from a superordinate level to the directly subordinate level within the development lifecycle. For example, relations can be derived from a requirements description for the data view in the form of an entity-relationship diagram and, in turn, concrete database descriptions for different database systems can be derived from these relations.

Since CASE systems support a specific design methodology by offering data models and function models (e.g., entity-relationship modeling or SADT), their metastructure has to reflect this methodology. Thus, they automatically provide an information model for the repository functionality of this system. Since these systems cannot really claim to provide a complete repository, they are sometimes also called "encyclopedias."

A third group encompasses standard software systems, which, since they offer the user greater flexibility with respect to customization and provide support for data management, include functions for creating and managing a (sub)repository and serve as a point of departure for software customization by incorporating tools for modeling the requirements definition.

Since these approaches focus on different aspects, none of the systems introduced thus far is suitable for handling the entire software development process from the analysis phase to support for software operation. Figure D.II.22 categorizes the three groups on the basis of their strengths. It also shows typical product examples, upon which the assessments are based. The analytical and modeling tools in the ARIS family of products feature an information model and, in a systems development environment, primarily support the phases of analysis, creation of the requirements definition and documentation, as well as system navigation. Various examples have already been cited in several

		Analysis and modeling tools (e.g. ARIS)	CASE tools (e.g. ADW)	Modern standard software (e.g. SAP R/3)
Repository management	Information model	high functionality	slightly existing	slightly existing
	Repository administration	scarcely existing	slightly existing	slightly existing
System development	Analysis	mean functionality	scarcely existing	scarcely existing
	Requirements definition	mean functionality	slightly existing	slightly existing
	Design specification	slightly existing	mean functionality (Generation)	mean functionality (Customizing)
	Implementation description	slightly existing	mean functionality (Generation)	mean functionality (Customizing)
	Documentation, navigation	high functionality	slightly existing	slightly existing
System usage	Active repository	slightly existing	slightly existing	slightly existing
	Active user interface	high functionality	scarcely existing	scarcely existing

Legend:
- ○ = scarcely existing
- ◔ = slightly existing
- ◐ = mean functionality
- ● = high functionality

Fig. D.II.22: Supporting tools for the information management

different contexts. The transformation of the requirements definitions into design specifications and implementation descriptions is established via interfaces to standard software systems (e.g., the FI-2 family, RI-2 production control software). At the same time, the information models for the requirements definition can also be transferred to CASE tools that then focus on software generation. The use of the information model and the modeling level for systems operation can be established via an active repository if it is linked with the subordinate application software. This is only possible in close cooperation with application software systems. Here, too, ARIS products feature interfaces to software systems. For example, when using the FI-2 software system in conjunction with the ARIS modeling tools, it is possible to directly route graphically performed process changes in the description of event-driven process chains to the application software control functions.

The use of the modeling level for direct system control can be established via dynamic user interfaces. The user is virtually "switched through" directly to the system functions and screen displays from the graphic process chain analysis.

CASE tools come into play relatively late in the development cycle and thus provide only minimal support for the analysis phase. Furthermore, they provide only graphical editing functions for the requirements definition level, but no comfortable functions for managing reference models, etc. Their focus, on the other hand, is primarily on the design specification and implementation description levels in that they generate data structures and software code from the subject-oriented descriptions. Application systems developed using CASE tools ensure that the repository can be used for application control, but not always in the case of various standard software systems, etc.

The modern standard software environment incorporates later-generation programming languages and data dictionaries. These tools, however, are closely oriented toward standard software. For this reason, the information model, which forms the basis for the data dictionary, relates to only a few aspects of the entire system description. Standard software typically provides only minimal support for the analysis and requirements definition levels. However, efforts aimed at improving requirements-definition documentation by publishing data and process models are apparent, in particular the R/3 system from SAP. The process of transferring customer-specific requirements that have been defined on the requirements definition level to the system has also been improved through the use of customization functions, e.g., by transferring parameter settings virtually automatically to the corresponding tables. However, the use of the repository for dynamic system control is limited to the data dictionary. Nor is a dynamic user interface from the modeling level possible at this time. In general, though, it must be noted that standard software, too, is opening up more and more to the modeling and analysis levels, and is endeavoring to support the entire systems development lifecycle through interaction with the appropriate tools. The planned integration between the ARIS Toolset and the R/3 system, however, will result in a corresponding change in the evaluation shown in Figure D.II.22.

Support in designing information models though the use of computerized tools can play a crucial role in increasing the efficiency of the development process. The advantages of computer support can be categorized as follows:

-       All relevant information is entered in a structured, easy-to-analyze form. This ensures uniform, complete documentation. The incorporation of a user-friendly graphical interface offers a comfortable means of creating and modifying the necessary diagrams. Changes in one part of the documentation are automatically updated in other locations and thus only need to be performed once.

-       Referencing stored design to its creation date enables the different versions to be managed in a comfortable fashion. Versions are overwritten only if the user expressly wishes it; otherwise, each modification is maintained as an independent version.

- The use of a tool facilitates conformance to a fixed procedural model. Consistency checks ensure that modeling activities are not permitted until the preceding level has been completely processed.

- The internal consistency of the draft model can be validated by using rule-based systems. The general system requirements must also be entered within the framework of tool application in order to ensure external consistency. This necessitates the use of a powerful tool that provides structured support for the entire lifecycle.

- Generation algorithms enable graphical representations to be derived from existing database structures. Likewise, the graphical tool interface enables the information objects to be categorized in a meaningful, content-related manner. However, since the aim of providing application-oriented data structuring is again based on content-related perspectives, it would be difficult for a tool to provide further support. In particular, reclassifying basic information units such as attributes into information objects that are more meaningful from a subject-oriented perspective is the virtual equivalent of redesigning the model.

Literature

ACTIS in Berlin GmbH (ed.): *DFÜ-Box Leistungsbeschreibung 1993*
DFÜ-Box Version 2.0, Leistungsbeschreibung, Berlin 1993.

ACTIS in Berlin GmbH (ed.): *DFÜ-Box 1992*
DFÜ-Box, Das leistungsstarke EDI-System für alle Branchen, Berlin 1992.

ACTIS in Stuttgart GmbH (ed.): *FORS 1993*
FORS, Flexible Fertigungsorganisation mit Fortschrittszahlen, Leistungsbeschreibung Produktionslogistik, Stuttgart 1993.

Adam, D.: *Produktions-Management 1993*
Produktions-Management, 7th ed., Wiesbaden 1993.

Adam, D.: *Produktionspolitik 1990*
Produktionspolitik, 6th ed., Wiesbaden 1990.

Adam, D.: *Fertigungssteuerung 1987*
Ansätze zu einem integrierten Konzept der Fertigungssteuerung bei Werkstattfertigung, in: Adam, D. (ed.): Neuere Entwicklungen in der Produktions- und Investitionspolitik, Wiesbaden 1987.

Adam, D.: *Produktionsplanung 1971*
Produktionsplanung bei Sortenfertigung, Wiesbaden 1971.

ADV-ORGA (ed.): *IPAS 1984*
Funktionsbeschreibung IPAS (Informatives Personalabrechnungssystem), Wilhelmshaven 1984.

Agthe, K.: *Die Abweichung in der Plankostenrechnung 1959*
Die Abweichungen in der Plankostenrechnung, Freiburg 1959.

Alpar, P.: *Expert Systems 1986*
Expert Systems in Marketing, Arbeitspapier am Department of Information and Decision Sciences, University of Illinios at Chicago 1986.

Alpar, P.: *Interaktive Methodenauswahl 1980*
Computergestützte interaktive Methodenauswahl, Dissertation, Frankfurt/Main 1980.

Anderl, R.: *STEP - Grundlagen, Entwurfsprinzipien und Aufbau 1992*
STEP - Grundlagen, Entwurfsprinzipien und Aufbau, in: Krause, F. L.; Ruland, D.; Hansen, J. (eds.): CAD 92, Neue Konzepte zur Realisierung anwendungsorientierter CAD-Systeme, Berlin 1992, pp. 361-381.

Anselstetter, R.: *Nutzeffekte der Datenverarbeitung 1986*
Betriebswirtschaftliche Nutzeffekte der Datenverarbeitung, 2nd ed., Berlin et al. 1986.

ANSI 1992
ANSI X3.135-1992.

Bachman, C.: *A CASE for Reverse Engineering 1988*
A CASE for Reverse Engineering, in: Datamation, 34 (1988) 13, pp. 49-56.

Back-Hock, A.: *Executive-Information-Systems 1990*
Executive-Information-Systems, Software für die Gestaltung von Controlling-Informationssystemen, in: Scheer, A.-W. (ed.): Rechnungswesen und EDV, 11. Saarbrücker Arbeitstagung, Heidelberg 1990, pp. 186-210.

Backhaus, K.: *Investitionsgütermarketing 1993*
Investitionsgütermarketing, in: Wittmann, W. (ed.): Handwörterbuch der Betriebswirtschaft, Teilbd. 2, 5th ed., Stuttgart 1993, pp. 1936-1951.

Balzert, H.: *Die Entwicklung von Software-Systemen 1982*
Die Entwicklung von Software-Systemen - Prinzipien, Methoden, Sprachen, Werkzeuge, Mannheim 1982.

Bechte, W.: *Belastungsorientierte Auftragsfreigabe 1980*
Steuerung der Durchlaufzeit durch belastungsorientierte Auftragsfreigabe bei Werkstattfertigung, Dissertation, Universität Hannover 1980.

Beitz, W.; Birkhofer, H.; Pahl, G.: *Konstruktionsmethodik in der Praxis 1992*
Konstruktionsmethodik in der Praxis, in: Konstruktion, 44 (1992), pp. 391-397.

Becker, J.; Rosemann, M.: *Logistik und CIM 1993*
Logistik und CIM - Die effiziente Material- und Informationsflußgestaltung im Industrieunternehmen, Berlin et al. 1993.

Becker, J.: *CIM-Integrationsmodell 1991*
CIM-Integrationsmodell - Die EDV-gestützte Verbindung betrieblicher Bereiche, Berlin et al. 1991.

Berkau, C.: *Datenstrukturen für die Prozeßkostenrechnung 1993*
Datenstrukturen für die Prozeßkostenrechnung, in: Scheer, A.-W. (ed.): Veröffentlichungen des Instituts für Wirtschaftsinformatik, Heft 103, Saarbrücken 1993.

Berthold, H. J.: *Aktionsdatenbanken 1983*
Aktionsdatenbanken in einem kommunikationsorientierten EDV-System, in: Informatik-Spektrum, 6 (1983) 6, pp. 20-26.

Biethahn, J.; Rohrig, N.: *Datenmanagement 1990*
Datenmanagement, in: Kurbel, K.; Strunz, H. (ed.): Handbuch Wirtschaftsinformatik, Stuttgart 1990, pp. 738-755.

Blazewicz, J.; Ecker, K.; Schmidt, G.; Weglarz, J.: *Scheduling in Computer and Manufacturing Systems 1993*
Scheduling in Computer and Manufacturing Systems, Berlin et al. 1993.

Bock, R.; Kube, Th.: *Weiterentwicklung der Leitstandkonzepte 1993*
Weiterentwicklung der Leitstandkonzepte: Der Engineering-Leitstand
in Verbindung mit dem Integrated Engineer, in: Scheer, A.-W. (ed.):
Beiträge zur Tagung der Wissenschaftlichen Kommission
Produktionswirtschaft, Saarbrücken 1993, pp. 63-77.

Bock, R.: *Simultane Produktentwicklung 1993*
Simultane Produktentwicklung - Konzepte und Realisierungsalterna-
tiven, in: Scheer, A.-W. (ed.): Handbuch Informationsmanagement:
Aufgaben - Konzepte - Praxislösungen, Wiesbaden 1993, pp. 221-
264.

Booch, G.: *Object-oriented Design with Applications 1991*
Object-Oriented Design with Applications, Redwood City 1991.

Brankamp, K.: *Terminplanungssystem 1973*
Ein Terminplanungssystem für Unternehmen der Einzel- und Kleinse-
rienfertigung - Voraussetzungen, Gesamtkonzeption und Durchführung mit EDV, 2nd ed., Würzburg-Wien 1973.

Brodie, M. L.: *Database Abstraction 1981*
A Database Abstraction for Semantic Modelling, in: Proceedings of
the 2nd International Entity-Relationship Conference, Washington
D.C. 1981.

Brombacher, R.; Scheer, A.-W.: *Marketinginformationssysteme 1985*
Marketinginformationssysteme in der Konsumgüterindustrie, in:
Thexis, 2 (1985) 3, pp. 3-11.

Brombacher, R.; Hars, A.; Scheer, A.-W.: *Informationsmodellierung 1993*
Informationsmodellierung, in: Scheer, A.-W. (ed.): Handbuch Informationsmanagement: Aufgaben - Konzept - Praxislösungen, Wiesbaden 1993, pp. 173-188.

Brombacher, R.: *Effizientes Informationsmanagement 1991*
Effizientes Informationsmanagement - Die Herausforderung von Ge-
genwart und Zukunft, in: SzU Schriften zur Unternehmensführung,
Band 44, Wiesbaden 1991, pp. 111-134.

Brombacher, R.: *Marketing-Management-Entscheidungsunterstützungssystem
1987*
Entscheidungsunterstützungssysteme für das Marketing-Management
- Gestaltungs- und Implementierungsansatz für die Konsumgüterindustrie, Berlin et al. 1988.

Budde, R. et al.: *Objektorientierter Entwurf von Informationssystemen 1992*
Objektorientierter Entwurf von Informationssystemen, in: Scheer, A.-
W. (ed.): Datenbanken 1992, Praxis und Tendenzen relationaler
Datenbanken, Anwendungserfahrungen, Entwicklungstrends, 4.
Fachtagung, Saarbrücken 1992, pp. 231-251.

Bullinger, H.-J.; Fähnrich, K.-P.; Erzberger, H.: *Werkstattorientierte Produktionsunterstützung 1990*
Werkstattorientierte Produktionsunterstützung, in: Bullinger, H.-J.
(ed.): Werkstattorientierte Produktionsunterstützung, Bd. T17, Berlin
et al. 1990, pp. 11-42.

Bullinger, H.-J.; Warnecke, H. J.; Lentes, H.-P.: *Factory of the Future 1985*
Towards the Factory of the Future, Opening Adress, in: Bullinger, H.-J.; Warnecke, H. J. (ed.); Kornwachs K. (Assistant ed.): Towards the Factory of the Future, pp. XXIX - LIV, Berlin et al. 1985.

Bullinger, H.J.: *Forschungs- und Entwicklungsmanagement in der deutschen Industrie 1992*
Forschungs- und Entwicklungsmanagement in der deutschen Industrie - Herausforderungen, Probleme, Lösungswege, in: Scheer, A.-W. (ed.): Simultane Produktentwicklung, München 1992, pp. 13-64.

Bungert, W.; Heß, H.: *Objektorientierte Geschäftsprozeßmodellierung 1995*
Objektorientierte Geschäftsprozeßmodellierung, in: IM Information Management, 10 (1995) 1, pp. 52-63.

Bürli, A. et al.: *Vorgehen beim Aufbau von CIM-Datenmodellen 1992*
Vorgehen beim Aufbau von CIM-Datenmodellen, in: io Management Zeitschrift, 61 (1992) 12, pp. 82-86.

Bussmann, K.-R.; Mertens, P. (ed.): *Instandhaltungsplanung 1968*
Operations Research und Datenverarbeitung bei der Instandhaltungs- planung, Stuttgart 1968.

Campbell, D.: *Entity-Relationship Modeling 1992*
Entity-Relationship Modeling: One Style Suits All?, in: Database, 23 (1992) 3, pp. 12 -18.

Chen, P. P.: *Entity-Relationship Approach 1981*
Entity-Relationship Approach to Information Modelling and Analysis, Proceedings of the 2nd International Conference on Entity-Relation- ship Approach (1981) Amsterdam, New York, Oxford 1981.

Chen, P.P.: *Entity-Relationship Model 1976*
Entity-Relationship Model: Towards a Unified View of Data, in: ACM Transactions on Database Systems, 1 (1976) 1, pp. 9-36.

Codd, E.F.: *Extending a Database Relational Model 1979*
Extending a Database Relational Model to Capture More Meaning, in: ACM Transactions on Database Systems, 4 (1979) 4, pp. 397-434.

Codd, E. F.: *Relational Model 1970*
A Relational Model for Large Shared Data Banks, in: Communicati- ons of the ACM, 13 (1970) 6, pp. 377-387.

Cooper, R.: *You Need a New Cost System When... 1989*
You Need a New Cost System When..., in: Havard Business Review, 67 (1989) 1, pp. 77-82.

Crowston, W. B.; Wagner, M.; Williams, J. F.: *Lot Size Determination 1973*
Economic Lot Size Determination in Multi-Stage-Assembly Systems, in: Management Science, 19 (1973), pp. 517 ff.

Dangelmeyer, W.: *Ereignisorientierte Fertigungssteuerung 1992*
Ansätze einer ereignisorientierten Fertigungssteuerung in CIM-Land- schaften, in: IM Information Management, 7 (1992) 3, pp. 52-57 und 7 (1992) 4, pp. 58-63.

Date, C. J.: *Twelve Rules for Distributed Databasesystem 1987*
Twelve Rules for Distributed Databasesystem, in: Computerworld, Juni 1987.

Date, C. J.: *An Introduction to Database Systems 1990*
An Introduction to Database Systems Volume I - The Systems Programming Series, Workingham et al. 1990.

Davis, C. G.; Jajodia, pp.; Ng, P. A.; Yeh, R. T. (ed.): *Entity-Relationship Approach 1983*
Entity-Relationship Approach to Software Engineering, Proceedings of the 3rd International Conference on Entity-Relationship Approach (1983), Amsterdam, New York, Oxford 1983.

DeMatteis, J. J.: *Lot-sizing Technique 1986*
An Economic Lot-sizing Technique, The Part-Period Algorithm, in: IBM Systems Journal, 7 (1968), pp. 30-38.

Diedenhoven, H.: *Informationsgehalt von CAD-Daten 1985*
Für die NC-Fertigung nutzbarer Informationsgehalt von CAD-Daten, in: CAE-Journal, 5 (1985), pp. 58-65.

Dinkelbach, W.: *Ablaufplanung in entscheidungstheoretischer Sicht 1976*
Ablaufplanung in entscheidungstheoretischer Sicht, Saarbrücken 1976.

Dittrich, K. R. et al.: *Datenbankunterstützung für den ingenieurwissenschaftlichen Entwurf 1985*
Datenbankunterstützung für den ingenieurwissenschaftlichen Entwurf, in: Informatik-Spektrum, 8 (1985) 3, pp. 113-125.

Dittrich, K. R.: *"Nachrelationale" Datenbanktechnologie 1990*
Objektorientiert, aktiv, erweiterbar: Stand und Tendenzen der "nachrelationalen" Datenbanktechnologie, in: Scheer, A-W. (ed.): Praxis relationaler Datenbanken 1990, Proceedings zur Fachtagung, Saarbrücken 1990, pp. 1-21.

Dogac, A.; Chen, P. P.: *Entity-Relationship Model 1983*
Entity Relationship Model in the ANSI/SPARC Framework, in: Chen, P. P. (ed.): Entity-Relationship Approach to Information Modelling and Analysis, Proceedings of the 2nd International Conference on Entity-Relationship Approach (1981), Amsterdam, New York, Oxford 1983, pp. 357-374.

Domsch, M.: *Simultane Personal- und Investitionsplanung im Produktionsbereich 1970*
Simultane Personal- und Investitionsplanung im Produktionsbereich, Bielefeld 1970.

Domsch, M.: *Systemgestützte Personalarbeit 1980*
Systemgestützte Personalarbeit, Wiesbaden 1980.

Dorbandt, J.; Fröhlich, J.; Schmelzer, H. J.; Schnopp, R.: *Ausgewählte Projektbeispiele zur Reduzierung der Entwicklungszeit 1990*
Ausgewählte Projektbeispiele zur Reduzierung der Entwicklungszeit, in: Reichwald, R.; Schmelzer, H. J. (ed.): Durchlaufzeiten in der Entwicklung: Praxis des industriellen F&E Managements, München 1990.

Dürmeyer, K.: *Informationsmodell AD/Cycle 1993*
Informationsmodell AD/Cycle, in: Scheer, A.-W. (ed.): Handbuch Informationsmanagement: Aufgaben - Konzepte - Lösungen, Wiesbaden 1993, pp. 143-172.

Eberle, P.; Heil, H.-G.: *Relativkosten-Informationen für die Konstruktion 1992*
Relativkosten-Informationen für die Konstruktion, in: Männel, W. (ed.): Handbuch Kostenrechnung, Wiesbaden 1992, pp. 782-790.

Eberlein, W.: *CAD-Datenbanksysteme 1984*
CAD-Datenbanksysteme: Architektur technischer Datenbanken für integrierte Ingenieursysteme, Berlin et al. 1984.

Ehrlenspiel, K.: *Kostengünstig Konstruieren 1985*
Kostengünstig Konstruieren, in: Pahl, G. (ed.): Konstruktionsbücher, Bd. 3, Berlin et al. 1985, pp. 247 f.

Encarnaçao, J. et al. (ed.): *CAD-Handbuch 1984*
CAD-Handbuch, Auswahl und Einführung von CAD-Systemen, Berlin et al. 1984.

Endl, R.; Fritz, B.: *Rezepte gegen Datenchaos 1993*
Rezepte gegen Datenchaos, in: Computerwoche FOCUS, 2 (1993), pp. 31-33.

Esch, F.-R.; Kroeber-Riel, W.: *Expertensysteme für die Werbung 1993*
Expertensysteme für die Werbung, München 1993.

Esch, F.-R.: *Expertensystem zur Beurteilung von Anzeigenwerbung 1990*
Expertensystem zur Beurteilung von Anzeigenwerbung, Heidelberg 1990.

Eversheim, W.: *Organisation in der Produktionstechnik 1989*
Organisation in der Produktionstechnik, Bd. 3: Arbeitsvorbereitung, 2nd Ed., Düsseldorf 1989.

Falk, J.; Spieck, pp.; Mertens, P.: *Teilintelligente Agenten in Lager- und Transportlogistik 1993*
Unterstützung der Lager- und Transportlogistik durch teilintelligente Agenten, in: IM Information Managment, 8 (1993) 2, pp. 26-31.

Fischer, J.: *Datenmanagement 1992*
Datenmanagement - Datenbanken und betriebliche Datenmodellierung, München-Wien 1992.

Fischer, W.: *Datenbank-Management in CAD/CAM-Systemen*
Datenbank-Management in CAD/CAM-Systemen: Anforderungen an CAD/CAM Datenbanken - Derzeitiges Marktangebot - Empfehlungen für effizientes DB-Management - Entwicklungstendenzen, Messerschmitt-Bölkow-Blohm GmbH, Ottobrunn o. J.

Forschungsinstitut für Rationalisierung an der TH Aachen (ed.): *Vergleich von Arbeitsplatzanforderungen und Personalfähigkeitsdaten 1975*
Ein Analyseinstrument zur Erfassung und zum Vergleich von Arbeitsplatzanforderungen und Personalfähigkeitsdaten, Aachen 1975.

Fox, E.: *OPT 1983*
OPT vs. MRP - Throughtware vs. Software, in: inventories & production, 3 (1983) 6.

Franz, K.-P.: *Prozeßkostenmanagement 1993*
Prozeßkostenmanagement: Skeptische Zurückhaltung, in: technologie & management, 42 (1993) 2, pp. 75-78.

Franz, K.-P.: *Target Costing 1993*
Target Costing - Konzept und kritische Bereiche, in: Controlling, 5 (1993) 3, pp. 124-130.

Gaul, W.; Baier, D.: *Marktforschung und Marketing Management 1993*
Marktforschung und Marketing-Management - Computerbasierte Entscheidungsunterstützung, 2nd Ed., München 1994.

Gerlach, J.: *Zentrale Auftragsabwicklung in Produktionsunternehmen 1983*
Entwicklung von Gestaltungsrichtlinien für eine zentrale Auftragsabwicklung in Produktionsunternehmen, Dissertation, Aachen 1983.

Gesellschaft für Fertigungssteuerung und Materialwirtschaft e.V. (ed.): *MRPS 1987*
MRPS - Ein neues System für das Produktmanagement, Lottenau 1987.

Gewald, K.; Kasper, K.; Schelle, H.: *Netzplantechnik 1972*
Netzplantechnik, Bd. 2: Kapazitätsoptimierung, München-Wien 1972.

Glaser, H.; Geiger W.; Rhode, V.: *Produktionsplanung und -steuerung 1992*
Produktionsplanung und -steuerung - Grundlagen, Konzepte, Anwendungen, 2nd Ed., Wiesbaden 1992.

Glaser, H.: *Prozeßkostenrechnung 1992*
Prozeßkostenrechnung - Darstellung und Kritik, in: Zeitschrift für betriebswirtschaftliche Forschung, 44 (1992), pp. 275-288.

Glaser, H.: *Verfahren zur Fertigungssteuerung in alternativen PPS-Systemen 1991*
Verfahren zur Fertigungssteuerung in alternativen PPS-Systemen - Eine kritische Analyse, in: Scheer, A.-W. (ed.): Fertigungssteuerung - Expertenwissen für die Praxis, München-Wien 1991, pp. 21-37.

Goldratt, E. M.; Cox, J.: *The Goal 1984*
The Goal, Excellence in Manufacturing, New York 1984.

Gora, W.: *MAP 1986*
MAP, in: Informatik-Spektrum, 9 (1986) 1, pp. 40-42.

Götzer, K. G.: *Bürokommunikation 1993*
Moderne Systeme für die Bürokommunikation, in: Management & Computer, 1 (1993) 1, pp. 45-52.

Götzer, K.: *Moderne Systeme für die Bürokommunikation 1993*
Bürokommunikation als integraler Bestandteil des Informationsmanagements, in: Scheer, A.-W. (ed.): Handbuch Informationsmanagement: Aufgaben - Konzepte - Praxislösungen, Wiesbaden 1993, pp. 433-462.

Grabowski, H.; Langlotz, G.; Rude, pp.: *25 Jahre CAD in Deutschland 1993*
25 Jahre CAD in Deutschland: Standortbestimmung und notwendige Entwicklungen, in: VDI-Gesellschaft Entwicklung-Konstruktion-Vertrieb (ed.): Jahrbuch 1993, Düsseldorf, pp. 133-162.

Grabowski, H.: *Entwerfen in Konstruktionsräumen zur Unterstützung der Teamarbeit 1992*
Entwerfen in Konstruktionsräumen zur Unterstützung der Teamarbeit, in: Scheer, A.-W. (ed.): Simultane Produktentwicklung, München 1992, pp. 123-160.

Grabowski, H.; Anderl, R.; Schilli, B.; Schmitt, M.: *STEP - Entwicklung einer Schnittstelle zum Produktdatenaustausch 1989*
STEP - Entwicklung einer Schnittstelle zum Produktdatenaustausch, in: VDI-Zeitung, 131 (1989) 9, pp. 68-76.

Grabowski, H.; Anderl, R.; Schmitt, M.: *Das Produktmodellkonzept von STEP 1989*
Das Produktmodellkonzept von STEP, in: VDI-Z, 131 (1989) 12, pp. 84-96.

Grabowski, H.; Glatz, R.: *Schnittstellen 1986*
Schnittstellen zum Austausch produktdefinierender Daten - Auf dem Weg zum internationalen Standard STEP, in: VDI-Zeitung 128 (1986), pp. 333-343.

Grochla, E.: *Materialwirtschaft 1992*
Grundlagen der Materialwirtschaft, Nachdruck der 3rd Ed., Wiesbaden 1992.

Grochla, E. et al.: *Gesamtmodelle der Datenverarbeitung 1974*
Integrierte Gesamtmodelle der Datenverarbeitung, München-Wien 1974.

Gröner, L.: *Entwicklungsbegleitende Vorkalkulation 1991*
Entwicklungsbegleitende Vorkalkulation, in: Hansen, H. R. et al. (ed.): Betriebs- und Wirtschaftsinformatik, Berlin-Heidelberg-New York 1991.

Gröner, L.; Roth, L.: *Konzeption eines CIM-Managers 1986*
Konzeption eines CIM-Managers, in: Logistik Heute, 10 (1986), pp. II - VI.

Große-Oetringhaus, W. F.: *Fertigungstypologie 1974*
Fertigungstypologie unter dem Gesichtspunkt der Fertigungsablaufplanung, Berlin 1974.

Grupp, B.: *Elektronische Stücklistenorganisation 1976*
Elektronische Stücklistenorganisation in der Praxis, Stuttgart-Wiesbaden, 1976.

Gutenberg, E.: *Der Absatz 1984*
Grundlagen der Betriebswirtschaftslehre, Bd. 2: Der Absatz, 17th Ed., Berlin et al. 1984.

Gutenberg, E.: *Die Produktion 1983*
Grundlagen der Betriebswirtschaftslehre, Bd. 1: Die Produktion, 24th Ed., Berlin et al. 1983.

Haas, A.: *Schlanke Fertigungs- und Qualitätssteuerung 1993*
Schlanke Fertigungs- und Qualitätssteuerung in einem mittelständischen Unternehmen, in: Scheer, A.-W. (ed.): CIM im Mittelstand, Fachtagung Saarbrücken 1993, Saarbrücken 1993.

Haberstock, L.: *Kostenrechnung I 1987*
Kostenrechnung I: Einführung, 8th Ed., Hamburg 1987.

Haberstock, L.: *Kostenrechnung II 1986*
Kostenrechnung II: (Grenz-)Plankostenrechnung, 7th Ed., Hamburg 1986.

Hackstein, R.: *PPS 1989*
Produktionsplanung und -steuerung (PPS): Ein Handbuch für die Betriebspraxis, 2nd Ed., Düsseldorf 1989.

Hahn, D.: *Computergestütztes Qualitätsinformationssystem 1992*
Computergestütztes Qualitätsinformationssystem, in: Scheer, A.-W. (ed.): Simultane Produktentwicklung, München 1992, pp. 161-192.

Hammer, M.; McLeod, D.: *Database Description 1981*
Database Description with SDM: A Semantic Database Model, in: ACM Transactions on Database Systems, 6 (1981) 3, pp. 351.

Hansen, H. R.: *Wirtschaftsinformatik I 1996*
Wirtschaftsinformatik I, Einführung in die betriebliche Datenverarbeitung, 7th Ed., Stuttgart 1996.

Hansmann, K.-W.: *Industrielles Management 1996*
Industrielles Management, 5th Ed., München-Wien 1996.

Hansmann, K.-W.: *Produktionssteuerung 1987*
PC-gestützte Produktionssteuerung bei Gruppen- oder Gemischtfertigung, in: Adam, D. (ed.): Neuere Entwicklungen in der Produktions- und Investitionspolitik, Wiesbaden 1987.

Härder, T.: *Grenzen und Erweiterungsmöglichkeiten relationaler Datenbanksysteme 1989*
Grenzen und Erweiterungsmöglichkeiten relationaler Datenbanksysteme für Nicht-Standard-Anwendungen, in: Scheer, A.-W. (ed.): Praxis relationaler Datenbanken 1989, Proceedings zur Fachtagung, Saarbrücken 1989, pp. 1-25.

Harrington, J.: *Computer Integrated Manufacturing 1973*
Computer Integrated Manufacturing, Reprint, Malabar (Florida) 1973.

Hars, A.: *Referenzdatenmodelle 1994*
Referenzdatenmodelle - Grundlagen effizienter Datenmodellierung, Wiesbaden 1994.

Hartmann, H.: *Materialwirtschaft - Organisation, Planung, Durchführung, Kontrolle 1992*
Materialwirtschaft - Organisation, Planung, Durchführung, Kontrolle, 6th Ed., Gernsbach 1992.

Hedrich, P. et al.: *Flexibilität in der Fertigungstechnik 1983*
Flexibilität in der Fertigungstechnik durch Computereinsatz, München 1983.

Heinen, E.; Kupsch, P. U.: *Rechnungslegung 1991*
Rechnungslegung, in: Heinen, E. (ed.): Industriebetriebslehre, 9th Ed., Wiesbaden 1991, pp. 1315-1516.

Heinen, E.; Dietel, B.: *Kostenrechnung 1991*
Kostenrechnung, in: Heinen, E. (ed.): Industriebetriebslehre, 9th Ed., Wiesbaden 1991, pp. 1157-1313.

Heinrich, L.; Burgholzer, P.: *Informationsmanagement 1996*
Informationsmanagement, 5th Ed., München-Wien 1996.

Heinrich, L. J.; Pils, M.: *Betriebsinformatik im Personalbereich 1983*
Betriebsinformatik im Personalbereich, in: Heinrich, L.J.; Baugut, G. (ed.): Methoden der Planung und Lenkung von Informationssystemen, Bd. 4, Würzburg-Wien 1983.

Heinz, K.: *Beispiel einer CAD-CAPP-Kopplung für die wissensbasierte Arbeitsplanerstellung 1992*
Beispiel einer CAD-CAPP-Kopplung für die wissensbasierte Arbeitsplanerstellung, in: Scheer, A.-W. (ed.): Simultane Produktentwicklung, München 1992, pp. 193-210.

Heinzelbecker, K.: *Marketinginformationssysteme 1985*
Marketinginformationssysteme, Stuttgart et al. 1985.

Heinzelbecker, K.: *Marketinginformationssysteme 1981*
Marketinginformationssysteme in der Investitionsgüterindustrie, in: Thome, R. (ed.): Datenverarbeitung im Marketing, Berlin-Heidelberg-New York 1981, pp. 169-199.

Henn, O.: *Schnittstellen für die Automatisierungstechnik 1990*
Schnittstellen für die Automatisierungstechnik: Evolution zu MAP/TOP 3.0, in: Krallmann, H. (ed.): CIM - Expertenwissen für die Praxis, München-Wien 1990, pp. 303-318.

Hentschel, B.: *Personaldatenbank 1976*
Anforderungen an eine Personaldatenbank, in: AWV-Papier 11, Frankfurt 1976.

Hermes, H.: *Syntax-Regeln für den elektronischen Datenaustausch 1988*
Syntaxregeln für den elektronischen Datenaustausch, in: DIN (ed.): Einführung in EDIFACT - Entwicklung, Grundlagen und Einsatz, Berlin 1988, pp. 7-12.

Herterich, R. P.: *Objektorientierte Leitstandsmodellierung 1993*
Objektorientierte Leitstandsmodellierung: Konzept und Organisation, Wiesbaden 1993.

Herterich, R. P.: *Datenmanagement in der Fertigung 1991*
Ein Lösungsansatz für das Datenmanagement in der Fertigung, in: Scheer, A.-W.: Fertigungssteuerung - Expertenwissen für die Praxis, München-Wien 1991, pp. 173-201.

Herzog, R.: *QS-Komponenten in Beschaffung und Materialfluß 1992*
QS-Komponenten in Beschaffung und Materialfluß, in: HMD - Theorie und Praxis der Wirtschaftsinformatik, 29 (1992) 168, pp. 50-60.

Heß, H.: *Wiederverwendung von Software 1993*
Wiederverwendung von Software: Framework für betriebliche Informationssysteme, Wiesbaden 1993.

Heß, H.; Hoffmann, W.; Houy, C.; Jung, pp.; Scheer, A.-W.: *INMAS - ein Tool zur Datenintegration über eine neutrale Schnittstelle 1992*
INMAS - ein Tool zur Datenintegration über eine neutrale Schnittstelle, in: Scheer, A.-W. (ed.): Praxis relationaler Datenbanken 1992, Proceedings zur Fachtagung, Saarbrücken 1992, pp. 65-84.

Heß, H.; Scheer, A.-W.: *Kopplung von CIM-Komponenten - ein europäisches Projekt 1991*
Kopplung von CIM-Komponenten - ein europäisches Projekt, in: Handbuch der modernen Datenverarbeitung 157, Wiesbaden 1991, pp. 22-34.

Hildebrand, R.; Mertens, P.: *PPS Controlling 1992*
PPS Controlling mit Kennzahlen und Checklisten, Berlin et al. 1992.

Hofmann, M.: *PPS - nichts für die chemische Industrie? 1992*
PPS - nichts für die chemische Industrie?, in: io Management, 61 (1992) 1, pp. 30-33.

Hoffmann, W.: *HP OpenCAM 1993*
HP OpenCAM - Offene Strukturen mit der ARIS Architektur, in: CIM-Management 9 (1993) 4.

Hoitsch, H.-J.: *Produktionswirtschaft 1993*
Produktionswirtschaft: Grundlagen einer industriellen Betriebswirtschaftslehre, München 1993.

Holley, W. H.; Jennings, K. M.: *Personnel Management 1983*
Personnel Management - Functions and Issues, New York 1983

Horton, F. W.: *Information Resource Management 1985*
Information Resource Management in Public Administration: A decade of progress, Aslib Proceedings, 37 (1985) 1, pp. 9-17.

Horváth, P.; Mayer, R.: *Prozeßkostenrechnung 1989*
Prozeßkostenrechnung - Der neue Weg zu mehr Kostentransparenz und wirkungsvolleren Unternehmensstrategien, in: Controlling, 4 (1989), pp. 214-219.

Horwitt, E.: *Exploning Expert Systems 1985*
Exploning Expert Systems, in: Business Computer Systems 1985.

Houy, Chr.: *Vernetzungsstrategien 1993*
Vernetzungsstrategien, in: Scheer, A.-W. (ed.): Handbuch Informationsmanagement: Aufgaben - Konzepte - Praxislösungen, Wiesbaden 1993, pp. 767-782.

Houy, Chr.; Scheer, A.-W.; Zimmermann, V.: *Anwendungsbereiche von Client/Server-Modellen 1992*
Anwendungsbereiche von Client/Server-Modellen, in: IM Information Management, 7 (1992) 3, pp. 14-23.

Howe, D. R.: *Data Base Design 1983*
Data Analysis for Data Base Design, London 1983.

Hubmann, E.: *Einsatz neuer Informations- und Kommunikationstechniken in der Beschaffung 1992*
Einsatz neuer Informations- und Kommunikationstechniken in der Beschaffung, in: HMD Theorie und Praxis der Wirtschaftsinformatik, Stuttgart, 29 (1992) 168, pp. 111-121.

Hubmann, E.: *Elektronisierung von Beschaffungsmärkten und Beschaffungs-hierarchien 1989*
Elektronisierung von Beschaffungsmärkten und Beschaffungshierarchien - Informationsverarbeitung im Beschaffungsmanagement unter dem Einfluß neuer Informations- und Kommunikationstechniken, München 1989.

Hübner, T.: *Electronic Commerce 1993*
Electronic Commerce, in: Management & Computer, 1 (1993) 1, pp. 19-24.

IBM (ed.): *CLASS*
CLASS (Capacity Loading and Sequencing System), IBM-Form 80 713-0.

IDS Prof. Scheer GmbH (ed.): *Produktbeschreibung Engineering Leitstand EI-2 1993*
Produktbeschreibung Engineering Leitstand EI-2, Saarbrücken 1993.

IDS Prof. Scheer GmbH (ed.): *ARIS - Analyser 1993*
ARIS - Analyser Handbuch, Version 1.1, Stand 03/93, Saarbrücken 1993.

IDS Prof. Scheer GmbH (ed.): *ARIS-Produkte 1997*
ARIS-Applications, ARIS-Analyser, ARIS-Link, ARIS-Modeller, ARIS-Navigator, ARIS-Promt, ARIS-Referenzmodelle, ARIS-Toolset, ARIS-Vorgehensmodelle, ARIS-Workflow, Saarbrücken 1997.

IDS Prof. Scheer CAM GmbH (ed.): *Der Fertigungsleitstand FI-2 1997*
Dezentrale Fertigungssteuerung, Der Fertigungsleitstand FI-2 - Systembeschreibung, Saarbrücken Januar 1997.

IFA (ed.): *Fertigungssteuerung 1984*
Statistisch orientierte Fertigungssteuerung, Hannover 1984.

ISA-dS88.01: *Batch Control Systems 1992*
Batch Control Systems - Models and Terminology, Draft 5, Dezember 1992.

Isermann, H.: *Generierung von Stapelplänen 1984*
Stapelung von rechteckigen Versandgebinden auf Paletten - Generierung von Stapelplänen im Dialog mit einem PC, in: Ohse, D. et al. (ed.): Operations Research, Proceedings 1984, Berlin-Heidelberg-New York-Tokyo 1985, pp. 354 ff.

Jacob, H.: *Industriebetriebslehre 1990*
Industriebetriebslehre, 4th Ed., Wiesbaden 1990.

Jacob, H.: *Produktionsplanung 1990*
Die Planung des Produktions- und Absatzprogramms, in: Jacob, H.; Adam, D. (ed.): Industriebetriebslehre, 4th Ed., Wiesbaden 1990, pp. 401-590.

Jost, W.: *EDV-gestützte CIM-Rahmenplanung 1992*
EDV-gestützte CIM-Rahmenplanung, Wiesbaden 1992.

Jost, W.: *Rechnergestützte CIM-Rahmenplanung 1992*
Rechnergestützte CIM-Rahmenplanung - Konzeption und Realisierung eines Werkzeugs zur Analyse und Planung von CIM-Systemen, Dissertation, Saarbrücken 1992.

Jost, W.; Keller, G.; Scheer, A.-W.: *Konzeption eines DV-Tools im Rahmen der CIM-Planung 1991*
Konzeption eines DV-Tools im Rahmen der CIM-Planung, in: ZfB 61 (1991) 1, pp. 22-64.

Jünemann, R.: *Materialfluß und Logistik 1990*
Materialfluß und Logistik - Systemtechnische Grundlagen mit Praxisbeispielen, in: Jünemann, R.; Pfohl, H. C. (ed.): Logistik in Industrie, Handel und Dienstleistungen, Berlin et al. 1989.

Karl, R.: *Prozeßorientierte Vorgangsbearbeitung 1993*
Prozeßorientierte Vorgangsbearbeitung, in: Office Management, 41 (1993) 3, pp. 45-47.

Kauffels, F.-J.: *Klassifizierung der lokalen Netze 1986*
Klassifizierung der lokalen Netze, in: Neumeier, H. (ed.): State of the Art: Lokale Netze, München 1986, pp. 5-13.

Kazmaier, E.: *Berücksichtigung der Belastungssituation eines neuen PPS-Systems 1984*
Berücksichtigung der Belastungssituation im Rahmen eines neuen PPS-Systems auf der Basis einer dialogorientierten Ablaufplanung, in: IFA (Institut für Fabrikanlagen der Universität Hannover) (ed.): Fachseminar Statistisch orientierte Fertigungssteuerung, Hannover 1984.

Keller, G.: *Informationsmanagement in objektorientierten Organisationsstrukturen 1993*
Informationsmanagement in objektorientierten Organisationsstrukturen - Ein methodischer Ansatz zur Neugestaltung der planenden Bereiche industrieller Unternehmen, Wiesbaden 1993.

Keller, G.; Hechler, H.-J.: *Informationsmodell 1991*
Konzeption eines integrierten Informationsmodells für die Kostenrechnung des SAP-Systems, in: Scheer, A.-W. (ed.): Rechnungswesen und EDV, 12. Saarbrücker Arbeitstagung, Heidelberg 1991, pp. 67-106.

Keller, G.; Meinhardt, St.: *DV-gestützte Beratung 1994*
DV-gestützte Beratung bei der SAP-Softwareeinführung, in: HMD - Theorie und Praxis der Wirtschaftsinformatik, 31 (1994) 175.

Kersting, F.-J.: *Betriebsleitsysteme zur Rezeptverwaltung und Produktionsdatenverarbeitung 1991*
Betriebsleitsysteme zur Rezeptverwaltung und Produktionsdatenverarbeitung, in: Chem.-Ing.-Tech. 63 (1991) 7, pp. 675-681.

Kettner, H.; Bechte, W.: *Belastungsorientierte Auftragsfreigabe 1981*
Neue Wege der Fertigungssteuerung durch belastungsorientierte Auftragsfreigabe, in: VDI-Zeitung 132 (1981) 11.

Kilger, W.; Vikas, K.: *Flexible Plankostenrechnung und Deckungsbeitragsrechnung 1993*
Flexible Plankostenrechnung und Deckungsbeitragsrechnung, 10th Ed., Wiesbaden 1993.

Kilger, W.: *Einführung in die Kostenrechnung 1987*
Einführung in die Kostenrechnung, 3rd Ed., Wiesbaden 1987.

Kilger, W.; Scheer, A.-W. (ed.): *Rechnungswesen und EDV 1980-1993*
Rechnungswesen und EDV, 1.-14. Saarbrücker Arbeitstagung, Bd. 1-14, Würzburg-Wien 1980-1985, Heidelberg 1986-1993.

Kilger, W.: *Optimale Produktions- und Absatzplanung 1973*
Optimale Produktions- und Absatzplanung, Opladen 1973.

Kinzer, D.: *Kapazitätsabgleich 1971*
Ein Verfahren zum mittelfristigen Kapazitätsabgleich bei Werkstattfertigung, Dissertation, Aachen 1971.

Kistner, K.-R.: *Betriebsstörungen 1978*
Elemente einer Theorie der Betriebsstörungen, Diskussionsarbeiten der Fakultät für Wirtschaftswissenschaften der Universität Bielefeld, Nr. 50, Bielefeld 1978.

Kittel, T.: *PPS im Klein- und Mittelbetrieb 1982*
Produktionsplanung und -steuerung im Klein- und Mittelbetrieb - Chancen und Risiken des EDV-Einsatzes, Grafenau 1982.

Klein, J.: *Datenintegrität in heterogenen Informationssystemen 1991*
Datenintegrität in heterogenen Informationssystemen - Ereignisorientierte Aktualisierung globaler Datenredundanzen, Dissertation, Saarbrücken 1991.

Kloock, J.: *Prozeßkostenrechnung als Rückschritt und Fortschritt der Kostenrechnung 1992*
Prozeßkostenrechnung als Rückschritt und Fortschritt der Kostenrechnung, in: Kostenrechnungspraxis, 4 (1992), pp. 183-193.

Kloock, J.: *Input-Output-Analyse 1969*
Betriebswirtschaftliche Input-Output-Analyse - Ein Beitrag zur Produktionstheorie, Wiesbaden 1969.

Knolmayer, G.; Myrach, T.: *Anforderungen an Tools 1990*
Anforderungen an Tools zur Darstellung und Analyse von Datenmodellen, in: HMD - Theorie und Praxis der Wirtschaftsinformatik, 27 (1990) 152, pp. 90-102.

Köhler, R.: *Strategische Marketingplanung 1981*
Grundproblem der strategischen Marketingplanung, in: Geist, M. N.; Köhler, R. (ed.): Die Führung des Betriebes, Stuttgart 1981.

König, W.; Wolf, pp.: *Objektorientierte Software-Entwicklung 1993*
Objektorientierte Software-Entwicklung - Anforderungen an das Informationsmanagement, in: Scheer, A.-W. (ed.): Handbuch Informationsmanagement: Aufgaben - Konzepte - Praxislösungen, Wiesbaden 1993, pp. 869-898.

Korson, T.; McGregor, J. D.: *Understanding Object Oriented 1990*
Understanding Object-Oriented: A Unifying Paradigm, in: Communications of the ACM, 33 (1990) 6, pp. 40-60.

Kotz, A. M.: *Triggermechanismen in Datenbanksystemen 1989*
Triggermechanismen in Datenbanksystemen, Berlin et al. 1989.

Kraemer, W.: *Effizientes Kostenmanagement 1993*
Effizientes Kostenmanagement, EDV-gestützte Datenanalyse und -interpretation durch den Controlling-Leitstand, Wiesbaden 1993.

Kraemer, W.: *Entwicklungspotentiale der EDV-gestützten Kostenauswertung 1993*
Entwicklungspotentiale der EDV-gestützten Kostenauswertung: Teil 1: Gründe für ein Lean Controlling, in: Management & Computer, 1 (1993) 1, pp. 33-4.

Kraemer, W.: *Wissensbasiertes Kostenmanagement 1993*
Entwicklungspotentiale der EDV-gestützten Kostenauswertung: Teil 2: Wissensbasiertes Kostenmanagement, in: Management & Computer, 1 (1993) 2, pp. 113-120.

Kraemer, W.; Wiechmann, D.: *Die Betriebsdatenerfassung als integraler Bestandteil der Fertigungssteuerung und Kostenrechnung 1991*
Die Betriebsdatenerfassung als integraler Bestandteil der Fertigungssteuerung und Kostenrechnung, in: Scheer, A.-W. (ed.): Fertigungssteuerung, Expertenwissen für die Praxis, München-Wien 1991.

Krallmann, H.; Huber, A.: *Constraint-basierte, heuristische Planung in der industriellen Produktion 1990*
Constraint-basierte, heuristische Planung in der industriellen Produktion, in: Krallmann, H. (ed.): CIM - Expertenwissen für die Praxis, München-Wien 1990, pp. 349-364.

Krallmann, H.: *Expertensysteme für CIM 1986*
Expertensysteme für die computerintegrierte Fertigung, in: Warnecke, H. H.; Bullinger H. J. (ed.): 18. Arbeitstagung des IPA (Institut für Produktionstechnik und Automatisierung), Berlin-Heidelberg 1986.

Krcmar, H; Elgass, P.: *Teams und Informationsmanagement 1993*
Teams und Informationsmanagement, in: Scheer, A.-W. (ed.): Handbuch Informationsmanagement: Aufgaben - Konzepte - Praxislösungen, Wiesbaden 1993, pp. 673-695.

Kroeber-Riel, W.: *Computer-Aided-Advertising-Systems 1993*
Wissensbasierte Computerprogramme zur kreativen Gestaltung und Beurteilung von Werbung (CAAS), in: Management & Computer, 1 (1993) 3, pp. 191-198.

Kroeber-Riel, W.; Weinberg, P.: *Konsumentenverhalten 1996*
Konsumentenverhalten, 7th Ed., München 1996.

Kruppke, H.: *Problematik bei der organisatorischen und technischen Integration von Fertigungsleitständen in die Unternehmenspraxis 1991*
Problematik bei der organisatorischen und technischen Integration von Fertigungsleitständen in die Unternehmenspraxis, in: Scheer, A.-W. (ed.): Fertigungssteuerung, Expertenwissen für die Praxis, München-Wien 1991.

Küpper, H.-U.: *Anforderungen der Kostenrechnung an moderne Unternehmensstrukturen 1992*

Anforderungen der Kostenrechnung an moderne Unternehmensstrukturen, in: Männel, W. (ed.): Handbuch Kostenrechnung,
Wiesbaden 1992, pp. 138-153

Kupsch, P. U.; Marr, R.: *Personalwirtschaft 1991*
Personalwirtschaft, in: Heinen, E. (ed.): Industriebetriebslehre, 9th Ed.,
Wiesbaden 1991, pp. 729-896.

Kurbel, K.: *Engpaßorientierte Auftragsterminierung und Kapazitätsdisposi-*
tion 1989
Engpaßorientierte Auftragsterminierung und Kapazitätsdisposition, in:
Kurbel, K.; Mertens, P.; Scheer, A.-W. (ed.): Interaktive be-
triebswirtschaftliche Informations- und Steuerungssysteme, Berlin-
New York 1989, pp. 69-87.

Kurbel, K.: *Software Engineering 1983*
Software Engineering im Produktionsbereich, Wiesbaden 1983.

Küting, K.; Weber, C.-P.: *Die Bilanzanalyse 1994*
Die Bilanzanalyse: Beurteilung von Einzel- und Konzernabschlüssen,
2nd Ed., Stuttgart 1994.

Lehner, F. et al.: *Organisationslehre für Wirtschaftsinformatiker 1991*
Organisationslehre für Wirtschaftsinformatiker, München-Wien 1991.

Lockemann, P. C.: *Weiterentwicklung relationaler Datenbanken 1991*
Weiterentwicklung relationaler Datenbanken für Nicht-Standard-Anwendungen, in: Scheer, A.-W. (ed.): Praxis relationaler Datenbanken
1991, Proceedings zur Fachtagung, Saarbrücken 1991, pp. 2-16.

Lockemann, P. C.; Rademacher, K.: *Konzepte, Methoden und Modelle zur*
Datenmodellierung 1990
Konzepte, Methoden und Modelle zur Datenmodellierung, in: HMD -
Theorie und Praxis der Wirtschaftsinformatik, 27 (1990) 152, pp. 3-
16.

Loos, P.: *Planungshierarchien für die dezentrale Auftragsabwicklung in der*
Prozeßindustrie 1993
Planungshierarchien für die dezentrale Auftragsabwicklung in der
Prozeßindustrie, Interner Forschungsbericht, Saarbrücken April 1993.

Loos, P.: *Offene Fertigungssteuerung nach dem Leitstandkonzept am Beispiel*
von FI-2 1993
Offene Fertigungssteuerung nach dem Leitstandkonzept am Beispiel
von FI-2, in: Scheer, A.-W. (ed.): Beiträge zur Tagung der wissenschaftlichen Kommission Produktionswirtschaft, Saarbrücken 1993,
pp. 37-49.

Loos, P.: *Produktionsplanung und -steuerung in der chemischen Industrie*
1993
Produktionsplanung und -steuerung in der chemischen Industrie, in:
Scheer, A.-W. (ed.): Beiträge zur Tagung der wissenschaftlichen
Kommission Produktionswirtschaft, Saarbrücken 1993, pp. 121-135.

Loos, P.: *Representation of Data Structures 1993*
Representation of Data Structures Using the Entity Relationship Model and the Transformation in Relational Databases, in: Scheer, A.-W.
(ed.): Institut für Wirtschaftsinformatik, Heft 100, Saarbrücken 1993.

Loos, P.: *Datenstrukturierung in der Fertigung 1992*
Datenstrukturierung in der Fertigung, München-Wien 1992.

Loos, P.: *Probleme des Datenbankeinsatzes in der Fertigung 1991*
Probleme des Datenbankeinsatzes in der Fertigung, in: Scheer, A.-W.
(ed.): Fertigungssteuerung - Expertenwissen für die Praxis, München-
Wien 1991, pp. 153-172.

Lorenz, W.: *Warteschlangenmodell 1984*
Entwicklung eines arbeitsstundenorientierten Warteschlangenmodells
zur Prozeßabbildung der Werkstattfertigung, Düsseldorf 1984.

Luber, A.: *How to Identify a True Process Industry Solution 1992*
How to Identify a True Process Industry Solution, in: Production and
Inventory Management 12 (1992) 2, pp. 16-17.

Männel, W.: *Anlagenerhaltung 1968*
Wirtschaftlichkeitsfragen der Anlagenerhaltung, Wiesbaden 1968.

Mattheis, P.: *Vorgehensmodell einer prozeßorientierten Informations- und
Organisationsstrategie 1993*
Vorgehensmodell einer prozeßorientierten Informations- und Organi-
sationsstrategie, Wiesbaden 1993.

Mayr, H. C.; Dittrich, K. R.; Lockemann, P. C.: *Datenbankentwurf 1987*
Datenbankentwurf, in: Lockemann, P. C.; Schmidt, J. W. (ed.):
Datenbank-Handbuch, Berlin et al. 1987, pp. 486-552.

mbp Industrie Software GmbH (ed.): *Factory Tower - Funktionen und Nutzen
1992*
Factory Tower - Funktionen und Nutzen, Überblick, Dortmund, Ok-
tober 1992.

McCarthy, W. E.: *Accounting Models 1979*
An Entity-Relationship View of Accounting Models, in: The Accounting Review, LIV (1979) 4, pp. 667-686.

McDermott, J.: *XSEL 1982*
XSEL: A computer salesperson's assistant, in: Hayes, J. E.; Michie,
D.; Pao, Y.-H. (ed.): Machine Intelligence 10, New York 1982, pp.
325-328.

Meffert, H.: *Konsumgütermarketing 1993*
Konsumgütermarketing, in: Wittmann, W. (ed.): Handwörterbuch der
Betriebswirtschaft, Teilbd. 2, 5th Ed., Stuttgart 1993, pp. 2241-2255.

Mertens, P.: *Integrierte Informationssysteme I 1993*
Integrierte Informationsverarbeitung, Bd. 1: Administrations- und
Dispositionssysteme in der Industrie, 10th Ed., Wiesbaden 1993.

Mertens, P.; Griese, J.: *Integrierte Informationssysteme II 1993*
Integrierte Informationssysteme, Bd. 2: Informations-, Planungs- und
Kontrollsysteme, 7th Ed., Wiesbaden 1993.

Mertens, P. et al. (ed.): *Lexikon der Wirtschaftsinformatik 1990*
Lexikon der Wirtschaftsinformatik, 2nd Ed., Berlin et al. 1990.

Mertens, P.; Steppan, G.: *Die Ausdehnung des CIM-Gedankens in den Vertrieb 1990*

Die Ausdehnung des CIM-Gedankens in den Vertrieb, in: Krallmann, H. (ed.): CIM - Expertenwissen für die Praxis, München-Wien 1990, pp. 198-208.

Mertens, P.: *Expertisesysteme als Variante der Expertensysteme zur Führungsinformation 1989*
Expertisesysteme als Variante der Expertensysteme zur Führungsinformation, in: zfbf Zeitschrift für betriebswirtschaftliche Forschung, 41 (1989) 10, pp. 835-854.

Mertens, P.; Hoffmann, I.: *Aktionsorientierte Datenverarbeitung 1983*
Aktionsorientierte Datenverarbeitung, in: Informatik-Spektrum, 9 (1983) 6, pp. 323-333.

Mertens, P.: *Zwischenbetriebliche Integration 1985*
Zwischenbetriebliche Integration der EDV, in: Informatik-Spektrum, 8 (1985) 2, pp. 81-90.

Mertens, P.; Puhl, W.: *Computereinsatz im Rechnungswesen 1981*
Computereinsatz im betrieblichen Rechnungswesen: Konzeption eines daten- und methodenbankorientierten Kostenrechnungssystems, in: Journal für Betriebswirtschaft, 31 (1981) 1, pp. 53-64.

Mertens, P.: *Prognoserechnung 1981*
Prognoserechnung, 4th Ed., Würzburg-Wien 1981.

Mertens, P.; Bodendorf, F.: *Methodenbanken 1979*
Interaktiv nutzbare Methodenbanken, Entwurfskriterien und Stand der Verwirklichung, in: Angewandte Informatik, 21 (1979), pp. 533-541.

Mertens, P.; Hansen, K.; Rackelmann, G.: *Selektionsentscheidungen im Rechnungswesen 1977*
Selektionsentscheidungen im Rechnungswesen - Überlegungen zu computergestützten Kosteninformationssystemen, in: Die Betriebswirtschaft, 37 (1977) 1, pp. 77-88.

Meyer, B. E.: *Informationssysteme 1987*
Logistische Ansätze für Informationssysteme in der Automobilindustrie, Vortrag auf der GI-Tagung "CIM-Realisierungen", 11. Juni, Frankfurt 1987.

Mülder, W.: *Organisatorische Implementierung von computergestützten Personalinformationssystemen 1984*
Organisatorische Implementierung von computergestützten Personalinformationssystemen - Probleme und Lösungen, Berlin et al. 1984.

Müller, E.: *Simultane Lagerdisposition und Fertigungsablaufplanung 1972*
Simultane Lagerdisposition und Fertigungsablaufplanung bei mehrstufiger Mehrproduktfertigung, Berlin-New York 1972.

Müller-Merbach, H.: *Optimale Losgrößen 1965*
Optimale Losgrößen bei mehrstufiger Fertigung, in: Zeitschrift für wirtschaftliche Fertigung, 60 (1965), pp. 113-118.

NAMUR Empfehlung NE33 1992
NAMUR Empfehlung NE33, Anforderungen an Systeme zur Rezeptfahrweise, Mai 1992.

Nassi, I.; Shneiderman, B.: *Flowchart Techniques 1973*
Flowchart Techniques for Structured Programming, in: ACM-SIG-PLAN Notices, 8 (1973), pp. 12-26.

Nedeß, C.: *Wissensbasierte FMEA-Erstellung zur Unterstützung der Simultanen Produktentwicklung 1992*
Wissensbasierte FMEA-Erstellung zur Unterstützung der Simultanen Produktentwicklung, in: Scheer, A.-W. (ed.): Simultane Produktentwicklung, München 1992, pp. 277-334.

Neibecker, B.: *Werbewirkungsanalyse mit Expertensystemen 1990*
Werbewirkungsanalyse mit Expertensystemen, Heidelberg 1990.

Niemeier, J.: *Analyse- und Gestaltungsmethoden für den Bürobereich 1991*
Analyse- und Gestaltungsmethoden für den Bürobereich, in: Bullinger, H.-J. (ed.): Handbuch des Informationsmanagements im Unternehmen: Technik, Organisation, Recht, Perspektiven, München 1991, pp. 925-966.

Nijssen, G. M.; Halpin, T. A.: *Conceptual Schema and Relational Database Design 1989*
Conceptual Schema and Relational Database Design - A Fact Oriented Approach, New York et al. 1989.

Nüttgens, M.; Scheer, A.-W.: *Integrierte Entsorgungssicherung als Bestandteil des betrieblichen Informationsmanagements 1993*
Integrierte Entsorgungssicherung als Bestandteil des betrieblichen Informationsmanagements, in: zfbf Zeitschrift für betriebswirtschaftliche Forschung, 45 (1993) 11, pp. 959-972.

Ochs, B.: *Methoden zur Verkürzung der Produktentstehungszeit 1992*
Methoden zur Verkürzung der Produktentstehungszeit, München-Wien 1992.

Oeldorf, G.; Olfert, K.: *Materialwirtschaft 1995*
Materialwirtschaft, 7th Ed., Ludwigshafen 1995.

Ohse, D.: *Transportprobleme 1992*
Transportprobleme, in: Gal, T. (ed.): Grundlagen des Operations Research, Bd. 2, 3rd Ed., Berlin et al. 1992, pp. 261-360.

Ohse, D.: *Lagerhaltungsmodelle 1969*
Lagerhaltungsmodelle für deterministisch schwankenden Absatz, in: Ablauf- und Planungsforschung, 10 (1969), pp. 309-322.

Opitz, H.: *Klassifizierungssystem 1966*
Werkstückbeschreibendes Klassifizierungssystem, Essen 1966.

Ordelheide, D.: *Instandhaltungsplanung 1973*
Instandhaltungsplanung (Simulationsmodelle für Instandhaltungsentscheidungen), Wiesbaden 1973.

Ortner, E.: *Semantische Modellierung 1985*
Semantische Modellierung - Datenbank auf der Ebene der Benutzer, in: Informatik-Spektrum, 8 (1985), pp. 23 ff.

Ortner, E.; Wedekind, H.: *Datenbank für die Kostenrechnung 1977*
Der Aufbau einer Datenbank für die Kostenrechnung, in: Arbeitspapiere des Instituts für Betriebswirtschaftslehre, Technische Hochschule Darmstadt 1977.

Österle, H.; Brenner, W.; Hilbers, K.: *Unternehmensführung und Informationssystem 1992*
Unternehmensführung und Informationssystem - Ansatz des St. Gallener Informationssystem-Managements, 2nd Ed., Stuttgart 1992.

Österle, G.: *Informationssysteme 1981*
Entwurf betrieblicher Informationssysteme, München-Wien 1981.

Overfeld, J.: *Produktionsplanung bei mehrstufiger Kampagnenfertigung 1990*
Produktionsplanung bei mehrstufiger Kampagnenfertigung: Untersuchung zur Losgrößen- und Ablaufplanung bei divergierenden Fertigungsprozessen, Frankfurt et al. 1990.

Parametric Technology Corporation (ed.): *Pro Engineer 1989*
Pro Engineer, User Guide, Waltham, USA, 1989.

Pfohl, H. C.: *Logistiksysteme 1990*
Logistiksysteme - Betriebswirtschaftliche Grundlagen, in: Jünemann, R.; Pfohl, H. C. (ed.): Logistik in Industrie, Handel und Dienstleistungen, 4th Ed., Berlin et al. 1990.

Picot, A.: *Organisationsstrukturen der Wirtschaft 1993*
Organisationsstrukturen der Wirtschaft und ihre Anforderungen an die Informations- und Kommunikationstechnik, in Scheer, A.-W. (ed.): Handbuch des Informationsmanagement: Aufgaben - Konzepte, Praxislösungen, Wiesbaden 1993, pp. 49-68.

Picot, A.; Reichwald, R.: *Bürokommunikation 1987*
Bürokommunikation: Leitsätze für den Anwender, München 1987.

Plattner, H.: *Client/Server-Architekturen 1993*
Client/Server-Architekturen, in: Scheer, A.-W. (ed.): Handbuch Informationsmanagement: Aufgaben - Konzepte - Praxislösungen, Wiesbaden 1993, pp. 923-937.

Plattner, H.; Kagermann, H.: *Einbettung eines Systems der Plankostenrechnung in ein EDV-Gesamtkonzept 1991*
Einbettung eines Systems der Plankostenrechnung in ein EDV-Gesamtkonzept, in: Scheer, A.-W. (ed.): Grenzplankostenrechnung - Stand und aktuelle Probleme, 2nd Ed., 1991, pp. 137-178.

Ploenzke Informatik (ed.): *Fertigungsleitstand-Report 1992*
Fertigungsleitstand-Report, Eine detaillierte Untersuchung von Fertigungsleitständen, 2nd Ed., Kiedrich 1992.

Ploenzke Informatik (ed.): *PPS Studie 1989*
PPS Studie, Eine detaillierte Untersuchung von Produktions-Planungs- und -Steuerungssystemen, 3rd Ed., Wiesbaden 1989.

Pocsay, A.: *Methoden- und Tooleinsatz 1991*
Methoden- und Tooleinsatz bei der Erarbeitung von Konzeptionen für die integrierte Informationsverarbeitung, in: SzU Schriften zur Unternehmensführung, Band 44, Wiesbaden 1991, pp. 65-80.

Poths, W.: *Integrierte Gesamtmodelle 1978*
Erfahrungen der Praxis mit Beschreibungsmodellen (Integrierte Gesamtmodelle), in: Angewandte Informatik, 20 (1978), pp. 293-298.

Pritsker, A. A. B.: *Papers - Experiences - Perspectives 1990*
Papers - Experiences - Perspectives, West Lafayette, In. 1990.

PSI (ed.): *PIUSS-Bedienerhandbuch 1987*
PIUSS Produktionsplanungs- und -steuerungssystem - Bedienerhandbuch, Berlin 1987.

Racke, W.; Effelsberg, W.: *X. 400-Empfehlungen 1986*
Die X. 400-Empfehlungen für Nachrichtenübermittlungssysteme, in: Informatik Spektrum, 9 (1986) 1, pp. 42-43.

Rauh, O.: *Die Gestaltung der individuellen Datenverarbeitung am Beispiel des Einkaufs 1992*
Die Gestaltung der individuellen Datenverarbeitung am Beispiel des Einkaufs, in: HMD - Theorie und Praxis der Wirtschaftsinformatik, 29 (1992) 168, pp. 61-72.

Rausch, W.; de Marne, K.-D.: *VDA-Flächenschnittstelle 1985*
Datenaustausch über die VDA-Flächenschnittstelle mit CAD/CAM-System STRIM 100, in: CAD/CAM, 1 (1986), pp. 95-102.

Reichmann, T.; Fritz, B.; Nölken, D.: *EIS-gestütztes Controlling 1993*
EIS-gestütztes Controlling: Schnittstelle zwischen Controlling und Informationsmanagement, in: Scheer, A.-W. (ed.): Handbuch Informationsmanagement: Augaben - Konzepte - Praxislösungen, Wiesbaden 1993, pp. 463-489.

Reitzle, W.: *Industrieroboter 1984*
Industrieroboter, München 1984.

Reuter, A.: *Verteilte Datenbanken 1991*
Verteilte Datenbanken - Ein Überblick, in: Scheer, A.-W. (ed.): Praxis relationaler Datenbanken 1991, Proceedings zur Fachtagung, Saarbrücken 1991, pp. 17-30.

Reuter, A.: *Maßnahmen zur Wahrung von Sicherheits- und Integritätsbedingungen 1987*
Maßnahmen zur Wahrung von Sicherheits- und Integritätsbedingungen, in: Lockemann, P. C.; Schmidt, J. W. (ed.): Datenbank-Handbuch, Berlin et al. 1987, pp. 342-441.

Reuter, A.: *Fehlerbehandlung in Datenbanksystemen 1982*
Fehlerbehandlung in Datenbanksystemen, München-Wien 1981.

Riebel, P.: *Einzelkosten- und Deckungsbeitragsrechnung 1994*
Einzelkosten- und Deckungsbeitragsrechnung, 7th Ed., Wiesbaden 1994.

Riebel, P.: *Industrielle Erzeugungsverfahren 1963*
Industrielle Erzeugungsverfahren in betriebswirtschaftlicher Sicht, Wiesbaden 1963.

Rieger, B.: *Vergleich ausgewählter EIS-Generatoren 1990*
Vergleich ausgewählter EIS-Generatoren, in: Wirtschaftsinformatik, 32 (1990) 6, pp. 503-518.

Robey, D.: *Designing Organizations 1990*
Designing Organizations, 3rd Ed., Homewood, IL. 1990.

Roschmann, K.: *Betriebsdatenerfassung im CIM-Konzept 1990*
Stand und Entwicklungstendenzen der Betriebsdatenerfassung im CIM-Konzept, in: Krallmann, H. (ed.): CIM - Expertenwissen für die Praxis, München-Wien 1990, pp. 167 -178.

Röske, W.; Gansera, H.: *Strategisches Marketing 1981*
Strategisches Marketing, in: Thome, R. (ed.): Datenverarbeitung im Marketing, Berlin-Heidelberg-New York 1981, pp. 25-97.

Rude, pp.: *Rechnerunterstützte Gestaltsfindung auf der Basis integrierter Produktmodelle 1991*
Rechnerunterstützte Gestaltsfindung auf der Basis integrierter Produktmodelle, Dissertation, Karlsruhe 1991.

Ruf, T.: *Featurebasierte Integration von CAD/CAM-Systemen 1991*
Featurebasierte Integration von CAD/CAM-Systemen, Berlin et al. 1991.

Ruffing, P.: *Informations- und Kommunikationssysteme 1991*
EDV-gestützte Informations- und Kommunikationssysteme als strategische Option für die Disposition von Modebekleidung im Handel, Dissertation, Saarbrücken 1991.

Ruffing, T.: *Integrierte Auftragsabwicklung 1991*
Die integrierte Auftragsabwicklung bei Fertigungsinseln - Grobplanung, Feinplanung, Überwachung, in: Scheer, A.-W. (ed.): Fertigungssteuerung - Expertenwissen für die Praxis, München-Wien 1991, pp. 65-86.

Rumbaugh, J. et al.: *Object-Oriented Modeling and Design 1991*
Object-Oriented Modeling and Design, Englewood Cliffs 1991.

Sakurai, M.: *Target Costing 1989*
Target Costing and How to use it, in: Journal of Cost Management 1989, pp. 39-50.

SAP (ed.): *System RM-MAT Funktionsbeschreibung 1993*
System RM-MAT, Funktionsbeschreibung, Walldorf 01.01.1993.

SAP (ed.): *System RM-PPS Funktionsbeschreibung 1993*
System RM-PPS, Funktionsbeschreibung, Walldorf 01.03.1993.

SAP (ed.): *DASS, Der Leitstand im SAP-System 1992*
DASS, Der Leitstand im SAP-System, Release 1.1, Walldorf 1992.

SAP (ed.): *SD-Grundfunktionen und Stammdaten 1992*
R/3-System, SD-Grundfunktionen und Stammdaten, Release 1.1, Vorabversion, Walldorf 1992.

SAP (ed.): *SD-Verkauf 1992*
R/3-System, SD-Verkauf, Release 1.1, Vorabversion, Walldorf 1992.

SAP (ed.): *SAP-System R/3 Architektur 1992*
SAP-System R/3 Architektur, Walldorf 1992.

SAP (ed.): *System R/3 - Funktionen im Detail 1992*
System R/3 - Funktionen im Detail: Das Finanzwesen der SAP, Release 1.1, September 1992.

SAP (ed.): *Das Finanzwesen der SAP 1992*
System R/3, Das Finanzwesen der SAP, Release 1.1, Walldorf 1992.

SAP (ed.): *System R/3, Die Personalwirtschaft der SAP 1992*
System R/3, Die Personalwirtschaft der SAP, Release 2.0, Walldorf 1992.

SAP (ed.): *System RK 1986*
System RK, Funktionsbeschreibung, Walldorf, 1986.

Schäfer, E.: *Der Industriebetrieb 1969*
Betriebswirtschaftslehre der Industrie auf typologischer Grundlage, Bd. 1, Köln 1969.

Schäfer, H.: *Technische Grundlagen der lokalen Netze 1986*
Technische Grundlagen der lokalen Netze, in: Neumeier, H. (ed.): State of the Art: Lokale Netze, 2/86, München 1986, pp. 14 - 23.

Scharek, B.; Schmitz, H.: *Dokumentationsverfahren betrieblicher Informationssysteme 1975*
Manuelle und computergestützte Dokumentationsverfahren betrieblicher Informationssysteme, Köln 1975.

Scheer, A.-W.; Brombacher, R.: *Klare Regeln und Abgrenzungen erforderlich - Wege zum Unternehmensdatenmodell 1993*
Klare Regeln und Abgrenzungen erforderlich: Wege zum Unternehmensdatenmodell, in: Computerwoche FOCUS, 2 (1993), pp. 20-22 und pp. 36.

Scheer, A.-W.: *Architektur integrierter Informationssysteme 1992*
Architektur integrierter Informationssysteme - Grundlagen der Unternehmensmodellierung, 2nd Ed., Berlin et al. 1992.

Scheer, A.-W.: *Neue Architekturen für PPS-Systeme 1992*
Neue Architekturen für PPS-Systeme, in: CIM-Management, 8 (1992) 1, pp. S1-S4.

Scheer, A.-W.: *Papierlose Beratung 1991*
Papierlose Beratung - Werkzeugunterstützung bei der DV-Beratung, in: Information Management, 6 (1991) 4, pp. 6-16.

Scheer, A.-W.: *EDV-orientierte Betriebswirtschaftslehre 1990*
EDV-orientierte Betriebswirtschaftslehre - Grundlagen für ein effizientes Informationsmanagement, 4th Ed., Berlin et al. 1990.

Scheer, A.-W.; Bock, M.; Bock, R.: *Expertensystem zur konstruktionsbegleitenden Kalkulation 1990*
Expertensystem zur konstruktionsbegleitenden Kalkulation, in: Scheer, A.-W. (ed.): Veröffentlichungen des Instituts für Wirtschaftsinformatik, Heft 73, Saarbrücken 1990.

Scheer, A.-W.: *CIM 1990*
CIM (Computer Integrated Manufacturing) - Der computergesteuerte Industriebetrieb, 4th Ed., Berlin et al. 1990.

Scheer, A.-W.; Bock, M.; Bock, R.: *Konstruktionsbegleitende Kalkulation in CIM-System aus betriebswirtschaftlicher Sicht 1989*
Konstruktionsbegleitende Kalkulation im CIM-System aus betriebswirtschaftlicher Sicht, in: Männel, W. (ed.): Perspektiven, Führungskonzepte und Instrumente der Anlagenwirtschaft, 1989, pp. 209-233.

Scheer, A.-W., Hoffmann, W., Wein, R.: *HP OpenCAM 1993*
HP OpenCAM - Offene Strukturen mit der ARIS-Architektur, in: CIM-Management 9 (1993) 2.

Scheer, A.-W.: *Neue PPS-Architekturen 1986*
Neue Architektur für EDV-Systeme zur Produktionsplanung und -steuerung, in: Scheer, A.-W. (ed.): Veröffentlichungen des Instituts für Wirtschaftsinformatik, Heft 53, Saarbrücken 1986.

Scheer, A.-W.: *Konstruktionsbegleitende Kalkulation in CIM-Systemen 1985*
Konstruktionsbegleitende Kalkulation in CIM-Systemen, in: Scheer, A.-W. (ed.): Veröffentlichungen des Instituts für Wirtschaftsinformatik, Heft 50, 1985.

Scheer, A.-W.: *Interaktive Methodenbanken 1984*
Interaktive Methodenbanken: Benutzerfreundliche Datenanalyse in der Marktforschung, in: Zentes, J. (ed.): Neue Informations- und Kommunikationstechnologien in der Marktforschung, Berlin et al. 1984, pp. 105 ff.

Scheer, A.-W.: *Schnittstellen zwischen betriebswirtschaftlicher und technischer Datenverarbeitung 1984*
Schnittstellen zwischen betriebswirtschaftlicher und technischer Datenverarbeitung in der Fabrik der Zukunft, in: Ehrlich, H. D. (ed.): GI-Proceedings-14. Jahrestagung, Braunschweig 1984, pp. 56-79.

Scheer, A.-W.: *Absatzprognosen 1983*
Absatzprognosen, Berlin et al. 1983.

Scheer, A.-W.: *Computergestützte Produktionsplanung und -steuerung 1983*
Stand und Trends der computergestützten Produktionsplanung und -steuerung (PPS) in der Bundesrepublik Deutschland, in: Zeitschrift für Betriebswirtschaft, 53 (1983), pp. 138-155.

Scheer, A.-W.: *Projektsteuerung 1978*
Projektsteuerung, Wiesbaden 1978.

Scheer, A.-W.: *Produktionsplanung 1976*
Produktionsplanung auf der Grundlage einer Datenbank des Fertigungsbereichs, München-Wien 1976.

Scheer, A.-W.: *Instandhaltungspolitik 1974*
Instandhaltungspolitik, Wiesbaden 1974.

Schlageter, G.; Stucky, W.: *Datenbanksysteme 1983*
Datenbanksysteme: Konzepte und Modelle, 2nd Ed., Stuttgart 1983.

Schmelzer, H. J.: *Steigerung der Effektivität und Effizienz durch Verkürzung von Entwicklungszeiten 1990*
Steigerung der Effektivität und Effizienz durch Verkürzung von Entwicklungszeiten, in: Reichwald, R.; Schmelzer, H.J. (ed.): Durchlaufzeiten in der Entwicklung: Praxis des industriellen F&E Managements, München 1990.

Schmidt, G.: *Fertigungsleitstände - ein Überblick 1992*
Fertigungsleitstände - ein Überblick, in: Scheer, A.-W. (ed.): AWF-IWi-Fachtagung: PPS - Software der 90er Jahre, Bad Soden 1992.

Schmidt, G.: *CAM: Algorithmen und Decision Support 1989*
CAM: Algorithmen und Decision Support für die Fertigungssteuerung, in: Hansen, H. R. et al. (ed.): Betriebs- und Wirtschaftsinformatik, Berlin et al. 1989.

Schneeweiß, C.: *Lagerhaltungssysteme 1981*
Modellierung industrieller Lagerhaltungssysteme. Einführung und Fallstudien, Berlin-Heidelberg- New York 1981.

Schönsleben, P.: *Flexible Produktionsplanung und -steuerung 1985*
Flexible Produktionsplanung und -steuerung mit dem Computer, München 1985.

Schumann, M.: *Bürokommunikationssysteme 1987*
Eingangspostbearbeitung in Bürokommunikationssystemen, Expertensystemansatz und Standardisierung, Berlin et al. 1987.

Schwyrz, G.: *ICASE 1993*
ICASE - Chancen und Risiken zur Lösung des Informations-Management-Problems, in: Scheer, A.-W. (ed.): Handbuch Informationsmanagement: Aufgaben - Konzepte - Praxislösungen, Wiesbaden 1993, pp. 737-763.

Seelbach, H. et al.: *Ablaufplanung 1975*
Ablaufplanung, Würzburg-Wien, 1975.

Seubert, M.: *SAP-Datenmodell 1991*
Entwicklungsstand und Konzeption des SAP-Datenmodells, in: Scheer, A.-W. (ed.): Praxis relationaler Datenbanken 1991, Proceedings zur Fachtagung, Saarbrücken 1991, pp. 87-109.

Siegwart, H.; Raas, F.: *CIM orientiertes Rechnungswesen 1991*
CIM-orientiertes Rechnungswesen: Bausteine zu einem System-Controlling, Stuttgart 1991.

Siemens (ed.): *UDS Entwerfen und Definieren 1982*
UDS Entwerfen und Definieren, Benutzerhandbuch V 3.2, 1982.

Simon, H.; Kucher, E.; Sebastian, K.-H.: *Scanner-Daten 1982*
Scanner-Daten in Marktforschung und Marketingentscheidung, in: Zeitschrift für Betriebswirtschaft, 52 (1982) 6, pp. 555-579.

Simon, T.: *Kommunikation in der automatisierten Fertigung 1986*
Kommunikation in der automatisierten Fertigung, in: Computer Magazin, 15 (1986) 6, pp. 38-42.

Sinz, E. J.: *Datenmodellierung im SERM 1993*
Datenmodellierung im Strukturierten Entity-Relationship-Modell (SERM), in: Müller-Ettrich, G. (ed.): Fachliche Modellierung von Informationssystemen - Methoden, Vorgehen, Werkzeuge, Bonn-Paris 1993, pp. 63-126.

Sinz, E. J.: *Das Entity-Relationship-Modell 1990*
Das Entity-Relationship-Modell und seine Erweiterungen, in: HMD Theorie und Praxis der Wirtschaftsinformatik, 27 (1990) 152, pp. 17-29.

Sinzig, W.: *Die Bedeutung relationaler Datenbanken 1992*
Die Bedeutung relationaler Datenbanken zur Unterstützung der entscheidungsorientierten Kostenrechnung, in: Männel, W. (ed.): Handbuch Kostenrechnung, Wiesbaden 1992, pp. 1251-1264

Sinzig, W.: *Rechnungswesen 1990*
Datenbankorientiertes Rechnungswesen - Grundzüge einer EDV-ge-stützten Realisierung der Einzelkosten- und Deckungsbeitragsrech-nung, 3rd Ed., Berlin et al. 1990.

Smith, G.: *Einsatz der OPT-Software 1985*
Einsatz der OPT Software bei Firma LUCAS BRYCE Ltd. Großbri-tannien, in: GF + M (ed.): Proceedings der Jahrestagung 1985 der Gesellschaft für Fertigungssteuerung und Materialwirtschaft e. V., Heidelberg 1985.

Smith, J. M.; Smith, D. C.: *Databases Abstractions 1977a*
Databases Abstractions: Aggregation and Generalization, in: ACM Transactions on Database Systems, 2 (1977) 2, pp. 105-133.

Smith, J. M.; Smith, D. C.: *Databases Abstractions 1977b*
Databases Abstractions: Aggregation, in: Communications of the ACM, 2 (1977) 6, pp. 405-413.

Sorgatz, U.; Hochfeld, H.-J.: *Austausch produktdefinierender Daten 1985*
Austausch produktdefinierender Daten im Anwendungsgebiet der Ka-rosseriekonstruktion, in: Informatik Spektrum, 8 (1985) 6, pp. 305-311.

Spang, pp.: *Informationsmodellierung im Investitionsgütermarketing 1993*
Informationsmodellierung im Investitionsgütermarketing, Wiesbaden 1993.

Spragne, R. H.; Carlson, E. D.: *Effective Decision Support Systems 1982*
Building Effective Decision Support Systems, Englewood Cliffs-New York 1982.

Spur, G.; Krause, F.-L.: *CAD-Technik 1984*
CAD-Technik, München-Wien 1984.

Stahlknecht, P.: *Wirtschaftsinformatik 1995*
Einführung in die Wirtschaftsinformatik, 7th Ed., Berlin et al. 1995.

Steinmann, D.: *Einsatzmöglichkeiten von Expertensystemen in integrierten Systemen der Produktionsplanung und -steuerung 1992*
Einsatzmöglichkeiten von Expertensystemen in integrierten Systemen der Produktionsplanung und -steuerung (PPS), Heidelberg 1992.

Steinmann, D.: *Expertensysteme in der Fertigungssteuerung 1991*
Expertensysteme in der Fertigungssteuerung, in: Scheer, A.-W. (ed.): Fertigungssteuerung, Expertenwissen für die Praxis, München-Wien 1991, pp. 371-386.

Stender, J.: *Expertensysteme in der Fertigungssteuerung 1991*
Expertensysteme im Marketing - Anwendungsmöglichkeiten und Per-spektiven, in: Handbuch der modernen Datenverarbeitung, 11 (1970), pp. 56-65.

Strack, M.: *Elektronische Leitstände - ein Thema für den Mittelstand 1989*
Elektronische Leitstände - ein Thema für den Mittelstand, in: Scheer (ed.): CIM im Mittelstand, Fachtagung Saarbrücken 1989, Berlin et al. 1989, pp. 29-46.

Suppan-Borowka, J.: *Anforderungen an MAP 1986*
    MAP unter der Lupe - Anforderungen an MAP, in: Technische Rundschau, 78 (1986), pp. 170 - 175.
Suppan-Borowka, J.; Simon, T.: *MAP in der automatisierten Fertigung 1986*
    MAP Datenkommunikation in der automatisierten Fertigung, Pulheim 1986.
Tanenbaum, A. pp.: *Computer Networks 1988*
    Computer Networks, 2nd Ed., Prentice Hall, Englewood Cliffs, NJ, 1988.
Tempelmeier, H.: *Material-Logistik 1992*
    Material-Logistik - Grundlagen der Bedarfs- und Losgrößenplanung in PPS-Systemen, Berlin et al. 1992.
Thome, R.: *Datenverarbeitung im Marketing 1981*
    Datenverarbeitung im Marketing, Berlin-Heidelberg-New York 1981.
Uhlig, R. J.: *Erstellen von Ablaufsteuerungen für Chargenprozesse mit wechselnden Rezepturen 1987*
    Erstellen von Ablaufsteuerungen für Chargenprozesse mit wechselnden Rezepturen, in: atp - Automatisierungstechnische Praxis, 29 (1987) 1, pp. 17-23.
Vatteroth, H.-C.: *Standard-Software für die computergestützte Personalplanung 1993*
    Standard-Software für die computergestützte Personalplanung - Resultate einer Längsschnittanalyse, in: IM Information Management, 8 (1993) 3, pp. 76-80.
Vazsonyi, A.: *Planungsrechnung 1962*
    Die Planungsrechnung in Wirtschaft und Industrie, München-Wien 1962.
VDI (ed.): *Produktionsplanung 1974*
    Elektronische Datenverarbeitung bei der Produktionsplanung und -steuerung, 2nd Ed., Düsseldorf 1974.
VDI (ed.): *VDI-Richtlinie 2222, Konstruktionsmethodik 1977*
    VDI-Richtlinie 2222, Blatt 1, Konstruktionsmethodik: Konzipieren technischer Produkte, Düsseldorf 1977.
Venitz, U.: *CIM und Logistik 1991*
    CIM und Logistik - Zwei Wege zum gleichen Ziel?, in: SzU Schriften zur Unternehmensführung, Band 44, Wiesbaden 1991, pp. 35-47.
Vetter, M.; Maddison, R. N.: *Database Design 1981*
    Database Design Methodology, London 1981.
Vormbaum, H.: *Grundlagen des betrieblichen Rechnungswesens 1977*
    Grundlagen des betrieblichen Rechnungswesens, Stuttgart et al. 1977.
Wagner, H. M.; Whithin, T. M.: *Economic Lot Size Model 1958*
    Dynamic Version of the Economic Lot Size Model, in: Management Science, 5 (1958), pp. 89-96.
Waidelich, R.: *Informationsmanagement in der Automobilindustrie 1993*
    Informationsmanagement in der Automobilindustrie, in: Scheer, A.-W. (ed.): Handbuch Informationsmanagement: Aufgaben - Konzepte - Praxislösungen, Wiesbaden 1993, pp. 265-297.

Warnecke, H.-J.; Huser, M.: *Die Fraktale Fabrik 1996*
Die Fraktale Fabrik - Revolution der Unternehmenskultur, 2nd Ed., Berlin-Heidelberg-New York 1996.

Wäscher, D.: *Prozeßorientiertes Gemeinkosten-Management im Material-und Logistik-Bereich eines Maschinenbau-Unternehmens 1991*
Prozeßorientiertes Gemeinkosten-Management im Material- und Logistik-Bereich eines Maschinenbau-Unternehmens, in: Scheer, A.-W. (ed.): Rechnungswesen und EDV, 12. Saarbrücker Arbeitstagung, Heidelberg 1991, pp. 190-200.

Webre, N. W.: *An Extended Entity-Relationship Model 1983*
An Extended Entity-Relationship Model and Its Use on a Defense Project, in: Chen, P. P. (ed.): Entity-Relationship Approach to Information Modelling and Analysis, Proceedings of the 2nd International Conference on Entity-Relationship Approach (1981), Amsterdam-New York-Oxford 1983, pp. 173-193.

Wedekind, H.: *Datenbanksysteme I 1991*
Datenbanksysteme I - Eine konstruktive Einführung in die Datenverarbeitung in Wirtschaft und Verwaltung, 3rd Ed., Mannheim-Wien-Zürich 1991.

Wedekind, H.; Müller, T.: *Stücklistenorganisation 1981*
Stücklistenorganisation bei einer großen Variantenzahl, in: Angewandte Informatik, 23 (1981) 9, pp. 377-382.

Wein, R.: *Integration technischer Subsysteme in die Fertigungssteuerung 1991*
Integration technischer Subsysteme in die Fertigungssteuerung, in: Scheer, A.-W. (ed.): Fertigungssteuerung - Expertenwissen für die Praxis, München-Wien 1991, pp. 293-309.

Westkämper, E. (Bd.-ed.): *Integrationspfad Qualität 1991*
Integrationspfad Qualität, in: Bey, I. (ed.): CIM-Fachmann, Berlin et al. 1991.

Wiendahl, H. P. (ed.): *Anwendung der belastungsorientierten Fertigungssteuerung 1991*
Anwendung der belastungsorientierten Fertigungssteuerung, München 1991.

Wiendahl, H.-P. (ed.).: *Analyse und Neuordnung der Fabrik 1991*
Analyse und Neuordnung der Fabrik, Berlin et al. 1991.

Wiendahl, H.-P.; Birnkraut, D.: *Ganzheitliche Fabrikplanung als Bestandteil des rechnerintegrierten Industriebetriebes 1990*
Ganzheitliche Fabrikplanung als Bestandteil des rechnerintegrierten Industriebetriebes, in: Krallmann, H. (ed.): CIM - Expertenwissen für die Praxis, München-Wien 1990, pp. 520-542.

Wiendahl, H.-P.: *Betriebsorganisation 1989*
Betriebsorganisation für Ingenieure, 3rd Ed., München 1989.

Wiendahl, H.-P.: *Belastungsorientierte Fertigungssteuerung 1987*
Belastungsorientierte Fertigungssteuerung, München 1987.

Wievelhove, W.: *Arbeitsplanerstellung für Varianten 1976*
Automatische Detaillierung, Zeichnungs- und Arbeitsplanerstellung
für Varianten, Dissertation, Aachen 1976.

Wildemann, H.: *Just-In-Time - Informationsflußgestaltung 1990*
Just-In-Time - Informationsflußgestaltung, in: Krallmann, H. (ed.):
CIM - Expertenwissen für die Praxis, München-Wien 1990, pp. 330-
344.

Wildemann, H. et al.: *Werkstattsteuerung 1984*
Flexible Werkstattsteuerung durch Integration von KANBAN-Prinzi-
pien, in: Wildemann, H. (ed.): Computergestütztes Produktions-
Management, Bd. 2, München 1984.

Wilkes, W.: *Versionsunterstützung in Datenbanken 1989*
Versionsunterstützung in Datenbanken, in: Informatik-Spektrum, 12
(1989) 3, pp. 166-169.

Witt, F. J.: *Beschaffungscontrolling 1992*
Beschaffungscontrolling, in HMD - Theorie und Praxis der Wirtschaftsinformatik, 29 (1992) 168, pp. 73-87.

Wollnik, M.: *Ein Referenzmodell des Informations-Managements 1988*
Ein Referenzmodell des Informations-Managements, in: Information
Management, 3 (1988) 3, pp. 34-43.

Zäpfel, G.: *Taktisches Produktions-Management 1989*
Taktisches Produktions-Management, Berlin New York 1989.

Zell, M.: *Simulationsgestützte Fertigungssteuerung 1992*
Simulationsgestützte Fertigungssteuerung, München-Wien 1992.

Zencke, P.: *Unterstützung des Lean-Production-Gedankens 1993*
Unterstützung des Lean-Production-Gedankens, in: Scheer, A.-W.
(ed.): CIM im Mittelstand, Fachtagung Saarbrücken 1993,
Saarbrücken 1993.

Zentes, J.: *Marketing-Informationssysteme 1993*
Marketing-Informationssysteme, in: Wittmann, W. (ed.): Handwörterbuch der Betriebswirtschaft, Teilbd. 2, 5th Ed., Stuttgart 1993,
pp. 2706-2720.

Zülch, G.; Grobel, Th.: *Schlanke Produktion - eine Herausforderung an die
Organisationsplanung 1993*
Schlanke Produktion - eine Herausforderung an die Organisationsplanung, in: Nedeß, Chr. (ed.): Produktion im Umbruch - Herausforderung an das Management, HAB-Forschungsbericht Nr. 5, St. Gallen
1993.

Zülch, G.: *Profilmethode bei der Personaleinsatzplanung 1976*
Anwendung der Profilmethode bei der qualitativen Personaleinsatzplanung, in: Zeitschrift für Arbeitswissenschaften, 30 (1976), pp. 226-
223.

Abbreviations

ABC	Activity-Based Costing
AIAG	Automative Industry Action Group
API	Application Programming Interface
APT	NC language
AWF	Ausschuß für Wirtschaftliche Fertigung
BMFT	Bundesministerium für Forschung und Technologie
BOMP	Bill of Material Processor
BREP	Boundary Representation
CAD	Computer Aided Design
CAE	Computer Aided Engineering
CAM	Computer Aided Manufacturing
CAP	Computer Aided Planning
CAPISCE	Computer Architecture for Production Information Systems in a Competitive Environment
CAPP	Computer Aided Process Planning
CAQ	Computer Aided Quality Assurance
CASE	Computer Aided Software Engineering
CIDAM	CIM System with Distributed Data Base and Configurable Moduls
CIM	Computer Integrated Manufacturing
CIP	Computer Integrated Processing
CNC	Computerized Numerical Control
CRA	Current Record of Area
CRR	Current Record of Record
CRS	Current Record of Set
CRU	Current Record of Run Unit
CSG	Constructive Solid Geometry
DBS	Data Base Management System
DDL	Data Description Language
DEVO	Datenerfassungsverordnung
DML	Data Manipulation Language
DNC	Direct Numerical Control
DSS	Decision Support System
DÜVO	Datenübermittlungsverordnung

DÜVO	Datenübermittlungsverordnung
DYNPRO	Dynamic Program
EDI	Electronic Data Interchange
EDIFACT	Electronic Data Interchange for Administration, Commerce and Transport
EDP	Electronic Data Processing
EIS	Executive Information System
EPA	Enhanced Performance Architecture
EPC	Event-Driven Process Chain
ERM	Entity-Relationship Model
ETM	Event/Trigger-Mechanism
FDE	Factory Data Entry
FIFO	First-In First-Out
FMEA	Failure Mode and Effects Analysis
FMS	Field Bus Message Specification
FTS	Fahrerlose Transportsysteme
GERT	Graphical Evaluation Revue Technique
GL	Generation Language
IDEF	I-CAM Definition Method No. 1 Extended
IGES	Initial Graphics Exchange Specification
INMAS	Interface Management System
ISO	International Organisation for Standardisation
ISO/OSI	International Organisation for Standardisation/ Open Systems Interconnection
JIT	Just-in-Time
LAN	Local Area Network
MAP	Manufacturing Automation Protocol
MDE	Machine Data Entry
MMS	Manufacturing Message Specification
MRP	Material Requirement Planning
MRP II	Management Resource Planning
NC	Numerical Control
NF^2	Non-First Normal Form
NIAM	Nijssen Analysis Method
OCR	Optical Character Recognition
ODETTE	Organisation for Data Exchange by Teletransmission in Europe
OEM	Original Equipment Manufacturer
OMT	Object Modeling Technique
ooDM	object-oriented Data Model
PC	Personal Computer
PCD	Process Chain Diagram
PDATIS	Personal Data Information System
PDI	Personal Data Information System
PERSIS	Personal Information System

PESIS	Personal Information System
PPC	Production Planning and Control
SADT	Structured Analysis and Design Technique
SEDAS	Standardregelungen für ein einheitliches Datenträgeraustauschsystem
SERM	Structured Entity-Relationship Model
SET	Standard d'Exchange et de Transfert
SIMO	Semantic Information Model
SPC	Statistical Process Control
SQL	Standard Query Language
STEP	Standard for the Exchange of Product Model Data
TCP/IP	Transmission Control Protocol/Internet Protocol
TOP	Technical Office Protocol
TQM	Total Quality Management
VDA	Verband deutscher Automobilindustrie
VDA-FS	Verband deutscher Automobilindustrie Freiformflächenschnittstelle
WOP	(Work-)Shop-Oriented Programming

Index

N

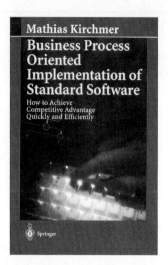

M. Kirchmer

Business Process Oriented Implementation of Standard Software

How to Achieve Competitive
Advantage Quickly and Efficiently

1998. XII, 233 pp. 107 figs. Hardcover
DM 128,-; öS 934,40; sFr 116,50
ISBN 3-540-63472-X

Companies must confront an increasingly tough competitive environment
with lean, flexible, and market-oriented structures. To accomplish this,
companies organize themselves according to their business processes
which are usually optimized by means of information technology.

Especially the use of standard software becomes an important element
of information system planning and implementation.

The author, with much experince in business consulting - mainly SAP R/3
implementations-, presents and explains necessary methods and tools
using case studies. Especially the efficient use of reference models is
described.

Springer

Springer-Verlag, P. O. Box 31 13 40, D-10643 Berlin, Fax 0 30 / 827 87 - 3 01 / 4 48 e-mail: orders@springer.de   rbw.BA.63867/1.SF

A.-W. Scheer

Business Process Engineering

Reference Models for Industrial Enterprises

2nd, completely rev. and enlarged ed. 1994. XXIV, 770 pp. 580 figs., 26 in colour
Hardcover **DM 128,-**; öS 934,40; sFr 116,50 ISBN 3-540-58234-7

The book affords researchers, users and students valuable assistance in implementing new organizational concepts through the employment of new information processing techniques.

The structure of the book follows the business of logistics, product development, information and coordination, and offers detailed examples of how outdated organizational structures can be reengineered. Examples from standard software systems (especially SAP R/3) demonstrate the book's down-to-earth practicality. The book develops in the views of the proven „Architecure of Integrated Information Systems" (ARIS) a comprehensive enterprise model, which serves as a reference model for engineering concrete business processes in industrial.

A.-W. Scheer

CIM Computer Integrated Manufacturing

Towards the Factory of the Future

3rd rev. and enl. ed. 1994. XV, 303 pp. 155 figs.
Hardcover **DM 85,-**; öS 620,50; sFr 77,50 ISBN 3-540-57964-8

Computer Integrated Manufacturing (CIM) is the computerized handling of integrated business processes among all different functions in an enterprise. The consistent application of information technology, along with modern manufacturing techniques and new organizational procedures, opens up great potential for speeding up processes. This book discusses the current state of applications and new demands arising from the integration principle. It mainly emphasizes on strategies for realization and implementation based on the author's concrete experience. The „Y-CIM information management" model is presented as a procedural method for implementing CIM. The third edition has been supplemented by up-to-date specified examples.

Springer

Price subject to change without notice.
In EU countries the local VAT is effective.

Springer-Verlag, Postfach 31 13 40, D-10643 Berlin, Fax 0 30 / 827 87 - 3 01/4 48 e-mail: orders@springer.de   rbw.BA.63867/2.SF